Contents

	Introduction	1
	Calendar of economic events: 1990–2010	12

Part 1 Main aggregates and summary accounts

Chapter 1:	Main aggregates and summary accounts		20
	The National Accounts at a glance		20
	Main aggregates and summary accounts		23
	1.1	Main aggregates: index numbers and values, 1997–2010	32
	1.2	UK Gross domestic product and national income, 1997–2010	34
	1.3	UK Gross domestic product chained volume measures, 1997–2010	36
	1.4	Indices of value, volume, prices and costs, 1997–2010	38
	1.5	Population, employment and GDP per head, 2002–2010	40
	1.6	United Kingdom summary accounts, 2002–2010	41
	1.7	Summary analysis by sector, 2007–2010	56
	1.7.1	Detailed analysis by sector, 2009	64
	1.8	Allocation of FISIM	84

Part 2 The industrial analyses

Chapter 2:	The industrial analyses		87
	The industrial analyses at a glance		87
	Explanation of industrial analyses		88
	2.1	Supply and Use Tables for the United Kingdom, 2007–2009	92
	2.2	Gross value added at current basic prices: output and capital formation, by industry and type of income, 2002–2009	98
	2.3	Gross value added at current basic prices by industry, 2002–2009	102
	2.4	Gross value added at basic prices by industry, 2002–2010	104
	2.5	Employment by industry, 2002–2010	106

Part 3 The sector accounts

	The sector accounts at a glance		108
	Sector accounts key indicators		110
	Explanation of the sector accounts		114
Chapter 3:	Non-financial corporations		115
	3.1	Non-financial corporations	116
	3.2	Public non-financial corporations	123
	3.3	Private non-financial corporations	130
Chapter 4:	Financial corporations		137
	4.1	Financial corporations	138

	4.2	Monetary financial institutions	145
	4.3	Other financial intermediaries and financial auxiliaries	152
	4.4	Insurance corporations and pension funds	159
	4.5	Financial derivatives	166
Chapter 5:	General government		173
	5.1	General government	174
	5.2	Central government	183
	5.3	Local government	193
Chapter 6:	Households and non-profit institutions serving households (NPISH)		203
	6.1	Combined households and NPISH sector	204
	6.2	Household final consumption expenditure at current market prices classified by purpose	214
	6.3	Household final consumption expenditure chained volume measures classified by purpose	215
	6.4	Individual consumption expenditure at current market prices by households, NPISH and general government	216
	6.5	Individual consumption expenditure chained volume measures by households, NPISH and general government	218
Chapter 7:	Rest of the world		220
	7.1	Rest of the world	221
Part 4	**Other analyses and derived statistics**		
Chapter 8:	Percentage distributions and growth rates		230
	8.1	Composition of UK gross domestic product at current market prices by category of expenditure	231
	8.2	Composition of UK gross domestic product at current market prices by category of income	231
	8.3	Gross value added at current basic prices analysed by Industry	232
	8.4	Annual increases in categories of expenditure (chained volume measures)	232
	8.5	Aggregates related to the gross national income	232
	8.6	Rates of change of GDP at current market prices	233
	8.7	Rates of change of GDP (chained volume measures)	234
	8.8	Rates of change of GDP at current market prices per capita	235
	8.9	Rates of change of GDP at chained volume measures per capita	235
	8.10	Rates of change of household disposable income (chained volume measures)	236
	8.11	Rates of change of household disposable income (chained volume measures)	237
Chapter 9:	Fixed capital formation supplementary tables		238
	9.1	Analysis of gross fixed capital formation at current purchasers' prices by type of asset and sector	239
	9.2	Analysis of gross fixed capital formation at current purchasers' prices by broad sector and type of asset	240

	9.3	Analysis of gross fixed capital formation at current purchasers' prices by type of asset	240
	9.4	Analysis of gross fixed capital formation at purchasers' prices (chained volume measures) by broad sector and type of asset	241
	9.5	Analysis of gross fixed capital formation at purchasers' prices (chained volume measures) by type of asset	241

Chapter 10: Non-financial balance sheets 242

Explanation of non-financial balance sheets 242

10.1	National balance sheet sector totals	243
10.2	National balance sheet asset totals	243
10.3	Non-financial corporations	244
10.4	Public non-financial corporations	244
10.5	Private non-financial corporations	245
10.6	Financial corporations	245
10.7	General government	246
10.8	Central government	246
10.9	Local government	247
10.10	Households & non-profit institutions serving households (NPISH)	247
10.11	Public sector	248

Chapter 11: Public sector supplementary tables 249

Explanation of public sector supplementary tables 249

11.1	Taxes paid by UK residents to general government and the European Union	250

Chapter 12: Statistics for European Union purposes 252

Explanation of statistics for European Union purposes 252

12.1	UK official transactions with institutions of the EU	253

Part 5   UK Environmental Accounts

Chapter 13: Environmental Accounts 255

The Environmental Accounts at a glance 255

Explanation of the UK Environmental Accounts 259

13.1	Estimates of recoverable oil and gas reserves	265
13.2	Oil and gas monetary balance sheet	266
13.3	Energy consumption	267
13.4	Atmospheric emissions, 2009	268
13.5	Greenhouse gas and acid rain precursor emissions	269
13.6	Material flows	270
13.7	Environmental protection expenditure in specified industries, 2009	271

Supplementary information

Glossary of terms 273

An introduction to the United Kingdom National Accounts

The *Blue Book* presents the full set of economic accounts, or National Accounts, for the United Kingdom. These accounts are compiled by the Office for National Statistics (ONS). They record and describe economic activity in the United Kingdom and as such are used to support the formulation and monitoring of economic and social policies.

This edition of the *Blue Book* presents estimates of the UK domestic and national product, income and expenditure. Data for 2010 are not yet available for the production account, the generation of income account, Input-Output Supply and Use Tables and for the full detailed industrial analysis of gross value added and its income components.

The accounts are based on the European System of Accounts 1995 (ESA95),[1] itself based on the System of National Accounts 1993 (SNA93),[2] which is being adopted by national statistical offices throughout the world. The UK National Accounts have been based on the ESA95 since September 1998. The 1998 edition of the *Blue Book* explains the main changes; a more detailed explanation of changes can be found in *Introducing the ESA95 in the UK*.[3] A detailed description of the structure for the accounts is provided in a separate National Statistics publication *National Accounts Concepts, Sources and Methods*.[4]

This introduction gives a brief overview of the accounts, explains their framework and sets out the main changes included in this edition of the *Blue Book*. Definitions of terms used throughout the accounts are included in the glossary. Explanations of more specific concepts are provided within the relevant parts.

The *Blue Book* comprises five parts:

- **Part 1** provides a summary of the UK National Accounts along with explanations and tables that cover the main national and domestic aggregates, for example gross domestic product (GDP) at current market prices and chained volume measures and the GDP deflator; gross value added (GVA) at basic prices; gross national income (GNI); gross national disposable income (GNDI); and where appropriate their equivalents net of capital consumption; population estimates; employment estimates and GDP per head; and the UK summary accounts (the goods and services account, production accounts, distribution and use of income accounts and accumulation accounts). It also includes details of revisions to the data.

- **Part 2** includes Input-Output Supply and Use Tables and analyses of gross value added at current market prices and chained volume measures, capital formation and employment, by industry.

- **Part 3** provides a description of the institutional sectors as well as explaining different types of transactions, the sequence of the accounts and the balance sheets. Explanation is also given of the statistical adjustment items needed to reconcile the accounts. This part comprises the fullest available set of accounts showing transactions by sectors and appropriate sub-sectors of the economy (including the rest of the world).

- **Part 4** covers other additional analyses. It includes tables showing the percentage growth rates of the main aggregates and supplementary tables for capital consumption, gross fixed capital formation, capital stock, non-financial balance sheets, public sector data, and GNI and GNP consistent with the ESA79 compiled for EU budgetary purposes.

- **Part 5** covers environmental accounts.

Overview of the accounts

In the UK, priority is given to the production of a single estimate of GDP using the income, production and expenditure data. The income analysis is available at current prices, expenditure is available at both current prices and chained volume measures, and value added on a quarterly basis is compiled in chained volume measures only. Income, capital and financial accounts are also produced for each of the institutional sectors: non-financial corporations, financial corporations, general government and the households and non-profit institutions serving households. The accounts are fully integrated, but with a statistical discrepancy, known as the statistical adjustment, shown for each sector account (reflecting the difference between the sector net borrowing or lending from the capital account, and the identified borrowing or lending in the financial accounts which should theoretically be equal). Financial transactions and balance sheets are also produced for the rest of the world sector in respect of its dealings with the UK.

Summary of Changes

While the structure in this edition of the *Blue Book* remains very close to last years publication, significant changes have been introduced; new industrial and product classifications (SIC 2007 and CPA 2008), improved methods of deflation and some additional improvements, largely in improved methods for the Financial Services and planned revisions to data. The reference year has been moved on two years, so that the latest base year for the chained volume measure of GDP is 2008.

The basic framework of the UK National Accounts

The accounting framework provides for a systematic and detailed description of the UK economy. It includes the sector accounts, which provide, by institutional sector, a description of the different stages of the economic process from production through income generation, distribution and use of income to capital accumulation and financing; and the Input-Output framework, which describes the production process in more detail. It contains all the elements required to compile aggregate measures such as GDP, gross national income (previously known as gross national product), saving and the current external balance (the balance of payments). The economic accounts provide the framework for a system of volume and price indices, so that chained volume measures of aggregates such as GDP can be produced. It should be noted that in this system, value added, from the production approach, is measured at basic prices (including other taxes less subsidies on production but not on products) rather than at factor cost (which excludes all taxes less subsidies on production). The system also encompasses measures of population and employment.

The whole economy is subdivided into institutional sectors. For each sector, current price accounts run in sequence from the production account through to the balance sheet.

The accounts for the whole UK economy and its counterpart, the rest of the world, follow a similar structure to the UK sectors, although several of the rest of the world accounts are collapsed into a single account because they can never be complete when viewed from a UK perspective.

The table numbering system is designed to show the relationships between the UK, its sectors and the rest of the world. A three–part numbering system (for example, 5.2.1) has been adopted for the accounts drawn directly from the ESA95. The first two digits denote the sector; the third digit denotes the ESA account. In this way for example, table 5.2.1 is the central government production account, table 5.3.1 is the local government production account and table 5.3.2 is the local government generation of income account. Not all sectors can have all types of account, so the numbering is not necessarily consecutive within each sector's chapter. For the rest of the world, the identified components of accounts 2–6 inclusive are given in a single account numbered 2. The UK whole economy accounts consistent with the ESA95 are given in section 1.6 as a time series, and in section 1.7 in detailed matrix format with all sectors, the rest of the world, and the UK total identified.

The ESA95 code for each series is shown in the left-hand column. The ESA95 codes use the prefix 'S' for the classification of institutional sectors. The ESA95 classification of transactions and other flows comprises transactions in products (prefix P), distributive transactions (prefix D), transactions in financial instruments (prefix F), and other accumulation entries (prefix K). Balancing items are classified using the prefix B. Within the financial balance sheets, financial assets/liabilities are classified using the prefix AF and non-financial assets/liabilities using the prefix AN.

What is an account? What is its purpose?

An account records and displays all of the flows and stocks for a given aspect of economic life. The sum of resources is equal to the sum of uses with a balancing item to ensure this equality. Normally the balancing item will be an economic measure which is itself of interest.

By employing a system of economic accounts we can build up accounts for different areas of the economy which highlight, for example, production, income and financial transactions. In many cases these accounts can be elaborated and set out for different institutional units and groups of units (or sectors). Usually a balancing item has to be introduced between the total resources and total uses of these units or sectors and, when summed across the whole economy, these balancing items constitute significant aggregates. Table A provides the structure of the accounts and shows how GDP estimates are derived as the balancing items.

The integrated economic accounts

The integrated economic accounts of the UK provide an overall view of the economy. Figure 1 presents a summary view of the accounts, balancing items and main aggregates and shows how they are expressed.

The accounting structure is uniform throughout the system and applies to all units in the economy, whether they are institutional units, sub-sectors, sectors or the whole economy, though some accounts (or transactions) may not be relevant for some sectors.

The accounts are grouped into four main categories: goods and services account, current accounts, accumulation accounts and balance sheets.

The goods and services account (Account 0)

The goods and services account is a transactions account which balances total resources, from output and imports, against the uses of these resources in consumption, investment, inventories and exports. As the resources are simply balanced with the uses, there is no balancing item. The goods and services account is discussed in detail in chapters 3 and 12 of *National Accounts Concepts, Sources and Methods*.[4]

Current accounts: the production accounts and the distribution of income accounts

Current accounts deal with production, distribution of income and use of income.

The production account (Account I)

The production account displays the transactions involved in the generation of income by the activity of producing goods and services. In this case the balancing item is value added (B.1). For the nation's accounts, the balancing item (the sum of value added for all industries) is, after the addition of taxes less subsidies on products, gross domestic product (GDP) at market prices or net domestic product when measured net of capital consumption. The production accounts are also shown for each institutional sector.

The production accounts are discussed in detail in Chapters 4 and 13 of *National Accounts Concepts, Sources and Methods*.[4]

Distribution and use of income account (Account II)

The distribution and use of income account shows the distribution of current income (in this case value added) carried forward from the production account, and has as its balancing item saving (B.8), which is the difference between income (disposable income) and expenditure (or final consumption). There are three sub-accounts which break down the distribution of income into the primary distribution of income, the secondary distribution of income and the redistribution of income in kind.

Primary incomes are those that accrue to institutional units as a consequence of their involvement in production, or their ownership of productive assets. They include property income (from lending or renting assets) and taxes on production and imports, but exclude taxes on income or wealth, social contributions or benefits and other current transfers. The primary distribution of income shows the way these are distributed among institutional units and sectors. The primary distribution account is itself divided into two sub-accounts – the generation and the allocation of primary incomes – but the further breakdown in the ESA95 of the allocation of primary income account into an entrepreneurial income account and an allocation of other primary income account has not been adopted in the UK.

The secondary distribution of income account shows how the balance of primary incomes for an institutional unit or sector is transformed into its disposable income by the receipt and payment of current transfers (excluding social transfers in kind). A further two sub-accounts – the use of disposable income and the use of adjusted disposable income – look at the use of income for either consumption or saving. These accounts are examined in detail in Chapters 5 and 14 of *National Accounts Concepts, Sources and Methods*.[4]

Aggregated across the whole economy the balance of the primary distribution of income provides national income (B.5) (which can be measured net or gross), the balance of the secondary distribution of income in kind provides national disposable income (B.6), and the balance of the use of income accounts provides national saving (B.8). These are shown in Figure 1.

The accumulation accounts (Accounts III and IV)

The accumulation accounts cover all changes in assets, liabilities and net worth (the difference for any sector between its assets and liabilities). The accounts are structured to allow various types of change in these elements to be distinguished.

The first group of accounts covers transactions which would correspond to all changes in assets/liabilities and net worth which result from transactions for example, savings and voluntary transfers of wealth (capital transfers). These accounts are the capital account and financial account which are distinguished in order to show the balancing item net lending/borrowing (B.9).

The second group of accounts relates to changes in assets, liabilities and net worth due to other factors (for example the discovery or re-evaluation of mineral reserves, or the reclassification of a body from one sector to another).

Capital account (Account III.1)

The capital account concerns the acquisition of non-financial assets (some of which will be income creating and others which are wealth only) such as fixed assets or inventories, financed out of saving, and capital transfers involving the redistribution of wealth. Capital transfers include for example, capital grants from private corporations to public corporations. This account shows how saving finances investment in the economy. In addition to gross fixed capital formation and changes in inventories, it shows the redistribution of capital assets between sectors of the economy and the rest of the world. The balance on the capital account, if negative, is designated net borrowing, and measures the net amount a unit or sector is obliged to borrow from others; if positive the balance is described as net lending, the amount the UK or a sector has available to lend to others. This balance is also referred to as the financial surplus or deficit and the net aggregate for the five sectors of the economy equals net lending/borrowing from the rest of the world.

Financial account (Account III.2)

The financial account shows how net lending and borrowing are achieved by transactions in financial instruments. The net acquisitions of financial assets are shown separately from the net incurrence of liabilities. The balancing item is again net lending or borrowing.

In principle net lending or borrowing in the capital account should be identical to net lending or borrowing on the financial account. However in practice, because of errors and omissions, this identity is very difficult to achieve for the sectors and the

Figure 1 Synoptic presentation of the accounts, balancing items and main aggregates

Accounts				Balancing items		Main aggregates [1]
Full sequence of accounts for institutional sectors						
Current accounts	I. Production account	I. Production account I		B.1	Value added	Domestic product (GDP/NDP)
	II. Distribution and use of income accounts	II.1. Primary distribution of income accounts	II.1.1. Generation of income account II	B.2	Operating surplus	National income (GNI, NNI)
				B.3	Mixed income	
			II.1.2. Allocation of primary income account	B.5	Balance of primary incomes	
		II.2. Secondary distribution of income account		B.6	Disposable income	National disposable income
		II.3. Redistribution of income in kind account		B.7	Adjusted disposable income	
		II.4. Use of income account				
		II.4.1. Use of disposable income account		B.8	Saving	National saving
		II.4.2. Use of adjusted disposable income account				
Accumulation accounts	III. Accumulation accounts	III.1. Capital account		B.10.1	(Changes in net worth, due to saving and capital transfers)	
				B.9	Net lending/Net borrowing	
		III.2. Financial account		B.9	Net lending/Net borrowing	
Balance sheets	IV. Financial balance sheets	IV.3. Closing balance sheet		B.90	Financial net worth	
Transaction accounts						
Goods and services account	0 Goods and services account					National expenditure
Rest of the world account (external transactions account)						
Current accounts	V. Rest of the world account	V.I. External account of goods and services		B.11	External balance of goods and services	External balance of goods and services
		V.II. External account of primary income and current transfers		B.12	Current external balance	Current external balance
Accumulation accounts		V.III. External accumulation accounts	V.III.1. Capital account	B.10.1	(Changes in net worth due to current external balance and capital transfers)	
				B.9	Net lending/Net borrowing	Net lending/Net borrowing of the nation
			V.III.2. Financial account	B.9	Net lending/Net borrowing	
Balance sheets		V.IV. External assets and liabilities account	V.IV.3. Closing balance sheet	B.90	Net worth	
				B.10	Changes in net worth	
				B.90	Net worth	

1/ Most balancing items and aggregates may be calculated gross or net.

economy as a whole. The difference is known as the statistical discrepancy (previously known as the balancing item).

The balance sheet (Account IV)

The sequence of accounts is completed by the second group of accumulation accounts. These include the balance sheets and a reconciliation of the changes that have brought about the change in net worth between the beginning and the end of the accounting period.

The opening and closing balance sheets show how total holdings of assets by the UK or its sectors match total liabilities and net worth (the balancing item). In detailed presentations of the balance sheets the various types of asset and liability can be shown. Changes between the opening and closing balance sheets for each group of assets and liabilities result from transactions and other flows recorded in the accumulation accounts, or reclassifications and revaluations. Net worth equals changes in assets less changes in liabilities.

Rest of the world account (Account V)

This account covers the transactions between resident and non-resident institutional units and the related stocks of assets and liabilities. The rest of the world plays a similar role to an institutional sector and the account is written from the point of view of the rest of the world. This account is discussed in detail in chapter 24 of *National Accounts Concepts, Sources and Methods*.[4]

Satellite accounts

Satellite accounts are accounts which involve areas or activities not dealt with in the central framework above, either because they add additional detail to an already complex system or because they actually conflict with the conceptual framework. The UK has begun work on a number of satellite accounts and one such – the UK environmental accounts – links environmental and economic data in order to show the interactions between the economy and the environment. Summary information from the environmental accounts is presented in part 5. More detailed information on the environmental accounts is available from the ONS website at: http://www.ons.gov.uk/ons/rel/environmental/environmental-accounts/2011/index.html

Some definitions

The text within Sections 1–3 explains the sources and methods used in the estimation of the UK economic accounts, but it is sensible to precede them with an explanation of some of the basic concepts and their 'UK specific' definitions, namely:

- the limits of the UK national economy: economic territory, residency and centre of economic interest
- economic activity: what production is included – the production boundary
- what price is used to value the products of economic activity
- estimation or imputation of values for non-monetary transactions
- the rest of the world: national and domestic

A full description of the accounting rules is provided in Chapter 2 of *National Accounts Concepts, Sources and Methods*.[4]

The limits of the national economy: economic territory, residence and centre of economic interest

The economy of the United Kingdom is made up of institutional units (see chapter 10 of *National Accounts Concepts, Sources and Methods*[4]) which have a centre of economic interest in the UK economic territory. These units are known as resident units and it is their transactions which are recorded in the UK National Accounts. The definitions of these terms are given below:

The UK economic territory is made up of:

- Great Britain and Northern Ireland (the geographic territory administered by the UK government within which persons, goods, services and capital move freely)
- any free zones, including bonded warehouses and factories under UK customs control
- the national airspace, UK territorial waters and the UK sector of the continental shelf

It excludes the offshore islands, the Channel Islands and the Isle of Man, which are not part of the United Kingdom or members of the European Union.

Within the ESA95 the definition of economic territory also includes:

- territorial enclaves in the rest of the world (embassies, military bases, scientific stations, information or immigration offices, aid agencies, used by the British government with the formal political agreement of the governments in which these units are located)

but excludes:

- any extra territorial enclaves (that is, parts of the UK geographic territory like embassies and US military bases used by general government agencies of other countries, by the institutions of the European Union or by international organisations under treaties or by agreement)

Centre of economic interest and residency

An institutional unit has a centre of economic interest and is a resident of the UK when, from a location (for example, a dwelling, place of production or premises) within the UK economic territory, it engages and intends to continue engaging (indefinitely or for a finite period; one year or more is used as a guideline) in economic activities on a significant scale. It follows that if a unit carries out transactions on the economic territory of several countries it has a centre of economic interest in each of them (for example, BP has an interest in many countries where it is involved in the exploration and production of oil and gas). Ownership of land and structures in the UK is enough to qualify the owner to have a centre of interest here.

Within the definition given above resident units are households, legal and social entities such as corporations and quasi corporations (for example, branches of foreign investors), non-profit institutions and government. Also included here however are so called 'notional residents'.

Travellers, cross border and seasonal workers, crews of ships and aircraft, and students studying overseas are all residents of their home countries and remain members of their households. However an individual who leaves the UK for a year or more (except students and patients receiving medical treatment) ceases to be a member of a resident household and becomes a non-resident even on home visits.

Economic activity: what production is included?

As GDP is defined as the sum of all economic activity taking place in UK territory, having defined the economic territory it is important to be clear about what is defined as economic activity. In its widest sense it could cover all activities resulting in the production of goods or services and so encompass some activities which are very difficult to measure. For example, estimates of smuggling of alcoholic drink and tobacco products, and the output, expenditure and income directly generated by that activity, have been included since the 2001 edition of the *Blue Book*.

In practice a 'production boundary' is defined, inside which are all the economic activities taken to contribute to economic performance. This economic production may be defined as activity carried out under the control of an institutional unit that uses inputs of labour or capital and goods and services to produce outputs of other goods and services. These activities range from agriculture and manufacturing through service producing activities (for example, financial services and hotels and catering) to the provision of health, education, public administration and defence; they are all activities where an output is owned and produced by an institutional unit, for which payment or other compensation has to be made to enable a change of ownership to take place. This omits purely natural processes.

The decision whether to include a particular activity within the production boundary takes into account the following:

- does the activity produce a useful output?
- is the product or activity marketable and does it have a market value?
- if the product does not have a meaningful market value can a market value be assigned (that is, can a value be imputed)?
- would exclusion (or inclusion) of the product of the activity make comparisons between countries or over time more meaningful?

In practice the ESA95 production boundary can be summarised as follows:

The production of all goods whether supplied to other units or retained by the producer for own final consumption or gross capital formation, and services only in so far as they are exchanged in the market and/or generate income for other economic units.

For households this has the result of including the production of goods on own-account, for example the produce of farms consumed by the farmer's own household (however, in practice produce from gardens or allotments has proved impossible to estimate in the United Kingdom). The boundary excludes the production of services for own final consumption (household domestic and personal services like cleaning, cooking, ironing and the care of children and the sick or infirm). Although the production of these services does take considerable time and effort, the activities are self-contained with limited repercussions for the rest of the economy and, as the vast majority of household domestic and personal services are not produced for the market, it is very difficult to value the services in a meaningful way.

What price is used to value the products of economic activity?

In the UK a number of different prices may be used to value inputs, outputs and purchases. The prices are different depending on the perception of the bodies engaged in the transaction, that is, the producer and user of a product will usually perceive the value of the product differently, with the result that the output prices received by producers can be distinguished from the prices paid by purchasers.

These different prices – purchasers' (or market) prices, basic prices and producers' prices – are looked at in turn below. They differ as a result of the treatment of taxes less subsidies on products, and trade and transport margins. Although the factor cost valuation (see explanation in Part 1) is not required under the SNA93 or the ESA95, ONS will continue to provide figures for gross value added at factor cost for as long as customers continue to find this analysis useful.

Basic prices

These prices are the preferred method of valuing output in the accounts. They reflect the amount received by the producer for a unit of goods or services, minus any taxes payable, and plus any subsidy receivable on that unit as a consequence of production or sale (that is, the cost of production including subsidies). As a result the only taxes included in the price will be taxes on the output process – for example business rates and vehicle excise duty – which are not specifically levied on the production of a unit of output. Basic prices exclude any transport charges invoiced separately by the producer. When a valuation at basic prices is not feasible then producers' prices may be used.

Producers' prices

Producers' prices equal basic prices plus those taxes paid per unit of output (other than taxes deductible by the purchaser, such as VAT, invoiced for output sold) less any subsidies received per unit of output.

Purchasers' or Market prices

These are the prices paid by the purchaser and include transport costs, trade margins and taxes (unless the taxes are deductible by the purchaser).

Purchasers' prices equal producers' prices plus any non-deductible VAT or similar tax payable by the purchaser, plus transport costs paid separately by the purchaser and not included in the producers' price.

'Purchaser's prices' are also referred to as 'market prices', for example 'GDP at market prices'.

The rest of the world: national and domestic

Domestic product (or income) includes production (or primary incomes generated and distributed) resulting from all activities taking place 'at home' or in the UK domestic territory. This will include production by any foreign owned company in the United Kingdom but exclude any income earned by UK residents from production taking place outside the domestic territory. Thus gross domestic product is also equal to the sum of primary incomes distributed by resident producer units.

The definition of gross national income can be introduced by considering the primary incomes distributed by the resident producer units above. These primary incomes, generated in the production activity of resident producer units, are distributed mostly to other residents' institutional units. For example, when a resident producer unit is owned by a foreign company, some of the primary incomes generated by the producer unit are likely to be paid abroad. Similarly, some primary incomes generated in the rest of the world may go to resident units. Thus, when looking at the income of the nation, it is necessary to exclude that part of resident producers' primary income paid abroad, but include the primary incomes generated abroad but paid to resident units; that is:

Gross domestic product (or income)

   less

   primary incomes payable to non-resident units

   plus

   primary incomes receivable from the rest of the world

   equals

   Gross national income

Thus gross national income (GNI) at market prices is the sum of gross primary incomes receivable by resident institutional units/sectors.

National income includes income earned by residents of the national territory, remitted (or deemed to be remitted in the case of direct investment) to the national territory, no matter where the income is earned; that is:

Real GDP (chained volume measures)

   plus

   trading gain

   equals

   Real gross domestic income (RGDI)

Real gross domestic income (RGDI)

   plus

   real primary incomes receivable from abroad

   less

   real primary incomes payable abroad

   equals

   Real gross national income (real GNI)

Real GNI (chained volume measures)

   plus

   real current transfers from abroad

   less

   real current transfers abroad

   equals

   Real gross national disposable income (real GNDI)

Receivables and transfers of primary incomes, and transfers to and from abroad are deflated using the index of gross domestic final expenditure.

Gross domestic product: the concept of net and gross

The term gross refers to the fact that when measuring domestic production we have not allowed for an important phenomenon: capital consumption or depreciation. Capital goods are different from the materials and fuels used up in the production process because they are not used up in the period of account but are instrumental in allowing that process to take place. However over time, capital goods wear out or become obsolete and in this sense gross domestic product does not give a true picture of value added in the economy. In other words, in calculating value added as the difference between output and costs we should include as a current cost that part of the capital goods used up in the production process; that is, the depreciation of the capital assets.

Net concepts are net of this capital depreciation, for example:

Gross domestic product

> *minus*
>
> consumption of fixed capital
>
> *equals*
>
> Net domestic product

However, because of the difficulties in obtaining reliable estimates of the consumption of fixed capital (depreciation), gross domestic product remains the most widely used measure of economic activity.

Symbols and conventions used

Symbols

In general, the following symbols are used:

> ..   not available
>
> –   nil or less than £500,000
>
> £ billion denotes £1,000 million.

Sign conventions

Resources and Uses

> Increase shown positive
>
> Decrease shown negative

Capital account

> Liabilities, net worth and Assets:
>
> Increase shown positive
>
> Decrease shown negative

Financial account

> Assets: net acquisition shown positive
>
> net disposal shown negative
>
> Liabilities: net acquisition shown positive
>
> net disposal shown negative

Balance sheet

> Assets and liabilities each shown positive
>
> Balance shown positive if net asset, negative if net liability

References

1. *Eurostat (1995) European System of Accounts 1995 (ESA95)*
   http://circa.europa.eu/irc/dsis/nfaccount/info/data/esa95/esa95-new.htm

2. UN, OECD, IMF, EU (1993) *System of National Accounts 1993 (SNA93)*
   http://unstats.un.org/unsd/nationalaccount/sna1993.asp

3. Office for National Statistics (1998) *Introducing the ESA95* in the UK. ISBN 0 11 621061 3. The Stationery Office: London.

4. Office for National Statistics (1998) *National Accounts Concepts, Sources and Methods*.
   http://www.ons.gov.uk/ons/rel/naa1-rd/national-accounts-concepts--sources-and-methods/1998-release/index.html

Articles

Akritidis L (2002) Accuracy assessment of National Accounts statistics. *Economic Trends*, No. 589.
http://www.ons.gov.uk/ons/rel/elmr/economic-trends--discontinued-/no--589--november-2002/index.html

Baxter M (2000) Developments in the measurement of general government output. *Economic Trends*, No. 562.
http://www.ons.gov.uk/ons/rel/elmr/economic-trends--discontinued-/no--562--september-2000/index.html

Clancy G and Gittins P (2011) Blue Book 2011: Improvements to Household Expenditure estimates
http://www.ons.gov.uk/ons/rel/consumer-trends/blue-book-2011--improvements-to-household-expenditure-estimates/q2-2011/art---blue-book-2011--improvements-to-household-expenditure-estimates.html

Drew S (2011) Deflation Improvements in the UK National Accounts
http://www.ons.gov.uk/ons/rel/naa1-rd/national-accounts-concepts--sources-and-methods/august-2011/deflation-improvements-in-the-uk-national-accounts.pdf

Drew S and Dunn M (2011) Blue Book 2011: Reclassification of the UK Supply and Use tables
http://www.ons.gov.uk/ons/rel/input-output/input-output-supply-and-use-tables/reclassification-of-the-uk-supply-and-use-tables/index.html

Duff H (2011) Blue Book 2011: Improvements to GDP(O), IoS and IoP
http://www.ons.gov.uk/ons/dcp171766_229044.pdf

Duff S (2011) Improving the coverage of derivatives data in the National Accounts and Balance of Payments
http://www.ons.gov.uk/ons/rel/naa1-rd/united-kingdom-economic-accounts/improving-the-coverage-of-derivatives-data-in-the-national-accounts-and-balance-of-payments/art-improving-the-coverage-of-derivatives-data-in-na-and-bop.html

Everett G (2011) Historic National Accounts data proposals for Blue Book 2011
http://www.ons.gov.uk/ons/rel/naa1-rd/united-kingdom-national-accounts/historic-national-accounts-data-proposals-for-blue-book-2011/ard-historic-national-accounts-data-proposals-fopr-blue-book-2011.pdf

Everett G (2011) Methods Changes in the 2011 Blue Book
http://www.ons.gov.uk/ons/rel/naa1-rd/united-kingdom-national-accounts/method-changes-in-blue-book-2011/ard-method-changes-in-blue-book-2011.pdf

Fletcher D and Williams M (2002) Index of Production redevelopment. *Economic Trends*, No. 587.
http://www.ons.gov.uk/ons/rel/elmr/economic-trends--discontinued-/no--587--september-2002/index.html

Jenkinson G (1997) Quarterly integrated economic accounts – The United Kingdom approach. *Economic Trends* Digest of Articles.
http://www.ons.gov.uk/ons/rel/elmr/economic-trends--discontinued-/economic-trends-digest-of-articles/index.html

Jones G (2000) The development of the annual business inquiry. *Economic Trends*, No. 564.
http://www.ons.gov.uk/ons/rel/elmr/economic-trends--discontinued-/no--564--november-2000/index.html

Lee P (2011) UK National Accounts - a short guide.
http://www.ons.gov.uk/ons/rel/naa1-rd/united-kingdom-national-accounts/2010-edition/uk-national-accounts---a-short-guide.pdf

Powell M and Swatch N (2002) An investigation into the coherence of deflation methods in the National Accounts. *Economic Trends*, No. 588.
http://www.ons.gov.uk/ons/rel/elmr/economic-trends--discontinued-/no--588--october-2002/index.html

Pritchard A (2003) Understanding government output and productivity. *Economic Trends*, No. 596.
http://www.ons.gov.uk/ons/rel/elmr/economic-trends--discontinued-/no--596-june-2003/index.html

Ruffles D, Tily G, Caplan D and Tudor S (2003) VAT missing trader intra-community fraud: The effect on balance of payments statistics and UK National Accounts. *Economic Trends*, No. 597.
http://www.ons.gov.uk/ons/rel/elmr/economic-trends--discontinued-/no--598--august-2003/vat-missing-trader-intra-community-fraud--the-effect-on-balance-of-payments-statistics---uk-national-accounts-.pdf

Sheerin C (2002) UK Material Flow Accounting. *Economic Trends*, No. 583.
http://www.ons.gov.uk/ons/rel/elmr/economic-trends--discontinued-/no--583--june-2002/index.html

Skipper H (2005) Early estimates of GDP: information content and forecasting methods. *Economic Trends*, No. 617.
http://www.ons.gov.uk/ons/rel/elmr/economic-trends--discontinued-/no--617--april-2005/index.html

Soo A and Charmokly Z (2003) The application of annual chain-linking to the Gross National Income system. *Economic Trends*, No. 593.
http://www.ons.gov.uk/ons/rel/elmr/economic-trends--discontinued-/no--593--march-2003/index.html

Tuke A and Beadle J (2003) The effect of annual chain-linking on Blue Book 2002 annual growth estimates. *Economic Trends*, No. 593.
http://www.ons.gov.uk/ons/rel/elmr/economic-trends--discontinued-/no--593--march-2003/index.html

A UK summary accounts, 2009
Total economy: all sectors and the rest of the world

£ million

		RESOURCES						USES	TOTAL
		UK total economy	Non-financial corporations	Financial corporations	General government	Households & NPISH	Not sector-ised	Rest of the world	Goods & services
		S.1	S.11	S.12	S.13	S.14+S.15	S.N	S.2	
	Current accounts								
I	**PRODUCTION / EXTERNAL**								
0	**ACCOUNT OF GOODS AND SERVICES**								
P.7	Imports of goods and services							421 225	421 225
P.6	Exports of goods and services							395 588	395 588
P.1	Output at basic prices	2 590 111	1 592 006	215 634	366 587	415 884			2 590 111
P.2	Intermediate consumption							1 333 179	1 333 179
D.21-D.31	Taxes less subsidies on products	136 922					136 922		136 922
II.1.1	**GENERATION OF INCOME**								
B.1g	**Gross domestic product, value added at market prices**	1 393 854	745 726	125 265	176 982	208 960	136 925		1 393 854
B.11	External balance of goods and services							25 637	25 637
II.1.2	**ALLOCATION OF PRIMARY INCOME**								
D.1	Compensation of employees	776 613				776 613		1 435	778 048
D.21-D.31	Taxes less subsidies on products	132 684			132 684			4 238	136 922
D.29-D.39	Other taxes less subsidies on production	17 472	18 274	2 559	–	–3 363		–3 411	14 061
B.2g	Operating surplus, gross	381 167	242 932	65 816	14 675	57 744			381 167
B.3g	Mixed income, gross	81 424				81 424			81 424
di	Statistical discrepancy between income components and GDP	–8					–8		–8
D.4	Property income	467 387	84 283	247 786	11 038	124 280		148 657	616 044
II.2	**SECONDARY DISTRIBUTION OF INCOME**								
B.5g	National income, balance of primary incomes, gross	1 413 417	181 741	50 236	149 105	1 032 343	–8		1 413 417
D.5	Current taxes on income, wealth etc	220 048			220 048			565	220 613
D.61	Social contributions	214 188	6 809	87 656	119 199	524		–	214 188
D.62	Social benefits other than social transfers in kind	277 534				277 534		2 251	279 785
D.7	Other current transfers	225 838	5 290	29 348	131 004	60 196		25 127	250 965
II.3	**REDISTRIBUTION OF INCOME IN KIND**								
B.6g	Disposable income, gross	1 399 127	147 711	71 262	237 019	943 143	–8		1 399 127
D.63	Social transfers in kind	242 776				242 776			242 776
II.4	**USE OF INCOME**								
B.7g	Adjusted disposable income, gross	1 399 127	147 711	71 262	30 106	1 150 056	–8		1 399 127
B.6g	Disposable income, gross	1 399 127	147 711	71 262	237 019	943 143	–8		1 399 127
P.4	Actual final consumption							1 221 454	1 221 454
P.3	Final consumption expenditure							1 221 454	1 221 454
D.8	Adjustment for change in households' net equity in pension funds	26 547				26 547		–41	26 506
	Accumulation accounts								
III.1.1	**CHANGE IN NET WORTH DUE TO SAVING AND CAPITAL TRANSFERS**								
B.8g	Saving, gross	177 714	147 711	44 756	–90 330	75 585	–8		177 714
B.12	Current external balance							20 316	20 316
D.9	Capital transfers receivable	55 540	13 128	10 120	18 922	13 370		1 058	56 598
D.9	Capital transfers payable	–52 276	–723	–1 981	–44 405	–5 167		–4 322	–56 598
III.1.2	**ACQUISITION ON NON-FINANCIAL ASSETS**								
	Changes in liabilities and net worth								
B.10.1.g	Changes in net worth due to saving and capital transfers	180 978	160 116	52 895	–115 813	83 788	–8	17 052	198 030
P.51	Gross fixed capital formation							209 253	209 253
-K.1	(Consumption of fixed capital)								
P.52	Changes in inventories							–11 651	–11 651
P.53	Acquisitions less disposals of valuables							429	429
K.2	Acquisitions less disposals of non-produced non-financial assets								
de	Statistical discrepancy between expenditure components and GDP							–	–
III.2	**FINANCIAL ACCOUNT**								
B.9	**Net lending(+) / net borrowing(-)**	–16 679	50 880	46 332	–151 967	38 084	–8	16 679	–
	Changes in liabilities								
F.2	Currency and deposits	276 700	–	267 559	9 141	–		–217 127	59 573
F.3	Securities other than shares	360 946	–8 888	148 275	221 770	–211		133 034	493 980
F.4	Loans	–211 995	–155 332	–44 822	–21 494	9 653		–161 651	–373 646
F.5	Shares and other equity	223 931	46 632	177 299		–		32 031	255 962
F.6	Insurance technical reserves	18 455		18 455					18 455
F.7	Other accounts payable	–6 788	–3 064	–2 589	–4 519	3 384		382	–6 406

A UK summary accounts, 2009
Total economy: all sectors and the rest of the world
continued

£ million

		USES						RESOURCES	TOTAL
		UK total economy	Non-financial corporations	Financial corporations	General government	Households & NPISH	Not sector-ised	Rest of the world	Goods & services
		S.1	S.11	S.12	S.13	S.14+S.15	S.N	S.2	
	Current accounts								
I	**PRODUCTION / EXTERNAL**								
0	**ACCOUNT OF GOODS AND SERVICES**								
P.7	Imports of goods and services							421 225	421 225
P.6	Exports of goods and services							395 588	395 588
P.1	Output at basic prices								2 590 111 2 590 111
P.2	Intermediate consumption	1 333 179	846 280	90 369	189 605	206 924			1 333 179
D.21-D.31	Taxes *less* subsidies on products								136 922 136 922
B.1g	**Gross domestic product, value added at market prices**	**1 393 854**	**745 726**	**125 265**	**176 982**	**208 960**	**136 925**		**1 393 854**
B.11	External balance of goods and services							25 637	25 637
II.1.1	**GENERATION OF INCOME**								
D.1	Compensation of employees	776 872	484 520	56 890	162 307	73 155		1 176	778 048
D.21-D.31	Taxes *less* subsidies on products	136 925					136 925		136 925
D.29-D.39	Other taxes *less* subsidies on production	17 472			17 472				17 472
B.2g	Operating surplus, gross	381 167	242 932	65 816	14 675	57 744			381 167
B.3g	Mixed income, gross	81 424				81 424			81 424
di	Statistical discrepancy between income components and GDP	–8					–8		–8
II.1.2	**ALLOCATION OF PRIMARY INCOME**								
D.4	Property income	446 731	145 474	263 366	30 173	7 718		169 313	616 044
B.5g	National income, balance of primary incomes, gross	1 413 417	181 741	50 236	149 105	1 032 343	–8		1 413 417
II.2	**SECONDARY DISTRIBUTION OF INCOME**								
D.5	Current taxes on income, wealth etc	219 941	33 542	5 400	1 189	179 810		672	220 613
D.61	Social contributions	214 016				214 016		172	214 188
D.62	Social benefits other than social transfers in kind	279 785	6 809	61 150	210 806	1 020			279 785
D.7	Other current transfers	238 156	5 778	29 428	170 342	32 608		12 809	250 965
B.6g	Disposable income, gross	1 399 127	147 711	71 262	237 019	943 143	–8		1 399 127
II.3	**REDISTRIBUTION OF INCOME IN KIND**								
B.7g	Adjusted disposable income, gross	1 399 127	147 711	71 262	30 106	1 150 056	–8		1 399 127
D.63	Social transfers in kind	242 776			206 913	35 863			242 776
II.4	**USE OF INCOME**								
B.6g	Disposable income, gross								
P.4	Actual final consumption	1 221 454			120 436	1 101 018			1 221 454
P.3	Final consumption expenditure	1 221 454			327 349	894 105			1 221 454
D.8	Adjustment for change in households' net equity in pension funds	26 506		26 506					26 506
B.8g	Saving, gross	177 714	147 711	44 756	–90 330	75 585	–8		177 714
B.12	Current external balance							20 316	20 316
	Accumulation accounts								
III.1.1	**CHANGE IN NET WORTH DUE TO SAVING AND CAPITAL TRANSFERS**								
D.9	Capital transfers receivable								
D.9	Capital transfers payable								
B.10.1.g	Changes in net worth due to saving and capital transfers	180 978	160 116	52 895	–115 813	83 788	–8	17 052	198 030
III.1.2	**ACQUISITION OF NON-FINANCIAL ASSETS**								
	Changes in assets								
P.51	Gross fixed capital formation	209 253	119 496	6 230	37 125	46 401			209 253
-K.1	(Consumption of fixed capital)	–159 862	–90 888	–6 924	–14 675	–47 375			–159 862
P.52	Changes in inventories	–11 651	–11 391	53	36	–349			–11 651
P.53	Acquisitions less disposals of valuables	429	153	264	12	–			429
K.2	Acquisitions less disposals of non-produced non-financial assets	–373	978	16	–1 019	–348		373	
de	Statistical discrepancy between expenditure components and GDP	–					–		–
B.9	**Net lending(+) / net borrowing(-)**	–16 679	50 880	46 332	–151 967	38 084	–8	16 679	–
III.2	**FINANCIAL ACCOUNT: changes in assets**								
F.1	Monetary gold and SDRs	–132			–132			132	
F.2	Currency and deposits	383 511	–33 934	392 824	9 674	14 947		–323 938	59 573
F.3	Securities other than shares	354 494	–6 138	355 515	1 883	3 234		139 486	493 980
F.4	Loans	–275 945	–46 465	–232 060	4 472	–1 892		–97 701	–373 646
F.5	Shares and other equity	162 292	24 132	87 240	37 352	13 568		93 670	255 962
F.6	Insurance technical reserves	18 778	–354	–37	–24	19 193		–323	18 455
F.7	Other accounts receivable	–6 514	–5 635	6 176	403	–7 458		108	–6 406
dB.9f	Statistical discrepancy between non-financial and financial transactions	8 086	–1 378	851	–697	9 318	–8	–8 086	–

Calendar of economic events: 1990–2010

1990

- Mar Budget introduces tax exempt savings accounts (TESSAs)
- Apr New Education Act brings in student loans
  Community Charge ('poll tax') introduced
- Aug Kuwait invaded by Iraq
- Oct Official reunification of Germany
  UK enters Exchange Rate Mechanism
- Nov John Major replaces Margaret Thatcher as Prime Minister
  Privatisation of electricity boards

1991

- Jan NHS internal market created
  Gulf War begins
- Feb Gulf War ends
- Mar Air Europe collapses
  Budget restricts mortgage interest relief to basic rate: Corporation Tax reduced and VAT increased
- Jul Bank of Credit and Commerce International closed by Bank of England
- Nov Maastricht agreement signed with UK opt-outs

1992

- Jan Russia agrees to join the IMF
- Feb 'Delors Package' raises EC's spending limits to 1.37 per cent of GDP to aid poorer member states
- Mar Budget raises lower rate of income tax to 20 per cent
- Apr Conservatives win General Election, John Major remains Prime Minister
- May Swiss vote in a referendum to join the IMF and International Bank for Reconstruction and Development
  Reform of EC Common Agricultural Policy agreed, switching from farm price support to income support
- Sep 'Black Wednesday': UK leaves Exchange Rate Mechanism
- Oct North American Free Trade Agreement (NAFTA) signed
- Nov Bill Clinton defeats George Bush in US presidential election

1993

- Jan Council Tax announced as replacement for Community Charge
- Mar Budget imposes VAT on domestic fuel
- Nov Parliament votes to relax Sunday trading rules
  First autumn Budget cuts public expenditure and increases taxes

1994

- Jan European Economic Area formed linking EU and European Free Trade Area
- Apr Eurotunnel opens
- Nov First draw of National Lottery
- Dec Coal industry privatised

1995

- Jan EU expanded to include Sweden, Finland and Austria
  World Trade Organisation succeeds General Agreement on Tariffs and Trade
- Feb Barings Bank collapses

1996

- Jan Gilt 'repo' market established
- Mar Rebates worth £1 billion paid to electricity consumers after break up of National Grid
- May Railtrack privatised, reducing public sector borrowing requirement (PSBR) by £1.1 billion
- Aug CREST clearing system initiated
- Sep Privatisation of National Power and PowerGen reduces PSBR by a further £1.0 billion

1997

- Apr Alliance and Leicester Building Society converts to bank
- May Labour Party wins general election, Tony Blair becomes Prime Minister
  Chancellor announces operational independence for the Bank of England, decisions on interest rates to be taken by a new Monetary Policy Committee
- Jun Halifax Building Society converts to a bank
  Norwich Union floated on the stock market
- Jul Gordon Brown presents his first Budget, setting inflation target of 2.5 per cent based on the Retail Prices Index excluding mortgage interest payments (RPIX)
  Woolwich Building Society converts to a bank

Bristol and West Building Society converts to a bank

Aug Stock market falls in Far East, Hang Seng Index ending 20 per cent lower than a year earlier

Economic and financial crisis in Russia

Dec The first instalment of the windfall tax on utilities (£2.6 billion) is paid

1998

Apr Sterling Exchange Rate Index hits its highest point since 1989

Mortgage payments rise as Mortgage Interest Relief at Source is cut from 15 per cent to 10 per cent

The New Deal for the unemployed is introduced

Jun The Bank of England's 'repo' rate is raised by 0.25 per cent to a peak of 7.5 per cent

Economic and Fiscal Strategy Report announces new format for public finances, distinguishing between current and capital spending

Aug BP merges with Amoco to create the UK's largest company

Oct The Working Time Directive, setting a 48-hour week, takes effect

Dec The second instalment of the windfall tax on utilities (£2.6 billion) is paid

Ten of the eleven countries about to enter the euro harmonise interest rates at 3.0 per cent

1999

Jan Introduction of Euro currency

Mar Allocation of new car registration letters switched from yearly in August to twice yearly

Energy tax announced at Budget

Apr Introduction of Individual Savings Accounts (ISAs) replaces Personal Equity Plans and TESSAs

Introduction of national minimum wage

Advanced Corporation tax abolished

Jun The Bank of England 'repo' rate reduced to low point of 5.0 per cent

2000

Feb House price growth peaks at 15 per cent in January and February

Oil price rises to highest level in 10 years

The UK company Vodafone takes over the German company Mannesman for £113 billion

Apr Government announces issue of 3G mobile phone spectrum licenses

May Share prices for internet companies start falling

Competition commission finds that UK car prices are high relative to EU prices

BMW sells Rover and Ford shuts Dagenham plant

June Inward investment in the UK hits record levels, with a large proportion made up of take-over deals

July Hauliers and farmers stage large scale protests over the price of fuel

Aug European banking regulators investigate £117 billion of new loans made to telecommunications companies, reflecting concerns that banks have overlent to the sector

Nov George W Bush elected US President

Dec US GDP growth slows sharply, following prolonged expansion

2001

Jan The US Federal Reserve cuts interest rates twice in one month, by 0.5 per cent each time

Feb The FTSE share price index falls below 6,000 points

Apr It emerges that Japan's bad debt problems are even worse than feared

May In the UK, business insolvencies are at a six-year high

Jun Pharmaceutical company Glaxo sheds 18,000 staff, 7 per cent of its UK workforce

Sep Terrorist attacks in United States. The World Trade Centre in New York is destroyed

Oct The US and its allies attack Afghanistan

Argentina devalues its currency and defaults on its debt of $155 billion, the biggest default in history

Railtrack collapses after the Government refuses to give further subsidies

Nov Bank of England cuts interest rates from 4.5 per cent to 4.0 per cent

Dec In the third quarter of 2001, US GDP shrinks for the first time in eight years

Enron, the 8th largest company in the United States, collapses leading to concerns about accountancy practices, banking involvement and financial market regulation

2002

Jan Euro notes and coins enter circulation

Apr UK tax rises announced to fund NHS

Jun	WorldCom collapses – the biggest corporate failure in history		Nov	George W Bush wins US election

2005

- Jun WorldCom collapses – the biggest corporate failure in history

   Network Rail takes over the running of the railways

- Aug IMF announces a $30 billion loan for Brazil, its biggest ever bailout of a struggling economy

- Oct UK housing boom peaks as house price inflation reaches 30 per cent

- Nov US Federal Reserve cuts interest rates to 1.25 per cent – a 40 year low

   Slowing UK economy forces doubling of the estimate of public borrowing

- Dec ECB cuts interest rates for the first time in more than a year, from 2.75 per cent to 2.5 per cent

   Stock markets around the world fall sharply over the second half of the year, with the FTSE 100 dropping below 4,000

2003

- Jan The FTSE 100 drops by nearly 50 per cent since its peak in 1999, reaching its lowest level since 1995

   UK economic growth at its lowest level since 1992, at 1.8 per cent per annum

   UK manufacturing jobs fall to their lowest level since records began

- Feb UK interest rates reduced by 0.25 per cent to 3.75 per cent due to weak internal and external demand

- Mar Second Gulf war begins

- Jul UK interest rates reduced by 0.25 per cent to 3.5 per cent, the lowest since January 1955, due to weak demand

- Nov UK interest rates raised by 0.25 per cent to 3.75 per cent

- Dec UK inflation target changes to 2.0 per cent based on the Consumer Prices Index (CPI)

2004

- Feb UK interest rates raised by 0.25 per cent to 4.0 per cent

- May UK interest rates rise 0.25 per cent to 4.25 per cent

   Price of oil breaches $40 barrier

   Petrol prices reach 80p a litre

- June The US Federal Reserve raises interest rates by 0.25 per cent to 1.25 per cent

   UK interest rates rise 0.25 per cent to 4.5 per cent

- July Gordon Brown releases 2004–05 Spending Review

- Aug Bank of England raises interest rates 0.25 per cent to 4.75 per cent

- Nov George W Bush wins US election

2005

- Mar The US Federal Reserve raise interest rates by 0.25 per cent to 2.75 per cent

- May Labour win general election, Tony Blair remains Prime Minister

- June Oil reaches near $60 a barrel – due to proposed strike in Norway

- July London wins right to host Olympics in 2012

   Terrorist attacks in London

- Aug Bank of England cuts interest rates by 0.25 per cent to 4.5 per cent

   Hurricane Katrina hits the US

   US crude oil prices breach $70 a barrel

- Oct UK house price inflation hits nine-year low of 2.2 per cent in October according to Office of the Deputy Prime Minister

- Dec European Central Bank (ECB) raises interest rates by 0.25 per cent to 2.5 per cent

   The US Federal Reserve raises interest rates for the 13th consecutive time by 0.25 per cent to 4.25 per cent

2006

- Jan Ukraine/Russia gas dispute leads to cuts in gas supplies to Europe

   The US Federal Reserve raises interest rates by 0.25 per cent to 4.5 per cent

- Mar ECB raises interest rates by 0.25 per cent to 2.5 per cent

   FTSE breaks 6,000 barrier

   The US Federal Reserve raises interest rates by 0.25 per cent to 4.75 per cent

- May The US Federal Reserve raises interest rates by 0.25 per cent to 5.0 per cent

   Oil prices rise above $73 a barrel

   State pension age to rise to 68 from 2044

- June Oil reaches $74 a barrel in response to Iran nuclear dispute

   ECB raises interest rates by 0.25 per cent to 2.75 per cent

   The US Federal Reserve raises interest rates by 0.25 per cent to 5.25 per cent

- July Israel–Lebanon conflict pushes oil to $78 a barrel

   Japan's Central Bank raises interest rate from 0.00 per cent to 0.25 per cent – the first increase in six years

Aug	Bank of England raises interest rates by 0.25 per cent to 4.75 per cent		The US Federal Reserve cut interest rates by 0.25 per cent to 4.25 per cent
	ECB raises interest rates by 0.25 per cent to 3.0 per cent	**2008**	
Sep	At $64.55, oil prices fall to their lowest level since the end of March	Jan	Gold prices rise above $900 a troy ounce for the first time ever as investors seek refuge from a weakening US dollar
	Greece announces 25 per cent increase in annual GDP after a new GDP calculation is applied		Stock markets in London and Europe suffer their biggest one-day falls since September 11th 2001
Oct	ECB lifts repo rate by 25 basis points to 3.25 per cent		Oil hits a new record high of $100 a barrel
	World output increases by 5.2 per cent in the year to the second quarter		The US Federal Reserve cuts interest rates to 3.0 per cent
Nov	Bank of England raises interest rates by 0.25 per cent to 5.0 per cent	Feb	Bank of England cuts the rate of interest by 0.25 per cent to 5.5 per cent
Dec	The pound surges against the dollar – sterling is at its highest level since Black Wednesday		Chancellor Alistair Darling announces the nationalisation of Northern Rock
	The ECB increases interest rates by 0.25 per cent to 3.5 per cent		Oil hits a new record high of $101 a barrel
	OPEC agrees to cut oil production from the 1st February 2007	Mar	US dollar falls to a record low as the euro moves to above $1.56
2007			The pound drops to a record low of £0.79 against the euro
Jan	Bank of England raises interest rates by 0.25 per cent to 5.25 per cent		The US Federal Reserve cuts interest rates by 75 basis points to 2.25 per cent
	The euro has displaced the US dollar as the world's leading currency in international bond markets	Apr	Oil prices surge to a record high above $122 a barrel
Feb	FTSE 100 hit a six-year high after a flurry of takeover speculation		Bank of England cuts interest rates by 0.25 per cent to 5.0 per cent
Mar	ECB lifts repo rate by 0.25 per cent to 3.75 per cent	May	Crude oil hits a new record high of $124 per barrel
Apr	Sterling moves past the $2 mark for the first time since 1992	Jun	Crude oil prices surged to a record high of $140.39 per barrel
May	Bank of England raises interest rates by 0.25 per cent to 5.5 per cent	Jul	ECB increases eurozone rates to seven-year high (up to 4.25 per cent)
June	Tony Blair resigns – Gordon Brown becomes Prime Minister	Aug	Oil prices fall below $120 for the first time in three months as fears on world growth intensify
Aug	The financial crisis begins with central banks intervening on a large scale as banks around the world stop lending to each other	Sep	Oil prices drop below $90 a barrel
Sep	Oil hits a new record high of $93.80 a barrel	Nov	Rates fall to a 54 year low. The Bank of England cuts base rates by 1.5 per cent to 3.0 per cent
	Sterling rises to a 26 year high of $2.0694 against the dollar		ECB cuts rates by 0.5 per cent to 3.25 per cent
Nov	Crude oil futures hit a record closing high, finishing above $98 a barrel	Dec	Bank of England announces a rate cut to 2.0 per cent, the joint lowest for Bank Rate not matched since 1951
	The three-month interbank interest rate hit 6.59 per cent		ECB cuts interest rates by 0.75 per cent to 2.5 per cent
	UK house prices recorded their biggest fall in 12 years	**2009**	
Dec	Bank of England cuts the rate of interest by 0.25 per cent to 5.5 per cent	Jan	Rates fall to a 315-year low. Bank of England cuts interest rates to 1.5 per cent
			ECB cuts interest rates by 0.5 per cent to 2.0 per cent

Feb　US Congress and Obama administration reach a deal on a $789 billion economic stimulus package

European leaders outline proposals to regulate financial markets and hedge funds and clamp down on tax havens

Mar　Share prices fall across the globe amid mounting fears over the financial health of banks and a spate of dividend cuts, Wall Street hits lowest levels since 1997

AIG reveals the depth of its financial plight with a $61.7 billion quarterly loss

The EC unveil new regulatory and legislative measures designed to beef up supervision of Europe's financial institutions

Bank of England introduce quantitative easing, £75 billion to pump into the economy over the next three months

ECB cuts interest rates by 0.5 per cent to 1.5 per cent

The IMF will have its $250 billion resources doubled to fight the financial crisis in emerging markets

Apr　G20 leaders unveil a $1,100 billion package of measures to tackle global downturn

Nine building societies, including Nationwide, have been down-graded by Moody's amid concern about their exposure to falling house prices and specialist mortgage loan

May　Bank of England boosts its quantitative easing program by announcing the availability of a further £50 billion in Bank money

ECB cuts its main target rate by 0.25 per cent to 1.0 per cent and announces plans to purchase £54 billion in covered bonds

Oil surges to $63 a barrel, with OPEC indicating that the global economy could withstand prices of between $75 and $80 a barrel

Jun　General Motors to file for Chapter 11 bankruptcy protection

Ireland's credit rating is cut to double A, with a negative outlook, from double A plus

Lloyds banking group is to repay £2.3 billion to the Treasury, aimed at repaying the government's $4 billion of preference shares

Bank of England announces that it will extend its Asset Purchase Facility to forms of working capital

ECB lends €442 billion to banks in bid to unlock credit markets

Jul　Spanish bank Santander announces plans to strengthen it's balance sheets and improve its capital structure by offering to swap a nominal €9.1 billion (£7.8 billion) in 30 securities for two new issues

Oil price drops below $60 per barrel for the first time since mid-May as markets continued to react to latest US inventories data

The pay and bonuses of hundreds of high-flying City traders and dealmakers will have to be publicly disclosed under a Treasury-backed plan to curb excessive and risky remuneration

Nissan is to build a plant in the UK to make Lithium-ion batteries for electrical vehicles in one of the biggest new investments by a carmaker since the industry entered its downturn last year

Aug　Oil increases to $73.50 a barrel as commodities prices hit their highest level for the year

Bank of England boosts its quantitative easing program to £175 billion

Sep　World Trade Organisation gives Brazil the go ahead to impose $295 million (£181 million) of sanctions on US goods over Washington's failure to scrap illegal subsidies to its cotton farmers

BP, the UK energy group, has discovered a 'giant' oil field in the Gulf Of Mexico that shows a new frontier opening up for US oil production

Gold prices hit a six-month high, approaching the $1,000 a troy ounce mark for the fifth time in two years

Dutch bankers are about to become the first in the world to cap bonuses paid to their most senior executives under a new code that will restrict such pay-outs to the equivalent of a year's salary

Oct　Aviva are set to sell their stake in Dutch subsidiary Delta Lloyd, the biggest initial public offering in Europe for at least 18 months

Oil prices face further upward pressure as they near $80 a barrel because of heavy trading in options contracts ahead of the year end

Nov　Gold increases to an all-time high after India bought 200 tonnes of the precious metal

Government gives £37 billion of new bail out cash to RBS and Lloyds

Bank of England MPC slows the rate of its asset purchase injections into the UK economy

Dubai World a sovereign backed holding group, requests a delay on repayment of its liabilities (around $60 billion)

Dec　Greece faces possible ratings downgrade

Gold prices fall for a fourth session and commodity markets remain under pressure

Greece's bond markets see the largest collapse in the history of the Eurozone

Standard & Poor's change Spain's outlook from 'stable' to 'negative'

OPEC indicate that it aims to keep oil prices at $70–$80 per barrel next year as it tries to support the economic recovery

Bank of England's injection of cash into the economy has so far fallen short of the desired result, according to the Monetary Policy Committee

Iceland's parliament approves an amended bill to repay more than $5 billion lost by savers in Britain and the Netherlands when the island's banks collapsed during the financial crisis

2010

Jan MPC votes to keep interest rates unchanged at 0.5 per cent

The recession has put a dent in future North Sea oil and gas production, with companies tapping fewer new oil reserves in 2009 than in previous years

Cadbury backs an improved £11.6 billion takeover bid from Kraft

Feb The European Union tell Greece to cut public sector wages and salaries and improve tax collection to prevent it's financial crisis from affecting the rest of the Eurozone

Hector Sants resigns as chief executive of the Financial Services Authority

House prices fall for the first time in 10 months

Sterling falls to a nine-month low against the dollar and it's weakest level against the yen in 11 months

Mar Greece announces it is prepared to turn to the IMF if the euro area does not provide the support it wants

Germany and France plan to launch a 'European Monetary Fund'

EU talks on hedge funds and the private equity industry are on hold until after the UK general election

Leaders have agreed a eurozone rescue mechanism for Greece, giving the IMF a major role

Global steel prices are set to increase by up to a third after miners and steelmakers agreed a ground-breaking change in the iron-ore pricing system

Mergers and Acquisitions boomed in Asia in contrast to a slump in Europe and the US

Apr Parliament will be dissolved on the 13th April and an election called for the 6th May

Copper prices crossed the key $8,000 a tonne barrier, leading other metals to their highest levels in 20 months

BA strike leads to a 15 per cent fall in passenger numbers in March, making it the worst March in a decade for passenger numbers

Eurozone members have committed to provide up to €30 billion in loans to Greece over the next year to stem the debt crisis

First live television debate between Labour, Conservative and Liberal Democrat leaders

Volcanic ash cloud strands passengers as air traffic across Europe's air space is halted

De Beers, the world's largest diamond miner, says the supply of the gems is running out over the long term

Standard & Poor downgrade Spain's debt, sparking fears that Greece's debt crisis will spread to other Eurozone countries

The US stepped up it's response to the BP oil spill in the Gulf of Mexico

May Eurozone agrees a €100 billion package of emergency loans aimed at averting sovereign default by Greece and preventing a confidence crisis spreading to countries such as Spain and Portugal

UK General Election results in a hung parliament, both Conservatives and Labour hold talks with the Liberal Democrats over power sharing

Gordon Brown announces he will quit as Labour leader. David Cameron takes power, as the Conservatives and Liberal Democrats agreed a deal to form Britain's first coalition government since the Second World War

The price of Gold hits an all-time high

George Osborne (Chancellor) creates an independent fiscal watchdog, the Office for Budget Responsibility, to provide independent analysis of the UK's public finances including producing forecasts for the economy and public sector finances twice a year

Some of the world's largest hedge funds have experienced significant losses after high levels of volatility across markets wiped billions from portfolios

Sterling fell sharply due to the fear that Britain's public finances were worse than expected

Prudential launches $21 billion rights issue to fund a takeover bid for the Asian businesses of AIG

Sanctions and under-investment have reduced Iran's oil production capacity by at least 300,000 barrels per day

George Osborne sets out plans for £6.2 billion of immediate public sector spending cuts

Share prices, commodities and the euro fell sharply

Calendar of economic events: 1990–2010

	President Obama orders a halt to the offshore drilling by oil companies following the BP spill
Jun	China's central bank warns that property problems are more severe than those in the US
	Pay freezes spread in the public sector
	Retailers warn over VAT rise impact which could cost the UK economy £24 billion
	Increase in the price of gold and demand for base metals drives growth of mining firms and share price in the FTSE 100
	Bank of England holds interest rates steady
	Oil drops after IEA forecasts oversupply
	G20 backs drive for crackdown on banks
Jul	UK group begins oil drilling in Arctic
	China drives German recovery – exports rise 9.2 per cent
	European banks in talks on bail-out fund
	BP suffering from share losses since the Gulf oil crisis
	Ministry of Defence looks at cutting 30,000 troops
	President Obama signs bill to overhaul Wall Street
	Emirates places $9 billion order for Boeing 777s
Aug	Wheat prices rise at fastest rate since 1973 as drought hits Russia
	BP faces $20 billion in penalties for oil leak
	Inflation remains above the Bank of England's target
	The coalition government set aside £2 billion to fight child poverty in the UK while the UK budget deficit as a proportion of GDP is 11 per cent
Sep	Fears grow over food supply as Russia announced a 12-month extension of its grain export ban. The UN's Food and Agricultural Organisation held an emergency meeting to discuss the wheat shortage
	ECB lifts eurozone growth forecast expecting the economy will grow 1.6 per cent in 2010 and 1.4 per cent in 2011, much higher than in the previous forecast
	President Obama in $50 billion plan to boost jobs
	Trade deficit rises to postwar record
	The CPI rate remains steady at 3.1 per cent partly because of higher commodity prices, in particular wheat which rose by 60 per cent since last year
	US census showed that poverty in the age group 18 to 64 rose 1.3 per cent and is now at 12.9 per cent of the US population
Oct	Ireland's deficit target reached 11.9 per cent of income and the government is expected to make further cuts
	Greece plans to cut it's budget deficit to 7 per cent reaching a deficit of €18.5 billion this year and €16.3 billion for 2011
	Iraq raises oil reserves by nearly 25 per cent
	President of the European Central Bank considers an exit strategy for emergency support to financial institutions following strong eurozone output data and the euro's rise by 5 per cent since August
	IMF report copper and tin price rises
	Eurozone output as a share of total world output is falling
	British Banker's Association announce a £1.5 billion equity fund will be created to ease funding constraints to small and medium-sized enterprises in the UK
	Cost of UK debt falls as Britain's borrowing costs have dropped to the lowest in a generation
	US home values decrease in August, home prices fell 0.2 per cent from August to September
Nov	Sugar prices soar to a 30 year high
	Bank of England keeps interest rates at 0.5 per cent and the quantitative easing package at £200 billion
	Decline in house prices continues, Halifax and Nationwide price indices declined by more than 1 per cent and Royal Institution of Chartered Surveyors housing price index dropped 0.2 per cent in October
	Ireland's borrowing costs rise sharply
	The price of copper reached $9,000 a tonne
	Food sales fell by 2.4 per cent in the three months to October
	EU agrees €85 billion Irish bail-out
Dec	Output grows at fastest rate in 16 years in the manufacturing sector
	China pledges to purchase Greek bonds and increase foreign investment in countries such as Portugal to help tackle the crisis in the eurozone
	Property prices fell by 4 per cent since June
	Private investment in the third quarter was 24 per cent higher than a year ago
	Copper rises to a record of $9,447 a tonne, increasing by more than 50 per cent since June

Main aggregates and summary accounts

Part 1

The Blue Book: 2011 edition

Chapter 1
National Accounts at a glance

Gross domestic product

In 2010 the output of the economy, as measured by the chained volume measure of **gross domestic product** (GDP), was 1.8 per cent higher than in 2009, compared with a fall of 4.4 per cent in 2009 over 2008. The chained volume measure of GDP rose by 52.8 per cent between 1990 and 2010.

Money GDP (at current market prices) increased by 4.6 per cent between 2009 and 2010, compared with a 2.8 per cent fall between 2008 over 2009. Since 1990, money GDP has grown by a factor of 2.6.

Annual changes GDP chained volume measures
Percentage change

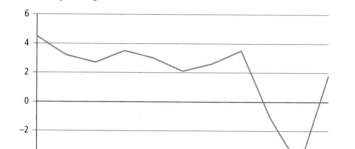

Gross domestic product deflator

This graph shows changes in the implied GDP deflator based on expenditure at market prices.

The annual rate of growth in the GDP expenditure deflator is 2.8 per cent between 2009 and 2010.

Annual changes in the GDP market prices deflator
Percentage change

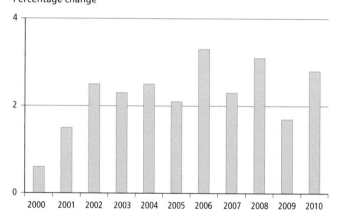

GDP: contribution of expenditure components to growth in 2010

The fall in real GDP of 1.8 per cent in 2010 can be split amongst the various expenditure components. This table shows what effect the change in each component would have had if all other components had remained unchanged. The changes in inventories and growth in households and NPISH final expenditure have been the strongest influences on positive growth. In contrast, net exports showed a negative influence on growth.

Contributions to annual growth in the chained volume measure of GDP, 2010

Component	Change in GDP	
	£ million	Per cent
Households and NPISH final expenditure	9,657	0.7
General government final expenditure	4,808	0.4
GFCF	5,434	0.4
Changes in inventories	17,412	1.3
Net exports	−11,037	−0.8
Other[1]	−2,125	−0.2
Total	24,149	1.8

1 Comprises acquisition of valuables and the statistical discrepancy between the expenditure measure and the average measure of GDP

20

Gross final expenditure at current prices: share by category of expenditure

Gross final expenditure (GFE) measures the sum of final uses of goods and services produced by, or imported to, the UK. In 2010 around 48 per cent of the total GFE was attributed to households and NPISH final consumption. Exports of goods and services accounted for around 23 per cent and the remainder was split between general government consumption (18 per cent) and gross capital formation (12 per cent).

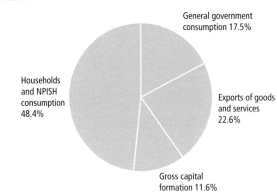

GFE at current prices: share by category of expenditure
Per cent

GDP at current prices: share by category of income

The income approach to GDP measures the income earned by individuals and corporations in the production of goods and services. In 2010 over half (55 per cent) of GDP at current market prices was accounted for by compensation of employees, which is largely comprised of wages and salaries. Total operating surplus, which includes corporations' gross trading profits, accounted for over a quarter (27 per cent). Taxes and subsidies on production and imports, included to convert the estimate to market prices, accounted for 12 per cent.

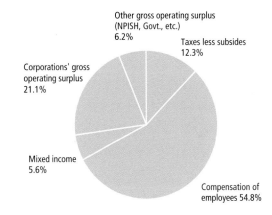

GDP at current market prices: share by category of income
Per cent

Gross value added at basic prices, by industry

In 2010 compared with 2009, the output of the production sector rose by 1.9 per cent, while the service sector rose by 1.2 per cent. The output of the agriculture sector fell by 1.5 per cent.

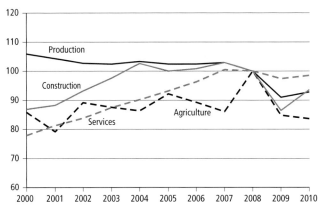

GVA at basic prices, by industry
Index 2008=100

Gross value added at basic prices, by industry, 2008

In 2008, the latest base year, just over 76 per cent of total gross value added was from the service sector, compared with 15 per cent from the production sector. Most of the remainder was attributed to the construction sector.

Gross value added at basic prices, by industry, 2008
Per cent

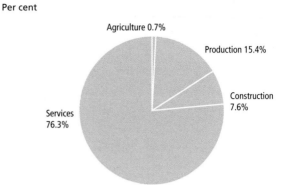

GDP per head

GDP chained volume measures per head rose by 1.4 per cent in 2010 compared with a fall of 5.0 per cent in 2009.

GDP per head
Percentage change

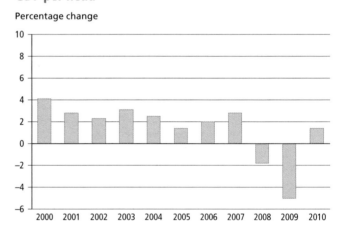

GDP and real household disposable income

Real household disposable income (RHDI) is the total resources available to the households sector after deductions and adjusting for the effects of inflation. RHDI rose by 0.1 per cent in 2010, while the chained volume measure of GDP rose by 1.8 per cent.

Comparison of GDP and real household disposable income
Index 2008=100

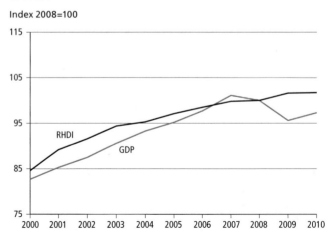

Main aggregates and summary accounts

UK GDP and national income
(Tables 1.1, 1.2, 1.3, 1.4)

Gross domestic product at current prices

The three approaches and the need for balancing

Gross Domestic Product (GDP) is arguably the most important aggregate or summary indicator for purposes of economic analysis and comparisons over time. It measures total domestic activity and can be defined in three different ways:

- GDP is the sum of gross value added of the institutional sectors or the industries *plus* taxes and *less* subsidies on products (which are not allocated to sectors and industries). It is also the balancing item in the total economy production account

- GDP is the sum of final uses of goods and services by resident institutional units (actual final consumption and gross capital formation), *plus* exports and *less* imports of goods and services

- GDP is the sum of uses in the total economy generation of income account (compensation of employees, taxes on production and imports *less* subsidies, gross operating surplus and gross mixed income of the total economy)

This is also the basis of estimating GDP. The use of three different methods which, as far as possible, use independent sources of information avoids sole reliance on one source and allows greater confidence in the overall estimation process.

The resulting estimates however, like all statistical estimates, contain errors and omissions; we obtain the best estimate of GDP (that is, the published figure) by reconciling the estimates obtained from all three approaches. On an annual basis this reconciliation is carried out through the construction of the input-output supply and use tables for the years for which data are available, and for subsequent periods by carrying forward the level of GDP set by the annual balancing process by using the quarterly movements in production, income and expenditure indicators.

For years in which no input-output balance has been struck a statistical discrepancy exists between estimates of the total expenditure components of GDP and the total income components of GDP after the balancing process has been carried out. This statistical discrepancy is made up of two components which are shown in the accounts, namely:

- **the statistical discrepancy (expenditure adjustment)**, which is the difference between the sum of the expenditure components and the definitive estimate of GDP, plus

- **the statistical discrepancy (income adjustment)**, which is the difference between the sum of the income components and the definitive estimate of GDP (with sign reversed)

As outlined in the framework above, the different approaches to the measurement of GDP provide various breakdowns useful for a wide range of economic analyses. These approaches are described in more detail below.

The income approach

The income approach provides estimates of GDP and its 'income' component parts at current market prices. The sources and methods of this approach are described in detail in chapter 14 of *National Accounts Concepts, Sources and Methods*.[1]

As it suggests, the income approach adds up all income earned by resident individuals or corporations in the production of goods and services and is therefore the sum of uses in the generation of income account for the total economy (or alternatively the sum of primary incomes distributed by resident producer units).

However some types of income are not included – these are transfer payments like unemployment benefit, child benefit or state pensions. Although they do provide individuals with money to spend, the payments are made out of, for example, taxes and national insurance contributions. Transfer payments are a **redistribution** of existing incomes and do not themselves represent any addition to current economic activity. To avoid double counting, these transfer payments and other current transfers (for example, taxes on income and wealth) are excluded from the calculation of GDP although they are recorded in the secondary distribution of income account.

In the UK the income approach to GDP is obtained by summing together:

- gross operating surplus
- gross mixed income
- compensation of employees (wages and salaries and employers' social contributions)
- taxes on production and imports

  less any subsidies on production

Mixed income is effectively the operating surplus of unincorporated enterprises owned by households, which implicitly includes remuneration for work done by the owner or other members of the household. This remuneration cannot be identified separately from the return to the owner as entrepreneur.

As most of these incomes are subject to tax, the figures are usually obtained from data collected for tax purposes by HM Revenue & Customs. However, because there is some delay in providing good quality estimates by this method, other sources are used to provide initial estimates.

The operating surplus and mixed income are measures of profit that exclude any holding gains. Holding gains result when, although no new goods or services have been produced, the value of inventories and fixed assets has increased simply as the result of an increase in the price of the item.

The Office for National Statistics (ONS) aims to cover the UK economy as comprehensively as possible. It is recognised that some income is not declared to the tax authorities, and to allow for this adjustments are routinely made to the GDP income measure. In 2008 the adjustment for undeclared income was about, £27.3 billion, approximately 1.9 per cent of GDP.

Although the income approach cannot be used to calculate chained volume measures directly (because it is not possible to separate income components into prices and quantities in the same way as for goods and services) some estimates are obtained indirectly. The expenditure-based **GDP deflator at market prices** (also known as the **index of total home costs**) is used to deflate the current market price estimates to provide a chained volume measure of the total income component of GDP for balancing purposes.

Data on the income components can be found in Table 1.2.

The expenditure approach

The expenditure approach measures total expenditure on finished or final goods and services produced in the domestic economy or, alternatively, the sum of final uses of goods and services by resident institutional units **less** the value of imports of goods and services.

The total is obtained from the sum of final consumption expenditure by households, non-profit institutions serving households and government on goods and services, gross capital formation (capital expenditure on tangible and intangible fixed assets, changes in inventories and acquisitions **less** disposals of valuables) and net exports of goods and services.

This approach can be represented by the following equation:

$$GDP = C + G + I + X - M$$

Where: C = final consumption expenditure by households and NPISH sectors,

G = government consumption expenditure,

I = investment or gross capital formation,

X = exports and M = imports.

The data for these categories are estimated from a wide variety of sources including expenditure surveys, the government's internal accounting system, surveys of traders and the administrative documents used in the importing and exporting of some goods.

To avoid double counting, in this approach it is important to classify consumption expenditures as either final or intermediate. **Final consumption** involves the consumption of goods purchased by or for the ultimate consumer or user. These expenditures are final because the goods are no longer part of the economic flow or being traded in the market place. **Intermediate consumption** on the other hand is consumption of goods and services which are used or consumed in the production process. Gross capital formation is treated separately from intermediate expenditure as the goods involved are not used up within the production process in an accounting period.

Exports include all sales to non-residents, and exports of both goods and services have to be regarded as final consumption expenditure, since they are final as far as the UK economy is concerned.

Imports of goods and services are deducted because although they are included directly or indirectly in final consumption expenditure they are not part of domestic production. What remains is what has been produced in the UK – gross domestic product using the expenditure approach.

Data on the current price expenditure components can be found in Table 1.2.

As well as GDP at current prices, the expenditure approach is used to estimate chained volume measures of GDP. The chained volume measure shows the change in GDP **after** the effects of inflation have been removed (see 'UK GDP Chained Volume Measures').

GDP at market prices (£ million)

	Current prices	Chained volume measures
1996	781,726	1,019,337
1997	830,013	1,054,232
1998	879,152	1,094,704
1999	928,871	1,134,723
2000	976,282	1,185,305
2001	1,021,625	1,222,650
2002	1,075,368	1,255,142
2003	1,139,441	1,299,381
2004	1,202,370	1,337,782
2005	1,254,292	1,365,685
2006	1,328,597	1,401,290
2007	1,405,796	1,449,861
2008	1,433,870	1,433,871
2009	1,393,854	1,371,163
2010	1,458,452	1,395,312

The reference year for the chained volume measure series in this edition of the *Blue Book* is 2008; the chained volume measure of GDP for 2008 is referenced to the annual current price estimate of GDP for 2008.

Two methods are used to remove the effects of inflation to obtain these chained volume measures. For some series, price indices for particular goods and services – such as components of the consumer prices index (CPI) or the producer price index (PPI) – are used to 'deflate' the current price series. For other series, chained volume measures are assumed to be proportional to the volume of goods or services. Chained volume measures of GDP and its main expenditure components can be found in Table 1.3; the calculation of these chained volume measures are explained below.

The production approach

The production approach to the estimation of GDP, which is also referred to as the output approach, looks at the contribution to production of each economic unit; that is the value (at basic prices) of their total output **less** the value of the inputs used up in the production process. The sum of these gross values added, **plus** taxes and **less** subsidies on products for all producers, is GDP at market prices: the production account balancing item. The following paragraphs give a brief overview of the methodology. It should be noted that the production approach concentrates on the basic price concept.

In theory, chained volume measures of value added should be estimated by double deflation; that is, deflating separately the inputs and the outputs of each economic unit (valued in chained volume measures) and then subtracting one from the other. But, because it is hard to get reliable data on intermediate consumption, double deflation is only used in the estimation of output for the agriculture and electricity industries. So for most industries, movements in the chained volume measures for gross value added are estimated by the use of output series. For industries whose outputs are goods, output can be estimated from the physical quantities of goods produced or from the value of output deflated by an index of price.

Apart from the use of output to estimate chained volume measures of value added, which accounts for around 80 per cent of the total of the production measure, a number of other kinds of indicator might be used as a proxy for the change in gross value added. For example, they may be estimated by changes in inputs, where the inputs chosen may be materials used, employment or some combination of these.

In the short-term it is reasonable to assume that movements in value added can be measured this way. However, changes in the ratio of output and inputs to gross value added can be caused by many factors: new production processes, new products made and inputs used, and changes in inputs from other industries will all occur over time. Aggregated over all industries the impact of these changes will be lessened. In the longer term all indicators are under constant review, with more suitable ones being used as they become available.

The estimate of gross value added for all industries (the proxy for the quarterly production approach to GDP) is finally obtained by combining or 'weighting together' the estimates for each industrial sector according to its relative importance (as established in the Input-Output Supply and Use tables). For each year these weights are based on supply and use data for the immediately preceding year, except for the most recent years where the weights are based on supply and use data for 2008 (see 'UK GDP Chained Volume Measures'). Data can be found in Table 2.4.

Headline GDP

The chained volume measure of **gross domestic product at market prices** provides the key indicator of change in the economy: this is sometimes called 'headline' GDP. The chained volume measure of **gross value added at basic prices** (GVA), another useful short-term indicator of growth in the economy, is the headline measure for the production approach. It is compiled in a way which is relatively free of short-term fluctuations due to uncertainties of timing. The construction of chained volume measures of **gross domestic product at factor cost** however, requires an adjustment for the relevant taxes and subsidies which can be subject to erratic changes. As a result the factor cost measure is less suitable as an indicator of short-term movements in the economy.

The figure below shows the distinction between market prices, basic prices and factor cost measures.

ESA95 code	
	Gross domestic product, at market prices
D.211	*Less* value added taxes (VAT) on products
D.212, D.214	*Less* other taxes on products (for example, alcohol duty)
D.31	*Plus* subsidies on products
	Gross value added, at basic prices
D.29	*less* taxes on production other than taxes on products (for example, business rates, vehicle excise duty paid by businesses and operating licences)
	Gross value added, at factor cost

GDP at market prices includes taxes on production, whilst GDP at basic prices includes only those taxes on production, such as business rates which are not taxes on products and GDP at factor cost excludes all taxes on production. A more detailed explanation of taxes follows.

Taxes

Taxes on production and imports including taxes on products (D.2), along with subsidies (D.3) (which can be regarded as negative taxes) make up the factor cost adjustment which represents the difference between GDP at market prices (sum of final expenditures) and GVA at factor cost (sum of incomes). This adjustment has to be added to the sum of incomes to obtain GDP at market prices. The basic price adjustment, which is the sum of **taxes on products** (D.21) *less* **subsidies on products** (D.31), is the difference between GVA at basic prices and GDP at market prices. Details of the taxes which comprise **taxes on production** are included in Table 11.1.

Taxes on production and imports (D.2) are taxes paid during the production or import of goods and services. They are paid irrespective of whether profits are made. They comprise taxes on products (D.21) and other taxes on production (D.29).

Taxes on products (D.21) are taxes paid per unit of good or service produced, sold, leased, transferred, exported or imported. They are included in the prices paid to suppliers of goods and services, so they are included in intermediate consumption at purchasers' prices (except for deductible VAT). Fuel duty is an example.

Deductible VAT differs from other **taxes on products**. It is levied like other **taxes on products** but producers are reimbursed by government for the amount they pay when goods and services are bought. Intermediate consumption at **purchasers' prices** is the price paid less deductible VAT refunded. The value of sales or production at **producers' prices** also excludes any deductible VAT charged.

Suppliers are required to pay to government any **taxes on products** included in their prices. So the supplier's net revenue from selling the good is the selling price less the taxes on products included in the selling price. This is the **basic price**. It is the price at which market output is measured since it represents the producers' actual revenue.

Other taxes on production (D.29) are taxes which producers have to pay but they are not paid when goods and services are bought and so are not included in intermediate consumption. They are levied separately and are usually linked to the use of fixed capital or to the right to undertake certain regulated activities. Examples are non-domestic rates, vehicle excise duty, and various licence fees where the fee is much higher than the cost of administering the licence and so, in effect, is classified as taxation.

Other aggregates – gross national income and gross national disposable income

In the discussions so far we have yet to consider the measure which represents the total **disposable income** of the country's residents. Gross national income (GNI) represents the **total income** of UK residents and is the balancing item of the UK allocation of primary income account. It can also be derived from GDP by adding net employment income and net property income from the rest of the world. However there are two other areas which affect UK residents' command over resources.

First, there are flows into and out of the country which are not concerned with economic production. These are current transfers from abroad and current transfers paid abroad. They include transactions with the European Union, overseas aid and private gifts. An estimate of gross national disposable income (GNDI) is reached by adjusting GNI by the amount of net income received. GNI and GNDI are shown in Table 1.1.

Second, disposable income is affected by the terms of trade effect. Some of the expenditure by UK residents is on imported goods and services; some of the income earned by residents is from exports of goods and services. If UK export prices fall relative to the price of imports then the terms of trade effect would move against the UK; that is, residents would have to sell more exports to be able to continue to buy the same amount of imports. The purchasing power of UK residents would be diminished to this extent. Similarly, if UK export prices rose relative to prices of imports then the effect would be opposite: the purchasing power of residents would rise. An adjustment is made specifically for the terms of trade effect in calculating the chained volume measure of GNDI, also shown in Table 1.1.

UK GDP chained volume measures (Tables 1.1, 1.3, 1.4)

When looking at the change in the economy over time, the main concern is usually whether more goods and services are actually being produced now than at some time in the past. Over time, changes in current price GDP show changes in the monetary value of the components of GDP. As these changes in value can reflect changes in both price and volume, it is difficult to establish how much of an increase in the series is due either to increased activity in the economy or to an increase in the price level. It is therefore useful to measure GDP in real terms (that is, excluding price effects) as well as at current prices. In most cases the revaluation of current price data to remove price effects (known as deflation) is carried out by using price indices such as component series of the consumer prices index or producer price index to deflate current price series at a detailed level of disaggregation. In the 2003 edition of the *Blue Book* a new method of measuring GDP in real terms, **annual chain-linking**, was introduced to replace fixed base chain-linking which was used in previous editions of the *Blue Book*. The real GDP time series produced by annual chain-linking are referred to as **chained volume measures**.

In the UK economic accounts the expenditure approach is used to provide current price and chained volume measures of GDP. Because of the difficulties in accounting for changes in labour productivity it is not possible to obtain direct chained volume measures of GDP from the income data. However, an approximate aggregate measure is calculated by deflating the current price estimates using the GDP deflator derived from the expenditure measure for balancing purposes. The production measure of GDP is largely based on output measures.

The introduction of annual chain-linking

The fixed-base chain-linking method, which was used in editions of the *Blue Book* prior to 2003, produced 'constant price' estimates of GDP whereby the price structure prevailing in 1995 was used to compile data from 1994 onwards. For years prior to 1994 more appropriate pricing structures were used and, in order to link all of the 'constant price' estimates to produce continuous time series, a process of chain-linking was used whereby blocks of constant price data with different price bases were linked together. In the link years, figures were calculated with reference to two consecutive base years to obtain a linking factor so that the whole time series could be shown with reference to the latest base year. This system of fixed-base chain-linking is described in more detail at pages 36 to 38 of the 2002 edition of the *Blue Book*.

In the 2003 edition of the *Blue Book*, the fixed-base chain-linking method was replaced with an annual chain-linking process which produces 'chained volume measures' of GDP. Chained volume measures are calculated by applying the price structure prevailing in the previous year for each year, except the most recent available years where chained volume measures are calculated by applying the price structure prevailing in 2008. The year 2008 is therefore the 'latest base year' for chained volume measures published in this edition of the *Blue Book*. Thus estimates for 2009 and 2010 are based on 2008 prices, estimates for 2008 are based on 2007 prices and so on. These 'previous years prices' data are chain-linked to produce continuous time series called 'chained volume measures', in a similar fashion to the fixed-based chain-linking described in the above paragraph.

These chained volume measure series are shown in £ million and referenced onto the 'latest base year' which is 2008 in this edition of the *Blue Book*. Current price data therefore equals chained volume measures annually in 2008. The process of annually chain-linking 'previous years prices' data onto a continuous time series referenced onto the latest base year results in a loss of additivity in the annual data prior to the latest base year. Thus chained volume measures prior to 2008 are non-additive in this edition of the *Blue Book*. Usually the 'latest base year' and therefore the 'reference year' will move forward by one year.

In the expenditure measure of GDP all of the components are annually chain-linked, as described above, and the chained volume measure of total GDP is aggregated from these. The output approach involves weighting together the detailed components using the contribution to current price GVA (or weight) in the immediately preceding year and annually chain-linking to produce a continuous time series. The application of annual chain-linking to the output measure of GDP is described in detail in an article published in the October 2001 edition of *Economic Trends*.[2]

Annual chain-linking provides more accurate measures of growth in the economy than that provided by the old method of fixed-base chain-linking because more up to date, and therefore more appropriate, price structures are used. The move to annual chain-linking is also consistent with international guidelines laid down in the *System of National Accounts 1993 (SNA93)*.

Index numbers and price indices

Some chained volume measure series are expressed as index numbers in which the series are simply scaled proportionately to a value of 100 in the reference year. These index numbers are volume indices of the 'base weighted' or 'Laspeyres' form (see chapter 2 of *National Accounts Concepts, Sources and Methods*[1]). Aggregate price indices are of the 'Paasche' or 'current-weighted' form. They are generally calculated indirectly by dividing the current price value by the corresponding chained volume measure and multiplying by 100. Examples are the GDP deflator and the households' consumption deflator.

Value indices are calculated by scaling current price values proportionately to a value of 100 in the reference year. By definition such a value index, if divided by the corresponding volume index and multiplied by 100, will give the corresponding price index.

Population, employment and GDP per head (Table 1.5)

Population and employment data are supplementary to the system of accounts. The estimated population of the UK is as at 30 June and includes all those resident in the UK, whatever their nationality. They include members of both UK and non-UK armed forces and their dependants stationed in the UK and exclude members of H.M. armed forces stationed in the rest of the world. This is recognised as not being in strict accord with ESA95 requirements, which are for all UK armed forces and dependants, wherever stationed, to be included and all non-UK ones to be excluded. At present, this is the most appropriate estimate available; it is used to calculate GDP per head.

The total employment data are from the UK Labour Force Survey (LFS) which is recognised as the most appropriate source for coherent national aggregate labour market estimates. The LFS is a household survey which uses definitions which are consistent with the International Labour Organisation recommendations and have been adopted by all EU member countries. The coverage of the LFS is people living in private households and, from 1992, student halls of residence and NHS accommodation; it is not precisely consistent with either the home population data or the ESA95 requirements.

The employment data in the table are estimates of people according to their economic and employment status. They are not comparable with estimates of jobs, as shown in Table 2.5, as some people have more than one job. The total employment figures include people on government sponsored training and employment programmes and unpaid family workers.

UK summary accounts (Tables 1.6.0 – 1.6.9)

The UK summary accounts show the full set of accounts for the UK total economy. The accounts comprise of the goods and services account, the production account, the distribution and use of income account and the accumulation accounts. The structure of the accounts is explained in the introduction.

UK summary accounts by sector (Tables 1.7.1 – 1.7.9)

The framework

As can be seen in Table 1.7, the UK sector accounts can be used to show the economic accounting framework in considerable detail by elaborating the accounts in three different dimensions:

- the institutional sectors
- the types of transaction
- the national and sector balance sheets

The institutional sectors

The first dimension involves the breakdown of the current account into institutional sectors grouped broadly according to their roles in the economy. Examples of these roles are: income distribution, income redistribution, private consumption, collective consumption, investment, financial intermediation, etc. Most units have more than one role but a natural classification is to distinguish between corporations, government and households. The rest of the world sector is also identified as having a role although it is obviously not part of the domestic economy.

The types of transaction

The second dimension is that of the type of transaction which relates to the particular account within which the transaction appears. These can be grouped broadly according to purpose, whether current, capital or financial.

Summary of the UK institutional sectors

Sectors and sub-sectors	ESA95	code
Non-financial corporations	**S.11**	
Public		S.11001
National private and foreign controlled		S.11002/3
Financial corporations	**S.12**	
Central bank		S.121
Other monetary financial institutions		S.122
Other financial intermediaries		S.123
Financial auxiliaries		S.124
Insurance corporations and pension funds		S.125
General government:	**S.13**	
Central government		S.1311
Local government		S.1313
Households	**S.14**	
Non-profit institutions serving households (NPISH)	**S.15**	
Rest of the world	**S.2**	

The balance sheets

To complete the full set of accounts the system includes balance sheets and a reconciliation of the changes that have brought about the change between the beginning and the end of the period. At present the UK does not compile the latter except for the general government sector which are available in the ONS public sector finances release.

In theory the net lending or borrowing from the capital account for each sector should equal the net borrowing or lending from the financial account. In practice, because of errors and omissions in the accounts, a balance is rarely achieved and the difference is known as the **statistical discrepancy** although, across all accounts, when an Input-Output balance is available, these sum to zero. Consolidating the current and accumulation accounts would provide a balanced account which would look like many of the presentations of commercial accounts.

Spurious accuracy and rounding to the nearest £ million

One final point must also be made about the reliability of the statistics. In most of the published tables no attempt is made to round estimates beyond the nearest £ million. In some instances this shows figures which appear to have more precision than evidence warrants.

The reasons for this presentation are as follows:

- rounded figures can distort differences over time or between items

- some of the estimates in the tables are fairly precise and, if such an estimate is small, rounding would unnecessarily distort what it shows; yet if such series were not rounded to the nearest £ million the major aggregates of which they are components would appear precise even though other components were heavily rounded

- not rounding beyond the nearest £ million aids users who prepare derived statistics, by avoiding the accumulation of rounding errors which can occur when a number of rounded numbers are manipulated

- in presenting numbers to the nearest £ million, the rounding is usually such that the components add to the total at current prices, so that the accounts balance. In particular the quarterly estimates, both before and after seasonal adjustment, add up to the calendar year totals. However, there are some small differences between the sum of component series and the total shown, due to rounding

Changes since last year's Blue Book

An analysis of revisions in current prices since last year's *Blue Book* is shown in Table B.

The revisions to the aggregate GDP levels and growth from 1997 to 2009 are as a result of balancing of those years through the supply and use framework and the incorporation of annual benchmark survey estimates, especially the Annual Business Survey. In this year's *Blue Book*, 1997 to 2008 have been re-balanced and 2009 has been balanced for the first time. More details can be found in chapter 2 of this publication. Current price data have been revised from 1997.

Chained volume estimates and index numbers have been updated as the reference year has been advanced from 2006 to 2008. This change has an impact on the entire time series for affected series.

References

1 Office for National Statistics (1998) *National Accounts Concepts, Sources and Methods.* The Stationery Office; London.
http://www.ons.gov.uk/ons/rel/naa1-rd/national-accounts-concepts--sources-and-methods/1998-release/national-accounts-concepts--sources-and-methods.pdf

2 Tuke A and Reed G (2001) The Effects of Annual Chain-linking on the Output Measure of GDP. *Economic Trends* No. 575.
http://www.ons.gov.uk/ons/rel/elmr/economic-trends--discontinued-/no--575--october-2001/the-effects-of-annual-chain-linking-on-the-output-measure-of-gdp.pdf

Blue Book 2011 Articles

Clancy G (2011) Improvements to Household Expenditure Estimates – Q2 2011
http://www.ons.gov.uk/ons/rel/consumer-trends/blue-book-2011--improvements-to-household-expenditure-estimates/q2-2011/art---blue-book-2011--improvements-to-household-expenditure-estimates.html

Drew S and Dunn M (2011) Blue Book 2011: Reclassification of the UK Supply and Use tables
http://www.ons.gov.uk/ons/rel/input-output/input-output-supply-and-use-tables/reclassification-of-the-uk-supply-and-use-tables/index.html

Drew S (2011) Deflation Improvements in the UK National Accounts
http://www.ons.gov.uk/ons/rel/naa1-rd/national-accounts-concepts--sources-and-methods/august-2011/deflation-improvements-in-the-uk-national-accounts.pdf

Duff H (2011) Blue Book 2011: Improvements to GDP(O), IoS and IoP
http://www.ons.gov.uk/ons/dcp171766_229044.pdf

Duff S (2011) Improving the coverage of derivatives in the National Accounts and Balance of Payments
http://www.ons.gov.uk/ons/rel/naa1-rd/united-kingdom-economic-accounts/improving-the-coverage-of-derivatives-data-in-the-national-accounts-and-balance-of-payments/art-improving-the-coverage-of-derivatives-data-in-na-and-bop.html

Economic Review: September 2011
http://www.ons.gov.uk/ons/dcp171766_237189.pdf

Everett G (2011) Content of Blue Book 2011
http://www.ons.gov.uk/ons/rel/naa1-rd/united-kingdom-national-accounts/2011-edition/content-of-blue-book.pdf

Everett G (2011) Historic National Accounts Data Proposals for Blue Book 2011
http://www.ons.gov.uk/ons/rel/naa1-rd/united-kingdom-national-accounts/historic-national-accounts-data-proposals-for-blue-book-2011/ard-historic-national-accounts-data-proposals-fopr-blue-book-2011.pdf

Everett G (2011) Methods Changes in Blue Book 2011
http://www.ons.gov.uk/ons/rel/naa1-rd/united-kingdom-national-accounts/method-changes-in-blue-book-2011/ard-method-changes-in-blue-book-2011.pdf

Lee P, Myers M (2011) Impact of changes in National Accounts and economic commentary for Q2 2011
http://www.ons.gov.uk/ons/rel/naa2/quarterly-national-accounts/impact-of-changes-in-national-accounts-and-economic-commentary-for-q2-2011/ard-impact-of-changes-in-the-national-accounts-and-economic-commentary-for-2011-quarter-2.pdf

McLaren C (2011) Blue Book 2011: Improvements to gross capital formation estimates
http://www.ons.gov.uk/ons/dcp171766_229111.pdf

National Accounts Publication Timetable: September
http://www.ons.gov.uk/ons/media-centre/statements/national-accounts-publication-timetable.html

Other articles

Simkins A (2010) Financial Crisis and Recession: How ONS has addressed the Statistical and Analytical Challenge.
http://www.ons.gov.uk/ons/rel/elmr/economic-and-labour-market-review/no--1--january-2010/financial-crisis-and-recession--how-ons-has-addressed-the-statistical-and-analytical-challenges.pdf

B Revisions since ONS Blue Book, 2010 edition

£ million

	2002	2003	2004	2005	2006	2007	2008	2009
National accounts aggregates								
At current prices								
Gross domestic product at market prices	−196	−305	−586	234	234	951	−11 710	1 149
less Basic price adjustment	−1	–	−4	–	−2	53	69	−59
Gross value added at basic prices	−195	−305	−582	234	236	898	−11 779	1 208
Expenditure components at current prices								
Domestic expenditure on goods and services at market prices								
Households	−315	−96	−260	9	−446	547	−14 170	−14 672
Non-profit making institutions serving households	–	–	–	–	–	−3	−65	−11
General government	−21	−208	−186	185	−25	−919	1 522	−333
Gross fixed capital formation	−18	59	15	−36	−62	519	1 003	4 190
Changes in inventories	117	259	4	−67	−40	409	1 416	3 322
Acquisitions less disposals of valuables	1	–	1	−1	–	91	−53	−148
Total exports	−82	−470	−184	273	1 065	29	−41	8 940
Statistical discrepancy (expenditure)	–	–	−1	–	−1	–	1	2 409
Total imports	−121	−150	−27	130	259	−278	1 323	2 554
Income components at current prices								
Compensation of employees	−553	−898	−345	39	505	−356	1 778	7 093
Gross operating surplus								
Public non-financial corporations	45	−48	−67	−188	78	−35	−133	−171
Private non-financial corporations	−1 112	−3 198	4	−229	−724	2 455	−9 163	−3 159
Financial corporations	73	−153	775	1 188	1 111	−2 090	−5 162	−1 175
General government	–	–	–	–	–	–	–	−127
Household sector	–	−1	−3	−3	−2	−19	−444	44
Mixed income	1 349	3 992	−947	−574	−732	938	1 492	−2 765
Taxes on production and imports	–	–	–	–	−4	19	−105	−823
less subsidies	−2	–	−5	–	–	38	27	77
Statistical discrepancy (income)	3	1	3	−2	−2	2	1	2 148

1.1 UK national and domestic product
Main aggregates: index numbers and values
Current prices and chained volume measures (reference year 2008)

			1997	1998	1999	2000	2001	2002	2003
	INDICES (2008=100)								
	VALUES AT CURRENT PRICES								
B.1*g	Gross domestic product at current market prices ("money GDP")	YBEU	57.9	61.3	64.8	68.1	71.2	75.0	79.5
B.1g	Gross value added at current basic prices	YBEX	57.6	60.9	64.1	67.3	70.7	74.5	79.0
	CHAINED VOLUME MEASURES								
B.1*g	Gross domestic product at market prices	YBEZ	73.5	76.3	79.1	82.7	85.3	87.5	90.6
B.6*g	Gross national disposable income at market prices	YBFP	71.9	75.6	77.5	80.8	84.3	87.5	90.6
B.1g	Gross value added at basic prices	CGCE	73.3	76.3	79.2	82.9	85.3	87.3	90.5
	PRICES								
	Implied deflator of GDP at market prices	YBGB	78.7	80.3	81.9	82.4	83.6	85.7	87.7
	VALUES AT CURRENT PRICES (£ million)								
	Gross measures (before deduction of fixed capital consumption) at current market prices								
B.1*g	Gross domestic product ("money GDP")	YBHA	830 013	879 152	928 871	976 282	1 021 625	1 075 368	1 139 441
D.1+D.4	Employment, property and entrepreneurial income from the rest of the world (receipts *less* payments)	YBGG	325	11 799	−1 042	1 963	9 425	18 503	17 770
−D.21+D.31	Subsidies (receipts) *less* taxes (payments) on products from/to the rest of the world	−QZOZ	−2 919	−3 651	−3 438	−4 098	−3 920	−2 890	−2 596
+D.29-D.39	Other subsidies on production from/to the rest of the world	−IBJL	208	241	338	335	582	519	592
B.5*g	Gross national income (GNI)	ABMX	827 623	887 543	924 729	974 484	1 027 712	1 091 500	1 155 207
D.5,6,7	Current transfers from the rest of the world (receipts *less* payments)	−YBGF	−2 816	−4 764	−4 224	−6 016	−3 182	−6 500	−7 835
B.6*g	Gross national disposable income	NQCO	824 807	882 779	920 505	968 468	1 024 530	1 085 000	1 147 372
	Adjustment to current basic prices								
B.1*g	Gross domestic product (at current market prices)	YBHA	830 013	879 152	928 871	976 282	1 021 625	1 075 368	1 139 441
−D.21 +D.31	Adjustment to current basic prices (*less* taxes *plus* subsidies on products)	−NQBU	−90 571	−97 115	−105 957	−112 246	−114 232	−118 469	−124 738
B.1g	Gross value added (at current basic prices)	ABML	739 442	782 037	822 914	864 036	907 393	956 899	1 014 703
−K.1	*Net measures (after deduction of fixed capital consumption) at current market prices*	−NQAE	−95 179	−98 960	−105 507	−111 251	−115 796	−121 914	−125 603
B.1*n	Net domestic product	NHRK	734 834	780 192	823 364	865 031	905 829	953 454	1 013 838
B.5*n	Net national income	NSRX	732 444	788 583	819 222	863 233	911 916	969 586	1 029 604
B.6*n	Net national disposable income	NQCP	729 628	783 819	814 998	857 217	908 734	963 086	1 021 769
	CHAINED VOLUME MEASURES (Reference year 2008, £ million)								
	Gross measures (before deduction of fixed capital consumption) at market prices								
B.1*g	Gross domestic product	ABMI	1 054 232	1 094 704	1 134 723	1 185 305	1 222 650	1 255 142	1 299 381
TGL	Terms of trade effect ("Trading gain or loss")	YBGJ	−3 113	129	2 257	−1 803	−1 764	5 106	8 274
GDI	Real gross domestic income	YBGL	1 051 119	1 094 833	1 136 980	1 183 502	1 220 886	1 260 248	1 307 655
D.1+D.4	Real employment, property and entrepreneurial income from the rest of the world (receipts *less* payments)	YBGI	411	14 665	−1 274	2 376	11 246	21 691	20 400
−D.21+D.31	Subsidies (receipts) *less* taxes (payments) on products from/to the rest of the world	−QZPB	−3 690	−4 541	−4 202	−4 961	−4 678	−3 388	−2 980
+D.29-D.39	Other subsidies on production from/to the rest of the world	−IBJN	263	300	413	406	695	608	680
B.5*g	Gross national income (GNI)	YBGM	1 048 092	1 105 279	1 131 908	1 181 318	1 228 158	1 279 184	1 325 782
D.5,6,7	Real current transfers from the rest of the world (receipts *less* payments)	−YBGP	−3 561	−5 926	−5 164	−7 283	−3 797	−7 621	−8 995
B.6*g	Gross national disposable income	YBGO	1 044 533	1 099 353	1 126 745	1 174 034	1 224 364	1 271 562	1 316 786
	Adjustment to basic prices								
B.1*g	Gross domestic product (at market prices)	ABMI	1 054 232	1 094 704	1 134 723	1 185 305	1 222 650	1 255 142	1 299 381
−D.21 +D.31	Adjustment to basic prices (*less* taxes *plus* subsidies on products)	−NTAQ	−113 807	−115 557	−117 819	−121 738	−127 762	−133 997	−137 875
B.1g	Gross value added (at basic prices)	ABMM	941 159	979 602	1 017 300	1 064 074	1 095 181	1 121 184	1 161 561
−K.1	*Net measures (after deduction of fixed capital consumption) at market prices[1]*	−CIHA	−109 124	−111 809	−117 106	−120 588	−123 867	−129 469	−130 493
B.5*n	Net national income at market prices	YBET	931 298	983 938	1 004 686	1 049 287	1 092 303	1 137 185	1 181 327
B.6*n	Net national disposable income at market prices	YBEY	927 748	978 013	999 526	1 042 001	1 088 519	1 129 564	1 172 330

1 Capital consumption CVM estimates are still referenced to 2006. Estimates for these series with CVM reference year 2008 will be published in the "Capital Stocks and Capital Consumption" statistical bulletin in 2012.

1.1 continued UK national and domestic product
Main aggregates: index numbers and values
Current prices and chained volume measures (reference year 2008)

			2004	2005	2006	2007	2008	2009	2010
	INDICES (2008=100)								
	VALUES AT CURRENT PRICES								
B.1*g	Gross domestic product at current market prices ("money GDP")	YBEU	83.9	87.5	92.7	98.0	100.0	97.2	101.7
B.1g	Gross value added at current basic prices	YBEX	83.4	87.0	92.2	97.6	100.0	97.9	101.3
	CHAINED VOLUME MEASURES								
B.1*g	Gross domestic product at market prices	YBEZ	93.3	95.2	97.7	101.1	100.0	95.6	97.3
B.6*g	Gross national disposable income at market prices	YBFP	93.2	94.7	96.4	100.5	100.0	94.6	96.0
B.1g	Gross value added at basic prices	CGCE	93.0	95.1	97.5	101.0	100.0	95.4	97.1
	PRICES								
	Implied deflator of GDP at market prices	YBGB	89.9	91.8	94.8	97.0	100.0	101.7	104.5
	VALUES AT CURRENT PRICES (£ million)								
	Gross measures (before deduction of fixed capital consumption) at current market prices								
B.1*g	Gross domestic product ("money GDP")	YBHA	1 202 370	1 254 292	1 328 597	1 405 796	1 433 870	1 393 854	1 458 452
D.1+D.4	Employment, property and entrepreneurial income from the rest of the world (receipts *less* payments)	YBGG	18 029	21 886	9 512	21 369	33 136	20 397	23 039
-D.21+D.31	Subsidies (receipts) *less* taxes (payments) on products from/to the rest of the world	-QZOZ	-1 234	-4 260	-4 496	-4 731	-4 906	-4 238	-5 186
+D.29-D.39	Other subsidies on production from/to the rest of the world	-IBJL	592	3 408	3 221	2 952	3 051	3 411	3 032
B.5*g	Gross national income (GNI)	ABMX	1 219 759	1 275 323	1 336 830	1 425 387	1 465 152	1 413 417	1 479 337
D.5,6,7	Current transfers from the rest of the world (receipts *less* payments)	-YBGF	-9 645	-11 052	-10 610	-11 804	-11 912	-14 290	-17 937
B.6*g	Gross national disposable income	NQCO	1 210 114	1 264 271	1 326 220	1 413 583	1 453 240	1 399 127	1 461 400
	Adjustment to current basic prices								
B.1*g	Gross domestic product (at current market prices)	YBHA	1 202 370	1 254 292	1 328 597	1 405 796	1 433 870	1 393 854	1 458 452
-D.21 +D.31	Adjustment to current basic prices (*less* taxes *plus* subsidies on products)	-NQBU	-132 001	-137 410	-144 657	-153 194	-149 986	-136 922	-157 334
B.1g	Gross value added (at current basic prices)	ABML	1 070 369	1 116 882	1 183 940	1 252 602	1 283 884	1 256 932	1 301 118
-K.1	*Net measures (after deduction of fixed capital consumption) at current market prices*	-NQAE	-135 067	-138 272	-147 323	-154 297	-151 370	-159 862	-164 006
B.1*n	Net domestic product	NHRK	1 067 303	1 116 020	1 181 274	1 251 499	1 282 500	1 233 992	1 294 446
B.5*n	Net national income	NSRX	1 084 692	1 137 051	1 189 507	1 271 090	1 313 782	1 253 555	1 315 331
B.6*n	Net national disposable income	NQCP	1 075 047	1 125 999	1 178 897	1 259 286	1 301 870	1 239 265	1 297 394
	CHAINED VOLUME MEASURES (Reference year 2008, £ million)								
	Gross measures (before deduction of fixed capital consumption) at market prices								
B.1*g	Gross domestic product	ABMI	1 337 782	1 365 685	1 401 290	1 449 861	1 433 871	1 371 163	1 395 312
TGL	Terms of trade effect ("Trading gain or loss")	YBGJ	8 337	280	2 495	2 016	-1	-2 023	-2 961
GDI	Real gross domestic income	YBGL	1 346 119	1 365 965	1 403 785	1 451 877	1 433 870	1 369 140	1 392 351
D.1+D.4	Real employment, property and entrepreneurial income from the rest of the world (receipts *less* payments)	YBGI	20 210	23 866	10 066	22 122	33 136	20 036	21 984
-D.21+D.31	Subsidies (receipts) *less* taxes (payments) on products from/to the rest of the world	-QZPB	-1 383	-4 646	-4 758	-4 898	-4 906	-4 163	-4 948
+D.29-D.39	Other subsidies on production from/to the rest of the world	-IBJN	664	3 716	3 408	3 056	3 051	3 351	2 893
B.5*g	Gross national income (GNI)	YBGM	1 365 637	1 388 923	1 412 542	1 472 183	1 465 151	1 388 364	1 412 280
D.5,6,7	Real current transfers from the rest of the world (receipts *less* payments)	-YBGP	-10 813	-12 054	-11 227	-12 220	-11 912	-14 037	-17 115
B.6*g	Gross national disposable income	YBGO	1 354 824	1 376 871	1 401 315	1 459 964	1 453 239	1 374 327	1 395 165
	Adjustment to basic prices								
B.1*g	Gross domestic product (at market prices)	ABMI	1 337 782	1 365 685	1 401 290	1 449 861	1 433 871	1 371 163	1 395 312
-D.21 +D.31	Adjustment to basic prices (*less* taxes *plus* subsidies on products)	-NTAQ	-144 020	-144 884	-149 352	-153 669	-149 983	-145 769	-149 232
B.1g	Gross value added (at basic prices)	ABMM	1 193 753	1 220 787	1 251 874	1 296 131	1 283 863	1 225 399	1 246 080
-K.1	*Net measures (after deduction of fixed capital consumption) at market prices[1]*	-CIHA	-138 887	-139 711	-146 702	-149 893	-144 846	-150 107	-149 928
B.5*n	Net national income at market prices	YBET	1 212 271	1 234 697	1 251 939	1 310 714	1 313 781	1 242 226	1 262 352
B.6*n	Net national disposable income at market prices	YBEY	1 201 458	1 222 647	1 240 710	1 298 495	1 301 869	1 228 189	1 245 237

[1] Capital consumption CVM estimates are still referenced to 2006. Estimates for these series with CVM reference year 2008 will be published in the "Capital Stocks and Capital Consumption" statistical bulletin in 2012.

1.2 UK gross domestic product and national income
Current prices

£ million

			1997	1998	1999	2000	2001	2002	2003
	GROSS DOMESTIC PRODUCT								
	Gross domestic product: Output								
B.1g	Gross value added, at basic prices								
P.1	Output of goods and services	KN26	1 509 576	1 596 513	1 684 293	1 777 510	1 860 987	1 939 727	2 040 249
-P.2	less intermediate consumption	-KN25	-770 134	-814 475	-861 379	-913 474	-953 594	-982 828	-1 025 546
B.1g	**Total Gross Value Added**	ABML	**739 442**	**782 037**	**822 914**	**864 036**	**907 393**	**956 899**	**1 014 703**
D.211	Value added taxes (VAT) on products	QYRC	54 964	56 541	61 512	64 189	67 097	71 059	77 335
D.212,4	Other taxes on products	NSUI	43 076	46 999	50 511	54 084	52 844	53 946	54 813
-D.31	less subsidies on products	-NZHC	-7 469	-6 425	-6 066	-6 027	-5 709	-6 536	-7 410
B.1*g	**Gross Domestic Product at market prices**	YBHA	**830 013**	**879 152**	**928 871**	**976 282**	**1 021 625**	**1 075 368**	**1 139 441**
	Gross domestic product: Expenditure								
P.3	Final consumption expenditure								
P.41	Actual individual consumption								
P.3	Household final consumption expenditure	ABPB	512 020	546 464	582 295	616 433	647 370	680 649	714 512
P.3	Final consumption expenditure of NPISH	ABNV	19 600	21 082	22 185	23 531	25 111	26 422	27 668
P.31	Individual govt. final consumption expenditure	NNAQ	90 925	96 432	104 385	110 746	119 718	132 003	143 649
P.41	Total actual individual consumption	NQEO	622 545	663 978	708 865	750 710	792 199	839 074	885 829
P.32	Collective govt. final consumption expenditure	NQEP	59 599	60 296	65 282	71 202	74 891	80 553	88 962
P.3	Total final consumption expenditure	ABKW	682 144	724 274	774 147	821 912	867 090	919 627	974 791
P.3	Households and NPISH	NSSG	531 620	567 546	604 480	639 964	672 481	707 071	742 180
P.3	Central government	NMBJ	93 897	97 156	103 594	110 829	118 778	130 348	142 658
P.3	Local government	NMMT	56 627	59 572	66 073	71 119	75 831	82 208	89 953
P.5	Gross capital formation								
P.51	Gross fixed capital formation	NPQX	138 814	156 369	161 846	167 063	171 785	180 533	186 759
P.52	Changes in inventories	ABMP	4 694	4 954	6 045	5 321	6 327	3 026	4 242
P.53	Acquisitions less disposals of valuables	NPJO	-28	430	229	4	396	215	-37
P.5	Total gross capital formation	NQFM	143 479	161 752	168 121	172 387	178 506	183 776	190 965
P.6	Exports of goods and services	KTMW	237 364	233 190	242 614	269 714	276 775	280 454	290 207
-P.7	less imports of goods and services	-KTMX	-232 976	-240 062	-256 009	-287 731	-300 747	-308 488	-316 522
B.11	External balance of goods and services	KTMY	4 388	-6 872	-13 395	-18 017	-23 972	-28 034	-26 315
de	Statistical discrepancy between expenditure components and GDP	RVFD	–	-1	–	–	–	–	–
B.1*g	**Gross Domestic Product at market prices**	YBHA	**830 013**	**879 152**	**928 871**	**976 282**	**1 021 625**	**1 075 368**	**1 139 441**
	Gross domestic product: Income								
B.2g	Operating surplus, gross								
	Non-financial corporations								
	Public non-financial corporations	NRJT	7 230	7 751	7 766	7 103	6 754	6 631	7 152
	Private non-financial corporations	NRJK	171 667	174 309	176 805	180 909	182 932	187 332	197 893
	Financial corporations	NQNV	21 936	17 714	18 552	12 016	13 699	27 198	33 065
	General government	NMXV	9 003	8 999	9 262	9 542	9 796	10 289	10 807
	Households and non-profit institutions serving households	QWLS	38 109	42 229	45 129	49 170	53 000	55 647	60 983
B.2g	Total operating surplus, gross	ABNF	247 945	251 002	257 514	258 740	266 181	287 097	309 900
B.3	Mixed income	QWLT	47 502	50 629	53 801	56 807	60 638	66 316	72 316
D.1	Compensation of employees	HAEA	429 761	465 640	496 097	532 315	564 253	586 843	615 995
D.2	Taxes on production and imports	NZGX	113 226	119 355	128 527	135 358	137 507	143 117	150 665
-D.3	less subsidies	-AAXJ	-8 419	-7 476	-7 067	-6 936	-6 953	-8 009	-9 436
di	Statistical discrepancy between income components and GDP	RVFC	-6	4	–	2	–	3	1
B.1*g	**Gross domestic product at market prices**	YBHA	**830 013**	**879 152**	**928 871**	**976 282**	**1 021 625**	**1 075 368**	**1 139 441**
	GROSS NATIONAL INCOME at market prices								
B.1*g	**Gross Domestic Product at market prices**	YBHA	**830 013**	**879 152**	**928 871**	**976 282**	**1 021 625**	**1 075 368**	**1 139 441**
D.1	Compensation of employees								
	receipts from the rest of the world (ROW)	KTMN	1 007	840	960	1 032	1 087	1 121	1 116
	less payments to the rest of the world (ROW)	-KTMO	-924	-850	-759	-882	-1 021	-1 054	-1 057
D.1	Total	KTMP	83	-10	201	150	66	67	59
-D.21+D.31	less Taxes on products paid to the ROW plus Subsidies received from the ROW	-QZOZ	-2 919	-3 651	-3 438	-4 098	-3 920	-2 890	-2 596
+D.29-D.39	Other subsidies on production	-IBJL	208	241	338	335	582	519	592
D.4	Property and entrepreneurial income								
	receipts from the rest of the world	HMBN	93 360	102 548	100 733	131 902	137 447	120 543	122 069
	less payments to the rest of the world	-HMBO	-93 118	-90 739	-101 976	-130 089	-128 088	-102 107	-104 358
D.4	Total	HMBM	242	11 809	-1 243	1 813	9 359	18 436	17 711
B.5*g	**Gross National Income at market prices**	ABMX	**827 623**	**887 543**	**924 729**	**974 484**	**1 027 712**	**1 091 500**	**1 155 207**

1.2 UK gross domestic product and national income
Current prices (continued)

£ million

			2004	2005	2006	2007	2008	2009	2010
	GROSS DOMESTIC PRODUCT								
	Gross domestic product: Output								
B.1g	Gross value added, at basic prices								
P.1	Output of goods and services[1]	KN26	2 140 984	2 258 356	2 398 550	2 537 820	2 630 445	2 590 111	..
-P.2	less intermediate consumption[1]	-KN25	-1 070 614	-1 141 474	-1 214 609	-1 285 218	-1 346 562	-1 333 179	..
B.1g	**Total Gross Value Added**	ABML	1 070 369	1 116 882	1 183 940	1 252 602	1 283 884	1 256 932	1 301 118
D.211	Value added taxes (VAT) on products	QYRC	81 544	83 425	87 758	92 017	91 952	79 900	95 964
D.212,4	Other taxes on products	NSUI	58 308	59 167	62 865	66 786	63 186	62 729	67 934
-D.31	less subsidies on products	-NZHC	-7 851	-5 182	-5 966	-5 609	-5 152	-5 707	-6 564
B.1*g	**Gross Domestic Product at market prices**	YBHA	**1 202 370**	**1 254 292**	**1 328 597**	**1 405 796**	**1 433 870**	**1 393 854**	**1 458 452**
	Gross domestic product: Expenditure								
P.3	Final consumption expenditure								
P.41	Actual individual consumption								
P.3	Household final consumption expenditure	ABPB	749 607	784 149	819 164	862 242	878 024	858 242	900 204
P.3	Final consumption expenditure of NPISH	ABNV	29 197	30 824	32 408	34 324	35 767	35 863	37 702
P.31	Individual govt. final consumption expenditure	NNAQ	147 751	159 195	172 489	181 762	194 621	206 913	212 764
P.41	Total actual individual consumption	NQEO	926 555	974 168	1 024 061	1 078 328	1 108 412	1 101 018	1 150 670
P.32	Collective govt. final consumption expenditure	NQEP	103 177	109 078	112 637	113 392	120 945	120 436	125 303
P.3	Total final consumption expenditure	ABKW	1 029 732	1 083 246	1 136 698	1 191 720	1 229 357	1 221 454	1 275 973
P.3	Households and NPISH	NSSG	778 804	814 973	851 572	896 566	913 791	894 105	937 906
P.3	Central government	NMBJ	152 274	161 329	173 416	178 058	191 348	199 649	207 349
P.3	Local government	NMMT	98 654	106 944	111 710	117 096	124 218	127 700	130 718
P.5	Gross capital formation								
P.51	Gross fixed capital formation	NPQX	200 430	209 722	227 172	250 036	241 364	209 253	217 108
P.52	Changes in inventories	ABMP	4 890	4 405	5 172	6 224	1 711	-11 651	6 832
P.53	Acquisitions less disposals of valuables	NPJO	-36	-377	285	465	561	429	638
P.5	Total gross capital formation	NQFM	205 285	213 750	232 630	256 725	243 634	198 035	224 577
P.6	Exports of goods and services	KTMW	303 612	331 067	379 091	374 032	422 864	395 588	436 796
-P.7	less imports of goods and services	-KTMX	-336 255	-373 771	-419 822	-416 681	-461 988	-421 225	-476 480
B.11	External balance of goods and services	KTMY	-32 643	-42 704	-40 731	-42 649	-39 124	-25 637	-39 684
de	Statistical discrepancy between expenditure components and GDP	RVFD	-1	–	-1	–	1	–	-2 415
B.1*g	**Gross Domestic Product at market prices**	YBHA	**1 202 370**	**1 254 292**	**1 328 597**	**1 405 796**	**1 433 870**	**1 393 854**	**1 458 452**
	Gross domestic product: Income								
B.2g	Operating surplus, gross								
	Non-financial corporations								
	Public non-financial corporations	NRJT	6 860	8 473	9 628	10 114	8 043	9 496	8 810
	Private non-financial corporations	NRJK	216 750	224 811	244 309	257 995	255 260	233 436	246 074
	Financial corporations	NQNV	33 654	34 323	39 098	43 643	57 758	65 816	52 898
	General government	NMXV	11 312	11 927	12 634	13 231	13 963	14 675	15 500
	Households and non-profit institutions serving households	QWLS	65 752	67 494	69 807	77 768	74 878	57 744	72 098
B.2g	Total operating surplus, gross	ABNF	334 328	347 028	375 476	402 751	409 902	381 167	395 380
B.3	Mixed income	QWLT	73 335	78 487	80 432	82 898	86 376	81 424	81 047
D.1	Compensation of employees	HAEA	646 006	677 517	713 513	751 858	770 969	776 872	799 974
D.2	Taxes on production and imports	NZGX	158 704	162 298	171 454	180 335	178 207	166 823	191 829
-D.3	less subsidies	-AAXJ	-10 005	-11 039	-12 280	-12 047	-11 584	-12 431	-12 819
di	Statistical discrepancy between income components and GDP	RVFC	3	-2	-2	2	1	-8	3 041
B.1*g	**Gross domestic product at market prices**	YBHA	**1 202 370**	**1 254 292**	**1 328 597**	**1 405 796**	**1 433 870**	**1 393 854**	**1 458 452**
	GROSS NATIONAL INCOME at market prices								
B.1*g	**Gross Domestic Product at market prices**	YBHA	1 202 370	1 254 292	1 328 597	1 405 796	1 433 870	1 393 854	1 458 452
D.1	Compensation of employees								
	receipts from the rest of the world (ROW)	KTMN	931	974	938	984	1 046	1 176	1 097
	less payments to the rest of the world (ROW)	-KTMO	-1 425	-1 584	-1 896	-1 718	-1 761	-1 435	-1 486
D.1	Total	KTMP	-494	-610	-958	-734	-715	-259	-389
	less Taxes on products paid to the ROW								
-D.21+D.31	plus Subsidies received from the ROW	-QZOZ	-1 234	-4 260	-4 496	-4 731	-4 906	-4 238	-5 186
+D.29-D.39	Other subsidies on production	-IBJL	592	3 408	3 221	2 952	3 051	3 411	3 032
D.4	Property and entrepreneurial income								
	receipts from the rest of the world	HMBN	137 380	185 640	237 505	291 614	262 842	169 313	162 366
	less payments to the rest of the world	-HMBO	-118 857	-163 144	-227 035	-269 511	-228 991	-148 657	-138 938
D.4	Total	HMBM	18 523	22 496	10 470	22 103	33 851	20 656	23 428
B.5*g	**Gross National Income at market prices**	ABMX	**1 219 759**	**1 275 323**	**1 336 830**	**1 425 387**	**1 465 152**	**1 413 417**	**1 479 337**

1 These series are not available for the latest year

1.3 UK gross domestic product
Chained volume measures (reference year 2008)

£ million

			1997	1998	1999	2000	2001	2002	2003
	GROSS DOMESTIC PRODUCT								
	Gross domestic product: expenditure approach								
P.3	Final consumption expenditure								
P.41	Actual individual consumption								
P.3	Household final consumption expenditure	ABPF	616 065	645 651	680 852	718 644	748 122	781 860	807 653
P.3	Final consumption expenditure of non-profit institutions serving households	ABNU	33 851	35 635	35 944	36 479	37 037	36 615	36 266
P.31	Individual government final consumption expenditure	NSZK	153 473	156 092	159 407	162 056	166 421	172 082	176 681
P.41	Total actual individual consumption	YBIO	798 100	832 937	873 110	915 463	950 375	989 940	1 020 298
P.32	Collective government final consumption expenditure	NSZL	83 729	85 188	90 628	96 429	98 783	103 486	111 027
P.3	Total final consumption expenditure	ABKX	882 203	918 691	964 196	1 012 225	1 049 625	1 093 862	1 131 451
P.5	Gross capital formation								
P.51	Gross fixed capital formation	NPQR	159 082	180 626	185 681	190 453	195 509	202 615	204 883
P.52	Changes in inventories	ABMQ	7 281	5 980	6 393	6 047	7 989	1 862	5 044
P.53	Acquisitions less disposals of valuables	NPJP	−148	550	274	4	457	236	−42
P.5	Total gross capital formation	NPQU	162 445	182 925	188 018	192 052	199 328	200 670	208 248
	Gross domestic final expenditure	YBIK	1 043 490	1 102 010	1 152 231	1 203 797	1 248 470	1 293 540	1 338 724
P.6	Exports of goods and services	KTMZ	265 377	275 661	285 142	312 442	322 079	328 327	334 505
	Gross final expenditure	ABME	1 310 420	1 378 839	1 438 466	1 517 859	1 572 158	1 623 417	1 674 822
−P.7	*less* imports of goods and services	−KTNB	−257 876	−283 985	−303 243	−331 623	−348 298	−366 783	−373 815
de	Statistical discrepancy between expenditure components and GDP	GIXS	–	−1	–	–	–	–	–
B.1*g	**Gross domestic product at market prices**	ABMI	**1 054 232**	**1 094 704**	**1 134 723**	**1 185 305**	**1 222 650**	**1 255 142**	**1 299 381**
B.11	*of which* External balance of goods and services	KTNC	7 501	−8 324	−18 101	−19 181	−26 219	−38 456	−39 310

1.3 UK gross domestic product
Chained volume measures (reference year 2008)

£ million

			2004	2005	2006	2007	2008	2009	2010
	GROSS DOMESTIC PRODUCT								
	Gross domestic product: expenditure approach								
P.3	Final consumption expenditure								
P.41	Actual individual consumption								
P.3	Household final consumption expenditure	ABPF	832 690	851 338	867 082	890 872	878 024	846 961	855 302
P.3	Final consumption expenditure of non-profit institutions serving households	ABNU	36 441	36 334	36 421	36 582	35 767	34 487	35 803
P.31	Individual government final consumption expenditure	NSZK	181 706	185 163	188 485	191 998	194 621	188 270	191 930
P.41	Total actual individual consumption	YBIO	1 050 668	1 072 795	1 091 991	1 119 538	1 108 412	1 069 718	1 083 035
P.32	Collective government final consumption expenditure	NSZL	115 879	118 881	120 132	118 558	120 945	127 111	128 260
P.3	Total final consumption expenditure	ABKX	1 166 570	1 191 701	1 212 138	1 238 115	1 229 353	1 196 821	1 211 287
P.5	Gross capital formation								
P.51	Gross fixed capital formation	NPQR	215 291	220 497	234 572	253 562	241 364	209 051	214 486
P.52	Changes in inventories	ABMQ	5 345	4 925	4 200	7 798	1 710	–12 474	4 940
P.53	Acquisitions less disposals of valuables	NPJP	–41	–412	312	489	561	418	604
P.5	Total gross capital formation	NPQU	218 872	223 272	237 272	260 714	243 635	196 996	220 028
	Gross domestic final expenditure	YBIK	1 384 657	1 414 155	1 449 024	1 499 124	1 472 988	1 393 817	1 431 315
P.6	Exports of goods and services	KTMZ	351 734	378 960	423 242	417 578	422 864	382 886	406 457
	Gross final expenditure	ABME	1 738 028	1 794 294	1 872 175	1 917 438	1 895 852	1 776 703	1 837 772
–P.7	*less* imports of goods and services	–KTNB	–398 915	–428 270	–471 768	–467 579	–461 988	–405 540	–440 151
de	Statistical discrepancy between expenditure components and GDP	GIXS	–1	–	–1	–	1	–	–2 312
B.1*g	**Gross domestic product at market prices**	ABMI	**1 337 782**	**1 365 685**	**1 401 290**	**1 449 861**	**1 433 871**	**1 371 163**	**1 395 312**
B.11	*of which* External balance of goods and services	KTNC	–47 181	–49 310	–48 526	–50 001	–39 124	–22 654	–33 694

1.4 Indices of value, volume, prices and costs

Indices 2008=100

			1997	1998	1999	2000	2001	2002	2003
	INDICES OF VALUE AT CURRENT PRICES								
	Gross measures, before deduction of fixed capital consumption								
	at current market prices								
B.1*g	Gross domestic product at current market prices ("money GDP")	YBEU	57.9	61.3	64.8	68.1	71.2	75.0	79.5
B.5*g	Gross national income at current market prices	YBEV	56.5	60.6	63.1	66.5	70.1	74.5	78.8
B.6*g	Gross national disposable income at current market prices	YBEW	56.8	60.7	63.3	66.6	70.5	74.7	79.0
	at current basic prices								
B.1g	Gross value added at current basic prices	YBEX	57.6	60.9	64.1	67.3	70.7	74.5	79.0
	CHAINED VOLUME INDICES ("real terms")								
	Gross measures, before deduction of fixed capital consumption at market prices								
B.1*g	Gross domestic product at market prices	YBEZ	73.5	76.3	79.1	82.7	85.3	87.5	90.6
	Categories of GDP expenditure								
P.3	Final consumption expenditure	YBFA	71.8	74.7	78.4	82.3	85.4	89.0	92.0
	by households and non-profit institutions serving households	YBFB	70.9	74.4	78.3	82.5	85.8	89.5	92.3
	by general government	YBFC	75.0	76.3	79.1	81.9	84.0	87.3	91.2
P.51	Gross fixed capital formation	YBFG	65.9	74.8	76.9	78.9	81.0	83.9	84.9
	Gross domestic final expenditure	YBFH	70.8	74.8	78.2	81.7	84.8	87.8	90.9
P.6	Exports of goods and services	YBFI	62.8	65.2	67.4	73.9	76.1	77.6	79.1
	of which, goods	YBFJ	71.9	73.2	75.0	83.6	85.4	86.2	86.3
	services	YBFK	48.6	53.1	56.2	59.2	62.4	64.9	68.4
	Gross final expenditure	YBFF	69.1	72.7	75.9	80.1	82.9	85.6	88.3
P.7	Imports of goods and services	YBFL	55.8	61.5	65.6	71.8	75.4	79.4	80.9
	of which, goods	YBFM	57.4	62.7	65.9	72.2	76.2	80.2	81.5
	services	YBFN	50.9	57.6	64.8	70.6	72.9	76.9	79.2
B.5*g	Gross national income at market prices	YBFO	71.5	75.4	77.3	80.6	83.8	87.3	90.5
B.6*g	Gross national disposable income at market prices	YBFP	71.9	75.6	77.5	80.8	84.3	87.5	90.6
	Adjustment to basic prices								
D.21-D.31	Taxes less subsidies on products	YBFQ	75.5	76.9	78.5	81.1	85.1	89.3	91.9
B.1g	Gross value added at basic prices	CGCE	73.3	76.3	79.2	82.9	85.3	87.3	90.5
	PRICE INDICES (IMPLIED DEFLATORS)[1]								
	Categories of GDP expenditure at market prices								
P.3	Final consumption expenditure	YBGA	77.3	78.8	80.3	81.2	82.6	84.1	86.2
	by households and non-profit institutions serving households	YBFS	82.0	83.5	84.5	84.9	85.8	86.4	88.0
	by general government	YBFT	63.6	65.1	67.9	70.4	73.4	77.1	80.8
P.51	Gross fixed capital formation	YBFU	87.3	86.6	87.2	87.7	87.9	89.1	91.2
	Total domestic expenditure	YBFV	79.1	80.4	81.8	82.6	83.8	85.3	87.1
P.6	Exports of goods and services	YBFW	89.4	84.6	85.1	86.3	86.0	85.4	86.8
	of which, goods	BQNK	94.8	88.8	87.9	89.1	87.8	85.8	86.5
	services	FKNW	78.8	76.3	79.6	80.8	82.3	84.7	87.2
	Total final expenditure	YBFY	81.1	81.2	82.4	83.3	84.1	85.2	86.9
P.7	Imports of goods and services	YBFZ	90.3	84.5	84.4	86.8	86.4	84.1	84.7
	of which, goods	BQNL	92.7	85.6	85.5	88.4	87.2	84.3	83.9
	services	FHMA	82.8	81.3	81.2	81.6	83.5	83.4	86.8
B.1*g	Gross domestic product at market prices	YBGB	78.7	80.3	81.9	82.4	83.6	85.7	87.7
	HOME COSTS PER UNIT OF OUTPUT[2]								
B.1*g	Total home costs (based on expenditure components of GDP)	YBGC	78.0	79.3	80.4	80.7	82.4	84.9	87.0
D.1	Compensation of employees	YBGD	75.8	79.1	81.3	83.5	85.8	87.0	88.2
B.2g,B.3g	Gross operating surplus and mixed income	YBGE	81.0	79.6	79.3	76.9	77.2	81.4	85.0

1 Implied deflators are derived by dividing the estimates for each component at current market prices by the corresponding chained volume estimate.
2 These index numbers show how employment and operating incomes relate to the implied deflator of GDP at market prices.

1.4 Indices of value, volume, prices and costs
continued

Indices 2008=100

			2004	2005	2006	2007	2008	2009	2010
	INDICES OF VALUE AT CURRENT PRICES								
	Gross measures, before deduction of fixed capital consumption								
	at current market prices								
B.1*g	Gross domestic product at current market prices ("money GDP")	YBEU	83.9	87.5	92.7	98.0	100.0	97.2	101.7
B.5*g	Gross national income at current market prices	YBEV	83.3	87.0	91.2	97.3	100.0	96.5	101.0
B.6*g	Gross national disposable income at current market prices	YBEW	83.3	87.0	91.3	97.3	100.0	96.3	100.6
	at current basic prices								
B.1g	Gross value added at current basic prices	YBEX	83.4	87.0	92.2	97.6	100.0	97.9	101.3
	CHAINED VOLUME INDICES ("real terms")								
	Gross measures, before deduction of fixed capital consumption at market prices								
B.1*g	Gross domestic product at market prices	YBEZ	93.3	95.2	97.7	101.1	100.0	95.6	97.3
	Categories of GDP expenditure								
P.3	Final consumption expenditure	YBFA	94.9	96.9	98.6	100.7	100.0	97.4	98.5
	by households and non-profit institutions serving households	YBFB	95.1	97.1	98.9	101.5	100.0	96.5	97.5
	by general government	YBFC	94.3	96.4	97.8	98.4	100.0	99.9	101.5
P.51	Gross fixed capital formation	YBFG	89.2	91.4	97.2	105.1	100.0	86.6	88.9
	Gross domestic final expenditure	YBFH	94.0	96.0	98.4	101.8	100.0	94.6	97.2
P.6	Exports of goods and services	YBFI	83.2	89.6	100.1	98.7	100.0	90.5	96.1
	of which, goods	YBFJ	87.4	94.9	107.3	98.1	100.0	88.0	97.1
	services	YBFK	76.8	81.6	89.2	99.7	100.0	94.3	94.7
	Gross final expenditure	YBFF	91.7	94.6	98.7	101.1	100.0	93.7	96.9
P.7	Imports of goods and services	YBFL	86.4	92.7	102.1	101.2	100.0	87.8	95.3
	of which, goods	YBFM	86.9	93.4	104.4	101.3	100.0	87.4	97.5
	services	YBFN	84.7	90.6	95.3	100.8	100.0	88.9	88.6
B.5*g	Gross national income at market prices	YBFO	93.2	94.8	96.4	100.5	100.0	94.8	96.4
B.6*g	Gross national disposable income at market prices	YBFP	93.2	94.7	96.4	100.5	100.0	94.6	96.0
	Adjustment to basic prices								
D.21-D.31	Taxes less subsidies on products	YBFQ	95.9	96.6	99.6	102.4	100.0	97.2	99.5
B.1g	Gross value added at basic prices	CGCE	93.0	95.1	97.5	101.0	100.0	95.4	97.1
	PRICE INDICES (IMPLIED DEFLATORS)[1]								
	Categories of GDP expenditure at market prices								
P.3	Final consumption expenditure	YBGA	88.3	90.9	93.8	96.3	100.0	102.1	105.3
	by households and non-profit institutions serving households	YBFS	89.6	91.8	94.3	96.7	100.0	101.4	105.3
	by general government	YBFT	84.3	88.2	92.4	95.0	100.0	103.8	105.6
P.51	Gross fixed capital formation	YBFU	93.1	95.1	96.8	98.6	100.0	100.1	101.2
	Total domestic expenditure	YBFV	89.2	91.7	94.5	96.6	100.0	101.8	104.8
P.6	Exports of goods and services	YBFW	86.3	87.4	89.6	89.6	100.0	103.3	107.5
	of which, goods	BQNK	86.6	88.4	90.0	89.1	100.0	102.9	108.7
	services	FKNW	85.9	85.8	88.9	90.2	100.0	103.9	105.7
	Total final expenditure	YBFY	88.5	90.7	93.4	95.0	100.0	102.2	105.4
P.7	Imports of goods and services	YBFZ	84.3	87.3	89.0	89.1	100.0	103.9	108.3
	of which, goods	BQNL	83.7	86.7	88.5	88.6	100.0	102.8	107.9
	services	FHMA	86.1	89.0	90.2	90.5	100.0	107.0	109.3
B.1*g	Gross domestic product at market prices	YBGB	89.9	91.8	94.8	97.0	100.0	101.7	104.5
	HOME COSTS PER UNIT OF OUTPUT[2]								
	Total home costs (based on expenditure								
B.1*g	components of GDP)	YBGC	89.4	91.5	94.6	96.7	100.0	102.6	104.0
D.1	Compensation of employees	YBGD	89.8	92.3	94.7	96.4	100.0	105.4	106.6
B.2g,B.3g	Gross operating surplus and mixed income	YBGE	88.0	90.0	94.0	96.8	100.0	97.5	98.7

1 Implied deflators are derived by dividing the estimates for each component at current market prices by the corresponding chained volume estimate.
2 These index numbers show how employment and operating incomes relate to the implied deflator of GDP at market prices.

1.5 Population, employment and GDP per head

			2002	2003	2004	2005	2006	2007	2008	2009	2010
	POPULATION AND EMPLOYMENT (thousands)[1]										
POP	Home population[4]	DYAY	59 319	59 552	59 842	60 235	60 584	60 986	61 398	61 792	62 181
	Household population aged 16+										
ESE	Self-employed[2]	MGRQ	3 336	3 564	3 618	3 634	3 735	3 805	3 823	3 843	3 962
EEM	Employees[2]	MGRN	24 385	24 424	24 642	24 924	25 095	25 212	25 408	24 924	24 852
ETO	Total employment[2,3]	MGRZ	27 920	28 182	28 480	28 770	29 025	29 228	29 440	28 960	29 035
EUN	Unemployed[2]	MGSC	1 529	1 490	1 426	1 467	1 674	1 654	1 783	2 394	2 479
	All economically active[2]	MGSF	29 448	29 672	29 907	30 237	30 698	30 882	31 222	31 355	31 513
	Economically inactive[2]	MGSI	17 344	17 421	17 549	17 644	17 582	17 810	17 862	18 090	18 318
	Total[2]	MGSL	46 792	47 093	47 456	47 881	48 280	48 691	49 084	49 445	49 831
	GROSS DOMESTIC PRODUCT PER HEAD £										
	At current prices										
	Gross domestic product at market prices[4]	IHXT	18 127	19 131	20 089	20 822	21 929	23 050	23 354	22 556	23 527
	Chained volume measures										
	Gross domestic product at market prices[4]	IHXW	21 158	21 817	22 354	22 671	23 130	23 774	23 354	22 190	22 509
	Gross value added at basic prices[4]	YBGT	18 900	19 503	19 947	20 266	20 663	21 253	20 911	19 832	20 100

1 Components may not sum to totals due to rounding.
2 These seasonally adjusted data are 4 quarter annual averages derived from quarterly Labour Force Survey, which does not include those resident in communal establishments except for those in student halls of residence and NHS accommodation.
3 Includes people on Government-supported training and employment programmes and unpaid family workers.
4 These data are consistent with the population estimates published on 23 June 2011.

1.6.0 UK summary accounts
Total economy ESA95 sector S.1

£ million

				2002	2003	2004	2005	2006	2007	2008	2009	2010
0	**GOODS AND SERVICES ACCOUNT**											
	Resources											
P.1	Output											
P.11	Market output[1]	NQAG		1 620 121	1 691 699	1 768 437	1 861 448	1 977 972	2 098 062	2 162 750	2 107 552	..
P.12	Output for own final use[1]	NQAH		80 628	88 271	92 422	97 811	103 044	110 280	116 362	119 347	..
P.13	Other non-market output[1]	NQAI		238 978	260 279	280 125	299 097	317 534	329 478	351 333	363 212	..
P.1	Total output[1]	KN26		1 939 727	2 040 249	2 140 984	2 258 356	2 398 550	2 537 820	2 630 445	2 590 111	..
D.21	Taxes on products	NZGW		125 004	132 148	139 851	142 592	150 623	158 804	155 138	142 629	163 898
-D.31	*less* Subsidies on products	-NZHC		−6 536	−7 410	−7 851	−5 182	−5 966	−5 609	−5 152	−5 707	−6 564
P.7	Imports of goods and services	KTMX		308 488	316 522	336 255	373 771	419 822	416 681	461 988	421 225	476 480
Total	Total resources[1]	NQBM		2 366 683	2 481 509	2 609 239	2 769 537	2 963 029	3 107 696	3 242 419	3 148 258	..
	Uses											
P.2	Intermediate consumption[1]	KN25		982 828	1 025 546	1 070 614	1 141 474	1 214 609	1 285 218	1 346 562	1 333 179	..
P.3	Final consumption expenditure											
P.31	By households	ABPB		680 649	714 512	749 607	784 149	819 164	862 242	878 024	858 242	900 204
P.31	By non-profit institutions serving households	ABNV		26 422	27 668	29 197	30 824	32 408	34 324	35 767	35 863	37 702
P.3	By government											
P.31	For individual consumption	NNAQ		132 003	143 649	147 751	159 195	172 489	181 762	194 621	206 913	212 764
P.32	For collective consumption	NQEP		80 553	88 962	103 177	109 078	112 637	113 392	120 945	120 436	125 303
P.3	Total by government	NMRK		212 556	232 611	250 928	268 273	285 126	295 154	315 566	327 349	338 067
P.3	Total final consumption expenditure[2]	ABKW		919 627	974 791	1 029 732	1 083 246	1 136 698	1 191 720	1 229 357	1 221 454	1 275 973
P.5	Gross capital formation											
P.51	Gross fixed capital formation	NPQX		180 533	186 759	200 430	209 722	227 172	250 036	241 364	209 253	217 108
P.52	Changes in inventories	ABMP		3 026	4 242	4 890	4 405	5 172	6 224	1 711	−11 651	6 832
P.53	Acquisitions less disposals of valuables	NPJO		215	−37	−36	−377	285	465	561	429	638
P.5	Total gross capital formation	NQFM		183 776	190 965	205 285	213 750	232 630	256 725	243 634	198 035	224 577
P.6	Exports of goods and services	KTMW		280 454	290 207	303 612	331 067	379 091	374 032	422 864	395 588	436 796
de	Statistical discrepancy between expenditure components and GDP	RVFD		–	–	−1	–	−1	–	1	–	−2 415
Total	Total uses[1]	NQBM		2 366 683	2 481 509	2 609 239	2 769 537	2 963 029	3 107 696	3 242 419	3 148 258	..

1 These series are not available for the latest year
2 For the total economy, total final consumption expenditure = P.4 actual final consumption

1.6.1 UK summary accounts
Total economy ESA95 sector S.1

£ million

			2002	2003	2004	2005	2006	2007	2008	2009
I	**PRODUCTION ACCOUNT**									
	Resources									
P.1	Output									
P.11	Market output	NQAG	1 620 121	1 691 699	1 768 437	1 861 448	1 977 972	2 098 062	2 162 750	2 107 552
P.12	Output for own final use	NQAH	80 628	88 271	92 422	97 811	103 044	110 280	116 362	119 347
P.13	Other non-market output	NQAI	238 978	260 279	280 125	299 097	317 534	329 478	351 333	363 212
P.1	Total output	KN26	1 939 727	2 040 249	2 140 984	2 258 356	2 398 550	2 537 820	2 630 445	2 590 111
D.21	Taxes on products	NZGW	125 004	132 148	139 851	142 592	150 623	158 804	155 138	142 629
-D.31	less Subsidies on products	-NZHC	-6 536	-7 410	-7 851	-5 182	-5 966	-5 609	-5 152	-5 707
Total	Total resources	NQBP	2 058 196	2 164 987	2 272 985	2 395 766	2 543 207	2 691 014	2 780 431	2 727 033
	Uses									
P.2	Intermediate consumption	KN25	982 828	1 025 546	1 070 614	1 141 474	1 214 609	1 285 218	1 346 562	1 333 179
B.1*g	**Gross domestic product**	YBHA	**1 075 368**	**1 139 441**	**1 202 370**	**1 254 292**	**1 328 597**	**1 405 796**	**1 433 870**	**1 393 854**
Total	Total uses	NQBP	2 058 196	2 164 987	2 272 985	2 395 766	2 543 207	2 691 014	2 780 431	2 727 033
B.1*g	**Gross domestic product**	YBHA	**1 075 368**	**1 139 441**	**1 202 370**	**1 254 292**	**1 328 597**	**1 405 796**	**1 433 870**	**1 393 854**
-K.1	less Fixed capital consumption	-NQAE	-121 914	-125 603	-135 067	-138 272	-147 323	-154 297	-151 370	-159 862
B.1*n	Net domestic product	NHRK	953 454	1 013 838	1 067 303	1 116 020	1 181 274	1 251 499	1 282 500	1 233 992

1.6.2 UK summary accounts
Total economy ESA95 sector S.1

£ million

			2002	2003	2004	2005	2006	2007	2008	2009
II	**DISTRIBUTION AND USE OF INCOME ACCOUNTS**									
II.1	**PRIMARY DISTRIBUTION OF INCOME ACCOUNT**									
II.1.1	**GENERATION OF INCOME ACCOUNT**									
	Resources									
B.1*g	Total resources (gross domestic product)	YBHA	1 075 368	1 139 441	1 202 370	1 254 292	1 328 597	1 405 796	1 433 870	1 393 854
	Uses									
D.1	Compensation of employees									
D.11	Wages and salaries	NQAU	508 704	526 755	549 369	570 242	598 506	632 856	650 573	649 163
D.12	Employers' social contributions	NQAV	78 139	89 240	96 637	107 275	115 007	119 002	120 396	127 709
D.1	Total	HAEA	586 843	615 995	646 006	677 517	713 513	751 858	770 969	776 872
D.2	Taxes on production and imports, paid									
D.21	Taxes on products and imports	QZPQ	125 004	132 148	139 851	142 592	150 627	158 804	155 140	142 632
D.29	Production taxes other than on products	NMYD	18 113	18 517	18 853	19 706	20 831	21 532	23 069	24 194
D.2	Total taxes on production and imports	NZGX	143 117	150 665	158 704	162 298	171 454	180 335	178 207	166 823
-D.3	less Subsidies, received									
-D.31	Subsidies on products	-NZHC	-6 536	-7 410	-7 851	-5 182	-5 966	-5 609	-5 152	-5 707
-D.39	Production subsidies other than on products	-LIUB	-1 473	-2 026	-2 154	-5 857	-6 312	-6 438	-6 432	-6 722
-D.3	Total subsidies on production	-AAXJ	-8 009	-9 436	-10 005	-11 039	-12 280	-12 047	-11 584	-12 431
B.2g	Operating surplus, gross	ABNF	287 097	309 900	334 328	347 028	375 476	402 751	409 902	381 167
B.3g	Mixed income, gross	QWLT	66 316	72 316	73 335	78 487	80 432	82 898	86 376	81 424
di	Statistical discrepancy between income components and GDP	RVFC	3	1	3	-2	-2	2	1	-8
B.1*g	Total uses (gross domestic product)	YBHA	1 075 368	1 139 441	1 202 370	1 254 292	1 328 597	1 405 796	1 433 870	1 393 854
-K.1	After deduction of fixed capital consumption:	-NQAE	-121 914	-125 603	-135 067	-138 272	-147 323	-154 297	-151 370	-159 862
B.2n	Operating surplus, net	NQAR	180 754	199 848	219 429	228 575	251 926	274 400	276 148	240 674
B.3n	Mixed income, net	QWLV	50 745	56 766	53 170	58 671	56 661	56 954	68 769	62 504

1.6.3 UK summary accounts
Total economy ESA95 sector S.1

£ million

				2003	2004	2005	2006	2007	2008	2009	2010
II.1.2	**ALLOCATION OF PRIMARY INCOME ACCOUNT**										
	Resources										
B.2g	Operating surplus, gross	ABNF		309 900	334 328	347 028	375 476	402 751	409 902	381 167	395 380
B.3g	Mixed income, gross	QWLT		72 316	73 335	78 487	80 432	82 898	86 376	81 424	81 047
D.1	Compensation of employees										
D.11	Wages and salaries	NQBI		526 814	548 875	569 632	597 548	632 122	649 858	648 904	661 379
D.12	Employers' social contributions	NQBJ		89 240	96 637	107 275	115 007	119 002	120 396	127 709	138 206
D.1	Total	NVCK		616 054	645 512	676 907	712 555	751 124	770 254	776 613	799 585
di	Statistical discrepancy between income components and GDP	RVFC		1	3	−2	−2	2	1	−8	3 041
D.2	Taxes on production and imports, received										
D.21	Taxes on products										
D.211	Value added tax (VAT)	NZGF		74 595	79 755	81 426	85 591	89 698	89 682	78 307	93 711
D.212	Taxes and duties on imports excluding VAT	NMBU		–	–	–	–	–	–	–	–
D.2121	Import duties	NMXZ		–	–	–	–	–	–	–	–
D.2122	Taxes on imports excluding VAT and import duties	NMBT		–	–	–	–	–	–	–	–
D.214	Taxes on products excluding VAT and import duties	NMYB		52 858	56 138	56 906	60 536	64 374	60 550	60 084	65 001
D.21	Total taxes on products	NVCE		127 453	135 893	138 332	146 127	154 072	150 232	138 391	158 712
D.29	Other taxes on production	NMYD		18 517	18 853	19 706	20 831	21 532	23 069	24 194	27 931
D.2	Total taxes on production and imports, received	NMYE		145 970	154 746	158 038	166 958	175 604	173 301	162 585	186 643
-D.3	*less* Subsidies, paid										
-D.31	Subsidies on products	-NMYF		−5 311	−5 126	−5 182	−5 966	−5 609	−5 152	−5 707	−6 564
-D.39	Other subsidies on production	-LIUF		−1 434	−1 562	−2 449	−3 093	−3 486	−3 381	−3 313	−3 223
-D.3	Total subsidies	-NMRL		−6 745	−6 688	−7 631	−9 059	−9 095	−8 533	−9 020	−9 787
D.4	Property income, received										
D.41	Interest	NHQY		204 963	251 136	310 890	409 825	529 922	518 511	209 477	175 469
D.42	Distributed income of corporations	NHQZ		150 803	157 859	168 948	180 759	183 960	176 995	176 418	175 828
D.43	Reinvested earnings on direct foreign investment	NHSK		21 456	31 076	43 555	47 878	63 738	38 394	13 241	22 920
D.44	Property income attributed to insurance policy holders	QYNF		55 460	55 049	64 703	67 278	72 045	75 551	66 799	63 848
D.45	Rent	NHRP		1 823	1 445	1 492	1 491	1 498	1 437	1 452	1 451
D.4	Total property income	NHRO		434 505	496 565	589 588	707 231	851 163	810 888	467 387	439 516
Total	Total resources	NQBR		1 572 001	1 697 801	1 842 415	2 033 591	2 254 447	2 242 189	1 860 148	1 895 425
	Uses										
D.4	Property income, paid										
D.41	Interest	NHQW		218 174	265 333	332 127	432 367	559 388	549 909	231 165	197 881
D.42	Distributed income of corporations	NHQX		132 665	146 556	157 167	172 387	172 078	147 757	142 385	152 337
D.43	Reinvested earnings on direct foreign investment	NHSJ		7 429	8 558	10 501	22 195	23 276	1 542	4 148	−14
D.44	Property income attributed to insurance policy holders	NQCG		56 703	56 150	65 805	68 321	72 820	76 392	67 581	64 433
D.45	Rent	NHRN		1 823	1 445	1 492	1 491	1 498	1 437	1 452	1 451
D.4	Total property income	NHRL		416 794	478 042	567 092	696 761	829 060	777 037	446 731	416 088
B.5*g	**Gross national income (GNI)**	ABMX		**1 155 207**	**1 219 759**	**1 275 323**	**1 336 830**	**1 425 387**	**1 465 152**	**1 413 417**	**1 479 337**
Total	Total uses	NQBR		1 572 001	1 697 801	1 842 415	2 033 591	2 254 447	2 242 189	1 860 148	1 895 425
-K.1	After deduction of fixed capital consumption	-NQAE		−125 603	−135 067	−138 272	−147 323	−154 297	−151 370	−159 862	−164 006
B.5*n	National income, net	NSRX		1 029 604	1 084 692	1 137 051	1 189 507	1 271 090	1 313 782	1 253 555	1 315 331

1.6.4 UK summary accounts
Total economy ESA95 sector S.1

£ million

				2002	2003	2004	2005	2006	2007	2008	2009	2010
II.2		**SECONDARY DISTRIBUTION OF INCOME OF INCOME ACCOUNT**										
		Resources										
B.5*g		Gross National Income	ABMX	1 091 500	1 155 207	1 219 759	1 275 323	1 336 830	1 425 387	1 465 152	1 413 417	1 479 337
	D.5	Current taxes on income, wealth, etc.										
	D.51	Taxes on income	NMZJ	142 842	144 234	154 127	172 498	192 600	199 851	207 597	185 160	191 342
	D.59	Other current taxes	NVCQ	23 664	26 016	28 001	29 443	30 908	32 697	34 032	34 888	35 847
	D.5	Total	NMZL	166 506	170 250	182 128	201 941	223 508	232 548	241 629	220 048	227 189
	D.61	Social contributions										
	D.611	Actual social contributions										
	D.6111	Employers' actual social contributions	NQDA	64 805	77 571	85 297	94 487	102 133	105 252	105 678	111 115	123 166
	D.6112	Employees' social contributions	NQDE	62 535	66 534	70 300	77 943	83 259	83 437	89 249	83 600	85 957
	D.6113	Social contributions by self- and non-employed persons	NQDI	2 318	2 595	2 727	2 825	2 930	2 861	3 053	2 879	2 576
	D.611	Total	NQCY	129 658	146 700	158 324	175 255	188 322	191 550	197 980	197 594	211 699
	D.612	Imputed social contributions	NQDK	13 334	11 669	11 340	12 788	12 874	13 750	14 718	16 594	15 040
	D.61	Total	NQCX	142 992	158 369	169 664	188 043	201 196	205 300	212 698	214 188	226 739
	D.62	Social benefits other than social transfers in kind	QZQP	182 030	193 573	198 972	212 540	226 994	227 926	252 054	277 534	287 196
	D.7	Other current transfers										
	D.71	Net non-life insurance premiums	NQBY	26 620	23 000	28 148	31 711	34 920	21 862	31 095	28 801	29 824
	D.72	Non-life insurance claims	NQDX	23 631	20 811	25 014	25 594	28 429	18 764	26 672	24 730	25 844
	D.73	Current transfers within general government	NQDY	77 592	85 224	94 720	101 369	110 407	113 108	117 867	124 622	132 444
	D.74	Current international cooperation from institutions of the EC	NQEA	3 112	3 570	3 673	3 726	3 674	3 684	4 996	5 522	3 179
	D.75	Miscellaneous current transfers	QYNA	33 748	35 401	35 599	38 568	39 335	41 074	40 162	42 163	44 147
	D.7	Total other current transfers	NQDU	164 703	168 006	187 154	200 968	216 765	198 492	220 792	225 838	235 438
Total		Total resources	NQBT	1 747 731	1 845 405	1 957 677	2 078 815	2 205 293	2 289 653	2 392 325	2 351 025	2 455 899
		Uses										
	D.5	Current taxes on income, wealth etc.										
	D.51	Taxes on income	NQCR	142 959	144 303	154 180	172 541	192 347	199 797	207 774	185 053	191 413
	D.59	Other current taxes	NQCU	23 664	26 016	28 001	29 443	30 908	32 697	34 032	34 888	35 847
	D.5	Total	NQCQ	166 623	170 319	182 181	201 984	223 255	232 494	241 806	219 941	227 260
	D.61	Social contributions										
	D.611	Actual social contributions										
	D.6111	Employers' actual social contributions	NQDB	64 805	77 571	85 297	94 487	102 133	105 252	105 678	111 115	123 166
	D.6112	Employees' actual social contributions	NQDF	62 458	66 490	70 264	77 929	83 203	83 411	89 181	83 428	85 874
	D.6113	Social contributions by self- and non-employed persons	NQDJ	2 318	2 595	2 727	2 825	2 930	2 861	3 053	2 879	2 576
	D.611	Total actual social contributions	NQCZ	129 581	146 656	158 288	175 241	188 266	191 524	197 912	197 422	211 616
	D.612	Imputed social contributions	QZQQ	13 334	11 669	11 340	12 788	12 874	13 750	14 718	16 594	15 040
	D.61	Total	NQBS	142 915	158 325	169 628	188 029	201 140	205 274	212 630	214 016	226 656
	D.62	Social benefits other than social transfers in kind	NQDN	183 472	195 050	200 593	214 237	228 752	229 787	254 083	279 785	289 420
	D.7	Other current transfers										
	D.71	Net non-life insurance premiums	NQDW	23 631	20 811	25 014	25 594	28 429	18 764	26 672	24 730	25 844
	D.72	Non-life insurance claims	NQBZ	26 620	23 000	28 148	31 711	34 920	21 862	31 095	28 801	29 824
	D.73	Current transfers within general government	NNAF	77 592	85 224	94 720	101 369	110 407	113 108	117 867	124 622	132 444
	D.74	Current international cooperation to institutions of the EC	NMDZ	2 362	2 433	3 080	3 255	3 632	3 930	4 292	5 011	5 683
	D.75	Miscellaneous current transfers	NUHK	39 516	42 871	44 199	48 365	48 538	50 851	50 640	54 992	57 368
		Of which: GNP based fourth own resource	NMFH	5 335	6 772	7 549	8 732	8 521	8 323	8 423	10 555	10 819
	D.7	Total other current transfers	NQDV	169 721	174 339	195 161	210 294	225 926	208 515	230 566	238 156	251 163
B.6*g		Gross national disposable income	NQCO	1 085 000	1 147 372	1 210 114	1 264 271	1 326 220	1 413 583	1 453 240	1 399 127	1 461 400
Total		Total uses	NQBT	1 747 731	1 845 405	1 957 677	2 078 815	2 205 293	2 289 653	2 392 325	2 351 025	2 455 899
	-K.1	After deduction of fixed capital consumption	-NQAE	−121 914	−125 603	−135 067	−138 272	−147 323	−154 297	−151 370	−159 862	−164 006
B.6*n		Disposable income, net	NQCP	963 086	1 021 769	1 075 047	1 125 999	1 178 897	1 259 286	1 301 870	1 239 265	1 297 394

1.6.5 UK summary accounts
Total economy ESA95 sector S.1

£ million

			2002	2003	2004	2005	2006	2007	2008	2009	2010
II.3	**REDISTRIBUTION OF INCOME IN KIND ACCOUNT**										
	Resources										
B.6*g	Gross national disposable income	NQCO	1 085 000	1 147 372	1 210 114	1 264 271	1 326 220	1 413 583	1 453 240	1 399 127	1 461 400
D.63	Social transfers in kind										
D.631	Social benefits in kind										
D.6313	Social assistance benefits in kind	NRNC	–	–	–	–	–	–	–	–	–
D.632	Transfers of individual non-market goods and services	NRNE	158 425	171 317	176 948	190 019	204 897	216 086	230 388	242 776	250 466
D.63	Total social transfers in kind	NRNF	158 425	171 317	176 948	190 019	204 897	216 086	230 388	242 776	250 466
Total	Total resources	NQCB	1 243 425	1 318 689	1 387 062	1 454 290	1 531 117	1 629 669	1 683 628	1 641 903	1 711 866
	Uses										
D.63	Social transfers in kind										
D.631	Social benefits in kind										
D.6313	Social assistance benefits in kind	NRNI	–	–	–	–	–	–	–	–	–
D.632	Transfers of individual non-market goods and services	NRNK	158 425	171 317	176 948	190 019	204 897	216 086	230 388	242 776	250 466
D.63	Total social transfers in kind	NRNL	158 425	171 317	176 948	190 019	204 897	216 086	230 388	242 776	250 466
B.7g	Adjusted disposable income, gross	NRNM	1 085 000	1 147 372	1 210 114	1 264 271	1 326 220	1 413 583	1 453 240	1 399 127	1 461 400
Total	Total uses	NQCB	1 243 425	1 318 689	1 387 062	1 454 290	1 531 117	1 629 669	1 683 628	1 641 903	1 711 866

1.6.6 UK summary accounts
Total economy ESA95 sector S.1

£ million

				2002	2003	2004	2005	2006	2007	2008	2009	2010
II.4		**USE OF INCOME ACCOUNT**										
II.4.1		**USE OF DISPOSABLE INCOME ACCOUNT**										
		Resources										
B.6g		Gross national disposable income	NQCO	1 085 000	1 147 372	1 210 114	1 264 271	1 326 220	1 413 583	1 453 240	1 399 127	1 461 400
D.8		Adjustment for the change in net equity of households in pension funds	NVCI	17 784	21 377	26 386	30 881	29 343	38 871	27 842	26 547	35 105
Total		Total resources	NVCW	1 102 784	1 168 749	1 236 500	1 295 152	1 355 563	1 452 454	1 481 082	1 425 674	1 496 505
		Uses										
P.3		Final consumption expenditure										
P.31		Individual consumption expenditure	NQEO	839 074	885 829	926 555	974 168	1 024 061	1 078 328	1 108 412	1 101 018	1 150 670
P.32		Collective consumption expenditure	NQEP	80 553	88 962	103 177	109 078	112 637	113 392	120 945	120 436	125 303
P.3		Total	ABKW	919 627	974 791	1 029 732	1 083 246	1 136 698	1 191 720	1 229 357	1 221 454	1 275 973
D.8		Adjustment for the change in net equity of households in pension funds	NQEL	17 783	21 373	26 375	30 826	29 334	38 834	27 840	26 506	35 095
B.8g		**Gross saving**	NQET	**165 374**	**172 585**	**180 393**	**181 080**	**189 531**	**221 900**	**223 885**	**177 714**	**185 437**
Total		Total uses	NVCW	1 102 784	1 168 749	1 236 500	1 295 152	1 355 563	1 452 454	1 481 082	1 425 674	1 496 505
-K.1		After deduction of fixed capital consumption	-NQAE	−121 914	−125 603	−135 067	−138 272	−147 323	−154 297	−151 370	−159 862	−164 006
B.8n		Saving, net	NQEJ	43 460	46 982	45 326	42 808	42 208	67 603	72 515	17 852	21 431
II.4.2		**USE OF ADJUSTED DISPOSABLE INCOME ACCOUNT**										
		Resources										
B.7g		Adjusted disposable income	NRNM	1 085 000	1 147 372	1 210 114	1 264 271	1 326 220	1 413 583	1 453 240	1 399 127	1 461 400
D.8		Adjustment for the change in net equity of households in pension funds	NVCI	17 784	21 377	26 386	30 881	29 343	38 871	27 842	26 547	35 105
Total		Total resources	NVCW	1 102 784	1 168 749	1 236 500	1 295 152	1 355 563	1 452 454	1 481 082	1 425 674	1 496 505
		Uses										
P.4		Actual final consumption										
P.41		Actual individual consumption	NQEO	839 074	885 829	926 555	974 168	1 024 061	1 078 328	1 108 412	1 101 018	1 150 670
P.42		Actual collective consumption	NRMZ	80 553	88 962	103 177	109 078	112 637	113 392	120 945	120 436	125 303
P.4		Total actual final consumption	NRMX	919 627	974 791	1 029 732	1 083 246	1 136 698	1 191 720	1 229 357	1 221 454	1 275 973
D.8		Adjustment for the change in net equity of households in pension funds	NQEL	17 783	21 373	26 375	30 826	29 334	38 834	27 840	26 506	35 095
B.8g		**Gross saving**	NQET	**165 374**	**172 585**	**180 393**	**181 080**	**189 531**	**221 900**	**223 885**	**177 714**	**185 437**
Total		Total uses	NVCW	1 102 784	1 168 749	1 236 500	1 295 152	1 355 563	1 452 454	1 481 082	1 425 674	1 496 505

1.6.7 UK summary accounts
Total economy ESA95 sector S.1

£ million

			2002	2003	2004	2005	2006	2007	2008	2009	2010
III	**ACCUMULATION ACCOUNTS**										
III.1	**CAPITAL ACCOUNT**										
III.1.1	**CHANGE IN NET WORTH DUE TO SAVING & CAPITAL TRANSFERS**										
	Changes in liabilities and net worth										
B.8g	Gross saving	NQET	165 374	172 585	180 393	181 080	189 531	221 900	223 885	177 714	185 437
D.9	Capital transfers receivable										
D.91	Capital taxes	NQEY	2 381	2 416	2 881	3 150	3 575	3 867	25 073	4 206	2 643
D.92	Investment grants	NQFB	13 679	17 614	16 898	21 076	21 443	25 092	25 924	33 816	32 194
D.99	Other capital transfers	NQFD	3 612	7 656	7 256	19 387	6 242	7 206	60 743	17 518	5 121
D.9	Total	NQEW	19 672	27 686	27 035	43 613	31 260	36 165	111 740	55 540	39 958
-D.9	*less* Capital transfers payable										
-D.91	Capital taxes	-NQCC	-2 381	-2 416	-2 881	-3 150	-3 575	-3 867	-25 073	-4 206	-2 643
-D.92	Investment grants	-NVDG	-13 646	-17 335	-16 176	-19 990	-21 163	-24 684	-25 026	-33 225	-31 393
-D.99	Other capital transfers	-NQCE	-2 581	-6 398	-5 595	-18 712	-5 555	-5 037	-58 360	-14 845	-2 271
-D.9	Total	-NQCF	-18 608	-26 149	-24 652	-41 852	-30 293	-33 588	-108 459	-52 276	-36 307
B.10.1g	Total change in liabilities and net worth	NQCT	166 438	174 122	182 776	182 841	190 498	224 477	227 166	180 978	189 088
	Changes in assets										
B.10.1g	Changes in net worth due to gross saving and capital transfers	NQCT	166 438	174 122	182 776	182 841	190 498	224 477	227 166	180 978	189 088
-K.1	After deduction of fixed capital consumption	-NQAE	-121 914	-125 603	-135 067	-138 272	-147 323	-154 297	-151 370	-159 862	-164 006
B.10.1n	Changes in net worth due to net saving and capital transfers	NQER	44 524	48 519	47 709	44 569	43 175	70 180	75 796	21 116	25 082
III.1.2	**ACQUISITION OF NON-FINANCIAL ASSETS ACCOUNT**										
	Changes in liabilities and net worth										
B.10.1n	Changes in net worth due to net saving and capital transfers	NQER	44 524	48 519	47 709	44 569	43 175	70 180	75 796	21 116	25 082
K.1	Consumption of fixed capital	NQAE	121 914	125 603	135 067	138 272	147 323	154 297	151 370	159 862	164 006
Total	Total change in liabilities and net worth	NQCT	166 438	174 122	182 776	182 841	190 498	224 477	227 166	180 978	189 088
	Changes in assets										
P.5	Gross capital formation										
P.51	Gross fixed capital formation	NPQX	180 533	186 759	200 430	209 722	227 172	250 036	241 364	209 253	217 108
P.52	Changes in inventories	ABMP	3 026	4 242	4 890	4 405	5 172	6 224	1 711	-11 651	6 832
P.53	Acquisitions less disposals of valuables	NPJO	215	-37	-36	-377	285	465	561	429	638
P.5	Total	NQFM	183 776	190 965	205 285	213 750	232 630	256 725	243 634	198 035	224 577
K.2	Acquisitions less disposals of non-produced non-financial assets	NQFJ	132	71	319	258	-8	11	40	-373	-57
de	Statistical discrepancy between expenditure components and GDP	RVFD	–	–	-1	–	-1	–	1	–	-2 415
B.9	**Net lending(+) / net borrowing(-)**	NQFH	-17 469	-16 914	-22 826	-31 164	-42 120	-32 260	-16 512	-16 679	-33 018
Total	Total change in assets	NQCT	166 438	174 122	182 776	182 841	190 498	224 477	227 166	180 978	189 088

1.6.8 UK summary accounts
Total economy ESA95 sector S.1 Unconsolidated

£ million

			2002	2003	2004	2005	2006
III.2	**FINANCIAL ACCOUNT**						
F.A	Net acquisition of financial assets						
F.1	Monetary gold and special drawing rights (SDRs)	NQAD	−240	−2	−37	−8	47
F.2	Currency and deposits						
F.21	Currency	NYPY	1 680	3 123	5 562	1 075	1 950
F.22	Transferable deposits						
F.221	Deposits with UK monetary financial institutions	NYQC	129 283	227 744	252 848	307 536	448 517
F.229	Deposits with rest of the world monetary financial institutions	NYQK	53 299	190 273	212 662	372 741	277 866
F.29	Other deposits	NYQM	2 464	2 498	3 318	6 109	4 754
F.2	Total currency and deposits	NQAK	186 726	423 638	474 390	687 461	733 087
F.3	Securities other than shares						
F.331	Short term: money market instruments						
F.3311	Issued by UK central government	NYQQ	10 510	442	−975	−2 879	−2 499
F.3312	Issued by UK local government	NYQY	–	–	–	–	–
F.3315	Issued by UK monetary financial institutions	NYRA	6 639	−11 824	46	1 034	8 535
F.3316	Issued by other UK residents	NYRK	−1 969	2 142	−3 136	2 846	6 298
F.3319	Issued by the rest of the world	NYRM	−6 133	12 224	−2 473	7 274	14 806
F.332	Medium (1 to 5 year) and long term (over 5 year) bonds						
F.3321	Issued by UK central government	NYRQ	5 189	20 278	21 568	9 159	16 177
F.3322	Issued by UK local government	NYRW	47	18	−226	213	360
F.3325	Medium term bonds issued by UK MFIs[1]	NYRY	2 463	11 387	11 063	15 105	14 499
F.3326	Other medium & long term bonds issued by UK residents	NYSE	24 816	37 610	32 570	34 342	44 585
F.3329	Long term bonds issued by the rest of the world	NYSG	9 900	818	88 345	84 691	102 366
F.34	Financial derivatives	NYSI	−1 433	5 136	6 752	−5 422	−20 911
F.3	Total securities other than shares	NQAL	50 030	78 230	153 534	146 363	184 216
F.4	Loans						
F.41	Short term loans						
F.411	Loans by UK monetary financial institutions, excluding loans secured on dwellings & financial leasing	NYSS	87 544	159 494	235 848	254 577	305 690
F.42	Long term loans						
F.421	Direct investment	NYTE	26 584	8 912	20 975	25 670	5 462
F.422	Loans secured on dwellings	NYTK	83 644	101 994	102 310	89 948	109 993
F.423	Finance leasing	NYTS	979	1 195	1 153	1 029	958
F.424	Other long-term loans by UK residents	NYTU	5 389	9 801	11 850	40 127	48 473
F.4	Total loans	NQAN	204 140	281 396	372 136	411 351	470 576
F.5	Shares and other equity						
F.51	Shares and other equity, excluding mutual funds' shares						
F.514	Quoted UK shares	NYUG	16 127	1 284	3 360	−54 651	−4 308
F.515	Unquoted UK shares	NYUI	2 159	8 375	11 066	8 149	18 242
F.516	Other UK equity (including direct investment in property)	NYUK	−3 064	−5 504	−3 803	−3 841	−3 529
F.517	UK shares and bonds issued by other UK residents	NSQJ	–	–	–	–	–
F.519	Shares and other equity issued by the rest of the world	NYUQ	55 592	61 972	107 366	119 152	94 291
F.52	Mutual funds' shares						
F.521	UK mutual funds' shares	NYUY	6 251	8 208	3 461	8 251	14 816
F.529	Rest of the world mutual funds' shares	NYVA	−8	41	536	1 810	783
F.5	Total shares and other equity	NQAP	77 057	74 376	121 986	78 870	120 295
F.6	Insurance technical reserves						
F.61	Net equity of households in life assurance and pension funds' reserves	NQAX	46 181	34 441	40 593	52 049	59 327
F.62	Prepayments of insurance premiums and reserves for outstanding claims	NQBD	1 446	2 058	2 454	1 294	1 588
F.6	Total insurance technical reserves	NQAW	47 627	36 499	43 047	53 343	60 915
F.7	Other accounts receivable	NQBK	19 944	11 064	14 663	13 956	81 813
F.A	**Total net acquisition of financial assets**	NQBL	585 284	905 201	1 179 719	1 391 336	1 650 949

1 UK monetary financial institutions

1.6.8 UK summary accounts
Total economy ESA95 sector S.1 Unconsolidated

continued

£ million

			2007	2008	2009	2010
III.2	**FINANCIAL ACCOUNT**					
F.A	**Net acquisition of financial assets**					
F.1	Monetary gold and special drawing rights (SDRs)	NQAD	−50	−24	−132	18
F.2	Currency and deposits					
F.21	Currency	NYPY	1 154	2 439	6 548	1 937
F.22	Transferable deposits					
F.221	Deposits with UK monetary financial institutions	NYQC	323 763	175 589	577 335	−24 482
F.229	Deposits with rest of the world monetary financial institutions	NYQK	516 077	−486 838	−217 063	220 619
F.29	Other deposits	NYQM	12 528	32 469	16 691	−8 823
F.2	Total currency and deposits	NQAK	853 522	−276 341	383 511	189 251
F.3	Securities other than shares					
F.331	Short term: money market instruments					
F.3311	Issued by UK central government	NYQQ	−4 914	841	25 388	−10 407
F.3312	Issued by UK local government	NYQY	–	–	–	–
F.3315	Issued by UK monetary financial institutions	NYRA	3 660	−12 858	−63 596	−19 414
F.3316	Issued by other UK residents	NYRK	−1 882	−1 516	−2 729	799
F.3319	Issued by the rest of the world	NYRM	−2 625	−22 891	14 204	−1 382
F.332	Medium (1 to 5 year) and long term (over 5 year) bonds					
F.3321	Issued by UK central government	NYRQ	11 661	67 523	172 349	91 710
F.3322	Issued by UK local government	NYRW	−9	−70	−83	−17
F.3325	Medium term bonds issued by UK MFIs[1]	NYRY	20 762	14 268	33 376	−1 262
F.3326	Other medium & long term bonds issued by UK residents	NYSE	27 959	136 040	56 755	−35 941
F.3329	Long term bonds issued by the rest of the world	NYSG	68 073	−43 385	148 024	79 734
F.34	Financial derivatives	NYSI	26 969	121 491	−29 194	−32 597
F.3	Total securities other than shares	NQAL	149 654	259 443	354 494	71 223
F.4	Loans					
F.41	Short term loans					
F.411	Loans by UK monetary financial institutions, excluding loans secured on dwellings & financial leasing	NYSS	516 578	26 321	−202 074	−19 767
F.42	Long term loans					
F.421	Direct investment	NYTE	56 427	118 539	−44 235	−6 853
F.422	Loans secured on dwellings	NYTK	107 776	39 822	10 527	6 204
F.423	Finance leasing	NYTS	1 144	546	410	620
F.424	Other long-term loans by UK residents	NYTU	33 783	−20 852	−40 573	15 969
F.4	Total loans	NQAN	715 708	164 376	−275 945	−3 827
F.5	Shares and other equity					
F.51	Shares and other equity, excluding mutual funds' shares					
F.514	Quoted UK shares	NYUG	−17 764	5 000	75 972	−193
F.515	Unquoted UK shares	NYUI	4 169	53 032	28 592	−13 545
F.516	Other UK equity (including direct investment in property)	NYUK	−2 156	−1 078	−539	−483
F.517	UK shares and bonds issued by other UK residents	NSQJ	–	–	–	–
F.519	Shares and other equity issued by the rest of the world	NYUQ	152 954	17 289	33 575	43 247
F.52	Mutual funds' shares					
F.521	UK mutual funds' shares	NYUY	−2 225	−4 618	26 236	43 092
F.529	Rest of the world mutual funds' shares	NYVA	−110	−376	−1 544	−185
F.5	Total shares and other equity	NQAP	134 868	69 249	162 292	71 933
F.6	Insurance technical reserves					
F.61	Net equity of households in life assurance and pension funds' reserves	NQAX	65 107	19 932	20 449	22 058
F.62	Prepayments of insurance premiums and reserves for outstanding claims	NQBD	−1 852	5 668	−1 671	1 150
F.6	Total insurance technical reserves	NQAW	63 255	25 600	18 778	23 208
F.7	Other accounts receivable	NQBK	−15 276	32 515	−6 514	13 576
F.A	**Total net acquisition of financial assets**	NQBL	1 901 681	274 818	636 484	365 382

1 UK monetary financial institutions

1.6.8 UK summary accounts
Total economy ESA95 sector S.1 Unconsolidated
continued

£ million

				2002	2003	2004	2005	2006
III.2		**FINANCIAL ACCOUNT** continued						
F.L		**Net acquisition of financial liabilities**						
F.2		Currency and deposits						
F.21		Currency	NYPZ	1 712	3 174	5 631	1 125	1 899
F.22		Transferable deposits						
F.221		Deposits with UK monetary financial institutions	NYQD	218 055	399 447	541 402	587 184	782 432
F.29		Other deposits	NYQN	2 440	2 730	2 441	6 052	5 228
F.2		Total currency and deposits	NQCK	222 207	405 351	549 474	594 361	789 559
F.3		Securities other than shares						
F.331		Short term: money market instruments						
F.3311		Issued by UK central government	NYQR	10 330	2 592	999	−3 902	−1 752
F.3312		Issued by UK local government	NYQZ	–	–	–	–	–
F.3315		Issued by UK monetary financial institutions	NYRB	25 599	−11 489	8 023	−3 490	53 189
F.3316		Issued by other UK residents	NYRL	8 850	−2 181	−3 043	217	2 800
F.332		Medium (1 to 5 year) and long term (over 5 year) bonds						
F.3321		Issued by UK central government	NYRR	1 555	31 474	34 176	39 820	41 100
F.3322		Issued by UK local government	NYRX	47	18	−226	213	360
F.3325		Medium term bonds issued by UK MFIs[1]	NYRZ	4 238	25 258	29 810	37 843	40 534
F.3326		Other medium & long term bonds issued by UK residents	NYSF	45 132	101 297	88 869	113 814	119 195
F.34		Financial derivatives	NYSJ	−274	−75	–	–	–
F.3		Total securities other than shares	NQCM	95 477	146 894	158 608	184 515	255 426
F.4		Loans						
F.41		Short term loans						
F.411		Loans by UK monetary financial institutions, excl loans secured on dwellings & financial leasing	NYST	70 027	88 503	123 812	119 769	185 854
F.419		Loans by rest of the world monetary financial institutions	NYTB	−33 874	70 716	135 773	221 923	16 120
F.42		Long term loans						
F.421		Direct investment	NYTF	50 445	12 927	18 354	44 408	37 337
F.422		Loans secured on dwellings	NYTL	83 644	101 994	102 310	89 948	109 993
F.423		Finance leasing	NYTT	979	1 195	1 153	1 029	958
F.424		Other long-term loans by UK residents	NYTV	6 847	10 093	11 919	41 750	51 644
F.429		Other long-term loans by the rest of the world	NYTX	−30	124	904	94	228
F.4		Total loans	NQCN	178 038	285 552	394 225	518 921	402 134
F.5		Shares and other equity						
F.51		Shares and other equity, excluding mutual funds' shares						
F.514		Quoted UK shares	NYUH	18 881	14 175	16 625	3 055	21 070
F.515		Unquoted UK shares	NYUJ	16 008	27 066	31 381	49 626	59 371
F.516		Other UK equity (including direct investment in property)	NYUL	−2 316	−5 109	−3 180	−3 244	−3 062
F.517		UK shares and bonds issued by other UK residents	NSQK	–	–	–	–	–
F.52		Mutual funds' shares						
F.521		UK mutual funds' shares	NYUZ	6 259	8 212	3 489	8 300	14 866
F.5		Total shares and other equity	NQCS	38 832	44 344	48 315	57 737	92 245
F.6		Insurance technical reserves						
F.61		Net equity of households in life assurance and pension funds' reserves	NQCD	46 180	34 437	40 582	51 994	59 318
F.62		Prepayments of insurance premiums and reserves for outstanding claims	NQDD	1 781	687	3 778	3 969	6 011
F.6		Total insurance technical reserves	NQCV	47 961	35 124	44 360	55 963	65 329
F.7		Other accounts payable	NQDG	18 974	10 497	14 201	15 074	80 232
F.L		**Total net acquisition of financial liabilities**	NQDH	601 489	927 762	1 209 183	1 426 571	1 684 925
B.9		**Net lending / borrowing**						
F.A		Total net acquisition of financial assets	NQBL	585 284	905 201	1 179 719	1 391 336	1 650 949
−F.L		*less* Total net acquisition of financial liabilities	−NQDH	−601 489	−927 762	−1 209 183	−1 426 571	−1 684 925
B.9f		Net lending (+) / net borrowing (−), from financial account	NQDL	−16 205	−22 561	−29 464	−35 235	−33 976
dB.9f		Statistical discrepancy between financial and non-financial accounts	NYVK	−1 264	5 647	6 638	4 071	−8 144
B.9		**Net lending (+) / net borrowing (−), from capital account**	NQFH	**−17 469**	**−16 914**	**−22 826**	**−31 164**	**−42 120**

1 UK monetary financial institutions

1.6.8 UK summary accounts
Total economy ESA95 sector S.1 Unconsolidated
continued

£ million

			2007	2008	2009	2010
III.2	**FINANCIAL ACCOUNT** continued					
F.L	**Net acquisition of financial liabilities**					
F.2	Currency and deposits					
F.21	Currency	NYPZ	1 165	2 495	6 445	2 140
F.22	Transferable deposits					
F.221	Deposits with UK monetary financial institutions	NYQD	1 004 812	−283 506	253 363	37 671
F.29	Other deposits	NYQN	12 229	32 187	16 892	−8 530
F.2	Total currency and deposits	NQCK	1 018 206	−248 824	276 700	31 281
F.3	Securities other than shares					
F.331	Short term: money market instruments					
F.3311	Issued by UK central government	NYQR	−1 367	13 494	25 975	−2 077
F.3312	Issued by UK local government	NYQZ	–	–	–	–
F.3315	Issued by UK monetary financial institutions	NYRB	17 860	−47 499	22 398	−85 918
F.3316	Issued by other UK residents	NYRL	1 040	1 621	−8 147	4 083
F.332	Medium (1 to 5 year) and long term (over 5 year) bonds					
F.3321	Issued by UK central government	NYRR	38 898	96 058	195 878	170 200
F.3322	Issued by UK local government	NYRX	−9	−70	−83	−17
F.3325	Medium term bonds issued by UK MFIs[1]	NYRZ	57 261	−8 674	60 343	3 031
F.3326	Other medium & long term bonds issued by UK residents	NYSF	149 773	316 106	64 582	26 219
F.34	Financial derivatives	NYSJ	–	–	–	–
F.3	Total securities other than shares	NQCM	263 456	371 036	360 946	115 521
F.4	Loans					
F.41	Short term loans					
F.411	Loans by UK monetary financial institutions, excl loans secured on dwellings & financial leasing	NYST	290 051	148 979	−84 674	−36 856
F.419	Loans by rest of the world monetary financial institutions	NYTB	55 061	−276 464	−54 457	154 843
F.42	Long term loans					
F.421	Direct investment	NYTF	8 696	86 748	−43 649	17 352
F.422	Loans secured on dwellings	NYTL	107 776	39 822	10 527	6 204
F.423	Finance leasing	NYTT	1 144	546	410	620
F.424	Other long-term loans by UK residents	NYTV	34 230	−20 517	−40 557	15 791
F.429	Other long-term loans by the rest of the world	NYTX	−25	414	405	−245
F.4	Total loans	NQCN	496 933	−20 472	−211 995	157 709
F.5	Shares and other equity					
F.51	Shares and other equity, excluding mutual funds' shares					
F.514	Quoted UK shares	NYUH	13 738	59 888	120 762	21 725
F.515	Unquoted UK shares	NYUJ	92 874	89 525	76 905	−240
F.516	Other UK equity (including direct investment in property)	NYUL	202	415	−7	49
F.517	UK shares and bonds issued by other UK residents	NSQK	–	–	–	–
F.52	Mutual funds' shares					
F.521	UK mutual funds' shares	NYUZ	−2 204	−4 607	26 271	43 136
F.5	Total shares and other equity	NQCS	104 610	145 221	223 931	64 670
F.6	Insurance technical reserves					
F.61	Net equity of households in life assurance and pension funds' reserves	NQCD	65 070	19 930	20 408	22 048
F.62	Prepayments of insurance premiums and reserves for outstanding claims	NQDD	−6 075	1 754	−1 953	1 344
F.6	Total insurance technical reserves	NQCV	58 995	21 684	18 455	23 392
F.7	Other accounts payable	NQDG	−15 537	32 158	−6 788	14 326
F.L	**Total net acquisition of financial liabilities**	NQDH	1 926 663	300 803	661 249	406 899
B.9	**Net lending / borrowing**					
F.A	Total net acquisition of financial assets	NQBL	1 901 681	274 818	636 484	365 382
-F.L	*less* Total net acquisition of financial liabilities	-NQDH	−1 926 663	−300 803	−661 249	−406 899
B.9f	Net lending (+) / net borrowing (-), from financial account	NQDL	−24 982	−25 985	−24 765	−41 517
dB.9f	Statistical discrepancy between financial and non-financial accounts	NYVK	−7 278	9 473	8 086	8 499
B.9	**Net lending (+) / net borrowing (-), from capital account**	NQFH	−32 260	−16 512	−16 679	−33 018

1 UK monetary financial institutions

1.6.9 UK summary accounts
Total economy ESA95 sector S.1 Unconsolidated

£ billion

			2002	2003	2004	2005	2006
IV.3	**FINANCIAL BALANCE SHEET** at end of period						
AN	**Non-financial assets**	CGJB	5 079.4	5 523.5	6 078.1	6 299.0	6 871.0
AF.A	**Financial assets**						
AF.1	Monetary gold and special drawing rights (SDRs)	NYVN	2.4	2.6	2.5	3.2	3.4
AF.2	Currency and deposits						
AF.21	Currency	NYVV	40.5	43.6	49.1	50.1	52.0
AF.22	Transferable deposits						
AF.221	Deposits with UK monetary financial institutions institutions	NYVZ	1 595.3	1 913.5	2 125.9	2 473.9	2 957.8
AF.229	Deposits with rest of the world monetary financial institutions	NYWH	1 203.3	1 399.9	1 605.3	2 055.5	2 189.5
AF.29	Other deposits	NYWJ	73.6	75.1	78.4	85.5	90.1
AF.2	Total currency and deposits	NYVT	2 912.7	3 432.0	3 858.7	4 665.0	5 289.4
AF.3	Securities other than shares						
AF.331	Short term: money market instruments						
AF.3311	Issued by UK central government	NYWP	21.2	22.1	21.2	18.3	15.8
AF.3312	Issued by UK local government	NYWX	–	–	–	–	–
AF.3315	Issued by UK monetary financial institutions	NYWZ	162.3	151.5	152.5	155.6	165.7
AF.3316	Issued by other UK residents	NYXJ	21.0	21.8	10.8	13.4	19.1
AF.3319	Issued by the rest of the world	NYXL	48.7	62.0	58.3	63.8	75.5
AF.332	Medium (1 to 5 year) and long term (over 5 year) bonds						
AF.3321	Issued by UK central government	NYXP	254.8	265.8	289.1	313.5	315.8
AF.3322	Issued by UK local government	NYXV	0.8	0.8	0.6	0.8	1.2
AF.3325	Medium term bonds issued by UK MFIs[1]	NYXX	37.4	53.3	63.8	80.0	91.0
AF.3326	Other medium & long term bonds issued by UK residents	NYYD	288.7	319.8	355.0	417.4	472.0
AF.3329	Long term bond issued by the rest of the world	NYYF	538.2	550.1	611.3	717.2	798.3
AF.34	Financial derivatives	NYYH	0.2	–	1 367.6	1 650.4	1 727.2
AF.3	Total securities other than shares	NYWL	1 373.4	1 447.4	2 930.3	3 430.4	3 681.7
AF.4	Loans						
AF.41	Short term loans						
AF.411	Loans by UK monetary financial institutions, excluding loans secured on dwellings & financial leasing	NYYT	1 142.5	1 283.9	1 487.7	1 754.5	1 969.0
AF.42	Long term loans						
AF.421	Direct investment	NYZF	176.2	175.3	205.5	222.6	224.1
AF.422	Loans secured on dwellings	NYZL	669.4	772.9	881.1	965.4	1 077.2
AF.423	Finance leasing	NYZT	27.2	28.3	29.5	30.5	31.5
AF.424	Other long-term loans by UK residents	NYZV	164.8	177.0	196.6	207.0	247.8
AF.4	Total loans	NYYP	2 180.0	2 437.5	2 800.3	3 180.0	3 549.6
AF.5	Shares and other equity						
AF.51	Shares and other equity, excluding mutual funds' shares						
AF.514	Quoted UK shares	NZAJ	707.4	833.6	891.4	985.1	1 065.3
AF.515	Unquoted UK shares	NZAL	373.3	414.8	456.1	504.7	549.3
AF.516	Other UK equity (including direct investment in property)	NZAN	97.2	105.8	114.6	130.8	122.1
AF.517	UK shares and bonds issued by other UK residents	NSRC	–	–	–	–	–
AF.519	Shares and other equity issued by the rest of the world	NZAT	931.3	1 049.0	1 128.8	1 348.3	1 459.0
AF.52	Mutual funds' shares						
AF.521	UK mutual funds' shares	NZBB	214.9	265.2	302.7	383.5	450.7
AF.529	Rest of the world mutual fund share	NZBD	1.4	1.4	1.7	4.1	6.0
AF.5	Total shares and other equity	NYZZ	2 325.5	2 669.8	2 895.4	3 356.6	3 652.4
AF.6	Insurance technical reserves						
AF.61	Net equity of households in life assurance and pension funds' reserves	NZBH	1 384.1	1 509.2	1 603.2	1 894.3	2 071.7
AF.62	Prepayments of insurance premiums and reserves for outstanding claims	NZBN	50.1	53.2	55.7	57.0	58.6
AF.6	Total insurance technical reserves	NZBF	1 434.2	1 562.4	1 658.9	1 951.3	2 130.3
AF.7	Other accounts receivable	NZBP	290.7	318.6	337.5	346.1	417.0
AF.A	**Total financial assets**	NZBV	10 518.9	11 870.3	14 483.6	16 932.6	18 723.8

1 UK monetary financial institutions

1.6.9 UK summary accounts
Total economy ESA95 sector S.1 Unconsolidated

£ billion

			2007	2008	2009	2010
IV.3	**FINANCIAL BALANCE SHEET** at end of period					
AN	**Non-financial assets**	CGJB	7 393.8	6 858.5	6 942.0	7 530.3
AF.A	**Financial assets**					
AF.1	Monetary gold and special drawing rights (SDRs)	NYVN	4.3	6.3	15.7	18.2
AF.2	Currency and deposits					
AF.21	Currency	NYVV	53.1	55.7	62.1	64.0
AF.22	Transferable deposits					
AF.221	Deposits with UK monetary financial institutions institutions	NYVZ	2 752.3	3 164.3	3 453.5	3 344.3
AF.229	Deposits with rest of the world monetary financial institutions	NYWH	2 768.0	3 029.5	2 589.6	2 798.0
AF.29	Other deposits	NYWJ	102.6	135.3	151.1	165.9
AF.2	Total currency and deposits	NYVT	5 676.0	6 384.8	6 256.3	6 372.2
AF.3	Securities other than shares					
AF.331	Short term: money market instruments					
AF.3311	Issued by UK central government	NYWP	10.8	10.5	38.0	27.5
AF.3312	Issued by UK local government	NYWX	–	–	–	–
AF.3315	Issued by UK monetary financial institutions	NYWZ	164.8	158.0	92.2	72.4
AF.3316	Issued by other UK residents	NYXJ	16.9	14.5	12.1	13.8
AF.3319	Issued by the rest of the world	NYXL	76.4	72.2	85.2	87.7
AF.332	Medium (1 to 5 year) and long term (over 5 year) bonds					
AF.3321	Issued by UK central government	NYXP	332.7	414.6	573.4	687.1
AF.3322	Issued by UK local government	NYXV	1.2	1.1	1.0	1.0
AF.3325	Medium term bonds issued by UK MFIs[1]	NYXX	118.4	157.4	181.2	180.6
AF.3326	Other medium & long term bonds issued by UK residents	NYYD	475.3	465.0	592.7	559.5
AF.3329	Long term bond issued by the rest of the world	NYYF	903.5	1 076.0	1 176.1	1 304.2
AF.34	Financial derivatives	NYYH	2 821.7	9 611.5	5 275.2	6 406.3
AF.3	Total securities other than shares	NYWL	4 921.6	11 980.7	8 027.2	9 340.0
AF.4	Loans					
AF.41	Short term loans					
AF.411	Loans by UK monetary financial institutions, excluding loans secured on dwellings & financial leasing	NYYT	2 537.7	2 990.4	2 504.8	2 472.8
AF.42	Long term loans					
AF.421	Direct investment	NYZF	269.9	376.1	369.7	362.8
AF.422	Loans secured on dwellings	NYZL	1 181.6	1 225.8	1 234.9	1 239.0
AF.423	Finance leasing	NYZT	32.6	33.2	33.7	34.3
AF.424	Other long-term loans by UK residents	NYZV	271.5	295.2	307.1	406.0
AF.4	Total loans	NYYP	4 293.3	4 920.6	4 450.2	4 514.9
AF.5	Shares and other equity					
AF.51	Shares and other equity, excluding mutual funds' shares					
AF.514	Quoted UK shares	NZAJ	1 008.6	599.7	845.9	928.2
AF.515	Unquoted UK shares	NZAL	541.2	528.2	626.1	665.6
AF.516	Other UK equity (including direct investment in property)	NZAN	120.5	123.7	119.0	118.1
AF.517	UK shares and bonds issued by other UK residents	NSRC	–	–	–	–
AF.519	Shares and other equity issued by the rest of the world	NZAT	1 620.1	1 596.0	1 648.7	1 799.3
AF.52	Mutual funds' shares					
AF.521	UK mutual funds' shares	NZBB	505.6	381.1	504.9	616.8
AF.529	Rest of the world mutual fund share	NZBD	4.5	2.3	0.8	0.7
AF.5	Total shares and other equity	NYZZ	3 800.5	3 231.0	3 745.4	4 128.7
AF.6	Insurance technical reserves					
AF.61	Net equity of households in life assurance and pension funds' reserves	NZBH	2 168.7	1 867.4	2 141.8	2 270.2
AF.62	Prepayments of insurance premiums and reserves for outstanding claims	NZBN	56.7	62.4	60.7	61.9
AF.6	Total insurance technical reserves	NZBF	2 225.4	1 929.8	2 202.5	2 332.0
AF.7	Other accounts receivable	NZBP	397.3	405.8	399.2	408.8
AF.A	**Total financial assets**	NZBV	21 318.5	28 859.1	25 096.5	27 114.8

1 UK monetary financial institutions

1.6.9 UK summary accounts
Total economy ESA95 sector S.1 Unconsolidated

continued

£ billion

			2002	2003	2004	2005	2006
IV.3	**FINANCIAL BALANCE SHEET** continued at end of period						
AF.L	**Financial liabilities**						
AF.2	Currency and deposits						
AF.21	Currency	NYVW	41.1	44.2	49.8	50.9	52.8
AF.22	Transferable deposits						
AF.221	Deposits with UK monetary financial institutions	NYWA	3 034.7	3 518.7	3 981.1	4 673.7	5 328.5
AF.29	Other deposits	NYWK	75.3	77.0	79.4	86.5	91.5
AF.2	Total currency and deposits	NYVU	3 151.1	3 639.9	4 110.4	4 811.0	5 472.7
AF.3	Securities other than shares						
AF.331	Short term: money market instruments						
AF.3311	Issued by UK central government	NYWQ	21.4	24.0	25.0	21.1	19.4
AF.3312	Issued by UK local government	NYWY	–	–	–	–	–
AF.3315	Issued by UK monetary financial institutions	NYXA	302.6	282.1	283.2	291.7	327.7
AF.3316	Issued by other UK residents	NYXK	51.6	45.6	33.3	35.5	35.4
AF.332	Medium (1 to 5 year) and long term (over 5 year) bonds						
AF.3321	Issued by UK central government	NYXQ	311.1	331.9	372.9	424.2	451.3
AF.3322	Issued by UK local government	NYXW	0.8	0.8	0.6	0.8	1.2
AF.3325	Medium term bonds issued by UK MFIs[1]	NYXY	81.0	107.0	134.7	175.4	205.8
AF.3326	Other medium & long term bonds issued by UK residents	NYYE	517.6	615.5	716.8	880.9	1 001.1
AF.34	Financial derivatives	NYYI	–	–	1 373.2	1 661.0	1 764.0
AF.3	Total securities other than shares	NYWM	1 286.2	1 407.0	2 939.8	3 490.8	3 805.9
AF.4	Loans						
AF.41	Short term loans						
AF.411	Loans by UK monetary financial institutions, excluding loans secured on dwellings & financial leasing	NYYU	814.1	885.5	991.3	1 112.5	1 259.9
AF.419	Loans by rest of the world monetary financial institutions	NYZC	438.9	512.2	637.6	887.3	872.3
AF.42	Long term loans						
AF.421	Direct investment	NYZG	284.1	280.6	305.1	358.7	376.8
AF.422	Loans secured on dwellings	NYZM	669.4	772.9	881.1	965.4	1 077.2
AF.423	Finance leasing	NYZU	27.2	28.3	29.5	30.5	31.5
AF.424	Other long-term loans by UK residents	NYZW	157.5	169.9	189.2	199.6	242.4
AF.429	Other long-term loans by the rest of the world	NYZY	2.0	2.2	3.2	3.2	3.4
AF.4	Total loans	NYYQ	2 393.2	2 651.6	3 037.0	3 557.2	3 863.5
AF.5	Shares and other equity						
AF.51	Shares and other equity, excluding mutual funds' shares						
AF.514	Quoted UK shares	NZAK	1 126.1	1 334.0	1 441.7	1 644.5	1 804.5
AF.515	Unquoted UK shares	NZAM	609.8	670.2	729.5	853.4	1 002.2
AF.516	Other UK equity (including direct investment in property)	NZAO	113.1	121.7	132.4	149.2	142.3
AF.517	UK shares and bonds issued by other UK residents	NSRD	–	–	–	–	–
AF.52	Mutual funds' shares						
AF.521	UK mutual funds' shares	NZBC	215.8	266.3	303.9	385.0	452.4
AF.5	Total shares and other equity	NZAA	2 064.7	2 392.2	2 607.5	3 032.1	3 401.4
AF.6	Insurance technical reserves						
AF.61	Net equity of households in life assurance and pension funds' reserves	NZBI	1 384.3	1 509.4	1 603.4	1 894.5	2 071.9
AF.62	Prepayments of insurance premiums and reserves for outstanding claims	NZBO	62.8	63.5	67.2	71.2	77.2
AF.6	Total insurance technical reserves	NZBG	1 447.1	1 572.9	1 670.6	1 965.7	2 149.1
AF.7	Other accounts payable	NZBQ	288.6	315.8	335.6	345.3	415.1
AF.L	**Total financial liabilities**	NZBW	10 630.9	11 979.4	14 700.9	17 202.2	19 107.6
BF.90	**Net financial assets / liabilities**						
AF.A	Total financial assets	NZBV	10 518.9	11 870.3	14 483.6	16 932.6	18 723.8
-AF.L	*less* Total financial liabilities	-NZBW	–10 630.9	–11 979.4	–14 700.9	–17 202.2	–19 107.6
BF.90	**Net financial assets (+) / liabilities (-)**	NQFT	–112.0	–109.2	–217.3	–269.6	–383.8
	Net worth						
AN	Non-financial assets	CGJB	5 079.4	5 523.5	6 078.1	6 299.0	6 871.0
BF.90	Net financial assets (+) / liabilities (-)	NQFT	–112.0	–109.2	–217.3	–269.6	–383.8
B.90	**Net worth**	CGDA	4 967.4	5 414.3	5 860.8	6 029.4	6 487.2

1 UK monetary financial institutions

1.6.9 UK summary accounts
Total economy ESA95 sector S.1 Unconsolidated

£ billion

			2007	2008	2009	2010
IV.3	**FINANCIAL BALANCE SHEET** continued at end of period					
AF.L	**Financial liabilities**					
AF.2	Currency and deposits					
AF.21	Currency	NYVW	53.9	56.3	62.7	64.7
AF.22	Transferable deposits					
AF.221	Deposits with UK monetary financial institutions	NYWA	5 895.8	6 761.5	6 429.8	6 412.9
AF.29	Other deposits	NYWK	103.7	136.1	152.1	167.3
AF.2	Total currency and deposits	NYVU	6 053.4	6 953.9	6 644.6	6 644.9
AF.3	Securities other than shares					
AF.331	Short term: money market instruments					
AF.3311	Issued by UK central government	NYWQ	18.0	31.5	57.5	55.4
AF.3312	Issued by UK local government	NYWY	–	–	–	–
AF.3315	Issued by UK monetary financial institutions	NYXA	348.5	360.3	360.1	278.3
AF.3316	Issued by other UK residents	NYXK	36.0	44.4	33.6	39.1
AF.332	Medium (1 to 5 year) and long term (over 5 year) bonds					
AF.3321	Issued by UK central government	NYXQ	492.8	618.2	797.7	996.2
AF.3322	Issued by UK local government	NYXW	1.2	1.1	1.0	1.0
AF.3325	Medium term bonds issued by UK MFIs[1]	NYXY	285.3	357.6	389.2	384.6
AF.3326	Other medium & long term bonds issued by UK residents	NYYE	1 081.2	1 222.7	1 447.2	1 407.8
AF.34	Financial derivatives	NYYI	2 835.7	9 486.5	5 195.6	6 338.4
AF.3	Total securities other than shares	NYWM	5 098.7	12 122.4	8 281.8	9 500.9
AF.4	Loans					
AF.41	Short term loans					
AF.411	Loans by UK monetary financial institutions, excluding loans secured on dwellings & financial leasing	NYYU	1 581.7	1 862.6	1 601.3	1 501.5
AF.419	Loans by rest of the world monetary financial institutions	NYZC	949.4	901.3	795.9	957.6
AF.42	Long term loans					
AF.421	Direct investment	NYZG	338.5	425.5	421.9	439.2
AF.422	Loans secured on dwellings	NYZM	1 181.6	1 225.8	1 234.9	1 239.0
AF.423	Finance leasing	NYZU	32.6	33.2	33.7	34.3
AF.424	Other long-term loans by UK residents	NYZW	266.3	288.1	301.2	399.9
AF.429	Other long-term loans by the rest of the world	NYZY	3.3	3.9	4.4	4.5
AF.4	Total loans	NYYQ	4 353.5	4 740.4	4 393.2	4 576.0
AF.5	Shares and other equity					
AF.51	Shares and other equity, excluding mutual funds' shares					
AF.514	Quoted UK shares	NZAK	1 791.8	1 134.7	1 599.3	1 789.8
AF.515	Unquoted UK shares	NZAM	1 063.1	1 119.5	1 225.2	1 291.1
AF.516	Other UK equity (including direct investment in property)	NZAO	145.3	147.7	143.6	144.6
AF.517	UK shares and bonds issued by other UK residents	NSRD	–	–	–	–
AF.52	Mutual funds' shares					
AF.521	UK mutual funds' shares	NZBC	507.3	382.1	506.2	618.4
AF.5	Total shares and other equity	NZAA	3 507.5	2 784.0	3 474.2	3 844.0
AF.6	Insurance technical reserves					
AF.61	Net equity of households in life assurance and pension funds' reserves	NZBI	2 168.9	1 867.6	2 142.0	2 270.4
AF.62	Prepayments of insurance premiums and reserves for outstanding claims	NZBO	71.1	72.9	70.9	72.3
AF.6	Total insurance technical reserves	NZBG	2 240.0	1 940.5	2 212.9	2 342.7
AF.7	Other accounts payable	NZBQ	393.8	401.6	393.9	403.6
AF.L	**Total financial liabilities**	NZBW	21 646.9	28 942.9	25 400.6	27 312.1
BF.90	**Net financial assets / liabilities**					
AF.A	Total financial assets	NZBV	21 318.5	28 859.1	25 096.5	27 114.8
-AF.L	*less* Total financial liabilities	-NZBW	–21 646.9	–28 942.9	–25 400.6	–27 312.1
BF.90	**Net financial assets (+) / liabilities (-)**	NQFT	–328.4	–83.8	–304.1	–197.3
	Net worth					
AN	Non-financial assets	CGJB	7 393.8	6 858.5	6 942.0	7 530.3
BF.90	Net financial assets (+) / liabilities (-)	NQFT	–328.4	–83.8	–304.1	–197.3
B.90	**Net worth**	CGDA	7 065.4	6 774.7	6 637.9	7 333.0

1 UK monetary financial institutions

1.7A UK summary accounts 2007

Total economy: all sectors and the rest of the world

£ million

		RESOURCES						USES	TOTAL
		UK total economy	Non-financial corporations	Financial corporations	General government	Households & NPISH	Not sector-ised	Rest of the world	Goods & services
		S.1	S.11	S.12	S.13	S.14+S.15	S.N	S.2	
	Current accounts								
I	**PRODUCTION / EXTERNAL**								
0	**ACCOUNT OF GOODS AND SERVICES**								
P.7	Imports of goods and services							416 681	416 681
P.6	Exports of goods and services								374 032 374 032
P.1	Output at basic prices	2 537 820	1 617 114	185 253	330 431	405 022			2 537 820
P.2	Intermediate consumption								1 285 218 1 285 218
D.21-D.31	Taxes less subsidies on products	153 194					153 194		153 194
II.1.1	**GENERATION OF INCOME**								
B.1g	Gross domestic product, value added at market prices	1 405 796	761 028	98 139	166 956	226 478	153 195		1 405 796
B.11	External balance of goods and services							42 649	42 649
II.1.2	**ALLOCATION OF PRIMARY INCOME**								
D.1	Compensation of employees	751 124				751 124		1 718	752 842
D.21-D.31	Taxes less subsidies on products	148 463			148 463			4 731	153 194
D.29-D.39	Other taxes less subsidies on production	15 094	16 310	1 676	–	–2 892		–2 952	12 142
B.2g	Operating surplus, gross	402 751	268 109	43 643	13 231	77 768			402 751
B.3g	Mixed income, gross	82 898				82 898			82 898
di	Statistical discrepancy between income components and GDP	2					2		2
D.4	Property income	851 163	120 666	537 305	12 915	180 277		269 511	1 120 674
II.2	**SECONDARY DISTRIBUTION OF INCOME**								
B.5g	National income, balance of primary incomes, gross	1 425 387	208 266	42 015	157 863	1 017 241	2		1 425 387
D.5	Current taxes on income, wealth etc	232 548			232 548			549	233 097
D.61	Social contributions	205 300	4 824	84 376	115 582	518		–	205 300
D.62	Social benefits other than social transfers in kind	227 926				227 926		1 861	229 787
D.7	Other current transfers	198 492	4 007	22 277	117 610	54 598		20 319	218 811
II.3	**REDISTRIBUTION OF INCOME IN KIND**								
B.6g	Disposable income, gross	1 413 583	169 375	70 903	290 907	882 396	2		1 413 583
D.63	Social transfers in kind	216 086				216 086			216 086
II.4	**USE OF INCOME**								
B.7g	Adjusted disposable income, gross	1 413 583	169 375	70 903	109 145	1 064 158	2		1 413 583
B.6g	Disposable income, gross	1 413 583	169 375	70 903	290 907	882 396	2		1 413 583
P.4	Actual final consumption								1 191 720 1 191 720
P.3	Final consumption expenditure								1 191 720 1 191 720
D.8	Adjustment for change in households' net equity in pension funds	38 871				38 871		–37	38 834
	Accumulation accounts								
III.1.1	**CHANGE IN NET WORTH DUE TO SAVING AND CAPITAL TRANSFERS**								
B.8g	Saving, gross	221 900	169 375	32 069	–4 247	24 701	2		221 900
B.12	Current external balance							34 826	34 826
D.9	Capital transfers receivable	36 165	8 420	388	16 918	10 439		1 233	37 398
D.9	Capital transfers payable	–33 588	–880	–388	–27 326	–4 994		–3 810	–37 398
III.1.2	**ACQUISITION ON NON-FINANCIAL ASSETS**								
	Changes in liabilities and net worth								
B.10.1.g	Changes in net worth due to saving and capital transfers	224 477	176 915	32 069	–14 655	30 146	2	32 249	256 726
P.51	Gross fixed capital formation								250 036 250 036
-K.1	(Consumption of fixed capital)								
P.52	Changes in inventories								6 224 6 224
P.53	Acquisitions less disposals of valuables								465 465
K.2	Acquisitions less disposals of non-produced non-financial assets								
de	Statistical discrepancy between expenditure components and GDP								– –
III.2	**FINANCIAL ACCOUNT**								
B.9	Net lending(+) / net borrowing(-)	–32 260	38 279	23 611	–38 331	–55 821	2	32 260	–
	Changes in liabilities								
F.2	Currency and deposits	1 018 206	–	1 010 154	8 052	–		516 111	1 534 317
F.3	Securities other than shares	263 456	24 652	199 702	37 522	1 580		92 417	355 873
F.4	Loans	496 933	128 830	244 956	2 015	121 132		282 507	779 440
F.5	Shares and other equity	104 610	60 222	44 388		–		152 844	257 454
F.6	Insurance technical reserves	58 995		58 995					58 995
F.7	Other accounts payable	–15 537	2 947	–9 953	–2 059	–6 472		506	–15 031

1.7A UK summary accounts 2007
Total economy: all sectors and the rest of the world
continued

£ million

		USES					RESOURCES	TOTAL
		UK total economy S.1	Non-financial corporations S.11	Financial corporations S.12	General government S.13	Households & NPISH S.14+S.15	Not sectorised S.N	Rest of the world S.2	Goods & services
	Current accounts								
I	**PRODUCTION / EXTERNAL**								
0	**ACCOUNT OF GOODS AND SERVICES**								
P.7	Imports of goods and services							416 681	416 681
P.6	Exports of goods and services							374 032	374 032
P.1	Output at basic prices								2 537 820	2 537 820
P.2	Intermediate consumption	1 285 218	856 086	87 114	163 475	178 544			1 285 218
D.21-D.31	Taxes *less* subsidies on products								153 194	153 194
B.1g	**Gross domestic product, value added at market prices**	**1 405 796**	**761 028**	**98 139**	**166 956**	**226 478**	**153 195**		**1 405 796**
B.11	External balance of goods and services							42 649	42 649
II.1.1	**GENERATION OF INCOME**								
D.1	Compensation of employees	751 858	476 609	52 820	153 725	68 704		984	752 842
D.21-D.31	Taxes *less* subsidies on products	153 195					153 195		153 195
D.29-D.39	Other taxes *less* subsidies on production	15 094			15 094				15 094
B.2g	Operating surplus, gross	402 751	268 109	43 643	13 231	77 768			402 751
B.3g	Mixed income, gross	82 898				82 898			82 898
di	Statistical discrepancy between income components and GDP	2					2		2
II.1.2	**ALLOCATION OF PRIMARY INCOME**								
D.4	Property income	829 060	180 509	538 933	34 792	74 826		291 614	1 120 674
B.5g	National income, balance of primary incomes, gross	1 425 387	208 266	42 015	157 863	1 017 241	2		1 425 387
II.2	**SECONDARY DISTRIBUTION OF INCOME**								
D.5	Current taxes on income, wealth etc	232 494	38 403	9 866	1 111	183 114		603	233 097
D.61	Social contributions	205 274				205 274		26	205 300
D.62	Social benefits other than social transfers in kind	229 787	4 824	45 542	178 407	1 014			229 787
D.7	Other current transfers	208 515	4 495	22 357	153 178	28 485		10 296	218 811
B.6g	Disposable income, gross	1 413 583	169 375	70 903	290 907	882 396	2		1 413 583
II.3	**REDISTRIBUTION OF INCOME IN KIND**								
B.7g	Adjusted disposable income, gross	1 413 583	169 375	70 903	109 145	1 064 158	2		1 413 583
D.63	Social transfers in kind	216 086			181 762	34 324			216 086
II.4	**USE OF INCOME**								
B.6g	Disposable income, gross								
P.4	Actual final consumption	1 191 720			113 392	1 078 328			1 191 720
P.3	Final consumption expenditure	1 191 720			295 154	896 566			1 191 720
D.8	Adjustment for change in households' net equity in pension funds	38 834		38 834					38 834
B.8g	Saving, gross	221 900	169 375	32 069	−4 247	24 701	2		221 900
B.12	Current external balance							34 826	34 826
	Accumulation accounts								
	CHANGE IN NET WORTH								
III.1.1	**DUE TO SAVING AND CAPITAL TRANSFERS**								
D.9	Capital transfers receivable								
D.9	Capital transfers payable								
B.10.1.g	Changes in net worth due to saving and capital transfers	224 477	176 915	32 069	−14 655	30 146	2	32 249	256 726
III.1.2	**ACQUISITION OF NON-FINANCIAL ASSETS**								
	Changes in assets								
P.51	Gross fixed capital formation	250 036	129 503	8 048	26 306	86 180			250 036
−K.1	(Consumption of fixed capital)	−154 297	−83 243	−5 919	−13 231	−51 904			−154 297
P.52	Changes in inventories	6 224	5 953	28	−14	257			6 224
P.53	Acquisitions less disposals of valuables	465	207	378	10	−130			465
K.2	Acquisitions less disposals of non-produced non-financial assets	11	2 973	4	−2 626	−340		−11	−
de	Statistical discrepancy between expenditure components and GDP	−					−		−
B.9	**Net lending(+) / net borrowing(−)**	−32 260	38 279	23 611	−38 331	−55 821	2	32 260	−
III.2	**FINANCIAL ACCOUNT: changes in assets**								
F.1	Monetary gold and SDRs	−50			−50			50	
F.2	Currency and deposits	853 522	98 425	653 137	10 126	91 834		680 795	1 534 317
F.3	Securities other than shares	149 654	−2 241	157 841	276	−6 222		206 219	355 873
F.4	Loans	715 708	52 177	667 354	5 803	−9 626		63 732	779 440
F.5	Shares and other equity	134 868	98 961	108 836	−8 525	−64 404		122 586	257 454
F.6	Insurance technical reserves	63 255	−3 571	−424	82	67 168		−4 260	58 995
F.7	Other accounts receivable	−15 276	1 764	−6 269	−1 414	−9 357		245	−15 031
dB.9f	Statistical discrepancy between non-financial and financial transactions	−7 278	9 415	−8 622	901	−8 974	2	7 278	−

1.7B UK summary accounts 2008

Total economy: all sectors and the rest of the world

£ million

		RESOURCES						USES	TOTAL
		UK total economy	Non-financial corporations	Financial corporations	General government	Households & NPISH	Not sector -ised	Rest of the world	Goods & services
		S.1	S.11	S.12	S.13	S.14+S.15	S.N	S.2	

Current accounts

I 0	**PRODUCTION / EXTERNAL ACCOUNT OF GOODS AND SERVICES**								
P.7	Imports of goods and services							461 988	461 988
P.6	Exports of goods and services							422 864	422 864
P.1	Output at basic prices	2 630 445	1 656 538	203 551	351 817	418 539			2 630 445
P.2	Intermediate consumption							1 346 562	1 346 562
D.21-D.31	Taxes *less* subsidies on products	149 986					149 986		149 986
II.1.1	**GENERATION OF INCOME**								
B.1g	**Gross domestic product, value added at market prices**	**1 433 870**	**770 684**	**112 222**	**171 632**	**229 346**	**149 988**		**1 433 870**
B.11	External balance of goods and services							39 124	39 124
II.1.2	**ALLOCATION OF PRIMARY INCOME**								
D.1	Compensation of employees	770 254				770 254		1 761	772 015
D.21-D.31	Taxes *less* subsidies on products	145 080			145 080			4 906	149 986
D.29-D.39	Other taxes *less* subsidies on production	16 637	17 562	2 076	–	–3 001		–3 051	13 586
B.2g	Operating surplus, gross	409 902	263 303	57 758	13 963	74 878			409 902
B.3g	Mixed income, gross	86 376				86 376			86 376
di	Statistical discrepancy between income components and GDP	1					1		1
D.4	Property income	810 888	109 895	511 749	14 659	174 585		228 991	1 039 879
II.2	**SECONDARY DISTRIBUTION OF INCOME**								
B.5g	National income, balance of primary incomes, gross	1 465 152	201 507	68 302	156 889	1 038 453	1		1 465 152
D.5	Current taxes on income, wealth etc	241 629			241 629			793	242 422
D.61	Social contributions	212 698	5 763	84 953	121 458	524		–	212 698
D.62	Social benefits other than social transfers in kind	252 054				252 054		2 029	254 083
D.7	Other current transfers	220 792	5 682	31 686	123 745	59 679		22 362	243 154
II.3	**REDISTRIBUTION OF INCOME IN KIND**								
B.6g	Disposable income, gross	1 453 240	160 174	84 417	293 553	915 095	1		1 453 240
D.63	Social transfers in kind	230 388				230 388			230 388
II.4	**USE OF INCOME**								
B.7g	Adjusted disposable income, gross	1 453 240	160 174	84 417	98 932	1 109 716	1		1 453 240
B.6g	Disposable income, gross	1 453 240	160 174	84 417	293 553	915 095	1		1 453 240
P.4	Actual final consumption							1 229 357	1 229 357
P.3	Final consumption expenditure							1 229 357	1 229 357
D.8	Adjustment for change in households' net equity in pension funds	27 842				27 842		–2	27 840

Accumulation accounts

III.1.1	**CHANGE IN NET WORTH DUE TO SAVING AND CAPITAL TRANSFERS**								
B.8g	Saving, gross	223 885	160 174	56 577	–22 013	29 146	1		223 885
B.12	Current external balance							19 753	19 753
D.9	Capital transfers receivable	111 740	9 278	27 187	40 171	35 104		1 308	113 048
D.9	Capital transfers payable	–108 459	–918	–22 034	–56 747	–28 760		–4 589	–113 048
III.1.2	**ACQUISITION ON NON-FINANCIAL ASSETS**								
	Changes in liabilities and net worth								
B.10.1.g	Changes in net worth due to saving and capital transfers	227 166	168 534	61 730	–38 589	35 490	1	16 472	243 638
P.51	Gross fixed capital formation							241 364	241 364
-K.1	(Consumption of fixed capital)								
P.52	Changes in inventories							1 711	1 711
P.53	Acquisitions less disposals of valuables							561	561
K.2	Acquisitions less disposals of non-produced non-financial assets								
de	Statistical discrepancy between expenditure components and GDP							1	1
III.2	**FINANCIAL ACCOUNT**								
B.9	Net lending(+) / net borrowing(-)	–16 512	31 231	52 755	–70 457	–30 040	–1	16 512	–
	Changes in liabilities								
F.2	Currency and deposits	–248 824	–	–269 813	20 989	–		–486 919	–735 743
F.3	Securities other than shares	371 036	3 552	257 177	109 482	825		55 215	426 251
F.4	Loans	–20 472	120 024	–205 711	17 665	47 550		–4 454	–24 926
F.5	Shares and other equity	145 221	31 307	113 914		–		16 913	162 134
F.6	Insurance technical reserves	21 684			21 684				21 684
F.7	Other accounts payable	32 158	–4 349	31 745	–4 649	9 411		532	32 690

1.7B UK summary accounts 2008 (continued)

Total economy: all sectors and the rest of the world £ million

		USES						RESOURCES	TOTAL
		UK total economy	Non-financial corporations	Financial corporations	General government	Households & NPISH	Not sector-ised	Rest of the world	Goods & services
		S.1	S.11	S.12	S.13	S.14+S.15	S.N	S.2	

		Current accounts							
I.0	**PRODUCTION / EXTERNAL ACCOUNT OF GOODS AND SERVICES**								
P.7	Imports of goods and services								461 988	461 988
P.6	Exports of goods and services							422 864		422 864
P.1	Output at basic prices								2 630 445	2 630 445
P.2	Intermediate consumption	1 346 562	885 854	91 329	180 185	189 193				1 346 562
D.21-D.31	Taxes less subsidies on products								149 986	149 986
B.1g	**Gross domestic product, value added at market prices**	**1 433 870**	**770 684**	**112 222**	**171 632**	**229 346**	**149 988**			**1 433 870**
B.11	External balance of goods and services							39 124		39 124
II.1.1	**GENERATION OF INCOME**									
D.1	Compensation of employees	770 969	489 819	52 388	157 669	71 093		1 046		772 015
D.21-D.31	Taxes less subsidies on products	149 988					149 988			149 988
D.29-D.39	Other taxes less subsidies on production	16 637			16 637					16 637
B.2g	Operating surplus, gross	409 902	263 303	57 758	13 963	74 878				409 902
B.3g	Mixed income, gross	86 376				86 376				86 376
di	Statistical discrepancy between income components and GDP	1					1			1
II.1.2	**ALLOCATION OF PRIMARY INCOME**									
D.4	Property income	777 037	171 691	501 205	36 501	67 640		262 842		1 039 879
B.5g	National income, balance of primary incomes, gross	1 465 152	201 507	68 302	156 889	1 038 453	1			1 465 152
II.2	**SECONDARY DISTRIBUTION OF INCOME**									
D.5	Current taxes on income, wealth etc	241 806	40 845	11 645	1 147	188 169		616		242 422
D.61	Social contributions	212 630				212 630		68		212 698
D.62	Social benefits other than social transfers in kind	254 083	5 763	57 113	190 187	1 020				254 083
D.7	Other current transfers	230 566	6 170	31 766	158 834	33 796		12 588		243 154
B.6g	Disposable income, gross	1 453 240	160 174	84 417	293 553	915 095	1			1 453 240
II.3	**REDISTRIBUTION OF INCOME IN KIND**									
B.7g	Adjusted disposable income, gross	1 453 240	160 174	84 417	98 932	1 109 716	1			1 453 240
D.63	Social transfers in kind	230 388			194 621	35 767				230 388
II.4	**USE OF INCOME**									
B.6g	Disposable income, gross									
P.4	Actual final consumption	1 229 357			120 945	1 108 412				1 229 357
P.3	Final consumption expenditure	1 229 357			315 566	913 791				1 229 357
D.8	Adjustment for change in households' net equity in pension funds	27 840		27 840						27 840
B.8g	Saving, gross	223 885	160 174	56 577	−22 013	29 146	1			223 885
B.12	Current external balance							19 753		19 753
	Accumulation accounts									
III.1.1	**CHANGE IN NET WORTH DUE TO SAVING AND CAPITAL TRANSFERS**									
D.9	Capital transfers receivable									
D.9	Capital transfers payable									
B.10.1.g	Changes in net worth due to saving and capital transfers	227 166	168 534	61 730	−38 589	35 490	1	16 472		243 638
III.1.2	**ACQUISITION OF NON-FINANCIAL ASSETS**									
	Changes in assets									
P.51	Gross fixed capital formation	241 364	134 071	8 704	32 860	65 729				241 364
-K.1	(Consumption of fixed capital)	−151 370	−86 127	−6 366	−13 963	−44 914				−151 370
P.52	Changes in inventories	1 711	1 744	−17	−41	25				1 711
P.53	Acquisitions less disposals of valuables	561	150	284	11	116				561
K.2	Acquisitions less disposals of non-produced non-financial assets	40	1 338	4	−962	−340		−40		−
de	Statistical discrepancy between expenditure components and GDP	1					1			1
B.9	**Net lending(+) / net borrowing(-)**	**−16 512**	**31 231**	**52 755**	**−70 457**	**−30 040**	**−1**	**16 512**		**−**
III.2	**FINANCIAL ACCOUNT: changes in assets**									
F.1	Monetary gold and SDRs	−24			−24			24		
F.2	Currency and deposits	−276 341	−30 498	−336 784	31 769	59 172		−459 402		−735 743
F.3	Securities other than shares	259 443	5 093	251 539	5 659	−2 848		166 808		426 251
F.4	Loans	164 376	100 474	50 246	7 301	6 355		−189 302		−24 926
F.5	Shares and other equity	69 249	121 151	21 837	10 866	−84 605		92 885		162 134
F.6	Insurance technical reserves	25 600	318	33	21	25 228		−3 916		21 684
F.7	Other accounts receivable	32 515	−5 064	7 345	16 689	13 545		175		32 690
dB.9f	Statistical discrepancy between non-financial and financial transactions	9 473	−9 709	7 535	749	10 899	−1	−9 473		−

1.7C UK summary accounts 2009
Total economy: all sectors and the rest of the world

£ million

		RESOURCES						USES	TOTAL
		UK total economy	Non-financial corporations	Financial corporations	General government	Households & NPISH	Not sector-ised	Rest of the world	Goods & services
		S.1	S.11	S.12	S.13	S.14+S.15	S.N	S.2	

Current accounts

I / 0 PRODUCTION / EXTERNAL ACCOUNT OF GOODS AND SERVICES

Code	Item	S.1	S.11	S.12	S.13	S.14+S.15	S.N	S.2	Total
P.7	Imports of goods and services							421 225	421 225
P.6	Exports of goods and services							395 588	395 588
P.1	Output at basic prices	2 590 111	1 592 006	215 634	366 587	415 884			2 590 111
P.2	Intermediate consumption							1 333 179	1 333 179
D.21-D.31	Taxes *less* subsidies on products	136 922					136 922		136 922

II.1.1 GENERATION OF INCOME

B.1g	**Gross domestic product, value added at market prices**	**1 393 854**	**745 726**	**125 265**	**176 982**	**208 960**	**136 925**		**1 393 854**
B.11	External balance of goods and services							25 637	25 637

II.1.2 ALLOCATION OF PRIMARY INCOME

D.1	Compensation of employees	776 613				776 613		1 435	778 048
D.21-D.31	Taxes *less* subsidies on products	132 684			132 684			4 238	136 922
D.29-D.39	Other taxes *less* subsidies on production	17 472	18 274	2 559	–	–3 363		–3 411	14 061
B.2g	Operating surplus, gross	381 167	242 932	65 816	14 675	57 744			381 167
B.3g	Mixed income, gross	81 424				81 424			81 424
di	Statistical discrepancy between income components and GDP	–8					–8		–8
D.4	Property income	467 387	84 283	247 786	11 038	124 280		148 657	616 044

II.2 SECONDARY DISTRIBUTION OF INCOME

B.5g	National income, balance of primary incomes, gross	1 413 417	181 741	50 236	149 105	1 032 343	–8		1 413 417
D.5	Current taxes on income, wealth etc	220 048			220 048			565	220 613
D.61	Social contributions	214 188	6 809	87 656	119 199	524		–	214 188
D.62	Social benefits other than social transfers in kind	277 534				277 534		2 251	279 785
D.7	Other current transfers	225 838	5 290	29 348	131 004	60 196		25 127	250 965

II.3 REDISTRIBUTION OF INCOME IN KIND

B.6g	Disposable income, gross	1 399 127	147 711	71 262	237 019	943 143	–8		1 399 127
D.63	Social transfers in kind	242 776				242 776			242 776

II.4 USE OF INCOME

B.7g	Adjusted disposable income, gross	1 399 127	147 711	71 262	30 106	1 150 056	–8		1 399 127
B.6g	Disposable income, gross	1 399 127	147 711	71 262	237 019	943 143	–8		1 399 127
P.4	Actual final consumption							1 221 454	1 221 454
P.3	Final consumption expenditure							1 221 454	1 221 454
D.8	Adjustment for change in households' net equity in pension funds	26 547				26 547		–41	26 506

Accumulation accounts

III.1.1 CHANGE IN NET WORTH DUE TO SAVING DUE TO SAVING AND CAPITAL TRANSFERS

B.8g	Saving, gross	177 714	147 711	44 756	–90 330	75 585	–8		177 714
B.12	Current external balance							20 316	20 316
D.9	Capital transfers receivable	55 540	13 128	10 120	18 922	13 370		1 058	56 598
D.9	Capital transfers payable	–52 276	–723	–1 981	–44 405	–5 167		–4 322	–56 598

III.1.2 ACQUISITION ON NON-FINANCIAL ASSETS

Changes in liabilities and net worth

B.10.1.g	Changes in net worth due to saving and capital transfers	180 978	160 116	52 895	–115 813	83 788	–8	17 052	198 030
P.51	Gross fixed capital formation							209 253	209 253
-K.1	(Consumption of fixed capital)								
P.52	Changes in inventories							–11 651	–11 651
P.53	Acquisitions less disposals of valuables							429	429
K.2	Acquisitions less disposals of non-produced non-financial assets								
de	Statistical discrepancy between expenditure components and GDP							–	–

III.2 FINANCIAL ACCOUNT

B.9	Net lending(+) / net borrowing(-)	–16 679	50 880	46 332	–151 967	38 084	–8	16 679	–
	Changes in liabilities								
F.2	Currency and deposits	276 700	–	267 559	9 141	–		–217 127	59 573
F.3	Securities other than shares	360 946	–8 888	148 275	221 770	–211		133 034	493 980
F.4	Loans	–211 995	–155 332	–44 822	–21 494	9 653		–161 651	–373 646
F.5	Shares and other equity	223 931	46 632	177 299		–		32 031	255 962
F.6	Insurance technical reserves	18 455		18 455					18 455
F.7	Other accounts payable	–6 788	–3 064	–2 589	–4 519	3 384		382	–6 406

1.7C UK summary accounts 2009
continued

Total economy: all sectors and the rest of the world

£ million

		USES						RESOURCES	TOTAL
		UK total economy	Non-financial corporations	Financial corporations	General government	Households & NPISH	Not sector -ised	Rest of the world	Goods & services
		S.1	S.11	S.12	S.13	S.14+S.15	S.N	S.2	
	Current accounts								
I	**PRODUCTION / EXTERNAL**								
0	**ACCOUNT OF GOODS AND SERVICES**								
P.7	Imports of goods and services							421 225	421 225
P.6	Exports of goods and services							395 588	395 588
P.1	Output at basic prices								2 590 111 2 590 111
P.2	Intermediate consumption	1 333 179	846 280	90 369	189 605	206 924			1 333 179
D.21-D.31	Taxes *less* subsidies on products								136 922 136 922
B.1g	**Gross domestic product, value added at market prices**	**1 393 854**	**745 726**	**125 265**	**176 982**	**208 960**	**136 925**		**1 393 854**
B.11	External balance of goods and services							25 637	25 637
II.1.1	**GENERATION OF INCOME**								
D.1	Compensation of employees	776 872	484 520	56 890	162 307	73 155		1 176	778 048
D.21-D.31	Taxes *less* subsidies on products	136 925					136 925		136 925
D.29-D.39	Other taxes *less* subsidies on production	17 472			17 472				17 472
B.2g	Operating surplus, gross	381 167	242 932	65 816	14 675	57 744			381 167
B.3g	Mixed income, gross	81 424				81 424			81 424
di	Statistical discrepancy between income components and GDP	–8					–8		–8
II.1.2	**ALLOCATION OF PRIMARY INCOME**								
D.4	Property income	446 731	145 474	263 366	30 173	7 718		169 313	616 044
B.5g	National income, balance of primary incomes, gross	1 413 417	181 741	50 236	149 105	1 032 343	–8		1 413 417
II.2	**SECONDARY DISTRIBUTION OF INCOME**								
D.5	Current taxes on income, wealth etc	219 941	33 542	5 400	1 189	179 810		672	220 613
D.61	Social contributions	214 016				214 016		172	214 188
D.62	Social benefits other than social transfers in kind	279 785	6 809	61 150	210 806	1 020			279 785
D.7	Other current transfers	238 156	5 778	29 428	170 342	32 608		12 809	250 965
B.6g	Disposable income, gross	1 399 127	147 711	71 262	237 019	943 143	–8		1 399 127
II.3	**REDISTRIBUTION OF INCOME IN KIND**								
B.7g	Adjusted disposable income, gross	1 399 127	147 711	71 262	30 106	1 150 056	–8		1 399 127
D.63	Social transfers in kind	242 776			206 913	35 863			242 776
II.4	**USE OF INCOME**								
B.6g	Disposable income, gross								
P.4	Actual final consumption	1 221 454			120 436	1 101 018			1 221 454
P.3	Final consumption expenditure	1 221 454			327 349	894 105			1 221 454
D.8	Adjustment for change in households' net equity in pension funds	26 506		26 506					26 506
B.8g	Saving, gross	177 714	147 711	44 756	–90 330	75 585	–8		177 714
B.12	Current external balance							20 316	20 316
	Accumulation accounts								
	CHANGE IN NET WORTH								
III.1.1	**DUE TO SAVING AND CAPITAL TRANSFERS**								
D.9	Capital transfers receivable								
D.9	Capital transfers payable								
B.10.1.g	Changes in net worth due to saving and capital transfers	180 978	160 116	52 895	–115 813	83 788	–8	17 052	198 030
III.1.2	**ACQUISITION OF NON-FINANCIAL ASSETS**								
	Changes in assets								
P.51	Gross fixed capital formation	209 253	119 496	6 230	37 125	46 401			209 253
-K.1	(Consumption of fixed capital)	–159 862	–90 888	–6 924	–14 675	–47 375			–159 862
P.52	Changes in inventories	–11 651	–11 391	53	36	–349			–11 651
P.53	Acquisitions less disposals of valuables	429	153	264	12	–			429
K.2	Acquisitions less disposals of non-produced non-financial assets	–373	978	16	–1 019	–348		373	–
de	Statistical discrepancy between expenditure components and GDP	–					–		–
B.9	**Net lending(+) / net borrowing(-)**	–16 679	50 880	46 332	–151 967	38 084	–8	16 679	–
III.2	**FINANCIAL ACCOUNT: changes in assets**								
F.1	Monetary gold and SDRs	–132			–132			132	–
F.2	Currency and deposits	383 511	–33 934	392 824	9 674	14 947		–323 938	59 573
F.3	Securities other than shares	354 494	–6 138	355 515	1 883	3 234		139 486	493 980
F.4	Loans	–275 945	–46 465	–232 060	4 472	–1 892		–97 701	–373 646
F.5	Shares and other equity	162 292	24 132	87 240	37 352	13 568		93 670	255 962
F.6	Insurance technical reserves	18 778	–354	–37	–24	19 193		–323	18 455
F.7	Other accounts receivable	–6 514	–5 635	6 176	403	–7 458		108	–6 406
dB.9f	Statistical discrepancy between non-financial and financial transactions	8 086	–1 378	851	–697	9 318	–8	–8 086	–

1.7D UK summary accounts 2010
Total economy: all sectors and the rest of the world

£ million

		RESOURCES						USES	TOTAL
		UK total economy S.1	Non-financial corporations S.11	Financial corporations S.12	General government S.13	Households & NPISH S.14+S.15	Not sector-ised S.N	Rest of the world S.2	Goods & services

Current accounts

I.0 PRODUCTION / EXTERNAL ACCOUNT OF GOODS AND SERVICES

Code	Item	S.1	S.11	S.12	S.13	S.14+S.15	S.N	S.2	Total
P.7	Imports of goods and services							476 480	476 480
P.6	Exports of goods and services							436 796	436 796
P.1	Output at basic prices	..	..	..	376 588	..			..
P.2	Intermediate consumption							..	..
D.21-D.31	Taxes *less* subsidies on products	157 334					157 334		157 334

II.1.1 GENERATION OF INCOME

Code	Item	S.1	S.11	S.12	S.13	S.14+S.15	S.N	S.2	Total
B.1g	Gross domestic product, value added at market prices	1 458 452	..	..	181 936	..160 376			1 458 452
B.11	External balance of goods and services							39 684	39 684

II.1.2 ALLOCATION OF PRIMARY INCOME

Code	Item	S.1	S.11	S.12	S.13	S.14+S.15	S.N	S.2	Total
D.1	Compensation of employees	799 585				799 585		1 486	801 071
D.21-D.31	Taxes *less* subsidies on products	152 148			152 148			5 186	157 334
D.29-D.39	Other taxes *less* subsidies on production	21 676	18 771	5 889	–	–2 984		–3 032	18 644
B.2g	Operating surplus, gross	395 380	254 884	52 898	15 500	72 098			395 380
B.3g	Mixed income, gross	81 047				81 047			81 047
di	Statistical discrepancy between income components and GDP	3 041					3 041		3 041
D.4	Property income	439 516	90 307	217 237	8 283	123 689		138 938	578 454

II.2 SECONDARY DISTRIBUTION OF INCOME

Code	Item	S.1	S.11	S.12	S.13	S.14+S.15	S.N	S.2	Total
B.5g	National income, balance of primary incomes, gross	1 479 337	214 886	35 441	155 323	1 070 646	3 041		1 479 337
D.5	Current taxes on income, wealth etc	227 189			227 189			638	227 827
D.61	Social contributions	226 739	4 399	98 367	123 445	528		–	226 739
D.62	Social benefits other than social transfers in kind	287 196				287 196		2 224	289 420
D.7	Other current transfers	235 438	5 714	30 391	136 579	62 754		26 651	262 089

II.3 REDISTRIBUTION OF INCOME IN KIND

Code	Item	S.1	S.11	S.12	S.13	S.14+S.15	S.N	S.2	Total
B.6g	Disposable income, gross	1 461 400	178 757	60 748	239 670	979 184	3 041		1 461 400
D.63	Social transfers in kind	250 466				250 466			250 466

II.4 USE OF INCOME

Code	Item	S.1	S.11	S.12	S.13	S.14+S.15	S.N	S.2	Total
B.7g	Adjusted disposable income, gross	1 461 400	178 757	60 748	26 906	1 191 948	3 041		1 461 400
B.6g	Disposable income, gross	1 461 400	178 757	60 748	239 670	979 184	3 041		1 461 400
P.4	Actual final consumption							1 275 973	1 275 973
P.3	Final consumption expenditure							1 275 973	1 275 973
D.8	Adjustment for change in households' net equity in pension funds	35 105				35 105		–10	35 095

Accumulation accounts

III.1.1 CHANGE IN NET WORTH DUE TO SAVING AND CAPITAL TRANSFERS

Code	Item	S.1	S.11	S.12	S.13	S.14+S.15	S.N	S.2	Total
B.8g	Saving, gross	185 437	178 757	25 653	–98 397	76 383	3 041		185 437
B.12	Current external balance							36 726	36 726
D.9	Capital transfers receivable	39 958	10 689	67	16 152	13 050		1 077	41 035
D.9	Capital transfers payable	–36 307	–456	–67	–32 297	–3 487		–4 728	–41 035

III.1.2 ACQUISITION ON NON-FINANCIAL ASSETS
Changes in liabilities and net worth

Code	Item	S.1	S.11	S.12	S.13	S.14+S.15	S.N	S.2	Total
B.10.1.g	Changes in net worth due to saving and capital transfers	189 088	188 990	25 653	–114 542	85 946	3 041	33 075	222 163
P.51	Gross fixed capital formation							217 108	217 108
-K.1	(Consumption of fixed capital)								
P.52	Changes in inventories							6 832	6 832
P.53	Acquisitions less disposals of valuables							638	638
K.2	Acquisitions less disposals of non-produced non-financial assets								
de	Statistical discrepancy between expenditure components and GDP							–2 415	–2 415

III.2 FINANCIAL ACCOUNT

Code	Item	S.1	S.11	S.12	S.13	S.14+S.15	S.N	S.2	Total
B.9	**Net lending(+) / net borrowing(-)**	–33 018	61 215	17 706	–150 151	32 757	5 455	33 018	–
	Changes in liabilities								
F.2	Currency and deposits	31 281	–	39 272	–7 991	–		220 479	251 760
F.3	Securities other than shares	115 521	–2 618	–49 995	168 106	28		45 755	161 276
F.4	Loans	157 709	26 368	109 768	–2 104	23 677		10 414	168 123
F.5	Shares and other equity	64 670	18 816	45 854		–		43 062	107 732
F.6	Insurance technical reserves	23 392		23 392					23 392
F.7	Other accounts payable	14 326	2 621	2 632	6 401	2 672		64	14 390

1.7D UK summary accounts 2010
continued
Total economy: all sectors and the rest of the world

£ million

		USES						RESOURCES	TOTAL
		UK total economy	Non-financial corporations	Financial corporations	General government	Households & NPISH	Not sector-ised	Rest of the world	Goods & services
		S.1	S.11	S.12	S.13	S.14+S.15	S.N	S.2	
	Current accounts								
I	**PRODUCTION / EXTERNAL**								
0	**ACCOUNT OF GOODS AND SERVICES**								
P.7	Imports of goods and services								476 480	476 480
P.6	Exports of goods and services							436 796		436 796
P.1	Output at basic prices								..	..
P.2	Intermediate consumption	..	..	..	194 652	..				
D.21-D.31	Taxes *less* subsidies on products								157 334	157 334
B.1g	**Gross domestic product, value added at market prices**	1 458 452	..	..	181 936	..160 376				1 458 452
B.11	External balance of goods and services							39 684		39 684
II.1.1	**GENERATION OF INCOME**									
D.1	Compensation of employees	799 974	499 091	58 805	166 436	75 642		1 097		801 071
D.21-D.31	Taxes *less* subsidies on products	157 334					157 334			157 334
D.29-D.39	Other taxes *less* subsidies on production	21 676			21 676					21 676
B.2g	Operating surplus, gross	395 380	254 884	52 898	15 500	72 098				395 380
B.3g	Mixed income, gross	81 047				81 047				81 047
di	Statistical discrepancy between income components and GDP	3 041					3 041			3 041
II.1.2	**ALLOCATION OF PRIMARY INCOME**									
D.4	Property income	416 088	130 305	234 694	45 316	5 773		162 366		578 454
B.5g	National income, balance of primary incomes, gross	1 479 337	214 886	35 441	155 323	1 070 646	3 041			1 479 337
II.2	**SECONDARY DISTRIBUTION OF INCOME**									
D.5	Current taxes on income, wealth etc	227 260	35 641	9 708	1 236	180 675		567		227 827
D.61	Social contributions	226 656				226 656		83		226 739
D.62	Social benefits other than social transfers in kind	289 420	4 399	63 272	220 725	1 024				289 420
D.7	Other current transfers	251 163	6 202	30 471	180 905	33 585		10 926		262 089
B.6g	Disposable income, gross	1 461 400	178 757	60 748	239 670	979 184	3 041			1 461 400
II.3	**REDISTRIBUTION OF INCOME IN KIND**									
B.7g	Adjusted disposable income, gross	1 461 400	178 757	60 748	26 906	1 191 948	3 041			1 461 400
D.63	Social transfers in kind	250 466			212 764	37 702				250 466
II.4	**USE OF INCOME**									
B.6g	Disposable income, gross									
P.4	Actual final consumption	1 275 973			125 303	1 150 670				1 275 973
P.3	Final consumption expenditure	1 275 973			338 067	937 906				1 275 973
D.8	Adjustment for change in households' net equity in pension funds	35 095		35 095						35 095
B.8g	Saving, gross	185 437	178 757	25 653	-98 397	76 383	3 041			185 437
B.12	Current external balance							36 726		36 726
	Accumulation accounts									
III.1.1	**CHANGE IN NET WORTH DUE TO SAVING AND CAPITAL TRANSFERS**									
D.9	Capital transfers receivable									
D.9	Capital transfers payable									
B.10.1.g	Changes in net worth due to saving and capital transfers	189 088	188 990	25 653	-114 542	85 946	3 041	33 075		222 163
III.1.2	**ACQUISITION OF NON-FINANCIAL ASSETS**									
	Changes in assets									
P.51	Gross fixed capital formation	217 108	119 937	7 578	36 434	53 158				217 108
-K.1	(Consumption of fixed capital)	-164 006	-94 636	-7 154	-15 500	-46 716				-164 006
P.52	Changes in inventories	6 832	6 668	55	43	66				6 832
P.53	Acquisitions less disposals of valuables	638	16	298	11	313				638
K.2	Acquisitions less disposals of non-produced non-financial assets	-57	1 154	16	-879	-348		57		–
de	Statistical discrepancy between expenditure components and GDP	-2 415					-2 415			-2 415
B.9	**Net lending(+) / net borrowing(-)**	-33 018	61 215	17 706	-150 151	32 757	5 455	33 018		–
III.2	**FINANCIAL ACCOUNT: changes in assets**									
F.1	Monetary gold and SDRs	18			18			-18		
F.2	Currency and deposits	189 251	51 388	113 000	-7 891	32 754		62 509		251 760
F.3	Securities other than shares	71 223	5 551	59 537	8 204	-2 069		90 053		161 276
F.4	Loans	-3 827	10 922	-25 363	9 356	1 258		171 950		168 123
F.5	Shares and other equity	71 933	31 912	44 016	1 011	-5 006		35 799		107 732
F.6	Insurance technical reserves	23 208	244	25	16	22 923		184		23 392
F.7	Other accounts receivable	13 576	5 679	2 568	3 290	2 039		814		14 390
dB.9f	Statistical discrepancy between non-financial and financial transactions	8 499	706	-5 154	257	7 235	5 455	-8 499		–

1.7.1 UK summary accounts 2009
Total economy: all sectors and the rest of the world
£ million

		UK total economy S.1	Non-financial corporations S.11	Financial corporations S.12	Monetary financial institutions S.121+S.122	Other financial intermediaries & auxiliaries S.123+S.124	Insurance corporations & pension funds S.125
I	**PRODUCTION ACCOUNT**						
	Resources						
P.1	Output						
P.11	Market output*	2 107 552	1 574 560	212 623			
P.12	Output for own final use	119 347	17 446	3 011			
P.13	Other non-market output	363 212					
P.1	Total output	2 590 111	1 592 006	215 634			
D.21	Taxes on products	142 629					
-D.31	less Subsidies on products	–5 707					
Total	Total resources	2 727 033	1 592 006	215 634			
	Uses						
P.2	Intermediate consumption	1 333 179	846 280	90 369			
B.1*g	**Gross domestic product**	**1 393 854**	**745 726**	**125 265**	**73 058**	**34 289**	**17 918**
Total	Total uses	2 727 033	1 592 006	215 634			
B.1*g	**Gross domestic product**	**1 393 854**	**745 726**	**125 265**	**73 058**	**34 289**	**17 918**
-K.1	less Fixed capital consumption	–159 862	–90 888	–6 924			
B.1*n	Net domestic product	1 233 992	654 838	118 341			

1.7.2 UK summary accounts 2009
Total economy: all sectors and the rest of the world
£ million

		UK total economy S.1	Non-financial corporations S.11	Financial corporations S.12	Monetary financial institutions S.121+S.122	Other financial intermediaries & auxiliaries S.123+S.124	Insurance corporations & pension funds S.125
II	**DISTRIBUTION AND USE OF INCOME ACCOUNTS**						
II.1	**PRIMARY DISTRIBUTION OF INCOME ACCOUNT**						
II.1.1	**GENERATION OF INCOME ACCOUNT**						
	Resources						
B.1*g	Total resources (gross domestic product) external balance of goods & services	1 393 854	745 726	125 265	73 058	34 289	17 918
	Uses						
D.1	Compensation of employees						
D.11	Wages and salaries	649 163	410 502	49 328	27 110	15 093	7 125
D.12	Employers' social contributions	127 709	74 018	7 562	3 529	2 712	1 321
D.1	Total	776 872	484 520	56 890	30 639	17 805	8 446
D.2	Taxes on production and imports, paid						
D.21	Taxes on products and imports	142 629					
D.29	Production taxes other than on products	24 194	21 587	2 559	1 290	750	519
D.2	Total taxes on production and imports	166 823	21 587	2 559	1 290	750	519
-D.3	less Subsidies, received						
-D.31	Subsidies on products	–5 707					
-D.39	Production subsidies other than on products	–6 722	–3 313	–	–	–	–
-D.3	Total subsidies on production	–12 431	–3 313	–	–	–	–
B.2g	Operating surplus, gross	381 167	242 932	65 816	41 129	15 734	8 953
B.3g	Mixed income, gross	81 424					
di	Statistical discrepancy between income components and GDP	–8					
B.1*g	**Total uses (gross domestic product)**	**1 393 854**	**745 726**	**125 265**	**73 058**	**34 289**	**17 918**
-K.1	After deduction of fixed capital consumption	–159 862	–90 888	–6 924			
B.2n	Operating surplus, net	240 674	152 044	58 892			
B.3n	Mixed income, net	62 504					

1.7.1 UK summary accounts 2009 (continued)
Total economy: all sectors and the rest of the world
£ million

		General government S.13	Central government S.1311	Local government S.1313	Households & NPISH S.14+S.15	Not sectorised S.N	Taxes less subsidies	Rest of the world S.2
I	**PRODUCTION ACCOUNT**							
	Resources							
P.1	Output							
P.11	Market output*	38 834	13 420	25 414	281 535			
P.12	Output for own final use	404	56	348	98 486			
P.13	Other non-market output	327 349	199 649	127 700	35 863			
P.1	Total output	366 587	213 125	153 462	415 884			
D.21	Taxes on products					142 629	142 629	
-D.31	*less* Subsidies on products					–5 707	–5 707	
Total	Total resources	366 587	213 125	153 462	415 884	136 922	136 922	
	Uses							
P.2	Intermediate consumption	189 605	118 188	71 417	206 924			
B.1*g	**Gross domestic product**	**176 982**	**94 937**	**82 045**	**208 960**	**136 925**	136 922	
Total	Total uses	366 587	213 125	153 462	415 884	136 922	136 922	
B.1*g	**Gross domestic product**	**176 982**	**94 937**	**82 045**	**208 960**	**136 925**	136 922	
-K.1	*less* Fixed capital consumption	–14 675	–7 232	–7 443	–47 375			
B.1*n	Net domestic product	162 307	87 705	74 602	161 585	136 922	136 922	

1.7.2 UK summary accounts 2009 (continued)
Total economy: all sectors and the rest of the world
£ million

		General government S.13	Central government S.1311	Local government S.1313	Households & NPISH S.14+S.15	Not sectorised S.N	Taxes less subsidies	Rest of the world S.2
II	**DISTRIBUTION AND USE OF INCOME ACCOUNTS**							
II.1	**PRIMARY DISTRIBUTION OF INCOME ACCOUNT**							
II.1.1	**GENERATION OF INCOME ACCOUNT**							
	Resources							
B.1*g	**Total resources (gross domestic product)**	176 982	94 937	82 045	208 960	136 925	136 922	
	external balance of goods & services							25 637
	Uses							
D.1	Compensation of employees							
D.11	Wages and salaries	127 294	70 165	57 129	62 039			1 176
D.12	Employers' social contributions	35 013	17 540	17 473	11 116			
D.1	Total	162 307	87 705	74 602	73 155			1 176
D.2	Taxes on production and imports, paid							
D.21	Taxes on products and imports					142 629	142 629	–
D.29	Production taxes other than on products	–	–	–	48			
D.2	Total taxes on production and imports	–	–	–	48	142 629	142 629	–
-D.3	*less* Subsidies, received							
-D.31	Subsidies on products					–5 707	–5 707	
-D.39	Production subsidies other than on products	–	–	–	–3 411			
-D.3	Total subsidies on production	–	–	–	–3 411	–5 707	–5 707	
B.2g	Operating surplus, gross	14 675	7 232	7 443	57 744			
B.3g	Mixed income, gross				81 424			
di	Statistical discrepancy between income components and GDP					–8		
B.1*g	**Total uses (gross domestic product)**	**176 982**	**94 937**	**82 045**	**208 960**	**136 925**	136 922	
-K.1	After deduction of fixed capital consumption	–14 675	–7 232	–7 443	–47 375			
B.2n	Operating surplus, net	–	–	–	29 738			
B.3n	Mixed income, net				62 504			

1.7.3 UK summary accounts 2009

Total economy: all sectors and the rest of the world

£ million

		UK total economy S.1	Non-financial corporations S.11	Financial corporations S.12	Monetary financial institutions S.121+S.122	Other financial intermediaries & auxiliaries S.123+S.124	Insurance corporations & pension funds S.125
II.1.2	**ALLOCATION OF PRIMARY INCOME ACCOUNT**						
	Resources						
B.2g	Operating surplus, gross	381 167	242 932	65 816	41 129	15 734	8 953
B.3g	Mixed income, gross	81 424					
D.1	Compensation of employees						
D.11	Wages and salaries	648 904					
D.12	Employers' social contributions	127 709					
D.1	Total	776 613					
di	Statistical discrepancy between income components and GDP	−8					
D.2	Taxes on production and imports, received						
D.21	Taxes on products						
D.211	Value added tax (VAT)	78 307					
D.212	Taxes and duties on imports excluding VAT	–					
D.2121	Import duties	–					
D.2122	Taxes on imports excluding VAT and import duties	–					
D.214	Taxes on products excluding VAT and import duties	60 084					
D.21	Total taxes on products	138 391					
D.29	Other taxes on production	24 194					
D.2	Total taxes on production and imports, received	162 585					
-D.3	*less* Subsidies, paid						
-D.31	Subsidies on products	−5 707					
-D.39	Other subsidies on production	−3 313					
-D.3	Total subsidies	−9 020					
D.4	Property income, received						
D.41	Interest	209 477	7 399	184 680	122 304	35 846	26 530
D.42	Distributed income of corporations	176 418	62 606	63 579	6 796	29 502	27 281
D.43	Reinvested earnings on direct foreign investment	13 241	13 783	−542	−832	1 561	−1 271
D.44	Property income attributed to insurance policy holders	66 799	363	38	10	8	20
D.45	Rent	1 452	132	31	–	–	31
D.4	Total property income	467 387	84 283	247 786	128 278	66 917	52 591
Total	Total resources	1 860 148	327 215	313 602	169 407	82 651	61 544
	Uses						
D.4	Property income, paid						
D.41	Interest	231 165	31 877	161 636	111 305	48 949	1 382
D.42	Distributed income of corporations	142 385	113 829	28 556	1 990	22 329	4 237
D.43	Reinvested earnings on direct foreign investment	4 148	−1 445	5 593	−1 075	6 535	133
D.44	Property income attributed to insurance policy holders	67 581		67 581			67 581
D.45	Rent	1 452	1 213	–	–	–	–
D.4	Total property income	446 731	145 474	263 366	112 220	77 813	73 333
B.5*g	**Gross national income (GNI)**	**1 413 417**	**181 741**	**50 236**	**57 187**	**4 838**	**−11 789**
Total	Total uses	1 860 148	327 215	313 602	169 407	82 651	61 544
-K.1	After deduction of fixed capital consumption	−159 862	−90 888	−6 924			
B.5*n	National income, net	1 253 555	90 853	43 312			

1.7.3 UK summary accounts 2009 continued

Total economy: all sectors and the rest of the world

£ million

		General government	Central government	Local government	Households & NPISH	Not sector-ised	Rest of the world
		S.13	S.1311	S.1313	S.14+S.15	S.N	S.2
II.1.2	**ALLOCATION OF PRIMARY INCOME ACCOUNT**						
	Resources						
B.2g	Operating surplus, gross	14 675	7 232	7 443	57 744		
B.3g	Mixed income, gross				81 424		
D.1	Compensation of employees						
D.11	Wages and salaries				648 904		1 435
D.12	Employers' social contributions				127 709		
D.1	Total				776 613		1 435
di	Statistical discrepancy between income components and GDP					−8	
D.2	Taxes on production and imports, received						
D.21	Taxes on products						
D.211	Value added tax (VAT)	78 307	78 307				1 593
D.212	Taxes and duties on imports excluding VAT						
D.2121	Import duties	–	–				2 645
D.2122	Taxes on imports excluding VAT and import duties	–	–				–
D.214	Taxes on products excluding VAT and import duties	60 084	60 084				–
D.21	Total taxes on products	138 391	138 391				4 238
D.29	Other taxes on production	24 194	23 877	317			
D.2	Total taxes on production and imports, received	162 585	162 268	317			4 238
−D.3	*less* Subsidies, paid						
−D.31	Subsidies on products	−5 707	−3 730	−1 977			–
−D.39	Other subsidies on production	−3 313	−1 820	−1 493			−3 411
−D.3	Total subsidies	−9 020	−5 550	−3 470			−3 411
D.4	Property income, received						
D.41	Interest	7 626	6 994	632	9 772		106 225
D.42	Distributed income of corporations	2 214	1 442	772	48 019		37 502
D.43	Reinvested earnings on direct foreign investment						4 148
D.44	Property income attributed to insurance policy holders	24		24	66 374		782
D.45	Rent	1 174	1 174	–	115		
D.4	Total property income	11 038	9 610	1 428	124 280		148 657
Total	Total resources	179 278	173 560	5 718	1 040 061	−8	
	Uses						
D.4	Property income, paid						
D.41	Interest	30 173	26 948	3 225	7 479		84 537
D.42	Distributed income of corporations						71 535
D.43	Reinvested earnings on direct foreign investment						13 241
D.44	Property income attributed to insurance policy holders						
D.45	Rent				239		
D.4	Total property income	30 173	26 948	3 225	7 718		169 313
B.5*g	**Gross national income (GNI)**	**149 105**	**146 612**	**2 493**	**1 032 343**	**−8**	
Total	Total uses	179 278	173 560	5 718	1 040 061	−8	
−K.1	After deduction of fixed capital consumption	−14 675	−7 232	−7 443	−47 375		
B.5*n	National income, net	134 430	139 380	−4 950	984 968	−8	

1.7.4 UK summary accounts 2009

Total economy: all sectors and the rest of the world

£ million

		UK total economy S.1	Non-financial corporations S.11	Financial corporations S.12	Monetary financial institutions S.121+S.122	Other financial intermediaries & auxiliaries S.123+S.124	Insurance corporations & pension funds S.125
II.2	**SECONDARY DISTRIBUTION OF INCOME ACCOUNT**						
	Resources						
B.5*g	**Gross national income**	1 413 417	181 741	50 236	57 187	4 838	–11 789
D.5	Current taxes on income, wealth etc.						
D.51	Taxes on income	185 160					
D.59	Other current taxes	34 888					
D.5	Total	220 048					
D.61	Social contributions						
D.611	Actual social contributions						
D.6111	Employers' actual social contributions	111 115		47 608			47 608
D.6112	Employees' social contributions	83 600		39 528			39 528
D.6113	Social contributions by self- and non-employed persons	2 879		–	–	–	–
D.611	Total	197 594		87 136	–		87 136
D.612	Imputed social contributions	16 594	6 809	520	257	179	84
D.61	Total	214 188	6 809	87 656	257	179	87 220
D.62	Social benefits other than social transfers in kind	277 534					
D.7	Other current transfers						
D.71	Net non-life insurance premiums	28 801		28 801			28 801
D.72	Non-life insurance claims	24 730	5 290	547	144	115	288
D.73	Current transfers within general government	124 622					
D.74	Current international cooperation from institutions of the EC	5 522					
D.75	Miscellaneous current transfers	42 163	–	–	–	–	–
D.7	Total, other current transfers	225 838	5 290	29 348	144	115	29 089
Total	Total resources	2 351 025	193 840	167 240	57 588	5 132	104 520
	Uses						
D.5	Current taxes on income, wealth etc.						
D.51	Taxes on income	185 053	33 542	5 400	1 841	763	2 796
D.59	Other current taxes	34 888					
D.5	Total	219 941	33 542	5 400	1 841	763	2 796
D.61	Social contributions						
D.611	Actual social contributions						
D.6111	Employers' actual social contributions	111 115					
D.6112	Employees' actual social contributions	83 428					
D.6113	Social contributions by self- and non-employed persons	2 879					
D.611	Total actual social contributions	197 422					
D.612	Imputed social contributions	16 594					
D.61	Total	214 016					
D.62	Social benefits other than social transfers in kind	279 785	6 809	61 150	257	179	60 714
D.7	Other current transfers						
D.71	Net non-life insurance premiums	24 730	5 290	547	144	115	288
D.72	Non-life insurance claims	28 801		28 801			28 801
D.73	Current transfers within general government	124 622					
D.74	Current international cooperation to institutions of the EC	5 011					
D.75	Miscellaneous current transfers	54 992	488	80	56	24	–
	Of which: GNP based fourth own resource	10 555					
D.7	Total other current transfers	238 156	5 778	29 428	200	139	29 089
B.6*g	**Gross national disposable income**	1 399 127	147 711	71 262	55 290	4 051	11 921
Total	Total uses	2 351 025	193 840	167 240	57 588	5 132	104 520
–K.1	After deduction of fixed capital consumption	–159 862	–90 888	–6 924			
B.6*n	Disposable income, net	1 239 265	56 823	64 338			

1.7.4 UK summary accounts 2009
Total economy: all sectors and the rest of the world

£ million

		General government S.13	Central government S.1311	Local government S.1313	Households & NPISH S.14+S.15	Not sector-ised S.N	Rest of the world S.2
II.2	**SECONDARY DISTRIBUTION OF INCOME ACCOUNT**						
	Resources						
B.5*g	**Gross national income**	149 105	146 612	2 493	1 032 343	–8	
D.5	Current taxes on income, wealth etc.						
D.51	Taxes on income	185 160	185 160				565
D.59	Other current taxes	34 888	9 814	25 074			
D.5	Total	220 048	194 974	25 074			565
D.61	Social contributions						
D.611	Actual social contributions						
D.6111	Employers' actual social contributions	63 507	63 507				
D.6112	Employees' social contributions	44 072	43 244	828			
D.6113	Social contributions by self- and non-employed persons	2 879	2 879				
D.611	Total	110 458	109 630	828			–
D.612	Imputed social contributions	8 741	5 652	3 089	524		
D.61	Total	119 199	115 282	3 917	524		–
D.62	Social benefits other than social transfers in kind				277 534		2 251
D.7	Other current transfers						
D.71	Net non-life insurance premiums						77
D.72	Non-life insurance claims	345	–	345	18 548		4 148
D.73	Current transfers within general government	124 622	–	124 622			
	Current international cooperation						5 011
D.74	from institutions of the EC	5 522	5 418	104			
D.75	Miscellaneous current transfers	515	515		41 648		15 891
	Of which: GNP based fourth own resource						10 555
D.7	Total, other current transfers	131 004	5 933	125 071	60 196		25 127
Total	Total resources	619 356	462 801	156 555	1 370 597	–8	
	Uses						
D.5	Current taxes on income, wealth etc.						
D.51	Taxes on income				146 111		672
D.59	Other current taxes	1 189		1 189	33 699		
D.5	Total	1 189		1 189	179 810		672
D.61	Social contributions						
D.611	Actual social contributions						
D.6111	Employers' actual social contributions				111 115		
D.6112	Employees' actual social contributions				83 428		172
D.6113	Social contributions by self- and non-employed persons				2 879		
D.611	Total actual social contributions				197 422		172
D.612	Imputed social contributions				16 594		
D.61	Total				214 016		172
D.62	Social benefits other than social transfers in kind	210 806	186 129	24 677	1 020		609
D.7	Other current transfers						
D.71	Net non-life insurance premiums	345	–	345	18 548		4 148
D.72	Non-life insurance claims						77
D.73	Current transfers within general government	124 622	124 622	–			
	Current international cooperation						5 522
D.74	to institutions of the EC	5 011	5 011				
D.75	Miscellaneous current transfers	40 364	40 338	26	14 060		3 062
	Of which: GNP based fourth own resource	10 555	10 555				
D.7	Total other current transfers	170 342	169 971	371	32 608		12 809
B.6*g	**Gross national disposable income**	237 019	106 701	130 318	943 143	–8	
Total	Total uses	619 356	462 801	156 555	1 370 597	–8	
-K.1	After deduction of fixed capital consumption	–14 675	–7 232	–7 443	–47 375		
B.6*n	Disposable income, net	222 344	99 469	122 875	895 768	–8	

1.7.5 UK summary accounts 2009

Total economy: all sectors and the rest of the world

£ million

		UK total economy S.1	Non-financial corporations S.11	Financial corporations S.12	Monetary financial institutions S.121+S.122	Other financial intermediaries & auxiliaries S.123+S.124	Insurance corporations & pension funds S.125
II.3	**REDISTRIBUTION OF INCOME IN KIND ACCOUNT**						
	Resources						
B.6*g	**Gross national disposable income**	1 399 127	147 711	71 262	55 290	4 051	11 921
D.63	Social transfers in kind						
D.631	Social benefits in kind						
D.6313	Social assistance benefits in kind	–					
D.632	Transfers of individual non-market goods and services	242 776					
D.63	Total social transfers in kind	242 776					
Total	Total resources	1 641 903	147 711	71 262	55 290	4 051	11 921
	Uses						
D.63	Social transfers in kind						
D.631	Social benefits in kind						
D.6313	Social assistance benefits in kind	–					
D.632	Transfers of individual non-market goods and services	242 776					
D.63	Total social transfers in kind	242 776					
B.7g	Adjusted disposable income, gross	1 399 127	147 711	71 262	55 290	4 051	11 921
Total	Total uses	1 641 903	147 711	71 262	55 290	4 051	11 921

1.7.5 UK summary accounts 2009
Total economy: all sectors and the rest of the world

£ million

		General government	Central government	Local government	Households & NPISH	Not sector-ised	Rest of the world
		S.13	S.1311	S.1313	S.14+S.15	S.N	S.2
II.3	**REDISTRIBUTION OF INCOME IN KIND ACCOUNT**						
	Resources						
B.6*g	**Gross national disposable income**	**237 019**	**106 701**	**130 318**	**943 143**	**−8**	
D.63	Social transfers in kind						
D.631	Social benefits in kind						
D.6313	Social assistance benefits in kind				−		
D.632	Transfers of individual non-market goods and services				242 776		
D.63	Total social transfers in kind				242 776		
Total	Total resources	**237 019**	**106 701**	**130 318**	**1 185 919**	**−8**	
	Uses						
D.63	Social transfers in kind						
D.631	Social benefits in kind						
D.6313	Social assistance benefits in kind				−		
D.632	Transfers of individual non-market goods and services	206 913	120 835	86 078	35 863		
D.63	Total social transfers in kind	206 913	120 835	86 078	35 863		
B.7g	Adjusted disposable income, gross	30 106	−14 134	44 240	1 150 056	−8	
Total	Total uses	**237 019**	**106 701**	**130 318**	**1 185 919**	**−8**	

1.7.6 UK summary accounts 2009
Total economy: all sectors and the rest of the world

£ million

		UK total economy S.1	Non-financial corporations S.11	Financial corporations S.12	Monetary financial institutions S.121+S.122	Other financial intermediaries & auxiliaries S.123+S.124	Insurance corporations & pension funds S.125
II.4	**USE OF INCOME ACCOUNT**						
II.4.1	**USE OF DISPOSABLE INCOME ACCOUNT**						
	Resources						
B.6g	**Gross national disposable income**	1 399 127	147 711	71 262	55 290	4 051	11 921
D.8	Adjustment for the change in net equity of households in pension funds	26 547					
Total	Total resources	1 425 674	147 711	71 262	55 290	4 051	11 921
	Uses						
P.3	Final consumption expenditure						
P.31	Individual consumption expenditure	1 101 018					
P.32	Collective consumption expenditure	120 436					
P.3	Total	1 221 454					
D.8	Adjustment for the change in net equity of households in pension funds	26 506		26 506			26 506
B.8g	**Gross saving**	177 714	147 711	44 756	55 290	4 051	−14 585
B.12	Current external balance						
Total	Total uses	1 425 674	147 711	71 262	55 290	4 051	11 921
-K.1	After deduction of fixed capital consumption	−159 862	−90 888	−6 924			
B.8n	Saving, net	17 852	56 823	37 832			
II.4.2	**USE OF ADJUSTED DISPOSABLE INCOME ACCOUNT**						
	Resources						
B.7g	Adjusted disposable income	1 399 127	147 711	71 262	55 290	4 051	11 921
D.8	Adjustment for the change in net equity of households in pension funds	26 547					
Total	Total resources	1 425 674	147 711	71 262	55 290	4 051	11 921
	Uses						
P.4	Actual final consumption						
P.41	Actual individual consumption	1 101 018					
P.42	Actual collective consumption	120 436					
P.4	Total actual final consumption	1 221 454					
D.8	Adjustment for the change in net equity of households in pension funds	26 506		26 506			26 506
B.8g	**Gross saving**	177 714	147 711	44 756	55 290	4 051	−14 585
Total	Total uses	1 425 674	147 711	71 262	55 290	4 051	11 921

1.7.6 UK summary accounts 2009 continued

Total economy: all sectors and the rest of the world

£ million

		General government	Central government	Local government	Households & NPISH	Not sector-ised	Rest of the world
		S.13	S.1311	S.1313	S.14+S.15	S.N	S.2
II.4	**USE OF INCOME ACCOUNT**						
II.4.1	**USE OF DISPOSABLE INCOME ACCOUNT**						
	Resources						
B.6g	Gross national disposable income	237 019	106 701	130 318	943 143	–8	
D.8	Adjustment for the change in net equity of households in pension funds				26 547		–41
Total	Total resources	237 019	106 701	130 318	969 690	–8	
	Uses						
P.3	Final consumption expenditure						
P.31	Individual consumption expenditure	206 913	120 835	86 078	894 105		
P.32	Collective consumption expenditure	120 436	78 814	41 622			
P.3	Total	327 349	199 649	127 700	894 105		
D.8	Adjustment for the change in net equity of households in pension funds						
B.8g	**Gross saving**	**–90 330**	**–92 948**	**2 618**	**75 585**	**–8**	
B.12	Current external balance						20 316
Total	Total uses	237 019	106 701	130 318	969 690	–8	
–K.1	After deduction of fixed capital consumption	–14 675	–7 232	–7 443	–47 375		
B.8n	Saving, net	–105 005	–100 180	–4 825	28 210	–8	
II.4.2	**USE OF ADJUSTED DISPOSABLE INCOME ACCOUNT**						
	Resources						
B.7g	Adjusted disposable income	30 106	–14 134	44 240	1 150 056	–8	
D.8	Adjustment for the change in net equity of households in pension funds				26 547		–41
Total	Total resources	30 106	–14 134	44 240	1 176 603	–8	
	Uses						
P.4	Actual final consumption						
P.41	Actual individual consumption				1 101 018		
P.42	Actual collective consumption	120 436	78 814	41 622			
P.4	Total actual final consumption	120 436	78 814	41 622	1 101 018		
D.8	Adjustment for the change in net equity of households in pension funds						
B.8g	**Gross saving**	**–90 330**	**–92 948**	**2 618**	**75 585**	**–8**	
Total	Total uses	30 106	–14 134	44 240	1 176 603	–8	

1.7.7 UK summary accounts 2009

Total economy: all sectors and the rest of the world

£ million

		UK total economy S.1	Non-financial corporations S.11	Financial corporations S.12	Monetary financial institutions S.121+S.122	Other financial intermediaries & auxiliaries S.123+S.124	Insurance corporations & pension funds S.125
III	**ACCUMULATION ACCOUNTS**						
III.1	**CAPITAL ACCOUNT**						
III.1.1	**CHANGE IN NET WORTH DUE TO SAVING & CAPITAL TRANSFERS**						
	Changes in liabilities and net worth						
B.8g	Gross Saving	177 714	147 711	44 756	55 290	4 051	−14 585
B.12	Current external balance						
D.9	Capital transfers receivable						
D.91	Capital taxes	4 206					
D.92	Investment grants	33 816	12 941				
D.99	Other capital transfers	17 518	187	10 120	9 944		176
D.9	Total	55 540	13 128	10 120	9 944		176
−D.9	*less* Capital transfers payable						
−D.91	Capital taxes	−4 206	−	−1 805	−1 805		
−D.92	Investment grants	−33 225					
−D.99	Other capital transfers	−14 845	−723	−176	−		−176
−D.9	Total	−52 276	−723	−1 981	−1 805		−176
B.10.1g	Total change in liabilities and net worth	180 978	160 116	52 895	63 429	4 051	−14 585
	Changes in assets						
B.10.1g	Changes in net worth due to gross saving and capital transfers	180 978	160 116	52 895	63 429	4 051	−14 585
−K.1	After deduction of fixed capital consumption	−159 862	−90 888	−6 924			
B.10.1n	Changes in net worth due to net saving and capital transfers	21 116	69 228	45 971			
III.1.2	**ACQUISITION OF NON-FINANCIAL ASSETS ACCOUNT**						
	Changes in liabilities and net worth						
B.10.1n	Changes in net worth due to net saving and capital transfers	21 116	69 228	45 971			
K.1	Consumption of fixed capital	159 862	90 888	6 924			
B.10.1g	Total change in liabilities and net worth	180 978	160 116	52 895	63 429	4 051	−14 585
	Changes in assets						
P.5	Gross capital formation						
P.51	Gross fixed capital formation	209 253	119 496	6 230	4 471	1 414	345
P.52	Changes in inventories	−11 651	−11 391	53	27	−	26
P.53	Acquisitions less disposals of valuables	429	153	264	−	−	264
P.5	Total	198 035	108 258	6 547	4 498	1 414	635
K.2	Acquisitions less disposals of non-produced non-financial assets	−373	978	16	−	28	−12
de	Statistical discrepancy between expenditure components and GDP	−					
B.9	**Net lending(+) / net borrowing(−)**	**−16 679**	**50 880**	**46 332**	**58 931**	**2 609**	**−15 208**
Total	Total change in assets	180 978	160 116	52 895	63 429	4 051	−14 585

1.7.7 UK summary accounts 2009 (continued)

Total economy: all sectors and the rest of the world

£ million

		General government	Central government	Local government	Households & NPISH	Not sector-ised	Rest of the world
		S.13	S.1311	S.1313	S.14+S.15	S.N	S.2
III	**ACCUMULATION ACCOUNTS**						
III.1	**CAPITAL ACCOUNT**						
III.1.1	**CHANGE IN NET WORTH DUE TO SAVING SAVING & CAPITAL TRANSFERS**						
	Changes in liabilities and net worth						
B.8g	Gross Saving	–90 330	–92 948	2 618	75 585	–8	
B.12	Current external balance						20 316
D.9	Capital transfers receivable						
D.91	Capital taxes	4 206	4 206				
D.92	Investment grants	13 407		13 407	7 468		264
D.99	Other capital transfers	1 309	322	987	5 902		794
D.9	Total	18 922	4 528	14 394	13 370		1 058
–D.9	*less* Capital transfers payable						
–D.91	Capital taxes				–2 401		
–D.92	Investment grants	–33 225	–30 179	–3 046			–855
–D.99	Other capital transfers	–11 180	–10 818	–362	–2 766		–3 467
–D.9	Total	–44 405	–40 997	–3 408	–5 167		–4 322
B.10.1g	Total change in liabilities and net worth	–115 813	–129 417	13 604	83 788	–8	17 052
	Changes in assets						
B.10.1g	Changes in net worth due to gross saving and capital transfers	–115 813	–129 417	13 604	83 788	–8	17 052
–K.1	After deduction of fixed capital consumption	–14 675	–7 232	–7 443	–47 375		
B.10.1n	Changes in net worth due to net saving and capital transfers	–130 488	–136 649	6 161	36 413	–8	
III.1.2	**ACQUISITION OF NON-FINANCIAL ASSETS ACCOUNT**						
	Changes in liabilities and net worth						
B.10.1n	Changes in net worth due to net saving and capital transfers	–130 488	–136 649	6 161	36 413	–8	
K.1	Consumption of fixed capital	14 675	7 232	7 443	47 375		
B.10.1g	Total change in liabilities and net worth	–115 813	–129 417	13 604	83 788	–8	17 052
	Changes in assets						
P.5	Gross capital formation						
P.51	Gross fixed capital formation	37 125	18 476	18 649	46 401		
P.52	Changes in inventories	36	36	–	–349		
P.53	Acquisitions less disposals of valuables	12	12		–		
P.5	Total	37 173	18 524	18 649	46 052		
K.2	Acquisitions less disposals of non-produced non-financial assets	–1 019	–63	–956	–348		373
de	Statistical discrepancy between expenditure components and GDP					–	
B.9	**Net lending(+) / net borrowing(–)**	–151 967	–147 878	–4 089	38 084	–8	16 679
Total	Total change in assets	–115 813	–129 417	13 604	83 788	–8	17 052

1.7.8 UK summary accounts 2009

Total economy: all sectors and the rest of the world. Unconsolidated

£ million

		UK total economy S.1	Non-financial corporations S.11	Financial corporations S.12	Monetary financial institutions S.121+S.122	Other financial intermediaries & auxiliaries S.123+S.124	Insurance corporations & pension funds S.125
III.2	**FINANCIAL ACCOUNT**						
F.A	**Net acquisition of financial assets**						
F.1	Monetary gold and special drawing rights (SDRs)	−132					
F.2	Currency and deposits						
F.21	Currency	6 548	521	2 476	2 476	–	
F.22	Transferable deposits						
F.221	Deposits with UK monetary financial institutions	577 335	20 106	535 802	442 679	95 565	−2 442
F.229	Deposits with rest of the world monetary financial institutions	−217 063	−54 252	−150 826	−147 423	1 570	−4 973
F.29	Other deposits	16 691	−309	5 372	–	5 372	–
F.2	Total currency and deposits	383 511	−33 934	392 824	297 732	102 507	−7 415
F.3	Securities other than shares						
F.331	Short term: money market instruments						
F.3311	Issued by UK central government	25 388	−245	25 556	19 749	3 697	2 110
F.3312	Issued by UK local authorities	–	–	–	–	–	–
F.3315	Issued by UK monetary financial institutions	−63 596	−62	−61 790	−40 887	−7 695	−13 208
F.3316	Issued by other UK residents	−2 729	−1 844	−924	−469	−52	−403
F.3319	Issued by the rest of the world	14 204	1 615	12 118	10 690	1 729	−301
F.332	Medium (1 to 5 year) and long term (over 5 year) bonds						
F.3321	Issued by UK central government	172 349	677	168 778	209 321	−50 227	9 684
F.3322	Issued by UK local authorities	−83	–	−139	–	–	−139
F.3325	Medium term bonds issued by UK monetary financial institutions	33 376	1 438	31 938	10 430	5 424	16 084
F.3326	Other medium & long term bonds issued by UK residents	56 755	−3 366	65 711	65 725	7 732	−7 746
F.3329	Long term bonds issued by the rest of the world	148 024	−1 103	141 205	−5 939	131 041	16 103
F.34	Financial derivatives	−29 194	−3 248	−26 938	−38 134	10 305	891
F.3	Total securities other than shares	354 494	−6 138	355 515	230 486	101 954	23 075
F.4	Loans						
F.41	Short term loans						
F.411	Loans by UK monetary financial institutions, excluding loans secured on dwellings & financial leasing	−202 074		−202 074	−202 074		
F.419	Loans by rest of the world monetary financial institutions						
F.42	Long term loans						
F.421	Direct investment	−44 235	−43 821	−414	–	−1 610	1 196
F.422	Loans secured on dwellings	10 527	–	9 862	35 765	−26 743	840
F.423	Finance leasing	410	−76	486	–	486	
F.424	Other long term loans	−40 573	−2 568	−39 920	191	−30 155	−9 956
F.429	Other long term loans by the rest of the world						
F.4	Total loans	−275 945	−46 465	−232 060	−166 118	−58 022	−7 920
F.5	Shares and other equity						
F.51	Shares and other equity, excluding mutual funds' shares						
F.514	Quoted UK shares	75 972	6 570	32 564	10 151	45 380	−22 967
F.515	Unquoted UK shares	28 592	8 657	25 455	26 711	−1 143	−113
F.516	Other UK equity (including direct investment in property)	−539					
F.517	UK shares and bonds issued by other UK residents	–	–	–	–	–	–
F.519	Shares and other equity issued by the rest of the world	33 575	8 894	21 294	12 308	7 139	1 847
F.52	Mutual funds' shares						
F.521	UK mutual funds' shares	26 236	11	7 927	35	94	7 798
F.529	Rest of the world mutual funds' shares	−1 544					
F.5	Total shares and other equity	162 292	24 132	87 240	49 205	51 470	−13 435
F.6	Insurance technical reserves						
F.61	Net equity of households in life assurance and pension funds' reserves	20 449					
F.62	Prepayments of insurance premiums and reserves for outstanding claims	−1 671	−354	−37	–	−17	−20
F.6	Total insurance technical reserves	18 778	−354	−37	–	−17	−20
F.7	Other accounts receivable	−6 514	−5 635	6 176	−43	644	5 575
F.A	**Total net acquisition of financial assets**	**636 484**	**−68 394**	**609 658**	**411 262**	**198 536**	**−140**

1.7.8 UK summary accounts 2009
continued
Total economy: all sectors and the rest of the world. Unconsolidated

£ million

		General government	Central government	Local government	Households & NPISH	Rest of the world
		S.13	S.1311	S.1313	S.14+S.15	S.2
III.2	**FINANCIAL ACCOUNT**					
F.A	**Net acquisition of financial assets**					
F.1	Monetary gold and special drawing rights (SDRs)	−132	−132			132
F.2	Currency and deposits					
F.21	Currency				3 551	−167
F.22	Transferable deposits					
F.221	Deposits with UK monetary financial institutions	40	6 958	−6 918	21 387	−323 972
F.229	Deposits with rest of the world monetary financial institutions	540	540		−12 525	
F.29	Other deposits	9 094	7 075	2 019	2 534	201
F.2	Total currency and deposits	9 674	14 573	−4 899	14 947	−323 938
F.3	Securities other than shares					
F.331	Short term: money market instruments					
F.3311	Issued by UK central government	77		77	–	587
F.3312	Issued by UK local authorities	–				–
F.3315	Issued by UK monetary financial institutions	−2 333	−2 144	−189	589	85 994
F.3316	Issued by other UK residents	39	882	−843	–	−5 418
F.3319	Issued by the rest of the world	471	471			
F.332	Medium (1 to 5 year) and long term (over 5 year) bonds					
F.3321	Issued by UK central government	28		28	2 866	23 529
F.3322	Issued by UK local authorities				56	–
F.3325	Medium term bonds issued by UK monetary financial institutions					26 967
F.3326	Other medium & long term bonds issued by UK residents	−5 236	−5 236	–	−354	7 827
F.3329	Long term bonds issued by the rest of the world	7 834	7 834		88	
F.34	Financial derivatives	1 003	1 003		−11	–
F.3	Total securities other than shares	1 883	2 810	−927	3 234	139 486
F.4	Loans					
F.41	Short term loans					
F.411	Loans by UK monetary financial institutions, excluding loans secured on dwellings & financial leasing					
F.419	Loans by rest of the world monetary financial institutions					−54 457
F.42	Long term loans					
F.421	Direct investment					−43 649
F.422	Loans secured on dwellings	665	–	665		
F.423	Finance leasing					
F.424	Other long-term loans by UK residents	3 807	3 688	119	−1 892	
F.429	Other long-term loans by the rest of the world					405
F.4	Total loans	4 472	3 688	784	−1 892	−97 701
F.5	Shares and other equity					
F.51	Shares and other equity, excluding mutual funds' shares					
F.514	Quoted UK shares	36 800	36 879	−79	38	44 790
F.515	Unquoted UK shares	−16	−16	–	−5 504	48 313
F.516	Other UK equity (including direct investment in property)	−539	–	−539	–	532
F.517	UK shares and bonds issued by other UK residents	–	–	–	–	–
F.519	Shares and other equity issued by the rest of the world	1 107	1 107		2 280	
F.52	Mutual funds' shares					
F.521	UK mutual funds' shares				18 298	35
F.529	Rest of the world mutual funds' shares				−1 544	
F.5	Total shares and other equity	37 352	37 970	−618	13 568	93 670
F.6	Insurance technical reserves					
F.61	Net equity of households in life assurance and pension funds' reserves				20 449	−41
F.62	Prepayments of insurance premiums and reserves for outstanding claims	−24		−24	−1 256	−282
F.6	Total insurance technical reserves	−24		−24	19 193	−323
F.7	Other accounts receivable	403	196	207	−7 458	108
F.A	**Total net acquisition of financial assets**	53 628	59 105	−5 477	41 592	−188 566

1.7.8 UK summary accounts 2009 continued

Total economy: all sectors and the rest of the world. Unconsolidated £ million

		UK total economy S.1	Non-financial corporations S.11	Financial corporations S.12	Monetary financial institutions S.121+S.122	Other financial intermediaries & auxiliaries S.123+S.124	Insurance corporations & pension funds S.125
III.2	**FINANCIAL ACCOUNT** continued						
F.L	**Net acquisition of financial liabilities**						
F.2	Currency and deposits						
F.21	Currency	6 445		6 330	6 330		
F.22	Transferable deposits						
F.221	Deposits with UK monetary financial institutions	253 363		253 363	253 363		
F.229	Deposits with rest of the world monetary financial institutions						
F.29	Other deposits	16 892	–	7 866		7 866	
F.2	Total currency and deposits	276 700	–	267 559	259 693	7 866	
F.3	Securities other than shares						
F.331	Short term: money market instruments						
F.3311	Issued by UK central government	25 975					
F.3312	Issued by UK local authorities	–					
F.3315	Issued by UK monetary financial institutions	22 398		22 398	22 398		
F.3316	Issued by other UK residents	–8 147	–5 803	–1 781		–1 781	
F.3319	Issued by the rest of the world						
F.332	Medium (1 to 5 year) and long term (over 5 year) bonds						
F.3321	Issued by UK central government	195 878					
F.3322	Issued by UK local authorities	–83					
F.3325	Medium term bonds issued by UK monetary financial institutions	60 343		60 343	60 343		
F.3326	Other medium & long term bonds issued by UK residents	64 582	–3 085	67 315	24 494	39 712	3 109
F.3329	Long term bonds issued by the rest of the world						
F.34	Financial derivatives	–					
F.3	Total securities other than shares	360 946	–8 888	148 275	107 235	37 931	3 109
F.4	Loans						
F.41	Short term loans						
	Loans by UK monetary financial institutions,						
F.411	excluding loans secured on dwellings & financial leasing	–84 674	–49 705	–12 152		–10 278	–1 874
F.419	Loans by rest of the world monetary financial institutions	–54 457	–42 123	–7 499		359	–7 858
F.42	Long term loans						
F.421	Direct investment	–43 649	–39 053	–4 596	–144	–4 369	–83
F.422	Loans secured on dwellings	10 527	3 226				
F.423	Finance leasing	410	219	141	81	60	
F.424	Other long-term loans by UK residents	–40 557	–27 892	–20 600		–14 297	–6 303
F.429	Other long-term loans by the rest of the world	405	–4	–116		–116	
F.4	Total loans	–211 995	–155 332	–44 822	–63	–28 641	–16 118
F.5	Shares and other equity						
F.51	Shares and other equity, excluding mutual funds' shares						
F.514	Quoted UK shares	120 762	32 864	87 898	–	87 383	515
F.515	Unquoted UK shares	76 905	13 775	63 130	–1 091	63 519	702
F.516	Other UK equity (including direct investment in property)	–7	–7	–	–		
F.517	UK shares and bonds issued by other UK residents	–	–	–		–	
F.519	Shares and other equity issued by the rest of the world						
F.52	Mutual funds' shares						
F.521	UK mutual funds' shares	26 271		26 271		26 271	
F.529	Rest of the world mutual funds' shares						
F.5	Total shares and other equity	223 931	46 632	177 299	–1 091	177 173	1 217
F.6	Insurance technical reserves						
	Net equity of households in life assurance and						
F.61	pension funds' reserves	20 408		20 408			20 408
	Prepayments of insurance premiums and reserves for						
F.62	outstanding claims	–1 953		–1 953			–1 953
F.6	Total insurance technical reserves	18 455		18 455			18 455
F.7	Other accounts payable	–6 788	–3 064	–2 589	–2 591	–85	87
F.L	**Total net acquisition of financial liabilities**	661 249	–120 652	564 177	363 183	194 244	6 750
B.9	**Net lending / borrowing**						
F.A	Total net acquisition of financial assets	636 484	–68 394	609 658	411 262	198 536	–140
-F.L	*less* Total net acquisition of financial liabilities	–661 249	120 652	–564 177	–363 183	–194 244	–6 750
B.9f	Net lending (+) / net borrowing (-), from financial account	–24 765	52 258	45 481	48 079	4 292	–6 890
dB.9f	Statistical discrepancy between financial & non-financial accounts	8 086	–1 378	851	10 852	–1 683	–8 318
B.9	**Net lending (+) / net borrowing (-), from capital account**	**–16 679**	**50 880**	**46 332**	**58 931**	**2 609**	**–15 208**

1.7.8 UK summary accounts 2009 (continued)

Total economy: all sectors and the rest of the world. Unconsolidated £ million

		General government S.13	Central government S.1311	Local government S.1313	Households & NPISH S.14+S.15	Not sector-ised S.N	Rest of the world S.2
III.2	**FINANCIAL ACCOUNT** continued						
F.L	**Net acquisition of financial liabilities**						
F.2	Currency and deposits						
F.21	Currency	115	115				–64
F.22	Transferable deposits						
F.221	Deposits with UK monetary financial institutions						
F.229	Deposits with rest of the world monetary financial institutions						–217 063
F.29	Other deposits	9 026	9 026				
F.2	Total currency and deposits	9 141	9 141				–217 127
F.3	Securities other than shares						
F.331	Short term: money market instruments						
F.3311	Issued by UK central government	25 975	25 975				
F.3312	Issued by UK local authorities	–		–			
F.3315	Issued by UK monetary financial institutions						
F.3316	Issued by other UK residents				–563		
F.3319	Issued by the rest of the world						14 204
F.332	Medium (1 to 5 year) and long term (over 5 year) bonds						
F.3321	Issued by UK central government	195 878	195 878				
F.3322	Issued by UK local authorities	–83		–83			
F.3325	Medium term bonds issued by UK monetary financial institutions						
F.3326	Other medium & long term bonds issued by UK residents				352		
F.3329	Long term bonds issued by the rest of the world						148 024
F.34	Financial derivatives						–29 194
F.3	Total securities other than shares	221 770	221 853	–83	–211		133 034
F.4	Loans						
F.41	Short term loans						
F.411	Loans by UK monetary financial institutions, excluding loans secured on dwellings & financial leasing	–20 281	–20 507	226	–2 536		–117 400
F.419	Loans by rest of the world monetary financial institutions	–	–	–	–4 835		
F.42	Long term loans						
F.421	Direct investment						–44 235
F.422	Loans secured on dwellings				7 301		
F.423	Finance leasing	50	50	–			–
F.424	Other long-term loans by UK residents	–1 788	–18	–1 770	9 723		–16
F.429	Other long-term loans by the rest of the world	525	5	520			
F.4	Total loans	–21 494	–20 470	–1 024	9 653		–161 651
F.5	Shares and other equity						
F.51	Shares and other equity, excluding mutual funds' shares						
F.514	Quoted UK shares						
F.515	Unquoted UK shares						
F.516	Other UK equity (including direct investment in property)						
F.517	UK shares and bonds issued by other UK residents						
F.519	Shares and other equity issued by the rest of the world						33 575
F.52	Mutual funds' shares						
F.521	UK mutual funds' shares						
F.529	Rest of the world mutual funds' shares						–1 544
F.5	Total shares and other equity						32 031
F.6	Insurance technical reserves						
F.61	Net equity of households in life assurance and pension funds' reserves						
F.62	Prepayments of insurance premiums and reserves for outstanding claims						
F.6	Total insurance technical reserves						
F.7	Other accounts payable	–4 519	–3 886	–633	3 384		382
F.L	**Total net acquisition of financial liabilities**	204 898	206 638	–1 740	12 826		–213 331
B.9	**Net lending / borrowing**						
F.A	Total net acquisition of financial assets	53 628	59 105	–5 477	41 592		–188 566
–F.L	*less* Total net acquisition of financial liabilities	–204 898	–206 638	1 740	–12 826		213 331
B.9f	Net lending (+) / net borrowing (–), from financial account	–151 270	–147 533	–3 737	28 766		24 765
dB.9f	Statistical discrepancy between financial & non-financial accounts	–697	–345	–352	9 318	–8	–8 086
B.9	**Net lending (+) / net borrowing (–), from capital account**	**–151 967**	**–147 878**	**–4 089**	**38 084**	**–8**	**16 679**

1.7.9 UK summary accounts 2009

Total economy: all sectors and the rest of the world. Unconsolidated

£ billion

		UK total economy S.1	Non-financial corporations S.11	Financial corporations S.12	Monetary financial institutions S.121+S.122	Other financial intermediaries & auxiliaries S.123+S.124	Insurance corporations & pension funds S.125
IV.3	**FINANCIAL BALANCE SHEET** at end of period						
AF.A	**Financial assets**						
AF.1	Monetary gold and special drawing rights (SDRs)	15.7					
AF.2	Currency and deposits						
AF.21	Currency	62.1	5.2	12.8	12.7	0.1	
AF.22	Transferable deposits						
AF.221	Deposits with UK monetary financial institutions	3 453.5	283.4	2 141.5	1 142.2	909.5	89.7
AF.229	Deposits with rest of the world monetary financial institutions	2 589.6	333.6	2 186.0	1 779.3	364.2	42.5
AF.29	Other deposits	151.1	8.9	16.9	–	16.9	–
AF.2	Total currency and deposits	6 256.3	631.1	4 357.2	2 934.2	1 290.7	132.3
AF.3	Securities other than shares						
AF.331	Short term: money market instruments						
AF.3311	Issued by UK central government	38.0	0.3	37.6	22.8	11.6	3.2
AF.3312	Issued by UK local authorities	–	–	–	–	–	
AF.3315	Issued by UK monetary financial institutions	92.2	11.5	73.5	32.0	29.1	12.4
AF.3316	Issued by other UK residents	12.1	6.4	4.3	–	0.3	4.0
AF.3319	Issued by the rest of the world	85.2	2.9	76.7	65.4	7.3	4.0
AF.332	Medium (1 to 5 year) and long term (over 5 year) bonds						
AF.3321	Issued by UK central government	573.4	2.6	560.6	228.8	81.4	250.4
AF.3322	Issued by UK local authorities	1.0	–	0.5	–	–	0.5
AF.3325	Medium term bonds issued by UK monetary financial institutions	181.2	4.8	176.4	54.3	31.1	91.0
AF.3326	Other medium & long term bonds issued by UK residents	592.7	3.6	582.9	318.8	98.6	165.6
AF.3329	Long term bonds issued by the rest of the world	1 176.1	18.2	1 128.6	504.0	291.5	333.1
AF.34	Financial derivatives	5 275.2	25.4	5 248.5	4 079.8	1 072.1	96.6
AF.3	Total securities other than shares	8 027.2	75.7	7 889.6	5 305.9	1 622.9	960.8
AF.4	Loans						
AF.41	Short term loans						
AF.411	Loans by UK monetary financial institutions, excluding loans secured on dwellings & financial leasing	2 504.8		2 504.8	2 504.8		
AF.419	Loans by rest of the world monetary financial institutions						
AF.42	Long term loans						
AF.421	Direct investment	369.7	329.3	40.4	–	32.4	8.0
AF.422	Loans secured on dwellings	1 234.9	–	1 230.9	922.0	306.4	2.4
AF.423	Finance leasing	33.7	5.0	28.7	2.6	26.1	
AF.424	Other long term loans	307.1	65.4	130.5	4.2	24.6	101.6
AF.429	Other long term loans by the rest of the world						
AF.4	Total loans	4 450.2	399.7	3 935.2	3 433.7	389.5	112.0
AF.5	Shares and other equity						
AF.51	Shares and other equity, excluding mutual funds' shares						
AF.514	Quoted UK shares	845.9	48.4	589.3	22.4	215.0	351.9
AF.515	Unquoted UK shares	626.1	72.9	326.1	113.3	207.8	4.9
AF.516	Other UK equity (including direct investment in property)	119.0					
AF.517	UK shares and bonds issued by other UK residents	–	–	–	–	–	
AF.519	Shares and other equity issued by the rest of the world	1 648.7	706.3	841.8	123.4	–	386.7
AF.52	Mutual funds' shares						
AF.521	UK mutual funds' shares	504.9	0.4	402.6	1.3	3.5	397.8
AF.529	Rest of the world mutual funds' shares	0.8					
AF.5	Total shares and other equity	3 745.4	828.1	2 159.7	260.3	758.1	1 141.3
AF.6	Insurance technical reserves						
AF.61	Net equity of households in life assurance and pension funds' reserves	2 141.8					
AF.62	Prepayments of insurance premiums and reserves for outstanding claims	60.7	12.8	1.3		0.6	0.7
AF.6	Total insurance technical reserves	2 202.5	12.8	1.3		0.6	0.7
AF.7	Other accounts receivable	399.2	136.5	68.2	0.2	17.9	50.1
AF.A	**Total financial assets**	25 096.5	2 083.9	18 411.3	11 934.3	4 079.8	2 397.2

1.7.9 UK summary accounts 2009 (continued)

Total economy: all sectors and the rest of the world. Unconsolidated

£ billion

		General government	Central government	Local government	Households & NPISH	Rest of the world
		S.13	S.1311	S.1313	S.14+S.15	S.2
IV.3	**FINANCIAL BALANCE SHEET** at end of period					
AF.A	**Financial assets**					
AF.1	Monetary gold and special drawing rights (SDRs)	15.7	15.7			
AF.2	Currency and deposits					
AF.21	Currency				44.1	1.4
AF.22	Transferable deposits					
AF.221	Deposits with UK monetary financial institutions	57.2	35.2	22.0	971.5	2 976.3
AF.229	Deposits with rest of the world monetary financial institutions	4.9	4.9		65.1	
AF.29	Other deposits	26.8	21.9	4.9	98.5	1.0
AF.2	Total currency and deposits	88.9	61.9	27.0	1 179.2	2 978.7
AF.3	Securities other than shares					
AF.331	Short term: money market instruments					
AF.3311	Issued by UK central government	0.1		0.1	–	19.4
AF.3312	Issued by UK local authorities	–			–	
AF.3315	Issued by UK monetary financial institutions	1.6	0.4	1.2	5.6	267.8
AF.3316	Issued by other UK residents	1.4	1.0	0.5	–	21.5
AF.3319	Issued by the rest of the world	5.6	5.6			
AF.332	Medium (1 to 5 year) and long term (over 5 year) bonds					
AF.3321	Issued by UK central government	0.2		0.2	10.0	224.3
AF.3322	Issued by UK local authorities	–	–		0.5	
AF.3325	Medium term bonds issued by UK monetary financial institutions					208.0
AF.3326	Other medium & long term bonds issued by UK residents	0.3	0.1	0.2	5.9	854.5
AF.3329	Long term bonds issued by the rest of the world	21.1	21.1		8.2	
AF.34	Financial derivatives	–1.4	–1.4		2.6	2 096.8
AF.3	Total securities other than shares	29.0	26.8	2.2	32.9	3 692.3
AF.4	Loans					
AF.41	Short term loans					
AF.411	Loans by UK monetary financial institutions, excluding loans secured on dwellings & financial leasing					
AF.419	Loans by rest of the world monetary financial institutions					795.9
AF.42	Long term loans					
AF.421	Direct investment					421.9
AF.422	Loans secured on dwellings	4.1	0.1	4.0		
AF.423	Finance leasing					
AF.424	Other long-term loans by UK residents	92.9	92.7	0.2	18.3	
AF.429	Other long-term loans by the rest of the world					4.4
AF.4	Total loans	97.0	92.7	4.2	18.3	1 222.2
AF.5	Shares and other equity					
AF.51	Shares and other equity, excluding mutual funds' shares					
AF.514	Quoted UK shares	54.6	54.1	0.5	153.6	753.3
AF.515	Unquoted UK shares	6.6	5.9	0.7	220.5	599.1
AF.516	Other UK equity (including direct investment in property)	117.7	3.8	113.9	1.4	24.5
AF.517	UK shares and bonds issued by other UK residents	–	–	–	–	–
AF.519	Shares and other equity issued by the rest of the world	12.3	12.3		88.3	
AF.52	Mutual funds' shares					
AF.521	UK mutual funds' shares				101.9	1.3
AF.529	Rest of the world mutual funds' shares				0.8	
AF.5	Total shares and other equity	191.1	76.0	115.1	566.5	1 378.3
AF.6	Insurance technical reserves					
AF.61	Net equity of households in life assurance and pension funds' reserves				2 141.8	0.2
AF.62	Prepayments of insurance premiums and reserves for outstanding claims	0.9		0.9	45.7	10.2
AF.6	Total insurance technical reserves	0.9		0.9	2 187.5	10.4
AF.7	Other accounts receivable	71.6	71.7	–0.1	123.0	2.6
AF.A	**Total financial assets**	494.1	344.9	149.2	4 107.2	9 284.5

1.7.9 UK summary accounts 2009 continued

Total economy: all sectors and the rest of the world. Unconsolidated

£ billion

		UK total economy S.1	Non-financial corporations S.11	Financial corporations S.12	Monetary financial institutions S.121+S.122	Other financial intermediaries & auxiliaries S.123+S.124	Insurance corporations & pension funds S.125
IV.3	**FINANCIAL BALANCE SHEET** continued at end of period						
AF.L	**Financial liabilities**						
AF.2	Currency and deposits						
AF.21	Currency	62.7		58.7	58.7		
AF.22	Transferable deposits						
AF.221	Deposits with UK monetary financial institutions	6 429.8		6 429.8	6 429.8		
AF.229	Deposits with rest of the world monetary financial institutions						
AF.29	Other deposits	152.1	–	25.2		25.2	
AF.2	Total currency and deposits	6 644.6	–	6 513.6	6 488.5	25.2	
AF.3	Securities other than shares						
AF.331	Short term: money market instruments						
AF.3311	Issued by UK central government	57.5					
AF.3312	Issued by UK local authorities	–					
AF.3315	Issued by UK monetary financial institutions	360.1		360.1	360.1		
AF.3316	Issued by other UK residents	33.6	22.5	10.7		10.7	
AF.3319	Issued by the rest of the world						
AF.332	Medium (1 to 5 year) and long term (over 5 year) bonds						
AF.3321	Issued by UK central government	797.7					
AF.3322	Issued by UK local authorities	1.0					
AF.3325	Medium term bonds issued by UK monetary financial institutions	389.2		389.2	389.2		
AF.3326	Other medium & long term bonds issued by UK residents	1 447.2	392.8	1 050.7	271.2	778.8	0.8
AF.3329	Long term bonds issued by the rest of the world						
AF.34	Financial derivatives	5 195.6	33.3	5 158.7	4 026.8	1 038.4	93.6
AF.3	Total securities other than shares	8 281.8	448.6	6 969.4	5 047.2	1 827.9	94.3
AF.4	Loans						
AF.41	Short term loans						
AF.411	Loans by UK monetary financial institutions, excluding loans secured on dwellings & financial leasing	1 601.3	479.0	925.0	–	919.3	5.7
AF.419	Loans by rest of the world monetary financial institutions	795.9	183.4	586.6		558.5	28.1
AF.42	Long term loans						
AF.421	Direct investment	421.9	366.9	54.9	1.0	45.2	8.7
AF.422	Loans secured on dwellings	1 234.9	43.5				
AF.423	Finance leasing	33.7	24.9	4.2	2.3	1.9	
AF.424	Other long-term loans by UK residents	301.2	117.7	89.4	–	88.9	0.5
AF.429	Other long-term loans by the rest of the world	4.4	0.9	0.5		0.5	
AF.4	Total loans	4 393.2	1 216.2	1 660.7	3.3	1 614.3	43.0
AF.5	Shares and other equity						
AF.51	Shares and other equity, excluding mutual funds' shares						
AF.514	Quoted UK shares	1 599.3	1 212.6	386.6	0.1	342.6	43.9
AF.515	Unquoted UK shares	1 225.2	633.5	591.7	158.7	418.6	14.4
AF.516	Other UK equity (including direct investment in property)	143.6	143.6				
AF.517	UK shares and bonds issued by other UK residents	–	–	–	–	–	
AF.519	Shares and other equity issued by the rest of the world						
AF.52	Mutual funds' shares						
AF.521	UK mutual funds' shares	506.2		506.2		506.2	
AF.529	Rest of the world mutual funds' shares						
AF.5	Total shares and other equity	3 474.2	1 989.7	1 484.5	158.8	1 267.4	58.3
AF.6	Insurance technical reserves						
AF.61	Net equity of households in life assurance and pension funds' reserves	2 142.0		2 142.0			2 142.0
AF.62	Prepayments of insurance premiums and reserves for outstanding claims	70.9		70.9			70.9
AF.6	Total insurance technical reserves	2 212.9		2 212.9			2 212.9
AF.7	Other accounts payable	393.9	161.6	103.6	24.6	2.7	76.3
AF.L	**Total financial liabilities**	25 400.6	3 816.1	18 944.8	11 722.4	4 737.5	2 484.9
BF.90	**Net financial assets / liabilities**						
AF.A	Total financial assets	25 096.5	2 083.9	18 411.3	11 934.3	4 079.8	2 397.2
-AF.L	*less* Total financial liabilities	−25 400.6	−3 816.1	−18 944.8	−11 722.4	−4 737.5	−2 484.9
BF.90	**Net financial assets (+) / liabilities (−)**	−304.1	−1 732.3	−533.4	212.0	−657.7	−87.7

1.7.9 UK summary accounts 2009 (continued)

Total economy: all sectors and the rest of the world. Unconsolidated £ billion

		General government	Central government	Local government	Households & NPISH	Rest of the world
		S.13	S.1311	S.1313	S.14+S.15	S.2
IV.3	**FINANCIAL BALANCE SHEET** continued at end of period					
AF.L	**Financial liabilities**					
AF.2	Currency and deposits					
AF.21	Currency	4.0	4.0			0.8
AF.22	Transferable deposits					
AF.221	Deposits with UK monetary financial institutions					
AF.229	Deposits with rest of the world monetary financial institutions					2 589.6
AF.29	Other deposits	127.0	127.0			
AF.2	Total currency and deposits	131.0	131.0			2 590.4
AF.3	Securities other than shares					
AF.331	Short term: money market instruments					
AF.3311	Issued by UK central government	57.5	57.5			
AF.3312	Issued by UK local authorities	–				
AF.3315	Issued by UK monetary financial institutions					
AF.3316	Issued by other UK residents				0.4	
AF.3319	Issued by the rest of the world					85.2
AF.332	Medium (1 to 5 year) and long term (over 5 year) bonds					
AF.3321	Issued by UK central government	797.7	797.7			
AF.3322	Issued by UK local authorities	1.0		1.0		
AF.3325	Medium term bonds issued by UK monetary financial institutions					
AF.3326	Other medium & long term bonds issued by UK residents			–	3.7	
AF.3329	Long term bonds issued by the rest of the world					1 176.1
AF.34	Financial derivatives				3.5	2 176.4
AF.3	Total securities other than shares	856.1	855.1	1.0	7.6	3 437.7
AF.4	Loans					
AF.41	Short term loans					
AF.411	Loans by UK monetary financial institutions, excluding loans secured on dwellings & financial leasing	16.1	5.0	11.0	181.2	903.5
AF.419	Loans by rest of the world monetary financial institutions	–	–	–	25.9	
AF.42	Long term loans					
AF.421	Direct investment					369.7
AF.422	Loans secured on dwellings				1 191.4	
AF.423	Finance leasing	4.6	4.5	0.1		
AF.424	Other long-term loans by UK residents	52.0	–	52.0	42.1	5.9
AF.429	Other long-term loans by the rest of the world	3.0	–	3.0		
AF.4	Total loans	75.8	9.6	66.2	1 440.6	1 279.1
AF.5	Shares and other equity					
AF.51	Shares and other equity, excluding mutual funds' shares					
AF.514	Quoted UK shares					
AF.515	Unquoted UK shares					
AF.516	Other UK equity (including direct investment in property)					
AF.517	UK shares and bonds issued by other UK residents					
AF.519	Shares and other equity issued by the rest of the world					1 648.7
AF.52	Mutual funds' shares					
AF.521	UK mutual funds' shares					
AF.529	Rest of the world mutual funds' shares					0.8
AF.5	Total shares and other equity					1 649.5
AF.6	Insurance technical reserves					
AF.61	Net equity of households in life assurance and pension funds' reserves					
AF.62	Prepayments of insurance premiums and reserves for outstanding claims					
AF.6	Total insurance technical reserves					
AF.7	Other accounts payable	45.3	36.7	8.6	83.4	8.0
AF.L	**Total financial liabilities**	1 108.1	1 032.4	75.8	1 531.6	8 964.7
BF.90	**Net financial assets / liabilities**					
AF.A	Total financial assets	494.1	344.9	149.2	4 107.2	9 284.5
-AF.L	less Total financial liabilities	-1 108.1	-1 032.4	-75.8	-1 531.6	-8 964.7
BF.90	**Net financial assets (+) / liabilities (-)**	−614.0	−687.4	73.4	2 575.7	319.8

1.8A FISIM[1,2] impact on UK gross domestic product and national income
Current prices

£ million

			2004	2005	2006	2007	2008	2009	2010
	IMPACT OF FISIM ON GROSS DOMESTIC PRODUCT								
	Gross domestic product: Output								
P.1	Output of services								
	Financial intermediaries	D8NH	39 100	43 445	49 232	49 491	68 551	80 873	73 522
	Non-Market	D8N9	591	349	283	142	162	–200	375
-P.2	Intermediate comsumption								
	Non-financial corporations	-G7VJ	–8 904	–11 035	–13 445	–15 041	–18 911	–18 231	–16 197
	Financial corporations	-D8OO	–593	55	–229	1 735	–119	–2 910	–2 957
	General Government	-C5PR	–142	–66	–31	58	–4	265	–176
	Households and NPISH	-IV8A	–7 820	–9 914	–10 930	–8 157	–16 582	–39 318	–36 182
B.1*g	**Gross domestic product at market prices**	C95M	22 232	22 834	24 880	28 228	33 097	20 479	18 385
	Gross domestic product: Expenditure								
P.3	Total Final consumption expenditure								
	Households and NPISH	IV8B	19 769	21 302	23 152	24 216	23 168	14 913	13 349
	General Government	C5PR	142	66	31	–58	4	–265	176
P.6	Exports of services	C6FD	4 943	5 288	6 103	9 210	15 652	10 362	9 259
-P.7	less imports of services	-C6F7	–2 622	–3 822	–4 406	–5 140	–5 727	–4 531	–4 399
B.1*g	**Gross domestic product at market prices**	C95M	22 232	22 834	24 880	28 228	33 097	20 479	18 385
	Gross domestic product: Income								
B.2g	Operating surplus, gross								
	Non-financial corporations	IV8H	–8 904	–11 035	–13 445	–15 041	–18 911	–18 231	–16 197
	Financial corporations	IV8I	38 507	43 500	49 003	51 226	68 432	77 963	70 565
	Households	IV8J	–7 371	–9 631	–10 678	–7 957	–16 424	–39 253	–35 983
B.1*g	**Gross domestic product at market prices**	C95M	22 232	22 834	24 880	28 228	33 097	20 479	18 385
	IMPACT OF FISIM ON GROSS NATIONAL INCOME								
B.1*g	Gross domestic product at market prices	C95M	22 232	22 834	24 880	28 228	33 097	20 479	18 385
D.4	Property and entrepreneurial income								
	receipts from the rest of the world	IV8E	–524	133	147	–597	–2 821	–2 045	–1 662
	less payments to the rest of the world (ROW)	-IV8F	–1 797	–1 599	–1 844	–3 473	–7 104	–3 786	–3 198
B.5*g	**Gross national income at market prices**	IV8G	19 911	21 368	23 183	24 158	23 172	14 648	13 525

1 FISIM = Financial intermediation services indirectly measured
2 In some sectors, including central government and local government, FISIM has been adjusted to avoid negative values for 2008. As 2008 is the reference year, negative values could distort the chained volume measures. The overall impact of these adjustments is small. A joint UN/Eurostat task force is reviewing the methodology for measurement of FISIM.

1.8B FISIM[1,2] impact on UK gross domestic product and national income
Chained volume measures (reference year 2008)

£ million

			2004	2005	2006	2007	2008	2009	2010
	IMPACT OF FISIM ON GROSS DOMESTIC PRODUCT								
	Gross domestic product: Expenditure								
P.3	Total Final consumption expenditure								
	Households and NPISH	IV8D	19 729	20 994	21 543	22 141	23 168	22 807	21 835
	General Government	C5Q9	2	2	2	3	4	4	3
P.6	Exports of services	C6FM	9 198	10 512	11 880	13 303	15 652	14 914	14 106
-P.7	less imports of services	-C6FL	–2 823	–4 038	–4 534	–5 155	–5 727	–5 204	–5 237
B.1*g	**Gross domestic product at market prices**	DZ4H	27 764	28 827	29 819	30 750	33 097	32 522	30 707

1 FISIM = Financial intermediation services indirectly measured
2 In some sectors, including central government and local government, FISIM has been adjusted to avoid negative values for 2008. As 2008 is the reference year, negative values could distort the chained volume measures. The overall impact of these adjustments is small. A joint UN/Eurostat task force is reviewing the methodology for measurement of FISIM.

1.8C FISIM[1,2] impact upon interest resources and uses by sector[3]
Current prices

£ million

			2004	2005	2006	2007	2008	2009	2010
	Public corporations								
	Resources								
	Unadjusted interest received	NENH	1 263	1 788	874	729	844	342	321
	plus FISIM	C7RL	-2	4	5	2	2	-29	-17
D.41	Interest received	CPBV	1 261	1 792	879	731	846	313	304
	Uses								
	Unadjusted interest paid	NENG	1 363	1 272	1 435	1 587	1 792	1 616	1 332
	less FISIM	D8KD	27	21	41	74	47	67	42
D.41	Interest paid	XAQZ	1 336	1 251	1 394	1 513	1 745	1 549	1 290
	Private non-financial corporations								
	Resources								
	Unadjusted interest received	I69R	9 917	12 075	19 993	24 868	19 348	5 640	4 875
	plus FISIM	IV87	2 963	3 513	4 519	4 922	4 372	1 446	1 741
D.41	Interest received	DSZR	12 880	15 588	24 512	29 790	23 720	7 086	6 616
	Uses								
	Unadjusted interest paid	I6A2	39 392	45 324	51 058	63 548	65 551	47 075	37 569
	less FISIM	IV86	5 916	7 497	8 880	10 043	14 490	16 747	14 431
D.41	Interest paid	DSZV	33 476	37 827	42 178	53 505	51 061	30 328	23 138
	Non-financial corporations								
	Resources								
	Unadjusted interest received	J4WQ	11 180	13 863	20 867	25 597	20 192	5 982	5 196
	plus FISIM	IV89	2 961	3 517	4 524	4 924	4 374	1 417	1 724
D.41	Interest received	EABC	14 141	17 380	25 391	30 521	24 566	7 399	6 920
	Uses								
	Unadjusted interest paid	J4WS	40 755	46 596	52 493	65 135	67 343	48 691	38 901
	less FISIM	IV88	5 943	7 518	8 921	10 117	14 537	16 814	14 473
D.41	Interest paid	EABG	34 812	39 078	43 572	55 018	52 806	31 877	24 428
	Financial corporations								
	Resources								
	Unadjusted interest received	J4WU	221 186	277 738	367 636	468 157	483 971	268 781	229 259
	plus FISIM	IV8Y	-25 834	-31 031	-34 431	-32 377	-50 988	-84 101	-75 881
D.41	Interest received	NHCK	195 352	246 707	333 205	435 780	432 983	184 680	153 378
	Uses								
	Unadjusted interest paid	J4WW	147 137	200 346	287 265	376 128	375 751	167 774	127 919
	plus FISIM	IV8Z	12 673	12 469	14 572	18 849	17 444	-6 138	-5 316
D.41	Interest paid	NHCM	159 810	212 815	301 837	394 977	393 195	161 636	122 603
	Central government								
	Resources								
	Unadjusted interest received	I69N	5 716	5 364	5 917	6 628	7 503	7 252	5 402
	plus FISIM	C6GA	39	37	16	-58	1	-258	-97
D.41	Interest received	NMCE	5 755	5 401	5 933	6 570	7 504	6 994	5 305
	Uses								
	Unadjusted interest paid	I69W	23 224	25 935	27 463	31 313	32 788	26 982	42 235
	less FISIM	C6G9	12	28	18	44	1	34	68
D.41	Interest paid	NUHA	23 212	25 907	27 445	31 269	32 787	26 948	42 167
	Local government								
	Resources								
	Unadjusted interest received	I69O	1 013	1 075	1 544	1 965	2 661	1 019	687
	plus FISIM	C6FQ	70	-5	-12	9	1	-387	-146
D.41	Interest received	NMKB	1 083	1 070	1 532	1 974	2 662	632	541
	Uses								
	Unadjusted interest paid	I69X	3 782	3 475	3 540	3 470	3 715	3 571	3 500
	less FISIM	C6FP	21	6	9	-53	1	346	351
D.41	Interest paid	NCBW	3 761	3 469	3 531	3 523	3 714	3 225	3 149
	Households & non-profit institutions serving households								
	Resources								
	Unadjusted interest received	J4WY	26 636	32 350	34 677	43 421	42 718	20 143	19 212
	plus FISIM	IV8W	8 169	7 982	9 087	11 656	8 078	-10 371	-9 887
D.41	Interest received	QWLZ	34 805	40 332	43 764	55 077	50 796	9 772	9 325
	Uses								
	Unadjusted interest paid	J4WZ	62 709	73 809	80 725	95 118	98 921	72 016	64 753
	less FISIM	IV8X	18 971	22 951	24 743	20 517	31 514	64 537	59 219
D.41	Interest paid	QWMG	43 738	50 858	55 982	74 601	67 407	7 479	5 534
	Rest of the world								
	Resources								
	Unadjusted interest received	I69V	76 886	112 129	156 724	203 820	196 884	102 439	86 407
	FISIM on interest paid to Rest of World	IV8F	1 797	1 599	1 844	3 473	7 104	3 786	3 198
D.41	Interest received	QYNG	78 683	113 728	158 568	207 293	203 988	106 225	89 605
	Uses								
	Unadjusted interest paid	I6A6	65 010	92 358	135 879	178 424	175 411	86 582	68 855
	FISIM on interest received from Rest of World	IV8E	-524	133	147	-597	-2 821	-2 045	-1 662
D.41	Interest paid	QYNJ	64 486	92 491	136 026	177 827	172 590	84 537	67 193

1 FISIM = Financial intermediation services indirectly measured
2 In some sectors, including central government and local government, FISIM has been adjusted to avoid negative values for 2008. As 2008 is the reference year, negative values could distort the chained volume measures. The overall impact of these adjustments is small. A joint UN/Eurostat task force is reviewing the methodology for measurement of FISIM.
3 Interest is recorded within the allocation of primary income account

The industrial analyses

Part 2

Chapter 2

The industrial analyses at a glance from Table 2.1

Gross value added at basic prices by industry

An analysis of the ten broad industrial groups shows that in 2009, the government, health and education industries provided the largest contribution to gross value added at current basic prices, at £253 billion out of a total of £1,256.9 billion (20.1 per cent). The distribution, transport, hotel and restaurant industries contributed 18.7 per cent; the production industries accounted for 15.0 per cent; and the professional and support activity industries 11.8 per cent.

Breakdown of gross value added at basic prices by industry for 2009

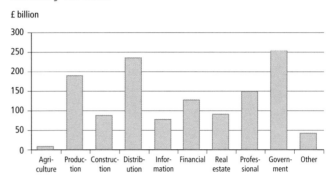

Final demand

In 2009, just under half (47.3 per cent) of all goods and services entering into final demand were purchased by consumers, 18.0 per cent were consumed by government, both central and local, and 21.8 per cent were exported. Gross capital formation by all sectors of the economy amounted to 10.9 per cent of the total.

Composition of final demand for 2009

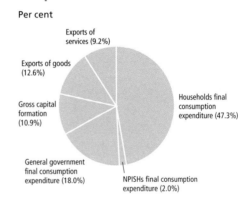

Compensation of employees by industry

The government, health and education industries showed the highest level of compensation of employees in 2009 at £220.1 billion (28.3 per cent). The second largest industry in terms of its contribution to total compensation of employees was the distribution, transport, hotel and restaurant industries at £161.3 billion (20.8 per cent).

Compensation of employees by industry, 2009

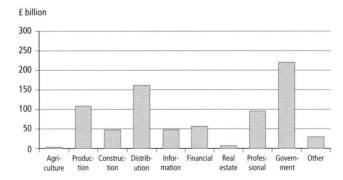

Explanation of industrial analyses

Input–Output Supply and Use tables

The annual estimates prepared for the *National Accounts Blue Book* incorporate the results of annual inquiries which become available in the first part of the year, although estimates for the latest year are still based largely on quarterly information. As new data are collected it is likely that revisions will be necessary. The process of reassessing these estimates involves the preparation of Supply and Use tables. This approach amalgamates all the available information on inputs, outputs, gross value added, income and expenditure. Similarly the production of the consolidated sector and financial accounts requires the preparation of 'top-to-bottom' sector and sub-sector accounts to identify discrepancies in the estimates relating to each sector.

In addition to methods changes, a significant reclassification exercise has been undertaken for this year's *Blue Book* with the introduction of the Standard Industrial Classification 2007 (SIC 2007) and the Classification of Product by Activity 2008 (CPA 2008). These replace SIC 2003 and CPA 2002 respectively. For previously published data, a conversion process has been implemented to provide a time series from 1997 to 2006 which is consistent with the new classifications. From 2007 to 2009, source data were supplied according to the new classifications and were balanced in the usual way. For further details see Drew and Dunn (2011)[1] and Everett (2011)[2].

GDP and the balancing of the annual accounts

There are three different approaches to the estimation of current price GDP in the UK: the income approach, the expenditure approach and the production approach. In theory the three different approaches should produce the same result. However, the different approaches are based on different surveys and administrative data sources and each produces estimates which, like all statistical estimates, are subject to errors and omissions. A definitive GDP estimate can only emerge after a process of balancing and adjustment. ONS believes that the most reliable 'definitive' estimate of the current price level of GDP is that derived using the annual Supply and Use tables framework. Thus, for the years when Supply and Use tables are available, GDP is set at the level derived from that year's balance. For periods subsequent to the latest Supply and Use tables, the level of GDP is carried forward using movements in income, expenditure and production totals.

The Supply and Use framework

The UK Supply and Use tables show the composition and value of goods and services entering into final demand, the outputs and incomes generated in the production process, as well as the intermediate transactions which form inputs into these processes.

The analyses are constructed to show a balanced and complete picture of the flows of products in the economy and illustrate the relationships between producers and consumers of goods and services. On an annual basis, Supply and Use tables are used to achieve consistency in the economic accounts' aggregates by linking the components of value added, inputs, outputs and final demand. As the income, production and expenditure measures of GDP can all be calculated from the Supply and Use tables, a single estimate of GDP can be derived by balancing the supply and demand for goods and services and reconciling them with the corresponding value added estimates. For the years 1989 to 2009, the balancing process has been used to set the level of current price GDP and has disposed of the need for statistical discrepancies in the form of a GDP expenditure adjustment and a GDP income adjustment.

Industrial analyses

The process, which produces Supply and Use tables annually, has been improved considerably over the last few years and can now produce the first balance for a year around 18 months after the end of that year. Both the full and summary Supply and Use tables, consistent with the *Blue Book*, are published as a separate web-only publication at the same time as the *Blue Book*. The latest annual Supply and Use tables[3] cover 1997 to 2009, with data for 2009 being balanced for the first time, and 2007 and 2008 being fully re-balanced. Figures for 1997 to 2006 have also been revised following the conversion of underlying data to new classifications and other methods changes.

Some background on the structure of the Supply and Use tables

The Supply and Use tables are based on a framework which incorporates estimates of industry inputs, outputs and value added. The tables consist of two matrices: the *Supply* table and the *Use* table, each of which breaks down and balances 112 different industries and 112 products at purchasers' prices. The following paragraphs summarise the methodology. For more detail see Akers and Clifton-Fearnside (2008).[4]

Supply table

At a very aggregate level the *Supply* table can be represented as follows:

	Output by industry	Imports of goods and services	Distributors' trading margins	Taxes *less* subsidies on products
Output by product				

The main part of the Supply table shows estimates of domestic industries' output (total sales adjusted for changes in inventories of work in progress and finished goods) compiled at basic prices. Basic prices value the goods leaving the factory gate but exclude any taxes on products and include any subsidies on products. However, for the balancing process, the estimates of supply of products are required at purchasers' prices, that is, those actually paid by the purchasers to take delivery of the goods, excluding any deductible VAT. To convert the estimates of domestic output valued at basic prices to the total supply of products valued at purchasers' prices requires the addition of:

- the value of imports of goods and services
- distributors' trading margins
- taxes on products (for example, VAT, excise duties, air passenger tax and insurance premium tax)

less

- subsidies on products (for example, agricultural and transport subsidies)

Use table

The Use table reveals the input structure of each industry in terms of combined domestic and imported goods and services. It also shows the product composition of final demand and, for each industry, the intermediate purchases adjusted for changes in inventories of materials and fuels. Consumption of products is represented in the rows of the balance while purchases by industries, and final demands, are represented in the columns. At the very aggregate level the Use table can be considered in three parts as at the bottom of the page.

The body of the matrix, which represents consumption of products, is at purchasers' prices and so already includes the product-specific taxes and subsidies separately added in the Supply table.

The Supply–Use balance is effectively achieved when:

For industries:

Inputs (from the *Use* table)

equals

Outputs (from the *Supply* table)

For products:

Supply (from the *Supply* table)

equals

Demand (from the *Use* table)

That is, when the data from the income, expenditure and production approaches used to fill the matrices all produce the same estimate of current price GDP at market prices. GDP at current market prices can be derived from the balances by taking the estimate of total gross value added at basic prices (from the Use table) and adding taxes on products and deducting subsidies on products (from the Supply table).

The balancing process

The supply and use tables produced this year use the same methods first employed in the 2008 edition of the *Blue Book* (see Akers and Clifton-Fearnside (2008)[4]). A detailed description of the methods and process used for the 2006, and earlier, editions of the *Blue Book* can be found in Mahajan (2006)[5].

Industry consumption/final demand table

	Industry consumption	Final demand
Products consumed	Shows consumption by each industry to produce their own output (that is, intermediate consumption)	Shows final demand categories (for example, households' expenditure, gross capital formation and exports) and the values of products going to these categories
Primary inputs	Shows the gross value added components of each industry, taxes *less* subsidies on production other than product specific taxes and subsidies, compensation of employees and gross operating surplus	

The current approach utilises new computing systems resulting from the ONS programme for the modernisation of its statistical systems and processes. Data compilers provide input to the balancing process. These individuals bring with them an understanding of the data that is being used to populate the Supply and Use framework. If we consider the Supply and Use framework as a column (industry) and row (product) matrix, the process of balancing consists of a series of alternating row and column confrontations of the data.

The **first stage** takes place before the Supply and Use framework is populated. It consists of an examination of each of the individual rows and columns within the framework being reviewed for plausibility independently of each other. For example, estimates of household consumption expenditure, by product, are produced and analysed to ensure the overall picture of household spending and its breakdown by product presents a credible story in their own right. Similarly, for those components with an industry dimension, such as output, the initial stage scrutinises these data to ensure the story for industries look plausible. This first stage is carried out by the compilers of the original data.

The **second stage** is a confrontation within the framework of the rows (products) in the Supply and Use framework. The accounting relationship that supply is equal to demand is tested for each product. This process identifies areas of inconsistency between the various sources which can then be investigated. Data within the row are then subsequently adjusted to achieve a balance. This adjustment process reviews the quality of the data used to populate the individual cells within a row and makes use of this information to adjust the original data.

The **third stage** of the balancing process is to confront the columns. Unlike the interrogation within the column, carried out during the first stage, this time it is carried out in the context of the Supply and Use framework. While the second stage of balancing results in a balance of the rows, it does not result in satisfying the accounting relationship for the columns. This needs to ensure that, for each industry, the inputs to the process of production equal its outputs. This third stage of balancing has the objective of confirming that this column identity is satisfied.

Once stage three is complete there is a strong probability that the row identities balanced during stage two of the process will have subsequently been broken. The process of repeating stages two and three continues until both the row and column identities are satisfied. This iterative process of row and column balancing effectively homes in on a position of balance by way of narrowing the degree of imbalance remaining in the Supply and Use framework after each balancing cycle. While the description above may seem to indicate a fairly mechanistic balancing approach, a significant amount of knowledge of the methods and quality of the basic data are used as part of the process. Alongside this, the evolving balance is reviewed at each stage to see how the economic story is developing and confirm that it is credible.

Current price analysis (Tables 2.1, 2.2 and 2.3)

The analyses of gross value added and other variables by industry shown in Tables 2.1, 2.2 and 2.3 reflect estimates based on the Standard Industrial Classification (SIC 2007). These tables are based on current price data reconciled through the Input–Output Supply and Use framework for 1997 to 2009.

Estimates of total output and gross value added are valued at basic prices, the method recommended by European System of Accounts 1995. Thus the only taxes included in the price will be taxes paid as part of the production process (such as business rates and vehicle excise duty), and not any taxes specifically levied on the production of a unit of output (such as VAT). Any subsidies on products received will also be included in the valuation of output.

Chained volume indices (2008=100) analyses (Table 2.4)

Table 2.4 shows chained volume estimates of gross value added at basic prices by industry. The source data for these estimates can be found in the GDP(O) source data guide on the ONS website:

http://www.ons.gov.uk/ons/guide-method/user-guidance/index-of-services-methodology/index.html

A more detailed explanation is in *National Accounts Concepts, Sources and Methods*.[6]

The output approach provides the lead indicator of economic change in the short-term. However, in the longer-term it is required to follow the annual path indicated by the expenditure measure of real GDP (usually to within 0.2 per cent of the average annual gross value added growth). To achieve this, balancing adjustments are sometimes applied to the output based gross value added estimates.

An examination of the chained volume gross value added and expenditure measures of GDP show what are considered to be excessive differences in growth for a number of recent years.

The output-based estimate grew less quickly than the expenditure measure in 2007 and 2009 but more quickly in 2008. The largest difference in growth between the output and expenditure GVA measure occurred in 2008.

To reduce these discrepancies, a number of balancing adjustments have been made to the chained volume gross value added annual growth rates.

Assigning adjustments: improvements for the 2011 *Blue Book*

For this year's *Blue Book*, balancing adjustments have been applied on the same basis as for the 2010 *Blue Book*. For technical and other reasons, the adjustments are not at present made to retail or the non-service industries for any years.

Applying the adjustments

ONS has developed an automatic function for assigning the annual adjustments to gross value added. This is designed to be as faithful as possible to the quarterly paths whilst adjusting the overall annual growth rate. Details of the new adjustments are given below.

An upwards adjustment of 0.6 per cent has been applied in 2007 to each of the series within the services sector, with the exception of retail. A downwards adjustment of 1.2 per cent has been applied in 2008 and an upwards adjustment of 0.5 per cent in 2009.

Workforce jobs by industry (Table 2.5)

Workforce Jobs (WFJ) is the preferred measure of the change in jobs by industry. The number of jobs is not the same as the number of people employed. This is because a person can have more than one job.

Table 2.5 breaks down WFJ into ten broad industry groupings on SIC 2007.

Employee jobs, the main component of WFJ are obtained mainly from surveys of businesses selected from the Inter-Departmental Business Register (IDBR). This is the same register used for all other business surveys collecting economic data.

Self-employment jobs come from the Labour Force Survey (LFS). This is a household survey which codes respondents according to their own view of the industry in which they work and so the industry breakdown is less reliable than the business surveys.

WFJ also includes Her Majesty's Forces (contained within industry section O) and government supported trainees from administrative sources (split by industry using the LFS).

References:

1 Drew S and Dunn M (2011) Blue Book 2011: Reclassification of UK Supply and Use Tables.
http://www.ons.gov.uk/ons/taxonomy/index.html?nscl=Supply+and+Use+Tables

2 Everett G (2011) Methods changes in the 2011 Blue Book.
http://www.ons.gov.uk/ons/rel/naa1-rd/united-kingdom-national-accounts/method-changes-in-blue-book-2011/ard-method-changes-in-blue-book-2011.pdf

3 Office for National Statistics (2011) Supply and Use Tables 1997–2009, 2011 Edition.
http://www.ons.gov.uk/ons/taxonomy/index.html?nscl=Supply+and+Use+Tables

4 Akers R and Clifton-Fearnside A (2008) Balanced Estimates of GDP using a Supply and Use Approach.
http://www.ons.gov.uk/ons/rel/input-output/input-output-supply-and-use-tables/2008-edition/balanced-estimates-of-gdp-using-a-supply-and-use-approach.pdf

5 Mahajan S (2006) Development, Compilation and Use of Input-Output Supply and Use Tables in the UK National Accounts *Economic Trends* No. 634.
http://www.ons.gov.uk/ons/rel/elmr/economic-trends--discontinued-/no--634--september-2006/development--compilation-and-use-of-input-output-suppy-and-use-tables.pdf

6 Office for National Statistics (1998) *National Accounts Concepts, Sources and Methods*, 1998 edition. The Stationery Office: London.
http://www.ons.gov.uk/ons/rel/naa1-rd/national-accounts-concepts--sources-and-methods/1998-release/index.html

2.1 Summary Supply and Use Tables for the United Kingdom, 2007

Supply Table

£ million

2007	SUPPLY OF PRODUCTS					
	Domestic output of products at basic prices	Imports		Distributors' trading margins	Taxes less subsidies on products	Total supply of products at purchasers' prices
		Goods	Services			
PRODUCTS[1]						
Agriculture [1-3]	21 148	7 689	449	5 042	352	34 680
Production [5-39]	541 946	297 775	17 376	230 008	90 598	1 177 703
Construction [41-43]	238 071	-	875	-	17 820	256 766
Distribution, transport, hotels and restaurants [45-56]	493 043	-	31 666	-242 378	13 486	295 817
Information and communication [58-63]	141 277	3 160	7 637	7 328	7 645	167 047
Financial and insurance [64-66]	172 625	-	12 993	-	6 866	192 484
Real estate [68.1-2-68.3]	164 180	-	1 010	-	401	165 591
Professional and support activities [69.1-82]	289 101	10	27 612	-	8 413	325 136
Government, health & education [84-88]	408 348	-	2 098	-	2 330	412 776
Other services [90-97]	68 081	2 318	4 013	-	5 283	79 695
Total	2 537 820	310 952	105 729	-	153 194	3 107 695
of which:						
Market output	2 098 062					
Output for own final use	110 280					
Other non-market output	329 478					

Use Table at Purchasers' prices

2007	INTERMEDIATE CONSUMPTION BY INDUSTRY GROUP[1][2]									
	1	2	3	4	5	6	7	8	9	10
	Agriculture	Production	Construction	Distribution transport, hotels and restaurants	Information and Communication	Financial and insurance	Real estate	Professional and support activities	Government, health and education	Other services
PRODUCTS[1]										
Agriculture [1-3]	2 992	11 567	291	1 586	8	-	-	16	98	22
Production [5-39]	6 783	298 762	37 831	65 173	14 328	6 075	606	10 879	60 693	6 227
Construction [41-43]	384	4 639	70 257	12 707	1 623	4 272	10 796	1 972	6 562	772
Distribution, transport, hotels and restaurants [45-56]	860	17 780	3 986	63 519	4 203	13 679	725	8 584	13 290	1 845
Information and communication [58-63]	219	6 755	1 609	18 690	16 376	14 107	1 133	9 689	9 001	3 424
Financial and insurance [64-66]	712	12 250	3 633	9 715	2 244	16 925	13 269	4 828	5 507	1 042
Real estate [68.1-2-68.3]	109	1 672	2 377	14 902	1 149	4 222	1 007	1 770	4 828	711
Professional and support activities [69.1-82]	608	25 242	18 824	43 677	19 697	26 285	4 146	72 208	28 982	11 385
Government, health & education [84-88]	25	2 372	1 224	4 574	1 039	2 617	2 915	7 695	41 514	782
Other services [90-97]	72	964	107	1 610	2 981	912	47	1 972	4 409	6 066
Total consumption	12 764	382 003	140 139	236 153	63 648	89 094	34 644	119 613	174 884	32 276
Taxes *less* subsidies on production	-2 773	3 773	815	8 655	1 231	1 676	-769	1 265	332	889
Compensation of employees	3 407	112 050	48 071	157 427	47 857	52 820	6 470	94 546	200 774	28 437
Gross operating surplus	8 014	78 801	48 011	74 005	28 226	44 517	104 606	55 479	32 175	11 815
Gross value added at basic prices[1]	8 648	194 624	96 897	240 087	77 314	99 013	110 307	151 290	233 281	41 141
Output at basic prices	21 412	576 627	237 036	476 240	140 962	188 107	144 951	270 903	408 165	73 417

2.1 Summary Supply and Use Tables for the United Kingdom, 2007
continued

Gross value added at basic prices
£ billion

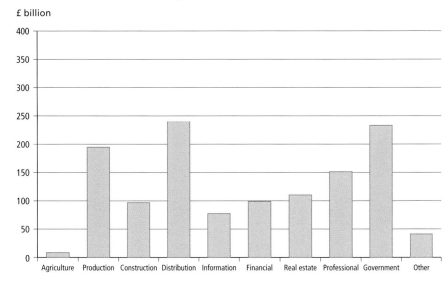

Components of final demand
Per cent

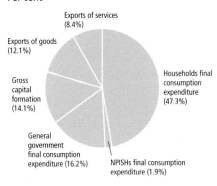

£ million

		FINAL CONSUMPTION EXPENDITURE[2]			GROSS CAPITAL FORMATION			EXPORTS		TOTAL
2007	Total intermediate consumption	Households	NPISHs	GGFC	GFCF	Valuables	Changes in inventories	Goods	Services	
PRODUCTS[1]										
Agriculture [1-3]	16 580	15 405	-	-	910	-	-143	1 794	134	34 680
Production [5-39]	507 357	373 437	-	-	69 602	-135	3 281	212 312	6 352	1 172 206
Construction [41-43]	113 984	7 633	-	-	131 708	-	2 403	-	1 038	256 766
Distribution, transport, hotels and restaurants [45-56]	128 471	136 669	-	-	1 283	600	180	-	28 614	295 817
Information and communication [58-63]	81 003	39 861	-	3 006	25 791	-	155	3 547	13 684	167 047
Financial and insurance [64-66]	70 125	70 262	-	-	50	-	77	-	51 970	192 484
Real estate [68.1-2-68.3]	32 747	125 820	-	-	6 543	-	-	-	481	165 591
Professional and support activities [69.1-82]	251 054	14 927	1 106	-	11 357	-	175	43	46 474	325 136
Government, health & education [84-88]	64 757	34 718	25 369	282 175	2 416	-	30	-	3 311	412 776
Other services [90-97]	19 140	43 510	7 849	4 476	376	-	66	2 651	1 627	79 695
Total consumption	1 285 218	862 242	34 324	295 154	250 036	465	6 224	220 347	153 685	3 107 695
Taxes *less* subsidies on production	15 094									
Compensation of employees	751 859									
Gross operating surplus	485 649									
Gross value added at basic prices[1]	1 252 602									
Output at basic prices	2 537 820									

Notes for information

(1) Some of the industry/product group headings have been truncated.
(2) Purchases of products by industry and by final consumption categories are valued at purchasers' prices.

NPISHs represents Non-Profit Institutions Serving Households.
GGFC represents General Government Final Consumption.
GFCF represents Gross Fixed Capital Formation.

Gross value added at basic prices *plus* taxes *less* subsidies on products gives GDP at market prices.
Gross operating surplus includes gross mixed income.
Changes in inventories includes materials and fuels, work-in-progress and finished goods.
Valuables include both 'transfer costs' and 'acquisitions less disposals'.

2.1 Summary Supply and Use Tables for the United Kingdom, 2008

Supply Table

£ million

2008	SUPPLY OF PRODUCTS					
	Domestic output of products at basic prices	Imports		Distributors' trading margins	Taxes less subsidies on products	Total supply of products at purchasers' prices
		Goods	Services			
PRODUCTS[1]						
Agriculture [1-3]	22 566	8 649	508	5 201	447	37 371
Production [5-39]	559 416	331 976	18 028	237 500	91 662	1 238 582
Construction [41-43]	232 228	-	1 169	-	13 452	246 849
Distribution, transport, hotels and restaurants [45-56]	505 741	-	33 044	-249 921	13 903	302 767
Information and communication [58-63]	144 164	3 211	8 761	7 220	7 577	170 933
Financial and insurance [64-66]	190 809	-	14 245	-	6 170	211 224
Real estate [68.1-2-68.3]	171 293	-	1 052	-	430	172 775
Professional and support activities [69.1-82]	300 093	7	32 242	-	8 509	340 851
Government, health & education [84-88]	434 309	-	2 475	-	2 480	439 264
Other services [90-97]	69 826	2 315	4 306	-	5 356	81 803
Total	2 630 445	346 158	115 830	-	149 986	3 242 419
of which:						
Market output	2 162 750					
Output for own final use	116 362					
Other non-market output	351 333					

Use Table at Purchasers' prices

2008	INTERMEDIATE CONSUMPTION BY INDUSTRY GROUP[1,2]									
	1	2	3	4	5	6	7	8	9	10
	Agriculture	Production	Construction	Distribution transport, hotels and restaurants	Information and Communication	Financial and insurance	Real estate	Professional and support activities	Government health and education	Other services
PRODUCTS[1]										
Agriculture [1-3]	3 342	12 291	304	1 662	8	-	-	18	99	23
Production [5-39]	7 105	312 343	37 859	69 481	13 742	6 231	644	11 931	67 153	6 690
Construction [41-43]	407	4 728	62 721	13 587	1 631	4 504	10 037	2 130	6 627	763
Distribution, transport, hotels and restaurants [45-56]	897	17 770	3 893	63 933	4 241	14 682	744	9 241	14 185	1 924
Information and communication [58-63]	211	6 547	1 594	19 148	16 631	14 112	1 259	10 168	9 677	3 490
Financial and insurance [64-66]	836	14 076	4 230	10 663	2 428	16 755	22 510	5 547	6 324	1 147
Real estate [68.1-2-68.3]	114	1 621	2 298	15 534	1 148	4 213	1 135	1 790	5 274	749
Professional and support activities [69.1-82]	725	25 275	18 726	46 033	20 307	28 540	4 633	78 362	31 880	12 408
Government, health & education [84-88]	26	2 436	1 385	4 726	1 078	2 618	2 860	7 866	44 820	822
Other services [90-97]	76	960	115	1 738	3 176	986	55	2 149	4 789	6 192
Total consumption	13 739	398 047	133 125	246 505	64 390	92 641	43 877	129 202	190 828	34 208
Taxes *less* subsidies on production	-2 885	4 134	906	9 339	1 149	2 076	-620	1 193	412	933
Compensation of employees	3 450	111 527	50 295	161 709	48 999	52 388	7 123	96 868	209 350	29 260
Gross operating surplus	8 531	81 969	46 672	69 595	29 006	59 413	101 550	54 788	33 297	11 456
Gross value added at basic prices[1]	9 096	197 630	97 873	240 643	79 154	113 877	108 053	152 849	243 059	41 649
Output at basic prices	22 835	595 677	230 998	487 148	143 544	206 518	151 930	282 051	433 887	75 857

2.1 Summary Supply and Use Tables for the United Kingdom, 2008
continued

Gross value added at basic prices
£ billion

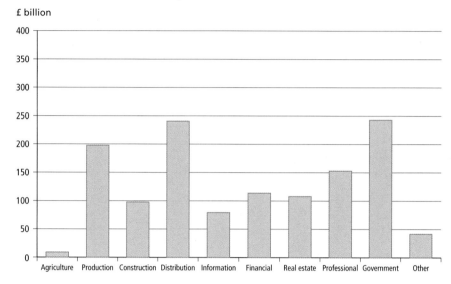

Components of final demand
Per cent

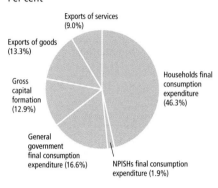

£ million

2008	Total intermediate consumption	FINAL CONSUMPTION EXPENDITURE[2]			GROSS CAPITAL FORMATION			EXPORTS		TOTAL
		Households	NPISHs	GGFC	GFCF	Valuables	Changes in inventories	Goods	Services	
PRODUCTS[1]										
Agriculture [1-3]	17 747	16 365	-	-	899	-	120	2 098	142	37 371
Production [5-39]	533 179	382 072	-	-	65 378	64	1 591	243 746	6 621	1 232 651
Construction [41-43]	107 135	7 445	-	-	131 467	-	-486	-	1 288	246 849
Distribution, transport, hotels and restaurants [45-56]	131 510	138 208	-	-	631	498	-212	-	32 132	302 767
Information and communication [58-63]	82 837	39 980	-	3 217	26 362	-	228	3 816	14 493	170 933
Financial and insurance [64-66]	84 516	65 659	-	-	42	-	78	-	60 929	211 224
Real estate [68.1-2-68.3]	33 876	133 037	-	-	5 335	-	-	-	527	172 775
Professional and support activities [69.1-82]	266 889	14 504	969	-	8 612	-	378	37	49 462	340 851
Government, health & education [84-88]	68 637	36 077	26 753	301 864	2 272	-	39	-	3 622	439 264
Other services [90-97]	20 236	44 677	8 045	4 554	366	-	-26	2 280	1 671	81 803
Total consumption	1 346 562	878 024	35 767	315 566	241 364	562	1 710	251 977	170 887	3 242 419
Taxes *less* subsidies on production	16 637									
Compensation of employees	770 969									
Gross operating surplus	496 277									
Gross value added at basic prices[1]	1 283 883									
Output at basic prices	2 630 445									

Notes for information

(1) Some of the industry/product group headings have been truncated.
(2) Purchases of products by industry and by final consumption categories are valued at purchasers' prices.

NPISHs represents Non-Profit Institutions Serving Households.
GGFC represents General Government Final Consumption.
GFCF represents Gross Fixed Capital Formation.

Gross value added at basic prices *plus* taxes *less* subsidies on products gives GDP at market prices.
Gross operating surplus includes gross mixed income.
Changes in inventories includes materials and fuels, work-in-progress and finished goods.
Valuables include both 'transfer costs' and 'acquisitions less disposals'.

2.1 Summary Supply and Use Tables for the United Kingdom, 2009

Supply Table

£ million

2009	SUPPLY OF PRODUCTS					
	Domestic output of products at basic prices	Imports		Distributors' trading margins	Taxes less subsidies on products	Total supply of products at purchasers' prices
		Goods	Services			
PRODUCTS[1]						
Agriculture [1-3]	21 680	8 690	431	5 261	337	36 399
Production [5-39]	530 349	297 755	16 349	231 502	86 969	1 162 924
Construction [41-43]	210 648	-	1 409	-	9 859	221 916
Distribution, transport, hotels and restaurants [45-56]	489 975	-	29 596	-243 674	12 138	288 035
Information and communication [58-63]	139 584	2 872	9 642	6 911	6 761	165 770
Financial and insurance [64-66]	203 556	-	11 823	-	5 452	220 831
Real estate [68.1-2-68.3]	176 182	-	909	-	404	177 495
Professional and support activities [69.1-82]	294 228	9	33 815	-	7 512	335 564
Government, health & education [84-88]	453 910	-	2 188	-	2 367	458 465
Other services [90-97]	69 999	1 652	4 085	-	5 123	80 859
Total	2 590 111	310 978	110 247	-	136 922	3 148 258
of which:						
Market output	2 107 552					
Output for own final use	119 347					
Other non-market output	363 212					

Use Table at Purchasers' prices

2009	INTERMEDIATE CONSUMPTION BY INDUSTRY GROUP[1][2]									
	1	2	3	4	5	6	7	8	9	10
	Agriculture	Production	Construction	Distribution transport, hotels and restaurants	Information and Communication	Financial and insurance	Real estate	Professional and support activities	Government health and education	Other services
PRODUCTS[1]										
Agriculture [1-3]	3 127	12 686	250	1 622	8	-	-	15	112	20
Production [5-39]	7 256	289 576	35 007	66 800	13 040	6 002	622	11 790	71 029	6 674
Construction [41-43]	426	4 722	57 324	13 139	1 639	4 300	9 765	2 075	6 725	784
Distribution, transport, hotels and restaurants [45-56]	974	17 089	3 467	60 804	4 062	13 401	696	9 064	14 481	1 855
Information and communication [58-63]	227	6 245	1 444	18 376	15 795	13 174	1 261	9 884	9 890	3 483
Financial and insurance [64-66]	863	14 741	4 369	11 293	2 729	20 750	44 549	5 918	6 781	1 233
Real estate [68.1-2-68.3]	139	1 558	1 980	15 065	1 157	3 938	1 139	1 723	5 356	723
Professional and support activities [69.1-82]	790	25 019	16 794	43 919	19 727	26 786	4 538	76 723	33 101	12 561
Government, health & education [84-88]	32	2 502	1 511	5 298	1 107	2 560	3 370	9 068	48 167	782
Other services [90-97]	77	938	100	1 725	3 085	939	51	2 201	4 869	6 628
Total consumption	13 911	375 076	122 246	238 041	62 349	91 850	65 991	128 461	200 511	34 743
Taxes *less* subsidies on production	-3 280	4 081	817	10 034	1 087	2 559	-533	1 157	380	1 168
Compensation of employees	3 394	108 572	47 246	161 281	47 434	56 890	6 794	95 617	220 102	29 542
Gross operating surplus	7 916	76 281	39 310	63 465	28 579	67 445	84 153	51 781	32 561	11 099
Gross value added at basic prices[1]	8 030	188 934	87 373	234 780	77 100	126 894	90 414	148 555	253 043	41 809
Output at basic prices	21 941	564 010	209 619	472 821	139 449	218 744	156 405	277 016	453 554	76 552

2.1 Summary Supply and Use Tables for the United Kingdom, 2009
continued

Gross value added at basic prices
£ billion

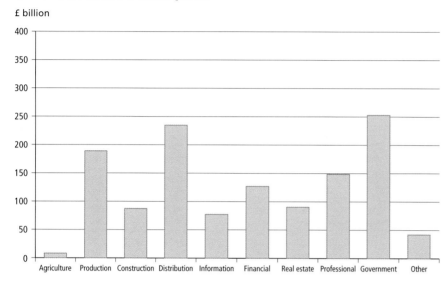

Components of final demand
Per cent

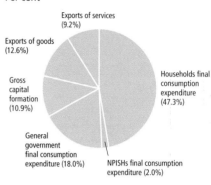

£ million

2009	Total intermediate consumption	FINAL CONSUMPTION EXPENDITURE[2]			GROSS CAPITAL FORMATION			EXPORTS		TOTAL
		Households	NPISHs	GGFC	GFCF	Valuables	Changes in inventories	Goods	Services	
PRODUCTS[1]										
Agriculture [1-3]	17 840	15 502	-	-	750	-	65	2 105	137	36 399
Production [5-39]	507 796	374 956	-	-	54 792	-4	-7 532	220 243	6 542	1 156 793
Construction [41-43]	100 899	7 167	-	-	115 366	-	-3 120	-	1 604	221 916
Distribution, transport, hotels and restaurants [45-56]	125 893	131 456	-	-	590	434	-222	-	29 884	288 035
Information and communication [58-63]	79 779	38 161	-	3 116	24 534	-	-162	3 937	16 405	165 770
Financial and insurance [64-66]	113 226	54 928	-	-	35	-	83	-	52 559	220 831
Real estate [68.1-2-68.3]	32 778	139 527	-	-	4 576	-	-	-	614	177 495
Professional and support activities [69.1-82]	259 958	14 453	934	-	6 750	-	-642	41	54 070	335 564
Government, health & education [84-88]	74 397	38 599	26 820	313 401	1 509	-	-78	-	3 817	458 465
Other services [90-97]	20 613	43 493	8 109	4 701	351	-	-38	1 800	1 830	80 859
Total consumption	1 333 179	858 242	35 863	327 349	209 253	430	-11 646	228 126	167 462	3 148 258
Taxes *less* subsidies on production	17 470									
Compensation of employees	776 872									
Gross operating surplus	462 590									
Gross value added at basic prices[1]	1 256 932									
Output at basic prices	2 590 111									

Notes for information

(1) Some of the industry/product group headings have been truncated.
(2) Purchases of products by industry and by final consumption categories are valued at purchasers' prices.

NPISHs represents Non-Profit Institutions Serving Households.
GGFC represents General Government Final Consumption.
GFCF represents Gross Fixed Capital Formation.

Gross value added at basic prices *plus* taxes *less* subsidies on products gives GDP at market prices.
Gross operating surplus includes gross mixed income.
Changes in inventories includes materials and fuels, work-in-progress and finished goods.
Valuables include both 'transfer costs' and 'acquisitions less disposals'.

2.2 Output and capital formation: by industry[1,2]
Gross value added at current basic prices

£ million

				2002	2003	2004	2005	2006	2007	2008	2009
	Agriculture										
	Output										
D.1	Compensation of employees	KLR2		2 892	3 008	3 047	3 151	3 347	3 407	3 450	3 394
D.29-D.39	Taxes *less* subsidies on production other than those on products	KLR3		−307	−350	−363	−2 864	−2 709	−2 773	−2 885	−3 280
B.2g/B.3g	Operating surplus/Mixed income, gross	KLR4		6 408	7 224	7 371	7 628	7 802	8 014	8 531	7 916
B.1g	Gross value added at basic prices	KLR5		8 993	9 882	10 055	7 915	8 440	8 648	9 096	8 030
P.2	Intermediate consumption at purchasers' prices	KLR6		10 974	11 260	12 034	11 929	11 956	12 764	13 739	13 911
P.1	Total output at basic prices	KLR7		19 967	21 142	22 089	19 844	20 396	21 412	22 835	21 941
P.5	Gross capital formation	KLR8		2 676	2 884	2 652	2 740	3 009	3 071	3 539	3 121
	Production										
	Output										
D.1	Compensation of employees	KLR9		100 981	101 867	102 675	104 098	106 646	112 050	111 527	108 572
D.29-D.39	Taxes *less* subsidies on production other than those on products	KLS4		3 996	3 981	3 789	3 731	3 925	3 773	4 134	4 081
B.2g/B.3g	Operating surplus/Mixed income, gross	KLS3		66 304	64 604	64 887	69 446	77 694	78 801	81 969	76 281
B.1g	Gross value added at basic prices	KLS5		171 281	170 452	171 351	177 275	188 265	194 624	197 630	188 934
P.2	Intermediate consumption at purchasers' prices	KLS6		302 709	307 696	317 411	339 924	363 872	382 003	398 047	375 076
P.1	Total output at basic prices	KLS7		473 990	478 148	488 762	517 199	552 137	576 627	595 677	564 010
P.5	Gross capital formation	KLS8		24 503	23 675	20 674	39 765	25 797	30 160	29 875	23 179
	Construction										
	Output										
D.1	Compensation of employees	KLS9		35 368	37 058	38 910	41 284	44 816	48 071	50 295	47 246
D.29-D.39	Taxes *less* subsidies on production other than those on products	KLT3		504	560	757	753	858	815	906	817
B.2g/B.g	Operating surplus/Mixed income, gross	KLT2		31 066	35 001	39 644	40 597	42 613	48 011	46 672	39 310
B.1g	Gross value added at basic prices	KLT4		66 938	72 619	79 311	82 634	88 287	96 897	97 873	87 373
P.2	Intermediate consumption at purchasers' prices	KLT5		91 065	98 141	106 413	115 712	124 438	140 139	133 125	122 246
P.1	Total output at basic prices	KLT6		158 003	170 760	185 724	198 346	212 725	237 036	230 998	209 619
P.5	Gross capital formation	KLT7		3 785	4 241	3 892	4 236	2 251	7 606	3 185	−2 807

1 The contribution of each industry to the gross domestic product before providing for consumption of fixed capital. The industrial composition in this table is consistent with the Supply-Use Tables in Table 2.1, which show data from 2007-2009.
2 Components may not sum to totals due to rounding.

2.2 Output and capital formation: by industry[1,2]
Gross value added at current basic prices
continued

£ million

			2002	2003	2004	2005	2006	2007	2008	2009
	Distribution, transport, hotels & restaurants									
	Output									
D.1	Compensation of employees	KLT8	127 636	131 939	137 907	142 835	149 312	157 427	161 709	161 281
D.29-D.39	Taxes *less* subsidies on production other than those on products	KLU2	8 081	8 070	8 119	8 829	8 897	8 655	9 339	10 034
B.2g/B.3g	Operating surplus/Mixed income, gross	KLT9	57 202	61 658	65 825	66 833	70 214	74 005	69 595	63 465
B.1g	Gross value added at basic prices	KLU3	192 919	201 667	211 851	218 497	228 423	240 087	240 643	234 780
P.2	Intermediate consumption at purchasers' prices	KLU4	189 575	200 002	208 229	217 341	225 204	236 153	246 505	238 041
P.1	Total output at basic prices	KLU5	382 494	401 669	420 080	435 838	453 627	476 240	487 148	472 821
P.5	Gross capital formation	KLU6	31 829	30 129	35 328	29 639	33 412	36 158	34 270	27 140
	Information and Communication									
	Output									
D.1	Compensation of employees	KLU7	37 616	39 226	41 828	42 480	42 711	47 857	48 999	47 434
D.29-D.39	Taxes *less* subsidies on production other than those on products	KLU9	1 145	1 201	1 037	1 113	1 254	1 231	1 149	1 087
B.2g/B.3g	Operating surplus/Mixed income, gross	KLU8	20 758	23 901	25 849	26 355	27 806	28 226	29 006	28 579
B.1g	Gross value added at basic prices	KLV2	59 519	64 328	68 714	69 948	71 771	77 314	79 154	77 100
P.2	Intermediate consumption at purchasers' prices	KLV3	54 069	56 439	56 487	58 759	61 296	63 648	64 390	62 349
P.1	Total output at basic prices	KLV4	113 588	120 767	125 201	128 707	133 067	140 962	143 544	139 449
P.5	Gross capital formation	KLV5	13 761	13 025	15 273	12 814	14 445	15 632	14 816	11 733
	Financial and insurance									
	Output									
D.1	Compensation of employees	KLV6	34 124	36 162	39 856	43 864	50 436	52 820	52 388	56 890
D.29-D.39	Taxes *less* subsidies on production other than those on products	KLV8	1 376	1 419	1 439	1 479	1 578	1 676	2 076	2 559
B.2g/B.3g	Operating surplus/Mixed income, gross	KLV7	27 763	33 802	34 186	34 696	39 464	44 517	59 413	67 445
B.1g	Gross value added at basic prices	KLV9	63 263	71 383	75 481	80 039	91 478	99 013	113 877	126 894
P.2	Intermediate consumption at purchasers' prices	KLW2	77 388	77 321	77 901	82 028	86 972	89 094	92 641	91 850
P.1	Total output at basic prices	KLW3	140 651	148 704	153 382	162 067	178 450	188 107	206 518	218 744
P.5	Gross capital formation	KLW4	1 414	1 471	972	1 244	1 303	1 385	1 433	978

1 The contribution of each industry to the gross domestic product before providing for consumption of fixed capital. The industrial composition in this table is consistent with the Supply-Use Tables in Table 2.1, which show data from 2007-2009.
2 Components may not sum to totals due to rounding.

2.2 Output and capital formation: by industry[1,2]
Gross value added at current basic prices
continued

£ million

				2002	2003	2004	2005	2006	2007	2008	2009
	Real estate										
	Output										
D.1	Compensation of employees	KLW5		4 071	4 200	4 697	5 200	5 478	6 470	7 123	6 794
D.29-D.39	Taxes *less* subsidies on production other than those on products	KLW7		−229	−224	−16	−888	−1 362	−769	−620	−533
B.2g/B.3g	Operating surplus/Mixed income, gross	KLW6		75 465	82 486	88 291	91 207	93 888	104 606	101 550	84 153
B.1g	Gross value added at basic prices	KLW8		79 307	86 462	92 972	95 519	98 004	110 307	108 053	90 414
P.2	Intermediate consumption at purchasers' prices	KLW9		25 591	27 170	28 333	32 234	35 826	34 644	43 877	65 991
P.1	Total output at basic prices	KLX2		104 898	113 632	121 305	127 753	133 830	144 951	151 930	156 405
P.5	Gross capital formation	KLX3		19 501	20 288	13 402	17 159	17 964	19 098	19 760	13 490
	Professional and support										
	Output										
D.1	Compensation of employees	KLX4		74 424	78 369	81 006	85 510	89 855	94 546	96 868	95 617
D.29-D.39	Taxes *less* subsidies on production other than those on products	KLX6		1 276	1 042	960	677	937	1 265	1 193	1 157
B.2g/B.3g	Operating surplus/Mixed income, gross	KLX5		36 812	39 312	43 248	47 906	53 175	55 479	54 788	51 781
B.1g	Gross value added at basic prices	KLX7		112 512	118 723	125 214	134 093	143 967	151 290	152 849	148 555
P.2	Intermediate consumption at purchasers' prices	KLX8		85 535	89 865	92 782	98 524	107 648	119 613	129 202	128 461
P.1	Total output at basic prices	KLX9		198 047	208 588	217 996	232 617	251 615	270 903	282 051	277 016
P.5	Gross capital formation	KLY2		12 061	12 547	8 289	10 613	11 110	11 812	12 221	8 343
	Government, health and education										
	Output										
D.1	Compensation of employees	KLY3		146 939	159 479	170 599	182 252	192 953	200 774	209 350	220 102
D.29-D.39	Taxes *less* subsidies on production other than those on products	KLY5		195	158	250	289	351	332	412	380
B.2g/B.3g	Operating surplus, Mixed income, gross	KLY4		22 613	24 423	27 104	29 217	31 417	32 175	33 297	32 561
B.1g	Gross value added at basic prices	KLY6		169 747	184 060	197 953	211 758	224 721	233 281	243 059	253 043
P.2	Intermediate consumption at purchasers' prices	KLY7		120 813	131 545	144 166	156 283	166 772	174 884	190 828	200 511
P.1	Total output at basic prices	KLY8		290 560	315 605	342 119	368 041	391 493	408 165	433 887	453 554
P.5	Gross capital formation	KLY9		17 130	20 622	25 816	11 629	29 430	32 382	41 701	48 488

1 The contribution of each industry to the gross domestic product before providing for consumption of fixed capital. The industrial composition in this table is consistent with the Supply-Use Tables in Table 2.1, which show data from 2007-2009.
2 Components may not sum to totals due to rounding.

2.2 Output and capital formation: by industry[1,2]
Gross value added at current basic prices
continued

£ million

			2002	2003	2004	2005	2006	2007	2008	2009
	Other services									
	Output									
D.1	Compensation of employees	KLZ2	22 793	24 688	25 483	26 844	27 961	28 437	29 260	29 542
	Taxes *less* subsidies on production other									
D.29-D.39	than those on products	KLZ4	603	634	727	730	788	889	933	1 168
B.2g/B.3g	Operating surplus/Mixed income, gross	KLZ3	9 024	9 805	11 258	11 630	11 836	11 815	11 456	11 099
B.1g	Gross value added at basic prices	KLZ5	32 420	35 127	37 468	39 204	40 585	41 141	41 649	41 809
	Intermediate consumption at									
P.2	purchasers' prices	KLZ6	25 109	26 107	26 858	28 740	30 625	32 276	34 208	34 743
P.1	Total output at basic prices	KLZ7	57 529	61 234	64 326	67 944	71 210	73 417	75 857	76 552
P.5	Gross capital formation	KLZ8	9 740	11 018	14 162	16 308	15 623	16 431	17 485	13 821
	Not allocated to industries									
P.5	Gross capital formation[3]	KN28	47 376	51 064	64 825	67 604	78 286	82 990	65 350	50 548
	All industries									
	Output									
D.1	Compensation of employees	KLZ9	586 844	615 996	646 008	677 518	713 515	751 859	770 969	776 872
	Taxes *less* subsidies on production other									
D.29-D.39	than those on products	KN22	16 640	16 491	16 699	13 849	14 517	15 094	16 637	17 470
B.2g	Operating surplus, gross	KN23	287 099	309 900	334 328	347 028	375 477	402 751	409 901	381 166
B.3g	Mixed income, gross	KN3C	66 316	72 316	73 335	78 487	80 432	82 898	86 376	81 424
	Statistical discrepancy between income									
di	and GDP	RVFC	3	1	3	−2	−2	2	1	−8
B.1g	Gross value added at basic prices	KN24	956 899	1 014 703	1 070 370	1 116 882	1 183 941	1 252 602	1 283 883	1 256 932
	Intermediate consumption at									
P.2	purchasers' prices	KN25	982 828	1 025 546	1 070 614	1 141 474	1 214 609	1 285 218	1 346 562	1 333 179
P.1	Total output at basic prices	KN26	1 939 727	2 040 249	2 140 984	2 258 356	2 398 550	2 537 820	2 630 445	2 590 111
	Gross capital formation									
P.51	Gross fixed capital formation	KN33	180 533	186 759	200 430	209 722	227 172	250 036	241 364	209 253
P.52	Changes in inventories	KN2Z	3 026	4 242	4 890	4 405	5 172	6 224	1 711	−11 651
P.53	Acquisitions less disposals of valuables	KN32	215	−37	−36	−377	285	465	561	429
P.5	Total gross capital formation	KN27	183 776	190 965	205 285	213 750	232 630	256 725	243 634	198 035

1 The contribution of each industry to the gross domestic product before providing for consumption of fixed capital. The industrial composition in this table is consistent with the Supply-Use Tables in Table 2.1, which show data from 2007-2009.
2 Components may not sum to totals due to rounding.
3 Includes investment in dwellings, transfer costs of land and existing buildings, and valuables.

2.3 Gross value added at current basic prices: by industry[1,2]

£ million

				2002	2003	2004	2005	2006	2007	2008	2009
A	**Agriculture**		KKD5	8 993	9 882	10 055	7 915	8 440	8 648	9 096	8 030
B - F	**Production and Construction**										
B - E	Production										
B	Mining and quarrying		KKD7	19 724	18 768	19 815	23 001	26 547	27 337	32 489	25 876
C	Manufacturing										
CA		Food products, beverages and tobacco	KKE5	20 984	21 648	22 147	22 039	21 869	22 544	22 139	22 465
CB		Textiles, wearing apparel and leather products	KKE7	4 882	4 450	4 278	4 225	4 315	4 439	4 220	4 089
CC		Wood, paper products and printing	KKE9	10 625	10 736	10 588	10 798	11 262	11 859	11 672	11 500
CD		Coke and refined petroleum products	KKF3	1 073	1 070	1 048	1 055	1 161	1 091	854	805
CE		Chemicals and chemical products	KKF5	10 638	10 624	10 138	10 853	11 749	11 806	10 915	10 610
CF		Basic pharmaceutical products and preparations	KKF7	4 875	4 921	5 545	6 230	6 951	7 304	9 632	11 199
CG		Rubber, plastic and other non-metallic mineral products	KKF9	11 297	11 222	10 867	10 364	10 420	10 648	9 832	9 127
CH		Basic metals and metal products	KKG3	17 342	17 096	16 942	18 216	17 679	18 590	18 415	16 609
CI		Computer, electronic and optical products	KKG5	8 970	8 593	8 286	8 600	9 167	9 791	9 674	8 776
CJ		Electrical equipment	KKG7	5 208	5 078	4 778	4 655	4 578	4 552	4 364	4 027
CK		Machinery and equipment n. e. c.	KKG9	8 408	8 544	8 392	8 124	8 322	8 534	8 643	8 455
CL		Transport equipment	KKH3	14 326	14 155	14 099	13 793	13 812	13 474	11 473	10 240
CM		Other manufacturing and repair	KKH5	9 511	9 014	9 317	9 272	9 544	10 079	9 724	8 837
C		Total manufacturing	KKE3	128 139	127 151	126 425	128 224	130 829	134 711	131 557	126 739
D	Electricity, gas, steam and air conditioning supply		KKH7	13 794	14 039	13 696	13 701	17 217	17 869	18 409	21 146
E	Water supply, sewerage, waste mgmt and remediation		KKH9	9 624	10 494	11 415	12 349	13 672	14 707	15 175	15 173
B - E	Total production		KKJ5	171 281	170 452	171 351	177 275	188 265	194 624	197 630	188 934
F	Construction		KKI3	66 938	72 619	79 311	82 634	88 287	96 897	97 873	87 373
B - F	Total production and construction		KKD9	238 219	243 071	250 662	259 909	276 552	291 521	295 503	276 307

1 Components may not sum to totals as a result of rounding.
2 Because of differences in the annual and monthly production inquiries, estimates of current price output and gross value added by industry derived from the current price Input-Output Supply and Use Tables are not consistent with the equivalent measures of chained volume measures growth given in 2.4. These differences do not affect GDP totals.

2.3 Gross value added at current basic prices: by industry[1,2]
continued

£ million

			2002	2003	2004	2005	2006	2007	2008	2009
G - T	**Services**									
G - I	Distribution, transport, hotels and restaurants									
G	Wholesale, retail, repair of motor vehicles and m/cycles	KKI5	113 177	119 069	126 337	129 357	135 244	142 041	139 782	137 682
H	Transportation and storage	KKI9	51 714	53 356	54 582	57 151	59 213	62 529	64 189	61 870
I	Accommodation and food service activities	KKJ3	28 028	29 242	30 932	31 989	33 966	35 517	36 672	35 228
G - I	Total distribution, transport, hotels and restaurants	KKI7	192 919	201 667	211 851	218 497	228 423	240 087	240 643	234 780
J	Information and communication									
JA	Publishing, audiovisual and broadcasting activities	KKK3	18 136	18 741	19 216	19 520	19 589	20 657	21 358	21 074
JB	Telecommunications	KKK5	20 885	22 213	23 002	23 155	23 215	24 142	24 451	23 534
JC	IT and other information service activities	KKK7	20 498	23 374	26 496	27 273	28 967	32 515	33 345	32 491
J	Total information and communication	KKJ9	59 519	64 328	68 714	69 948	71 771	77 314	79 154	77 099
K	Financial and insurance	KKK9	63 263	71 383	75 481	80 039	91 478	99 013	113 877	126 894
L	Real estate	KKL3	79 307	86 462	92 971	95 519	98 003	110 307	108 054	90 415
M - N	Professional and support									
M	Professional, scientific and technical activities									
MA	Legal, accounting, mgmt, architect, engineering etc	KKL9	50 060	53 251	56 375	60 016	65 854	70 095	71 959	70 378
MB	Scientific research and development	KKM3	3 747	3 952	4 199	4 686	5 057	4 746	4 268	4 321
MC	Other professional, scientific and technical activities	KKM5	13 509	14 043	14 554	16 225	17 243	17 706	18 582	17 755
M	Total professional, scientific and technical activities	KKL5	67 316	71 246	75 128	80 927	88 154	92 547	94 809	92 454
N	Administrative and support service activities	KKM7	45 196	47 477	50 086	53 166	55 813	58 743	58 040	56 101
M - N	Total professional and support	KKL7	112 512	118 723	125 214	134 093	143 967	151 290	152 849	148 555
O - Q	Government, health and education									
O	Public admin, defence, compulsory social security	KKM9	47 298	51 449	55 312	59 889	62 154	63 403	65 243	68 037
P	Education	KKN5	58 740	62 360	65 891	70 367	75 306	79 537	83 398	85 677
Q	Human health and social work activities									
QA	Human health activities	KKN9	45 689	50 570	55 939	59 286	63 746	65 654	67 452	70 669
QB	Residential care and social work activities	KKO3	18 020	19 681	20 811	22 216	23 515	24 687	26 966	28 660
Q	Total human health and social work activities	KKN7	63 709	70 251	76 750	81 502	87 261	90 341	94 418	99 329
O - Q	Total government, health and education	KKN3	169 747	184 060	197 953	211 758	224 721	233 281	243 059	253 043
R - T	Other services									
R	Arts, entertainment and recreation	KKO5	15 680	17 105	18 143	18 914	19 677	19 572	19 571	19 405
S	Other service activities	KKO9	12 225	13 170	14 377	15 092	15 609	16 280	16 242	17 089
T	Activities of households as employers, undiff. goods	KKP3	4 515	4 852	4 948	5 198	5 299	5 289	5 836	5 315
R - T	Total other services	KKO7	32 420	35 127	37 468	39 204	40 585	41 141	41 649	41 809
G - T	Total service industries	KKJ7	709 687	761 750	809 652	849 058	898 948	952 433	979 285	972 595
B.1g	**All industries**	ABML	956 899	1 014 703	1 070 369	1 116 882	1 183 940	1 252 602	1 283 884	1 256 932

1 Components may not sum to totals as a result of rounding.
2 Because of differences in the annual and monthly production inquiries, estimates of current price output and gross value added by industry derived from the current price Input-Output Supply and Use Tables are not consistent with the equivalent measures of chained volume measures growth given in 2.4. These differences do not affect GDP totals.

2.4 Gross value added at basic prices: by industry[1,2,3]
Chained volume indices

Indices 2008=100

		Weight per 1000[1] 2008		2002	2003	2004	2005	2006	2007	2008	2009	2010
A	**Agriculture**	7.1	L2KL	89.2	87.6	86.4	92.2	89.3	86.1	100.0	84.8	83.6
B - F	**Production and Construction**											
B - E	Production											
B	Mining and quarrying	25.3	L2KR	148.2	141.0	129.8	118.7	109.7	107.0	100.0	91.0	86.4
C	Manufacturing											
CA	Food products, beverages and tobacco	17.2	KN3D	103.6	101.6	103.2	104.0	103.0	102.4	100.0	98.4	101.8
CB	Textiles, wearing apparel and leather products	3.3	KN3E	116.7	115.5	103.2	101.0	101.6	99.8	100.0	90.3	93.3
CC	Wood, paper products and printing	9.1	KN3F	109.0	107.8	107.6	105.8	104.4	104.0	100.0	93.1	92.2
CD	Coke and refined petroleum products	0.7	KN3G	111.2	109.8	115.7	108.5	102.2	101.5	100.0	94.0	92.2
CE	Chemicals and chemical products	8.5	KN3H	96.5	94.5	98.0	97.4	98.7	100.6	100.0	86.3	82.4
CF	Basic pharmaceutical products and preparations	7.5	KN3I	84.9	89.5	91.6	98.1	103.3	98.9	100.0	106.0	100.6
CG	Rubber, plastic and other non-metallic mineral products	7.7	KN3J	97.8	100.0	101.8	100.6	104.9	104.5	100.0	86.3	86.5
CH	Basic metals and metal products	14.3	KN3K	94.1	95.3	98.7	99.6	102.0	104.3	100.0	80.5	84.3
CI	Computer, electronic and optical products	7.5	KN3L	109.8	105.9	110.5	105.1	106.0	106.5	100.0	94.1	88.5
CJ	Electrical equipment	3.4	KN3M	102.1	96.4	97.2	95.5	100.1	102.2	100.0	77.8	85.5
CK	Machinery and equipment n. e. c.	6.7	KN3N	89.2	88.8	91.7	93.4	98.4	100.9	100.0	79.4	95.5
CL	Transport equipment	8.9	KN3O	90.3	94.3	97.8	97.0	98.1	101.4	100.0	88.9	111.2
CM	Other manufacturing and repair	7.6	KN3P	98.3	96.7	98.4	98.6	101.7	103.9	100.0	93.7	96.2
C	Total manufacturing	102.5	L2KX	98.6	98.4	100.4	100.2	101.9	102.7	100.0	90.4	93.8
D	Electricity, gas, steam and air conditioning supply	14.3	L2MW	95.9	97.7	99.2	98.9	98.7	99.5	100.0	95.2	98.6
E	Water supply, sewerage, waste mgmt and remediation	11.8	L2N2	91.7	96.0	97.2	101.6	98.8	101.8	100.0	91.9	90.4
B - E	Total production	153.9	L2KQ	102.7	102.4	103.3	102.4	102.4	102.9	100.0	91.0	92.8
F	Construction	76.2	L2N8	93.2	97.6	102.6	100.0	100.8	102.9	100.0	86.5	93.6
B - F	Total production and construction	230.2	L2KP	99.8	100.9	103.0	101.6	101.9	102.9	100.0	89.5	93.0

1 The weights shown are in proportion to total gross value added (GVA) in 2008 and are used to combine the industry output indices to calculate the totals. For 2007 and earlier, totals are calculated using the equivalent weights for the previous year (e.g. totals for 2007 use 2006 weights). Weights may not sum to totals due to rounding.

2 As GVA is expressed in index number form, it is inappropriate to show as a statistical adjustment any divergence from the other measures of GDP. Such an adjustment does, however, exist implicitly.

3 See footnote 2 to Table 2.3.

2.4 Gross value added at basic prices: by industry[1,2,3]
Chained volume indices

continued

Indices 2008=100

			Weight per 1000[1]										
			2008		2002	2003	2004	2005	2006	2007	2008	2009	2010
G - T	**Services**												
G - I	Distribution, transport, hotels and restaurants												
G	Wholesale, retail, repair of motor vehicles and m/cycles	108.9	L2NE	89.5	91.6	95.4	94.7	98.0	103.0	100.0	95.4	96.9
H	Transportation and storage	50.0	L2NI	92.9	94.4	96.0	97.6	98.1	101.7	100.0	91.4	89.5
I	Accommodation and food service activities	28.6	L2NQ	87.8	90.3	92.0	94.7	98.9	102.6	100.0	95.5	97.5
G - I	Total distribution, transport, hotels and restaurants	187.4	L2ND	90.1	92.1	95.1	95.4	98.2	102.6	100.0	94.3	95.0
J	Information and communication												
JA	Publishing, audiovisual and broadcasting activities	16.6	L2NU	102.0	100.6	98.7	94.8	97.0	100.8	100.0	92.1	106.5
JB	Telecommunications	19.0	L2NZ	66.2	71.9	77.8	86.6	89.9	98.3	100.0	103.7	111.2
JC	IT and other information service activities	26.0	L2O3	71.1	78.1	82.5	87.1	90.7	98.4	100.0	94.3	106.3
J	Total information and communication	61.7	L2NT	76.8	81.3	84.8	88.9	92.1	99.0	100.0	96.6	107.8
K	Financial and insurance	88.7	L2O6	78.6	84.3	86.5	89.4	95.7	101.5	100.0	95.1	89.9
L	Real estate	84.2	L2OC	88.8	92.5	93.8	97.5	99.7	100.6	100.0	104.2	103.5
M - N	Professional and support												
M	Professional, scientific and technical activities												
MA	Legal, accounting, mgmt, architect, engineering etc	56.0	L2OJ	61.3	66.3	69.4	76.2	84.7	97.1	100.0	91.8	85.3
MB	Scientific research and development	3.3	L2OQ	62.5	69.1	83.7	91.6	97.2	102.3	100.0	94.1	103.2
MC	Other professional, scientific and technical activities	14.5	L2OS	90.8	94.0	95.1	100.6	98.4	100.9	100.0	90.1	96.1
M	Total professional, scientific and technical activities	73.8	L2OI	66.0	70.9	74.3	81.1	87.7	98.0	100.0	91.6	88.2
N	Administrative and support service activities	45.2	L2OX	75.6	78.3	82.1	88.1	93.2	101.0	100.0	87.7	100.4
M - N	Total professional and support	119.1	L2OH	69.6	73.7	77.3	83.7	89.8	99.2	100.0	90.1	92.8
O - Q	Government, health and education												
O	Public admin, defence, compulsory social security	50.8	L2P8	83.3	93.7	95.6	97.1	96.1	95.7	100.0	104.2	102.8
P	Education	65.0	L2PA	98.8	99.5	99.9	102.5	101.5	101.3	100.0	101.1	100.8
Q	Human health and social work activities												
QA	Human health activities	52.5	L2PD	79.8	83.2	86.7	90.6	93.3	97.9	100.0	104.9	109.2
QB	Residential care and social work activities	21.0	L2PF	90.1	94.0	97.5	100.2	101.9	103.4	100.0	100.3	103.9
Q	Total human health and social work activities	73.5	L2PC	82.4	85.9	89.5	93.1	95.5	99.4	100.0	103.6	107.7
O - Q	Total government, health and education	189.3	L2P7	87.8	92.4	94.5	97.2	97.6	99.0	100.0	102.9	104.0
R - T	Other services												
R	Arts, entertainment and recreation	15.2	L2PJ	93.9	100.6	103.9	102.4	104.1	108.0	100.0	97.6	99.7
S	Other service activities	12.7	L2PP	96.8	92.7	93.0	96.8	102.7	98.6	100.0	103.9	97.7
T	Activities of households as employers, undiff. goods	4.5	L2PT	111.6	113.6	114.5	120.4	115.4	102.5	100.0	91.6	106.7
R - T	Total other services	32.4	L2PI	96.6	98.6	100.4	101.9	104.6	103.4	100.0	99.2	99.9
G - T	Total service industries	762.8	L2NC	83.8	87.5	90.2	93.2	96.3	100.5	100.0	97.4	98.5
B.1g	**All industries**	1 000.0	CGCE	87.3	90.5	93.0	95.1	97.5	101.0	100.0	95.4	97.1

1 The weights shown are in proportion to total gross value added (GVA) in 2008 and are used to combine the industry output indices to calculate the totals. For 2007 and earlier, totals are calculated using the equivalent weights for the previous year (e.g. totals for 2007 use 2006 weights). Weights may not sum to totals due to rounding.

2 As GVA is expressed in index number form, it is inappropriate to show as a statistical adjustment any divergence from the other measures of GDP. Such an adjustment does, however, exist implicitly.

3 See footnote 2 to Table 2.3.

2.5 Workforce jobs by Industry (SIC 2007)[1]

United Kingdom (thousands), not seasonally adjusted

				2002	2003	2004	2005	2006	2007	2008	2009	2010
A	**Agriculture, hunting & forestry; fishing**											
ESE	Self-employment jobs		L42V	139	150	143	160	154	162	177	193	217
EEM	Employee jobs & government supported trainees		L42K	229	222	234	240	239	228	229	214	242
ETO	Workforce jobs		L428	369	372	377	400	393	390	406	408	458
B-E	**Production industries, including energy**											
ESE	Self-employment jobs		L42W	245	248	256	243	256	246	243	211	219
EEM	Employee jobs & government supported trainees		L42L	3 689	3 484	3 308	3 167	3 062	3 026	2 902	2 772	2 690
ETO	Workforce jobs		L429	3 935	3 733	3 564	3 410	3 318	3 272	3 145	2 983	2 909
F	**Construction**											
ESE	Self-employment jobs		L42Y	767	827	876	898	898	940	945	887	872
EEM	Employee jobs & government supported trainees		L42N	1 252	1 256	1 286	1 346	1 394	1 398	1 389	1 341	1 260
ETO	Workforce jobs		L42B	2 019	2 082	2 163	2 244	2 293	2 338	2 335	2 228	2 133
G-I	**Wholesale & retail trade (including motor trade)**											
ESE	Self-employment jobs		L42Z	836	857	848	825	823	835	830	825	810
EEM	Employee jobs & government supported trainees		L42O	7 476	7 512	7 595	7 660	7 664	7 694	7 730	7 471	7 323
ETO	Workforce jobs		L42C	8 312	8 369	8 443	8 485	8 488	8 530	8 560	8 296	8 134
J	**Information & communication**											
ESE	Self-employment jobs		L432	173	194	177	178	195	203	175	164	176
EEM	Employee jobs & government supported trainees		L42P	1 016	1 008	980	986	1 010	1 014	1 022	1 005	950
ETO	Workforce jobs		L42E	1 189	1 202	1 157	1 165	1 206	1 218	1 197	1 168	1 126
K	**Financial & insurance activities**											
ESE	Self-employment jobs		L433	48	56	60	60	50	56	62	78	80
EEM	Employee jobs & government supported trainees		L42Q	1 137	1 125	1 105	1 097	1 101	1 112	1 130	1 082	1 043
ETO	Workforce jobs		L42F	1 185	1 181	1 164	1 157	1 150	1 168	1 192	1 160	1 123
L	**Real estate activities**											
ESE	Self-employment jobs		L434	60	60	62	62	59	66	59	53	62
EEM	Employee jobs & government supported trainees		L42R	246	254	271	298	326	356	388	398	380
ETO	Workforce jobs		L42G	305	314	334	360	386	422	448	452	442
M-N	**Professional, scientific, technical**											
ESE	Self-employment jobs		L435	579	635	628	647	644	653	662	746	795
EEM	Employee jobs & government supported trainees		L42S	3 408	3 441	3 591	3 764	3 920	4 070	4 124	3 904	3 916
ETO	Workforce jobs		L42H	3 986	4 076	4 219	4 411	4 564	4 722	4 786	4 651	4 711
O-Q	**Public administration and defence**											
ESE	Self-employment jobs		L436	388	417	424	424	475	476	497	579	620
EEM	Employee jobs, HM Forces & government supported trainees		L42T	6 886	7 120	7 334	7 514	7 584	7 577	7 648	7 824	7 886
ETO	Workforce jobs		L42I	7 274	7 538	7 758	7 938	8 060	8 054	8 146	8 403	8 506
R-S	**Arts, entertainment and recreation**											
ESE	Self-employment jobs		L437	459	486	495	496	531	523	517	469	488
EEM	Employee jobs & government supported trainees		L42U	1 232	1 240	1 240	1 260	1 273	1 252	1 262	1 216	1 182
ETO	Workforce jobs		L42J	1 690	1 726	1 735	1 756	1 805	1 776	1 779	1 685	1 670
A-S	**All industries**											
ESE	Self-employment jobs		I8FH	3 694	3 930	3 969	3 994	4 086	4 162	4 167	4 206	4 341
EEM	Employee jobs, HM Forces & government supported trainees		I8F9	26 571	26 663	26 944	27 332	27 576	27 728	27 826	27 229	26 871
ETO	Workforce jobs		I8EZ	30 265	30 593	30 913	31 326	31 662	31 890	31 993	31 434	31 213

1 Data sources are: Labour Force Survey for self-employment jobs; employer surveys for employee jobs; administrative sources for HM forces and government supported trainees. Figures as at June of each year.

The sector accounts

Part 3

The sector accounts at a glance

Net lending/borrowing

Net borrowing by general government decreased in 2010 to £150.2 billion compared with net borrowing of £152.0 billion in 2009. The non-financial corporations sector was a net lender of £61.2 billion in 2010 and a net lender of £50.9 billion in 2009. The households and non-profit institutions serving households (NPISH) sector was a net lender of £32.8 billion in 2010 compared with a net lender of £38.1 billion in 2009. Financial corporations were net lenders in 2010 at £17.7 billion, from net lending of £46.3 billion in 2009. Rest of the world sector net lending was £33.0 billion in 2010 compared with £16.7 billion in 2009.

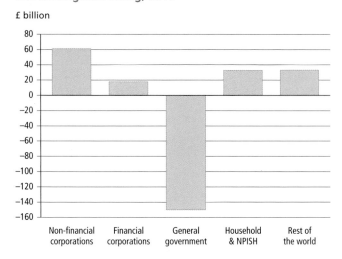

Net lending/borrowing, 2010
£ billion

Net financial transactions

Net financial transactions by general government showed a deficit of £150.4 billion in 2010 compared with a £151.3 billion deficit in 2009. The non-financial corporations show a surplus of £60.5 billion in 2010 compared with a £52.3 billion surplus in 2009. Households and NPISH showed a surplus of £25.5 billion in 2010 compared with a surplus of £28.8 billion in 2009. In 2010 financial corporations showed a surplus of £22.9 billion, following on from a surplus of £45.5 billion in 2009. The rest of the world sector shows a surplus of £41.5 billion in 2010 compared with £24.8 billion in 2009.

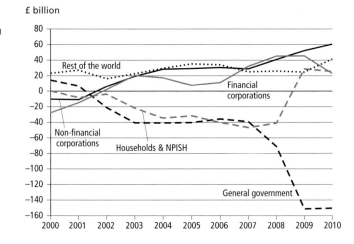

Net financial transactions
£ billion

Gross trading profits of private non-financial corporations

Gross trading profit is the largest component of private non-financial corporations' gross operating surplus. Profits increased by 6.7 per cent between 2009 and 2010 compared with a decrease of 8.6 per cent between 2008 and 2009.

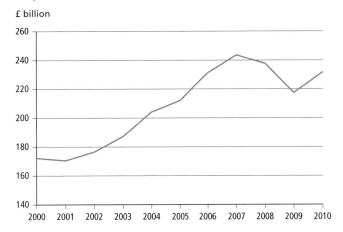

Gross trading profits of private non-financial corporations
£ billion

Real household disposable income

Real household disposable income (RHDI) is the amount of money in real terms the households sector has available for spending after taxes and other deductions. Between 2009 and 2010 RHDI increased by 0.1 per cent compared with an increase of 1.6 per cent between 2008 and 2009.

Annual changes in real household disposable income
Per cent

Household saving ratio

The household saving ratio reflects household gross savings as a percentage of their total available resources (the amount available to invest or save). Household resources rose by 4.6 per cent between 2009 and 2010. Households and NPISH final consumption expenditure increased by 4.9 per cent in the same period. As a consequence the household saving ratio decreased to 7.5 in 2010 from 7.8 in 2009

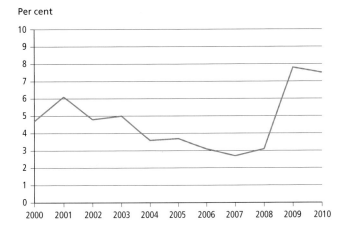

Household saving ratio
Per cent

The sector accounts

The sector accounts show the relationships between different sectors of the economy and different types of transactions. They summarise the transactions of particular groups of institutions in the economy, showing how the income from production is distributed and redistributed, and how savings are used to add wealth through investment in physical or financial assets. This section introduces the tables in Chapters 3 to 7 which deal with individual areas and subdivisions of the accounts. This introduction to the sector accounts has been divided into the following areas:

- framework of the accounts
- institutional sectors
- types of transactions
- sequence of accounts
- statistical adjustment items
- balance sheets

Framework of the accounts

The framework of national accounts detailed in Part 1 highlights the five main types of accounts; goods and services, production, distribution and use of income, capital and financial. The production account records the activity of producing goods and services. The distribution and use of income accounts record how the incomes generated by production are distributed to institutional units with claims on the value added created by production, redistributed among institutional units, and eventually used by households, government units or non-profit institutions serving households for purposes of final consumption or saving. The capital account records the flows of non-financial assets acquired and disposed. The financial account shows how the net lending or borrowing on the capital account is financed by transactions in financial instruments.

The distribution and use of income accounts can be elaborated to form a consistent set of sector accounts. This is done in two dimensions, by sectors and types of transaction. A third dimension, related to capital and financial transactions, is that of asset and liability levels on the national and sector balance sheets. The sectors and types of transaction are described below.

Institutional sectors

The system identifies two kinds of institutions: consuming units (mostly households) and production units (mainly corporations and non-profit institutions or government). Units can own goods and assets, incur liabilities and engage in economic activities and transactions with other units in their own right. All units within the country are put in one of the sectors. Also, the rest of the world is treated as a sector in respect of its dealings with the United Kingdom.

Non-financial corporations are those which exist to produce goods and non-financial services. They are, in the UK, mainly public limited companies, private companies and partnerships. They are mostly owned privately but there are some public corporations which are shown separately.

Financial corporations are those engaged primarily in financial activities and are subdivided into monetary financial institutions, other financial intermediaries and financial auxiliaries and insurance corporations and pension funds.

General government comprises central government and local government.

The household sector contains all the resident people of the United Kingdom as receivers of income and consumers of products. It includes individuals such as prisoners as well as conventional family units. It also contains unincorporated enterprises (except quasi-corporations). This sector currently includes non-profit institutions serving households which include productive units such as charities and universities.

The rest of the world sector comprises those units that are not in the United Kingdom. The accounts for the rest of the world only record transactions between units in the rest of the world and units in the UK, and are equivalent to the balance of payments.

The tables in Chapters 3 to 7 are based on the sector classification detailed above. More detailed definitions of these sectors are given in the appropriate chapters of the *UK National Accounts Concepts, Sources and Methods* and, in full detail, in the National Accounts *Sector Classification area* of the ONS website.

Types of transactions

The other dimension is that of the types of transactions. There are three main types:

- **Transactions in products** are related to goods and services. They include output, intermediate and final consumption, gross capital formation and exports and imports

- **Distributive transactions** transfer income or wealth between units of the economy. They include property income, taxes and subsidies, social contributions and benefits and other current or capital transfers

- **Financial transactions** differ from distributive transactions in that they relate to transactions in financial claims by one unit on another, whereas distributive transactions are unrequited. The main categories in the classification of financial instruments are monetary gold and special drawing rights; currency and deposits; securities other than shares; loans; shares and other equity; insurance and pension funds reserves; and other accounts receivable/payable.

Sequence of accounts

Transactions can be grouped broadly according to purpose in the production, distribution and use of income, capital, or financial accounts. These are described briefly below:

Production account

The production account displays the transactions involved in the generation of income by the production of goods and services. This account is produced for the UK total economy (Table 1.6.1) and for the first four sectors (Tables 3.1.1, 4.1.1 etc.); the rest of the world does not have a production account. For each of the four sectors, the balancing item gross value added is shown as output *less* intermediate consumption. Gross value added at basic prices for each sector differs from gross domestic product for the UK total economy in that taxes *less* subsidies on products are not taken into the production accounts by sector but they are included within resources for the UK total economy. The sum of gross value added and taxes *less* subsidies on products for the UK economy is GDP at market prices.

Distribution and use of income account

The distribution and use of income accounts exist for all the main institutional sectors. To obtain the disposable income and savings of each sector we need to take account of transfers in and out of the sector. The accounts are not consolidated, so that in the whole economy account, transfers such as social contributions and benefits appear in both uses and resources.

These accounts describe the distribution and redistribution of income and its use in the form of final consumption. The distribution and use of income are analysed in four stages, each of which is presented as a separate account:

- generation of income account
- allocation of primary income account
- secondary distribution of income account
- use of disposable income account

Generation of income account

This is the first of the distribution and use of income accounts. It shows the sectors, sub-sectors and industries which are the source, rather than the destination, of income. It shows the derivation of the 'profit' arising from production, called the operating surplus (or mixed income in the case of unincorporated businesses in the households sector). The industry dimension is shown in Part 2, Table 2.1.

This account analyses the degree to which value added covers the compensation of employees (their wages and salaries, etc.) and other taxes *less* subsidies on production. It therefore gives a figure for the operating surplus: the surplus (or deficit) on production activities before distributions such as interest, rent and income tax charges have been considered. Hence the operating surplus is the income which units obtain from their own use of the production facilities.

Note that taxes on production and imports are shown as a use by producing sectors in this account but not as a resource of government. This is because they do not relate to productive activity by government and cannot therefore contribute to its operating surplus. They become a resource of government in the allocation of primary income account which follows.

Allocation of primary income account

This account shows the resident units and institutional sectors as recipients rather than producers of primary income. It demonstrates the extent to which operating surpluses are distributed (for example by dividends) to the owners of the enterprises. Also recorded in this account is the property income received by an owner of a financial asset in return for providing funds to, or putting a tangible non-produced asset at the disposal of, another unit. The receipt by government of taxes on production *less* subsidies is shown in resources.

The resources side of the allocation of primary income accounts includes the components of the income approach to measurement of gross domestic product and this is the starting point for the quarterly sector accounts. The accounts also include property income recorded as both resources for receipts and uses for payments.

The balance of this account is the gross balance of primary income (B.5g) for each sector, and if the gross balance of primary income is aggregated across all sectors of the UK economy the result is gross national income.

Secondary distribution of income account

This account describes how the balance of primary income for each institutional sector is allocated by redistribution; through transfers such as taxes on income, social contributions and benefits and other current transfers. It excludes social transfers in kind.

The balancing item of this account is gross disposable income (B.6g) which reflects current transactions and explicitly excludes capital transfers, real holding gains and losses, and the consequences of events such as natural disasters.

Use of disposable income account

This account illustrates how disposable income is split between final consumption expenditure and saving. In the system for recording economic accounts, only the government and the households and non-profit institutions serving households (NPISH) sectors have final consumption. In addition, for households and pension funds, there is an adjustment item in the account which reflects the way that transactions between households and pension funds are recorded (this adjustment is D.8: Adjustment for the changes in the net equity of households in pension funds reserves).

The balancing item for this account, and thus for this whole group of distribution and use of income accounts, is gross saving (B.8g).

Thus it is only in the case of non-financial corporations (public and private) that undistributed income and saving are equivalent.

Capital account

The capital account is presented in two parts.

The first part shows that saving (B.8g) the balance between national disposable income and final consumption expenditure from the production and distribution and use of income accounts is reduced or increased by the balance of capital transfers (D.9) to provide an amount available for financing investment (in both non-financial and financial assets).

In the second part, total investment in non-financial assets is the sum of gross fixed capital formation (P.51), changes in inventories (P.52), acquisitions *less* disposals of valuables (P.53) and acquisitions *less* disposals of non-financial non-produced assets (K.2). The balance on the capital account is known as net lending or borrowing. Conceptually this net lending or borrowing for all the domestic sectors represents net lending or borrowing to the rest of the world sector.

Thus, if investment is lower than the amount available for investment, the balance will be positive and is regarded as lending (if negative the balance is borrowing). Where the capital accounts relate to the individual institutional sectors, the net lending/borrowing of a particular sector represents the amounts available for lending or borrowing to other sectors. The value of net lending/borrowing is the same irrespective of whether the accounts are shown before or after deduction of fixed capital consumption (K.1), provided a consistent approach is adopted throughout.

Financial account

The financial account elaborates the acquisition and disposal of financial assets and liabilities. Examples of financial assets include: bank deposits (which are assets of the depositors and liabilities of the banks), unit trust units (assets of the holders and liabilities of unit trusts), and Treasury Bills (assets of the holders and a liability of central government). The balance of all transactions in the financial account is net lending or borrowing.

The statistical adjustment items

Although in theory the net lending/borrowing from the financial account and the net lending/borrowing from the capital account for each sector should be equal, in practice they are not. This is because of the (sometimes substantial) errors and omissions in the accounts. The difference between the two balances is known as the statistical adjustment item.

Part of the balancing process for the economic accounts statistics for years before the latest one shown (that is, for years t−1 and earlier) involves assessing and modifying the component variables so that the estimates of net lending/borrowing made from the income and capital accounts, and from the financial accounts, are the same at the level of the whole economy, and reasonably close to each other at the sector level.

The sectoral statistical adjustment items are shown in Table D. They provide a measure of the reliability of the accounts.

Balance sheets

A financial balance sheet for each sector has been compiled using the same financial instrument classification as that used for financial transactions. The changes in the end period levels in the financial balance sheets do not equal the financial transactions because of holding gains or losses and reclassifications of units between sectors. Non-financial balance sheets for the ESA95 sectors are now included.

Further information

In addition to the articles and publications mentioned in Part 1, further information relating to the sector accounts and in particular the financial accounts can be found in the following publication:

Office for National Statistics (2011) *'Financial Statistics: Explanatory Handbook* 2011 Edition'
http://www.ons.gov.uk/ons/rel/fin-stats/financial-statistics-explanatory-handbook/2011/index.html

Articles relating to Public Sector Finances

Golland J, Savage D, Pike T and Pike S (1999) 'Monthly Statistics on Public Sector Finances. A Methodological Guide'
http://ons.gov.uk/ons/guide-method/method-quality/specific/economy/public-sector-statistics/monthly-statistics-on-public-sector-finances--a-methodological-guide.pdf

'Government and Public Sector Debt Measures'
http://ons.gov.uk/ons/guide-method/method-quality/specific/economy/public-sector-statistics/government-and-public-sector-debt-measures.pdf

Hobbs (2010) 'Wider Measures of Public Sector Debt'
http://ons.gov.uk/ons/rel/psa/wider-measures-of-public-sector-debt/july-2010/wider-measures-of-public-sector-debt.pdf

Kellaway M, (2009) 'Public Sector Interventions in the Financial Crisis'
http://ons.gov.uk/ons/rel/psa/financial-crisis-and-statitical-classification/public-sector-interventions-in-the-financial-crisis/public-sector-interventions-in-the-financial-crisis-.pdf

Kellaway M, Shanks H, (2006) 'National Accounts Classification of London & Continental Railways (LCR)'
http://ons.gov.uk/ons/rel/na-classification/national-accounts-sector-classification/national-accounts-classification-of-london---continental-railways--lcr-/national-accounts-classification-of-london---continental-railways--lcr--.pdf

O'Donoghue J (2008) 'Inclusion of Bank of England and Northern Rock in Public Sector Finance Statistics'
http://ons.gov.uk/ons/rel/psa/public-sector-statistics/forthcoming-revisions-to-the-public-sector-finances---explanatory-note/forthcoming-revisions-to-the-public-sector-finances---explanatory-note-.pdf

O'Donoghue J (2009) 'The Public Sector Balance Sheet' *Economic & Labour Market Review*, vol 3, no 7, pp. 37–42. Palgrave Macmillan, Basingstoke.
http://ons.gov.uk/ons/rel/elmr/economic-and-labour-market-review/no--7july-2009/the-public-sector-balance-sheet.pdf

O'Donoghue J (2010) 'Public Sector Finances excluding Financial Sector Interventions'
http://ons.gov.uk/ons/rel/psa/public-sector-statistics/including-finance-lease-liabilities-in-public-sector-net-debt--pfi-and-other/including-finance-lease-liabilities-in-public-sector-net-debt--pfi-and-other-.pdf

Article relating to monetary aggregates (M0, M4)

Bank of England (1993) 'Divisia Measures of Money' *Bank of England Quarterly Bulletin*, May 1993.
http://www.bankofengland.co.uk/mfsd/iadb/noteslADB/divisia.htm

C The sector accounts: Key economic indicators

£ million

			2002	2003	2004	2005	2006	2007	2008	2009	2010
	Net lending/borrowing by:										
B.9	Non-financial corporations	EABO	14 749	28 670	39 532	37 967	40 086	38 279	31 231	50 880	61 215
B.9	Financial corporations	NHCQ	4 062	11 011	17 533	7 110	2 649	23 611	52 755	46 332	17 706
B.9	General government	NNBK	−20 163	−40 965	−41 707	−40 341	−35 020	−38 331	−70 457	−151 967	−150 151
B.9	Households and NPISH's	NSSZ	−16 120	−15 632	−38 188	−35 899	−49 834	−55 821	−30 040	38 084	32 757
B.9	Rest of the world	NHRB	17 469	16 914	22 826	31 164	42 120	32 260	16 512	16 679	33 018
	Private non-financial corporations										
	Gross trading profits										
	Continental shelf profits	CAGD	16 038	15 331	16 029	19 299	22 352	23 309	27 851	21 256	32 926
	Others	CAED	160 468	172 079	188 092	192 831	209 067	220 310	209 870	196 111	198 987
	Rental of buildings	DTWR	13 818	14 709	15 288	16 882	17 005	19 233	22 353	21 317	22 562
	less Holding gains of inventories	-DLRA	−2 992	−4 226	−2 659	−4 201	−4 115	−4 857	−4 814	−5 248	−8 401
B.2g	Gross operating surplus	CAER	187 332	197 893	216 750	224 811	244 309	257 995	255 260	233 436	246 074
	Households and NPISH										
B.6g	Household gross disposable income	QWND	724 815	759 820	781 573	815 311	849 789	882 396	915 095	943 143	979 184
	Implied deflator of household and NPISH individual consumption expenditure index (2008=100)[1]	YBFS	86.4	88.0	89.6	91.8	94.3	96.7	100.0	101.4	105.3
	Real household disposable income:										
	Chained volume measures (Reference year 2008)	RVGK	838 455	863 663	872 030	887 943	901 557	912 788	915 095	929 792	930 323
	Index (2008=100)	OSXR	91.6	94.4	95.3	97.0	98.5	99.7	100.0	101.6	101.7
B.8g	Gross saving	NSSH	35 528	39 017	29 155	31 219	27 560	24 701	29 146	75 585	76 383
	Households total resources	NSSJ	874 602	924 846	955 710	1 005 387	1 051 621	1 103 029	1 137 558	1 176 603	1 227 053
	Saving ratio, per cent	RVGL	4.8	5.0	3.6	3.7	3.1	2.7	3.1	7.8	7.5

1 Rounded to one decimal place

D Table D: Sector statistical adjustments

£ million

		2002	2003	2004	2005	2006	2007	2008	2009	2010
Households sector	NZDV	−12 419	6 024	−3 700	−4 328	−9 621	−8 974	10 899	9 318	7 235
Private non-financial corporations	NYPM	8 926	8 749	10 434	8 496	10 348	9 790	−9 424	−2 350	1 458
Financial corporations	NYOX	1 736	−9 373	166	−443	−8 677	−8 622	7 535	851	−5 154
Public corporations	NYPI	−410	575	652	259	−896	−375	−285	972	−752
Central government	NZDW	818	11	64	−860	62	840	265	−345	126
Local government	NYPC	82	−341	−982	948	641	61	484	−352	131
Rest of the world	NYPO	1 265	−5 647	−6 637	−4 071	8 144	7 278	−9 473	−8 086	−8 499
Total[1]	-RVFE	−3	−2	−4	1	1	−2	1	8	−5 455

1 Equals, but opposite in sign to, the residual error observed between GDP measured by the income approach and GDP measured by the expenditure approach

Chapter 3

Non-financial corporations

3.1.1 Non-financial corporations
ESA95 sector S.11

£ million

			2002	2003	2004	2005	2006	2007	2008	2009
I	**PRODUCTION ACCOUNT**									
	Resources									
P.1	Output									
P.11	Market output	FAIN	1 243 999	1 294 692	1 359 734	1 429 082	1 511 371	1 599 297	1 638 185	1 574 560
P.12	Output for own final use	FAIO	12 032	13 896	13 456	14 628	16 014	17 817	18 353	17 446
P.1	Total resources	FAFA	1 256 031	1 308 588	1 373 190	1 443 710	1 527 385	1 617 114	1 656 538	1 592 006
	Uses									
P.2	Intermediate consumption	FAIQ	659 226	687 681	718 979	764 756	808 675	856 086	885 854	846 280
B.1g	**Gross Value Added**	FAIS	**596 805**	**620 907**	**654 211**	**678 954**	**718 710**	**761 028**	**770 684**	**745 726**
Total	Total uses	FAFA	1 256 031	1 308 588	1 373 190	1 443 710	1 527 385	1 617 114	1 656 538	1 592 006
B.1g	**Gross Value Added**	FAIS	**596 805**	**620 907**	**654 211**	**678 954**	**718 710**	**761 028**	**770 684**	**745 726**
-K.1	less Consumption of fixed capital	-DBGF	–70 547	–72 598	–75 559	–77 277	–80 365	–83 243	–86 127	–90 888
B.1n	Value added, net	FAIT	526 258	548 309	578 652	601 677	638 345	677 785	684 557	654 838

3.1.2 Non-financial corporations
ESA95 sector S.11

£ million

			2002	2003	2004	2005	2006	2007	2008	2009
II	**DISTRIBUTION AND USE OF INCOME ACCOUNTS**									
II.1	**PRIMARY DISTRIBUTION OF INCOME ACCOUNT**									
II.1.1	**GENERATION OF INCOME ACCOUNT** before deduction of fixed capital consumption									
	Resources									
B.1g	**Total resources (Gross Value Added)**	FAIS	596 805	620 907	654 211	678 954	718 710	761 028	770 684	745 726
	Uses									
D.1	Compensation of employees									
D.11	Wages and salaries	FAKT	339 650	344 920	356 176	365 485	379 802	406 658	419 524	410 502
D.12	Employers' social contributions	FAKU	47 467	55 339	58 641	64 475	68 862	69 951	70 295	74 018
D.1	Total	FCFV	387 117	400 259	414 817	429 960	448 664	476 609	489 819	484 520
D.2	Taxes on production and imports, paid									
D.29	Production taxes other than on products	EACJ	16 679	17 037	17 346	18 159	19 202	19 796	20 943	21 587
-D.3	less Subsidies, received									
-D.39	Production subsidies other than on products	-JQJV	–954	–1 434	–1 562	–2 449	–3 093	–3 486	–3 381	–3 313
B.2g	Operating surplus, gross	NQBE	193 963	205 045	223 610	233 284	253 937	268 109	263 303	242 932
B.1g	**Total uses (Gross Value Added)**	FAIS	**596 805**	**620 907**	**654 211**	**678 954**	**718 710**	**761 028**	**770 684**	**745 726**
-K.1	After deduction of fixed capital consumption	-DBGF	–70 547	–72 598	–75 559	–77 277	–80 365	–83 243	–86 127	–90 888
B.2n	Operating surplus, net	FAIR	123 416	132 447	148 051	156 007	173 572	184 866	177 176	152 044

3.1.3 Non-financial corporations
ESA95 sector S.11

£ million

			2002	2003	2004	2005	2006	2007	2008	2009	2010
II.1.2	**ALLOCATION OF PRIMARY INCOME ACCOUNT** before deduction of fixed capital consumption										
	Resources										
B.2g	Operating surplus, gross	NQBE	193 963	205 045	223 610	233 284	253 937	268 109	263 303	242 932	254 884
D.4	Property income, received										
D.41	Interest	EABC	9 330	9 727	14 141	17 380	25 391	30 521	24 566	7 399	6 920
D.42	Distributed income of corporations	EABD	30 550	50 263	42 964	46 687	43 893	38 953	47 124	62 606	55 915
D.43	Reinvested earnings on direct foreign investment	WEYD	26 931	12 559	22 868	33 354	36 725	50 760	37 714	13 783	27 043
D.44	Attributed property income of insurance policy-holders	FAOF	300	398	368	582	545	309	365	363	299
D.45	Rent	FAOG	118	120	122	122	124	123	126	132	130
D.4	Total	FAKY	67 229	73 067	80 463	98 125	106 678	120 666	109 895	84 283	90 307
Total	Total resources	FBXJ	261 192	278 112	304 073	331 409	360 615	388 775	373 198	327 215	345 191
	Uses										
D.4	Property income, paid										
D.41	Interest	EABG	28 871	29 395	34 812	39 078	43 572	55 018	52 806	31 877	24 428
D.42	Distributed income of corporations	NVCS	85 619	89 102	93 788	104 875	108 471	109 167	114 025	113 829	105 286
D.43	Reinvested earnings on direct foreign investment	HDVB	1 614	3 955	6 325	4 983	15 452	15 051	3 656	−1 445	−621
D.45	Rent	FBXO	1 939	1 603	1 221	1 268	1 265	1 273	1 204	1 213	1 212
D.4	Total	FBXK	118 043	124 055	136 146	150 204	168 760	180 509	171 691	145 474	130 305
B.5g	**Balance of primary incomes, gross**	NQBG	**143 149**	**154 057**	**167 927**	**181 205**	**191 855**	**208 266**	**201 507**	**181 741**	**214 886**
Total	Total uses	FBXJ	261 192	278 112	304 073	331 409	360 615	388 775	373 198	327 215	345 191
-K.1	After deduction of fixed capital consumption	-DBGF	−70 547	−72 598	−75 559	−77 277	−80 365	−83 243	−86 127	−90 888	−94 636
B.5n	Balance of primary incomes, net	FBXQ	72 602	81 459	92 368	103 928	111 490	125 023	115 380	90 853	120 250

3.1.4 Non-financial corporations
ESA95 sector S.11

£ million

			2002	2003	2004	2005	2006	2007	2008	2009	2010
II.2	**SECONDARY DISTRIBUTION OF INCOME ACCOUNT**										
	Resources										
B.5g	**Balance of primary incomes, gross**	NQBG	**143 149**	**154 057**	**167 927**	**181 205**	**191 855**	**208 266**	**201 507**	**181 741**	**214 886**
D.61	Social contributions										
D.612	Imputed social contributions	NSTJ	3 932	4 206	4 121	4 392	4 560	4 824	5 763	6 809	4 399
D.7	Current transfers other than taxes, social contributions and benefits										
D.72	Non-life insurance claims	FCBP	5 396	5 999	6 522	7 261	7 476	4 007	5 682	5 290	5 714
D.75	Miscellaneous current transfers	CY8C	147	124	28	–	–	–	–	–	–
D.7	Total	NRJB	5 543	6 123	6 550	7 261	7 476	4 007	5 682	5 290	5 714
Total	Total resources	FCBR	152 624	164 386	178 598	192 858	203 891	217 097	212 952	193 840	224 999
	Uses										
D.5	Current taxes on income, wealth etc.										
D.51	Taxes on income	FCBS	24 038	23 702	27 366	33 618	37 184	38 403	40 845	33 542	35 641
D.62	Social benefits other than social transfers in kind	NSTJ	3 932	4 206	4 121	4 392	4 560	4 824	5 763	6 809	4 399
D.7	Current transfers other than taxes, social contributions and benefits										
D.71	Net non-life insurance premiums	FCBY	5 396	5 999	6 522	7 261	7 476	4 007	5 682	5 290	5 714
D.75	Miscellaneous current transfers	CY8B	480	462	451	488	477	488	488	488	488
D.7	Total, other current transfers	FCBX	5 876	6 461	6 973	7 749	7 953	4 495	6 170	5 778	6 202
B.6g	**Gross Disposable Income**	NRJD	**118 778**	**130 017**	**140 138**	**147 099**	**154 194**	**169 375**	**160 174**	**147 711**	**178 757**
Total	Total uses	FCBR	152 624	164 386	178 598	192 858	203 891	217 097	212 952	193 840	224 999
-K.1	After deduction of fixed capital consumption	-DBGF	−70 547	−72 598	−75 559	−77 277	−80 365	−83 243	−86 127	−90 888	−94 636
B.6n	Disposable income, net	FCCF	48 231	57 419	64 579	69 822	73 829	86 132	74 047	56 823	84 121

3.1.6 Non-financial corporations
ESA95 sector S.11

£ million

			2002	2003	2004	2005	2006	2007	2008	2009	2010
II.4.1	**USE OF DISPOSABLE INCOME ACCOUNT**										
	Resources										
B.6g	Total resources (Gross Disposable Income)	NRJD	118 778	130 017	140 138	147 099	154 194	169 375	160 174	147 711	178 757
	Uses										
B.8g	Total uses (Gross Saving)	NRJD	118 778	130 017	140 138	147 099	154 194	169 375	160 174	147 711	178 757
-K.1	After deduction of fixed capital consumption	-DBGF	–70 547	–72 598	–75 559	–77 277	–80 365	–83 243	–86 127	–90 888	–94 636
B.8n	Saving, net	FCCF	48 231	57 419	64 579	69 822	73 829	86 132	74 047	56 823	84 121

3.1.7 Non-financial corporations
ESA95 sector S.11

£ million

			2002	2003	2004	2005	2006	2007	2008	2009	2010
III	**ACCUMULATION ACCOUNTS**										
III.1	**CAPITAL ACCOUNT**										
III.1.1	**CHANGE IN NET WORTH DUE TO SAVING AND CAPITAL TRANSFERS**										
	Changes in liabilities and net worth										
B.8g	Gross Saving	NRJD	118 778	130 017	140 138	147 099	154 194	169 375	160 174	147 711	178 757
D.9	Capital transfers receivable										
D.92	Investment grants	FCCO	3 895	5 563	5 722	6 798	7 672	8 154	7 454	12 941	10 612
D.99	Other capital transfers	LNZN	184	148	136	11 801	449	266	1 824	187	77
D.9	Total	FCCQ	4 079	5 711	5 858	18 599	8 121	8 420	9 278	13 128	10 689
-D.9	*less* Capital transfers payable										
-D.91	Capital taxes	-QYKB	–	–	–	–	–	–	–	–	–
-D.99	Other capital transfers	-JRWI	–492	–575	–419	–1 256	–630	–880	–918	–723	–456
-D.9	Total	-JRWJ	–492	–575	–419	–1 256	–630	–880	–918	–723	–456
B.10.1g	Total change in liabilities and net worth	FCCY	122 365	135 153	145 577	164 442	161 685	176 915	168 534	160 116	188 990
	Changes in assets										
B.10.1g	Changes in net worth due to gross saving and capital transfers	FCCY	122 365	135 153	145 577	164 442	161 685	176 915	168 534	160 116	188 990
-K.1	After deduction of fixed capital consumption	-DBGF	–70 547	–72 598	–75 559	–77 277	–80 365	–83 243	–86 127	–90 888	–94 636
B.10.1n	Changes in net worth due to net saving and capital transfers	FCCV	51 818	62 555	70 018	87 165	81 320	93 672	82 407	69 228	94 354
III.1.2	**ACQUISITION OF NON-FINANCIAL ASSETS ACCOUNT**										
	Changes in liabilities and net worth										
B.10.1n	Changes in net worth due to net saving and capital transfers	FCCV	51 818	62 555	70 018	87 165	81 320	93 672	82 407	69 228	94 354
K.1	Consumption of fixed capital	DBGF	70 547	72 598	75 559	77 277	80 365	83 243	86 127	90 888	94 636
B.10.1g	Total change in liabilities and net worth	FCCY	122 365	135 153	145 577	164 442	161 685	176 915	168 534	160 116	188 990
	Changes in assets										
P.5	Gross capital formation										
P.51	Gross fixed capital formation	DBGP	103 275	101 362	99 341	120 315	114 976	129 503	134 071	119 496	119 937
P.52	Changes in inventories	DBGM	2 742	3 708	4 835	4 218	5 085	5 953	1 744	–11 391	6 668
P.53	Acquisitions less disposals of valuables	NPOV	168	172	184	197	157	207	150	153	16
P.5	Total gross capital formation	FCCZ	106 185	105 242	104 360	124 730	120 218	135 663	135 965	108 258	126 621
K.2	Acquisitions less disposals of non-produced non-financial assets	FCFY	1 431	1 241	1 685	1 745	1 381	2 973	1 338	978	1 154
B.9	**Net lending(+) / net borrowing(-)**	EABO	**14 749**	**28 670**	**39 532**	**37 967**	**40 086**	**38 279**	**31 231**	**50 880**	**61 215**
Total	Total change in assets	FCCY	122 365	135 153	145 577	164 442	161 685	176 915	168 534	160 116	188 990

3.1.8 Non-financial corporations
ESA95 sector S.11 Unconsolidated

£ million

III.2 FINANCIAL ACCOUNT

F.A Net acquisition of financial assets

			2002	2003	2004	2005	2006	2007	2008	2009	2010
F.2	Currency and deposits										
F.21	Currency	NGIJ	10	338	–49	182	260	277	–40	521	225
F.22	Transferable deposits										
F.221	Deposits with UK monetary financial institutions	NGIL	8 570	14 866	14 282	22 824	26 667	18 183	–20 318	20 106	15 168
F.2212	*of which* Foreign currency deposits	NGIN	–274	3 840	2 559	2 640	2 653	3 078	–5 684	9 612	11 929
F.229	Deposits with rest of the world monetary financial institutions	NGIP	9 947	38 367	54 849	39 482	36 771	79 870	–9 841	–54 252	38 179
F.29	Other deposits	NGIQ	1 109	–398	454	663	718	95	–299	–309	–2 184
F.2	Total currency and deposits	NGII	19 636	53 173	69 536	63 151	64 416	98 425	–30 498	–33 934	51 388
F.3	Securities other than shares										
F.331	Short term: money market instruments										
F.3311	Issued by UK central government	NGIT	–	2	–4	1	–	408	161	–245	17
F.3312	Issued by UK local government	NGIX	–	–	–	–	–	–	–	–	–
F.3315	Issued by UK monetary financial institutions	NGIY	230	622	77	–786	1 508	3 472	1 053	–62	–1 002
F.3316	Issued by other UK residents	NGJD	–2 108	821	–710	–1 731	3 284	–547	2 264	–1 844	1 433
F.3319	Issued by the rest of the world	NGJE	1 110	3 798	615	1 078	4 758	–9 820	–5 055	1 615	1 936
F.332	Medium (1 to 5 year) and long term (over 5 year) bonds										
F.3321	Issued by UK central government	NGJG	148	–335	32	–902	–2 000	492	680	677	773
F.3322	Issued by UK local government	NGJJ	–	–	–	–	–	–	–	–	–
F.3325	Medium term bonds issued by UK monetary financial institutions	NGJK	42	167	–23	395	466	658	991	1 438	488
F.3326	Other medium & long term bonds issued by UK residents	NGJN	559	–685	–390	–3 421	–265	3 303	1 301	–3 366	218
F.3329	Long term bonds issued by the rest of the world	NGJO	–601	2 213	437	892	–1 093	1 663	2 968	–1 103	3 271
F.34	Financial derivatives	NGJQ	10	9	–1 339	–2 216	–288	–1 870	730	–3 248	–1 583
F.3	Total securities other than shares	NGIR	–610	6 612	–1 305	–6 690	6 370	–2 241	5 093	–6 138	5 551
F.4	Loans										
F.42	Long term loans										
F.421	Direct investment	NGKB	21 891	9 678	17 775	22 347	3 648	54 924	115 830	–43 821	–7 119
F.422	Loans secured on dwellings	NGKE	–	–	–	–	–	–	–	–	–
F.423	Finance leasing	NGKI	221	471	444	478	292	528	58	–76	147
F.424	Other long-term loans by UK residents	NGKJ	–27	–4 863	614	13 664	39 022	–3 275	–15 414	–2 568	17 894
F.4	Total loans	NGJT	22 085	5 286	18 833	36 489	42 962	52 177	100 474	–46 465	10 922
F.5	Shares and other equity										
F.51	Shares and other equity, excluding mutual funds' shares										
F.514	Quoted UK shares	NGKQ	13 999	4 944	12 620	11 640	17 786	11 794	19 505	6 570	–233
F.515	Unquoted UK shares	NGKR	7 557	9 425	9 278	16 002	9 917	11 255	37 183	8 657	3 721
F.517	UK shares and bonds issued by other UK residents	NSQC	–	–	–	–	–	–	–	–	–
F.519	Shares and other equity issued by the rest of the world	NGKV	49 469	19 394	26 461	41 057	49 980	75 905	64 460	8 894	28 410
F.52	Mutual funds' shares										
F.521	UK mutual funds' shares	NGKZ	3	1	9	17	17	7	3	11	14
F.5	Total shares and other equity	NGKL	71 028	33 764	48 368	68 716	77 700	98 961	121 151	24 132	31 912
F.6	Insurance technical reserves										
F.62	Prepayments of insurance premiums and reserves for outstanding claims	NGLE	363	170	–1 035	1 839	–856	–3 571	318	–354	244
F.7	Other accounts receivable	NGLF	2 881	918	–1 709	1 562	6 902	1 764	–5 064	–5 635	5 679
F.A	Total net acquisition of financial assets	NRGP	115 383	99 923	132 688	165 067	197 494	245 515	191 474	–68 394	105 696

3.1.8 Non-financial corporations
ESA95 sector S.11 Unconsolidated
continued

£ million

			2002	2003	2004	2005	2006	2007	2008	2009	2010
III.2	**FINANCIAL ACCOUNT** continued										
F.L	**Net acquisition of financial liabilities**										
F.2	Currency and deposits										
F.29	Other deposits	-A4VS	18	–	–	–	–	–	–	–	–
F.2	Total currency and deposits	-A4VR	18	–	–	–	–	–	–	–	–
F.3	Securities other than shares										
F.331	Short term: money market instruments										
F.3316	Issued by UK residents other than government or monetary financial institutions	NGMH	8 543	–1 541	–3 157	–178	672	695	1 366	–5 803	3 898
F.332	Medium (1 to 5 year) and long term (over 5 year) bonds										
F.3326	Other medium & long term bonds issued by UK residents or monetary financial institutions	NGMR	15 330	19 426	8 550	12 420	11 252	23 957	2 186	–3 085	–6 516
F.34	Financial derivatives	CY7W	–204	–138	–	–	–	–	–	–	–
F.3	Total securities other than shares	NGLV	23 669	17 747	5 393	12 242	11 924	24 652	3 552	–8 888	–2 618
F.4	Loans										
F.41	Short term loans										
F.411	Loans by UK monetary financial institutions, excluding loans secured on dwellings & financial leasing	NGMZ	20 861	7 140	20 484	46 281	55 200	83 033	40 883	–49 705	–25 265
F.419	Loans by rest of the world monetary financial institutions	NGND	–1 297	32 248	43 762	–2 962	36 371	–14 134	–1 590	–42 123	51 886
F.42	Long term loans										
F.421	Direct investment	NGNF	43 802	10 162	15 667	49 740	35 753	1 323	83 660	–39 053	16 302
F.422	Secured on dwellings	G9JS	–	–	–	2 591	3 812	3 830	5 752	3 226	1 095
F.423	Finance leasing	NGNM	291	389	510	379	464	545	309	219	331
F.424	Other long-term loans by UK residents	NGNN	490	4 611	583	6 087	5 046	54 239	–8 981	–27 892	–17 981
F.429	Other long-term loans by the rest of the world	NGNO	–	–	283	–7	–12	–6	–9	–4	–
F.4	Total loans	NGMX	64 147	54 550	81 289	102 109	136 634	128 830	120 024	–155 332	26 368
F.5	Shares and other equity										
F.51	Shares and other equity, excluding mutual funds' shares										
F.514	Quoted UK shares	NGNU	16 508	–748	7 286	–4 608	–3 737	5 342	4 321	32 864	11 623
F.515	Unquoted UK shares	NGNV	4 834	11 348	10 843	22 690	19 790	54 678	26 571	13 775	7 144
F.516	Other UK equity (including direct investment in property)	NGNW	–2 348	–5 100	–3 172	–3 244	–3 062	202	415	–7	49
F.517	UK shares and bonds issued by other UK residents	NSQD	–	–	–	–	–	–	–	–	–
F.5	Total shares and other equity	NGNP	18 994	5 500	14 957	14 838	12 991	60 222	31 307	46 632	18 816
F.7	Other accounts payable	NGOJ	2 322	2 780	2 603	6 666	5 311	2 947	–4 349	–3 064	2 621
F.L	**Total net acquisition of financial liabilities**	NRGR	109 150	80 577	104 242	135 855	166 860	216 651	150 534	–120 652	45 187
B.9	**Net lending / borrowing**										
F.A	Total net acquisition of financial assets	NRGP	115 383	99 923	132 688	165 067	197 494	245 515	191 474	–68 394	105 696
-F.L	*less* Total net acquisition of financial liabilities	-NRGR	–109 150	–80 577	–104 242	–135 855	–166 860	–216 651	–150 534	120 652	–45 187
B.9f	Net lending (+) / net borrowing (-), from financial account	NYNT	6 233	19 346	28 446	29 212	30 634	28 864	40 940	52 258	60 509
dB.9f	Statistical discrepancy	NYPF	8 516	9 324	11 086	8 755	9 452	9 415	–9 709	–1 378	706
B.9	**Net lending (+) / net borrowing (-), from capital account**	EABO	**14 749**	**28 670**	**39 532**	**37 967**	**40 086**	**38 279**	**31 231**	**50 880**	**61 215**

3.1.9 Non-financial corporations
ESA95 sector S.11 Unconsolidated

£ billion

				2002	2003	2004	2005	2006	2007	2008	2009	2010
IV.3	**FINANCIAL BALANCE SHEET** at end of period											
AN	**Non-financial assets**		CGES	1 315.4	1 356.4	1 434.0	1 451.4	1 547.0	1 563.5	1 532.3	1 487.9	1 781.8
AF.A	**Financial assets**											
AF.2	Currency and deposits											
AF.21	Currency		NNZG	3.8	4.1	4.1	4.3	4.5	4.8	4.9	5.2	5.4
AF.22	Transferable deposits											
AF.221	Deposits with UK monetary financial institutions		NNZI	177.9	191.4	205.4	230.4	253.6	274.3	267.3	283.4	303.1
AF.2212	*of which* Foreign currency deposits		NNZK	23.7	26.5	28.1	32.0	31.9	36.3	43.5	48.7	62.2
AF.229	Deposits with rest of the world monetary financial institutions		NNZM	65.1	121.1	194.2	255.4	286.9	361.1	416.8	333.6	371.9
AF.29	Other deposits		NNZN	8.0	6.7	7.1	8.7	9.4	9.5	9.2	8.9	7.3
AF.2	Total currency and deposits		NNZF	254.8	323.4	410.8	498.7	554.4	649.7	698.3	631.1	687.8
AF.3	Securities other than shares											
AF.331	Short term: money market instruments											
AF.3311	Issued by UK central government		NNZQ	–	–	–	–	0.1	0.4	0.6	0.3	0.3
AF.3312	Issued by UK local government		NNZU	–	–	–	–	–	–	–	–	–
AF.3315	Issued by UK monetary financial institutions		NNZV	5.0	5.4	5.8	5.2	7.0	9.8	12.0	11.5	10.6
AF.3316	Issued by other UK residents		NOLO	13.9	13.8	5.0	3.3	6.3	5.7	8.2	6.4	7.8
AF.3319	Issued by the rest of the world		NOLP	6.0	9.8	10.4	11.4	16.2	6.4	1.3	2.9	4.9
AF.332	Medium (1 to 5 year) and long term (over 5 year) bonds											
AF.3321	Issued by UK central government		NOLR	3.5	3.2	3.6	2.7	0.7	1.2	1.9	2.6	3.3
AF.3322	Issued by UK local government		NOLU	–	–	–	–	–	–	–	–	–
AF.3325	Medium term bonds issued by UK monetary financial institutions	NOLV	0.3	0.9	1.0	1.5	1.9	2.5	3.6	4.8	4.6
AF.3326	Other medium & long term bonds issued by UK residents		NOLY	6.1	5.2	5.1	1.4	1.6	5.3	7.6	3.6	4.8
AF.3329	Long term bonds issued by the rest of the world		NOLZ	29.3	30.0	12.8	14.6	12.1	11.0	16.0	18.2	22.9
AF.34	Financial derivatives		JXK2	..	..	13.7	17.8	19.0	15.7	46.2	25.4	26.0
AF.3	Total securities other than shares		NNZO	64.1	68.2	57.3	57.8	64.8	58.1	97.4	75.7	85.3
AF.4	Loans											
AF.42	Long term loans											
AF.421	Direct investment		NOMM	163.3	159.1	180.3	193.7	201.4	246.8	349.5	329.3	322.2
AF.422	Loans secured on dwellings		NOMP	–	–	–	–	–	–	–	–	–
AF.423	Finance leasing		NOMT	2.7	3.2	3.6	4.1	4.4	4.9	4.9	5.0	5.1
AF.424	Other long-term loans by UK residents		NOMU	29.6	28.7	28.1	33.6	46.8	49.8	77.7	65.4	121.2
AF.4	Total loans		NOME	195.7	191.0	211.9	231.4	252.6	301.4	432.1	399.7	448.5
AF.5	Shares and other equity											
AF.51	Shares and other equity, excluding mutual funds' shares											
AF.514	Quoted UK shares		NONB	8.9	9.6	9.0	16.9	32.9	35.1	34.7	48.4	47.5
AF.515	Unquoted UK shares		NONC	39.9	46.6	50.3	57.4	61.2	63.3	59.5	72.9	71.3
AF.517	UK shares and bonds issued by other UK residents		NSQW	–	–	–	–	–	–	–	–	–
AF.519	Shares and other equity issued by the rest of the world		NONG	522.3	565.7	550.8	593.3	605.3	657.1	782.7	706.3	757.5
AF.52	Mutual funds' shares											
AF.521	UK mutual funds' shares		NONK	0.3	0.3	0.4	0.5	0.6	0.6	0.3	0.4	0.5
AF.5	Total shares and other equity		NOMW	571.4	622.3	610.5	668.1	700.0	756.1	877.2	828.1	876.8
AF.6	Insurance technical reserves											
AF.62	Prepayments of insurance premiums and reserves for outstanding claims		NONP	12.8	15.7	15.5	17.3	16.4	12.9	13.2	12.8	13.1
AF.7	Other accounts receivable		NONQ	116.8	119.9	134.9	133.0	137.6	138.4	137.2	136.5	135.9
AF.A	**Total financial assets**		NNZB	1 215.5	1 340.4	1 440.8	1 606.2	1 725.9	1 916.6	2 255.4	2 083.9	2 247.4

3.1.9 Non-financial corporations
ESA95 sector S.11 Unconsolidated
continued

£ billion

			2002	2003	2004	2005	2006	2007	2008	2009	2010
IV.3	**FINANCIAL BALANCE SHEET** continued at end of period										
AF.L	**Financial liabilities**										
	Currency and deposits										
AF.29	Other deposits	NOOF	–	–	–	–	–	–	–	–	–
AF.2	Total currency and deposits	NONX	–	–	–	–	–	–	–	–	–
AF.3	Securities other than shares										
AF.331	Short term: money market instruments										
AF.3316	Issued by UK residents other than government or monetary financial institutions	NOOS	30.4	26.0	21.8	23.8	21.7	22.2	31.1	22.5	27.7
AF.332	Medium (1 to 5 year) and long term (over 5 year) bonds										
AF.3326	Other medium & long term bonds issued by UK residents or monetary financial institutions	NOPC	233.1	255.4	260.4	308.1	342.1	339.8	328.1	392.8	326.6
AF.34	Financial derivatives	JX27	..	..	14.8	21.1	22.5	21.0	51.1	33.3	36.6
AF.3	Total securities other than shares	NOOG	263.4	281.4	297.1	353.0	386.2	383.0	410.4	448.6	390.9
AF.4	Loans										
AF.41	Short term loans										
AF.411	Loans by UK monetary financial institutions, excluding loans secured on dwellings & financial leasing	NOPK	285.5	286.1	299.0	346.6	397.6	477.6	538.9	479.0	440.4
AF.419	Loans by rest of the world monetary financial institutions	NOPO	62.7	100.4	143.3	150.8	198.2	186.4	240.8	183.4	231.2
AF.42	Long term loans										
AF.421	Direct investment	NOPQ	249.9	241.6	250.6	308.4	325.4	282.5	381.0	366.9	383.2
AF.422	Loans secured on dwellings	G9JO	–	–	–	27.1	30.9	34.8	40.2	43.5	40.7
AF.423	Finance leasing	NOPX	22.0	22.3	22.9	23.2	23.7	24.2	24.5	24.9	25.2
AF.424	Other long-term loans by UK residents	NOPY	55.8	70.9	83.6	77.5	95.7	111.5	94.4	117.7	123.4
AF.429	Other long-term loans by the rest of the world	NOPZ	0.4	0.4	0.8	0.8	0.8	0.8	0.9	0.9	0.9
AF.4	Total loans	NOPI	676.4	721.7	800.2	934.4	1 072.3	1 117.9	1 320.8	1 216.2	1 245.1
AF.5	Shares and other equity										
AF.51	Shares and other equity, excluding mutual funds' shares										
AF.514	Quoted UK shares	NOQF	857.8	1 002.0	1 080.2	1 235.4	1 318.7	1 366.1	917.9	1 212.6	1 373.7
AF.515	Unquoted UK shares	NOQG	353.0	393.2	423.9	515.0	611.1	672.6	625.3	633.5	683.1
AF.516	Other UK equity (including direct investment in property)	NOQH	113.1	121.7	132.4	149.2	142.3	145.3	147.7	143.6	144.6
AF.517	UK shares and bonds issued by other UK residents	NSQX	–	–	–	–	–	–	–	–	–
AF.5	Total shares and other equity	NOQA	1 323.9	1 517.0	1 636.6	1 899.6	2 072.1	2 184.0	1 690.9	1 989.7	2 201.4
AF.7	Other accounts payable	NOQU	143.0	145.4	154.7	159.6	162.4	162.7	162.1	161.6	163.9
AF.L	**Total financial liabilities**	NONT	2 406.7	2 665.5	2 888.5	3 346.6	3 693.0	3 847.7	3 584.2	3 816.1	4 001.2
BF.90	**Net financial assets / liabilities**										
AF.A	Total financial assets	NNZB	1 215.5	1 340.4	1 440.8	1 606.2	1 725.9	1 916.6	2 255.4	2 083.9	2 247.4
-AF.L	*less* Total financial liabilities	-NONT	-2 406.7	-2 665.5	-2 888.5	-3 346.6	-3 693.0	-3 847.7	-3 584.2	-3 816.1	-4 001.2
BF.90	**Net financial assets (+) / liabilities (-)**	NYOM	-1 191.2	-1 325.0	-1 447.7	-1 740.3	-1 967.0	-1 931.1	-1 328.8	-1 732.3	-1 753.9
	Net worth										
AN	Non-financial assets	CGES	1 315.4	1 356.4	1 434.0	1 451.4	1 547.0	1 563.5	1 532.3	1 487.9	1 781.8
BF.90	Net financial assets(+)/ liabilities(-)	NYOM	-1 191.2	-1 325.0	-1 447.7	-1 740.3	-1 967.0	-1 931.1	-1 328.8	-1 732.3	-1 753.9
B.90	**Net worth**	CGRV	124.2	31.4	-13.7	-288.9	-420.0	-367.7	203.5	-244.4	28.0

3.2.1 Public non-financial corporations[1]
ESA95 sector S.11001

£ million

			2002	2003	2004	2005	2006	2007	2008	2009
I	**PRODUCTION ACCOUNT**									
	Resources									
P.1	Output									
P.11	Market output	FCZI	34 091	37 553	40 313	43 679	43 498	41 508	40 894	38 602
P.12	Output for own final use	GIRZ	224	205	97	57	10	1	1	–
P.1	Total resources	FCZG	34 315	37 758	40 410	43 736	43 508	41 509	40 895	38 602
	Uses									
P.2	Intermediate consumption	QZLQ	15 573	18 436	20 495	22 661	22 098	19 925	21 145	16 912
B.1g	**Gross Value Added**	FACW	**18 742**	**19 322**	**19 915**	**21 075**	**21 410**	**21 584**	**19 750**	**21 690**
Total	Total uses	FCZG	34 315	37 758	40 410	43 736	43 508	41 509	40 895	38 602
B.1g	**Gross Value Added**	FACW	**18 742**	**19 322**	**19 915**	**21 075**	**21 410**	**21 584**	**19 750**	**21 690**
-K.1	*less* Consumption of fixed capital	-NSRM	–3 900	–4 068	–4 077	–4 287	–4 424	–4 528	–4 676	–4 809
B.1n	Value added, net	FACX	14 842	15 254	15 838	16 788	16 986	17 056	15 074	16 881

1 Public financial corporations are also included to avoid disclosure of commercial information

3.2.2 Public non-financial corporations[1]
ESA95 sector S.11001

£ million

			2002	2003	2004	2005	2006	2007	2008	2009
II	**DISTRIBUTION AND USE OF INCOME ACCOUNTS**									
II.1	**PRIMARY DISTRIBUTION OF INCOME ACCOUNT**									
II.1.1	**GENERATION OF INCOME ACCOUNT** before deduction of fixed capital consumption									
	Resources									
B.1g	**Total resources (Gross Value Added)**	FACW	18 742	19 322	19 915	21 075	21 410	21 584	19 750	21 690
	Uses									
D.1	Compensation of employees									
D.11	Wages and salaries	FAIZ	10 523	10 513	11 414	11 802	11 603	11 562	11 547	11 729
D.12	Employers' social contributions	FAOH	1 859	1 855	2 016	2 081	2 046	2 022	2 029	2 040
D.1	Total	FDDI	12 382	12 368	13 430	13 883	13 649	13 584	13 576	13 769
D.2	Taxes on production and imports, paid									
D.29	Production taxes other than on products	FAOK	95	95	95	86	85	84	84	86
-D.3	*less* Subsidies, received									
-D.39	Production subsidies other than on products	-ARDD	–366	–293	–470	–1 367	–1 952	–2 198	–1 953	–1 661
B.2g	Operating surplus, gross	NRJT	6 631	7 152	6 860	8 473	9 628	10 114	8 043	9 496
B.1g	**Total uses (Gross Value Added)**	FACW	**18 742**	**19 322**	**19 915**	**21 075**	**21 410**	**21 584**	**19 750**	**21 690**
-K.1	After deduction of fixed capital consumption	-NSRM	–3 900	–4 068	–4 077	–4 287	–4 424	–4 528	–4 676	–4 809
B.2n	Operating surplus, net	FAOO	2 731	3 084	2 783	4 186	5 204	5 586	3 367	4 687

1 Public financial corporations are also included to avoid disclosure of commercial information

3.2.3 Public non-financial corporations[1]
ESA95 sector S.11001

£ million

			2002	2003	2004	2005	2006	2007	2008	2009	2010
II.1.2	**ALLOCATION OF PRIMARY INCOME ACCOUNT** before deduction of fixed capital consumption										
	Resources										
B.2g	Operating surplus, gross	NRJT	6 631	7 152	6 860	8 473	9 628	10 114	8 043	9 496	8 810
D.4	Property income, received										
D.41	Interest	CPBV	813	771	1 261	1 792	879	731	846	313	304
D.42	Distributed income of corporations	FACT	59	79	62	41	38	491	735	25	14
D.43	Property income reinvested earnings on foreign investments	WUHM	38	67	155	155	214	151	–176	118	115
D.44	Property income attributed to insurance policy-holders	FAOT	–	–	–	–	–	–	–	–	–
D.4	Total	FAOP	910	917	1 478	1 988	1 131	1 373	1 405	456	433
Total	Total resources	FAOU	7 541	8 069	8 338	10 461	10 759	11 487	9 448	9 952	9 243
	Uses										
D.4	Property income, paid										
D.41	Interest	XAQZ	649	722	1 336	1 251	1 394	1 513	1 745	1 549	1 290
D.42	Distributed income of corporations	ZOYB	1 729	1 443	867	808	693	649	601	738	538
D.45	Rent	FAOZ	–	–	–	–	–	–	–	–	–
D.4	Total	FAOV	2 378	2 165	2 203	2 059	2 087	2 162	2 346	2 287	1 828
B.5g	**Balance of primary incomes, gross**	NRJX	**5 163**	**5 904**	**6 135**	**8 402**	**8 672**	**9 325**	**7 102**	**7 665**	**7 415**
Total	Total uses	FAOU	7 541	8 069	8 338	10 461	10 759	11 487	9 448	9 952	9 243
-K.1	After deduction of fixed capital consumption	-NSRM	–3 900	–4 068	–4 077	–4 287	–4 424	–4 528	–4 676	–4 809	–4 968
B.5n	Balance of primary incomes, net	FARX	1 263	1 836	2 058	4 115	4 248	4 797	2 426	2 856	2 447

1 Public financial corporations are also included to avoid disclosure of commercial information

3.2.4 Public non-financial corporations[1]
ESA95 sector S.11001

£ million

			2002	2003	2004	2005	2006	2007	2008	2009	2010
II.2	**SECONDARY DISTRIBUTION OF INCOME ACCOUNT**										
	Resources										
B.5g	Balance of primary incomes, gross	NRJX	5 163	5 904	6 135	8 402	8 672	9 325	7 102	7 665	7 415
D.61	Social contributions										
D.612	Imputed social contributions	EWRS	138	131	132	132	135	137	140	140	144
D.7	Current transfers other than taxes, social contributions and benefits										
D.72	Net non-life insurance claims	FDDF	–	–	–	–	–	–	–	–	–
D.75	Miscellaneous current transfers	CY89	147	124	28	–	–	–	–	–	–
D.7	Total	FDEK	147	124	28	–	–	–	–	–	–
Total	Total resources	FDDH	5 448	6 159	6 295	8 534	8 807	9 462	7 242	7 805	7 559
	Uses										
D.5	Current taxes on income, wealth etc.										
D.51	Taxes on income	FCCS	61	94	75	141	372	225	254	272	283
D.62	Social benefits other than social transfers in kind	EWRS	138	131	132	132	135	137	140	140	144
D.7	Current transfers other than taxes, social contributions and benefits										
D.71	Net non-life insurance premiums	FDDM	–	–	–	–	–	–	–	–	–
D.75	Miscellaneous current transfers	CY87	58	28	5	–	–	–	–	–	–
D.7	Total	FDDL	58	28	5	–	–	–	–	–	–
B.6g	**Gross Disposable Income**	NRKD	**5 191**	**5 906**	**6 083**	**8 261**	**8 300**	**9 100**	**6 848**	**7 393**	**7 132**
Total	Total uses	FDDH	5 448	6 159	6 295	8 534	8 807	9 462	7 242	7 805	7 559
-K.1	After deduction of fixed capital consumption	-NSRM	–3 900	–4 068	–4 077	–4 287	–4 424	–4 528	–4 676	–4 809	–4 968
B.6n	Disposable income, net	FDDP	1 291	1 838	2 006	3 974	3 876	4 572	2 172	2 584	2 164

1 Public financial corporations are also included to avoid disclosure of commercial information

3.2.6 Public non-financial corporations[1]
ESA95 sector S.11001

£ million

			2002	2003	2004	2005	2006	2007	2008	2009	2010
II.4.1	**USE OF DISPOSABLE INCOME ACCOUNT**										
	Resources										
B.6g	Total resources (Gross Disposable Income)	NRKD	5 191	5 906	6 083	8 261	8 300	9 100	6 848	7 393	7 132
	Uses										
B.8g	Total uses (Gross Saving)	NRKD	5 191	5 906	6 083	8 261	8 300	9 100	6 848	7 393	7 132
-K.1	After deduction of fixed capital consumption	-NSRM	-3 900	-4 068	-4 077	-4 287	-4 424	-4 528	-4 676	-4 809	-4 968
B.8n	Saving, net	FDDP	1 291	1 838	2 006	3 974	3 876	4 572	2 172	2 584	2 164

1 Public financial corporations are also included to avoid disclosure of commercial information

3.2.7 Public non-financial corporations[1]
ESA95 sector S.11001

£ million

			2002	2003	2004	2005	2006	2007	2008	2009	2010
III	**ACCUMULATION ACCOUNTS**										
III.1	**CAPITAL ACCOUNT**										
III.1.1	**CHANGE IN NET WORTH DUE TO SAVING AND CAPITAL TRANSFERS**										
	Changes in liabilities and net worth										
B.8g	Gross Saving	NRKD	5 191	5 906	6 083	8 261	8 300	9 100	6 848	7 393	7 132
D.9	Capital transfers receivable										
D.92	Investment grants	FDBV	764	504	794	1 658	1 566	504	470	1 896	1 786
D.99	Other capital transfers	NZGD	91	42	42	11 682	333	155	1 888	162	80
D.9	Total	FDBU	855	546	836	13 340	1 899	659	2 358	2 058	1 866
-D.9	*less* Capital transfers payable										
-D.99	Other capital transfers	-ZMLL	–	–	–	-800	-122	-187	-68	–	–
B.10.1g	Total change in liabilities and net worth	FDEG	6 046	6 452	6 919	20 801	10 077	9 572	9 138	9 451	8 998
	Changes in assets										
B.10.1g	Changes in net worth due to gross saving and capital transfers	FDEG	6 046	6 452	6 919	20 801	10 077	9 572	9 138	9 451	8 998
-K.1	After deduction of fixed capital consumption	-NSRM	-3 900	-4 068	-4 077	-4 287	-4 424	-4 528	-4 676	-4 809	-4 968
B.10.1n	Changes in net worth due to net saving and capital transfers	FDED	2 146	2 384	2 842	16 514	5 653	5 044	4 462	4 642	4 030
III.1.2	**ACQUISITION OF NON-FINANCIAL ASSETS ACCOUNT**										
	Changes in liabilities and net worth										
B.10.1n	Changes in net worth due to net saving and capital transfers	FDED	2 146	2 384	2 842	16 514	5 653	5 044	4 462	4 642	4 030
K.1	Consumption of fixed capital	NSRM	3 900	4 068	4 077	4 287	4 424	4 528	4 676	4 809	4 968
B.10.1g	Total change in liabilities and net worth	FDEG	6 046	6 452	6 919	20 801	10 077	9 572	9 138	9 451	8 998
	Changes in assets										
P.5	Gross capital formation										
P.51	Gross fixed capital formation	FCCJ	3 830	1 857	1 260	20 575	5 440	6 148	7 296	8 177	8 141
P.52	Changes in inventories	DHHL	2	-5	-17	-101	70	-5	-49	330	203
P.5	Total	FDEH	3 832	1 852	1 243	20 474	5 510	6 143	7 247	8 507	8 344
K.2	Acquisitions less disposals of non-produced non-financial assets	FDEJ	176	282	346	428	512	484	484	484	484
B.9g	Net lending (+) / net borrowing (-)	CPCM	2 038	4 318	5 330	-101	4 055	2 945	1 407	460	170
Total	Total change in assets	FDEG	6 046	6 452	6 919	20 801	10 077	9 572	9 138	9 451	8 998

1 Public financial corporations are also included to avoid disclosure of commercial information

3.2.8 Public non-financial corporations
ESA95 sector S.11001 Unconsolidated

£ million

			2002	2003	2004	2005	2006	2007	2008	2009	2010
III.2	**FINANCIAL ACCOUNT**										
F.A	**Net acquisition of financial assets**										
F.2	Currency and deposits										
F.21	Currency	NCXV	−143	141	−295	−16	23	55	−111	13	29
F.22	Transferable deposits										
F.221	Deposits with UK monetary financial institutions	NCXX	−52	−333	−352	−12	1 501	−2 071	−772	144	−353
F.2212	*of which* Foreign currency deposits	NCXZ	−42	29	−3	33	1 201	−1 191	−13	191	−159
F.229	Deposits with rest of the world monetary financial institutions	NCYB	−30	3	−3	–	–	–	–	–	–
F.29	Other deposits	NCYC	477	−626	592	534	345	61	−173	70	−679
F.2	Total currency and deposits	NCXU	252	−815	−58	506	1 869	−1 955	−1 056	227	−1 003
F.3	Securities other than shares										
F.331	Short term: money market instruments										
F.3311	Issued by UK central government	NCYF	–	–	–	–	–	400	2	−86	8
F.3315	Issued by UK monetary financial institutions	NCYK	–	–	–	–	–	–	–	–	–
F.3316	Issued by other UK residents	NCYP	223	104	−943	240	396	−109	−651	−230	−21
F.332	Medium (1 to 5 year) and long term (over 5 year) bonds										
F.3321	Issued by UK central government	NCYS	−67	−196	74	−789	−1 971	217	488	101	1
F.3326	Other medium & long term bonds issued by UK residents	NCYZ	–	–	–	–	–	–	–	–	–
F.3329	Long term bonds issued by the rest of the world	NCZA	–	–	–	–	–	−28	–	−5	–
F.34	Financial derivatives	NSSK	10	9	8	1	1	10	3	–	–
F.3	Total securities other than shares	NCYD	166	−83	−861	−548	−1 574	490	−158	−220	−12
F.4	Loans										
F.42	Long term loans										
F.421	Direct investment loans	CFZI	120	−10	2	–	−348	21	−18	–	–
F.422	Loans secured on dwellings	NCZQ	–	–	–	–	–	–	–	–	–
F.424	Other long-term loans by UK residents	NCZV	−489	−380	−368	−1 735	−2 724	−394	−288	−216	69
F.4	Total loans	NCZF	−369	−390	−366	−1 735	−3 072	−373	−306	−216	69
F.5	Shares and other equity										
F.51	Shares and other equity, excluding mutual funds' shares										
F.514	Quoted UK shares	NEBC	23	24	24	−243	–	–	–	–	–
F.515	Unquoted UK shares	NEBD	510	−2	−2	–	−1 248	−56	−87	–	–
F.517	UK shares and bonds issued by other UK residents	NSPN	–	–	–	–	–	–	–	–	–
F.519	Shares and other equity issued by the rest of the world	NEBH	158	−151	−64	14	−1 763	75	−176	118	115
F.5	Total shares and other equity	NCZX	691	−129	−42	−229	−3 011	19	−263	118	115
F.6	Insurance technical reserves										
F.62	Prepayments of insurance premiums and reserves for outstanding claims	NEBQ	–	–	–	–	–	–	–	–	–
F.7	Other accounts receivable	NEBR	328	899	3 413	916	5 141	1 382	388	−4 790	1 671
F.A	**Total net acquisition of financial assets**	NCXQ	1 068	−518	2 086	−1 090	−647	−437	−1 395	−4 881	840

3.2.8 Public non-financial corporations
ESA95 sector S.11001 Unconsolidated

continued

£ million

				2002	2003	2004	2005	2006	2007	2008	2009	2010
III.2	FINANCIAL ACCOUNT continued											
F.L	**Net acquisition of financial liabilities**											
F.2	Currency & deposits											
F.29	Other deposits		WUGZ	18	–	–	–	–	–	–	–	–
	Total currency & deposits		-A4FK	18	–	–	–	–	–	–	–	–
F.3	Securities other than shares											
F.332	Medium (1 to 5 year) and long term (over 5 year) bonds											
F.3326	Other medium & long term bonds issued by UK residents or monetary financial institutions		NEOF	–1 541	–	–	856	–631	–54	–1 035	–600	–
F.34	Financial derivatives		CY7U	–204	–138	–	–	–	–	–	–	–
F.3	Total securities other than shares		NENJ	–1 745	–138	–	856	–631	–54	–1 035	–600	–
F.4	Loans											
F.41	Short term loans											
F.411	Loans by UK monetary financial institutions, excluding loans secured on dwellings & financial leasing		NEON	321	–112	332	–276	12	194	–96	–1 196	62
F.42	Long term loans											
F.421	Direct investment		-CFZJ	–	–	–	–	–108	–136	118	6	–
F.423	Finance leasing		NEPA	–56	–41	–6	–29	–10	118	–28	–126	2
F.424	Other long-term loans by UK residents		NEPB	3 019	1 661	452	–172	–152	27	–517	21	658
F.429	Other long-term loans by the rest of the world		NEPC	–	–	283	–7	–12	–6	–9	–4	–
F.4	Total loans		NEOL	3 284	1 508	1 061	–484	–270	197	–532	–1 299	722
F.5	Shares and other equity											
F.51	Shares and other equity, excluding mutual funds' shares											
F.515	Unquoted UK shares		NEPJ	–	–	28	–495	46	–2 060	–600	–	–
F.516	Other UK equity (including direct investment in property)		NEPK	–3 096	–5 495	–3 795	–3 841	–3 529	–2 156	–1 078	–539	–483
F.517	UK shares and bonds issued by other UK residents		NSPO	–	–	–	–	–	–	–	–	–
F.5	Total shares and other equity		NEPD	–3 096	–5 495	–3 767	–4 336	–3 483	–4 216	–1 678	–539	–483
F.7	Other accounts payable		NEPX	159	–136	114	3 234	–1 214	316	158	–1 931	–321
F.L	**Total net acquisition of financial liabilities**		NEBU	–1 380	–4 261	–2 592	–730	–5 598	–3 757	–3 087	–4 369	–82
B.9	**Net lending / borrowing**											
F.A	Total net acquisition of financial assets		NCXQ	1 068	–518	2 086	–1 090	–647	–437	–1 395	–4 881	840
-F.L	*less* Total net acquisition of financial liabilities		-NEBU	1 380	4 261	2 592	730	5 598	3 757	3 087	4 369	82
B.9f	Net lending (+) / net borrowing (-), from financial account		NZEC	2 448	3 743	4 678	–360	4 951	3 320	1 692	–512	922
dB.9f	Statistical discrepancy		NYPI	–410	575	652	259	–896	–375	–285	972	–752
B.9g	**Net lending (+) / net borrowing (-), from capital account**		CPCM	**2 038**	**4 318**	**5 330**	**–101**	**4 055**	**2 945**	**1 407**	**460**	**170**

3.2.9 Public non-financial corporations
ESA95 sector S.11001 Unconsolidated

£ billion

			2002	2003	2004	2005	2006	2007	2008	2009	2010
IV.3	**FINANCIAL BALANCE SHEET** at end of period										
AN	**Non-financial assets**	CGGN	157.7	160.0	173.3	185.6	177.4	185.5	190.1	199.5	193.0
AF.A	**Financial assets**										
AF.2	Currency and deposits										
AF.21	Currency	NKDS	0.8	0.9	0.6	0.6	0.6	0.7	0.6	0.6	0.6
AF.22	Transferable deposits										
AF.221	Deposits with UK monetary financial institutions	NKDU	6.0	4.6	4.9	4.8	6.0	3.9	2.6	2.8	2.7
AF.2212	*of which* Foreign currency deposits	NKDV	5.8	4.4	4.7	4.6	4.7	3.8	2.5	2.5	2.5
AF.229	Deposits with rest of the world monetary financial institutions	NKDY	–	–	–	–	–	–	–	–	–
AF.29	Other deposits	NKDZ	3.1	1.5	2.1	3.5	3.9	3.9	3.7	3.8	3.2
AF.2	Total currency and deposits	NKDR	10.0	7.0	7.6	9.0	10.5	8.5	7.0	7.2	6.5
AF.3	Securities other than shares										
AF.331	Short term: money market instruments										
AF.3311	Issued by UK central government	NKEC	–	–	–	–	–	0.4	0.4	0.3	0.3
AF.3315	Issued by UK monetary financial institutions	NKEH	0.4	0.4	0.4	0.4	0.4	0.4	0.4	0.4	0.4
AF.3316	Issued by other UK residents	NKEM	0.2	0.3	1.3	1.5	1.9	1.7	0.9	0.7	0.6
AF.332	Medium (1 to 5 year) and long term (over 5 year) bonds										
AF.3321	Issued by UK central government	NKEP	3.1	2.9	3.3	2.5	0.5	0.7	1.2	1.3	1.3
AF.3322	Issued by UK local government	NKES	–	–	–	–	–	–	–	–	–
AF.3326	Other medium & long term bonds issued by UK residents	NKEW	–	–	–	–	–	–	–	–	–
AF.3329	Long term bonds issued by rest of the world	NKIQ	–	–	–	–	–	–	–	0.1	0.1
AF.3	Total securities other than shares	NKEA	3.7	3.6	4.9	4.4	2.8	3.3	2.9	2.8	2.8
AF.4	Loans										
AF.42	Long term loans										
AF.421	Direct investment loans	ZYBN	0.5	0.4	0.3	0.3	–	0.1	0.1	–	–
AF.422	Loans secured on dwellings	NKFN	–	–	–	–	–	–	–	–	–
AF.424	Other long-term loans by UK residents	NKFS	3.9	4.0	4.0	3.8	2.7	2.4	2.5	2.3	2.2
AF.4	Total loans	NKFC	4.4	4.5	4.4	4.1	2.7	2.4	2.6	2.3	2.2
AF.5	Shares and other equity										
AF.51	Shares and other equity, excluding mutual funds' shares										
AF.514	Quoted UK shares	NKFZ	0.2	0.2	0.2	–	–	–	–	–	–
AF.515	Unquoted UK shares	NKGA	0.3	0.3	0.3	0.3	0.3	0.3	0.3	0.3	0.3
AF.517	UK shares and bonds issued by other UK residents	NSOL	–	–	–	–	–	–	–	–	–
AF.519	Shares and other equity issued by the rest of the world	NKGE	1.0	1.1	1.6	0.5	0.5	0.5	0.3	0.4	0.6
AF.5	Total shares and other equity	NKFU	1.5	1.6	2.1	0.8	0.8	0.8	0.6	0.8	0.9
AF.6	Insurance technical reserves										
AF.62	Prepayments of insurance premiums and reserves for outstanding claims	NKGN	–	–	–	–	–	–	–	–	–
AF.7	Other accounts receivable	NKGO	6.4	7.5	10.9	11.1	16.2	17.6	17.3	19.5	20.4
AF.A	**Total financial assets**	NKFB	26.0	24.3	29.9	29.3	33.0	32.6	30.3	32.5	32.7

3.2.9 Public non-financial corporations
ESA95 sector S.11001 Unconsolidated

continued

£ billion

IV.3 FINANCIAL BALANCE SHEET continued
at end of period

				2002	2003	2004	2005	2006	2007	2008	2009	2010
AF.L	**Financial liabilities**											
AF.2	Currency & deposits											
AF.29	Other deposits		NKHD	–	–	–	–	–	–	–	–	–
AF.2	Total currency & deposits		NKGV	–	–	–	–	–	–	–	–	–
AF.3	Securities other than shares											
AF.332	Medium (1 to 5 year) and long term (over 5 year) bonds											
AF.3326	Other medium & long term bonds issued by UK residents or monetary financial institutions		NKIA	0.9	1.3	5.8	7.0	6.5	7.2	7.4	17.3	11.7
AF.3	Total securities other than shares		NKHE	0.9	1.3	5.8	7.0	6.5	7.2	7.4	17.3	11.7
AF.4	Loans											
AF.41	Short term loans											
AF.411	Loans by UK monetary financial institutions, excluding loans secured on dwellings & financial leasing		NKII	0.6	0.5	0.5	0.5	0.6	0.7	0.6	0.6	0.5
AF.419	Loans by rest of the world monetary financial institutions		ZMEW	–	–	–	–	–	–	–	–	–
AF.42	Long term loans											
AF.421	Direct investment		ZYBO	–	–	–	–	0.2	0.1	0.2	0.6	0.6
AF.423	Finance leasing		NKIV	0.4	0.4	0.4	0.3	0.3	0.4	0.4	0.4	0.4
AF.424	Other long-term loans by UK residents		NKIW	11.3	3.3	4.7	4.6	4.4	4.4	3.6	3.1	3.2
AF.429	Other long-term loans by the rest of the world		NKIX	–	–	0.4	0.4	0.4	0.4	0.4	0.4	0.4
AF.4	Total loans		NKIG	12.3	4.1	6.0	5.9	5.9	6.1	5.3	5.0	5.1
AF.5	Shares and other equity											
AF.51	Shares and other equity, excluding mutual funds' shares											
AF.514	Quoted UK shares		C3O8	–	–	–	3.0	3.2	5.6	7.9	12.4	12.4
AF.515	Unquoted UK shares		NKJE	0.8	0.8	1.8	1.8	4.3	2.7	2.3	2.2	2.2
AF.516	Other UK equity		H4O6	95.8	104.4	113.3	129.5	120.7	119.1	122.3	117.7	116.7
AF.517	UK shares and bonds issued by other UK residents		NSOM	–	–	–	–	–	–	–	–	–
AF.5	Total shares and other equity		NKIY	96.6	105.3	115.1	134.3	128.2	127.4	132.6	132.3	131.3
AF.7	Other accounts payable		NKJS	13.7	13.8	14.7	16.8	15.6	15.8	15.9	14.0	13.7
AF.L	**Total financial liabilities**		NKIF	123.6	124.4	141.5	163.9	156.2	156.5	161.2	168.6	161.7
BF.90	**Net financial assets / liabilities**											
AF.A	Total financial assets		NKFB	26.0	24.3	29.9	29.3	33.0	32.6	30.3	32.5	32.7
-AF.L	*less* Total financial liabilities		-NKIF	−123.6	−124.4	−141.5	−163.9	−156.2	−156.5	−161.2	−168.6	−161.7
BF.90	**Net financial assets (+) / liabilities (-)**		NYOP	−97.6	−100.2	−111.6	−134.6	−123.2	−123.9	−130.9	−136.1	−129.0
	Net worth											
AN	Non-financial assets		CGGN	157.7	160.0	173.3	185.6	177.4	185.5	190.1	199.5	193.0
BF.90	Net financial assets (+) / liabilities (-)		NYOP	−97.6	−100.2	−111.6	−134.6	−123.2	−123.9	−130.9	−136.1	−129.0
B.90	**Net worth**		CGRW	60.1	59.8	61.7	51.0	54.2	61.6	59.2	63.4	64.0

3.3.1 Private non-financial corporations
ESA95 sectors S.11002 National controlled and S.11003 Foreign controlled

£ million

			2002	2003	2004	2005	2006	2007	2008	2009
I	**PRODUCTION ACCOUNT**									
	Resources									
P.1	Output									
P.11	Market output	FBXS	1 209 908	1 257 139	1 319 421	1 385 403	1 467 873	1 557 789	1 597 291	1 535 958
P.12	Output for own final use	FDCG	11 808	13 691	13 359	14 571	16 004	17 816	18 352	17 446
P.1	Total resources	FBXR	1 221 716	1 270 830	1 332 780	1 399 974	1 483 877	1 575 605	1 615 643	1 553 404
	Uses									
P.2	Intermediate consumption	FARP	643 653	669 245	698 484	742 095	786 577	836 161	864 709	829 368
B.1g	**Gross Value Added**	FARR	**578 063**	**601 585**	**634 296**	**657 879**	**697 300**	**739 444**	**750 934**	**724 036**
Total	Total uses	FBXR	1 221 716	1 270 830	1 332 780	1 399 974	1 483 877	1 575 605	1 615 643	1 553 404
B.1g	**Gross Value Added**	FARR	**578 063**	**601 585**	**634 296**	**657 879**	**697 300**	**739 444**	**750 934**	**724 036**
-K.1	*less* Consumption of fixed capital	-NSRK	−66 647	−68 530	−71 482	−72 990	−75 941	−78 715	−81 451	−86 079
B.1n	Value added, net	FARS	511 416	533 055	562 814	584 889	621 359	660 729	669 483	637 957

3.3.2 Private non-financial corporations
ESA95 sectors S.11002 National controlled and S.11003 Foreign controlled

£ million

			2002	2003	2004	2005	2006	2007	2008	2009
II	**DISTRIBUTION AND USE OF INCOME ACCOUNTS**									
II.1	**PRIMARY DISTRIBUTION OF INCOME ACCOUNT**									
II.1.1	**GENERATION OF INCOME ACCOUNT** before deduction of fixed capital consumption									
	Resources									
B.1g	Total resources (Gross Value Added)	FARR	578 063	601 585	634 296	657 879	697 300	739 444	750 934	724 036
	Uses									
D.1	Compensation of employees									
D.11	Wages and salaries	FAAX	329 127	334 407	344 762	353 683	368 199	395 096	407 977	398 773
D.12	Employers' social contributions	FABH	45 608	53 484	56 625	62 394	66 816	67 929	68 266	71 978
D.1	Total	FBDA	374 735	387 891	401 387	416 077	435 015	463 025	476 243	470 751
D.2	Taxes on production and imports, paid									
D.29	Production taxes other than on products	FACQ	16 584	16 942	17 251	18 073	19 117	19 712	20 859	21 501
-D.39	Production subsidies other than on products	-JQJW	−588	−1 141	−1 092	−1 082	−1 141	−1 288	−1 428	−1 652
B.2g	Operating surplus, gross	NRJK	187 332	197 893	216 750	224 811	244 309	257 995	255 260	233 436
B.1g	**Total uses (Gross Value Added)**	FARR	**578 063**	**601 585**	**634 296**	**657 879**	**697 300**	**739 444**	**750 934**	**724 036**
-K.1	After deduction of fixed capital consumption	-NSRK	−66 647	−68 530	−71 482	−72 990	−75 941	−78 715	−81 451	−86 079
B.2n	Operating surplus, net	FACU	120 685	129 363	145 268	151 821	168 368	179 280	173 809	147 357

3.3.3 Private non-financial corporations
ESA95 sectors S.11002 National controlled and S.11003 Foreign controlled

£ million

			2002	2003	2004	2005	2006	2007	2008	2009	2010
II.1.2	**ALLOCATION OF PRIMARY INCOME ACCOUNT**										
	before deduction of fixed capital consumption										
	Resources										
B.2g	Operating surplus, gross[1]	NRJK	187 332	197 893	216 750	224 811	244 309	257 995	255 260	233 436	246 074
D.4	Property income, received										
D.41	Interest	DSZR	8 517	8 956	12 880	15 588	24 512	29 790	23 720	7 086	6 616
D.42	Distributed income of corporations	DSZS	30 491	50 184	42 902	46 646	43 855	38 462	46 389	62 581	55 901
D.43	Reinvested earnings on direct foreign investment	HDVR	26 893	12 492	22 713	33 199	36 511	50 609	37 890	13 665	26 928
D.44	Property income attributed to insurance policy-holders	FCFP	300	398	368	582	545	309	365	363	299
D.45	Rent	FAOL	118	120	122	122	124	123	126	132	130
D.4	Total	FACV	66 319	72 150	78 985	96 137	105 547	119 293	108 490	83 827	89 874
Total	Total resources	FCFQ	253 651	270 043	295 735	320 948	349 856	377 288	363 750	317 263	335 948
	Uses										
D.4	Property income, paid										
D.41	Interest	DSZV	28 222	28 673	33 476	37 827	42 178	53 505	51 061	30 328	23 138
D.42	Distributed income of corporations	NVDC	83 890	87 659	92 921	104 067	107 778	108 518	113 424	113 091	104 748
	Of which: Dividend payments	NETZ	61 580	71 096	72 689	82 891	83 684	83 909	88 150	85 816	75 883
D.43	Reinvested earnings on direct foreign investment	HDVB	1 614	3 955	6 325	4 983	15 452	15 051	3 656	−1 445	−621
D.45	Rent	FCFU	1 939	1 603	1 221	1 268	1 265	1 273	1 204	1 213	1 212
D.4	Total	FCFR	115 665	121 890	133 943	148 145	166 673	178 347	169 345	143 187	128 477
B.5g	**Balance of primary incomes, gross**	NRJM	**137 986**	**148 153**	**161 792**	**172 803**	**183 183**	**198 941**	**194 405**	**174 076**	**207 471**
Total	Total uses	FCFQ	253 651	270 043	295 735	320 948	349 856	377 288	363 750	317 263	335 948
-K.1	After deduction of fixed capital consumption	-NSRK	−66 647	−68 530	−71 482	−72 990	−75 941	−78 715	−81 451	−86 079	−89 668
B.5n	Balance of primary incomes, net	FCFW	71 339	79 623	90 310	99 813	107 242	120 226	112 954	87 997	117 803

1 Companies gross trading profits and rental of buildings less holding gains of inventories, details of which are shown at Table C: The Sector Accounts Key Economic Indicators.

3.3.4 Private non-financial corporations
ESA95 sectors S.11002 National controlled and S.11003 Foreign controlled

£ million

			2002	2003	2004	2005	2006	2007	2008	2009	2010
II.2	**SECONDARY DISTRIBUTION OF INCOME ACCOUNT**										
	Resources										
B.5g	**Balance of primary incomes, gross**	NRJM	**137 986**	**148 153**	**161 792**	**172 803**	**183 183**	**198 941**	**194 405**	**174 076**	**207 471**
D.61	Social contributions										
D.612	Imputed social contributions	EWRT	3 794	4 075	3 989	4 260	4 425	4 687	5 623	6 669	4 255
D.7	Current transfers other than taxes, social contributions and benefits										
D.72	Net non-life insurance claims	FDBA	5 396	5 999	6 522	7 261	7 476	4 007	5 682	5 290	5 714
Total	Total resources	FDBC	147 176	158 227	172 303	184 324	195 084	207 635	205 710	186 035	217 440
	Uses										
D.5	Current taxes on income, wealth etc.										
D.51	Taxes on income	FCCP	23 977	23 608	27 291	33 477	36 812	38 178	40 591	33 270	35 358
D.62	Social benefits other than social transfers in kind	EWRT	3 794	4 075	3 989	4 260	4 425	4 687	5 623	6 669	4 255
D.7	Current transfers other than taxes, social contributions and benefits										
D.71	Net non-life insurance premiums	FDBH	5 396	5 999	6 522	7 261	7 476	4 007	5 682	5 290	5 714
D.75	Miscellaneous current transfers	CY88	422	434	446	488	477	488	488	488	488
D.7	Total	FCCN	5 818	6 433	6 968	7 749	7 953	4 495	6 170	5 778	6 202
B.6g	**Gross Disposable Income**	NRJQ	**113 587**	**124 111**	**134 055**	**138 838**	**145 894**	**160 275**	**153 326**	**140 318**	**171 625**
Total	Total uses	FDBC	147 176	158 227	172 303	184 324	195 084	207 635	205 710	186 035	217 440
-K.1	After deduction of fixed capital consumption	-NSRK	−66 647	−68 530	−71 482	−72 990	−75 941	−78 715	−81 451	−86 079	−89 668
B.6n	Disposable income, net	FDBK	46 940	55 581	62 573	65 848	69 953	81 560	71 875	54 239	81 957

3.3.6 Private non-financial corporations
ESA95 sectors S.11002 National controlled and S.11003 Foreign controlled

£ million

			2002	2003	2004	2005	2006	2007	2008	2009	2010
II.4.1	**USE OF DISPOSABLE INCOME ACCOUNT**										
	Resources										
B.6g	Total resources (Gross Disposable Income)	NRJQ	113 587	124 111	134 055	138 838	145 894	160 275	153 326	140 318	171 625
	Uses										
B.8g	Total uses (Gross Saving)	NRJQ	113 587	124 111	134 055	138 838	145 894	160 275	153 326	140 318	171 625
-K.1	After deduction of fixed capital consumption	-NSRK	−66 647	−68 530	−71 482	−72 990	−75 941	−78 715	−81 451	−86 079	−89 668
B.8n	Saving, net	FDBK	46 940	55 581	62 573	65 848	69 953	81 560	71 875	54 239	81 957

3.3.7 Private non-financial corporations
ESA95 sectors S.11002 National controlled and S.11003 Foreign controlled

£ million

			2002	2003	2004	2005	2006	2007	2008	2009	2010
III	**ACCUMULATION ACCOUNTS**										
III.1	**CAPITAL ACCOUNT**										
III.1.1	**CHANGE IN NET WORTH DUE TO SAVING AND CAPITAL TRANSFERS**										
	Changes in liabilities and net worth										
B.8g	Gross Saving	NRJQ	113 587	124 111	134 055	138 838	145 894	160 275	153 326	140 318	171 625
D.9	Capital transfers receivable										
D.92	Investment grants	AIBR	3 131	5 059	4 928	5 140	6 106	7 650	6 984	11 045	8 826
D.99	Other capital transfers	LNZM	93	106	94	119	116	111	−64	25	−3
-D.9	*less* Capital transfers payable										
-D.91	Capital taxes	-QYKB	–	–	–	–	–	–	–	–	–
-D.99	Other capital transfers	-CISB	−492	−575	−419	−456	−508	−693	−850	−723	−456
-D.9	Total	-FCFX	−492	−575	−419	−456	−508	−693	−850	−723	−456
B.10.1g	Total change in liabilities and net worth	NRMG	116 319	128 701	138 658	143 641	151 608	167 343	159 396	150 665	179 992
	Changes in assets										
B.10.1g	Changes in net worth due to gross saving and capital transfers	NRMG	116 319	128 701	138 658	143 641	151 608	167 343	159 396	150 665	179 992
-K.1	After deduction of fixed capital consumption	-NSRK	−66 647	−68 530	−71 482	−72 990	−75 941	−78 715	−81 451	−86 079	−89 668
B.10.1n	Changes in net worth due to net saving and capital transfers	FDCH	49 672	60 171	67 176	70 651	75 667	88 628	77 945	64 586	90 324
III.1.2	**ACQUISITION OF NON-FINANCIAL ASSETS ACCOUNT**										
	Changes in liabilities and net worth										
B.10.1n	Changes in net worth due to net saving and capital transfers	FDCH	49 672	60 171	67 176	70 651	75 667	88 628	77 945	64 586	90 324
K.1	Consumption of fixed capital	NSRK	66 647	68 530	71 482	72 990	75 941	78 715	81 451	86 079	89 668
B.10.1g	Total change in liabilities and net worth	NRMG	116 319	128 701	138 658	143 641	151 608	167 343	159 396	150 665	179 992
	Changes in assets										
P.5	Gross capital formation										
P.51	Gross fixed capital formation	FDBM	99 445	99 505	98 081	99 740	109 536	123 355	126 775	111 319	111 796
P.52	Changes in inventories	DLQX	2 740	3 713	4 852	4 319	5 015	5 958	1 793	−11 721	6 465
P.53	Acquisitions less disposals of valuables	NPOV	168	172	184	197	157	207	150	153	16
P.5	Total	FDCL	102 353	103 390	103 117	104 256	114 708	129 520	128 718	99 751	118 277
K.2	Acquisitions less disposals of non-produced non-financial assets	FDCN	1 255	959	1 339	1 317	869	2 489	854	494	670
B.9	Net lending (+) / net borrowing (-)	DTAL	12 711	24 352	34 202	38 068	36 031	35 334	29 824	50 420	61 045
Total	Total change in assets	NRMG	116 319	128 701	138 658	143 641	151 608	167 343	159 396	150 665	179 992

3.3.8 Private non-financial corporations
ESA95 sectors S.11002 National controlled and S.11003 Foreign controlled. Unconsolidated

£ million

III.2 FINANCIAL ACCOUNT

F.A Net acquisition of financial assets

			2002	2003	2004	2005	2006	2007	2008	2009	2010
F.2	Currency and deposits										
F.21	Currency	NEQF	153	197	246	198	237	222	71	508	196
F.22	Transferable deposits										
F.221	Sterling deposits with UK MFIs	NEQH	8 622	15 199	14 634	22 836	25 166	20 254	–19 546	19 962	15 521
F.2212	*of which* Foreign currency deposits	NEQJ	–232	3 811	2 562	2 607	1 452	4 269	–5 671	9 421	12 088
F.229	Deposits with rest of the world monetary financial institutions	NEQL	9 977	38 364	54 852	39 482	36 771	79 870	–9 841	–54 252	38 179
F.29	Other deposits	NEQM	632	228	–138	129	373	34	–126	–379	–1 505
F.2	Total currency and deposits	NEQE	19 384	53 988	69 594	62 645	62 547	100 380	–29 442	–34 161	52 391
F.3	Securities other than shares										
F.331	Short term: money market instruments										
F.3311	Issued by UK central government	NEQP	–	2	–4	1	–	8	159	–159	9
F.3315	Issued by UK monetary financial institutions	NEQU	230	622	77	–786	1 508	3 472	1 053	–62	–1 002
F.3316	Issued by other UK residents	NEQZ	–2 331	717	233	–1 971	2 888	–438	2 915	–1 614	1 454
F.3319	Issued by the rest of the world	NERA	1 110	3 798	615	1 078	4 758	–9 820	–5 055	1 615	1 936
F.332	Medium (1 to 5 year) and long term (over 5 year) bonds										
F.3321	Issued by UK central government	NERC	215	–139	–42	–113	–29	275	192	576	772
F.3325	Medium term bonds issued by UK monetary financial institutions	NERG	42	167	–23	395	466	658	991	1 438	488
F.3326	Other medium & long term bonds issued by UK residents	NERJ	559	–685	–390	–3 421	–265	3 303	1 301	–3 366	218
F.3329	Long term bonds issued by the rest of the world	NERK	–601	2 213	437	892	–1 093	1 691	2 968	–1 098	3 271
F.34	Financial derivatives	J8XO	..	..	–1 347	–2 217	–289	–1 880	727	–3 248	–1 583
F.3	Total securities other than shares	NEQN	–776	6 695	–444	–6 142	7 944	–2 731	5 251	–5 918	5 563
F.4	Loans										
F.42	Long term loans										
F.4211	Outward direct investment	NERY	16 366	10 155	13 053	13 713	–44	42 688	88 740	–31 909	–8 715
F.4212	Inward direct investment	NERZ	5 405	–467	4 720	8 634	4 040	12 215	27 108	–11 912	1 596
F.423	Finance leasing	F8Y9	221	471	444	478	292	528	58	–76	147
F.424	Other long-term loans by UK residents	NESF	462	–4 483	982	15 399	41 746	–2 881	–15 126	–2 352	17 825
F.4	Total loans	NERP	22 454	5 676	19 199	38 224	46 034	52 550	100 780	–46 249	10 853
F.5	Shares and other equity										
F.51	Shares and other equity, excluding mutual funds' shares										
F.514	Quoted UK shares	NESM	13 976	4 920	12 596	11 883	17 786	11 794	19 505	6 570	–233
F.515	Unquoted UK shares	NESN	7 047	9 427	9 280	16 002	11 165	11 311	37 270	8 657	3 721
F.517	UK shares and bonds issued by other UK residents	NSPP	–	–	–	–	–	–	–	–	–
F.519	Shares and other equity issued by the rest of the world	NESR	49 311	19 545	26 525	41 043	51 743	75 830	64 636	8 776	28 295
F.52	Mutual funds' shares										
F.521	UK mutual funds' shares	NESV	3	1	9	17	17	7	3	11	14
F.5	Total shares and other equity	NESH	70 337	33 893	48 410	68 945	80 711	98 942	121 414	24 014	31 797
F.6	Insurance technical reserves										
F.62	Prepayments of insurance premiums and reserves for outstanding claims	NETA	363	170	–1 035	1 839	–856	–3 571	318	–354	244
F.7	Other accounts receivable	NETB	2 553	19	–5 122	646	1 761	382	–5 452	–845	4 008
F.A	Total net acquisition of financial assets	NEQA	114 315	100 441	130 602	166 157	198 141	245 952	192 869	–63 513	104 856

3.3.8 Private non-financial corporations
ESA95 sectors S.11002 National controlled and S.11003 Foreign controlled. Unconsolidated

continued

£ million

				2002	2003	2004	2005	2006	2007	2008	2009	2010
III.2	**FINANCIAL ACCOUNT** continued											
F.L	**Net acquisition of financial liabilities**											
F.3	Securities other than shares											
F.331	Short term: money market instruments											
F.3316	Issued by UK residents other than government or monetary financial institutions		NEUD	8 543	−1 541	−3 157	−178	672	695	1 366	−5 803	3 898
F.332	Medium (1 to 5 year) and long term (over 5 year) bonds											
F.3326	Other medium & long term bonds issued by UK residents or monetary financial institutions		NEUN	16 871	19 426	8 550	11 564	11 883	24 011	3 221	−2 485	−6 516
F.3	Total securities other than shares		NETR	25 414	17 885	5 393	11 386	12 555	24 706	4 587	−8 288	−2 618
F.4	Loans											
F.41	Short term loans											
F.411	Loans by UK monetary financial institutions,		NEUV	20 540	7 252	20 152	46 557	55 188	82 839	40 979	−48 509	−25 327
F.419	Loans by rest of the world monetary financial institutions		-ZMFI	−1 297	32 248	43 762	−2 962	36 371	−14 134	−1 590	−42 123	51 886
F.42	Long term loans											
F.4211	Outward direct investment		NEVC	38 989	12 030	9 173	27 467	27 684	4 623	63 630	−37 499	15 797
F.4212	Inward direct investment		NEVD	4 813	−1 868	6 494	22 273	8 177	−3 164	19 912	−1 560	505
F.422	Secured on dwellings		G9JQ	–	–	–	2 591	3 812	3 830	5 752	3 226	1 095
F.423	Finance leasing		NEVI	347	430	516	408	474	427	337	345	329
F.424	Other long-term loans by UK residents		NEVJ	−2 529	2 950	131	6 259	5 198	54 212	−8 464	−27 913	−18 639
F.429	Other long-term loans by the rest of the world		NEVK	–	–	–	–	–	–	–	–	–
F.4	Total loans		NEUT	60 863	53 042	80 228	102 593	136 904	128 633	120 556	−154 033	25 646
F.5	Shares and other equity											
F.51	Shares and other equity, excluding mutual funds' shares											
F.514	Quoted UK shares		NEVQ	16 508	−748	7 286	−4 608	−3 737	5 342	4 321	32 864	11 623
F.515	Unquoted UK shares		NEVR	4 834	11 348	10 815	23 185	19 744	56 738	27 171	13 775	7 144
F.516	Other UK equity (including direct investment in property)		NEVS	748	395	623	597	467	2 358	1 493	532	532
F.517	UK shares and bonds issued by other UK residents		NSPQ	–	–	–	–	–	–	–	–	–
F.5	Total shares and other equity		NEVL	22 090	10 995	18 724	19 174	16 474	64 438	32 985	47 171	19 299
F.7	Other accounts payable		NEWF	2 163	2 916	2 489	3 432	6 525	2 631	−4 507	−1 133	2 942
F.L	**Total net acquisition of financial liabilities**		NETE	110 530	84 838	106 834	136 585	172 458	220 408	153 621	−116 283	45 269
B.9	**Net lending / borrowing**											
F.A	Total net acquisition of financial assets		NEQA	114 315	100 441	130 602	166 157	198 141	245 952	192 869	−63 513	104 856
-F.L	*less* Total net acquisition of financial liabilities		-NETE	−110 530	−84 838	−106 834	−136 585	−172 458	−220 408	−153 621	116 283	−45 269
B.9f	Net lending (+) / net borrowing (-), from financial account		NYOA	3 785	15 603	23 768	29 572	25 683	25 544	39 248	52 770	59 587
dB.9f	Statistical discrepancy		NYPM	8 926	8 749	10 434	8 496	10 348	9 790	−9 424	−2 350	1 458
B.9	**Net lending (+) / net borrowing (-), from capital account**		DTAL	12 711	24 352	34 202	38 068	36 031	35 334	29 824	50 420	61 045

3.3.9 Private non-financial corporations
ESA95 sectors S.11002 National controlled and S.11003 Foreign controlled. Unconsolidated

£ billion

			2002	2003	2004	2005	2006	2007	2008	2009	2010
IV.3	**FINANCIAL BALANCE SHEET** at end of period										
AN	**Non-financial assets**	TMPL	1 157.7	1 196.4	1 260.7	1 265.9	1 369.6	1 378.0	1 342.2	1 288.4	1 588.8
AF.A	**Financial assets**										
AF.2	Currency and deposits										
AF.21	Currency	NKKA	3.0	3.2	3.4	3.6	3.8	4.1	4.3	4.6	4.8
AF.22	Transferable deposits										
AF.221	Sterling deposits with UK monetary financial institutions	NKKC	171.9	186.9	200.5	225.6	247.6	270.4	264.7	280.6	300.5
AF.2212	*of which* Foreign currency deposits	NKKE	23.7	26.4	28.0	31.9	30.7	36.2	43.4	48.5	62.1
AF.229	Deposits with rest of the world monetary financial institutions	NKKG	65.1	121.1	194.2	255.4	286.9	361.1	416.8	333.6	371.9
AF.29	Other deposits	NKKH	4.9	5.1	5.0	5.1	5.5	5.6	5.5	5.1	4.0
AF.2	Total currency and deposits	NKJZ	244.8	316.3	403.2	489.7	543.9	641.1	691.3	623.9	681.2
AF.3	Securities other than shares										
AF.331	Short term: money market instruments										
AF.3311	Issued by UK central government	NKKK	–	–	–	–	–	–	0.2	–	–
AF.3315	Issued by UK monetary financial institutions	NKKP	4.6	5.0	5.4	4.8	6.6	9.4	11.6	11.1	10.2
AF.3316	Issued by other UK residents	NKKU	13.7	13.5	3.8	1.8	4.4	4.0	7.3	5.7	7.2
AF.3319	Issued by the rest of the world	NKKV	6.0	9.8	10.4	11.4	16.2	6.4	1.3	2.9	4.9
AF.332	Medium (1 to 5 year) and long term (over 5 year) bonds										
AF.3321	Issued by UK central government	NKKX	0.5	0.3	0.3	0.2	0.2	0.5	0.7	1.3	2.0
AF.3322	Issued by UK local government	NKLA	–	–	–	–	–	–	–	–	–
AF.3325	Medium term bonds issued by UK monetary financial institutions	NKLB	0.3	0.9	1.0	1.5	1.9	2.5	3.6	4.8	4.6
AF.3326	Other medium & long term bonds issued by UK residents	NKLE	6.1	5.2	5.1	1.4	1.6	5.3	7.6	3.6	4.8
AF.3329	Long term bonds issued by the rest of the world	NKLF	29.3	30.0	12.8	14.6	12.1	11.0	16.0	18.1	22.8
AF.34	Financial derivatives	JS3W	..	..	13.7	17.8	19.0	15.7	46.2	25.4	26.0
AF.3	Total securities other than shares	NKKI	60.4	64.6	52.4	53.4	62.1	54.8	94.5	73.0	82.5
AF.4	Loans										
AF.42	Long term loans										
AF.4211	Outward direct investment	NKXH	110.5	110.7	124.5	125.9	129.2	178.4	262.3	273.7	265.0
AF.4212	Inward direct investment	NKXI	52.2	48.0	55.5	67.4	72.2	68.4	87.1	55.6	57.2
AF.423	Finance leasing	F8YG	2.7	3.2	3.6	4.1	4.4	4.9	4.9	5.0	5.1
AF.424	Other long-term loans by UK residents	NKXO	25.7	24.6	24.0	29.8	44.2	47.4	75.2	63.1	118.9
AF.4	Total loans	NKWY	191.2	186.5	207.5	227.3	249.9	299.0	429.5	397.4	446.2
AF.5	Shares and other equity										
AF.51	Shares and other equity, excluding mutual funds' shares										
AF.514	Quoted UK shares	NKXV	8.7	9.4	8.8	16.9	32.9	35.1	34.7	48.4	47.5
AF.515	Unquoted UK shares	NKXW	39.6	46.3	50.0	57.1	60.9	63.0	59.2	72.6	71.0
AF.517	UK shares and bonds issued by other UK residents	NSON	–	–	–	–	–	–	–	–	–
AF.519	Shares and other equity issued by the rest of the world	NKYA	521.3	564.6	549.2	592.8	604.8	656.7	782.3	705.9	756.9
AF.52	Mutual funds' shares										
AF.521	UK mutual funds' shares	NKYE	0.3	0.3	0.4	0.5	0.6	0.6	0.3	0.4	0.5
AF.5	Total shares and other equity	NKXQ	569.9	620.7	608.3	667.3	699.2	755.3	876.6	827.3	876.0
AF.6	Insurance technical reserves										
AF.62	Prepayments of insurance premiums and reserves for outstanding claims	NKYJ	12.8	15.7	15.5	17.3	16.4	12.9	13.2	12.8	13.1
AF.7	Other accounts receivable	NKYK	110.4	112.3	124.0	121.9	121.4	120.8	119.9	117.0	115.6
AF.A	**Total financial assets**	NKWX	1 189.5	1 316.2	1 410.9	1 576.9	1 692.9	1 884.0	2 225.1	2 051.3	2 214.6

3.3.9 Private non-financial corporations
ESA95 sectors S.11002 National controlled and S.11003 Foreign controlled. Unconsolidated
continued

£ billion

IV.3 FINANCIAL BALANCE SHEET continued
at end of period

AF.L Financial liabilities

			2002	2003	2004	2005	2006	2007	2008	2009	2010
AF.3	Securities other than shares										
AF.331	Short term: money market instruments										
AF.3316	Issued by UK residents other than government or monetary financial institutions	NKZM	30.4	26.0	21.8	23.8	21.7	22.2	31.1	22.5	27.7
AF.332	Medium (1 to 5 year) and long term (over 5 year) bonds										
AF.3326	Other medium & long term bonds issued by UK residents or monetary financial institutions	NKZW	232.2	254.1	254.7	301.2	335.6	332.6	320.7	375.5	314.9
AF.34	Financial derivatives	JS3X	..	..	14.8	21.1	22.5	21.0	51.1	33.3	36.6
AF.3	Total securities other than shares	NKZA	262.5	280.2	291.3	346.0	379.7	375.9	402.9	431.4	379.2
AF.4	Loans										
AF.41	Short term loans										
AF.411	Sterling loans by UK monetary financial institutions	NLBE	285.0	285.6	298.5	346.0	397.0	476.9	538.3	478.5	439.9
AF.4112	*of which* Foreign currency loans	NLBG	40.3	32.7	31.8	42.4	43.1	66.9	97.3	59.9	54.4
AF.419	Loans by rest of the world monetary financial institutions	ZMEV	62.7	100.4	143.3	150.8	198.2	186.4	240.8	183.4	231.2
AF.42	Long term loans										
AF.4211	Outward direct investment	NLBL	125.0	124.2	125.6	159.2	168.6	152.9	225.9	228.4	244.2
AF.4212	Inward direct investment	NLBM	124.9	117.4	125.0	149.3	156.6	129.5	154.9	138.0	138.5
AF.422	Secured on dwellings	G9JM	–	–	–	27.1	30.9	34.8	40.2	43.5	40.7
AF.423	Finance leasing	NLBR	21.5	22.0	22.5	22.9	23.4	23.8	24.1	24.5	24.8
AF.424	Other long-term loans by UK residents	NLBS	44.5	67.6	78.9	72.9	91.3	107.1	90.8	114.5	120.2
AF.429	Other long-term loans by the rest of the world	NLBT	0.4	0.4	0.4	0.4	0.4	0.4	0.5	0.5	0.5
AF.4	Total loans	NLBC	664.0	717.7	794.2	928.6	1 066.3	1 111.8	1 315.5	1 211.2	1 240.0
AF.5	Shares and other equity										
AF.51	Shares and other equity, excluding mutual funds' shares										
AF.514	Quoted UK shares	NLBZ	857.8	1 002.0	1 080.2	1 232.3	1 315.5	1 360.5	910.0	1 200.3	1 361.3
AF.515	Unquoted UK shares	NLCA	352.2	392.4	422.1	513.2	606.8	669.9	623.0	631.2	680.9
AF.516	Other UK equity (including direct investment in property)	NLCB	17.3	17.3	19.2	19.7	21.6	26.2	25.4	25.9	27.9
AF.517	UK shares and bonds issued by other UK residents	NSOO	–	–	–	–	–	–	–	–	–
AF.5	Total shares and other equity	NLBU	1 227.2	1 411.7	1 521.5	1 765.3	1 943.9	2 056.6	1 558.3	1 857.4	2 070.1
AF.7	Other accounts payable	NLCO	129.3	131.5	140.0	142.7	146.8	146.9	146.2	147.5	150.1
AF.L	**Total financial liabilities**	NLBB	2 283.1	2 541.0	2 747.0	3 182.6	3 536.8	3 691.2	3 423.0	3 647.5	3 839.5

BF.90 Net financial assets / liabilities

			2002	2003	2004	2005	2006	2007	2008	2009	2010
AF.A	Total financial assets	NKWX	1 189.5	1 316.2	1 410.9	1 576.9	1 692.9	1 884.0	2 225.1	2 051.3	2 214.6
-AF.L	*less* Total financial liabilities	-NLBB	-2 283.1	-2 541.0	-2 747.0	-3 182.6	-3 536.8	-3 691.2	-3 423.0	-3 647.5	-3 839.5
BF.90	**Net financial assets (+) / liabilities (-)**	NYOT	-1 093.7	-1 224.9	-1 336.1	-1 605.8	-1 843.8	-1 807.2	-1 197.9	-1 596.1	-1 624.9

Net worth

			2002	2003	2004	2005	2006	2007	2008	2009	2010
AN	Non-financial assets	TMPL	1 157.7	1 196.4	1 260.7	1 265.9	1 369.6	1 378.0	1 342.2	1 288.4	1 588.8
BF.90	Net financial assets(+)/liabilities(-)	NYOT	-1 093.7	-1 224.9	-1 336.1	-1 605.8	-1 843.8	-1 807.2	-1 197.9	-1 596.1	-1 624.9
BF.90	**Net worth**	TMPN	64.1	-28.4	-75.4	-339.9	-474.2	-429.3	144.3	-307.8	-36.0

Chapter 4

Financial corporations

4.1.1 Financial corporations
ESA95 sector S.12

£ million

				2002	2003	2004	2005	2006	2007	2008	2009
I	**PRODUCTION ACCOUNT**										
	Resources										
P.1	Output										
P.11	Market output		NHCV	135 747	143 578	147 829	156 238	172 225	181 772	199 806	212 623
P.12	Output for own final use		NHCW	2 755	2 867	3 178	3 337	3 475	3 481	3 745	3 011
P.1	Total resources		NHCT	138 502	146 445	151 007	159 575	175 700	185 253	203 551	215 634
	Uses										
P.2	Intermediate consumption		NHCX	75 804	75 799	76 054	79 909	84 588	87 114	91 329	90 369
B.1g	**Gross Value Added**		NHDB	**62 698**	**70 646**	**74 953**	**79 666**	**91 112**	**98 139**	**112 222**	**125 265**
Total	Total uses		NHCT	138 502	146 445	151 007	159 575	175 700	185 253	203 551	215 634
B.1g	**Gross Value Added**		NHDB	**62 698**	**70 646**	**74 953**	**79 666**	**91 112**	**98 139**	**112 222**	**125 265**
-K.1	less Consumption of fixed capital		-NHCE	−5 035	−5 295	−5 687	−5 811	−5 740	−5 919	−6 366	−6 924
B.1n	Value added, net of fixed capital consumption		NHDC	57 663	65 351	69 266	73 855	85 372	92 220	105 856	118 341

4.1.2 Financial corporations
ESA95 sector S.12

£ million

			2002	2003	2004	2005	2006	2007	2008	2009
II	**DISTRIBUTION AND USE OF INCOME ACCOUNTS**									
II.1	**PRIMARY DISTRIBUTION OF INCOME ACCOUNT**									
II.1.1	**GENERATION OF INCOME ACCOUNT**									
	Resources										
B.1g	Total resources (Gross Value Added)	NHDB	62 698	70 646	74 953	79 666	91 112	98 139	112 222	125 265
	Uses										
D.1	Compensation of employees									
D.11	Wages and salaries	NHCC	30 105	31 361	34 308	37 291	42 775	44 785	45 222	49 328
D.12	Employers' social contributions	NHCD	4 019	4 801	5 548	6 573	7 661	8 035	7 166	7 562
D.1	Total	NHCR	34 124	36 162	39 856	43 864	50 436	52 820	52 388	56 890
D.2	Taxes on production and imports, paid									
D.29	Production taxes other than on products	NHCS	1 376	1 419	1 443	1 479	1 578	1 676	2 076	2 559
-D.3	less Subsidies, received									
-D.39	Production subsidies other than on products	-NHCA	–	–	–	–	–	–	–	–
B.2g	Operating surplus, gross	NQNV	27 198	33 065	33 654	34 323	39 098	43 643	57 758	65 816
B.1g	**Total uses (Gross Value Added)**	NHDB	**62 698**	**70 646**	**74 953**	**79 666**	**91 112**	**98 139**	**112 222**	**125 265**
-K.1	After deduction of fixed capital consumption	-NHCE	−5 035	−5 295	−5 687	−5 811	−5 740	−5 919	−6 366	−6 924
B.2n	Operating surplus, net	NHDA	22 163	27 770	27 967	28 512	33 358	37 724	51 392	58 892

4.1.3 Financial corporations
ESA95 sector S.12

£ million

			2002	2003	2004	2005	2006	2007	2008	2009	2010
II.1.2	**ALLOCATION OF PRIMARY INCOME ACCOUNT**										
	Resources										
B.2g	Operating surplus, gross	NQNV	27 198	33 065	33 654	34 323	39 098	43 643	57 758	65 816	52 898
D.4	Property income, received										
D.41	Interest	NHCK	162 003	160 854	195 352	246 707	333 205	435 780	432 983	184 680	153 378
D.42	Distributed income of corporations	NHCL	51 990	56 471	65 273	70 120	82 903	88 483	78 015	63 579	67 918
D.43	Reinvested earnings on direct foreign investment	NHEM	5 278	8 897	8 208	10 201	11 153	12 978	680	−542	−4 123
D.44	Attributed property income of insurance policy-holders	NHDG	34	44	39	66	59	32	39	38	32
D.45	Rent	NHDH	30	30	31	31	31	32	32	31	32
D.4	Total	NHDF	219 335	226 296	268 903	327 125	427 351	537 305	511 749	247 786	217 237
Total	Total resources	NQNW	246 533	259 361	302 557	361 448	466 449	580 948	569 507	313 602	270 135
	Uses										
D.4	Property income, paid										
D.41	Interest	NHCM	133 962	129 891	159 810	212 815	301 837	394 977	393 195	161 636	122 603
D.42	Distributed income of corporations	NHCN	37 599	43 563	52 768	52 292	63 916	62 911	33 732	28 556	47 051
D.43	Reinvested earnings on direct foreign investment	NHEO	2 033	3 474	2 233	5 518	6 743	8 225	−2 114	5 593	607
D.44	Attributed property income of insurance policy-holders	NQCG	53 652	56 703	56 150	65 805	68 321	72 820	76 392	67 581	64 433
D.45	Rent	NHDK	–	–	–	–	–	–	–	–	–
D.4	Total	NHDI	227 246	233 631	270 961	336 430	440 817	538 933	501 205	263 366	234 694
B.5g	**Balance of primary incomes, gross**	NQNY	**19 287**	**25 730**	**31 596**	**25 018**	**25 632**	**42 015**	**68 302**	**50 236**	**35 441**
Total	Total uses	NQNW	246 533	259 361	302 557	361 448	466 449	580 948	569 507	313 602	270 135
-K.1	After deduction of fixed capital consumption	-NHCE	−5 035	−5 295	−5 687	−5 811	−5 740	−5 919	−6 366	−6 924	−7 154
B.5n	Balance of primary incomes, net	NHDL	14 252	20 435	25 909	19 207	19 892	36 096	61 936	43 312	28 287

4.1.4 Financial corporations
ESA95 sector S.12

£ million

			2002	2003	2004	2005	2006	2007	2008	2009	2010
II.2	**SECONDARY DISTRIBUTION OF INCOME ACCOUNT**										
	Resources										
B.5g	**Balance of primary incomes, gross**	NQNY	**19 287**	**25 730**	**31 596**	**25 018**	**25 632**	**42 015**	**68 302**	**50 236**	**35 441**
D.61	Social contributions										
D.611	Actual social contributions										
D.6111	Employers' actual social contributions	NQOB	26 025	32 504	35 807	41 635	46 093	44 516	40 754	47 608	57 292
D.6112	Employees' social contributions	NQOC	32 967	32 158	31 238	36 107	38 868	39 346	43 679	39 528	40 551
D.6113	Social contributions by self-employed persons	NQOD	–	–	–	–	–	–	–	–	–
D.611	Total	NQOA	58 992	64 662	67 045	77 742	84 961	83 862	84 433	87 136	97 843
D.612	Imputed social contributions	NHDR	524	502	503	507	511	514	520	520	524
D.61	Total	NQNZ	59 516	65 164	67 548	78 249	85 472	84 376	84 953	87 656	98 367
D.7	Other current transfers										
D.71	Net non-life insurance premiums	NQOF	26 620	23 000	28 148	31 711	34 920	21 862	31 095	28 801	29 824
D.72	Non-life insurance claims	NHDN	588	645	675	806	802	415	591	547	567
D.75	Miscellaneous current transfers	NQOG	58	28	5	–	–	–	–	–	–
D.7	Total	NQOE	27 266	23 673	28 828	32 517	35 722	22 277	31 686	29 348	30 391
Total	Total resources	NQOH	106 069	114 567	127 972	135 784	146 826	148 668	184 941	167 240	164 199
	Uses										
D.5	Current taxes on income and wealth										
D.51	Taxes on income	NHDO	6 750	7 514	7 223	8 723	15 478	9 866	11 645	5 400	9 708
D.62	Social benefits other than social transfers in kind	NHDQ	41 733	43 791	41 172	47 423	56 137	45 542	57 113	61 150	63 272
D.7	Other current transfers										
D.71	Net non-life insurance premiums	NHDU	588	645	675	806	802	415	591	547	567
D.72	Non-life insurance claims	NQOI	26 620	23 000	28 148	31 711	34 920	21 862	31 095	28 801	29 824
D.75	Miscellaneous current transfers	NHEK	227	204	108	80	80	80	80	80	80
D.7	Total	NHDT	27 435	23 849	28 931	32 597	35 802	22 357	31 766	29 428	30 471
B.6g	**Gross Disposable Income**	NQOJ	**30 151**	**39 413**	**50 646**	**47 041**	**39 409**	**70 903**	**84 417**	**71 262**	**60 748**
Total	Total uses	NQOH	106 069	114 567	127 972	135 784	146 826	148 668	184 941	167 240	164 199
-K.1	After deduction of fixed capital consumption	-NHCE	−5 035	−5 295	−5 687	−5 811	−5 740	−5 919	−6 366	−6 924	−7 154
B.6n	Disposable income, net	NHDV	25 116	34 118	44 959	41 230	33 669	64 984	78 051	64 338	53 594

4.1.6 Financial corporations
ESA95 sector S.12

£ million

			2002	2003	2004	2005	2006	2007	2008	2009	2010
II.4.1	**USE OF DISPOSABLE INCOME ACCOUNT**										
	Resources										
B.6g	Total resources (Gross Disposable Income)	NQOJ	30 151	39 413	50 646	47 041	39 409	70 903	84 417	71 262	60 748
	Uses										
D.8	Adjustment for the change in net equity of households in pension funds	NQOK	17 783	21 373	26 375	30 826	29 334	38 834	27 840	26 506	35 095
B.8g	Gross Saving	NQOL	12 368	18 040	24 271	16 215	10 075	32 069	56 577	44 756	25 653
B.6g	Total uses (Gross Disposable Income)	NQOJ	30 151	39 413	50 646	47 041	39 409	70 903	84 417	71 262	60 748
-K.1	After deduction of fixed capital consumption	-NHCE	-5 035	-5 295	-5 687	-5 811	-5 740	-5 919	-6 366	-6 924	-7 154
B.8n	Saving, net	NQOM	7 333	12 745	18 584	10 404	4 335	26 150	50 211	37 832	18 499

4.1.7 Financial corporations
ESA95 sector S.12

£ million

			2002	2003	2004	2005	2006	2007	2008	2009	2010
III	**ACCUMULATION ACCOUNTS**										
III.1	**CAPITAL ACCOUNT**										
III.1.1	**CHANGE IN NET WORTH DUE TO SAVING & CAPITAL TRANSFERS**										
	Changes in liabilities and net worth										
B.8g	Gross Saving	NQOL	12 368	18 040	24 271	16 215	10 075	32 069	56 577	44 756	25 653
D.9	Capital transfers receivable										
D.99	Other capital transfers	NHEB	412	391	328	321	446	388	27 187	10 120	67
D.9	Total	NHDZ	412	391	328	321	446	388	27 187	10 120	67
-D.9	*less* Capital transfers payable										
-D.91	Capital taxes	-NHBW	–	–	–	–	–	–	-21 816	-1 805	–
-D.99	Other capital transfers	-NHCB	-412	-391	-328	-321	-446	-388	-218	-176	-67
-D.9	Total	-NHEC	-412	-391	-328	-321	-446	-388	-22 034	-1 981	-67
B.10.1g	Total change in liabilities and net worth	NQON	12 368	18 040	24 271	16 215	10 075	32 069	61 730	52 895	25 653
	Changes in assets										
B.10.1g	Changes in net worth due to gross saving and capital transfers	NQON	12 368	18 040	24 271	16 215	10 075	32 069	61 730	52 895	25 653
-K.1	After deduction of fixed capital consumption	-NHCE	-5 035	-5 295	-5 687	-5 811	-5 740	-5 919	-6 366	-6 924	-7 154
B.10.1n	Changes in net worth due to net saving and capital transfers	NHEF	7 333	12 745	18 584	10 404	4 335	26 150	55 364	45 971	18 499
III.1.2	**ACQUISITION OF NON-FINANCIAL ASSETS ACCOUNT**										
	Changes in liabilities and net worth										
B.10.1n	Changes in net worth due to net saving and capital transfers	NHEF	7 333	12 745	18 584	10 404	4 335	26 150	55 364	45 971	18 499
K.1	Consumption of fixed capital	NHCE	5 035	5 295	5 687	5 811	5 740	5 919	6 366	6 924	7 154
Total	Total change in liabilities and net worth	NQON	12 368	18 040	24 271	16 215	10 075	32 069	61 730	52 895	25 653
	Changes in assets										
P.5	Gross capital formation										
P.51	Gross fixed capital formation	NHCJ	8 025	6 717	6 398	8 744	7 106	8 048	8 704	6 230	7 578
P.52	Changes in inventories	NHCI	11	11	16	12	24	28	-17	53	55
P.53	Acquisitions less disposals of valuables	NPQI	306	304	330	350	290	378	284	264	298
P.5	Total	NHEG	8 342	7 032	6 744	9 106	7 420	8 454	8 971	6 547	7 931
K.2	Acquisitions less disposals of non-produced non-financial assets	NHEI	-36	-3	-6	-1	6	4	4	16	16
B.9	**Net lending(+) / net borrowing(-)**	NHCQ	**4 062**	**11 011**	**17 533**	**7 110**	**2 649**	**23 611**	**52 755**	**46 332**	**17 706**
Total	Total change in assets	NQON	12 368	18 040	24 271	16 215	10 075	32 069	61 730	52 895	25 653

4.1.8 Financial corporations
ESA95 sector S.12. Unconsolidated

£ million

				2002	2003	2004	2005	2006	2007	2008	2009	2010
III.2	**FINANCIAL ACCOUNT**											
F.A	**Net acquisition of financial assets**											
F.2	Currency and deposits											
F.21	Currency		NFCV	165	903	3 071	–1 104	–168	–1 413	–538	2 476	–181
F.22	Transferable deposits											
F.221	Deposits with UK monetary financial institutions		NFCX	78 123	159 371	180 289	226 682	349 702	228 824	135 125	535 802	–59 337
F.229	Deposits with rest of the world monetary financial institutions		NFDB	41 276	147 457	151 263	330 582	235 204	423 478	–479 150	–150 826	178 848
F.29	Other deposits		NFDC	1 263	–1 064	1 387	1 392	–2 083	2 248	7 779	5 372	–6 330
F.2	Total currency and deposits		NFCU	120 827	306 667	336 010	557 552	582 655	653 137	–336 784	392 824	113 000
F.3	Securities other than shares											
F.331	Short term: money market instruments											
F.3311	Issued by UK central government		NFDF	10 651	478	–912	–2 894	–2 481	–5 271	657	25 556	–11 218
F.3312	Issued by UK local government		NFDJ	–	–	–	–	–	–	–	–	–
F.3315	Issued by UK monetary financial institutions		NFDK	7 138	–12 219	–693	2 497	4 734	2 049	–16 790	–61 790	–16 053
F.3316	Issued by other UK residents		NFDP	–603	2 386	–2 436	4 379	1 097	–865	–4 067	–924	–2 012
F.3319	Issued by the rest of the world		NFDQ	–5 667	9 413	–3 194	4 731	8 685	5 070	–16 807	12 118	–3 784
F.332	Medium (1 to 5 year) and long term (over 5 year) bonds											
F.3321	Issued by UK central government		NFDS	4 364	16 765	27 915	19 585	45 453	18 641	69 308	168 778	90 899
F.3322	Issued by UK local government		NFDV	59	14	–92	139	230	–30	–10	–139	–30
F.3325	Issued by UK monetary financial institutions		NFDW	2 421	11 220	11 086	14 710	14 033	20 104	13 277	31 938	–1 750
F.3326	Issued by UK residents		NFDZ	24 061	38 256	32 777	36 474	45 227	24 913	130 147	65 711	–35 303
F.3329	Issued by the rest of the world		NFEA	8 133	–1 093	86 269	83 341	104 225	64 167	–45 356	141 205	70 551
F.34	Financial derivatives		NFEB	–1 205	5 263	8 275	–3 101	–20 514	29 063	121 180	–26 938	–31 763
F.3	Total securities other than shares		NFDD	49 352	70 483	158 995	159 861	200 689	157 841	251 539	355 515	59 537
F.4	Loans											
F.41	Short term loans											
F.411	Loans by UK monetary financial institutions, excluding loans secured on dwellings & financial leasing		NFEH	87 544	159 494	235 848	254 577	305 690	516 578	26 321	–202 074	–19 767
F.42	Long term loans											
F.421	Direct investment		NFEN	4 693	–766	3 200	3 323	1 814	1 503	2 709	–414	266
F.422	Loans secured on dwellings		NFEQ	83 438	101 808	102 306	89 696	109 653	107 254	38 631	9 862	5 799
F.423	Finance leasing		NFEU	758	724	709	551	666	616	488	486	473
F.424	Other long term loans		NFEV	3 798	10 120	10 306	19 161	8 962	41 403	–17 903	–39 920	–12 134
F.4	Total loans		NFEF	180 231	271 380	352 369	367 308	426 785	667 354	50 246	–232 060	–25 363
F.5	Shares and other equity											
F.51	Shares and other equity, excluding mutual funds' shares											
F.514	Quoted UK shares		NFFC	–13 763	–1 726	529	–42 246	–13 330	13 128	–10 957	32 564	–1 275
F.515	Unquoted UK shares		NFFD	–208	747	7 519	5 162	19 394	11 119	78 044	25 455	–844
F.517	UK shares and bonds issued by other UK residents		NSPS	–	–	–	–	–	–	–	–	–
F.519	Shares and other equity issued by the rest of the world		NFFH	5 074	38 706	76 289	68 350	41 726	72 976	–50 276	21 294	11 292
F.52	Mutual funds' shares											
F.521	UK mutual funds' shares		NFFL	3 370	901	391	11 844	12 271	11 613	5 026	7 927	34 843
F.5	Total shares and other equity		NFEX	–5 527	38 628	84 728	43 110	60 061	108 836	21 837	87 240	44 016
F.6	Insurance technical reserves											
F.62	Prepayments of insurance premiums and reserves for outstanding claims		NFFQ	42	20	–164	309	–146	–424	33	–37	25
F.7	Other accounts receivable		NFFR	15 697	8 439	4 367	3 434	41 392	–6 269	7 345	6 176	2 568
F.A	**Total net acquisition of financial assets**		NFCQ	360 622	695 617	936 305	1 131 574	1 311 436	1 580 475	–5 784	609 658	193 783

4.1.8 Financial corporations
ESA95 sector S.12. Unconsolidated
continued

£ million

				2002	2003	2004	2005	2006	2007	2008	2009	2010
III.2	**FINANCIAL ACCOUNT** continued											
F.L	**Net acquisition of financial liabilities**											
F.2	Currency and deposits											
F.21	Currency		NFFZ	1 532	2 958	5 460	945	1 745	1 043	2 332	6 330	1 988
F.22	Transferable deposits											
F.221	Deposits with UK monetary financial institutions		NFGB	218 055	399 447	541 402	587 184	782 432	1 004 812	–283 506	253 363	37 671
F.29	Other deposits		NFGG	476	–536	18	550	–12	4 299	11 361	7 866	–387
F.2	Total currency and deposits		NFFY	220 063	401 869	546 880	588 679	784 165	1 010 154	–269 813	267 559	39 272
F.3	Securities other than shares											
F.331	Short term: money market instruments											
F.3315	Issued by UK monetary financial institutions		NFGO	25 599	–11 489	8 023	–3 490	53 189	17 860	–47 499	22 398	–85 918
F.3316	Issued by other non-government UK residents		NFGT	267	–567	118	238	1 421	–1 235	–570	–1 781	–64
F.332	Medium (1 to 5 year) and long term (over 5 year) bonds											
F.3325	Issued by UK monetary financial institutions		NFHA	4 238	25 258	29 810	37 843	40 534	57 261	–8 674	60 343	3 031
F.3326	Issued by UK residents		NFHD	29 802	81 671	80 252	101 363	107 543	125 816	313 920	67 315	32 956
F.34	Financial derivatives		NFHF	–70	63	–	–	–	–	–	–	–
F.3	Total securities other than shares		NFGH	59 836	94 936	118 203	135 954	202 687	199 702	257 177	148 275	–49 995
F.4	Loans											
F.41	Short term loans											
F.411	Loans by UK monetary financial institutions, excluding loans secured on dwellings & financial leasing		NFHL	26 966	62 182	72 308	52 941	116 603	195 810	87 625	–12 152	–4 520
F.419	Loans by rest of the world monetary financial institutions		NFHP	–33 073	34 636	86 354	224 800	–25 425	69 936	–274 510	–7 499	96 640
F.42	Long term loans											
F.421	Direct investment		NFHR	6 643	2 765	2 687	–5 332	1 584	7 373	3 088	–4 596	1 050
F.423	Finance leasing		NFHY	411	294	193	143	192	189	151	141	144
F.424	Other long-term loans by UK residents		NFHZ	2 474	4 358	5 712	24 843	40 554	–28 378	–22 010	–20 600	16 379
F.429	Other long-term loans by the rest of the world		NFIA	–21	–42	10	29	–	26	–55	–116	75
F.4	Total loans		NFHJ	3 400	104 193	167 264	297 424	133 508	244 956	–205 711	–44 822	109 768
F.5	Shares and other equity											
F.51	Shares and other equity, excluding mutual funds' shares											
F.514	Quoted UK shares		NFIG	2 373	14 923	9 339	7 663	24 807	8 396	55 567	87 898	10 102
F.515	Unquoted UK shares		NFIH	11 174	15 718	20 538	26 936	39 581	38 196	62 954	63 130	–7 384
F.516	Other UK equity (including direct investment in property)		NFII	32	–9	–8	–	–	–	–	–	–
F.517	UK shares and bonds issued by other UK residents		NSPT	–	–	–	–	–	–	–	–	–
F.52	Mutual funds' shares											
F.521	UK mutual funds' shares		NFIP	6 259	8 212	3 489	8 300	14 866	–2 204	–4 607	26 271	43 136
F.5	Total shares and other equity		NFIB	19 838	38 844	33 358	42 899	79 254	44 388	113 914	177 299	45 854
F.6	Insurance technical reserves											
F.61	Net equity of households in life assurance and pension funds' reserves		NFIR	46 180	34 437	40 582	51 994	59 318	65 070	19 930	20 408	22 048
F.62	Prepayments of insurance premiums and reserves for outstanding claims		NFIU	1 781	687	3 778	3 969	6 011	–6 075	1 754	–1 953	1 344
F.6	Total insurance technical reserves		NPWS	47 961	35 124	44 360	55 963	65 329	58 995	21 684	18 455	23 392
F.7	Other accounts payable		NFIV	7 198	267	8 873	3 102	35 167	–9 953	31 745	–2 589	2 632
F.L	**Total net acquisition of financial liabilities**		NFFU	358 296	675 233	918 938	1 124 021	1 300 110	1 548 242	–51 004	564 177	170 923
B.9	**Net lending / borrowing**											
F.A	Total net acquisition of financial assets		NFCQ	360 622	695 617	936 305	1 131 574	1 311 436	1 580 475	–5 784	609 658	193 783
–F.L	*less* Total net acquisition of financial liabilities		–NFFU	–358 296	–675 233	–918 938	–1 124 021	–1 300 110	–1 548 242	51 004	–564 177	–170 923
B.9f	Net lending (+) / net borrowing (-), from financial account		NYNL	2 326	20 384	17 367	7 553	11 326	32 233	45 220	45 481	22 860
dB.9f	Statistical discrepancy		NYOX	1 736	–9 373	166	–443	–8 677	–8 622	7 535	851	–5 154
B.9	**Net lending (+) / net borrowing (-), from capital account**		NHCQ	**4 062**	**11 011**	**17 533**	**7 110**	**2 649**	**23 611**	**52 755**	**46 332**	**17 706**

4.1.9 Financial corporations
ESA95 sector S.12. Unconsolidated

£ billion

IV.3 FINANCIAL BALANCE SHEET
at end of period

			2002	2003	2004	2005	2006	2007	2008	2009	2010
AN	Non-financial assets	CGDB	122.1	128.7	139.7	142.9	147.1	154.1	137.8	136.6	145.9
AF.A	**Financial assets**										
AF.2	Currency and deposits										
AF.21	Currency	NLJE	7.4	8.3	11.3	10.2	10.1	8.7	8.1	12.8	10.4
AF.22	Transferable deposits										
AF.221	Deposits with UK monetary financial institutions	NLJG	790.9	1 041.7	1 180.6	1 446.1	1 833.6	1 533.5	1 888.6	2 141.5	2 011.8
AF.229	Deposits with rest of the world monetary financial institutions	NLJK	1 099.7	1 233.1	1 357.0	1 740.4	1 838.1	2 330.3	2 526.2	2 186.0	2 352.7
AF.29	Other deposits	NLJL	1.9	0.8	2.2	3.6	1.5	3.8	11.5	16.9	10.6
AF.2	Total currency and deposits	NLJD	1 899.8	2 283.9	2 551.1	3 200.4	3 683.3	3 876.2	4 434.4	4 357.2	4 385.4
AF.3	Securities other than shares										
AF.331	Short term: money market instruments										
AF.3311	Issued by UK central government	NLJO	21.0	21.9	21.1	18.2	15.7	10.3	9.8	37.6	26.2
AF.3312	Issued by UK local government	NLJS	–	–	–	–	–	–	–	–	–
AF.3315	Issued by UK monetary financial institutions	NLJT	151.1	140.0	139.8	144.1	150.4	148.1	135.9	73.5	56.0
AF.3316	Issued by other UK residents	NLJY	5.3	7.3	5.1	9.4	10.3	9.4	5.1	4.3	3.0
AF.3319	Issued by the rest of the world	NLJZ	41.6	52.1	47.6	50.6	56.3	64.5	65.5	76.7	76.8
AF.332	Medium (1 to 5 year) and long term (over 5 year) bonds										
AF.3321	Issued by UK central government	NLKB	210.5	227.3	254.3	273.1	296.9	319.1	401.5	560.6	671.3
AF.3322	Issued by UK local government	NLKE	0.5	0.5	0.4	0.4	0.5	0.3	0.2	0.5	0.6
AF.3325	Issued by UK monetary financial institutions	NLKF	37.1	52.4	62.8	78.5	89.0	115.9	153.8	176.4	176.0
AF.3326	Issued by UK residents	NLKI	278.0	309.9	345.0	409.8	464.6	464.0	446.1	582.9	548.3
AF.3329	Long term bonds issued by the rest of the world	NLKJ	484.4	496.2	573.7	677.4	763.4	866.6	1 027.1	1 128.6	1 245.9
AF.34	Financial derivatives	NLKK	–	–	1 353.7	1 631.2	1 706.9	2 805.1	9 566.2	5 248.5	6 376.3
AF.3	Total securities other than shares	NLJM	1 229.6	1 307.6	2 803.5	3 292.8	3 553.9	4 803.4	11 811.4	7 889.6	9 180.3
AF.4	Loans										
AF.41	Short term loans										
AF.411	Loans by UK monetary financial institutions, excluding loans secured on dwellings & financial leasing	NLKQ	1 142.5	1 283.9	1 487.7	1 754.5	1 969.0	2 537.7	2 990.4	2 504.8	2 472.8
AF.42	Long term loans										
AF.421	Direct investment	NLKW	12.8	16.2	25.3	28.9	22.7	23.2	26.6	40.4	40.7
AF.422	Loans secured on dwellings	NLKZ	668.5	771.8	880.0	964.1	1 075.5	1 179.4	1 222.4	1 230.9	1 234.1
AF.423	Finance leasing	NLLD	24.5	25.2	25.9	26.4	27.1	27.7	28.2	28.7	29.2
AF.424	Other long term loans	NLLE	60.0	75.0	91.9	91.8	115.8	128.2	109.8	130.5	165.3
AF.4	Total loans	NLKO	1 908.2	2 172.1	2 510.8	2 865.7	3 210.1	3 896.2	4 377.5	3 935.2	3 942.0
AF.5	Shares and other equity										
AF.51	Shares and other equity, excluding mutual funds' shares										
AF.514	Quoted UK shares	NLLL	532.9	625.9	678.0	752.6	805.9	779.2	432.6	589.3	653.3
AF.515	Unquoted UK shares	NLLM	209.5	231.8	263.9	280.6	332.1	313.7	336.0	326.1	362.3
AF.517	UK shares and bonds issued by other UK residents	NSQL	–	–	–	–	–	–	–	–	–
AF.519	Shares and other equity issued by the rest of the world	NLLQ	376.4	441.7	526.5	682.2	771.0	870.8	720.4	841.8	937.1
AF.52	Mutual funds' shares										
AF.521	UK mutual funds' shares	NLLU	106.3	146.0	164.1	243.3	286.0	342.1	303.9	402.6	473.5
AF.5	Total shares and other equity	NLLG	1 225.1	1 445.3	1 632.5	1 958.6	2 195.1	2 306.0	1 792.9	2 159.7	2 426.2
AF.6	Insurance technical reserves										
AF.62	Prepayments of insurance premiums and reserves for outstanding claims	NLLZ	1.4	1.7	1.6	1.9	1.8	1.4	1.4	1.3	1.4
AF.7	Other accounts receivable	NLMA	47.6	63.2	62.4	63.8	99.2	91.4	69.9	68.2	69.9
AF.A	**Total financial assets**	NLIZ	6 311.8	7 273.8	9 561.8	11 383.2	12 743.3	14 974.4	22 487.4	18 411.3	20 005.2

4.1.9 Financial corporations
ESA95 sector S.12. Unconsolidated
continued

£ billion

IV.3 FINANCIAL BALANCE SHEET continued
at end of period

AF.L Financial liabilities

			2002	2003	2004	2005	2006	2007	2008	2009	2010
AF.2	Currency and deposits										
AF.21	Currency	NLMI	37.9	40.8	46.3	47.2	49.0	50.0	52.3	58.7	60.7
AF.22	Transferable deposits										
AF.221	Deposits with UK monetary financial institutions	NLMK	3 034.7	3 518.7	3 981.1	4 673.7	5 328.5	5 895.8	6 761.5	6 429.8	6 412.9
AF.29	Other deposits	NLMP	0.8	0.3	0.3	1.8	1.6	5.9	17.3	25.2	47.7
AF.2	Total currency and deposits	NLMH	3 073.3	3 559.8	4 027.7	4 722.7	5 379.1	5 951.7	6 831.2	6 513.6	6 521.2
AF.3	Securities other than shares										
AF.331	Short term: money market instruments										
AF.3315	Issued by UK monetary financial institutions	NLMX	302.6	282.1	283.2	291.7	327.7	348.5	360.3	360.1	278.3
AF.3316	Issued by other non-government UK residents	NLNC	21.1	19.4	11.4	11.6	13.0	12.6	12.0	10.7	10.9
AF.332	Medium (1 to 5 year) and long term (over 5 year) bonds										
AF.3325	Issued by UK monetary financial institutions	NLNJ	81.0	107.0	134.7	175.4	205.8	285.3	357.6	389.2	384.6
AF.3326	Issued by UK residents	NLNM	281.7	357.1	453.3	569.6	655.9	738.2	891.3	1 050.7	1 077.7
AF.34	Financial derivatives	NLNO	–	–	1 358.2	1 638.8	1 740.8	2 813.5	9 432.0	5 158.7	6 296.8
AF.3	Total securities other than shares	NLMQ	686.4	765.7	2 240.8	2 687.2	2 943.2	4 198.1	11 053.3	6 969.4	8 048.5
AF.4	Loans										
AF.41	Short term loans										
AF.411	Loans by UK monetary financial institutions, excluding loans secured on dwellings & financial leasing	NLNU	357.2	421.9	490.0	550.9	642.6	877.8	1 094.5	925.0	873.2
AF.419	Loans by rest of the world monetary financial institutions	NLNY	368.0	398.9	475.8	716.6	647.7	737.0	627.9	586.6	694.7
AF.42	Long term loans										
AF.421	Direct investment	NLOA	34.1	39.0	54.5	50.3	51.5	56.0	44.6	54.9	55.9
AF.423	Finance leasing	NLOH	2.9	3.2	3.4	3.5	3.7	3.9	4.1	4.2	4.3
AF.424	Other long-term loans by UK residents	NLOI	32.4	32.7	36.0	48.3	68.1	70.3	101.5	89.4	174.1
AF.429	Other long-term loans by the rest of the world	NLOJ	0.5	0.5	0.5	0.5	0.5	0.5	0.5	0.5	0.5
AF.4	Total loans	NLNS	795.1	896.1	1 060.2	1 370.1	1 414.1	1 745.4	1 872.9	1 660.7	1 802.7
AF.5	Shares and other equity										
AF.51	Shares and other equity, excluding mutual funds' shares										
AF.514	Quoted UK shares	NLOP	268.3	332.0	361.5	409.2	485.7	425.7	216.8	386.6	416.1
AF.515	Unquoted UK shares	NLOQ	256.7	277.0	305.5	338.4	391.1	390.5	494.2	591.7	608.0
AF.517	UK shares and bonds issued by other UK residents	NSQM	–	–	–	–	–	–	–	–	–
AF.52	Mutual funds' shares										
AF.521	UK mutual funds' shares	NLOY	215.8	266.3	303.9	385.0	452.4	507.3	382.1	506.2	618.4
AF.5	Total shares and other equity	NLOK	740.8	875.2	971.0	1 132.6	1 329.3	1 323.5	1 093.1	1 484.5	1 642.6
AF.6	Insurance technical reserves										
AF.61	Net equity of households in life assurance and pension funds' reserves	NLPA	1 384.3	1 509.4	1 603.4	1 894.5	2 071.9	2 168.9	1 867.6	2 142.0	2 270.4
AF.62	Prepayments of insurance premiums and reserves for outstanding claims	NLPD	62.8	63.5	67.2	71.2	77.2	71.1	72.9	70.9	72.3
AF.6	Total insurance technical reserves	NPYI	1 447.1	1 572.9	1 670.6	1 965.7	2 149.1	2 240.0	1 940.5	2 212.9	2 342.7
AF.7	Other accounts payable	NLPE	33.8	41.9	49.5	52.3	82.6	67.6	101.0	103.6	108.8
AF.L	**Total financial liabilities**	NLMD	6 776.5	7 711.7	10 019.7	11 930.5	13 297.4	15 526.3	22 891.9	18 944.8	20 466.5

BF.90 Net financial assets / liabilities

			2002	2003	2004	2005	2006	2007	2008	2009	2010
AF.A	Total financial assets	NLIZ	6 311.8	7 273.8	9 561.8	11 383.2	12 743.3	14 974.4	22 487.4	18 411.3	20 005.2
-AF.L	*less* Total financial liabilities	-NLMD	-6 776.5	-7 711.7	-10 019.7	-11 930.5	-13 297.4	-15 526.3	-22 891.9	-18 944.8	-20 466.5
BF.90	**Net financial assets (+) / liabilities (-)**	NYOE	-464.7	-437.8	-457.9	-547.3	-554.1	-551.9	-404.5	-533.4	-461.3
	Net worth										
AN	Non-financial assets	CGDB	122.1	128.7	139.7	142.9	147.1	154.1	137.8	136.6	145.9
BF.90	Net financial assets (+) / liabilities (-)	NYOE	-464.7	-437.8	-457.9	-547.3	-554.1	-551.9	-404.5	-533.4	-461.3
BF.90	**Net worth**	CGRU	-342.6	-309.2	-318.2	-404.4	-407.0	-397.8	-266.7	-396.8	-315.5

4.2.2 Monetary financial institutions
ESA95 sectors S.121 Central bank & S.122 Other monetary financial institutions

£ million

			2002	2003	2004	2005	2006	2007	2008	2009
II	**DISTRIBUTION AND USE OF INCOME ACCOUNTS**									
II.1	**PRIMARY DISTRIBUTION OF INCOME ACCOUNT**									
II.1.1	**GENERATION OF INCOME ACCOUNT** *before deduction of fixed capital consumption*									
	Resources									
B.1g	Total resources (Gross Value Added)	NHJN	41 109	44 119	47 131	50 766	54 623	57 878	74 664	73 058
	Uses									
D.1	Compensation of employees									
D.11	Wages and salaries	NHDJ	20 019	19 295	19 757	21 858	21 400	23 257	24 927	27 110
D.12	Employers' social contributions	NHDM	2 666	2 806	3 725	4 255	3 946	4 331	4 909	3 529
D.1	Total	NHFL	22 685	22 101	23 482	26 113	25 346	27 588	29 836	30 639
D.2	Taxes on production and imports, paid									
D.29	Production taxes other than on products	NHJE	801	761	795	796	709	799	1 211	1 290
-D.3	*less* Subsidies, received									
-D.39	Production subsidies other than on products	-NHET	–	–	–	–	–	–	–	–
B.2g	Operating surplus, gross	NHBX	17 623	21 257	22 854	23 857	28 568	29 491	43 617	41 129
B.1g	**Total uses (Gross Value Added)**	NHJN	**41 109**	**44 119**	**47 131**	**50 766**	**54 623**	**57 878**	**74 664**	**73 058**

4.2.3 Monetary financial institutions
ESA95 sectors S.121 Central bank & S.122 Other monetary financial institutions

£ million

			2002	2003	2004	2005	2006	2007	2008	2009	2010
II.1.2	**ALLOCATION OF PRIMARY INCOME ACCOUNT**										
	Resources										
B.2g	Operating surplus, gross	NHBX	17 623	21 257	22 854	23 857	28 568	29 491	43 617	41 129	31 389
D.4	Property income, received										
D.41	Interest	NHFE	120 356	117 237	142 671	184 319	255 077	336 318	326 943	122 304	98 237
D.42	Distributed income of corporations	NHFF	6 660	8 076	10 862	10 447	13 506	12 362	2 744	6 796	6 761
D.43	Reinvested earnings on direct foreign investment	NHKY	2 411	3 321	4 130	4 927	5 938	3 686	1 310	–832	–8 845
D.44	Property income attributed to insurance policy-holders	NHJS	8	11	9	17	15	8	10	10	9
D.45	Rent	NHJT	–	–	–	–	–	–	–	–	–
D.4	Total	NHJR	129 435	128 645	157 672	199 710	274 536	352 374	331 007	128 278	96 162
Total	Total resources	NRKH	147 058	149 902	180 526	223 567	303 104	381 865	374 624	169 407	127 551
	Uses										
D.4	Property income, paid										
D.41	Interest	NHFG	105 418	102 067	124 945	166 017	243 646	316 472	310 109	111 305	83 590
D.42	Distributed income of corporations	NHFH	13 399	18 384	23 385	21 426	26 663	18 075	–269	1 990	11 522
D.43	Reinvested earnings on direct foreign investment	NHLB	1 215	1 948	499	2 692	1 487	2 062	–3 954	–1 075	–191
D.45	Rent	NHJW	–	–	–	–	–	–	–	–	–
D.4	Total	NHJU	120 032	122 399	148 829	190 135	271 796	336 609	305 886	112 220	94 921
B.5g	**Balance of primary incomes, gross**	NRKI	**27 026**	**27 503**	**31 697**	**33 432**	**31 308**	**45 256**	**68 738**	**57 187**	**32 630**
Total	Total uses	NRKH	147 058	149 902	180 526	223 567	303 104	381 865	374 624	169 407	127 551

4.2.4 Monetary financial institutions
ESA95 sectors S.121 Central bank & S.122 Other monetary financial institutions

£ million

			2002	2003	2004	2005	2006	2007	2008	2009	2010
II.2	**SECONDARY DISTRIBUTION OF INCOME ACCOUNT**										
	Resources										
B.5g	**Balance of primary incomes, gross**	NRKI	27 026	27 503	31 697	33 432	31 308	45 256	68 738	57 187	32 630
D.61	Social contributions										
D.612	Imputed social contributions	NHKD	227	224	238	246	256	257	258	257	263
D.7	Other current transfers										
D.72	Non-life insurance claims	NHJZ	134	161	168	210	210	109	155	144	149
D.75	Miscellaneous current transfers	CY8D	58	28	5	–	–	–	–	–	–
D.7	Total	NRKN	192	189	173	210	210	109	155	144	149
Total	Total resources	NRKP	27 445	27 916	32 108	33 888	31 774	45 622	69 151	57 588	33 042
	Uses										
D.5	Current taxes on income, wealth etc.										
D.51	Taxes on income	NHKA	4 054	4 131	3 378	3 924	5 224	3 322	2 547	1 841	2 149
D.62	Social benefits other than social transfers in kind	NHKC	227	224	238	246	256	257	258	257	263
D.7	Other current transfers										
D.71	Net non-life insurance premiums	NHKG	134	161	168	210	210	109	155	144	149
D.75	Miscellaneous current transfers	NHKW	203	180	84	56	56	56	56	56	56
D.7	Total	NHKF	337	341	252	266	266	165	211	200	205
B.6g	**Gross Disposable Income**	NRKQ	22 827	23 220	28 240	29 452	26 028	41 878	66 135	55 290	30 425
Total	Total uses	NRKP	27 445	27 916	32 108	33 888	31 774	45 622	69 151	57 588	33 042

4.2.6 Monetary financial institutions
ESA95 sectors S.121 Central bank & S.122 Other monetary financial institutions

£ million

			2002	2003	2004	2005	2006	2007	2008	2009	2010
II.4.1	**USE OF DISPOSABLE INCOME ACCOUNT**										
	Resources										
B.6g	**Total resources (Gross Disposable Income)**	NRKQ	22 827	23 220	28 240	29 452	26 028	41 878	66 135	55 290	30 425
	Uses										
B.8g	**Total uses (Gross Saving)**	NRKT	22 827	23 220	28 240	29 452	26 028	41 878	66 135	55 290	30 425

4.2.7 Monetary financial institutions
ESA95 sectors S.121 Central bank & S.122 Other monetary financial institutions

£ million

			2002	2003	2004	2005	2006	2007	2008	2009	2010
III	ACCUMULATION ACCOUNTS										
III.1	**CAPITAL ACCOUNT**										
III.1.1	CHANGE IN NET WORTH DUE TO SAVING & CAPITAL TRANSFERS ACCOUNT										
	Changes in liabilities and net worth										
B.8g	Gross Saving	NRKT	22 827	23 220	28 240	29 452	26 028	41 878	66 135	55 290	30 425
D.9	Capital transfers receivable										
D.99	Other capital transfers	J97X	–	–	–	–	–	–	26 969	9 944	–
D.9	Total	J97Y	–	–	–	–	–	–	26 969	9 944	–
-D.9	*less* Capital transfers payable										
-D.91	Capital taxes	-NRXX	–	–	–	–	–	–	–21 816	–1 805	–
-D.99	Other capital transfers	-NHEV	–	–	–	–	–	–	–	–	–
-D.9	Total	-NHKP	–	–	–	–	–	–	–21 816	–1 805	–
B.10.1g	Total change in liabilities and net worth	NRMH	22 827	23 220	28 240	29 452	26 028	41 878	71 288	63 429	30 425
	Changes in assets										
B.10.1g	Changes in net worth due to saving and capital transfers before deduction of fixed capital consumption	NRMH	22 827	23 220	28 240	29 452	26 028	41 878	71 288	63 429	30 425
III.1.2	**ACQUISITION OF NON-FINANCIAL ASSETS ACCOUNT**										
B.10.1g	Total changes in liabilities and net worth due to saving & capital transfers	NRMH	22 827	23 220	28 240	29 452	26 028	41 878	71 288	63 429	30 425
	Changes in assets										
P.5	Gross capital formation										
P.51	Gross fixed capital formation	NHFD	5 110	4 741	3 855	5 879	4 419	5 217	4 862	4 471	5 457
P.52	Changes in inventories	NHFC	6	6	9	7	12	15	–9	27	29
P.53	Acquisitions less disposals of valuables	NHKT	–	–	–	–	–	–	–	–	–
P.5	Total	NHKS	5 116	4 747	3 864	5 886	4 431	5 232	4 853	4 498	5 486
K.2	Acquisitions less disposals of non-produced non-financial assets	NHKU	–	–	–	–	–	–	–	–	–
B.9	**Net lending (+) / net borrowing (-)**	NHFK	**17 711**	**18 473**	**24 376**	**23 566**	**21 597**	**36 646**	**66 435**	**58 931**	**24 939**
B.10.1g	Total change in assets	NRMH	22 827	23 220	28 240	29 452	26 028	41 878	71 288	63 429	30 425

4.2.8 Monetary financial institutions
ESA95 sectors S.121 Central bank and S.122 Other monetary financial institutions. Unconsolidated

£ million

				2002	2003	2004	2005	2006	2007	2008	2009	2010
III.2	**FINANCIAL ACCOUNT**											
F.A	**Net acquisition of financial assets**											
F.2	Currency and deposits											
F.21	Currency		NGCB	165	903	3 071	−1 104	−168	−1 413	−538	2 476	−181
F.22	Transferable deposits											
F.221	Deposits with UK MFIs[1]		NGCD	75 820	128 363	131 912	129 309	231 824	96 409	−46 119	442 679	11 253
F.229	Deposits with rest of the world monetary financial institutions		NGCH	52 742	87 727	105 775	157 873	177 587	375 378	−146 485	−147 423	123 070
F.29	Other deposits		NGCI	−2	−1	−6	–	–	−11	–	–	–
F.2	Total currency and deposits		NGCA	128 725	216 992	240 752	286 078	409 243	470 363	−193 142	297 732	134 142
F.3	Securities other than shares											
F.331	Short term: money market instruments											
F.3311	Issued by UK central government		NGCL	10 798	−1 655	−2 362	−304	−3 746	−6 513	−2 466	19 749	−11 765
F.3312	Issued by UK local government		NGCP	–	–	–	–	–	–	–	–	–
F.3315	Issued by UK MFIs[1]		NGCQ	330	−14 166	1 810	3 728	3 112	−8 677	−18 542	−40 887	−11 494
F.3316	Issued by other UK residents		NGCV	−225	2 139	−1 166	909	2 239	−3 768	−571	−469	−36
F.3319	Issued by the rest of the world		NGCW	−3 982	7 432	−4 461	2 039	5 321	8 534	−14 888	10 690	−831
F.332	Medium (1 to 5 year) and long term (over 5 year) bonds											
F.3321	Issued by UK central government		NGCY	−4 805	−5 030	5 124	−1 528	−4 828	1 738	30 874	209 321	49 983
F.3322	Issued by UK local government		NGDB	–	–	–	–	–	–	–	–	−3
F.3325	Medium term bonds issued by UK MFIs[1]		NGDC	−860	2 590	2 525	1 640	−58	1 090	16 852	10 430	−6 401
F.3326	Other medium & long term bonds issued by UK residents		NGDF	−1 748	8 423	12 290	26 008	45 046	27 888	94 323	65 725	−30 604
F.3329	Long term bonds issued by the rest of the world		NGDG	3 768	−14 511	58 782	62 434	100 968	43 168	−159 678	−5 939	−23 547
F.34	Financial derivatives		NGDH	−1 205	5 263	11 308	1 563	−11 501	33 775	78 940	−38 134	−27 103
F.3	Total securities other than shares		NGCJ	2 071	−9 515	83 850	96 489	136 553	97 235	24 844	230 486	−61 801
F.4	Loans											
F.41	Short term loans											
F.411	Loans by UK MFIs[1], excluding loans secured on dwellings & financial leasing		NGDN	87 544	159 494	235 848	254 577	305 690	516 578	26 321	−202 074	−19 767
F.42	Long term loans											
F.421	Direct investment		NGDT	−52	−4	–	–	–	–	–	–	–
F.422	Loans secured on dwellings		NGDW	59 962	66 529	60 004	46 301	46 430	26 718	−37 923	35 765	15 132
F.423	Finance leasing		NGEA	8	−21	−13	−14	−4	−6	−24	–	−19
F.424	Other long term loans		NGEB	−1 017	113	231	−106	−478	−168	42	191	306
F.4	Total loans		NGDL	146 445	226 111	296 070	300 758	351 638	543 122	−11 584	−166 118	−4 348
F.5	Shares and other equity											
F.51	Shares and other equity, excluding mutual funds' shares											
F.514	Quoted UK shares		NGEI	−10 446	6 243	1 505	8 198	6 084	3 635	−13 135	10 151	1 020
F.515	Unquoted UK shares		NGEJ	347	2 564	8 433	4 207	21 094	10 308	56 243	26 711	−15 802
F.517	UK shares and bonds issued by other UK residents		NSQA	–	–	–	–	–	–	–	–	–
F.519	Shares and other equity issued by the rest of the world		NGEN	−9 268	22 544	46 981	46 341	34 106	20 686	−60 710	12 308	9 117
F.52	Mutual funds' shares											
F.521	UK mutual funds' shares		NGER	8	4	28	49	50	21	11	35	44
F.5	Total shares and other equity		NGED	−19 359	31 355	56 947	58 795	61 334	34 650	−17 591	49 205	−5 621
F.7	Other accounts receivable		NGEX	−180	−143	−47	25	−68	−47	−1	−43	−2
F.A	**Total net acquisition of financial assets**		NGBW	257 702	464 800	677 572	742 145	958 700	1 145 323	−197 474	411 262	62 370

1 UK monetary financial institutions

4.2.8 Monetary financial institutions
ESA95 sectors S.121 Central bank and S.122 Other monetary financial institutions. Unconsolidated

£ million

			2002	2003	2004	2005	2006	2007	2008	2009	2010
III.2	**FINANCIAL ACCOUNT** continued										
F.L	**Net acquisition of financial liabilities**										
F.2	Currency and deposits										
F.21	Currency	NGFF	1 532	2 958	5 460	945	1 745	1 043	2 332	6 330	1 988
F.22	Transferable deposits										
F.221	Deposits with UK MFIs[1]	NGFH	218 055	399 447	541 402	587 184	782 432	1 004 812	–283 506	253 363	37 671
F.2	Total currency and deposits	NGFE	219 587	402 405	546 862	588 129	784 177	1 005 855	–281 174	259 693	39 659
F.3	Securities other than shares										
F.331	Short term: money market instruments										
F.3315	Issued by UK MFIs[1]	NGFU	25 599	–11 489	8 023	–3 490	53 189	17 860	–47 499	22 398	–85 918
F.332	Medium (1 to 5 year) and long term (over 5 year) bonds										
F.3325	Medium term bonds issued by UK MFIs[1]	NGGG	4 238	25 258	29 810	37 843	40 534	57 261	–8 674	60 343	3 031
F.3326	Other medium & long term bonds issued by UK residents	NGGJ	8 801	26 069	7 931	16 364	–10 087	–12 682	156 340	24 494	49 837
F.34	Financial derivatives	NGGL	–70	63	–	–	–	–	–	–	–
F.3	Total securities other than shares	NGFN	38 568	39 901	45 764	50 717	83 636	62 439	100 167	107 235	–33 050
F.4	Loans										
F.42	Long term loans										
F.421	Direct investment	NGGX	–92	171	137	27	–7	–56	–87	–144	–68
F.423	Finance leasing	NGHE	275	190	98	72	111	110	87	81	84
F.4	Total loans	NGGP	183	361	235	99	104	54	–	–63	16
F.5	Shares and other equity										
F.51	Shares and other equity, excluding mutual funds' shares										
F.514	Quoted UK shares	NGHM	2 041	2 979	–85	–2	–387	2 995	37	–	–
F.515	Unquoted UK shares	NGHN	1 756	2 755	476	2 692	1 487	2 062	–4 566	–1 091	–191
F.516	Other UK equity (including direct investment in property)	NGHO	32	–9	–8	–	–	–	–	–	–
F.517	UK shares and bonds issued by other UK residents	NSQB	–	–	–	–	–	–	–	–	–
F.5	Total shares and other equity	NGHH	3 829	5 725	383	2 690	1 100	5 057	–4 529	–1 091	–191
F.7	Other accounts payable	NGIB	–571	221	1 020	978	649	1 780	18 904	–2 591	593
F.L	**Total net acquisition of financial liabilities**	NGFA	261 596	448 613	594 264	642 613	869 666	1 075 185	–166 632	363 183	7 027
B.9	**Net lending / borrowing**										
F.A	Total net acquisition of financial assets	NGBW	257 702	464 800	677 572	742 145	958 700	1 145 323	–197 474	411 262	62 370
-F.L	*less* Total net acquisition of financial liabilities	-NGFA	–261 596	–448 613	–594 264	–642 613	–869 666	–1 075 185	166 632	–363 183	–7 027
B.9f	Net lending (+) / net borrowing (-), from financial account	NYNS	–3 894	16 187	83 308	99 532	89 034	70 138	–30 842	48 079	55 343
dB.9f	Statistical discrepancy	NYPE	21 605	2 286	–58 932	–75 966	–67 437	–33 492	97 277	10 852	–30 404
B.9	**Net lending (+) / net borrowing (-), from capital account**	NHFK	17 711	18 473	24 376	23 566	21 597	36 646	66 435	58 931	24 939

1 UK monetary financial institutions

4.2.9 Monetary financial institutions
ESA95 sectors S.121 Central bank and S.122 Other monetary financial institutions. Unconsolidated

£ billion

				2002	2003	2004	2005	2006	2007	2008	2009	2010
IV.3		**FINANCIAL BALANCE SHEET** at end of period										
AF.A		**Financial assets**										
	AF.2	Currency and deposits										
	AF.21	Currency	NNSY	7.3	8.2	11.3	10.2	10.0	8.6	8.0	12.7	10.3
	AF.22	Transferable deposits										
	AF.221	Deposits with UK MFIs[1]	NNTA	509.1	736.4	831.9	1 000.5	1 282.2	842.7	924.6	1 142.2	938.5
	AF.229	Deposits with rest of the world monetary financial institutions	NNTE	843.0	921.4	1 006.9	1 199.7	1 286.0	1 714.1	2 092.6	1 779.3	1 876.3
	AF.29	Other deposits	NNTF	–	–	–	–	–	–	–	–	–
	AF.2	Total currency and deposits	NNSX	1 359.5	1 666.1	1 850.1	2 210.4	2 578.1	2 565.5	3 025.3	2 934.2	2 825.0
	AF.3	Securities other than shares										
	AF.331	Short term: money market instruments										
	AF.3311	Issued by UK central government	NNTI	19.3	18.4	16.1	15.8	12.1	5.6	3.1	22.8	10.7
	AF.3312	Issued by UK local government	NNTM	–	–	–	–	–	–	–	–	–
	AF.3315	Issued by UK MFIs[1]	NNTN	102.5	89.8	90.9	96.1	98.4	88.7	72.5	32.0	21.0
	AF.3316	Issued by other UK residents	NNTS	1.1	3.2	1.9	2.9	5.0	1.3	0.5	–	–
	AF.3319	Issued by the rest of the world	NNTT	34.6	42.8	37.0	39.6	42.8	53.8	57.1	65.4	65.0
	AF.332	Medium (1 to 5 year) and long term (over 5 year) bonds										
	AF.3321	Issued by UK central government	NNTV	–1.0	–6.3	–1.4	–2.8	–7.7	–5.5	25.7	228.8	290.4
	AF.3322	Issued by UK local government	NNTY	–	–	–	–	–	–	–	–	–
	AF.3325	Medium term bonds issued by UK MFIs[1]	NNTZ	18.5	21.1	23.4	25.2	24.5	25.2	43.0	54.3	57.2
	AF.3326	Other medium & long term bonds issued by UK residents	NNUC	50.9	65.9	90.0	133.6	189.4	209.5	230.5	318.8	313.9
	AF.3329	Long term bonds issued by the rest of the world	NNUD	336.3	327.3	359.7	413.7	479.1	555.6	568.5	504.0	480.7
	AF.34	Financial derivatives	NNUE	–	–	1 166.9	1 407.5	1 481.4	2 368.4	7 634.7	4 079.8	4 242.0
	AF.3	Total securities other than shares	NNTG	562.2	562.2	1 784.6	2 131.6	2 325.0	3 302.7	8 635.6	5 305.9	5 481.0
	AF.4	Loans										
	AF.41	Short term loans										
	AF.411	Loans by UK MFIs[1], excluding loans secured on dwellings & financial leasing	NNUK	1 142.5	1 283.9	1 487.7	1 754.5	1 969.0	2 537.7	2 990.4	2 504.8	2 472.8
	AF.42	Long term loans										
	AF.421	Direct investment	NNUQ	–	–	–	–	–	–	–	–	–
	AF.422	Loans secured on dwellings	NNUT	591.2	653.4	708.4	749.0	795.5	829.7	795.1	922.0	1 045.4
	AF.423	Finance leasing	NNUX	2.7	2.7	2.6	2.6	2.6	2.6	2.6	2.6	2.6
	AF.424	Other long term loans	NNUY	3.8	3.7	4.2	4.3	3.4	3.3	4.5	4.2	4.6
	AF.4	Total loans	NNUI	1 740.2	1 943.6	2 202.9	2 510.4	2 770.5	3 373.3	3 792.6	3 433.7	3 525.8
	AF.5	Shares and other equity										
	AF.51	Shares and other equity, excluding mutual funds' shares										
	AF.514	Quoted UK shares	NNVF	3.3	9.6	8.6	16.6	22.7	26.2	11.8	22.4	22.0
	AF.515	Unquoted UK shares	NNVG	70.7	89.4	108.8	113.8	153.0	123.2	124.5	113.3	135.6
	AF.517	UK shares and bonds issued by other UK residents	NSQU	–	–	–	–	–	–	–	–	–
	AF.519	Shares and other equity issued by the rest of the world	NNVK	26.4	44.2	87.4	129.1	156.3	177.5	100.7	123.4	136.1
	AF.52	Mutual funds' shares										
	AF.521	UK mutual funds' shares	NNVO	0.9	1.0	1.2	1.5	1.7	1.7	1.0	1.3	1.6
	AF.5	Total shares and other equity	NNVA	101.3	144.2	205.9	261.1	333.8	328.5	238.0	260.3	295.3
	AF.7	Other accounts receivable	NNVU	0.8	0.6	0.5	0.5	0.3	0.2	0.2	0.2	0.2
AF.A		**Total financial assets**	NNST	3 763.9	4 316.6	6 044.1	7 113.9	8 007.7	9 570.1	15 691.6	11 934.3	12 127.3

1 UK monetary financial institutions

4.2.9 Monetary financial institutions
ESA95 sectors S.121 Central bank and S.122 Other monetary financial institutions. Unconsolidated

£ billion

				2002	2003	2004	2005	2006	2007	2008	2009	2010
IV.3	**FINANCIAL BALANCE SHEET** continued at end of period											
AF.L	**Financial liabilities**											
AF.2	Currency and deposits											
AF.21	Currency		NNWC	37.9	40.8	46.3	47.2	49.0	50.0	52.3	58.7	60.7
AF.22	Transferable deposits											
AF.221	Deposits with UK MFIs[1]		NNWE	3 034.7	3 518.7	3 981.1	4 673.7	5 328.5	5 895.8	6 761.5	6 429.8	6 412.9
AF.2	Total currency and deposits		NNWB	3 072.5	3 559.6	4 027.4	4 720.9	5 377.5	5 945.8	6 813.9	6 488.5	6 473.6
AF.3	Securities other than shares											
AF.331	Short term: money market instruments											
AF.3315	Issued by UK MFIs[1]		NNWR	302.6	282.1	283.2	291.7	327.7	348.5	360.3	360.1	278.3
AF.332	Medium (1 to 5 year) and long term (over 5 year) bonds											
AF.3325	Medium term bonds issued by UK MFIs[1]		NNXD	81.0	107.0	134.7	175.4	205.8	285.3	357.6	389.2	384.6
AF.3326	Other medium & long term bonds issued by UK residents		NNXG	92.2	113.2	119.4	138.8	142.3	108.5	221.5	271.2	337.2
AF.34	Financial derivatives		NNXI	–	–	1 167.6	1 406.5	1 499.3	2 357.1	7 517.6	4 026.8	4 204.2
AF.3	Total securities other than shares		NNWK	475.8	502.4	1 705.0	2 012.6	2 175.1	3 099.4	8 457.0	5 047.2	5 204.4
AF.4	Loans											
AF.41	Short term loans											
AF.411	Loans by UK MFIs[1], excluding loans secured on dwellings & financial leasing		NNXO	–	–	–	–	–	–	–	–	–
AF.42	Long term loans											
AF.421	Direct investment		NNXU	0.9	1.2	1.3	1.3	1.3	1.3	1.2	1.0	1.0
AF.423	Finance leasing		NNYB	1.5	1.7	1.8	1.9	2.0	2.1	2.2	2.3	2.3
AF.424	Other long-term loans by UK residents		NNYC	–	–	–	–	–	–	–	–	–
AF.4	Total loans		NNXM	2.4	2.9	3.1	3.2	3.3	3.3	3.3	3.3	3.3
AF.5	Shares and other equity											
AF.51	Shares and other equity, excluding mutual funds' shares											
AF.514	Quoted UK shares		NNYJ	19.4	20.8	14.0	11.2	13.5	5.0	0.1	0.1	0.2
AF.515	Unquoted UK shares		NNYK	109.1	108.0	119.8	124.5	127.7	133.8	151.9	158.7	162.4
AF.517	UK shares and bonds issued by other UK residents		NSQV	–	–	–	–	–	–	–	–	–
AF.5	Total shares and other equity		NNYE	128.5	128.8	133.8	135.7	141.2	138.9	152.0	158.8	162.5
AF.7	Other accounts payable		NNYY	3.9	4.0	4.9	5.8	6.3	7.7	26.7	24.6	25.8
AF.L	**Total financial liabilities**		NNVX	3 683.1	4 197.7	5 874.2	6 878.2	7 703.3	9 195.1	15 452.9	11 722.4	11 869.6
BF.90	**Net financial assets / liabilities**											
AF.A	Total financial assets		NNST	3 763.9	4 316.6	6 044.1	7 113.9	8 007.7	9 570.1	15 691.6	11 934.3	12 127.3
-AF.L	less Total financial liabilities		-NNVX	-3 683.1	-4 197.7	-5 874.2	-6 878.2	-7 703.3	-9 195.1	-15 452.9	-11 722.4	-11 869.6
BF.90	**Net financial assets (+) / liabilities (-)**		NYOL	80.8	118.9	169.9	235.8	304.4	375.0	238.7	212.0	257.7

1 UK monetary financial institutions

4.3.2 Other financial intermediaries and financial auxiliaries
ESA95 sectors S.123 Other financial intermediaries & S.124 Financial auxiliaries

£ million

			2002	2003	2004	2005	2006	2007	2008	2009
II		DISTRIBUTION AND USE OF INCOME ACCOUNTS								
II.1		PRIMARY DISTRIBUTION OF INCOME ACCOUNT								
II.1.1		GENERATION OF INCOME ACCOUNT *before deduction of fixed capital consumption*								
		Resources								
B.1g		Total resources (Gross Value Added)	NHMH	7 929	10 415	11 736	15 030	19 909	22 083	24 936	34 289
		Uses								
D.1		Compensation of employees									
D.11		Wages and salaries	NHED	5 956	7 751	7 785	8 977	14 721	14 052	13 135	15 093
D.12		Employers' social contributions	NHEE	775	1 295	1 027	1 447	2 595	2 568	1 299	2 712
D.1		Total	NHLX	6 731	9 046	8 812	10 424	17 316	16 620	14 434	17 805
D.2		Taxes on production and imports, paid									
D.29		Production taxes other than on products	NHLY	238	312	299	318	485	482	374	750
-D.3		*less* Subsidies, received									
-D.39		Production subsidies other than on products	-NHLF	–	–	–	–	–	–	–	–
B.2g		Operating surplus, gross	NHBY	960	1 057	2 625	4 288	2 108	4 981	10 128	15 734
B.1g		**Total uses (Gross Value Added)**	NHMH	**7 929**	**10 415**	**11 736**	**15 030**	**19 909**	**22 083**	**24 936**	**34 289**

4.3.3 Other financial intermediaries and financial auxiliaries
ESA95 sectors S.123 Other financial intermediaries & S.124 Financial auxiliaries

£ million

			2002	2003	2004	2005	2006	2007	2008	2009	2010
II.1.2		ALLOCATION OF PRIMARY INCOME ACCOUNT									
		Resources									
B.2g		Operating surplus, gross	NHBY	960	1 057	2 625	4 288	2 108	4 981	10 128	15 734	11 259
D.4		Property income, received										
D.41		Interest	NHLQ	18 173	18 158	24 286	34 988	50 340	67 901	77 231	35 846	30 603
D.42		Distributed income of corporations	NHLR	23 601	27 882	32 508	35 371	42 284	47 533	44 686	29 502	33 774
D.43		Reinvested earnings on direct foreign investment	NHNS	2 942	4 004	1 381	2 166	2 600	6 590	1 587	1 561	2 663
D.44		Property income attributed to insurance policy-holders	NHMM	8	9	9	15	13	6	8	8	6
D.45		Rent	NHMN	–	–	–	–	–	–	–	–	–
D.4		Total	NHML	44 724	50 053	58 184	72 540	95 237	122 030	123 512	66 917	67 046
Total		Total resources	NRKX	45 684	51 110	60 809	76 828	97 345	127 011	133 640	82 651	78 305
		Uses										
D.4		Property income										
D.41		Interest	NHLS	27 549	26 884	33 481	44 862	55 720	75 581	80 309	48 949	37 847
D.42		Distributed income of corporations	NHLT	21 399	22 035	25 125	26 946	31 947	37 925	29 116	22 329	31 198
D.43		Reinvested earnings on direct foreign investment	NHNU	873	991	814	1 958	3 611	6 140	2 319	6 535	734
D.45		Rent	NHMQ	–	–	–	–	–	–	–	–	–
D.4		Total	NHMO	49 821	49 910	59 420	73 766	91 278	119 646	111 744	77 813	69 779
B.5g		**Balance of primary incomes, gross**	NRKZ	**–4 137**	**1 200**	**1 389**	**3 062**	**6 067**	**7 365**	**21 896**	**4 838**	**8 526**
Total		Total uses	NRKX	45 684	51 110	60 809	76 828	97 345	127 011	133 640	82 651	78 305

4.3.4 Other financial intermediaries and financial auxiliaries
ESA95 sectors S.123 Other financial intermediaries & S.124 Financial auxiliaries

£ million

			2002	2003	2004	2005	2006	2007	2008	2009	2010
II.2	**SECONDARY DISTRIBUTION OF INCOME ACCOUNT**										
	Resources										
B.5g	**Balance of primary incomes, gross**	NRKZ	–4 137	1 200	1 389	3 062	6 067	7 365	21 896	4 838	8 526
D.61	Social contributions										
D.612	Imputed social contributions	NHMX	172	158	167	171	178	180	179	179	184
D.7	Other current transfers										
D.72	Non-life insurance claims	NHMT	134	138	141	179	174	87	124	115	120
D.75	Miscellaneous current transfers	NRLD	–	–	–	–	–	–	–	–	–
D.7	Total	NRLE	134	138	141	179	174	87	124	115	120
Total	Total resources	NRLF	–3 831	1 496	1 697	3 412	6 419	7 632	22 199	5 132	8 830
	Uses										
D.5	Current taxes on income, wealth etc.										
D.51	Taxes on income	NHMU	5 042	1 499	317	–243	6 637	4 858	14 085	763	4 756
D.62	Social benefits other than social transfers in kind	NHMW	172	158	167	171	178	180	179	179	184
D.7	Other current transfers										
D.71	Net non-life insurance premiums	NHNA	134	138	141	179	174	87	124	115	120
D.75	Miscellaneous current transfers	NHNQ	24	24	24	24	24	24	24	24	24
D.7	Total	NHMZ	158	162	165	203	198	111	148	139	144
B.6g	**Gross Disposable Income**	NRLG	–9 203	–323	1 048	3 281	–594	2 483	7 787	4 051	3 746
Total	Total uses	NRLF	–3 831	1 496	1 697	3 412	6 419	7 632	22 199	5 132	8 830

4.3.6 Other financial intermediaries and financial auxiliaries
ESA95 sectors S.123 Other financial intermediaries & S.124 Financial auxiliaries

£ million

			2002	2003	2004	2005	2006	2007	2008	2009	2010
II.4.1	**USE OF DISPOSABLE INCOME ACCOUNT**										
	Resources										
B.6g	Total resources (Gross Disposable Income)	NRLG	–9 203	–323	1 048	3 281	–594	2 483	7 787	4 051	3 746
	Uses										
B.8g	Total uses (Gross Saving)	NRLJ	–9 203	–323	1 048	3 281	–594	2 483	7 787	4 051	3 746

4.3.7 Other financial intermediaries and financial auxiliaries
ESA95 sectors S.123 Other financial intermediaries & S.124 Financial auxiliaries

£ million

			2002	2003	2004	2005	2006	2007	2008	2009	2010
III	**ACCUMULATION ACCOUNTS**										
III.1	**CAPITAL ACCOUNT**										
III.1.1	**CHANGE IN NET WORTH DUE TO SAVING & CAPITAL TRANSFERS ACCOUNT**										
	Changes in liabilities and net worth										
B.8g	Gross Saving	NRLJ	−9 203	−323	1 048	3 281	−594	2 483	7 787	4 051	3 746
B.10.1g	Total change in liabilities and net worth	NRMI	−9 203	−323	1 048	3 281	−594	2 483	7 787	4 051	3 746
	Changes in assets										
B.10.1g	Change in net worth due to saving and capital transfers before deduction of fixed capital consumption	NRMI	−9 203	−323	1 048	3 281	−594	2 483	7 787	4 051	3 746
III.1.2	**ACQUISITION OF NON-FINANCIAL ASSETS ACCOUNT**										
B.10.1g	**Total changes in liabilities and net worth due to saving and capital transfers**	NRMI	−9 203	−323	1 048	3 281	−594	2 483	7 787	4 051	3 746
	Changes in assets										
P.5	Gross capital formation										
P.51	Gross fixed capital formation	NHLP	1 515	1 247	1 263	1 788	1 911	2 177	2 746	1 414	1 708
P.52	Changes in inventories	NHLO	−	−	−	−	−	−	−	−	−
P.53	Acquisitions less disposals of valuables	NHNN	−	−	−	−	−	−	−	−	−
P.5	Total	NHNM	1 515	1 247	1 263	1 788	1 911	2 177	2 746	1 414	1 708
K.2	Acquisitions less disposals of non-produced non-financial assets	NHNO	6	11	18	20	20	20	20	28	28
B.9	**Net lending (+) / net borrowing (−)**	NHLW	−10 724	−1 581	−233	1 473	−2 525	286	5 021	2 609	2 010
Total	Total change in assets	NRMI	−9 203	−323	1 048	3 281	−594	2 483	7 787	4 051	3 746

4.3.8 Other financial intermediaries and financial auxiliaries
ESA95 sectors S.123 and S.124. Unconsolidated

£ million

				2002	2003	2004	2005	2006	2007	2008	2009	2010
III.2	**FINANCIAL ACCOUNT**											
F.A	Net acquisition of financial assets											
F.2	Currency and deposits											
F.21	Currency		NFJD	–	–	–	–	–	–	–	–	–
F.22	Transferable deposits											
F.221	Sterling deposits with UK MFIs		NFJE	−7 730	83 054	79 430	268 799	159 526	152 398	−152 634	97 135	−8 936
F.2212	o/w Foreign currency deposits		NFJH	−970	26 864	15 439	30 800	38 916	49 521	−20 345	−20 527	−4 707
F.229	Deposits with rest of the world monetary financial institutions		NFJJ	−12 963	52 104	37 303	167 116	50 338	36 409	−337 101	1 570	45 393
F.29	Other deposits		NFJK	1 265	−1 063	1 393	1 392	−2 083	2 259	7 779	5 372	−6 330
F.2	Total currency and deposits		NFJC	−6 465	81 991	80 823	270 191	157 443	154 657	−144 855	102 507	−15 266
F.3	Securities other than shares											
F.331	Short term: money market instruments											
F.3311	Issued by UK central government		NFJN	−413	2 492	1 074	−2 053	1 041	1 257	2 724	3 697	2 523
F.3312	Issued by UK local government		NFJR	–	–	–	–	–	–	–	–	–
F.3315	Issued by UK monetary financial institutions		NFJS	4 125	−1 155	−4 509	472	−2 586	9 198	6 972	−7 695	−1 711
F.3316	Issued by other UK residents		NFJX	−429	118	223	−144	768	648	−2 017	−52	−322
F.3319	Issued by the rest of the world		NFJY	−2 018	1 911	665	1 273	3 920	−3 618	−2 616	1 729	−2 879
F.332	Medium (1 to 5 year) and long term (over 5 year) bonds											
F.3321	Issued by UK central government		NFKA	5 932	2 024	2 731	−6 005	24 793	25 157	51 552	−50 227	28 269
F.3322	Issued by UK local government		NFKD	39	9	8	–	–	–	–	–	–
F.3325	Medium term bonds issued by UK MFIs[1]		NFKE	839	2 191	2 189	3 312	3 565	4 802	−849	5 424	1 206
F.3326	Other medium & long term bonds issued by UK residents		NFKH	4 064	15 705	8 650	9 624	−4 420	−3 960	7 630	7 732	6 260
F.3329	Long term bonds issued by the rest of the world		NFKI	−464	12 422	23 431	14 666	−18 987	−14 564	97 265	131 041	84 455
F.34	Financial derivatives		JS3D	..	..	−2 509	−3 967	−7 845	−4 092	37 830	10 305	−6 196
F.3	Total securities other than shares		NFJL	11 675	35 717	31 953	17 178	249	14 828	198 491	101 954	111 605
F.4	Loans											
F.42	Long term loans											
F.421	Direct investment		NFKV	3 705	−2 731	2 031	2 575	1 048	2 989	1 207	−1 610	−749
F.422	Loans secured on dwellings		NFKY	23 641	35 070	42 268	43 823	63 435	80 539	75 776	−26 743	−9 556
F.423	Finance leasing		NFLC	750	745	722	565	670	622	512	486	492
F.424	Other long-term loans by UK residents		NFLD	4 253	4 978	2 307	9 991	5 156	58 400	−13 457	−30 155	−22 047
F.4	Total loans		NFKN	32 349	38 062	47 328	56 954	70 309	142 550	64 038	−58 022	−31 860
F.5	Shares and other equity											
F.51	Shares and other equity, excluding mutual funds' shares											
F.514	Quoted UK shares		NFLK	10 921	11 619	16 629	1 953	6 956	43 319	21 317	45 380	26 892
F.515	Unquoted UK shares		NFLL	−876	−585	−1 103	1 842	−635	1 469	21 858	−1 143	14 870
F.517	UK shares and bonds issued by other UK residents		NSPJ	–	–	–	–	–	–	–	–	–
F.519	Shares and other equity issued by the rest of the world		NFLP	−5 177	13 651	13 219	−9 410	−2 762	40 391	19 034	7 139	1 645
F.52	Mutual funds' shares											
F.521	UK mutual funds' shares		NFLT	41	16	76	143	131	40	37	94	114
F.5	Total shares and other equity		NFLF	4 909	24 701	28 821	−5 472	3 690	85 219	62 246	51 470	43 521
F.6	Insurance technical reserves											
F.62	Prepayments of insurance premiums and reserves for outstanding claims		NFLY	20	10	−86	186	−76	−208	15	−17	11
F.7	Other accounts receivable		NFLZ	618	605	644	643	645	645	631	644	644
F.A	**Total net acquisition of financial assets**		NFIY	43 106	181 086	189 483	339 680	232 260	397 691	180 566	198 536	108 655

1 UK monetary financial institutions

4.3.8 Other financial intermediaries and financial auxiliaries
ESA95 sectors S.123 and S.124. Unconsolidated
continued

£ million

			2002	2003	2004	2005	2006	2007	2008	2009	2010
III.2	**FINANCIAL ACCOUNT** continued										
F.L	**Net acquisition of financial liabilities**										
F.2	Currency and deposits	NFMG	476	−536	18	550	−12	4 299	11 361	7 866	−387
F.3	Securities other than shares										
F.331	Short term: money market instruments										
F.3316	Issued by UK residents other than monetary financial institutions and government	NFNB	267	−567	118	238	1 421	−1 235	−570	−1 781	−64
F.332	Medium (1 to 5 year) and long term (over 5 year) bonds										
F.3326	Other medium & long term bonds issued by UK residents institutions and government	NFNL	20 662	53 255	70 726	83 767	117 569	137 784	157 024	39 712	−17 131
F.3	Total securities other than shares	NFMP	20 929	52 688	70 844	84 005	118 990	136 549	156 454	37 931	−17 195
F.4	Loans										
F.41	Short term loans										
F.411	Sterling loans by UK MFIs	NFNT	28 423	61 532	67 212	54 931	115 945	195 401	93 350	−10 278	−3 802
F.4112	o/w Foreign currency loans	NFNV	16 548	40 304	33 834	16 585	60 688	86 043	−67 636	−8 600	37 448
F.419	Loans by rest of the world monetary financial institutions	NFNX	−34 727	31 085	81 096	224 344	−34 043	70 612	−274 446	359	92 461
F.42	Long term loans										
F.421	Direct investment	NFNZ	6 554	2 200	1 872	−7 370	−905	8 174	3 225	−4 369	1 991
F.423	Finance leasing	NFOG	136	104	95	71	81	79	64	60	60
F.424	Other long-term loans by UK residents	NFOH	−292	−6 416	795	17 150	38 739	−18 027	−14 501	−14 297	18 469
F.429	Other long-term loans by the rest of the world	NFOI	−21	−42	10	29	–	26	−55	−116	75
F.4	Total loans	NFNR	73	88 463	151 080	289 155	119 817	256 265	−192 363	−28 641	109 254
F.5	Shares and other equity										
F.51	Shares and other equity, excluding mutual funds' shares										
F.514	Quoted UK shares	NFOO	−809	10 711	7 490	6 799	14 905	4 468	54 708	87 383	9 660
F.515	Unquoted UK shares	NFOP	7 234	12 217	18 484	23 533	36 218	35 867	67 421	63 519	−9 713
F.517	UK shares and bonds issued by other UK residents	NSPK	–	–	–	–	–	–	–	–	–
F.52	Mutual funds' shares										
F.521	UK mutual funds' shares	NFOX	6 259	8 212	3 489	8 300	14 866	−2 204	−4 607	26 271	43 136
F.5	Total shares and other equity	NFOJ	12 684	31 140	29 463	38 632	65 989	38 131	117 522	177 173	43 083
F.7	Other accounts payable	NFPD	500	−614	−173	143	107	−996	−70	−85	−189
F.L	**Total net acquisition of financial liabilities**	NFMC	34 662	171 141	251 232	412 485	304 891	434 248	92 904	194 244	134 566
B.9	**Net lending / borrowing**										
F.A	Total net acquisition of financial assets	NFIY	43 106	181 086	189 483	339 680	232 260	397 691	180 566	198 536	108 655
-F.L	*less* Total net acquisition of financial liabilities	-NFMC	−34 662	−171 141	−251 232	−412 485	−304 891	−434 248	−92 904	−194 244	−134 566
B.9f	Net lending (+) / net borrowing (-), from financial account	NYNM	8 444	9 945	−61 749	−72 805	−72 631	−36 557	87 662	4 292	−25 911
dB.9f	Statistical discrepancy	NYOY	−19 168	−11 526	61 516	74 278	70 106	36 843	−82 641	−1 683	27 921
B.9	**Net lending (+) / net borrowing (-), from capital account**	NHLW	−10 724	−1 581	−233	1 473	−2 525	286	5 021	2 609	2 010

4.3.9 Other financial intermediaries and financial auxiliaries
ESA95 sectors S.123 and S.124. Unconsolidated

£ billion

			2002	2003	2004	2005	2006	2007	2008	2009	2010
IV.3	**FINANCIAL BALANCE SHEET** at end of period										
AF.A	**Financial assets**										
AF.2	Currency and deposits										
AF.21	Currency	NLPM	0.1	0.1	0.1	0.1	0.1	0.1	0.1	0.1	0.1
AF.22	Transferable deposits										
AF.221	Sterling deposits with UK MFIs	NLPO	222.1	247.9	284.3	385.8	483.9	606.4	881.9	909.5	1 000.1
AF.2212	o/w Foreign currency deposits	NLPQ	103.7	128.2	140.9	173.1	200.9	265.3	330.7	273.8	267.7
AF.229	Deposits with rest of the world monetary financial institutions	NLPS	248.5	296.2	324.8	506.9	514.8	570.7	380.1	364.2	429.3
AF.29	Other deposits	NLPT	1.8	0.8	2.2	3.5	1.5	3.7	11.5	16.9	10.5
AF.2	Total currency and deposits	NLPL	472.5	545.0	611.3	896.3	1 000.2	1 180.9	1 273.6	1 290.7	1 440.1
AF.3	Securities other than shares										
AF.331	Short term: money market instruments										
AF.3311	Issued by UK central government	NLPW	0.9	3.1	4.0	1.9	2.9	4.1	5.7	11.6	14.3
AF.3312	Issued by UK local government	NLQA	–	–	–	–	–	–	–	–	–
AF.3315	Issued by UK monetary financial institutions	NLQB	27.1	25.6	22.3	23.1	22.9	28.7	38.0	29.1	25.4
AF.3316	Issued by other UK residents	NLQG	0.9	0.7	1.2	1.0	1.6	2.3	0.2	0.3	0.7
AF.3319	Issued by the rest of the world	NLQH	5.6	7.8	8.5	7.5	10.5	7.6	4.6	7.3	7.8
AF.332	Medium (1 to 5 year) and long term (over 5 year) bonds										
AF.3321	Issued by UK central government	NLQJ	27.3	31.3	31.1	44.9	63.4	84.0	137.5	81.4	85.4
AF.3322	Issued by UK local government	NLQM	–	–	–	–	–	–	–	–	–
AF.3325	Medium term bonds issued by UK MFIs[1]	NLQN	5.0	8.2	10.2	13.8	16.6	23.2	28.3	31.1	30.4
AF.3326	Other medium & long term bonds issued by UK residents	NLQQ	56.0	69.7	79.5	89.9	97.0	92.0	70.9	98.6	95.2
AF.3329	Long term bonds issued by the rest of the world	NLQR	38.8	50.3	71.8	95.4	71.5	53.0	172.2	291.5	382.5
AF.34	Financial derivatives	JS3S	..	..	154.8	195.9	200.5	387.9	1 782.9	1 072.1	2 047.8
AF.3	Total securities other than shares	NLPU	161.5	196.7	383.4	473.3	487.0	682.8	2 240.3	1 622.9	2 689.4
AF.4	Loans										
AF.42	Long term loans										
AF.421	Direct investment	NLRE	7.1	11.3	18.4	20.7	17.4	19.7	20.6	32.4	31.6
AF.422	Loans secured on dwellings	NLRH	76.1	117.1	170.1	214.1	279.3	348.9	425.7	306.4	185.7
AF.423	Finance leasing	NLRL	21.8	22.5	23.2	23.8	24.5	25.1	25.6	26.1	26.6
AF.424	Other long-term loans by UK residents	NLRM	4.8	6.3	3.0	1.3	5.0	13.9	12.1	24.6	20.1
AF.4	Total loans	NLQW	109.8	157.2	214.8	259.8	326.2	407.6	484.1	389.5	264.0
AF.5	Shares and other equity										
AF.51	Shares and other equity, excluding mutual funds' shares										
AF.514	Quoted UK shares	NLRT	131.9	173.0	201.6	250.0	289.6	282.6	125.0	215.0	269.4
AF.515	Unquoted UK shares	NLRU	131.1	135.6	150.6	161.5	176.2	186.4	206.8	207.8	220.8
AF.517	UK shares and bonds issued by other UK residents	NSOH	–	–	–	–	–	–	–	–	–
AF.519	Shares and other equity issued by the rest of the world	NLRY	142.7	169.9	183.6	202.7	224.6	289.2	279.5	331.7	370.9
AF.52	Mutual funds' shares										
AF.521	UK mutual funds' shares	NLSC	2.4	2.9	3.2	4.2	4.6	4.5	2.7	3.5	4.4
AF.5	Total shares and other equity	NLRO	408.1	481.4	539.0	618.4	695.1	762.8	614.0	758.1	865.5
AF.6	Insurance technical reserves										
AF.62	Prepayments of insurance premiums and reserves for outstanding claims	NLSH	0.7	0.8	0.7	0.9	0.8	0.6	0.7	0.6	0.6
AF.7	Other accounts receivable	NLSI	11.4	11.9	12.4	13.1	13.2	15.2	16.5	17.9	19.2
AF.A	**Total financial assets**	NLPH	1 163.9	1 393.0	1 761.7	2 261.8	2 522.5	3 050.0	4 629.1	4 079.8	5 278.8

1 UK monetary financial institutions

4.3.9 Other financial intermediaries and financial auxiliaries
ESA95 sectors S.123 and S.124. Unconsolidated

continued £ billion

				2002	2003	2004	2005	2006	2007	2008	2009	2010
IV.3		**FINANCIAL BALANCE SHEET** continued at end of period										
AF.L		**Financial liabilities**										
	AF.2	Currency and deposits	NLSP	0.8	0.3	0.3	1.8	1.6	5.9	17.3	25.2	47.7
	AF.3 AF.331 AF.3316	Securities other than shares Short term: money market instruments Issued by UK residents other than monetary financial institutions and government	NLTK	21.1	19.4	11.4	11.6	13.0	12.6	12.0	10.7	10.9
	AF.332 AF.3326	Medium (1 to 5 year) and long term (over 5 year) bonds Other medium & long term bonds issued by UK residents institutions and government	NLTU	189.4	243.6	333.3	430.4	512.8	628.0	667.8	778.8	739.7
	AF.34	Financial derivatives	JS3T	..	..	157.9	203.3	214.8	405.4	1 767.2	1 038.4	2 009.1
	AF.3	Total securities other than shares	NLSY	210.5	263.1	502.6	645.4	740.6	1 046.0	2 447.0	1 827.9	2 759.7
	AF.4 AF.41 AF.411	Loans Short term loans Short-term loans by UK MFIs	NLUC	348.7	412.8	475.8	538.6	629.7	864.5	1 086.9	919.3	868.2
	AF.4112	o/w Foreign currency loans	NLUE	163.5	202.9	226.7	253.1	289.4	382.7	453.8	376.8	408.7
	AF.419	Loans by rest of the world monetary financial institutions	NLUG	357.8	384.3	456.2	695.3	616.3	706.0	590.1	558.5	662.8
	AF.42 AF.421	Long term loans Direct investment	NLUI	25.6	29.9	44.6	38.6	38.4	43.8	33.0	45.2	47.2
	AF.423	Finance leasing	NLUP	1.4	1.5	1.6	1.7	1.7	1.8	1.9	1.9	2.0
	AF.424	Other long-term loans by UK residents	NLUQ	32.0	32.2	35.5	47.8	67.7	69.8	101.0	88.9	173.7
	AF.429	Other long-term loans by the rest of the world	NLUR	0.5	0.5	0.5	0.5	0.5	0.5	0.5	0.5	0.5
	AF.4	Total loans	NLUA	765.9	861.2	1 014.1	1 322.4	1 354.3	1 686.3	1 813.3	1 614.3	1 754.3
	AF.5 AF.51 AF.514	Shares and other equity Shares and other equity, excluding mutual funds' shares Quoted UK shares	NLUX	215.6	274.2	303.7	341.0	399.2	353.4	177.1	342.6	368.0
	AF.515	Unquoted UK shares	NLUY	135.9	155.3	176.0	204.0	245.0	243.2	324.7	418.6	427.8
	AF.517	UK shares and bonds issued by other UK residents	NSOI	–	–	–	–	–	–	–	–	–
	AF.52 AF.521	Mutual funds' shares UK mutual funds' shares	NLVG	215.8	266.3	303.9	385.0	452.4	507.3	382.1	506.2	618.4
	AF.5	Total shares and other equity	NLUS	567.3	695.8	783.6	930.0	1 096.6	1 103.9	883.9	1 267.4	1 414.3
	AF.7	Other accounts payable	NLVM	1.8	2.3	2.2	2.1	2.5	0.6	0.3	2.7	2.4
AF.L		**Total financial liabilities**	NLSL	1 546.3	1 822.7	2 302.8	2 901.6	3 195.7	3 842.8	5 161.8	4 737.5	5 978.4
BF.90		**Net financial assets / liabilities**										
	AF.A	Total financial assets	NLPH	1 163.9	1 393.0	1 761.7	2 261.8	2 522.5	3 050.0	4 629.1	4 079.8	5 278.8
	-AF.L	*less* Total financial liabilities	-NLSL	-1 546.3	-1 822.7	-2 302.8	-2 901.6	-3 195.7	-3 842.8	-5 161.8	-4 737.5	-5 978.4
BF.90		**Net financial assets (+) / liabilities (-)**	NYOF	–382.4	–429.7	–541.1	–639.8	–673.1	–792.8	–532.7	–657.7	–699.6

4.4.2 Insurance corporations and pension funds
ESA95 sector S.125

£ million

			2002	2003	2004	2005	2006	2007	2008	2009
II	**DISTRIBUTION AND USE OF INCOME ACCOUNTS**									
II.1	**PRIMARY DISTRIBUTION OF INCOME ACCOUNT**									
II.1.1	**GENERATION OF INCOME ACCOUNT**									
	Resources									
B.1g	Total resources (Gross Value Added)	NRHH	13 660	16 112	16 086	13 870	16 580	18 178	12 622	17 918
	Uses									
D.1	Compensation of employees									
D.11	Wages and salaries	NHEJ	4 130	4 315	6 766	6 456	6 654	7 476	7 160	7 125
D.12	Employers' social contributions	NHEL	578	700	796	871	1 120	1 136	958	1 321
D.1	Total	NSCV	4 708	5 015	7 562	7 327	7 774	8 612	8 118	8 446
D.2	Taxes on production and imports, paid									
D.29	Production taxes other than on products	NHOS	337	346	349	365	384	395	491	519
-D.3	*less* Subsidies, received									
-D.39	Production subsidies other than on products	-NHNZ	–	–	–	–	–	–	–	–
B.2g	Operating surplus, gross	NHBZ	8 615	10 751	8 175	6 178	8 422	9 171	4 013	8 953
B.1g	**Total uses (Gross Value Added)**	NRHH	**13 660**	**16 112**	**16 086**	**13 870**	**16 580**	**18 178**	**12 622**	**17 918**

4.4.3 Insurance corporations and pension funds
ESA95 sector S.125

£ million

			2002	2003	2004	2005	2006	2007	2008	2009
II.1.2	**ALLOCATION OF PRIMARY INCOME ACCOUNT**									
	Resources									
B.2g	Operating surplus, gross	NHBZ	8 615	10 751	8 175	6 178	8 422	9 171	4 013	8 953
D.4	Property income, received									
D.41	Interest	NHOK	23 474	25 459	28 395	27 400	27 788	31 561	28 809	26 530
D.42	Distributed income of corporations	NHOL	21 729	20 513	21 903	24 302	27 113	28 588	30 585	27 281
D.43	Reinvested earnings on direct foreign investment	NHQM	–75	1 572	2 697	3 108	2 615	2 702	–2 217	–1 271
D.44	Property income attributed to insurance policy-holders	NHPG	18	24	21	34	31	18	21	20
D.45	Rent	NHPH	30	30	31	31	31	32	32	31
D.4	Total	NHPF	45 176	47 598	53 047	54 875	57 578	62 901	57 230	52 591
Total	Total resources	NRMN	53 791	58 349	61 222	61 053	66 000	72 072	61 243	61 544
	Uses									
D.4	Property income									
D.41	Interest	NHOM	995	940	1 384	1 936	2 471	2 924	2 777	1 382
D.42	Distributed income of corporations	NHON	2 801	3 144	4 258	3 920	5 306	6 911	4 885	4 237
D.43	Reinvested earnings on direct foreign investment	NHQO	–55	535	920	868	1 645	23	–479	133
D.44	Property income attributed to insurance policy-holders	NQCG	53 652	56 703	56 150	65 805	68 321	72 820	76 392	67 581
D.45	Rent	NHPK	–	–	–	–	–	–	–	–
D.4	Total	NHPI	57 393	61 322	62 712	72 529	77 743	82 678	83 575	73 333
B.5g	**Balance of primary incomes, gross**	NRMO	**–3 602**	**–2 973**	**–1 490**	**–11 476**	**–11 743**	**–10 606**	**–22 332**	**–11 789**
Total	Total uses	NRMN	53 791	58 349	61 222	61 053	66 000	72 072	61 243	61 544

4.4.4 Insurance corporations and pension funds
ESA95 sector S.125

£ million

				2002	2003	2004	2005	2006	2007	2008	2009	2010
II.2	**SECONDARY DISTRIBUTION OF INCOME ACCOUNT**											
	Resources											
B.5g	**Balance of primary incomes, gross**		NRMO	−3 602	−2 973	−1 490	−11 476	−11 743	−10 606	−22 332	−11 789	−5 715
D.61	Social contributions											
D.611	Actual social contributions											
D.6111	Employers' actual contributions		NSAR	26 025	32 504	35 807	41 635	46 093	44 516	40 754	47 608	57 292
D.6112	Employees social contributions		NSAS	32 967	32 158	31 238	36 107	38 868	39 346	43 679	39 528	40 551
D.6113	Social contributions by the self-employed		NSAT	–	–	–	–	–	–	–	–	–
D.611	Total		NSCN	58 992	64 662	67 045	77 742	84 961	83 862	84 433	87 136	97 843
D.612	Imputed social contributions		NHPR	125	120	98	90	77	77	83	84	77
D.61	Total		NRMP	59 117	64 782	67 143	77 832	85 038	83 939	84 516	87 220	97 920
D.7	Other current transfers											
D.71	Net non-life insurance premiums		NSCT	26 620	23 000	28 148	31 711	34 920	21 862	31 095	28 801	29 824
D.72	Non-life insurance claims		NHPN	320	346	366	417	418	219	312	288	298
D.7	Total		NRMR	26 940	23 346	28 514	32 128	35 338	22 081	31 407	29 089	30 122
Total	Total resources		NRMS	82 455	85 155	94 167	98 484	108 633	95 414	93 591	104 520	122 327
	Uses											
D.5	Current taxes on income, wealth, etc.											
D.51	Taxes on income		NHPO	−2 346	1 884	3 528	5 042	3 617	1 686	−4 987	2 796	2 803
D.62	Social benefits other than social transfers in kind											
D.622	Private funded social benefits		SBDW	41 209	43 289	40 669	46 916	55 626	45 028	56 593	60 630	62 748
D.623	Unfunded employee social benefits		NHPR	125	120	98	90	77	77	83	84	77
D.62	Total		NHPQ	41 334	43 409	40 767	47 006	55 703	45 105	56 676	60 714	62 825
D.7	Other current transfers											
D.71	Net non-life insurance premiums		NHPU	320	346	366	417	418	219	312	288	298
D.72	Non-life insurance claims		NSCS	26 620	23 000	28 148	31 711	34 920	21 862	31 095	28 801	29 824
D.75	Miscellaneous current transfers		NHQK	–	–	–	–	–	–	–	–	–
D.7	Total		NHPT	26 940	23 346	28 514	32 128	35 338	22 081	31 407	29 089	30 122
B.6g	**Gross Disposable Income**		NRMT	**16 527**	**16 516**	**21 358**	**14 308**	**13 975**	**26 542**	**10 495**	**11 921**	**26 577**
Total	Total uses		NRMS	82 455	85 155	94 167	98 484	108 633	95 414	93 591	104 520	122 327

4.4.6 Insurance corporations and pension funds
ESA95 sector S.125

£ million

				2002	2003	2004	2005	2006	2007	2008	2009	2010
II.4.1	**USE OF DISPOSABLE INCOME ACCOUNT**											
	Resources											
B.6g	**Total resources (Gross Disposable Income)**		NRMT	16 527	16 516	21 358	14 308	13 975	26 542	10 495	11 921	26 577
	Uses											
D.8	Adjustment for the change in net equity of households in pension funds		NRYH	17 783	21 373	26 375	30 826	29 334	38 834	27 840	26 506	35 095
B.8g	**Gross Saving**		NRMV	−1 256	−4 857	−5 017	−16 518	−15 359	−12 292	−17 345	−14 585	−8 518
B.6g	**Total uses (Gross Disposable Income)**		NRMT	16 527	16 516	21 358	14 308	13 975	26 542	10 495	11 921	26 577

4.4.7 Insurance corporations and pension funds
ESA95 sector S.125

£ million

			2002	2003	2004	2005	2006	2007	2008	2009	2010
III	**ACCUMULATION ACCOUNTS**										
III.1	**CAPITAL ACCOUNT**										
III.1.1	**CHANGE IN NET WORTH DUE TO SAVING & CAPITAL TRANSFERS**										
	Changes in liabilities and net worth										
B.8g	Gross Saving	NRMV	−1 256	−4 857	−5 017	−16 518	−15 359	−12 292	−17 345	−14 585	−8 518
D.9	Capital transfers receivable										
D.99	Other capital transfers	NHQB	412	391	328	321	446	388	218	176	67
D.9	Total	NHPZ	412	391	328	321	446	388	218	176	67
-D.9	*less* Capital transfers payable										
-D.99	Other capital transfers	-NHOB	−412	−391	−328	−321	−446	−388	−218	−176	−67
-D.9	Total	-NHQD	−412	−391	−328	−321	−446	−388	−218	−176	−67
B.10.1g	Total change in liabilities and net worth	NRYI	−1 256	−4 857	−5 017	−16 518	−15 359	−12 292	−17 345	−14 585	−8 518
	Changes in assets										
B.10.1g	Change in net worth due to saving and capital transfers before deduction of fixed capital consumption	NRYI	−1 256	−4 857	−5 017	−16 518	−15 359	−12 292	−17 345	−14 585	−8 518
III.1.2	**ACQUISITION OF NON-FINANCIAL ASSETS ACCOUNT**										
B.10.1g	Total changes in liabilities and net worth due to saving and capital transfers	NRYI	−1 256	−4 857	−5 017	−16 518	−15 359	−12 292	−17 345	−14 585	−8 518
	Changes in assets										
P.5	Gross capital formation										
P.51	Gross fixed capital formation	NHOJ	1 400	729	1 280	1 077	776	654	1 096	345	413
P.52	Changes in inventories	NHOI	5	5	7	5	12	13	−8	26	26
P.53	Acquisitions less disposals of valuables	NHQH	306	304	330	350	290	378	284	264	298
P.5	Total	NHQG	1 711	1 038	1 617	1 432	1 078	1 045	1 372	635	737
K.2	Acquisitions less disposals of non-produced non-financial assets	NHQI	−42	−14	−24	−21	−14	−16	−16	−12	−12
B.9	**Net lending (+) / net borrowing (-)**	NHOQ	**−2 925**	**−5 881**	**−6 610**	**−17 929**	**−16 423**	**−13 321**	**−18 701**	**−15 208**	**−9 243**
Total	Total change in assets	NRYI	−1 256	−4 857	−5 017	−16 518	−15 359	−12 292	−17 345	−14 585	−8 518

4.4.8 Insurance corporations and pension funds
ESA95 sector S.125. Unconsolidated

£ million

			2002	2003	2004	2005	2006	2007	2008	2009	2010
III.2	**FINANCIAL ACCOUNT**										
F.A	**Net acquisition of financial assets**										
F.2	Currency and deposits										
F.22	Transferable deposits										
F.221	Sterling deposits with UK monetary financial institutions	NBSJ	-2 930	58	6 250	-4 310	8 690	16 426	-3 223	-2 442	-16 261
F.2212	*of which* Foreign Currency Deposits	IE2X	-2 241	1 509	842	-786	2 384	790	625	-823	-1 084
F.229	Deposits with rest of the world monetary financial institutions	NBSN	1 497	7 626	8 185	5 593	7 279	11 691	4 436	-4 973	10 385
F.29	Other deposits	NBSO	–	–	–	–	–	–	–	–	–
F.2	Total currency and deposits	NBSG	-1 433	7 684	14 435	1 283	15 969	28 117	1 213	-7 415	-5 876
F.3	Securities other than shares										
F.331	Short term: money market instruments										
F.3311	Issued by UK central government	NBSR	266	-359	376	-537	224	-15	399	2 110	-1 976
F.3315	Issued by UK monetary financial institutions	NBSW	2 683	3 102	2 006	-1 703	4 208	1 528	-5 220	-13 208	-2 848
F.3316	Issued by other UK residents	NBTB	51	129	-1 493	3 614	-1 910	2 255	-1 479	-403	-1 654
F.3319	Issued by the rest of the world	NBTC	333	70	602	1 419	-556	154	697	-301	-74
F.332	Medium (1 to 5 year) and long term (over 5 year) bonds										
F.3321	Issued by UK central government	NBTE	3 237	19 771	20 060	27 118	25 488	-8 254	-13 118	9 684	12 647
F.3322	Issued by UK local government	NBTH	20	5	-100	139	230	-30	-10	-139	-27
F.3325	Issued by UK monetary financial institutions	NBTI	2 442	6 439	6 372	9 758	10 526	14 212	-2 726	16 084	3 445
F.3326	Other medium & long term bonds issued by UK residents	NBTL	21 745	14 128	11 837	842	4 601	985	28 194	-7 746	-10 959
F.3329	Long term bonds issued by the rest of the world	NBTM	4 829	996	4 056	6 241	22 244	35 563	17 057	16 103	9 643
F.34	Financial derivatives	JS3C	..	..	-524	-697	-1 168	-620	4 410	891	1 536
F.3	Total securities other than shares	NBSP	35 606	44 281	43 192	46 194	63 887	45 778	28 204	23 075	9 733
F.4	Loans										
F.42	Long term loans										
F.421	Direct investment	NBTZ	1 040	1 969	1 169	748	766	-1 486	1 502	1 196	1 015
F.422	Loans secured on dwellings	NBUC	-165	209	34	-428	-212	-3	778	840	223
F.424	Other long-term loans by UK residents	NBUH	562	5 029	7 768	9 276	4 284	-16 829	-4 488	-9 956	9 607
F.4	Total loans	NBTR	1 437	7 207	8 971	9 596	4 838	-18 318	-2 208	-7 920	10 845
F.5	Shares and other equity										
F.51	Shares and other equity, excluding mutual funds' shares										
F.514	Quoted UK shares	NBUO	-14 238	-19 588	-17 605	-52 397	-26 370	-33 826	-19 139	-22 967	-29 187
F.515	Unquoted UK shares	NBUP	321	-1 232	189	-887	-1 065	-658	-57	-113	88
F.517	UK shares and bonds issued by other UK residents	NSPC	–	–	–	–	–	–	–	–	–
F.519	Shares and other equity issued by the rest of the world	NBUT	19 519	2 511	16 089	31 419	10 382	11 899	-8 600	1 847	530
F.52	Mutual funds' shares										
F.521	UK mutual funds' shares	NBUX	3 321	881	287	11 652	12 090	11 552	4 978	7 798	34 685
F.5	Total shares and other equity	NBUJ	8 923	-17 428	-1 040	-10 213	-4 963	-11 033	-22 818	-13 435	6 116
F.6	Insurance technical reserves										
F.62	Prepayments of insurance premiums and reserves for outstanding claims	NBVC	22	10	-78	123	-70	-216	18	-20	14
F.7	Other accounts receivable	NBVD	15 259	7 977	3 770	2 766	40 815	-6 867	6 715	5 575	1 926
F.A	**Total net acquisition of financial assets**	NBSC	59 814	49 731	69 250	49 749	120 476	37 461	11 124	-140	22 758

4.4.8 Insurance corporations and pension funds
ESA95 sector S.125. Unconsolidated

continued

£ million

				2002	2003	2004	2005	2006	2007	2008	2009	2010
III.2	**FINANCIAL ACCOUNT** continued											
	F.L	**Net acquisition of financial liabilities**										
	F.3	Securities other than shares										
	F.332	Medium (1 to 5 year) and long term (over 5 year) bonds										
	F.3326	Other medium & long term bonds issued by UK residents institutions and government	NBWP	339	2 347	1 595	1 232	61	714	556	3 109	250
	F.3	Total securities other than shares	NBVT	339	2 347	1 595	1 232	61	714	556	3 109	250
	F.4	Loans										
	F.41	Short term loans										
	F.411	Loans by UK monetary financial institutions, excluding loans secured on dwellings & financial leasing	NBWX	–1 457	650	5 096	–1 990	658	409	–5 725	–1 874	–718
	F.419	Loans by rest of the world monetary financial institutions	ZMFP	1 654	3 551	5 258	456	8 618	–676	–64	–7 858	4 179
	F.42	Long term loans										
	F.421	Direct investment	NBXD	181	394	678	2 011	2 496	–745	–50	–83	–873
	F.424	Other long-term loans by UK residents	NBXL	2 766	10 774	4 917	7 693	1 815	–10 351	–7 509	–6 303	–2 090
	F.4	Total loans	NBWV	3 144	15 369	15 949	8 170	13 587	–11 363	–13 348	–16 118	498
	F.5	Shares and other equity										
	F.51	Shares and other equity, excluding mutual funds' shares										
	F.514	Quoted UK shares	NBXS	1 141	1 233	1 934	866	10 289	933	822	515	442
	F.515	Unquoted UK shares	NBXT	2 184	746	1 578	711	1 876	267	99	702	2 520
	F.5	Total shares and other equity	NBXN	3 325	1 979	3 512	1 577	12 165	1 200	921	1 217	2 962
	F.6	Insurance technical reserves										
	F.61	Net equity of households in life assurance and pension funds' reserves	NBYD	46 180	34 437	40 582	51 994	59 318	65 070	19 930	20 408	22 048
	F.62	Prepayments of insurance premiums and reserves for outstanding claims	NBYG	1 781	687	3 778	3 969	6 011	–6 075	1 754	–1 953	1 344
	F.6	Total insurance technical reserves	NPWC	47 961	35 124	44 360	55 963	65 329	58 995	21 684	18 455	23 392
	F.7	Other accounts payable	NBYH	7 269	660	8 026	1 981	34 411	–10 737	12 911	87	2 228
	F.L	**Total net acquisition of financial liabilities**	NBVG	62 038	55 479	73 442	68 923	125 553	38 809	22 724	6 750	29 330
	B.9	**Net lending / borrowing**										
	F.A	Total net acquisition of financial assets	NBSC	59 814	49 731	69 250	49 749	120 476	37 461	11 124	–140	22 758
	-F.L	*less* Total net acquisition of financial liabilities	-NBVG	–62 038	–55 479	–73 442	–68 923	–125 553	–38 809	–22 724	–6 750	–29 330
	B.9f	Net lending (+) / net borrowing (-), from financial account	NYNN	–2 224	–5 748	–4 192	–19 174	–5 077	–1 348	–11 600	–6 890	–6 572
	dB.9f	Statistical discrepancy	NYPB	–701	–133	–2 418	1 245	–11 346	–11 973	–7 101	–8 318	–2 671
	B.9	**Net lending (+) / net borrowing (-), from capital account**	NHOQ	**–2 925**	**–5 881**	**–6 610**	**–17 929**	**–16 423**	**–13 321**	**–18 701**	**–15 208**	**–9 243**

4.4.9 Insurance corporations and pension funds
ESA95 sector S.125. Unconsolidated

£ billion

IV.3 FINANCIAL BALANCE SHEET
at end of period

AF.A Financial assets

			2002	2003	2004	2005	2006	2007	2008	2009	2010
AF.2	Currency and deposits										
AF.22	Transferable deposits										
AF.221	Sterling deposits with UK monetary financial institutions	NIYG	59.7	57.4	64.4	59.8	67.6	84.4	82.1	89.7	73.2
AF.2212	*of which* Foreign currency deposits	IE2Y	3.3	4.8	5.6	4.8	7.2	8.0	8.6	7.8	6.7
AF.229	Deposits with rest of the world monetary financial institutions	NIYK	8.1	15.5	25.3	33.9	37.4	45.4	53.4	42.5	47.1
AF.29	Other deposits	NIYL	–	–	–	–	–	–	–	–	–
AF.2	Total currency and deposits	NIYD	67.9	72.9	89.7	93.7	104.9	129.8	135.5	132.3	120.3
AF.3	Securities other than shares										
AF.331	Short term: money market instruments										
AF.3311	Issued by UK central government	NIYO	0.8	0.5	1.0	0.4	0.7	0.6	1.0	3.2	1.2
AF.3315	Issued by UK monetary financial institutions	NIYT	21.5	24.6	26.6	24.9	29.1	30.6	25.4	12.4	9.6
AF.3316	Issued by other UK residents	NIYY	3.3	3.4	1.9	5.5	3.6	5.9	4.4	4.0	2.3
AF.3319	Issued by the rest of the world	NIYZ	1.4	1.5	2.1	3.5	3.0	3.1	3.8	4.0	3.9
AF.332	Medium (1 to 5 year) and long term (over 5 year) bonds										
AF.3321	Issued by UK central government	NIZB	184.3	202.4	224.6	231.0	241.1	240.7	238.2	250.4	295.5
AF.3322	Issued by UK local government	NIZE	0.5	0.4	0.3	0.4	0.5	0.3	0.2	0.5	0.6
AF.3325	Medium term bonds issued by UK monetary financial institutions	NIZF	13.7	23.1	29.1	39.5	47.9	67.5	82.6	91.0	88.4
AF.3326	Other medium & long term bonds issued by UK residents	NIZI	171.1	174.2	175.4	186.4	178.2	162.4	144.7	165.6	139.2
AF.3329	Long term bonds issued by the rest of the world	NIZJ	109.3	118.6	142.3	168.3	212.8	258.0	286.5	333.1	382.7
AF.34	Financial derivatives	JS3Q	..	..	32.0	27.9	25.0	48.8	148.5	96.6	86.5
AF.3	Total securities other than shares	NIYM	505.8	548.7	635.4	688.0	742.0	818.0	935.5	960.8	1 009.9
AF.4	Loans										
AF.42	Long term loans										
AF.421	Direct investment	NIZW	5.7	4.8	6.9	8.2	5.3	3.4	6.0	8.0	9.0
AF.422	Loans secured on dwellings	NIZZ	1.2	1.4	1.4	1.0	0.8	0.8	1.5	2.4	2.6
AF.424	Other long-term loans by UK residents	NJAE	51.4	65.1	84.7	86.3	107.3	111.0	93.3	101.6	140.5
AF.4	Total loans	NIZO	58.3	71.3	93.0	95.5	113.4	115.3	100.9	112.0	152.1
AF.5	Shares and other equity										
AF.51	Shares and other equity, excluding mutual funds' shares										
AF.514	Quoted UK shares	NJAL	397.7	443.3	467.8	486.0	493.6	470.5	295.8	351.9	362.0
AF.515	Unquoted UK shares	NJAM	7.7	6.7	4.5	5.2	2.9	4.1	4.7	4.9	5.9
AF.517	UK shares and bonds issued by other UK residents	NSOC	–	–	–	–	–	–	–	–	–
AF.519	Shares and other equity issued by the rest of the world	NJAQ	207.3	227.6	255.4	350.4	390.1	404.1	340.2	386.7	430.1
AF.52	Mutual funds' shares										
AF.521	UK mutual funds' shares	NJAU	103.1	142.0	159.8	237.6	279.7	335.9	300.2	397.8	467.5
AF.5	Total shares and other equity	NJAG	715.8	819.7	887.5	1 079.2	1 166.2	1 214.7	940.9	1 141.3	1 265.5
AF.6	Insurance technical reserves										
AF.62	Prepayments of insurance premiums and reserves for outstanding claims	NJAZ	0.8	0.9	0.9	1.0	0.9	0.7	0.7	0.7	0.7
AF.7	Other accounts receivable	NJBA	35.5	50.7	49.5	50.2	85.6	75.9	53.2	50.1	50.5
AF.A	Total financial assets	NIZN	1 384.0	1 564.2	1 756.0	2 007.5	2 213.1	2 354.3	2 166.7	2 397.2	2 599.1

4.4.9 Insurance corporations and pension funds
ESA95 sector S.125. Unconsolidated

£ billion

				2002	2003	2004	2005	2006	2007	2008	2009	2010
IV.3	**FINANCIAL BALANCE SHEET** continued at end of period											
AF.L	**Financial liabilities**											
AF.3	Securities other than shares											
AF.332	Medium (1 to 5 year) and long term (over 5 year) bonds											
AF.3326	Other medium & long term bonds issued by UK residents institutions and government		NJCM	0.1	0.3	0.6	0.3	0.8	1.7	2.0	0.8	0.8
AF.34	Financial derivatives		JS3R	..	..	32.6	29.0	26.8	51.0	147.2	93.6	83.6
AF.3	Total securities other than shares		NJBQ	0.1	0.3	33.2	29.3	27.6	52.7	149.2	94.3	84.4
AF.4	Loans											
AF.41	Short term loans											
AF.411	Loans by UK monetary financial institutions, excluding loans secured on dwellings & financial leasing		NJCU	8.5	9.1	14.2	12.3	12.9	13.3	7.6	5.7	5.0
AF.419	Loans by Rest of World monetary financial institutions		C657	10.1	14.5	19.7	21.4	31.4	31.0	37.8	28.1	31.9
AF.42	Long term loans											
AF.421	Direct investment		NJDA	7.6	7.9	8.6	10.4	11.7	11.0	10.4	8.7	7.8
AF.424	Other long-term loans by UK residents		NJDI	0.5	0.5	0.5	0.5	0.5	0.5	0.5	0.5	0.5
AF.4	Total loans		NJCS	26.7	32.0	43.0	44.5	56.5	55.7	56.3	43.0	45.2
AF.5	Shares and other equity											
AF.51	Shares and other equity, excluding mutual funds' shares											
AF.514	Quoted UK shares		NJDP	33.4	37.0	43.8	56.9	73.1	67.3	39.6	43.9	47.9
AF.515	Unquoted UK shares		NJDQ	11.7	13.6	9.8	9.9	18.4	13.4	17.6	14.4	17.8
AF.517	UK shares and bonds issued by other UK residents		NSOD	–	–	–	–	–	–	–	–	–
AF.5	Total shares and other equity		NJDK	45.1	50.6	53.6	66.9	91.5	80.7	57.2	58.3	65.8
AF.6	Insurance technical reserves											
AF.61	Net equity of households in life assurance and pension funds' reserves		NJEA	1 384.3	1 509.4	1 603.4	1 894.5	2 071.9	2 168.9	1 867.6	2 142.0	2 270.4
AF.62	Prepayments of insurance premiums and reserves for outstanding claims		NJED	62.8	63.5	67.2	71.2	77.2	71.1	72.9	70.9	72.3
AF.6	Total insurance technical reserves		NPXS	1 447.1	1 572.9	1 670.6	1 965.7	2 149.1	2 240.0	1 940.5	2 212.9	2 342.7
AF.7	Other accounts payable		NJEE	28.1	35.5	42.3	44.4	73.8	59.2	74.1	76.3	80.6
AF.L	**Total financial liabilities**		NJCR	1 547.1	1 691.3	1 842.7	2 150.8	2 398.5	2 488.4	2 277.2	2 484.9	2 618.5
BF.90	**Net financial assets / liabilities**											
AF.A	Total financial assets		NIZN	1 384.0	1 564.2	1 756.0	2 007.5	2 213.1	2 354.3	2 166.7	2 397.2	2 599.1
-AF.L	*less* Total financial liabilities		-NJCR	-1 547.1	-1 691.3	-1 842.7	-2 150.8	-2 398.5	-2 488.4	-2 277.2	-2 484.9	-2 618.5
BF.90	**Net financial assets (+) / liabilities (-)**		NYOI	-163.1	-127.1	-86.7	-143.3	-185.4	-134.1	-110.5	-87.7	-19.5

4.5 Financial derivatives: Gross positions of UK banks, securities dealers & other institutions by counterparty

£ million

	MFIs[1]		Other Financial[2]		Other UK[3]		Rest of World		
	Sterling	Other currencies	Sterling	Other currencies	Sterling	Other currencies	Sterling	Other currencies	Total
2003									
FINANCIAL BALANCE SHEET									
Assets									
UK banks[4]	40 068	155 012	21 256	101 044	9 185	4 983	44 141	579 275	954 964
Securities dealers[5]	6 201	19 410	9 367	17 133	511	474	10 640	144 041	207 777
Total	46 269	174 422	30 623	118 177	9 361	5 457	54 781	723 316	1 162 741
Liabilities									
UK banks[4]	28 991	164 651	20 418	100 278	6 023	7 812	32 391	600 008	960 572
Securities dealers[5]	8 048	23 431	13 619	18 402	540	244	13 971	149 960	228 215
Total	37 039	188 082	34 037	118 680	6 563	8 056	46 362	749 968	1 188 787

	UK	Rest of World	Total
2003			
FINANCIAL BALANCE SHEET			
Assets			
Insurance[6]	4 445	204	4 649
Pension Funds[7]	3 089	561	3 650
Insurance and Pension Funds Total	7 534	765	8 299
Other Financial Intermediaries[8]	5 253	1 136	6 389
Total	12 787	1 901	14 688
Liabilities			
Insurance[6]	877	215	1 092
Pension Funds[7]	1 817	437	2 254
Insurance and Pension Funds Total	2 694	652	3 346
Other Financial Intermediaries[8]	3 540	700	4 240
Total	6 234	1 352	7 586

Source: ONS, Bank of England and Financial Services Authority

KEY:

These data are not included in the aggregates shown in the main tables. From 2010, ONS has improved it's data collection of financial derivatives and the new data has been incorporated into the main tables. Table 4.5 will therefore be removed from Blue Book 2012.

1 MFIs = Monetary financial institutions covers banks and building societies.
2 Other Financial = Other financial institutions and insurance corporations and pension funds.
3 Other UK = Government, private and public non-financial corporations and households.
4 UK banks = Collected by the Bank of England.
5 Securities dealers = Collected by ONS.
6 Insurance = Includes both general and long-term insurance, and are collected by ONS.
7 Pension Funds = Relates to self administered pension funds only, and are collected by ONS.
8 Other Financial Intermediaries = This does not include securities dealers (see above), includes unit trusts, investment trusts, OEICS, finance leasing, credit grantors and factoring companies all collected by ONS. This also includes Building Societies data collected by the Financial Services Authority.

Further information about the data on financial derivatives collected by ONS, including transactions, can be obtained from an article in the May 2005 edition of Economic Trends.

4.5 Financial derivatives: Gross positions of UK banks, securities dealers & other institutions by counterparty
continued

£ million

	MFIs[1]		Other Financial[2]		Other UK[3]		Rest of World		
	Sterling	Other currencies	Sterling	Other currencies	Sterling	Other currencies	Sterling	Other currencies	Total
2004									
FINANCIAL BALANCE SHEET									
Assets									
UK banks[4]	37 727	207 204	35 908	154 678	10 469	4 755	46 078	663 302	1 160 121
Securities dealers[5]	11 669	54 662	7 350	13 764	507	347	11 485	104 670	204 454
Total	49 396	261 866	43 258	168 442	10 976	5 102	57 563	767 972	1 364 575
Liabilities									
UK banks[4]	27 833	223 191	34 316	152 452	6 506	7 695	36 268	678 753	1 167 014
Securities dealers[5]	17 958	61 129	8 642	11 592	712	517	14 034	112 155	226 739
Total	45 791	284 320	42 958	164 044	7 218	8 212	50 302	790 908	1 393 753

	UK	Rest of World	Total
2004			
FINANCIAL BALANCE SHEET			
Assets			
Insurance[6]	3 862	3	3 865
Pension Funds[7]	10 235	2 962	13 197
Insurance and Pension Funds Total	14 097	2 965	17 062
Other Financial Intermediaries[8]	3 490	408	3 898
Total	17 587	3 373	20 960
Liabilities			
Insurance[6]	692	141	833
Pension Funds[7]	7 873	3 082	10 955
Insurance and Pension Funds Total	8 565	3 223	11 788
Other Financial Intermediaries[8]	2 641	137	2 778
Total	11 206	3 360	14 566

Source: ONS, Bank of England and Financial Services Authority

KEY:

These data are not included in the aggregates shown in the main tables. From 2010, ONS has improved it's data collection of financial derivatives and the new data has been incorporated into the main tables. Table 4.5 will therefore be removed from Blue Book 2012.

1 MFIs = Monetary financial institutions covers banks and building societies.
2 Other Financial = Other financial institutions and insurance corporations and pension funds.
3 Other UK = Government, private and public non-financial corporations and households.
4 UK banks = Collected by the Bank of England.
5 Securities dealers = Collected by ONS.
6 Insurance = Includes both general and long-term insurance, and are collected by ONS.
7 Pension Funds = Relates to self administered pension funds only, and are collected by ONS.
8 Other Financial Intermediaries = This does not include securities dealers (see above), includes unit trusts, investment trusts, OEICS, finance leasing, credit grantors and factoring companies all collected by ONS. This also includes Building Societies data collected by the Financial Services Authority.

Further information about the data on financial derivatives collected by ONS, including transactions, can be obtained from an article in the May 2005 edition of Economic Trends.

4.5 Financial derivatives: Gross positions of UK banks, securities dealers & other institutions by counterparty
continued

£ million

	MFIs[1]		Other Financial[2]		Other UK[3]		Rest of World		
	Sterling	Other currencies	Sterling	Other currencies	Sterling	Other currencies	Sterling	Other currencies	Total
2005									
FINANCIAL BALANCE SHEET									
Assets									
UK banks[4]	51 702	262 038	36 522	195 784	14 750	7 762	51 327	768 752	1 388 637
Securities dealers[5]	11 869	102 410	6 509	20 674	1 048	1 168	15 002	186 531	345 211
Total	63 571	364 448	43 031	216 458	15 798	8 930	66 329	955 283	1 733 848
Liabilities									
UK banks[4]	59 243	272 352	30 422	193 338	10 667	8 666	66 286	764 817	1 405 791
Securities dealers[5]	24 491	119 426	12 739	18 797	1 368	11 487	18 190	183 147	389 645
Total	83 734	391 778	43 161	212 135	12 035	20 153	84 476	947 964	1 795 436

	UK	Rest of World	Total
2005			
FINANCIAL BALANCE SHEET			
Assets			
Insurance[6]	5 830	–47	5 783
Pension Funds[7]	22 157	2 668	24 825
Insurance and Pension Funds Total	27 987	2 621	30 608
Other Financial Intermediaries[8]	6 141	538	6 679
Total	34 128	3 159	37 287
Liabilities			
Insurance[6]	773	12	785
Pension Funds[7]	16 818	2 785	19 603
Insurance and Pension Funds Total	17 591	2 797	20 388
Other Financial Intermediaries[8]	3 815	111	3 926
Total	21 406	2 908	24 314

Source: ONS, Bank of England and Financial Services Authority

KEY:

These data are not included in the aggregates shown in the main tables. From 2010, ONS has improved it's data collection of financial derivatives and the new data has been incorporated into the main tables. Table 4.5 will therefore be removed from Blue Book 2012.

1 MFIs = Monetary financial institutions covers banks and building societies.
2 Other Financial = Other financial institutions and insurance corporations and pension funds.
3 Other UK = Government, private and public non-financial corporations and households.
4 UK banks = Collected by the Bank of England.
5 Securities dealers = Collected by ONS.
6 Insurance = Includes both general and long-term insurance, and are collected by ONS.
7 Pension Funds = Relates to self administered pension funds only, and are collected by ONS.
8 Other Financial Intermediaries = This does not include securities dealers (see above), includes unit trusts, investment trusts, OEICS, finance leasing, credit grantors and factoring companies all collected by ONS. This also includes Building Societies data collected by the Financial Services Authority.

Further information about the data on financial derivatives collected by ONS, including transactions, can be obtained from an article in the May 2005 edition of Economic Trends.

4.5 continued Financial derivatives: Gross positions of UK banks, securities dealers & other institutions by counterparty

£ million

	MFIs[1]		Other Financial[2]		Other UK[3]		Rest of World		
	Sterling	Other currencies	Sterling	Other currencies	Sterling	Other currencies	Sterling	Other currencies	Total
2006									
FINANCIAL BALANCE SHEET									
Assets									
UK banks[4]	65 931	281 076	44 398	197 161	18 263	5 570	62 865	790 853	1 466 117
Securities dealers[5]	16 415	45 918	19 134	33 419	2 630	2 111	28 596	234 529	382 752
Total	82 346	326 994	63 532	230 580	20 893	7 681	91 461	1 025 382	1 848 869
Liabilities									
UK banks[4]	61 786	299 782	30 659	194 813	11 620	8 840	62 364	828 112	1 497 976
Securities dealers[5]	23 552	85 572	13 407	28 463	1 676	2 884	23 625	234 353	413 532
Total	85 338	385 354	44 066	223 276	13 296	11 724	85 989	1 062 465	1 911 508

	UK	Rest of World	Total
2006			
FINANCIAL BALANCE SHEET			
Assets			
Insurance[6]	5 957	25	5 982
Pension Funds[7]	24 357	5 995	30 352
Insurance and Pension Funds Total	30 314	6 020	36 334
Other Financial Intermediaries[8]	6 030	156	6 186
Total	36 344	6 176	42 520
Liabilities			
Insurance[6]	2 932	−10	2 922
Pension Funds[7]	17 231	7 036	24 267
Insurance and Pension Funds Total	20 163	7 026	27 189
Other Financial Intermediaries[8]	5 003	23	5 026
Total	25 166	7 049	32 215

Source: ONS, Bank of England and Financial Services Authority

KEY:

These data are not included in the aggregates shown in the main tables. From 2010, ONS has improved it's data collection of financial derivatives and the new data has been incorporated into the main tables. Table 4.5 will therefore be removed from Blue Book 2012.

1 MFIs = Monetary financial institutions covers banks and building societies.
2 Other Financial = Other financial institutions and insurance corporations and pension funds.
3 Other UK = Government, private and public non-financial corporations and households.
4 UK banks = Collected by the Bank of England.
5 Securities dealers = Collected by ONS.
6 Insurance = Includes both general and long-term insurance, and are collected by ONS.
7 Pension Funds = Relates to self administered pension funds only, and are collected by ONS.
8 Other Financial Intermediaries = This does not include securities dealers (see above), includes unit trusts, investment trusts, OEICS, finance leasing, credit grantors and factoring companies all collected by ONS. This also includes Building Societies data collected by the Financial Services Authority.

Further information about the data on financial derivatives collected by ONS, including transactions, can be obtained from an article in the May 2005 edition of Economic Trends.

4.5 Financial derivatives: Gross positions of UK banks, securities dealers & other institutions by counterparty
continued

£ million

	MFIs[1]		Other Financial[2]		Other UK[3]		Rest of World		
	Sterling	Other currencies	Sterling	Other currencies	Sterling	Other currencies	Sterling	Other currencies	Total
2007									
FINANCIAL BALANCE SHEET									
Assets									
UK banks[4]	55 109	443 358	62 808	393 583	14 910	8 848	84 155	1 293 991	2 356 762
Securities dealers[5]	18 836	128 945	12 440	35 816	10 569	33 800	38 623	400 621	679 650
Total	73 945	572 303	75 248	429 399	25 479	42 648	122 778	1 694 612	3 036 412
Liabilities									
UK banks[4]	65 472	442 702	73 625	363 075	10 126	10 560	82 261	1 309 945	2 357 766
Securities dealers[5]	37 350	160 787	23 571	37 011	5 875	44 516	40 171	392 473	741 754
Total	102 822	603 489	97 196	400 086	16 001	55 076	122 432	1 702 418	3 099 520

	UK	Rest of World	Total
2007			
FINANCIAL BALANCE SHEET			
Assets			
Insurance[6]	5 139	274	5 413
Pension Funds[7]	29 789	8 652	38 441
Insurance and Pension Funds Total	34 928	8 926	43 854
Other Financial Intermediaries[8]	7 458	1 895	9 353
Total	42 386	10 821	53 207
Liabilities			
Insurance[6]	2 080	352	2 432
Pension Funds[7]	26 187	11 275	37 462
Insurance and Pension Funds Total	28 267	11 627	39 894
Other Financial Intermediaries[8]	6 327	1 819	8 146
Total	34 594	13 446	48 040

Source: ONS, Bank of England and Financial Services Authority

KEY:

These data are not included in the aggregates shown in the main tables. From 2010, ONS has improved it's data collection of financial derivatives and the new data has been incorporated into the main tables. Table 4.5 will therefore be removed from Blue Book 2012.

1 MFIs = Monetary financial institutions covers banks and building societies.
2 Other Financial = Other financial institutions and insurance corporations and pension funds.
3 Other UK = Government, private and public non-financial corporations and households.
4 UK banks = Collected by the Bank of England.
5 Securities dealers = Collected by ONS.
6 Insurance = Includes both general and long-term insurance, and are collected by ONS.
7 Pension Funds = Relates to self administered pension funds only, and are collected by ONS.
8 Other Financial Intermediaries = This does not include securities dealers (see above), includes unit trusts, investment trusts, OEICS, finance leasing, credit grantors and factoring companies all collected by ONS. This also includes Building Societies data collected by the Financial Services Authority.

Further information about the data on financial derivatives collected by ONS, including transactions, can be obtained from an article in the May 2005 edition of Economic Trends.

4.5 Financial derivatives: Gross positions of UK banks, securities dealers & other institutions by counterparty
continued

£ million

	MFIs[1]		Other Financial[2]		Other UK[3]		Rest of World		
	Sterling	Other currencies	Sterling	Other currencies	Sterling	Other currencies	Sterling	Other currencies	Total
2008									
FINANCIAL BALANCE SHEET									
Assets									
UK banks[4]	173 397	1 442 731	207 240	1 707 147	32 472	24 990	180 246	3 859 947	7 628 170
Securities dealers[5]	44 732	314 466	21 383	43 453	24 304	127 093	83 676	849 376	1 508 483
Total	218 129	1 757 197	228 623	1 750 600	56 776	152 083	263 922	4 709 323	9 136 653
Liabilities									
UK banks[4]	205 601	1 412 019	259 880	1 671 593	32 170	18 888	258 247	3 657 029	7 515 427
Securities dealers[5]	75 303	325 083	44 209	43 375	19 855	143 452	86 332	740 752	1 478 361
Total	280 904	1 737 102	304 089	1 714 968	52 025	162 340	344 579	4 397 781	8 993 788

	UK	Rest of World	Total
2008			
FINANCIAL BALANCE SHEET			
Assets			
Insurance[6]	16 451	2 126	18 577
Pension Funds[7]	35 194	5 835	41 029
Insurance and Pension Funds Total	51 645	7 961	59 606
Other Financial Intermediaries[8]	14 721	2 610	17 331
Total	66 366	10 571	76 937
Liabilities			
Insurance[6]	10 210	2 301	12 511
Pension Funds[7]	27 533	6 335	33 868
Insurance and Pension Funds Total	37 743	8 636	46 379
Other Financial Intermediaries[8]	11 389	2 227	13 616
Total	49 132	10 863	59 995

Source: ONS, Bank of England and Financial Services Authority

KEY:

These data are not included in the aggregates shown in the main tables. From 2010, ONS has improved it's data collection of financial derivatives and the new data has been incorporated into the main tables. Table 4.5 will therefore be removed from Blue Book 2012.

1 MFIs = Monetary financial institutions covers banks and building societies.
2 Other Financial = Other financial institutions and insurance corporations and pension funds.
3 Other UK = Government, private and public non-financial corporations and households.
4 UK banks = Collected by the Bank of England.
5 Securities dealers = Collected by ONS.
6 Insurance = Includes both general and long-term insurance, and are collected by ONS.
7 Pension Funds = Relates to self administered pension funds only, and are collected by ONS.
8 Other Financial Intermediaries = This does not include securities dealers (see above), includes unit trusts, investment trusts, OEICS, finance leasing, credit grantors and factoring companies all collected by ONS. This also includes Building Societies data collected by the Financial Services Authority.

Further information about the data on financial derivatives collected by ONS, including transactions, can be obtained from an article in the May 2005 edition of Economic Trends.

4.5 Financial derivatives: Gross positions of UK banks, securities dealers & other institutions by counterparty
continued

£ million

	MFIs[1]		Other Financial[2]		Other UK[3]		Rest of World		
	Sterling	Other currencies	Sterling	Other currencies	Sterling	Other currencies	Sterling	Other currencies	Total
2009									
FINANCIAL BALANCE SHEET									
Assets									
UK banks[4]	110 814	625 374	125 952	1 006 023	25 880	11 679	111 986	2 064 400	4 082 108
Securities dealers[5]	24 720	175 441	10 454	40 716	4 810	62 073	35 731	456 859	810 804
Total	135 534	800 815	136 406	1 046 739	30 690	73 752	147 717	2 521 259	4 892 912
Liabilities									
UK banks[4]	118 765	611 330	136 453	1 032 190	18 650	10 776	124 784	1 972 028	4 024 976
Securities dealers[5]	45 572	197 786	21 996	38 580	4 882	63 423	38 948	414 276	825 463
Total	164 337	809 116	158 449	1 070 770	23 532	74 199	163 732	2 386 304	4 850 439

	UK	Rest of World	Total
2009			
FINANCIAL BALANCE SHEET			
Assets			
Insurance[6]	8 517	2 255	10 772
Pension Funds[7]	61 862	20 534	82 396
Insurance and Pension Funds Total	70 379	22 789	93 168
Other Financial Intermediaries[8]	17 611	2 591	20 202
Total	87 990	25 380	113 370
Liabilities			
Insurance[6]	7 161	1 080	8 241
Pension Funds[7]	37 689	41 110	78 799
Insurance and Pension Funds Total	44 850	42 190	87 040
Other Financial Intermediaries[8]	13 499	3 198	16 697
Total	58 349	45 388	103 737

Source: ONS, Bank of England and Financial Services Authority

KEY:

These data are not included in the aggregates shown in the main tables. From 2010, ONS has improved it's data collection of financial derivatives and the new data has been incorporated into the main tables. Table 4.5 will therefore be removed from Blue Book 2012.

1 MFIs = Monetary financial institutions covers banks and building societies.
2 Other Financial = Other financial institutions and insurance corporations and pension funds.
3 Other UK = Government, private and public non-financial corporations and households.
4 UK banks = Collected by the Bank of England.
5 Securities dealers = Collected by ONS.
6 Insurance = Includes both general and long-term insurance, and are collected by ONS.
7 Pension Funds = Relates to self administered pension funds only, and are collected by ONS.
8 Other Financial Intermediaries = This does not include securities dealers (see above), includes unit trusts, investment trusts, OEICS, finance leasing, credit grantors and factoring companies all collected by ONS. This also includes Building Societies data collected by the Financial Services Authority.

Further information about the data on financial derivatives collected by ONS, including transactions, can be obtained from an article in the May 2005 edition of Economic Trends.

Chapter 5

General government

5.1.1 General government
ESA95 sector S.13 Unconsolidated

£ million

				2002	2003	2004	2005	2006	2007	2008	2009
I	**PRODUCTION ACCOUNT**										
	Resources										
P.1	Output										
P.11	Market output		NMXJ	19 464	20 780	26 510	30 631	32 699	34 835	35 850	38 834
P.12	Output for own final use		NMXK	424	447	428	371	462	442	401	404
P.13	Other non-market output		NMYK	212 556	232 611	250 928	268 273	285 126	295 154	315 566	327 349
P.1	Total resources		NMXL	232 444	253 838	277 866	299 275	318 287	330 431	351 817	366 587
	Uses										
P.2	Intermediate consumption		NMXM	111 206	121 210	134 636	145 922	156 447	163 475	180 185	189 605
B.1g	**Gross Value Added**		NMXN	**121 238**	**132 628**	**143 230**	**153 353**	**161 840**	**166 956**	**171 632**	**176 982**
Total	Total uses		NMXL	232 444	253 838	277 866	299 275	318 287	330 431	351 817	366 587
B.1g	**Gross Value Added**		NMXN	**121 238**	**132 628**	**143 230**	**153 353**	**161 840**	**166 956**	**171 632**	**176 982**
K.1	*less* Consumption of fixed capital		-NMXO	–10 289	–10 807	–11 312	–11 927	–12 634	–13 231	–13 963	–14 675
B.1n	Value added, net of fixed capital consumption		NMXP	110 949	121 821	131 918	141 426	149 206	153 725	157 669	162 307

5.1.2 General government
ESA95 sector S.13 Unconsolidated

£ million

				2002	2003	2004	2005	2006	2007	2008	2009
II	**DISTRIBUTION AND USE OF INCOME ACCOUNTS**										
II.1	**PRIMARY DISTRIBUTION OF INCOME ACCOUNT**										
II.1.1	**GENERATION OF INCOME ACCOUNT**										
	Resources										
B.1g	**Total resources (Gross Value Added)**		NMXN	**121 238**	**132 628**	**143 230**	**153 353**	**161 840**	**166 956**	**171 632**	**176 982**
	Uses										
D.1	Compensation of employees										
D.11	Wages and salaries		NMXQ	90 952	100 671	107 883	114 578	120 718	122 863	124 934	127 294
D.12	Employers' social contributions		NMXR	19 997	21 150	24 035	26 848	28 488	30 862	32 735	35 013
D.1	Total		NMXS	110 949	121 821	131 918	141 426	149 206	153 725	157 669	162 307
D.2	Taxes on production and imports, paid										
D.29	Production taxes other than on products		NMXT	–	–	–	–	–	–	–	–
D.3	*less* Subsidies, received										
D.39	Production subsidies other than on products		-NMXU	–	–	–	–	–	–	–	–
B.2g	Operating surplus, gross		NMXV	10 289	10 807	11 312	11 927	12 634	13 231	13 963	14 675
B.1g	**Total uses (Gross Value Added)**		NMXN	**121 238**	**132 628**	**143 230**	**153 353**	**161 840**	**166 956**	**171 632**	**176 982**
K.1	After deduction of fixed capital consumption		-NMXO	–10 289	–10 807	–11 312	–11 927	–12 634	–13 231	–13 963	–14 675
B.2n	Operating surplus, net		NMXW	–	–	–	–	–	–	–	–

5.1.3 General government
ESA95 sector S.13 Unconsolidated

£ million

			2002	2003	2004	2005	2006	2007	2008	2009	2010
II.1.2	**ALLOCATION OF PRIMARY INCOME ACCOUNT**										
	Resources										
B.2g	Operating surplus, gross	NMXV	10 289	10 807	11 312	11 927	12 634	13 231	13 963	14 675	15 500
D.2	Taxes on production and imports, received										
D.21	Taxes on products										
D.211	Value added tax (VAT)	NZGF	68 251	74 595	79 755	81 426	85 591	89 698	89 682	78 307	93 711
D.212	Taxes and duties on imports excluding VAT										
D.2121	Import duties	NMXZ	–	–	–	–	–	–	–	–	–
D.2122	Taxes on imports excluding VAT and import duties	NMBT	–	–	–	–	–	–	–	–	–
D.214	Taxes on products excluding VAT and import duties	NMYB	52 002	52 858	56 138	56 906	60 536	64 374	60 550	60 084	65 001
D.21	Total taxes on products	NVCC	120 253	127 453	135 893	138 332	146 127	154 072	150 232	138 391	158 712
D.29	Other taxes on production	NMYD	18 113	18 517	18 853	19 706	20 831	21 532	23 069	24 194	27 931
D.2	Total taxes on production and imports, received	NMYE	138 366	145 970	154 746	158 038	166 958	175 604	173 301	162 585	186 643
-D.3	*less* Subsidies, paid										
-D.31	Subsidies on products	-NMYF	–4 674	–5 311	–5 126	–5 182	–5 966	–5 609	–5 152	–5 707	–6 564
-D.39	Other subsidies on production	-LIUF	–954	–1 434	–1 562	–2 449	–3 093	–3 486	–3 381	–3 313	–3 223
-D.3	Total	-NMRL	–5 628	–6 745	–6 688	–7 631	–9 059	–9 095	–8 533	–9 020	–9 787
D.4	Property income, received										
D.41	Total Interest	NMYL	6 683	7 131	6 838	6 471	7 465	8 544	10 166	7 626	5 846
D.42	Distributed income of corporations	NMYM	3 290	3 027	2 794	2 900	2 566	3 118	3 305	2 214	1 245
D.44	Property income attributed to insurance policy holders	NMYO	18	19	19	27	25	20	24	24	20
D.45	Rent from sectors other than general government	NMYR	1 901	1 565	1 182	1 229	1 226	1 233	1 164	1 174	1 172
D.4	Total	NMYU	11 892	11 742	10 833	10 627	11 282	12 915	14 659	11 038	8 283
Total	Total resources	NMYV	154 919	161 774	170 203	172 961	181 815	192 655	193 390	179 278	200 639
	Uses										
D.4	Property income, paid										
D.41	Total interest	NRKB	25 410	26 913	26 973	29 376	30 976	34 792	36 501	30 173	45 316
D.4	Total	NMYY	25 410	26 913	26 973	29 376	30 976	34 792	36 501	30 173	45 316
B.5g	**Balance of primary incomes, gross**	NMZH	**129 509**	**134 861**	**143 230**	**143 585**	**150 839**	**157 863**	**156 889**	**149 105**	**155 323**
Total	Total uses	NMYV	154 919	161 774	170 203	172 961	181 815	192 655	193 390	179 278	200 639
K.1	After deduction of fixed capital consumption	-NMXO	–10 289	–10 807	–11 312	–11 927	–12 634	–13 231	–13 963	–14 675	–15 500
B.5n	Balance of primary incomes, net	NMZI	119 220	124 054	131 918	131 658	138 205	144 632	142 926	134 430	139 823

5.1.4 General government
ESA95 sector S.13 Unconsolidated

£ million

			2002	2003	2004	2005	2006	2007	2008	2009	2010
II.2	**SECONDARY DISTRIBUTION OF INCOME ACCOUNT**										
	Resources										
B.5g	Balance of primary incomes, gross	NMZH	129 509	134 861	143 230	143 585	150 839	157 863	156 889	149 105	155 323
D.5	Current taxes on income, wealth, etc.										
D.51	Taxes on income	NMZJ	142 842	144 234	154 127	172 498	192 600	199 851	207 597	185 160	191 342
D.59	Other current taxes	NVCM	23 664	26 016	28 001	29 443	30 908	32 697	34 032	34 888	35 847
D.5	Total	NMZL	166 506	170 250	182 128	201 941	223 508	232 548	241 629	220 048	227 189
D.61	Social contributions										
D.611	Actual social contributions										
D.6111	Employers' actual social contributions	NMZM	38 780	45 067	49 490	52 852	56 040	60 736	64 924	63 507	65 874
D.6112	Employees' social contributions	NMZN	29 568	34 376	39 062	41 836	44 391	44 091	45 570	44 072	45 406
D.6113	Social contributions by self- and non-employed persons	NMZO	2 318	2 595	2 727	2 825	2 930	2 861	3 053	2 879	2 576
D.611	Total	NMZP	70 666	82 038	91 279	97 513	103 361	107 688	113 547	110 458	113 856
D.612	Imputed social contributions	NMZQ	8 348	6 456	6 218	7 383	7 289	7 894	7 911	8 741	9 589
D.61	Total	NMZR	79 014	88 494	97 497	104 896	110 650	115 582	121 458	119 199	123 445
D.7	Other current transfers										
D.72	Non-life insurance claims	NMZS	320	276	338	328	349	262	374	345	359
D.73	Current transfers within general government	NMZT	77 592	85 224	94 720	101 369	110 407	113 108	117 867	124 622	132 444
D.74	Current international cooperation	NMZU	3 112	3 570	3 673	3 726	3 674	3 684	4 996	5 522	3 179
D.75	Miscellaneous current transfers from sectors other than general government	NMZX	502	562	721	728	606	556	508	515	597
D.7	Other current transfers	NNAA	81 526	89 632	99 452	106 151	115 036	117 610	123 745	131 004	136 579
Total	Total resources	NNAB	456 555	483 237	522 307	556 573	600 033	623 603	643 721	619 356	642 536
	Uses										
D.59	Other current taxes	EBFQ	876	842	924	1 022	1 075	1 111	1 147	1 189	1 236
D.62	Social benefits other than social transfers in kind	NNAD	136 801	146 066	154 313	161 422	167 045	178 407	190 187	210 806	220 725
D.7	Other current transfers										
D.71	Net non-life insurance premiums	NNAE	320	276	338	328	349	262	374	345	359
D.73	Current transfers within general government	NNAF	77 592	85 224	94 720	101 369	110 407	113 108	117 867	124 622	132 444
D.74	Current international cooperation	NNAG	2 362	2 433	3 080	3 255	3 632	3 930	4 292	5 011	5 683
D.75	Miscellaneous current transfers to sectors other than general government	NNAI	27 351	30 275	31 178	34 355	34 695	35 878	36 301	40 364	42 419
	Of which: GNP based fourth own resource	NMFH	5 335	6 772	7 549	8 732	8 521	8 323	8 423	10 555	10 819
D.7	Other current transfers	NNAN	107 625	118 208	129 316	139 307	149 083	153 178	158 834	170 342	180 905
B.6g	**Gross Disposable Income**	**NNAO**	**211 253**	**218 121**	**237 754**	**254 822**	**282 830**	**290 907**	**293 553**	**237 019**	**239 670**
Total	Total uses	NNAB	456 555	483 237	522 307	556 573	600 033	623 603	643 721	619 356	642 536
K.1	After deduction of fixed capital consumption	-NMXO	–10 289	–10 807	–11 312	–11 927	–12 634	–13 231	–13 963	–14 675	–15 500
B.6n	Disposable income, net	NNAP	200 964	207 314	226 442	242 895	270 196	277 676	279 590	222 344	224 170

5.1.5 General government
ESA95 sector S.13 Unconsolidated

£ million

			2002	2003	2004	2005	2006	2007	2008	2009	2010
II.3	**REDISTRIBUTION OF INCOME IN KIND ACCOUNT**										
	Resources										
B.6g	Total resources (Gross Disposable Income)	NNAO	211 253	218 121	237 754	254 822	282 830	290 907	293 553	237 019	239 670
	Uses										
D.63	Social transfers in kind										
D.632	Transfers of individual non-market goods and services	NSZE	132 003	143 649	147 751	159 195	172 489	181 762	194 621	206 913	212 764
B.7g	Adjusted disposable income, gross	NSZI	79 250	74 472	90 003	95 627	110 341	109 145	98 932	30 106	26 906
B.6g	**Total uses (Gross Disposable Income)**	**NNAO**	**211 253**	**218 121**	**237 754**	**254 822**	**282 830**	**290 907**	**293 553**	**237 019**	**239 670**

5.1.6 General government
ESA95 sector S.13 Unconsolidated

£ million

			2002	2003	2004	2005	2006	2007	2008	2009	2010
II.4	**USE OF INCOME ACCOUNT**										
II.4.1	**USE OF DISPOSABLE INCOME ACCOUNT**										
	Resources										
B.6g	Total resources (Gross Disposable Income)	NNAO	211 253	218 121	237 754	254 822	282 830	290 907	293 553	237 019	239 670
	Uses										
P.3	Final consumption expenditure										
P.31	Individual consumption expenditure	NNAQ	132 003	143 649	147 751	159 195	172 489	181 762	194 621	206 913	212 764
P.32	Collective consumption expenditure	NQEP	80 553	88 962	103 177	109 078	112 637	113 392	120 945	120 436	125 303
P.3	Total	NMRK	212 556	232 611	250 928	268 273	285 126	295 154	315 566	327 349	338 067
B.8g	Gross Saving	NNAU	–1 303	–14 490	–13 174	–13 451	–2 296	–4 247	–22 013	–90 330	–98 397
B.6g	**Total uses (Gross Disposable Income)**	NNAO	211 253	218 121	237 754	254 822	282 830	290 907	293 553	237 019	239 670
-K.1	After deduction of fixed capital consumption	-NMXO	–10 289	–10 807	–11 312	–11 927	–12 634	–13 231	–13 963	–14 675	–15 500
B.8n	Saving, net	NNAV	–11 592	–25 297	–24 486	–25 378	–14 930	–17 478	–35 976	–105 005	–113 897
II.4.2	**USE OF ADJUSTED DISPOSABLE INCOME ACCOUNT**										
	Resources										
B.7g	Total resources, adjusted disposable income, gross	NSZI	79 250	74 472	90 003	95 627	110 341	109 145	98 932	30 106	26 906
	Uses										
P.4	Actual final consumption										
P.42	Actual collective consumption	NRMZ	80 553	88 962	103 177	109 078	112 637	113 392	120 945	120 436	125 303
B.8g	Gross Saving	NNAU	–1 303	–14 490	–13 174	–13 451	–2 296	–4 247	–22 013	–90 330	–98 397
Total	Total uses	NSZI	79 250	74 472	90 003	95 627	110 341	109 145	98 932	30 106	26 906

5.1.7 General government
ESA95 sector S.13 Unconsolidated

£ million

				2002	2003	2004	2005	2006	2007	2008	2009	2010
III	**ACCUMULATION ACCOUNTS**											
III.1	**CAPITAL ACCOUNT**											
III.1.1	**CHANGE IN NET WORTH DUE TO SAVING & CAPITAL TRANSFERS**											
	Changes in liabilities and net worth											
B.8g	Gross Saving		NNAU	−1 303	−14 490	−13 174	−13 451	−2 296	−4 247	−22 013	−90 330	−98 397
D.9	Capital transfers receivable											
D.91	Capital taxes											
	from sectors other than general government		NMGI	2 381	2 416	2 881	3 150	3 575	3 867	25 073	4 206	2 643
D.92	Investment grants		NSZF	6 328	7 360	6 804	7 582	8 515	9 960	11 359	13 407	13 061
D.99	Other capital transfers		NNAX	1 147	5 161	3 961	4 510	2 345	3 091	3 739	1 309	448
D.9	Total capital transfers receivable		NNAY	9 856	14 937	13 646	15 242	14 435	16 918	40 171	18 922	16 152
-D.9	*less* Capital transfers payable											
-D.92	Investment grants		-NNAW	−13 646	−17 335	−16 176	−19 990	−21 163	−24 684	−25 026	−33 225	−31 393
-D.99	Other capital transfers		-NNBB	−683	−4 494	−3 896	−16 208	−3 322	−2 642	−31 721	−11 180	−904
-D.9	Total capital transfers payable		-NNBC	−14 329	−21 829	−20 072	−36 198	−24 485	−27 326	−56 747	−44 405	−32 297
B.10.1g	Total change in liabilities and net worth		NMWG	−5 776	−21 382	−19 600	−34 407	−12 346	−14 655	−38 589	−115 813	−114 542
	Changes in assets											
B.10.1g	Changes in net worth due to gross saving and capital transfers		NMWG	−5 776	−21 382	−19 600	−34 407	−12 346	−14 655	−38 589	−115 813	−114 542
K.1	After deduction of fixed capital consumption		-NMXO	−10 289	−10 807	−11 312	−11 927	−12 634	−13 231	−13 963	−14 675	−15 500
B.10.1n	Changes in net worth due to net saving and capital transfers		NNBD	−16 065	−32 189	−30 912	−46 334	−24 980	−27 886	−52 552	−130 488	−130 042
III.1.2	**ACQUISITION OF NON-FINANCIAL ASSETS ACCOUNT**											
	Changes in liabilities and net worth											
B.10.1n	Changes in net worth due to net saving and capital transfers		NNBD	−16 065	−32 189	−30 912	−46 334	−24 980	−27 886	−52 552	−130 488	−130 042
K.1	Consumption of fixed capital		NMXO	10 289	10 807	11 312	11 927	12 634	13 231	13 963	14 675	15 500
B.10.1g	Total change in liabilities and net worth		NMWG	−5 776	−21 382	−19 600	−34 407	−12 346	−14 655	−38 589	−115 813	−114 542
	Changes in assets											
P.5	Gross capital formation											
P.51	Gross fixed capital formation		NNBF	15 452	20 509	23 219	7 091	23 701	26 306	32 860	37 125	36 434
P.52	Changes in inventories		NNBG	–	15	−48	−7	−4	−14	−41	36	43
P.53	Acquisitions less disposals of valuables		NPOZ	22	16	20	16	14	10	11	12	11
P.5	Total		NNBI	15 474	20 540	23 191	7 100	23 711	26 302	32 830	37 173	36 488
K.2	Acquisitions less disposals of non-produced non-financial assets		NNBJ	−1 087	−957	−1 084	−1 166	−1 037	−2 626	−962	−1 019	−879
B.9g	**Net lending(+) / net borrowing(-)**		NNBK	**−20 163**	**−40 965**	**−41 707**	**−40 341**	**−35 020**	**−38 331**	**−70 457**	**−151 967**	**−150 151**
Total	Total change in assets		NMWG	−5 776	−21 382	−19 600	−34 407	−12 346	−14 655	−38 589	−115 813	−114 542

5.1.8 General government
ESA95 sector S.13 Unconsolidated

£ million

			2002	2003	2004	2005	2006	2007	2008	2009	2010
III.2	**FINANCIAL ACCOUNT**										
F.A	**Net acquisition of financial assets**										
F.1	Monetary gold and special drawing rights (SDRs)	NFPH	−240	−2	−37	−8	47	−50	−24	−132	18
F.2	Currency and deposits										
F.22	Transferable deposits with monetary financial institutions										
F.221	UK institutions	NFPN	−3 479	2 476	1 397	334	7 631	6 363	15 697	40	−5 747
F.229	Rest of the world institutions	NFPR	−299	−916	−1 407	−1 516	−671	−579	2 913	540	423
F.29	Other deposits	NFPS	644	−546	−67	−75	−47	4 342	13 159	9 094	−2 567
F.2	Total currency and deposits	NFPK	−3 134	1 014	−77	−1 257	6 913	10 126	31 769	9 674	−7 891
F.3	Securities other than shares										
F.331	Short term: money market instruments										
F.3311	Issued by UK central government	NFPV	−141	−38	−59	14	−18	−51	23	77	794
F.3312	Issued by UK local government	NFPZ	–	–	–	–	–	–	–	–	–
F.3315	Issued by UK monetary financial institutions	NFQA	−233	−75	519	54	801	−2 991	1 755	−2 333	−569
F.3316	Issued by other UK residents	NFQF	741	−1 067	10	197	1 917	−472	469	39	1 378
F.3319	Issued by the rest of the world	NFQG	−1 576	−987	106	1 465	1 363	2 125	−1 029	471	466
F.332	Medium (1 to 5 year) and long term (over 5 year) bonds										
F.3321	Issued by UK central government	NFQI	−264	−101	−98	7	75	−126	45	28	26
F.3326	Other medium & long term bonds issued by UK residents	NFQP	−17	–	–	1 071	−601	−21	4 978	−5 236	–
F.3329	Long term bonds issued by the rest of the world	NFQQ	2 280	−390	1 551	370	−854	2 155	−1 085	7 834	5 824
F.34	Financial derivatives	NFQR	−238	−136	−173	137	−419	−343	503	1 003	285
F.3	Total securities other than shares	NFPT	552	−2 794	1 856	3 315	2 264	276	5 659	1 883	8 204
F.4	Loans										
F.42	Long term loans										
F.422	Loans secured on dwellings	NFRG	206	186	4	252	340	522	1 191	665	405
F.424	Other long-term loans by UK residents	NFRL	−314	−994	2 540	4 911	4 151	5 281	6 110	3 807	8 951
F.429	Other long-term loans by the rest of the world	NFRM	–	–	–	–	–	–	–	–	–
F.4	Total loans	NFQV	−108	−808	2 544	5 163	4 491	5 803	7 301	4 472	9 356
F.5	Shares and other equity										
F.51	Shares and other equity, excluding mutual funds' shares										
F.514	Quoted UK shares	NFRS	−218	45	−116	138	182	−4 874	12 207	36 800	229
F.515	Unquoted UK shares	NFRT	–	−29	−1	−550	3	−2 188	−1 212	−16	–
F.516	Other UK equity (including direct investment in property)	NFRU	−3 064	−5 504	−3 803	−3 841	−3 529	−2 156	−1 078	−539	−483
F.517	UK shares and bonds issued by other UK residents	NSPW	–	–	–	–	–	–	–	–	–
F.519	Shares and other equity issued by the rest of the world	NFRX	409	234	283	656	792	693	949	1 107	1 265
F.5	Total shares and other equity	NFRN	−2 873	−5 254	−3 637	−3 597	−2 552	−8 525	10 866	37 352	1 011
F.6	Insurance technical reserves										
F.62	Prepayments of insurance premiums and reserves for outstanding claims	NFSG	27	8	45	−24	−11	82	21	−24	16
F.7	Other accounts receivable	NFSH	−1 819	3 058	2 781	5 691	2 645	−1 414	16 689	403	3 290
F.A	**Total net acquisition of financial assets**	NFPG	−7 595	−4 778	3 475	9 283	13 797	6 298	72 281	53 628	14 004

5.1.8 General government
ESA95 sector S.13 Unconsolidated
continued

£ million

				2002	2003	2004	2005	2006	2007	2008	2009	2010
III.2	**FINANCIAL ACCOUNT** continued											
F.L	**Net acquisition of financial liabilities**											
F.2	Currency and deposits											
F.21	Currency		NFSP	180	216	171	180	154	122	163	115	152
F.29	Non-transferable deposits		NFSW	1 946	3 266	2 423	5 502	5 240	7 930	20 826	9 026	−8 143
F.2	Total currency and deposits		NFSO	2 126	3 482	2 594	5 682	5 394	8 052	20 989	9 141	−7 991
F.3	Securities other than shares											
F.331	Short term: money market instruments											
F.3311	Issued by UK central government		NFSZ	10 330	2 592	999	−3 902	−1 752	−1 367	13 494	25 975	−2 077
F.3312	Issued by UK local government		NFTD	–	–	–	–	–	–	–	–	–
F.332	Medium (1 to 5 year) and long term (over 5 year) bonds											
F.3321	Issued by UK central government		NFTM	1 555	31 474	34 176	39 820	41 100	38 898	96 058	195 878	170 200
F.3322	Issued by UK local government		NFTP	47	18	−226	213	360	−9	−70	−83	−17
F.3	Total securities other than shares		NFSX	11 932	34 084	34 949	36 131	39 708	37 522	109 482	221 770	168 106
F.4	Loans											
F.41	Short term loans											
F.411	Loans by UK monetary financial institutions, excluding loans secured on dwellings & financial leasing		NFUB	1 731	1 109	7 406	3 070	−1 825	385	13 941	−20 281	−4 335
F.419	Loans by rest of the world monetary financial institutions		NFUF	−14	−7	−6	−3	−1	–	–	–	–
F.42	Long term loans											
F.423	Finance leasing		NFUO	277	512	450	507	302	410	86	50	145
F.424	Other long-term loans by UK residents		NFUP	−1 727	−3 912	507	2 608	2 638	1 265	3 160	−1 788	2 406
F.429	Other long-term loans by the rest of the world		NFUQ	−9	166	611	72	240	−45	478	525	−320
F.4	Total loans		NFTZ	258	−2 132	8 968	6 254	1 354	2 015	17 665	−21 494	−2 104
F.7	Other accounts payable		NFVL	−848	423	−2 247	1 645	3 064	−2 059	−4 649	−4 519	6 401
F.L	**Total net acquisition of financial liabilities**		NFSK	13 468	35 857	44 264	49 712	49 520	45 530	143 487	204 898	164 412
B.9	**Net lending / borrowing**											
F.A	Total net acquisition of financial assets		NFPG	−7 595	−4 778	3 475	9 283	13 797	6 298	72 281	53 628	14 004
−F.L	*less* Total net acquisition of financial liabilities		−NFSK	−13 468	−35 857	−44 264	−49 712	−49 520	−45 530	−143 487	−204 898	−164 412
B.9f	Net lending (+) / net borrowing (−), from financial account		NYNO	−21 063	−40 635	−40 789	−40 429	−35 723	−39 232	−71 206	−151 270	−150 408
dB.9f	Statistical discrepancy		NYOZ	900	−330	−918	88	703	901	749	−697	257
B.9g	**Net lending (+) / net borrowing (−), from capital account**		NNBK	**−20 163**	**−40 965**	**−41 707**	**−40 341**	**−35 020**	**−38 331**	**−70 457**	**−151 967**	**−150 151**

5.1.9 General government
ESA95 S.13 Unconsolidated

£ billion

IV.3 FINANCIAL BALANCE SHEET
at end of period

			2002	2003	2004	2005	2006	2007	2008	2009	2010
AN	Non-financial assets	CGIX	506.8	547.3	602.3	657.5	705.4	758.6	736.7	696.0	721.3
AF.A	**Financial assets**										
AF.1	Monetary gold and special drawing rights (SDRs)	NIFC	2.4	2.6	2.5	3.2	3.4	4.3	6.3	15.7	18.2
AF.2	Currency and deposits										
AF.22	Transferable deposits										
AF.221	Deposits with UK monetary financial institutions	NLVW	20.3	23.9	26.9	27.1	34.6	41.0	57.4	57.2	30.6
AF.229	Deposits with rest of the world monetary financial institutions	NLWA	5.9	4.9	3.3	2.0	1.2	1.0	4.6	4.9	6.0
AF.29	Other deposits	NLWB	1.0	0.4	0.4	0.4	0.2	4.6	17.7	26.8	47.1
AF.2	Total currency and deposits	NLUT	27.1	29.2	30.6	29.4	35.9	46.6	79.7	88.9	83.7
AF.3	Securities other than shares										
AF.331	Short term: money market instruments										
AF.3311	Issued by UK central government	NLWE	0.2	0.2	0.1	0.1	0.1	0.1	0.1	0.1	0.9
AF.3312	Issued by UK local government	NLWI	–	–	–	–	–	–	–	–	–
AF.3315	Issued by UK monetary financial institutions	NLWJ	3.9	3.9	4.4	4.5	5.2	2.3	3.9	1.6	1.0
AF.3316	Issued by other UK residents	NLWO	1.3	0.2	0.2	0.3	2.1	1.3	1.5	1.4	2.8
AF.3319	Issued by the rest of the world	NLWP	1.2	0.2	0.3	1.7	3.0	5.5	5.3	5.6	6.1
AF.332	Medium (1 to 5 year) and long term (over 5 year) bonds										
AF.3321	Issued by UK central government	NLWR	0.4	0.3	0.2	0.2	0.2	0.1	0.2	0.2	0.2
AF.3322	Issued by UK local government	NLWU	–	–	–	–	–	–	–	–	–
AF.3326	Other medium & long term bonds issued by UK residents	NLWY	0.1	0.1	0.1	1.1	0.5	0.5	5.5	0.3	0.3
AF.3329	Long term bonds issued by the rest of the world	NLWZ	16.8	16.2	17.1	17.5	15.3	18.2	24.4	21.1	27.1
AF.34	Financial derivatives	NLXA	0.2	–	0.2	0.6	0.7	–0.4	–3.5	–1.4	1.3
AF.3	Total securities other than shares	NLWC	24.0	20.9	22.5	26.0	27.2	27.6	37.4	29.0	39.8
AF.4	Loans										
AF.42	Long term loans										
AF.422	Loans secured on dwellings	NLXP	0.9	1.1	1.1	1.4	1.7	2.2	3.4	4.1	4.9
AF.424	Other long-term loans by UK residents	NLXU	68.5	66.5	69.6	74.5	78.0	83.6	89.4	92.9	101.2
AF.4	Total loans	NLXE	69.4	67.6	70.7	75.9	79.6	85.8	92.8	97.0	106.0
AF.5	Shares and other equity										
AF.51	Shares and other equity, excluding mutual funds' shares										
AF.514	Quoted UK shares	NLYB	1.0	1.2	0.8	1.1	1.6	1.4	13.1	54.6	54.9
AF.515	Unquoted UK shares	NLYC	1.3	1.3	2.1	2.1	4.7	3.0	6.7	6.6	6.5
AF.516	Other UK equity	H4O9	95.8	104.4	113.3	129.5	120.7	119.1	122.3	117.7	116.7
AF.517	UK shares and bonds issued by other UK residents	NSQP	–	–	–	–	–	–	–	–	–
AF.519	Shares and other equity issued by the rest of the world	NLYG	7.5	7.7	8.0	8.7	9.5	10.2	11.2	12.3	13.5
AF.5	Total shares and other equity	NLXW	105.6	114.7	124.2	141.4	136.5	133.8	153.3	191.1	191.7
AF.6	Insurance technical reserves										
AF.62	Prepayments of insurance premiums and reserves for outstanding claims	NLYP	0.9	0.8	0.8	0.8	0.8	0.9	0.9	0.9	0.9
AF.7	Other accounts receivable	NLYQ	41.5	45.4	47.5	53.4	56.2	53.6	69.6	71.6	75.2
AF.A	**Total financial assets**	NPUP	271.0	281.2	298.8	330.1	339.7	352.6	440.0	494.1	515.4

5.1.9 General government
ESA95 S.13 Unconsolidated

£ billion

				2002	2003	2004	2005	2006	2007	2008	2009	2010
IV.3	**FINANCIAL BALANCE SHEET** continued at end of period											
AF.L	**Financial liabilities**											
AF.2	Currency and deposits											
AF.21	Currency		NLYY	3.3	3.4	3.5	3.7	3.8	3.9	3.9	4.0	4.1
AF.29	Non-transferable deposits		NLZF	74.5	76.7	79.1	84.7	89.9	97.8	118.8	127.0	119.6
AF.2	Total currency and deposits		NLYX	77.8	80.1	82.7	88.4	93.7	101.6	122.7	131.0	123.7
AF.3	Securities other than shares											
AF.331	Short term: money market instruments											
AF.3311	Issued by UK central government		NLZI	21.4	24.0	25.0	21.1	19.4	18.0	31.5	57.5	55.4
AF.3312	Issued by UK local government		NLZM	–	–	–	–	–	–	–	–	–
AF.332	Medium (1 to 5 year) and long term (over 5 year) bonds											
AF.3321	Issued by UK central government		NLZV	311.1	331.9	372.9	424.2	451.3	492.8	618.2	797.7	996.2
AF.3322	Issued by UK local government		NLZY	0.8	0.8	0.6	0.8	1.2	1.2	1.1	1.0	1.0
AF.3	Total securities other than shares[1]		NLZG	333.4	356.8	398.5	446.1	471.8	512.0	650.8	856.1	1 054.5
AF.4	Loans											
AF.41	Short term loans											
AF.411	Loans by UK monetary financial institutions, excluding loans secured on dwellings & financial leasing		NNKY	22.8	25.0	32.6	35.7	34.1	34.8	37.4	16.1	14.4
AF.419	Loans by rest of the world monetary financial institutions		NNLC	–	–	–	–	–	–	–	–	–
AF.42	Long term loans											
AF.423	Finance leasing		NNLL	2.3	2.8	3.2	3.8	4.1	4.5	4.5	4.6	4.7
AF.424	Other long-term loans by UK residents		NNLM	48.3	44.5	45.6	48.0	49.8	50.7	53.8	52.0	54.7
AF.429	Other long-term loans by the rest of the world		NNLN	1.2	1.3	1.9	1.9	2.1	2.1	2.5	3.0	3.2
AF.4	Total loans		NNKW	74.7	73.7	83.2	89.4	90.1	92.0	98.3	75.8	77.1
AF.7	Other accounts payable		NNMI	39.3	42.7	45.7	45.5	48.7	46.7	44.8	45.3	45.6
AF.L	**Total financial liabilities**		NPVQ	525.1	553.2	610.2	669.4	704.3	752.3	916.6	1 108.1	1 300.8
AF.A	Total financial assets		NPUP	271.0	281.2	298.8	330.1	339.7	352.6	440.0	494.1	515.4
-AF.L	*less* Total financial liabilities		-NPVQ	–525.1	–553.2	–610.2	–669.4	–704.3	–752.3	–916.6	–1 108.1	–1 300.8
BF.90	**Net financial assets (+) / liabilities (-)**		NYOG	–254.1	–272.1	–311.4	–339.3	–364.6	–399.7	–476.6	–614.0	–785.5
	Net worth											
AN	Non-financial assets		CGIX	506.8	547.3	602.3	657.5	705.4	758.6	736.7	696.0	721.3
BF.90	Net financial assets (+) / liabilities (-)		NYOG	–254.1	–272.1	–311.4	–339.3	–364.6	–399.7	–476.6	–614.0	–785.5
BF.90	**Net worth**		CGRX	252.6	275.2	290.9	318.2	340.8	358.9	260.1	81.9	–64.1

1 This total includes financial derivatives which are not presented separately.

5.2.1 Central government
ESA95 sector S.1311

£ million

			2002	2003	2004	2005	2006	2007	2008	2009
I	**PRODUCTION ACCOUNT**									
	Resources									
P.1	Output									
P.11	Market output	NMIW	3 480	3 514	6 972	8 881	9 321	11 090	11 454	13 420
P.12	Output for own final use	QYJV	42	44	–	–	3	21	22	56
P.13	Other non-market output	NMBJ	130 348	142 658	152 274	161 329	173 416	178 058	191 348	199 649
P.1	Total resources	NMAE	133 870	146 216	159 246	170 210	182 740	189 169	202 824	213 125
	Uses									
P.2	Intermediate consumption	NMAF	68 890	74 383	81 551	87 773	95 068	99 297	111 156	118 188
B.1g	**Gross Value Added**	NMBR	**64 980**	**71 833**	**77 695**	**82 437**	**87 672**	**89 872**	**91 668**	**94 937**
Total	Total uses	NMAE	133 870	146 216	159 246	170 210	182 740	189 169	202 824	213 125
B.1g	**Gross Value Added**	NMBR	**64 980**	**71 833**	**77 695**	**82 437**	**87 672**	**89 872**	**91 668**	**94 937**
-K.1	*less* Consumption of fixed capital	-NSRN	–5 636	–5 902	–5 998	–6 108	–6 269	–6 533	–6 905	–7 232
B.1n	Value added, net of fixed capital consumption	NMAH	59 344	65 931	71 697	76 329	81 403	83 339	84 763	87 705

5.2.2 Central government
ESA95 sector S.1311

£ million

			2002	2003	2004	2005	2006	2007	2008	2009
II	**DISTRIBUTION AND USE OF INCOME ACCOUNTS**									
II.1	**PRIMARY DISTRIBUTION OF INCOME ACCOUNT**									
II.1.1	**GENERATION OF INCOME ACCOUNT**									
	Resources									
B.1g	**Total resources (Gross Value Added)**	NMBR	**64 980**	**71 833**	**77 695**	**82 437**	**87 672**	**89 872**	**91 668**	**94 937**
	Uses									
D.1	Compensation of employees									
D.11	Wages and salaries	NMAI	48 648	54 514	59 926	62 822	67 310	68 098	68 811	70 165
D.12	Employers' social contributions	NMAL	10 696	11 417	11 771	13 507	14 093	15 241	15 952	17 540
D.1	Total	NMBG	59 344	65 931	71 697	76 329	81 403	83 339	84 763	87 705
D.2	Taxes on production and imports, paid									
D.29	Production taxes other than on products	NMAN	–	–	–	–	–	–	–	–
-D.3	*less* Subsidies, received									
-D.39	Production subsidies other than on products	-NMAO	–	–	–	–	–	–	–	–
B.2g	Operating surplus, gross	NRLN	5 636	5 902	5 998	6 108	6 269	6 533	6 905	7 232
B.1g	**Total uses (Gross Value Added)**	NMBR	**64 980**	**71 833**	**77 695**	**82 437**	**87 672**	**89 872**	**91 668**	**94 937**
-K.1	After deduction of fixed capital consumption	-NSRN	–5 636	–5 902	–5 998	–6 108	–6 269	–6 533	–6 905	–7 232
B.2n	Operating surplus, net	NMAP	–	–	–	–	–	–	–	–

5.2.3 Central government
ESA95 sector S.1311

£ million

			2002	2003	2004	2005	2006	2007	2008	2009	2010
II.1.2	**ALLOCATION OF PRIMARY INCOME ACCOUNT**										
	Resources										
B.2g	Operating surplus, gross	NRLN	5 636	5 902	5 998	6 108	6 269	6 533	6 905	7 232	7 587
D.2	Taxes on production and imports, received										
D.21	Taxes on products										
D.211	Value added tax (VAT)	NZGF	68 251	74 595	79 755	81 426	85 591	89 698	89 682	78 307	93 711
D.212	Taxes and duties on imports excluding VAT										
D.2121	Import duties	NMXZ	–	–	–	–	–	–	–	–	–
D.2122	Taxes on imports excluding VAT and import duties	NMBT	–	–	–	–	–	–	–	–	–
D.214	Taxes on products excluding VAT and import duties	NMYB	52 002	52 858	56 138	56 906	60 536	64 374	60 550	60 084	65 001
D.21	Total taxes on products	NMYC	120 253	127 453	135 893	138 332	146 127	154 072	150 232	138 391	158 712
D.29	Other taxes on production	NMBX	17 940	18 329	18 690	19 524	20 629	21 265	22 768	23 877	27 602
D.2	Total taxes on production and imports, received	NMBY	138 193	145 782	154 583	157 856	166 756	175 337	173 000	162 268	186 314
-D.3	*less* Subsidies, paid										
-D.31	Subsidies on products	-NMCB	–3 636	–4 030	–3 542	–3 491	–4 235	–3 767	–3 510	–3 730	–4 349
-D.39	Other subsidies on production	-NMCC	–937	–1 416	–1 323	–1 383	–1 432	–1 961	–1 670	–1 820	–1 728
-D.3	Total	-NMCD	–4 573	–5 446	–4 865	–4 874	–5 667	–5 728	–5 180	–5 550	–6 077
D.4	Property income										
D.41	Total Interest	NMCE	5 865	6 331	5 755	5 401	5 933	6 570	7 504	6 994	5 305
D.42	Distributed income of corporations	NMCH	1 789	1 773	2 074	2 167	1 863	2 429	2 667	1 442	693
D.45	Rent from sectors other than general government	NMCK	1 901	1 565	1 182	1 229	1 226	1 233	1 164	1 174	1 172
D.4	Total	NMCL	9 555	9 669	9 011	8 797	9 022	10 232	11 335	9 610	7 170
Total	Total resources	NMCM	148 811	155 907	164 727	167 887	176 380	186 374	186 060	173 560	194 994
	Uses										
D.4	Property income										
D.41	Total Interest	RVFK	21 429	22 421	23 212	25 907	27 445	31 269	32 787	26 948	42 167
D.4	Total property income	NUHA	21 429	22 421	23 212	25 907	27 445	31 269	32 787	26 948	42 167
B.5g	**Balance of primary incomes, gross**	NRLP	**127 382**	**133 486**	**141 515**	**141 980**	**148 935**	**155 105**	**153 273**	**146 612**	**152 827**
Total	Total uses	NMCM	148 811	155 907	164 727	167 887	176 380	186 374	186 060	173 560	194 994
-K.1	After deduction of fixed capital consumption	-NSRN	–5 636	–5 902	–5 998	–6 108	–6 269	–6 533	–6 905	–7 232	–7 587
B.5n	Balance of primary incomes, net	NMCT	121 746	127 584	135 517	135 872	142 666	148 572	146 368	139 380	145 240

5.2.4 Central government
ESA95 sector S.1311

£ million

			2002	2003	2004	2005	2006	2007	2008	2009	2010
II.2	**SECONDARY DISTRIBUTION OF INCOME ACCOUNT**										
	Resources										
B.5g	**Balance of primary incomes, gross**	NRLP	**127 382**	**133 486**	**141 515**	**141 980**	**148 935**	**155 105**	**153 273**	**146 612**	**152 827**
D.5	Current taxes on income, wealth, etc.										
D.51	Taxes on income	NMCU	142 842	144 234	154 127	172 498	192 600	199 851	207 597	185 160	191 342
D.59	Other current taxes	NMCV	7 133	7 534	7 991	8 330	8 689	9 346	9 635	9 814	10 237
D.5	Total	NMCP	149 975	151 768	162 118	180 828	201 289	209 197	217 232	194 974	201 579
D.61	Social contributions										
D.611	Actual social contributions										
D.6111	Employers' actual social contributions	NMCY	38 780	45 067	49 490	52 852	56 040	60 736	64 924	63 507	65 874
D.6112	Employees' social contributions	NMDB	28 931	33 717	38 359	41 078	43 594	43 289	44 764	43 244	44 553
D.6113	Social contributions by self- and non-employed persons	NMDE	2 318	2 595	2 727	2 825	2 930	2 861	3 053	2 879	2 576
D.611	Total	NMCX	70 029	81 379	90 576	96 755	102 564	106 886	112 741	109 630	113 003
D.612	Imputed social contributions	QYJS	6 282	4 311	3 997	5 073	4 863	5 369	5 160	5 652	6 343
D.61	Total	NMCW	76 311	85 690	94 573	101 828	107 427	112 255	117 901	115 282	119 346
D.7	Other current transfers										
D.72	Non-life insurance claims	NMDJ	–	–	–	–	–	–	–	–	–
D.73	Current transfers within general government	NMDK	–	–	–	–	–	–	–	–	–
D.74	Current international cooperation	NMDL	3 112	3 570	3 604	3 668	3 594	3 600	4 892	5 418	3 061
D.75	Miscellaneous current transfers from sectors other than general government	NMEZ	502	562	721	728	606	556	508	515	597
D.7	Other current transfers	NMDI	3 614	4 132	4 325	4 396	4 200	4 156	5 400	5 933	3 658
Total	Total resources	NMDN	357 282	375 076	402 531	429 032	461 851	480 713	493 806	462 801	477 410
	Uses										
D.62	Social benefits other than social transfers in kind	NMDR	120 938	129 606	137 370	143 501	147 985	158 244	168 523	186 129	193 836
D.7	Other current transfers										
D.71	Net non-life insurance premiums	NMDX	–	–	–	–	–	–	–	–	–
D.73	Current transfers within general government	QYJR	77 592	85 224	94 720	101 369	110 407	113 108	117 867	124 622	132 444
D.74	Current international cooperation	NMDZ	2 362	2 433	3 080	3 255	3 632	3 930	4 292	5 011	5 683
D.75	Miscellaneous current transfers to sectors other than general government										
	GNP based fourth own resource	NMFH	5 335	6 772	7 549	8 732	8 521	8 323	8 423	10 555	10 819
	NHS trusts compensation payments	MJTI	572	606	758	863	850	891	743	1 427	272
	Misc grants to non profit institutions	DFT8	21 421	22 873	22 842	24 735	25 299	26 636	27 106	28 356	31 302
D.75	Total	NMFC	27 328	30 251	31 149	34 330	34 670	35 850	36 272	40 338	42 393
D.7	Other current transfers	NMDW	107 282	117 908	128 949	138 954	148 709	152 888	158 431	169 971	180 520
B.6g	**Gross Disposable Income**	NRLR	**129 062**	**127 562**	**136 212**	**146 577**	**165 157**	**169 581**	**166 852**	**106 701**	**103 054**
Total	Total uses	NMDN	357 282	375 076	402 531	429 032	461 851	480 713	493 806	462 801	477 410
-K.1	After deduction of fixed capital consumption	-NSRN	–5 636	–5 902	–5 998	–6 108	–6 269	–6 533	–6 905	–7 232	–7 587
B.6n	Disposable income, net	NMEB	123 426	121 660	130 214	140 469	158 888	163 048	159 947	99 469	95 467

5.2.4S Central government Social contributions and benefits
ESA95 sector S.1311

£ million

	Part	SECONDARY DISTRIBUTION OF INCOME (further detail of certain items)		2002	2003	2004	2005	2006	2007	2008	2009	2010
		Resources										
	D.61	Social contributions										
		National Insurance Contributions (NICs)										
	D.611	Actual social contributions										
	D.61111	Employers' NICs	CEAN	35 735	39 890	43 874	46 824	49 568	53 765	57 080	54 387	56 089
	D.61121	Employees' NICs	GCSE	25 357	29 055	32 623	34 810	37 052	36 584	38 186	37 179	38 500
	D.61131	Self- and non-employed persons' NICs	NMDE	2 318	2 595	2 727	2 825	2 930	2 861	3 053	2 879	2 576
	D.61	Total national insurance contributions	AIIH	63 410	71 540	79 224	84 459	89 550	93 210	98 319	94 445	97 165
		Pension schemes[1]										
	D.611	Actual social contributions										
	D.61112	Employers' contributions	GCMP	3 045	5 177	5 616	6 028	6 472	6 971	7 844	9 120	9 785
	D.61122	Employees' contributions	CX3X	3 574	4 662	5 736	6 268	6 542	6 705	6 578	6 065	6 053
	D.612	Imputed social contributions	QYJS	6 282	4 311	3 997	5 073	4 863	5 369	5 160	5 652	6 343
	D.61	Total pension schemes	FAD5	12 901	14 150	15 349	17 369	17 877	19 045	19 582	20 837	22 181
	D.61	Total social contributions	NMCW	76 311	85 690	94 573	101 828	107 427	112 255	117 901	115 282	119 346
		Uses										
	D.62	Social benefits										
	D.621	Social security benefits in cash										
		National insurance fund										
		Retirement pensions	CSDG	43 967	46 098	48 495	50 929	53 200	56 727	60 743	66 412	67 536
		Widows' and guardians' allowances	CSDH	1 096	1 027	939	882	807	748	699	650	620
		Unemployment benefit	CSDI	–2	–	–1	–4	–	–	–	–	–
		Jobseeker's allowance	CJTJ	512	519	454	486	474	435	469	1 223	821
		Sickness benefit	CSDJ	–	–	–	–	–	–	–	–	–
		Invalidity benefit	CSDK	–	–	–	–	–	–	–	–	–
		Incapacity benefit	CUNL	6 754	6 792	6 674	6 618	6 545	6 590	6 568	6 657	6 546
		Maternity benefit	CSDL	66	107	146	162	172	230	308	336	341
		Death grant	CSDM	–	–	–	–	–	–	–	–	–
		Statutory sick pay	CSDQ	19	58	75	78	83	94	75	96	96
		Statutory maternity pay	GTKZ	711	1 130	1 336	1 249	1 319	1 684	1 767	1 655	1 694
		Payment in lieu of benefits foregone	GTKV	–	–	–	–	–	–	–	–	–
		Total national insurance fund benefits	ACHH	53 123	55 731	58 118	60 400	62 600	66 508	70 629	77 029	77 654
		Redundancy fund benefit	GTKN	278	245	169	274	200	178	267	522	139
		Maternity fund benefit	GTKO	–	–	–	–	–	–	–	–	–
		Social fund benefit	GTLQ	1 910	2 135	2 240	2 232	2 253	2 351	2 975	3 275	3 684
		Benefits paid to overseas residents	FJVZ	1 338	1 404	1 539	1 596	1 675	1 774	1 946	2 048	2 160
	D.621	Total social security benefits in cash	QYRJ	56 649	59 515	62 066	64 502	66 728	70 811	75 817	82 874	83 637
	D.623	Total unfunded social benefits	QYJT	14 744	15 602	16 615	17 617	18 744	21 677	22 376	24 545	25 953
	D.624	Social assistance benefits in cash										
		War pensions and allowances	CSDD	1 173	1 108	1 079	1 018	995	966	1 006	1 020	953
		Income support	CSDE	14 400	14 986	15 946	15 595	15 633	15 866	16 205	16 574	16 161
		Income tax credits and reliefs	RYCQ	6 344	8 805	11 329	12 418	14 006	15 252	17 778	21 288	23 157
		Child Benefit	EKY3	8 906	9 281	9 623	9 627	10 124	10 414	10 919	11 882	12 041
		Non-contributory job seekers' allowance	EKY4	2 112	2 098	1 931	1 848	2 067	2 054	2 032	3 513	3 851
		Care allowances	EKY5	5 174	5 379	5 839	6 123	6 427	6 840	7 121	7 724	8 001
		Disability benefits	EKY6	7 716	8 249	8 716	9 248	9 841	10 621	11 125	12 010	12 779
		Other benefits	EKY7	3 670	4 535	4 169	5 451	3 374	3 688	4 091	4 648	7 303
		Benefits paid to overseas residents	RNNF	50	48	57	54	46	55	53	51	–
	D.624	Total social assistance benefits in cash	NZGO	49 545	54 489	58 689	61 382	62 513	65 756	70 330	78 710	84 246
	D.62	Total social benefits	NMDR	120 938	129 606	137 370	143 501	147 985	158 244	168 523	186 129	193 836

1 Mainly civil service, armed forces', teachers' and NHS pension schemes

5.2.5 Central government
ESA95 sector S.1311

£ million

			2002	2003	2004	2005	2006	2007	2008	2009	2010
II.3	**REDISTRIBUTION OF INCOME IN KIND ACCOUNT**										
	Resources										
B.6g	Total resources (Gross Disposable Income)	NRLR	129 062	127 562	136 212	146 577	165 157	169 581	166 852	106 701	103 054
	Uses										
D.63	Social transfers in kind										
D.631	Social benefits in kind										
D.632	Transfers of individual non-market goods and services	NMED	75 408	83 215	83 371	89 549	98 257	103 769	112 208	120 835	123 480
B.7g	Adjusted disposable income, gross	NSVS	53 654	44 347	52 841	57 028	66 900	65 812	54 644	−14 134	−20 426
B.6g	**Total uses (Gross Disposable Income)**	NRLR	129 062	127 562	136 212	146 577	165 157	169 581	166 852	106 701	103 054

5.2.6 Central government
ESA95 sector S.1311

£ million

			2002	2003	2004	2005	2006	2007	2008	2009	2010
II.4	**USE OF INCOME ACCOUNT**										
II.4.1	**USE OF DISPOSABLE INCOME ACCOUNT**										
	Resources										
B.6g	Total resources (Gross Disposable Income)	NRLR	129 062	127 562	136 212	146 577	165 157	169 581	166 852	106 701	103 054
	Uses										
P.3	Final consumption expenditure										
P.31	Individual consumption expenditure	NMED	75 408	83 215	83 371	89 549	98 257	103 769	112 208	120 835	123 480
P.32	Collective consumption expenditure	NMEE	54 940	59 443	68 903	71 780	75 159	74 289	79 140	78 814	83 869
P.3	Total	NMBJ	130 348	142 658	152 274	161 329	173 416	178 058	191 348	199 649	207 349
B.8g	**Gross Saving**	NRLS	−1 286	−15 096	−16 062	−14 752	−8 259	−8 477	−24 496	−92 948	−104 295
B.6g	**Total uses (Gross Disposable Income)**	NRLR	129 062	127 562	136 212	146 577	165 157	169 581	166 852	106 701	103 054
−K.1	After deduction of fixed capital consumption	−NSRN	−5 636	−5 902	−5 998	−6 108	−6 269	−6 533	−6 905	−7 232	−7 587
B.8n	Saving, net	NMEG	−6 922	−20 998	−22 060	−20 860	−14 528	−15 010	−31 401	−100 180	−111 882
II.4.2	**USE OF ADJUSTED DISPOSABLE INCOME ACCOUNT**										
	Resources										
B.7g	Total resources, adjusted disposable income, gross	NSVS	53 654	44 347	52 841	57 028	66 900	65 812	54 644	−14 134	−20 426
	Uses										
P.4	Actual final consumption										
P.42	Actual collective consumption	NMEE	54 940	59 443	68 903	71 780	75 159	74 289	79 140	78 814	83 869
B.8g	**Gross Saving**	NRLS	−1 286	−15 096	−16 062	−14 752	−8 259	−8 477	−24 496	−92 948	−104 295
Total	Total uses	NSVS	53 654	44 347	52 841	57 028	66 900	65 812	54 644	−14 134	−20 426

5.2.7 Central government
ESA95 sector S.1311

£ million

				2002	2003	2004	2005	2006	2007	2008	2009	2010
III	**ACCUMULATION ACCOUNTS**											
III.1	**CAPITAL ACCOUNT**											
III.1.1	**CHANGE IN NET WORTH DUE TO SAVINGS AND CAPITAL TRANSFERS**											
	Changes in liabilities and net worth											
B.8g	Gross Saving	NRLS		–1 286	–15 096	–16 062	–14 752	–8 259	–8 477	–24 496	–92 948	–104 295
D.9	Capital transfers receivable											
D.91	Capital taxes from sectors other than general government	NMGI		2 381	2 416	2 881	3 150	3 575	3 867	25 073	4 206	2 643
D.92	Investment grants	GCMT		–	–	–	–	–	–	–	–	–
D.99	Other capital transfers	NMEK		412	391	1 679	2 496	1 204	1 350	780	322	196
D.9	Total capital transfers receivable	NMEH		2 793	2 807	4 560	5 646	4 779	5 217	25 853	4 528	2 839
-D.9	*less* Capital transfers payable											
-D.92	Investment grants	-NMEN		–12 807	–16 170	–15 049	–18 427	–19 528	–22 595	–22 643	–30 179	–27 819
-D.99	Other capital transfers	-NMEO		–678	–4 489	–2 649	–14 883	–2 721	–1 682	–29 511	–10 818	–424
-D.9	Total capital transfers payable	-NMEL		–13 485	–20 659	–17 698	–33 310	–22 249	–24 277	–52 154	–40 997	–28 243
B.10.1g	Total change in liabilities and net worth	NMEP		–11 978	–32 948	–29 200	–42 416	–25 729	–27 537	–50 797	–129 417	–129 699
	Changes in assets											
B.10.1g	Changes in net worth due to gross saving and capital transfers	NMEP		–11 978	–32 948	–29 200	–42 416	–25 729	–27 537	–50 797	–129 417	–129 699
-K.1	After deduction of fixed capital consumption	-NSRN		–5 636	–5 902	–5 998	–6 108	–6 269	–6 533	–6 905	–7 232	–7 587
B.10.1n	Changes in net worth due to net saving and capital transfers	NMEQ		–17 614	–38 850	–35 198	–48 524	–31 998	–34 070	–57 702	–136 649	–137 286
III.1.2	**ACQUISITION OF NON-FINANCIAL ASSETS ACCOUNT**											
	Changes in liabilities and net worth											
B.10.1n	Changes in net worth due to saving and capital transfers	NMEQ		–17 614	–38 850	–35 198	–48 524	–31 998	–34 070	–57 702	–136 649	–137 286
K.1	Consumption of fixed capital	NSRN		5 636	5 902	5 998	6 108	6 269	6 533	6 905	7 232	7 587
B.10.1g	Total changes in liabilities and net worth	NMEP		–11 978	–32 948	–29 200	–42 416	–25 729	–27 537	–50 797	–129 417	–129 699
	Changes in assets											
P.5	Gross capital formation											
P.51	Gross fixed capital formation	NMES		7 506	6 372	8 328	–6 425	9 894	11 977	15 643	18 476	17 896
P.52	Changes in inventories	NMFE		–	15	–48	–7	–4	–14	–41	36	43
P.53	Acquisitions less disposals of valuables	NPPD		22	16	20	16	14	10	11	12	11
P.5	Total	NMER		7 528	6 403	8 300	–6 416	9 904	11 973	15 613	18 524	17 950
K.2	Acquisitions less disposals of non-produced non-financial assets	NMFG		–327	–157	–227	–264	–90	–1 698	–42	–63	64
B.9g	**Net lending(+) / net borrowing(-)**	NMFJ		**–19 179**	**–39 194**	**–37 273**	**–35 736**	**–35 543**	**–37 812**	**–66 368**	**–147 878**	**–147 713**
Total	Total change in assets	NMEP		–11 978	–32 948	–29 200	–42 416	–25 729	–27 537	–50 797	–129 417	–129 699

5.2.8 Central government
ESA95 sector S.1311 Unconsolidated

£ million

			2002	2003	2004	2005	2006	2007	2008	2009	2010
III.2	**FINANCIAL ACCOUNT**										
F.A	**Net acquisition of financial assets**										
F.1	Monetary gold and special drawing rights (SDRs)	NWXM	−240	−2	−37	−8	47	−50	−24	−132	18
F.2	Currency and deposits										
F.22	Transferable deposits										
F.221	Sterling deposits with UK MFIs	NART	−4 809	1 163	−2 488	256	2 246	2 024	18 238	6 958	−6 702
F.2212	o/w Foreign currency deposits	NARV	−356	−41	−947	−329	542	297	12	−633	28
F.229	Deposits with rest of the world monetary financial institutions	NARX	−299	−916	−1 407	−1 516	−671	−579	2 913	540	423
F.29	Other deposits national savings & tax	RYWO	376	−681	–	–	161	3 761	11 021	7 075	−1 248
F.2	Total currency and deposits	NARQ	−4 732	−434	−3 895	−1 260	1 736	5 206	32 172	14 573	−7 527
F.3	Securities other than shares										
F.331	Short term: money market instruments										
F.3315	Issued by UK MFI's	NSUN	−720	−99	751	213	1 768	−2 038	1 974	−2 144	−400
F.3316	Issued by other UK residents	NSRI	730	−1 029	–	–	1 192	−1 142	–	882	1 349
F.3319	Issued by the rest of the world	NASM	−1 576	−987	106	1 465	1 363	2 125	−1 029	471	466
F.332	Medium (1 to 5 year) and long term (over 5 year) bonds										
F.3326	Other medium & long term bonds issued by UK residents	NASV	−17	–	–	856	−601	−21	4 978	−5 236	–
F.3329	Long term bonds issued by the rest of the world	NASW	2 280	−390	1 551	370	−854	2 155	−1 085	7 834	5 824
F.34	Financial derivatives	CFZG	−238	−136	−173	137	−419	−343	503	1 003	285
F.3	Total securities other than shares	NARZ	459	−2 641	2 235	3 041	2 449	736	5 341	2 810	7 524
F.4	Loans										
F.42	Long term loans										
F.422	Loans secured on dwellings	NATM	–	–	–	–	–	–	–	–	–
F.424	Other long-term loans by UK residents	NATR	−231	−976	2 568	4 711	4 174	5 539	6 148	3 688	8 462
F.429	Other long-term loans by the rest of the world	NATS	–	–	–	–	–	–	–	–	–
F.4	Total loans	NATB	−231	−976	2 568	4 711	4 174	5 539	6 148	3 688	8 462
F.5	Shares and other equity										
F.51	Shares and other equity, excluding mutual funds' shares										
F.514	Quoted UK shares	NATY	–	–	–	295	25	−4 706	12 258	36 879	24
F.515	Unquoted UK shares	NATZ	–	−29	–	−550	–	−2 060	−1 212	−16	–
F.516	Other UK equity (including direct investment in property)	NAUA	−204	−25	−117	−1 249	−1 356	−76	–	–	–
F.517	UK shares and bonds issued by other UK residents	NSOX	–	–	–	–	–	–	–	–	–
F.519	Shares and other equity issued by the rest of the world	NAUD	409	234	283	656	792	693	949	1 107	1 265
F.5	Total shares and other equity	NATT	205	180	166	−848	−539	−6 149	11 995	37 970	1 289
F.7	Other accounts receivable	NAUN	−696	2 777	2 826	5 491	2 672	−1 392	16 599	196	2 771
F.A	**Total net acquisition of financial assets**	NARM	−5 235	−1 096	3 863	11 127	10 539	3 890	72 231	59 105	12 537

5.2.8 Central government
ESA95 sector S.1311 Unconsolidated

£ million

			2002	2003	2004	2005	2006	2007	2008	2009	2010
III.2	**FINANCIAL ACCOUNT** continued										
F.L	**Net acquisition of financial liabilities**										
F.2	Currency and deposits										
F.21	Currency	NAUV	180	216	171	180	154	122	163	115	152
F.29	Non-transferable deposits	NAVC	1 946	3 266	2 423	5 502	5 240	7 930	20 826	9 026	−8 143
F.2	Total currency and deposits	NAUU	2 126	3 482	2 594	5 682	5 394	8 052	20 989	9 141	−7 991
F.3	Securities other than shares										
F.331	Short term: money market instruments										
F.3311	Issued by UK central government	NAVF	10 330	2 592	999	−3 902	−1 752	−1 367	13 494	25 975	−2 077
F.332	Medium (1 to 5 year) and long term (over 5 year) bonds										
F.33211	British government securities	NAVT	4 701	29 748	34 162	39 803	41 087	38 873	97 548	195 885	170 173
F.33212	Other central government bonds	NAVU	−3 146	1 726	14	17	13	25	−1 490	−7	27
F.3	Total securities other than shares	NAVD	11 885	34 066	35 175	35 918	39 348	37 531	109 552	221 853	168 123
F.4	Loans										
F.41	Short term loans										
F.411	Loans by UK monetary financial institutions, excluding loans secured on dwellings & financial leasing	NAWH	915	−53	5 878	2 336	−2 996	−1 069	13 941	−20 507	−4 699
F.419	Loans by rest of the world monetary financial institutions	NAWL	−1	–	–	–	–	–	–	–	–
F.42	Long term loans										
F.423	Finance leasing	NAWU	259	497	450	502	299	410	86	50	145
F.424	Other long-term loans by UK residents	NAWV	−18	−19	−14	−12	−7	−6	−7	−18	−9
F.429	Other long-term loans by the rest of the world	NAWW	−48	−45	−46	−65	7	−3	32	5	−495
F.4	Total loans	NAWF	1 107	380	6 268	2 761	−2 697	−668	14 052	−20 470	−5 058
F.7	Other accounts payable	NAXR	−356	181	−2 837	1 642	4 099	−2 373	−5 729	−3 886	5 302
F.L	**Total net acquisition of financial liabilities**	NAUQ	14 762	38 109	41 200	46 003	46 144	42 542	138 864	206 638	160 376
B.9	**Net lending / borrowing**										
F.A	Total net acquisition of financial assets	NARM	−5 235	−1 096	3 863	11 127	10 539	3 890	72 231	59 105	12 537
−F.L	*less* Total net acquisition of financial liabilities	−NAUQ	−14 762	−38 109	−41 200	−46 003	−46 144	−42 542	−138 864	−206 638	−160 376
B.9f	Net lending (+) / net borrowing (−), from financial account	NZDX	−19 997	−39 205	−37 337	−34 876	−35 605	−38 652	−66 633	−147 533	−147 839
dB.9f	Statistical discrepancy	NZDW	818	11	64	−860	62	840	265	−345	126
B.9g	**Net lending (+) / net borrowing (−), from capital account**	NMFJ	−19 179	−39 194	−37 273	−35 736	−35 543	−37 812	−66 368	−147 878	−147 713

5.2.9 Central government
ESA95 sector S.1311 Unconsolidated

£ billion

			2002	2003	2004	2005	2006	2007	2008	2009	2010
IV.3	**FINANCIAL BALANCE SHEET** at end of period										
AN	Non-financial assets	CGIY	197.8	211.8	221.1	250.6	269.1	281.4	291.9	294.2	310.1
AF.A	**Financial assets**										
AF.1	Monetary gold and special drawing rights (SDRs)	NIFC	2.4	2.6	2.5	3.2	3.4	4.3	6.3	15.7	18.2
AF.2	Currency and deposits										
AF.22	Transferable deposits										
AF.221	Deposits with UK monetary financial institutions	NIFI	4.6	6.8	5.5	5.6	7.7	9.8	28.5	35.2	7.7
AF.2212	o/w Foreign currency deposits	NIFK	0.9	1.7	1.9	1.4	1.6	1.7	2.2	1.2	1.1
AF.229	Deposits with rest of the world monetary financial institutions	NIFM	5.9	4.9	3.3	2.0	1.2	1.0	4.6	4.9	6.0
AF.29	Other deposits	NIFN	0.7	–	–	–	–	3.8	14.8	21.9	43.5
AF.2	Total currency and deposits	NIFF	11.2	11.7	8.8	7.6	8.9	14.6	47.9	61.9	57.1
AF.3	Securities other than shares										
AF.331	Short term: money market instruments										
AF.3315	Issued by UK MFI's	NSUO	0.1	–	0.8	1.0	2.7	0.8	2.6	0.4	–
AF.3316	Issued by other UK residents	NSRH	1.1	–	–	–	1.2	0.1	0.1	1.0	2.3
AF.3319	Issued by the rest of the world	NIGB	1.2	0.2	0.3	1.7	3.0	5.5	5.3	5.6	6.1
AF.332	Medium (1 to 5 year) and long term (over 5 year) bonds										
AF.3322	Issued by UK local government	NIGG	–	–	–	–	–	–	–	–	–
AF.3326	Other medium & long term bonds issued by UK residents	NIGK	0.1	0.1	0.1	0.9	0.3	0.3	5.3	0.1	0.1
AF.3329	Long term bonds issued by the rest of the world	NIGL	16.8	16.2	17.1	17.5	15.3	18.2	24.4	21.1	27.1
AF.34	Financial derivatives	ZYBQ	0.2	–	0.2	0.6	0.7	−0.4	−3.5	−1.4	1.3
AF.3	Total securities other than shares	NIFO	19.4	16.4	18.4	21.8	23.3	24.4	34.1	26.8	36.9
AF.4	Loans										
AF.42	Long term loans										
AF.422	Loans secured on dwellings	NIHB	0.1	0.1	0.1	0.1	0.1	0.1	0.1	0.1	0.1
AF.424	Other long-term loans by UK residents	NIHG	68.2	66.2	69.4	74.3	77.7	83.3	89.2	92.7	100.9
AF.4	Total loans	NIGQ	68.3	66.3	69.4	74.4	77.8	83.4	89.3	92.7	101.0
AF.5	Shares and other equity										
AF.51	Shares and other equity, excluding mutual funds' shares										
AF.514	Quoted UK shares	NIHN	–	–	–	0.3	0.6	0.5	12.8	54.1	54.1
AF.515	Unquoted UK shares	NIHO	0.9	0.9	1.4	1.4	3.9	2.3	5.9	5.9	5.8
AF.516	Other UK equity	H407	9.8	9.3	7.1	12.7	9.8	7.8	8.9	3.8	2.6
AF.517	UK shares and bonds issued by other UK residents	NSNX	–	–	–	–	–	–	–	–	–
AF.519	Shares and other equity issued by the rest of the world	NIHS	7.5	7.7	8.0	8.7	9.5	10.2	11.2	12.3	13.5
AF.5	Total shares and other equity	NIHI	18.2	18.0	16.5	23.1	23.8	20.8	38.8	76.0	76.1
AF.7	Other accounts receivable	NIIC	41.2	44.5	47.2	52.5	55.1	53.7	70.4	71.7	75.4
AF.A	**Total financial assets**	NIGP	160.6	159.5	162.8	182.4	192.3	201.4	286.8	344.9	364.5

5.2.9 Central government
ESA95 sector S.1311 Unconsolidated

£ billion

			2002	2003	2004	2005	2006	2007	2008	2009	2010
IV.3	**FINANCIAL BALANCE SHEET** continued at end of period										
AF.L	**Financial liabilities**										
AF.2	Currency and deposits										
AF.21	Currency	NIIK	3.3	3.4	3.5	3.7	3.8	3.9	3.9	4.0	4.1
AF.29	Non-transferable deposits	NIIR	74.5	76.7	79.1	84.7	89.9	97.8	118.8	127.0	119.6
AF.2	Total currency and deposits	NIIJ	77.8	80.1	82.7	88.4	93.7	101.6	122.7	131.0	123.7
AF.3	Securities other than shares										
AF.331	Short term: money market instruments										
AF.33111	Sterling Treasury bills	NIIV	21.4	24.0	25.0	21.1	19.4	18.0	31.5	57.5	55.4
AF.33112	ECU Treasury bills	NIIW	–	–	–	–	–	–	–	–	–
AF.332	Medium (1 to 5 year) and long term (over 5 year) bonds										
AF.33211	British government securities	NIJI	309.3	330.3	370.1	421.3	448.4	490.0	616.9	796.3	994.9
AF.33212	Other central government bonds	NIJJ	1.8	1.6	2.8	3.0	2.9	2.8	1.4	1.3	1.4
AF.3	Total securities other than shares[1]	NIIS	332.5	355.9	397.9	445.3	470.6	510.8	649.7	855.1	1 053.5
AF.4	Loans										
AF.41	Short term loans										
AF.411	Loans by UK monetary financial institutions, excluding loans secured on dwellings & financial leasing	NIJW	20.0	20.8	26.3	28.1	25.0	24.5	26.5	5.0	2.8
AF.419	Loans by rest of the world monetary financial institutions	ZMFG	–	–	–	–	–	–	–	–	–
AF.42	Long term loans										
AF.423	Finance leasing	NIKJ	2.3	2.8	3.2	3.7	4.0	4.4	4.5	4.5	4.7
AF.424	Other long-term loans by UK residents	NIKK	–	0.1	0.1	0.1	0.1	–	–	–	–
AF.429	Other long-term loans by the rest of the world	NIKL	0.4	0.2	0.1	0.1	–	–	–	–	–
AF.4	Total loans	NIJU	22.6	23.8	29.8	31.9	29.1	29.0	31.0	9.6	7.4
AF.7	Other accounts payable	NILG	30.0	32.9	34.9	34.6	37.4	37.2	35.9	36.7	37.1
AF.L	**Total financial liabilities**	NIJT	462.9	492.8	545.3	600.1	630.7	678.6	839.3	1 032.4	1 221.7
BF.90	**Net financial assets / liabilities**										
AF.A	Total financial assets	NIGP	160.6	159.5	162.8	182.4	192.3	201.4	286.8	344.9	364.5
-AF.L	*less* Total financial liabilities	-NIJT	–462.9	–492.8	–545.3	–600.1	–630.7	–678.6	–839.3	–1 032.4	–1 221.7
BF.90	**Net financial assets (+) / liabilities (-)**	NZDZ	–302.3	–333.3	–382.5	–417.7	–438.5	–477.2	–552.5	–687.4	–857.2
	Net worth										
AN	Non-financial assets	CGIY	197.8	211.8	221.1	250.6	269.1	281.4	291.9	294.2	310.1
BF.90	Net financial assets (+) / liabilities (-)	NZDZ	–302.3	–333.3	–382.5	–417.7	–438.5	–477.2	–552.5	–687.4	–857.2
BF.90	**Net worth**	CGRY	–104.4	–121.5	–161.5	–167.0	–169.4	–195.9	–260.6	–393.3	–547.1

1 This total includes financial derivatives which are not presented separately.

5.3.1 Local government
ESA95 sector S.1313

£ million

			2002	2003	2004	2005	2006	2007	2008	2009
I	**PRODUCTION ACCOUNT**									
	Resources									
P.1	Output									
P.11	Market output	NMIX	15 984	17 266	19 538	21 750	23 378	23 745	24 396	25 414
P.12	Output for own final use	QYJW	382	403	428	371	459	421	379	348
P.13	Other non-market output	NMMT	82 208	89 953	98 654	106 944	111 710	117 096	124 218	127 700
P.1	Total resources	NMIZ	98 574	107 622	118 620	129 065	135 547	141 262	148 993	153 462
	Uses									
P.2	Intermediate consumption	NMJA	42 316	46 827	53 085	58 149	61 379	64 178	69 029	71 417
B.1g	**Gross Value Added**	NMJB	**56 258**	**60 795**	**65 535**	**70 916**	**74 168**	**77 084**	**79 964**	**82 045**
Total	Total uses	NMIZ	98 574	107 622	118 620	129 065	135 547	141 262	148 993	153 462
B.1g	**Gross Value Added**	NMJB	**56 258**	**60 795**	**65 535**	**70 916**	**74 168**	**77 084**	**79 964**	**82 045**
-K.1	less Consumption of fixed capital	-NSRO	–4 653	–4 905	–5 314	–5 819	–6 365	–6 698	–7 058	–7 443
B.1n	Value added, net of fixed capital consumption	NMJD	51 605	55 890	60 221	65 097	67 803	70 386	72 906	74 602

5.3.2 Local government
ESA95 sector S.1313

£ million

			2002	2003	2004	2005	2006	2007	2008	2009
II	**DISTRIBUTION AND USE OF INCOME ACCOUNTS**									
II.1	**PRIMARY DISTRIBUTION OF INCOME ACCOUNT**									
II.1.1	**GENERATION OF INCOME ACCOUNT**									
	Resources									
B.1g	**Total resources (Gross Value Added)**	NMJB	**56 258**	**60 795**	**65 535**	**70 916**	**74 168**	**77 084**	**79 964**	**82 045**
	Uses									
D.1	Compensation of employees									
D.11	Wages and salaries	NMJF	42 304	46 157	47 957	51 756	53 408	54 765	56 123	57 129
D.12	Employers' social contributions	NMJG	9 301	9 733	12 264	13 341	14 395	15 621	16 783	17 473
D.1	Total	NMJE	51 605	55 890	60 221	65 097	67 803	70 386	72 906	74 602
D.2	Taxes on production and imports, paid									
D.29	Production taxes other than on products	NMHY	–	–	–	–	–	–	–	–
-D.3	less Subsidies, received									
-D.39	Production subsidies other than on products	-NMJL	–	–	–	–	–	–	–	–
B.2g	Operating surplus, gross	NRLT	4 653	4 905	5 314	5 819	6 365	6 698	7 058	7 443
B.1g	**Total uses (Gross Valued Added)**	NMJB	**56 258**	**60 795**	**65 535**	**70 916**	**74 168**	**77 084**	**79 964**	**82 045**
-K.1	After deduction of fixed capital consumption	-NSRO	–4 653	–4 905	–5 314	–5 819	–6 365	–6 698	–7 058	–7 443
B.2n	Operating surplus, net	NMJM	–	–	–	–	–	–	–	–

5.3.3 Local government
ESA95 sector S.1313

£ million

			2002	2003	2004	2005	2006	2007	2008	2009	2010
II.1.2	**ALLOCATION OF PRIMARY INCOME ACCOUNT**										
	Resources										
B.2g	Operating surplus, gross	NRLT	4 653	4 905	5 314	5 819	6 365	6 698	7 058	7 443	7 913
D.2	Taxes on production and imports, received										
D.29	Taxes on production other than on products	NMYH	173	188	163	182	202	267	301	317	329
-D.3	*less* Subsidies, paid										
-D.31	Subsidies on products	-LIUA	−1 038	−1 281	−1 584	−1 691	−1 731	−1 842	−1 642	−1 977	−2 215
-D.39	Other subsidies on production	-LIUC	−17	−18	−239	−1 066	−1 661	−1 525	−1 711	−1 493	−1 495
D.4	Property income										
D.41	Total interest	NMKB	818	800	1 083	1 070	1 532	1 974	2 662	632	541
D.42	Distributed income of corporations	FDDA	1 501	1 254	720	733	703	689	638	772	552
D.44	Property income attributed to insurance policy holders	NMKK	18	19	19	27	25	20	24	24	20
D.45	Rent										
	from sectors other than general government	NMKM	–	–	–	–	–	–	–	–	–
D.4	Total property income	NMJZ	2 337	2 073	1 822	1 830	2 260	2 683	3 324	1 428	1 113
Total	Total resources	NMKN	6 108	5 867	5 476	5 074	5 435	6 281	7 330	5 718	5 645
	Uses										
D.4	Property income										
D.41	Total interest	NCBW	3 981	4 492	3 761	3 469	3 531	3 523	3 714	3 225	3 149
D.4	Total property income	NUHI	3 981	4 492	3 761	3 469	3 531	3 523	3 714	3 225	3 149
B.5g	**Balance of primary incomes, gross**	NRLU	**2 127**	**1 375**	**1 715**	**1 605**	**1 904**	**2 758**	**3 616**	**2 493**	**2 496**
Total	Total uses	NMKN	6 108	5 867	5 476	5 074	5 435	6 281	7 330	5 718	5 645
-K.1	After deduction of fixed capital consumption	-NSRO	−4 653	−4 905	−5 314	−5 819	−6 365	−6 698	−7 058	−7 443	−7 913
B.5n	Balance of primary incomes, net	NMKZ	−2 526	−3 530	−3 599	−4 214	−4 461	−3 940	−3 442	−4 950	−5 417

5.3.4 Local government
ESA95 sector S.1313

£ million

			2002	2003	2004	2005	2006	2007	2008	2009	2010
II.2	**SECONDARY DISTRIBUTION OF INCOME ACCOUNT**										
	Resources										
B.5g	**Balance of primary incomes, gross**	NRLU	**2 127**	**1 375**	**1 715**	**1 605**	**1 904**	**2 758**	**3 616**	**2 493**	**2 496**
D.5	Current taxes on income, wealth etc.										
D.59	Current taxes other than on income	NMIS	16 531	18 482	20 010	21 113	22 219	23 351	24 397	25 074	25 610
D.61	Social contributions										
D.611	Actual social contributions										
D.6112	Employees' social contributions	NMWM	637	659	703	758	797	802	806	828	853
D.612	Imputed social contributions	GCMN	2 066	2 145	2 221	2 310	2 426	2 525	2 751	3 089	3 246
D.61	Total	NSMM	2 703	2 804	2 924	3 068	3 223	3 327	3 557	3 917	4 099
D.7	Other current transfers										
D.72	Non-life insurance claims	NMLR	320	276	338	328	349	262	374	345	359
D.73	Current transfers within general government	QYJR	77 592	85 224	94 720	101 369	110 407	113 108	117 867	124 622	132 444
D.74	Current grants from rest of the world	GNK9	–	–	69	58	80	84	104	104	118
D.7	Other current transfers	NMLO	77 912	85 500	95 127	101 755	110 836	113 454	118 345	125 071	132 921
Total	Total resources	NMLX	99 273	108 161	119 776	127 541	138 182	142 890	149 915	156 555	165 126
	Uses										
D.59	Other current taxes	EBFS	876	842	924	1 022	1 075	1 111	1 147	1 189	1 236
D.62	Social benefits other than social transfers in kind	NSMN	15 863	16 460	16 943	17 921	19 060	20 163	21 664	24 677	26 889
D.7	Other current transfers										
D.71	Net non-life insurance premiums	NMMI	320	276	338	328	349	262	374	345	359
D.73	Current transfers within general government	NMDK	–	–	–	–	–	–	–	–	–
D.75	Miscellaneous current transfers	EBFE	23	24	29	25	25	28	29	26	26
D.7	Other current transfers	NMMF	343	300	367	353	374	290	403	371	385
B.6g	**Gross Disposable Income**	NRLW	**82 191**	**90 559**	**101 542**	**108 245**	**117 673**	**121 326**	**126 701**	**130 318**	**136 616**
Total	Total uses	NMLX	99 273	108 161	119 776	127 541	138 182	142 890	149 915	156 555	165 126
-K.1	After deduction of fixed capital consumption	-NSRO	-4 653	-4 905	-5 314	-5 819	-6 365	-6 698	-7 058	-7 443	-7 913
B.6n	Disposable income, net	NMMQ	77 538	85 654	96 228	102 426	111 308	114 628	119 643	122 875	128 703

5.3.4S Local government
Social contributions and benefits
ESA95 sector S.1313

£ million

Part			2002	2003	2004	2005	2006	2007	2008	2009	2010
	SECONDARY DISTRIBUTION OF INCOME (further detail of certain items)										
	Resources										
D.61	Social contributions										
	Unfunded pension schemes[1]										
D.611	Actual social contributions										
D.61122	Employees' voluntary contributions	NMWM	637	659	703	758	797	802	806	828	853
D.612	Imputed social contributions										
D.612	Employers' contributions	GCMN	2 066	2 145	2 221	2 310	2 426	2 525	2 751	3 089	3 246
D.61	Total social contributions	NSMM	2 703	2 804	2 924	3 068	3 223	3 327	3 557	3 917	4 099
	Uses										
D.62	Social benefits										
D.623	Unfunded employee social benefits										
	Unfunded pensions paid[1]	NMWK	2 192	2 317	2 446	2 585	2 736	2 836	3 057	3 417	3 596
	Other unfunded employee benefits	EWRN	511	487	478	483	487	491	500	500	503
D.623	Total unfunded social benefits	GCMO	2 703	2 804	2 924	3 068	3 223	3 327	3 557	3 917	4 099
D.624	Social assistance benefits in cash										
	Student grants	GCSI	1 082	1 208	1 037	1 094	1 207	1 327	1 345	1 488	1 690
	Rent rebates	CTML	5 232	5 120	5 158	5 249	5 344	5 433	5 388	5 449	5 390
	Rent allowances	GCSR	6 846	7 328	7 824	8 510	9 286	10 076	11 374	13 823	15 710
	Total other transfers	ZXHZ	–	–	–	–	–	–	–	–	–
D.624	Total social assistance benefits in cash	ADAL	13 160	13 656	14 019	14 853	15 837	16 836	18 107	20 760	22 790
D.62	Total social benefits	NSMN	15 863	16 460	16 943	17 921	19 060	20 163	21 664	24 677	26 889

1 Mainly police and firefighters' schemes

5.3.5 Local government
ESA95 sector S.1313

£ million

			2002	2003	2004	2005	2006	2007	2008	2009	2010
II.3	**REDISTRIBUTION OF INCOME IN KIND ACCOUNT**										
	Resources										
B.6g	Total resources (Gross Disposable Income)	NRLW	**82 191**	**90 559**	**101 542**	**108 245**	**117 673**	**121 326**	**126 701**	**130 318**	**136 616**
	Uses										
D.63	Social transfers in kind										
D.631	Social benefits in kind										
D.632	Transfers of individual non-market goods and services	NMMU	56 595	60 434	64 380	69 646	74 232	77 993	82 413	86 078	89 284
B.7g	Adjusted disposable income, gross	NSXL	25 596	30 125	37 162	38 599	43 441	43 333	44 288	44 240	47 332
B.6g	Total uses (Gross Disposable Income)	NRLW	**82 191**	**90 559**	**101 542**	**108 245**	**117 673**	**121 326**	**126 701**	**130 318**	**136 616**

5.3.6 Local government
ESA95 sector S.1313

£ million

			2002	2003	2004	2005	2006	2007	2008	2009	2010
II.4	**USE OF INCOME ACCOUNT**										
II.4.1	**USE OF DISPOSABLE INCOME ACCOUNT**										
	Resources										
B.6g	Total resources (Gross Disposable Income)	NRLW	**82 191**	**90 559**	**101 542**	**108 245**	**117 673**	**121 326**	**126 701**	**130 318**	**136 616**
	Uses										
P.3	Final consumption expenditure										
P.31	Individual consumption expenditure	NMMU	56 595	60 434	64 380	69 646	74 232	77 993	82 413	86 078	89 284
P.32	Collective consumption expenditure	NMMV	25 613	29 519	34 274	37 298	37 478	39 103	41 805	41 622	41 434
P.3	Total	NMMT	82 208	89 953	98 654	106 944	111 710	117 096	124 218	127 700	130 718
B.8g	**Gross Saving**	NRLX	**–17**	**606**	**2 888**	**1 301**	**5 963**	**4 230**	**2 483**	**2 618**	**5 898**
B.6g	Total uses (Gross Disposable Income)	NRLW	**82 191**	**90 559**	**101 542**	**108 245**	**117 673**	**121 326**	**126 701**	**130 318**	**136 616**
-K.1	After deduction of fixed capital consumption	-NSRO	–4 653	–4 905	–5 314	–5 819	–6 365	–6 698	–7 058	–7 443	–7 913
B.8n	Saving, net	NMMX	–4 670	–4 299	–2 426	–4 518	–402	–2 468	–4 575	–4 825	–2 015
II.4.2	**USE OF ADJUSTED DISPOSABLE INCOME ACCOUNT**										
	Resources										
B.7g	Total resources, adjusted disposable income, gross	NSXL	25 596	30 125	37 162	38 599	43 441	43 333	44 288	44 240	47 332
	Uses										
P.4	Actual final consumption										
P.42	Actual collective consumption	NMMV	25 613	29 519	34 274	37 298	37 478	39 103	41 805	41 622	41 434
B.8g	**Gross Saving**	NRLX	**–17**	**606**	**2 888**	**1 301**	**5 963**	**4 230**	**2 483**	**2 618**	**5 898**
Total	Total uses	NSXL	25 596	30 125	37 162	38 599	43 441	43 333	44 288	44 240	47 332

5.3.7 Local government
ESA95 sector S.1313

£ million

			2002	2003	2004	2005	2006	2007	2008	2009	2010
III	**ACCUMULATION ACCOUNTS**										
III.1	**CAPITAL ACCOUNT**										
III.1.1	**CHANGE IN NET WORTH DUE TO SAVINGS AND CAPITAL TRANSFERS**										
	Changes in liabilities and net worth										
B.8g	Gross Saving	NRLX	–17	606	2 888	1 301	5 963	4 230	2 483	2 618	5 898
D.9	Capital transfers receivable										
D.92	Investment grants	NMNE	6 328	7 360	6 804	7 582	8 515	9 960	11 359	13 407	13 061
D.99	Other capital transfers	NMNH	735	4 770	2 282	2 014	1 141	1 741	2 959	987	252
D.9	Total capital transfers receivable	NMMY	7 063	12 130	9 086	9 596	9 656	11 701	14 318	14 394	13 313
-D.9	*less* Capital transfers payable										
-D.92	Investment grants	-NMNR	–839	–1 165	–1 127	–1 563	–1 635	–2 089	–2 383	–3 046	–3 574
-D.99	Other capital transfers	-NMNU	–5	–5	–1 247	–1 325	–601	–960	–2 210	–362	–480
-D.9	Total capital transfers payable	-NMNL	–844	–1 170	–2 374	–2 888	–2 236	–3 049	–4 593	–3 408	–4 054
B.10.1g	Total change in liabilities and net worth	NRMJ	6 202	11 566	9 600	8 009	13 383	12 882	12 208	13 604	15 157
	Changes in assets										
B.10.1g	Changes in net worth due to gross saving and capital transfers	NRMJ	6 202	11 566	9 600	8 009	13 383	12 882	12 208	13 604	15 157
-K.1	After deduction of fixed capital consumption	-NSRO	–4 653	–4 905	–5 314	–5 819	–6 365	–6 698	–7 058	–7 443	–7 913
B.10.1n	Changes in net worth due to net saving and capital transfers	NMNX	1 549	6 661	4 286	2 190	7 018	6 184	5 150	6 161	7 244
III.1.2	**ACQUISITION OF NON-FINANCIAL ASSETS ACCOUNT**										
	Changes in liabilities and net worth										
B.10.1n	Changes in net worth due to saving and capital transfers	NMNX	1 549	6 661	4 286	2 190	7 018	6 184	5 150	6 161	7 244
K.1	Consumption of fixed capital	NSRO	4 653	4 905	5 314	5 819	6 365	6 698	7 058	7 443	7 913
B.10.1g	Total changes in liabilities and net worth	NRMJ	6 202	11 566	9 600	8 009	13 383	12 882	12 208	13 604	15 157
	Changes in assets										
P.5	Gross capital formation										
P.51	Gross fixed capital formation	NMOA	7 946	14 137	14 891	13 516	13 807	14 329	17 217	18 649	18 538
P.52	Changes in inventories	NMOB	–	–	–	–	–	–	–	–	–
P.5	Total	NMNZ	7 946	14 137	14 891	13 516	13 807	14 329	17 217	18 649	18 538
K.2	Acquisitions less disposals of non-produced non-financial assets	NMOD	–760	–800	–857	–902	–947	–928	–920	–956	–943
B.9g	**Net lending(+) / net borrowing(-)**	NMOE	**–984**	**–1 771**	**–4 434**	**–4 605**	**523**	**–519**	**–4 089**	**–4 089**	**–2 438**
Total	Total change in assets	NRMJ	6 202	11 566	9 600	8 009	13 383	12 882	12 208	13 604	15 157

5.3.8 Local government
ESA95 sector S.1313 Unconsolidated

£ million

				2002	2003	2004	2005	2006	2007	2008	2009	2010
III.2	**FINANCIAL ACCOUNT**											
F.A	**Net acquisition of financial assets**											
F.2	Currency and deposits											
F.22	Transferable deposits											
F.221	Sterling deposits with UK monetary financial institutions	NBYR		1 330	1 313	3 885	78	5 385	4 339	–2 541	–6 918	955
F.2212	*of which* Foreign currency deposits	NBYT		–1	–9	1	28	–20	2	1	46	9
F.29	Other deposits	NBYW		268	135	–67	–75	–208	581	2 138	2 019	–1 319
F.2	Total currency and deposits	NBYO		1 598	1 448	3 818	3	5 177	4 920	–403	–4 899	–364
F.3	Securities other than shares											
F.331	Short term: money market instruments											
F.3311	Issued by UK central government	NBYZ		–141	–38	–59	14	–18	–51	23	77	794
F.3315	Issued by UK monetary financial institutions	NBZE		487	24	–232	–159	–967	–953	–219	–189	–169
F.3316	Issued by other UK residents	NBZJ		11	–38	10	197	725	670	469	–843	29
F.332	Medium (1 to 5 year) and long term (over 5 year) bonds											
F.3321	Issued by UK central government	NBZM		–264	–101	–98	7	75	–126	45	28	26
F.3326	Issued by other UK residents	E55E		–	–	–	215	–	–	–	–	–
F.3	Total securities other than shares	NBYX		93	–153	–379	274	–185	–460	318	–927	680
F.4	Loans											
F.42	Long term loans											
F.422	Loans secured on dwellings	NCAK		206	186	4	252	340	522	1 191	665	405
F.424	Other long-term loans by UK residents	NCAP		–83	–18	–28	200	–23	–258	–38	119	489
F.4	Total loans	NBZZ		123	168	–24	452	317	264	1 153	784	894
F.5	Shares and other equity											
F.51	Shares and other equity, excluding mutual funds' shares											
F.514	Quoted UK shares	NCAW		–218	45	–116	–157	157	–168	–51	–79	205
F.515	Unquoted UK shares	NCAX		–	–	–1	–	3	–128	–	–	–
F.516	Other UK equity	HN68		–2 860	–5 479	–3 686	–2 592	–2 173	–2 080	–1 078	–539	–483
F.517	UK shares and bonds issued by other UK residents	NSPE		–	–	–	–	–	–	–	–	–
F.5	Total shares and other equity	NCAR		–3 078	–5 434	–3 803	–2 749	–2 013	–2 376	–1 129	–618	–278
F.6	Insurance technical reserves											
F.62	Prepayments of insurance premiums and reserves for outstanding claims	NCBK		27	8	45	–24	–11	82	21	–24	16
F.7	Other accounts receivable	NCBL		–1 123	281	–45	200	–27	–22	90	207	519
F.A	**Total net acquisition of financial assets**	NBYK		–2 360	–3 682	–388	–1 844	3 258	2 408	50	–5 477	1 467

5.3.8 Local government
ESA95 sector S.1313 Unconsolidated
continued

£ million

			2002	2003	2004	2005	2006	2007	2008	2009	2010
III.2	**FINANCIAL ACCOUNT** continued										
F.L	Net acquisition of financial liabilities										
F.3	Securities other than shares										
F.331	Short term: money market instruments										
F.3312	Issued by UK local government	NCCH	–	–	–	–	–	–	–	–	–
F.332	Medium (1 to 5 year) and long term (over 5 year) bonds										
F.3322	Issued by UK local authorities	NCCT	47	18	–226	213	360	–9	–70	–83	–17
F.3	Total securities other than shares	NCCB	47	18	–226	213	360	–9	–70	–83	–17
F.4	Loans										
F.41	Short term loans										
F.411	Loans by UK monetary financial institutions, excluding loans secured on dwellings & financial leasing	NCDF	816	1 162	1 528	734	1 171	1 454	–	226	364
F.419	Loans by rest of the world monetary financial institutions	NCDJ	–13	–7	–6	–3	–1	–	–	–	–
F.42	Long term loans										
F.423	Finance leasing	NCDS	18	15	–	5	3	–	–	–	–
F.424	Other long-term loans by UK residents	NCDT	–1 709	–3 893	521	2 620	2 645	1 271	3 167	–1 770	2 415
F.429	Other long-term loans by the rest of the world	NCDU	39	211	657	137	233	–42	446	520	175
F.4	Total loans	NCDD	–849	–2 512	2 700	3 493	4 051	2 683	3 613	–1 024	2 954
F.7	Other accounts payable	NCEP	–492	242	590	3	–1 035	314	1 080	–633	1 099
F.L	**Total net acquisition of financial liabilities**	NCBO	–1 294	–2 252	3 064	3 709	3 376	2 988	4 623	–1 740	4 036
B.9	Net lending / borrowing										
F.A	Total net acquisition of financial assets	NBYK	–2 360	–3 682	–388	–1 844	3 258	2 408	50	–5 477	1 467
-F.L	*less* Total net acquisition of financial liabilities	-NCBO	1 294	2 252	–3 064	–3 709	–3 376	–2 988	–4 623	1 740	–4 036
B.9f	Net lending (+) / net borrowing (-), from financial account	NYNQ	–1 066	–1 430	–3 452	–5 553	–118	–580	–4 573	–3 737	–2 569
dB.9f	Statistical discrepancy	NYPC	82	–341	–982	948	641	61	484	–352	131
B.9g	**Net lending (+) / net borrowing (-), from capital account**	NMOE	–984	–1 771	–4 434	–4 605	523	–519	–4 089	–4 089	–2 438

5.3.9 Local government
ESA95 sector S.1313 Unconsolidated

£ billion

			2002	2003	2004	2005	2006	2007	2008	2009	2010
IV.3	**FINANCIAL BALANCE SHEET** at end of period										
AN	**Non-financial assets**	CGIZ	308.9	335.5	381.2	406.8	436.3	477.2	444.8	401.8	411.2
AF.A	**Financial assets**										
AF.2	Currency and deposits										
AF.22	Transferable deposits										
AF.221	Sterling deposits with UK monetary financial institutions	NJEO	15.6	17.1	21.4	21.5	26.9	31.2	28.9	22.0	23.0
AF.2212	*of which* Foreign currency deposits	NJEQ	–	–	–	–	–	–	0.1	0.1	0.1
AF.29	Other deposits	NJET	0.3	0.4	0.4	0.4	0.2	0.8	2.9	4.9	3.6
AF.2	Total currency and deposits	NJEL	15.9	17.6	21.8	21.9	27.1	32.0	31.8	27.0	26.6
AF.3	Securities other than shares										
AF.331	Short term: money market instruments										
AF.3311	Issued by UK central government	NJEW	0.2	0.2	0.1	0.1	0.1	0.1	0.1	0.1	0.9
AF.3315	Issued by UK monetary financial institutions	NJFB	3.8	3.9	3.6	3.5	2.5	1.6	1.3	1.2	1.0
AF.3316	Issued by other UK residents	NJFG	0.2	0.2	0.1	0.3	0.8	1.3	1.4	0.5	0.5
AF.332	Medium (1 to 5 year) and long term (over 5 year) bonds										
AF.3321	Issued by UK central government	NJFJ	0.4	0.3	0.2	0.2	0.2	0.1	0.2	0.2	0.2
AF.3326	Issued by other UK residents	E55D	–	–	–	0.2	0.2	0.2	0.2	0.2	0.2
AF.3	Total securities other than shares	NJEU	4.7	4.5	4.1	4.3	3.9	3.2	3.2	2.2	2.9
AF.4	Loans										
AF.42	Long term loans										
AF.422	Loans secured on dwellings	NJGH	0.8	1.0	1.0	1.3	1.6	2.1	3.3	4.0	4.8
AF.424	Other long-term loans by UK residents	NJGM	0.3	0.3	0.3	0.2	0.2	0.2	0.2	0.2	0.3
AF.4	Total loans	NJFW	1.1	1.3	1.3	1.5	1.8	2.4	3.5	4.2	5.1
AF.5	Shares and other equity										
AF.51	Shares and other equity, excluding mutual funds' shares										
AF.514	Quoted UK shares	NJGT	1.0	1.2	0.8	0.8	1.0	0.9	0.3	0.5	0.8
AF.515	Unquoted UK shares	NJGU	0.4	0.4	0.8	0.8	0.8	0.7	0.7	0.7	0.7
AF.516	Other UK equity	HN69	86.0	95.1	106.2	116.7	110.9	111.4	113.5	113.9	114.1
AF.517	UK shares and bonds issued by other UK residents	NSOE	–	–	–	–	–	–	–	–	–
AF.5	Total shares and other equity	NJGO	87.4	96.7	107.7	118.3	112.7	113.0	114.5	115.1	115.6
AF.6	Insurance technical reserves										
AF.62	Prepayments of insurance premiums and reserves for outstanding claims	NJHH	0.9	0.8	0.8	0.8	0.8	0.9	0.9	0.9	0.9
AF.7	Other accounts receivable	NJHI	0.3	0.8	0.3	0.9	1.1	–0.2	–0.8	–0.1	–0.2
AF.A	**Total financial assets**	NJFV	110.4	121.7	136.0	147.7	147.4	151.3	153.2	149.2	150.8

5.3.9 Local government
ESA95 sector S.1313 Unconsolidated

£ billion

				2002	2003	2004	2005	2006	2007	2008	2009	2010
IV.3	**FINANCIAL BALANCE SHEET** continued at end of period											
AF.L	**Financial liabilities**											
AF.3	Securities other than shares											
AF.331	Short term: money market instruments											
AF.3312	Issued by UK local government	NJIE		–	–	–	–	–	–	–	–	–
AF.332	Medium (1 to 5 year) and long term (over 5 year) bonds											
AF.3322	Issued by UK local government	NJIQ		0.8	0.8	0.6	0.8	1.2	1.2	1.1	1.0	1.0
AF.3326	Issued by UK residents	IH3I		–	–	–	–	–	–	–	–	–
AF.3	Total securities other than shares	NJHY		0.8	0.8	0.6	0.8	1.2	1.2	1.1	1.0	1.0
AF.4	Loans											
AF.41	Short term loans											
AF.411	Loans by UK monetary financial institutions, excluding loans secured on dwellings & financial leasing	NJJC		2.9	4.3	6.3	7.6	9.1	10.3	10.9	11.0	11.7
AF.419	Loans by rest of the world monetary financial institutions	ZMFC		–	–	–	–	–	–	–	–	–
AF.42	Long term loans											
AF.423	Finance leasing	NJJP		–	–	–	0.1	0.1	0.1	0.1	0.1	0.1
AF.424	Other long-term loans by UK residents	NJJQ		48.4	44.5	45.5	48.0	49.8	50.6	53.8	52.0	54.7
AF.429	Other long-term loans by the rest of the world	NJJR		0.8	1.1	1.7	1.9	2.1	2.1	2.5	3.0	3.2
AF.4	Total loans	NJJA		52.1	49.9	53.5	57.5	61.1	63.1	67.3	66.2	69.6
AF.7	Other accounts payable	NJKM		9.3	9.7	10.8	11.0	11.3	9.5	9.0	8.6	8.5
AF.L	**Total financial liabilities**	NJIZ		62.2	60.4	64.9	69.3	73.6	73.7	77.3	75.8	79.1
BF.90	**Net financial assets / liabilities**											
AF.A	Total financial assets	NJFV		110.4	121.7	136.0	147.7	147.4	151.3	153.2	149.2	150.8
-AF.L	*less* Total financial liabilities	-NJIZ		−62.2	−60.4	−64.9	−69.3	−73.6	−73.7	−77.3	−75.8	−79.1
BF.90	**Net financial assets (+) / liabilities (-)**	NYOJ		48.2	61.3	71.1	78.4	73.8	77.5	75.8	73.4	71.7
	Net worth											
AN	Non-financial assets	CGIZ		308.9	335.5	381.2	406.8	436.3	477.2	444.8	401.8	411.2
BF.90	Net financial assets (+) / liabilities (-)	NYOJ		48.2	61.3	71.1	78.4	73.8	77.5	75.8	73.4	71.7
BF.90	**Net worth**	CGRZ		357.1	396.8	452.4	485.2	510.2	554.7	520.6	475.2	483.0

Chapter 6

Households and non-profit institutions serving households (NPISH)

6.1.1 Households and non-profit institutions serving households
ESA95 sectors S.14 and S.15

£ million

			2002	2003	2004	2005	2006	2007	2008	2009
I	**PRODUCTION ACCOUNT**									
	Resources									
P.1	Output									
P.11	Market output	QWLF	220 911	232 649	234 364	245 497	261 677	282 158	288 909	281 535
P.12	Output for own final use	QWLG	65 417	71 061	75 360	79 475	83 093	88 540	93 863	98 486
P.13	Other non-market output	QWLH	26 422	27 668	29 197	30 824	32 408	34 324	35 767	35 863
P.1	Total resources	QWLI	312 750	331 378	338 921	355 796	377 178	405 022	418 539	415 884
	Uses									
P.2	Intermediate consumption	QWLJ	136 595	140 857	140 947	150 888	164 902	178 544	189 193	206 924
B.1g	**Gross Value Added**	QWLK	**176 155**	**190 521**	**197 974**	**204 908**	**212 276**	**226 478**	**229 346**	**208 960**
Total	Total uses	QWLI	312 750	331 378	338 921	355 796	377 178	405 022	418 539	415 884
B.1g	**Gross Value Added**	QWLK	**176 155**	**190 521**	**197 974**	**204 908**	**212 276**	**226 478**	**229 346**	**208 960**
-K.1	*less* Consumption of fixed capital	-QWLL	−36 043	−36 903	−42 509	−43 257	−48 584	−51 904	−44 914	−47 375
B.1n	Value added, net	QWLM	140 112	153 618	155 465	161 651	163 692	174 574	184 432	161 585

6.1.2 Households and non-profit institutions serving households
ESA95 sectors S.14 and S.15

£ million

			2002	2003	2004	2005	2006	2007	2008	2009
II	**DISTRIBUTION AND USE OF INCOME ACCOUNTS**									
II.1	**PRIMARY DISTRIBUTION OF INCOME ACCOUNT**									
II.1.1	**GENERATION OF INCOME ACCOUNT**									
	before deduction of fixed capital consumption									
	Resources									
B.1g	**Total resources (Gross Value Added)**	QWLK	**176 155**	**190 521**	**197 974**	**204 908**	**212 276**	**226 478**	**229 346**	**208 960**
	Uses									
D.1	Compensation of employees									
D.11	Wages and salaries	QWLN	47 997	49 803	51 002	52 888	55 211	58 550	60 893	62 039
D.12	Employers' social contributions	QWLO	6 656	7 950	8 413	9 379	9 996	10 154	10 200	11 116
D.1	Total	QWLP	54 653	57 753	59 415	62 267	65 207	68 704	71 093	73 155
D.2	Taxes on production and imports, paid									
D.29	Production taxes other than on products	QWLQ	58	61	64	68	51	60	50	48
-D.3	*less* Subsidies received									
-D.39	Production subsidies other than on products	-QWLR	−519	−592	−592	−3 408	−3 221	−2 952	−3 051	−3 411
B.2g	Operating surplus, gross	QWLS	55 647	60 983	65 752	67 494	69 807	77 768	74 878	57 744
B.3g	Mixed income, gross	QWLT	66 316	72 316	73 335	78 487	80 432	82 898	86 376	81 424
B.1g	**Total uses (Gross Value Added)**	QWLK	**176 155**	**190 521**	**197 974**	**204 908**	**212 276**	**226 478**	**229 346**	**208 960**
-K.1	After deduction of fixed capital consumption	-QWLL	−36 043	−36 903	−42 509	−43 257	−48 584	−51 904	−44 914	−47 375
B.2n	Operating surplus, net	QWLU	35 175	39 631	43 411	44 056	44 996	51 810	47 580	29 738
B.3n	Mixed income, net	QWLV	50 745	56 766	53 170	58 671	56 661	56 954	68 769	62 504

6.1.3 Households and non-profit institutions serving households
ESA95 sectors S.14 and S.15

£ million

			2002	2003	2004	2005	2006	2007	2008	2009	2010
II.1.2	**ALLOCATION OF PRIMARY INCOME ACCOUNT**										
	before deduction of fixed capital consumption										
	Resources										
B.2g	Operating surplus, gross	QWLS	55 647	60 983	65 752	67 494	69 807	77 768	74 878	57 744	72 098
B.3g	Mixed income, gross	QWLT	66 316	72 316	73 335	78 487	80 432	82 898	86 376	81 424	81 047
D.1	Compensation of employees										
D.11	Wages and salaries	QWLW	508 771	526 814	548 875	569 632	597 548	632 122	649 858	648 904	661 379
D.12	Employers' social contributions	QWLX	78 139	89 240	96 637	107 275	115 007	119 002	120 396	127 709	138 206
D.1	Total	QWLY	586 910	616 054	645 512	676 907	712 555	751 124	770 254	776 613	799 585
D.4	Property income, received										
D.41	Interest	QWLZ	26 658	27 251	34 805	40 332	43 764	55 077	50 796	9 772	9 325
D.42	Distributed income of corporations	QWMA	42 517	41 042	46 828	49 241	51 397	53 406	48 551	48 019	50 750
D.44	Attributed property income of insurance policy holders	QWMC	52 104	54 999	54 623	64 028	66 649	71 684	75 123	66 374	63 497
D.45	Rent	QWMD	106	108	110	110	110	110	115	115	117
D.4	Total	QWME	121 385	123 400	136 366	153 711	161 920	180 277	174 585	124 280	123 689
Total	Total resources	QWMF	830 258	872 753	920 965	976 599	1 024 714	1 092 067	1 106 093	1 040 061	1 076 419
	Uses										
D.4	Property income, paid										
D.41	Interest	QWMG	30 490	31 975	43 738	50 858	55 982	74 601	67 407	7 479	5 534
D.45	Rent	QWMH	216	220	224	224	226	225	233	239	239
D.4	Total	QWMI	30 706	32 195	43 962	51 082	56 208	74 826	67 640	7 718	5 773
B.5g	**Balance of primary incomes, gross**	QWMJ	**799 552**	**840 558**	**877 003**	**925 517**	**968 506**	**1 017 241**	**1 038 453**	**1 032 343**	**1 070 646**
Total	Total uses	QWMF	830 258	872 753	920 965	976 599	1 024 714	1 092 067	1 106 093	1 040 061	1 076 419
-K.1	After deduction of fixed capital consumption	-QWLL	−36 043	−36 903	−42 509	−43 257	−48 584	−51 904	−44 914	−47 375	−46 716
B.5n	Balance of primary incomes, net	QWMK	763 509	803 655	834 494	882 260	919 922	965 337	993 539	984 968	1 023 930

6.1.4 Households and non-profit institutions serving households
ESA95 sectors S.14 and S.15

£ million

				2002	2003	2004	2005	2006	2007	2008	2009	2010
II.2	**SECONDARY DISTRIBUTION OF INCOME ACCOUNT**											
	Resources											
B.5g	Balance of primary incomes, gross	QWMJ		799 552	840 558	877 003	925 517	968 506	1 017 241	1 038 453	1 032 343	1 070 646
D.612	Imputed social contributions	RVFH		530	505	498	506	514	518	524	524	528
D.62	Social benefits other than social transfers in kind	QWML		182 030	193 573	198 972	212 540	226 994	227 926	252 054	277 534	287 196
D.7	Other current transfers											
D.72	Non-life insurance claims	QWMM		17 327	13 891	17 479	17 199	19 802	14 080	20 025	18 548	19 204
D.75	Miscellaneous current transfers	QWMN		33 041	34 687	34 845	37 840	38 729	40 518	39 654	41 648	43 550
D.7	Total	QWMO		50 368	48 578	52 324	55 039	58 531	54 598	59 679	60 196	62 754
	Total resources	QWMP		1 032 480	1 083 214	1 128 797	1 193 602	1 254 545	1 300 283	1 350 710	1 370 597	1 421 124
	Uses											
D.5	Current taxes on income, wealth, etc											
D.51	Taxes on income	QWMQ		112 171	113 087	119 591	130 200	139 685	151 528	155 284	146 111	146 064
D.59	Other current taxes	NVCO		22 788	25 174	27 077	28 421	29 833	31 586	32 885	33 699	34 611
D.5	Total	QWMS		134 959	138 261	146 668	158 621	169 518	183 114	188 169	179 810	180 675
D.61	Social contributions											
D.611	Actual social contributions											
D.6111	Employers' actual social contributions	QWMT		64 805	77 571	85 297	94 487	102 133	105 252	105 678	111 115	123 166
D.6112	Employees' social contributions	QWMU		62 458	66 490	70 264	77 929	83 203	83 411	89 181	83 428	85 874
D.6113	Social contributions by self- and non-employed	QWMV		2 318	2 595	2 727	2 825	2 930	2 861	3 053	2 879	2 576
D.611	Total	QWMW		129 581	146 656	158 288	175 241	188 266	191 524	197 912	197 422	211 616
D.612	Imputed social contributions	QWMX		13 334	11 669	11 340	12 788	12 874	13 750	14 718	16 594	15 040
D.61	Total	QWMY		142 915	158 325	169 628	188 029	201 140	205 274	212 630	214 016	226 656
D.62	Social benefits other than social transfers in kind	QWMZ		1 006	987	987	1 000	1 010	1 014	1 020	1 020	1 024
D.7	Other current transfers											
D.71	Net non-life insurance premiums	QWNA		17 327	13 891	17 479	17 199	19 802	14 080	20 025	18 548	19 204
D.75	Miscellaneous current transfers	QWNB		11 458	11 930	12 462	13 442	13 286	14 405	13 771	14 060	14 381
D.7	Total	QWNC		28 785	25 821	29 941	30 641	33 088	28 485	33 796	32 608	33 585
B.6g	**Gross Disposable Income**[1]	QWND		724 815	759 820	781 573	815 311	849 789	882 396	915 095	943 143	979 184
	Total uses	QWMP		1 032 480	1 083 214	1 128 797	1 193 602	1 254 545	1 300 283	1 350 710	1 370 597	1 421 124
-K.1	After deduction of fixed capital consumption	-QWLL		–36 043	–36 903	–42 509	–43 257	–48 584	–51 904	–44 914	–47 375	–46 716
B.6n	Disposable income, net	QWNE		688 772	722 917	739 064	772 054	801 205	830 492	870 181	895 768	932 468

1 Gross household disposable income revalued by the implied households and NPISH's final consumption expenditure deflator is as follows:

		2002	2003	2004	2005	2006	2007	2008	2009	2010
Real household disposable income: (Chained volume measures)										
£ million (Reference year 2008)	RVGK	838 455	863 663	872 030	887 943	901 557	912 788	915 095	929 792	930 323
Index (2008 = 100)	OSXR	91.6	94.4	95.3	97.0	98.5	99.7	100.0	101.6	101.7

6.1.4S Households and non-profit institutions serving households
Social benefits and contributions
ESA 95 sectors S.14 and S.15

£ million

Part			2002	2003	2004	2005	2006	2007	2008	2009	2010
	SECONDARY DISTRIBUTION OF INCOME (further detail of certain items)										
	Benefits										
	Resources										
D.62	Social benefits										
D.621	Social security benefits in cash										
	National insurance fund benefits[1]	ACHH	53 123	55 731	58 118	60 400	62 600	66 508	70 629	77 029	77 654
	Redundancy fund benefit	GTKN	278	245	169	274	200	178	267	522	139
	Social fund benefit	GTLQ	1 910	2 135	2 240	2 232	2 253	2 351	2 975	3 275	3 684
	Maternity fund benefits	GTKO	–	–	–	–	–	–	–	–	–
D.621	Total social security benefits in cash	HAYQ	55 311	58 111	60 527	62 906	65 053	69 037	73 871	80 826	81 477
D.622	Private funded social benefits										
	Funded social benefits	D3N3	40 225	42 121	39 375	45 469	54 131	43 494	55 013	58 880	61 038
	Employee benefits from employers' liability insurance	NRXD	930	1 143	1 269	1 400	1 458	1 502	1 550	1 598	1 646
D.622	Total private funded social benefits	HAYR	41 155	43 264	40 644	46 869	55 589	44 996	56 563	60 478	62 684
D.623	Unfunded employee social benefits										
	Unfunded central government pensions paid[2]	E8AF	14 345	15 221	16 240	17 238	18 361	21 292	21 988	24 157	25 567
	Unfunded local government pensions paid[3]	NMWK	2 192	2 317	2 446	2 585	2 736	2 836	3 057	3 417	3 596
	Other unfunded employee benefits[4]	EWRM	5 896	6 081	5 974	6 267	6 455	6 732	7 695	8 741	6 340
D.623	Total unfunded social benefits	RVFF	22 433	23 619	24 661	26 090	27 552	30 860	32 740	36 315	35 503
D.624	Social assistance benefits in cash										
	Received from central government	LNJT	49 495	54 441	58 632	61 328	62 467	65 701	70 277	78 659	84 246
	Received from local government	ADAL	13 160	13 656	14 019	14 853	15 837	16 836	18 107	20 760	22 790
	Received from NPISHs	HABJ	476	482	489	494	496	496	496	496	496
D.624	Total social assistance benefits in cash	HAYU	63 131	68 579	73 140	76 675	78 800	83 033	88 880	99 915	107 532
D.62	Total social benefits	QWML	182 030	193 573	198 972	212 540	226 994	227 926	252 054	277 534	287 196
	Uses										
D.62	Social benefits	QWMZ	1 006	987	987	1 000	1 010	1 014	1 020	1 020	1 024
	Contributions										
	Resources										
D.612	Imputed social contributions	RVFH	530	505	498	506	514	518	524	524	528
	Uses										
D.61	Social Contributions										
D.611	Actual social contributions										
D.6111	Employers' actual social contributions										
	National Insurance contributions	CEAN	35 735	39 890	43 874	46 824	49 568	53 765	57 080	54 387	56 089
	Notionally funded pension schemes	GCMP	3 045	5 177	5 616	6 028	6 472	6 971	7 844	9 120	9 785
	Funded pension schemes	RIUO	26 025	32 504	35 807	41 635	46 093	44 516	40 754	47 608	57 292
D.6111	Total employers' actual social contributions	QWMT	64 805	77 571	85 297	94 487	102 133	105 252	105 678	111 115	123 166
D.6112	Employees' actual social contributions										
	National Insurance contributions	GCSE	25 357	29 055	32 623	34 810	37 052	36 584	38 186	37 179	38 500
	Unfunded central government pension schemes	E8AA	3 550	4 639	5 714	6 246	6 514	6 674	6 538	6 004	6 024
	Unfunded local government pension schemes	NMWM	637	659	703	758	797	802	806	828	853
	Funded pension schemes	GCRR	32 914	32 137	31 224	36 115	38 840	39 351	43 651	39 417	40 497
D.6112	Total employees' actual social contributions	QWMU	62 458	66 490	70 264	77 929	83 203	83 411	89 181	83 428	85 874
D.6113	Social contributions by self and non-employed	QWMV	2 318	2 595	2 727	2 825	2 930	2 861	3 053	2 879	2 576
D.611	Total actual social contributions	QWMW	129 581	146 656	158 288	175 241	188 266	191 524	197 912	197 422	211 616
D.612	Imputed social contributions										
	Employers imputed contributions to unfunded central government pension schemes	E8AC	5 883	3 930	3 622	4 694	4 480	4 984	4 772	5 264	5 957
	Employers imputed contributions to unfunded local government pension schemes	NMWL	1 555	1 658	1 743	1 827	1 939	2 034	2 251	2 589	2 743
	Other imputed unfunded employers' contributions	EWRM	5 896	6 081	5 974	6 267	6 455	6 732	7 695	8 741	6 340
D.612	Total imputed social contributions	QWMX	13 334	11 669	11 340	12 788	12 874	13 750	14 718	16 594	15 040
D.61	Total social contributions	QWMY	142 915	158 325	169 628	188 029	201 140	205 274	212 630	214 016	226 656

1 For a more detailed analysis see table 5.2.4S
2 Mainly civil service, armed forces', teachers' and NHS staff
3 Mainly police and fire fighters
4 Such as payments whilst absent from work due to illness

6.1.5 Households and non-profit institutions serving households
ESA95 sectors S.14 and S.15

£ million

				2002	2003	2004	2005	2006	2007	2008	2009	2010
II.3	**REDISTRIBUTION OF INCOME IN KIND ACCOUNT**											
	Resources											
B.6g	Gross Disposable Income	QWND		724 815	759 820	781 573	815 311	849 789	882 396	915 095	943 143	979 184
D.63	Social transfers in kind											
D.631	Social benefits in kind											
D.6313	Social assistance benefits in kind	QWNH		–	–	–	–	–	–	–	–	–
D.632	Transfers of individual non-market goods and services	NSSA		158 425	171 317	176 948	190 019	204 897	216 086	230 388	242 776	250 466
D.63	Total social transfers in kind	NSSB		158 425	171 317	176 948	190 019	204 897	216 086	230 388	242 776	250 466
Total	Total resources	NSSC		883 240	931 137	958 521	1 005 330	1 054 686	1 098 482	1 145 483	1 185 919	1 229 650
	Uses											
D.63	Social transfers in kind											
D.631	Social benefits in kind											
D.6313	Social assistance benefits in kind	HAEJ		–	–	–	–	–	–	–	–	–
D.632	Transfers of individual non-market goods and services	HABK		26 422	27 668	29 197	30 824	32 408	34 324	35 767	35 863	37 702
D.63	Total social transfers in kind	HAEK		26 422	27 668	29 197	30 824	32 408	34 324	35 767	35 863	37 702
B.7g	Adjusted disposable income, gross	NSSD		856 818	903 469	929 324	974 506	1 022 278	1 064 158	1 109 716	1 150 056	1 191 948
Total	Total uses	NSSC		883 240	931 137	958 521	1 005 330	1 054 686	1 098 482	1 145 483	1 185 919	1 229 650

6.1.6 Households and non-profit institutions serving households
ESA95 sectors S.14 and S.15

£ million

				2002	2003	2004	2005	2006	2007	2008	2009	2010
II.4	**USE OF INCOME ACCOUNT**											
II.4.1	**USE OF DISPOSABLE INCOME ACCOUNT**											
	Resources											
B.6g	Gross Disposable Income	QWND		724 815	759 820	781 573	815 311	849 789	882 396	915 095	943 143	979 184
D.8	Adjustment for the change in net equity of households in pension funds	NSSE		17 784	21 377	26 386	30 881	29 343	38 871	27 842	26 547	35 105
Total	Total resources	NSSF		742 599	781 197	807 959	846 192	879 132	921 267	942 937	969 690	1 014 289
	Uses											
P.3	Final consumption expenditure											
P.31	Individual consumption expenditure	NSSG		707 071	742 180	778 804	814 973	851 572	896 566	913 791	894 105	937 906
B.8g	Gross Saving	NSSH		35 528	39 017	29 155	31 219	27 560	24 701	29 146	75 585	76 383
Total	Total uses	NSSF		742 599	781 197	807 959	846 192	879 132	921 267	942 937	969 690	1 014 289
-K.1	After deduction of fixed capital consumption	-QWLL		–36 043	–36 903	–42 509	–43 257	–48 584	–51 904	–44 914	–47 375	–46 716
B.8n	Saving, net	NSSI		–515	2 114	–13 354	–12 038	–21 024	–27 203	–15 768	28 210	29 667
II.4.2	**USE OF ADJUSTED DISPOSABLE INCOME ACCOUNT**											
	Resources											
B.7g	Adjusted disposable income, gross	NSSD		856 818	903 469	929 324	974 506	1 022 278	1 064 158	1 109 716	1 150 056	1 191 948
D.8	Adjustment for the change in net equity of households in pension funds	NSSE		17 784	21 377	26 386	30 881	29 343	38 871	27 842	26 547	35 105
Total	Total resources	NSSJ		874 602	924 846	955 710	1 005 387	1 051 621	1 103 029	1 137 558	1 176 603	1 227 053
	Uses											
P.4	Actual final consumption											
P.41	Actual individual consumption	NQEO		839 074	885 829	926 555	974 168	1 024 061	1 078 328	1 108 412	1 101 018	1 150 670
B.8g	Gross Saving[1]	NSSH		35 528	39 017	29 155	31 219	27 560	24 701	29 146	75 585	76 383
Total	Total uses	NSSJ		874 602	924 846	955 710	1 005 387	1 051 621	1 103 029	1 137 558	1 176 603	1 227 053

1 Households' saving as a percentage of total available households' resources is as follows:

			2002	2003	2004	2005	2006	2007	2008	2009	2010
Households' saving ratio (per cent)	RVGL		4.8	5.0	3.6	3.7	3.1	2.7	3.1	7.8	7.5

6.1.7 Households and non-profit institutions serving households
ESA95 sectors S.14 and S.15

£ million

			2002	2003	2004	2005	2006	2007	2008	2009	2010
III	**ACCUMULATION ACCOUNTS**										
III.1	**CAPITAL ACCOUNT**										
III.1.1	**CHANGE IN NET WORTH DUE TO SAVING & CAPITAL TRANSFERS ACCOUNT**										
	Changes in liabilities and net worth										
B.8g	Gross Saving	NSSH	35 528	39 017	29 155	31 219	27 560	24 701	29 146	75 585	76 383
D.9	Capital transfers receivable										
D.92	Investment grants	NSSL	3 456	4 691	4 372	6 696	5 256	6 978	7 111	7 468	8 521
D.99	Other capital transfers	NSSM	1 869	1 956	2 831	2 755	3 002	3 461	27 993	5 902	4 529
D.9	Total	NSSN	5 325	6 647	7 203	9 451	8 258	10 439	35 104	13 370	13 050
-D.9	*less* Capital transfers payable										
-D.91	Capital taxes	-NSSO	–2 381	–2 416	–2 881	–3 150	–3 575	–3 867	–3 257	–2 401	–2 643
-D.99	Other capital transfers	-NSSQ	–994	–938	–952	–927	–1 157	–1 127	–25 503	–2 766	–844
-D.9	Total	-NSSR	–3 375	–3 354	–3 833	–4 077	–4 732	–4 994	–28 760	–5 167	–3 487
B.10.1g	Total change in liabilities and net worth	NSSS	37 478	42 310	32 525	36 593	31 086	30 146	35 490	83 788	85 946
	Changes in assets										
B.10.1g	Changes in net worth due to gross saving and capital transfers	NSSS	37 478	42 310	32 525	36 593	31 086	30 146	35 490	83 788	85 946
-K.1	After deduction of fixed capital consumption	-QWLL	–36 043	–36 903	–42 509	–43 257	–48 584	–51 904	–44 914	–47 375	–46 716
B.10.1n	Changes in net worth due to saving and capital transfers	NSST	1 435	5 407	–9 984	–6 664	–17 498	–21 758	–9 424	36 413	39 230
III.1.2	**ACQUISITION OF NON-FINANCIAL ASSETS ACCOUNT**										
	Changes in liabilities and net worth										
B.10.1n	Changes in net worth due to saving and capital transfers	NSST	1 435	5 407	–9 984	–6 664	–17 498	–21 758	–9 424	36 413	39 230
K.1	Consumption of fixed capital	QWLL	36 043	36 903	42 509	43 257	48 584	51 904	44 914	47 375	46 716
B.10.1g	Total change in liabilities and net worth	NSSS	37 478	42 310	32 525	36 593	31 086	30 146	35 490	83 788	85 946
	Changes in assets										
P.5	Gross capital formation										
P.51	Gross fixed capital formation	NSSU	53 782	58 173	71 472	73 570	81 387	86 180	65 729	46 401	53 158
P.52	Changes in inventories	NSSV	273	508	87	182	67	257	25	–349	66
P.53	Acquisitions less disposals of valuables	NSSW	–281	–529	–570	–940	–176	–130	116	–	313
P.5	Total gross capital formation	NSSX	53 774	58 152	70 989	72 812	81 278	86 307	65 870	46 052	53 537
K.2	Acquisitions less disposals of non-produced non-financial assets	NSSY	–176	–210	–276	–320	–358	–340	–340	–348	–348
B.9	Net lending (+) / net borrowing (-)	NSSZ	–16 120	–15 632	–38 188	–35 899	–49 834	–55 821	–30 040	38 084	32 757
Total	Total change in assets	NSSS	37 478	42 310	32 525	36 593	31 086	30 146	35 490	83 788	85 946

6.1.8 Households and non-profit institutions serving households
ESA95 sectors S.14 and S.15 Unconsolidated

£ million

			2002	2003	2004	2005	2006	2007	2008	2009	2010
III.2	**FINANCIAL ACCOUNT**										
F.A	**Net acquisition of financial assets**										
F.2	Currency and deposits										
F.21	Currency	NFVT	1 505	1 882	2 540	1 997	1 858	2 290	3 017	3 551	1 893
F.22	Transferable deposits										
F.221	Deposits with UK monetary financial institutions	NFVV	46 069	51 031	56 880	57 696	64 517	70 393	45 085	21 387	25 434
F.2212	*of which* Foreign currency deposits	NFVX	62	489	602	101	809	1 052	−286	−42	−153
F.229	Deposits with rest of the world monetary financial institutions	NFVZ	2 375	5 365	7 957	4 193	6 562	13 308	−760	−12 525	3 169
F.29	Other deposits	NFWA	−552	4 506	1 544	4 129	6 166	5 843	11 830	2 534	2 258
F.2	Total currency and deposits	NFVS	49 397	62 784	68 921	68 015	79 103	91 834	59 172	14 947	32 754
F.3	Securities other than shares										
F.331	Short term: money market instruments										
F.3311	Issued by UK central government	NFWD	–	–	–	–	–	–	–	–	–
F.3312	Issued by UK local authorities	NFWH	–	–	–	–	–	–	–	–	–
F.3315	Issued by UK monetary financial institutions	NFWI	−496	−152	143	−731	1 492	1 130	1 124	589	−1 790
F.3316	Issued by other UK residents	NFWN	1	2	–	1	–	2	−182	–	–
F.332	Medium (1 to 5 year) and long term (over 5 year) bonds										
F.3321	Issued by UK central government	NFWQ	941	3 949	−6 281	−9 531	−27 351	−7 346	−2 510	2 866	12
F.3322	Issued by UK local authorities	NFWT	−12	4	−134	74	130	21	−60	56	13
F.3326	Other medium & long term bonds issued by UK residents	NFWX	213	39	183	218	224	−236	−386	−354	−856
F.3329	Long term bonds issued by the rest of the world	NFWY	88	88	88	88	88	88	88	88	88
F.34	Financial derivatives	NFWZ	–	–	−11	−242	310	119	−922	−11	464
F.3	Total securities other than shares	NFWB	736	3 929	−6 012	−10 123	−25 107	−6 222	−2 848	3 234	−2 069
F.4	Loans										
F.42	Long term loans										
F.424	Other long-term loans by UK residents	NFXT	1 932	5 538	−1 610	2 391	−3 662	−9 626	6 355	−1 892	1 258
F.4	Total loans	NFXD	1 932	5 538	−1 610	2 391	−3 662	−9 626	6 355	−1 892	1 258
F.5	Shares and other equity										
F.51	Shares and other equity, excluding mutual funds' shares										
F.514	Quoted UK shares	NFYA	16 109	−1 979	−9 673	−24 183	−8 946	−37 812	−15 755	38	1 086
F.515	Unquoted UK shares	NFYB	−5 190	−1 768	−5 730	−12 465	−11 072	−16 017	−60 983	−5 504	−16 422
F.516	Other UK equity (including direct investment in property)	NFYC	–	–	–	–	–	–	–	–	–
F.517	UK shares and bonds issued by other UK residents	NSPY	–	–	–	–	–	–	–	–	–
F.519	Shares and other equity issued by the rest of the world	NFYF	640	3 638	4 333	9 089	1 793	3 380	2 156	2 280	2 280
F.52	Mutual funds' shares										
F.521	UK mutual funds' shares	NFYJ	2 878	7 306	3 061	−3 610	2 528	−13 845	−9 647	18 298	8 235
F.529	Rest of the world mutual funds' shares	NFYK	−8	41	536	1 810	783	−110	−376	−1 544	−185
F.5	Total shares and other equity	NFXV	14 429	7 238	−7 473	−29 359	−14 914	−64 404	−84 605	13 568	−5 006
F.6	Insurance technical reserves										
F.61	Net equity of households in life assurance and pension funds' reserves	NFYL	46 181	34 441	40 593	52 049	59 327	65 107	19 932	20 449	22 058
F.62	Prepayments of insurance premiums and reserves for outstanding claims	NFYO	1 014	1 860	3 608	−830	2 601	2 061	5 296	−1 256	865
F.6	Total insurance technical reserves	NPWX	47 195	36 301	44 201	51 219	61 928	67 168	25 228	19 193	22 923
F.7	Other accounts receivable	NFYP	3 185	−1 351	9 224	3 269	30 874	−9 357	13 545	−7 458	2 039
F.A	**Total net acquisition of financial assets**	NFVO	116 874	114 439	107 251	85 412	128 222	69 393	16 847	41 592	51 899

6.1.8 Households and non-profit institutions serving households
ESA95 sectors S.14 and S.15 Unconsolidated
continued

£ million

			2002	2003	2004	2005	2006	2007	2008	2009	2010
III.2	**FINANCIAL ACCOUNT** continued										
F.L	**Net acquisition of financial liabilities**										
F.3	Securities other than shares										
F.331	Short term: money market instruments										
F.3316	Issued by UK residents other than monetary financial institutions and general government	NFZR	40	−73	−4	157	707	1 580	825	−563	249
F.332	Medium (1 to 5 year) and long term (over 5 year) bonds										
F.3326	Other medium & long term bonds issued by UK residents institutions and general government	NGAB	–	200	67	31	400	–	–	352	−221
F.34	Financial derivatives	NGAD	–	–	–	–	–	–	–	–	–
F.3	Total securities other than shares	NFZF	40	127	63	188	1 107	1 580	825	−211	28
F.4	Loans										
F.41	Short term loans										
F.411	Short-term loans by UK monetary financial institutions	NGAJ	20 469	18 072	23 614	17 477	15 876	10 823	6 530	−2 536	−2 736
F.4112	*of which* Foreign currency loans	NGAL	141	82	178	103	336	280	70	−162	−161
F.419	Loans by rest of the world monetary financial institutions	NGAN	510	3 839	5 663	88	5 175	−741	−364	−4 835	6 317
F.42	Long term loans										
F.422	Loans secured on dwellings by UK monetary financial institutions	NGAS	83 644	101 994	102 310	87 357	106 181	103 946	34 070	7 301	5 109
F.424	Other long-term loans by UK residents	NGAX	5 610	5 036	5 117	8 212	3 406	7 104	7 314	9 723	14 987
F.4	Total loans	NGAH	110 233	128 941	136 704	113 134	130 638	121 132	47 550	9 653	23 677
F.7	Other accounts payable	NGBT	10 302	7 027	4 972	3 661	36 690	−6 472	9 411	3 384	2 672
F.L	**Total net acquisition of financial liabilities**	NFYS	120 575	136 095	141 739	116 983	168 435	116 240	57 786	12 826	26 377
B.9	**Net lending / borrowing**										
F.A	Total net acquisition of financial assets	NFVO	116 874	114 439	107 251	85 412	128 222	69 393	16 847	41 592	51 899
-F.L	*less* Total net acquisition of financial liabilities	-NFYS	−120 575	−136 095	−141 739	−116 983	−168 435	−116 240	−57 786	−12 826	−26 377
B.9f	Net lending (+) / net borrowing (-), from financial account	NZDY	−3 701	−21 656	−34 488	−31 571	−40 213	−46 847	−40 939	28 766	25 522
dB.9f	Statistical discrepancy	NZDV	−12 419	6 024	−3 700	−4 328	−9 621	−8 974	10 899	9 318	7 235
B.9	**Net lending (+) / net borrowing (-), from capital account**	NSSZ	**−16 120**	**−15 632**	**−38 188**	**−35 899**	**−49 834**	**−55 821**	**−30 040**	**38 084**	**32 757**

6.1.9 Households and non-profit institutions serving households
ESA95 sectors S.14 and S.15   Unconsolidated

£ billion

				2002	2003	2004	2005	2006	2007	2008	2009	2010
IV.3		**FINANCIAL BALANCE SHEET** at end of period										
AN.2		Non-financial assets	CGCZ	3 135.1	3 491.1	3 902.2	4 047.2	4 471.4	4 917.6	4 451.7	4 621.5	4 881.3
AF.A		**Financial assets**										
AF.2		Currency and deposits										
AF.21		Currency	NNMQ	29.3	31.2	33.7	35.6	37.4	39.7	42.7	44.1	48.2
AF.22		Transferable deposits										
AF.221		Deposits with UK monetary financial institutions	NNMS	606.2	656.4	713.0	770.3	836.0	903.5	951.0	971.5	998.7
AF.2212		*of which* Foreign currency deposits	NNMU	2.2	2.6	3.1	3.4	3.9	4.9	6.3	5.7	5.6
AF.229		Deposits with rest of the world monetary financial institutions	NNMW	32.7	40.7	50.8	57.7	63.3	75.6	82.0	65.1	67.4
AF.29		Other deposits	NNMX	62.7	67.2	68.7	72.9	79.0	84.8	96.8	98.5	101.0
AF.2		Total currency and deposits	NNMP	731.0	795.5	866.2	936.5	1 015.8	1 103.6	1 172.5	1 179.2	1 215.4
AF.3		Securities other than shares										
AF.331		Short term: money market instruments										
AF.3311		Issued by UK central government	NNNA	–	–	–	–	–	–	–	–	–
AF.3312		Issued by UK local authorities	NNNE	–	–	–	–	–	–	–	–	–
AF.3315		Issued by UK monetary financial institutions	NNNF	2.3	2.3	2.5	1.9	3.1	4.6	6.2	5.6	4.7
AF.3316		Issued by other UK residents	NNNK	0.5	0.5	0.5	0.4	0.5	0.4	–0.3	–	0.1
AF.332		Medium (1 to 5 year) and long term (over 5 year) bonds										
AF.3321		Issued by UK central government	NNNN	40.3	35.0	31.0	37.5	18.0	12.2	11.1	10.0	12.2
AF.3322		Issued by UK local authorities	NNNQ	0.3	0.4	0.3	0.4	0.7	0.9	0.9	0.5	0.4
AF.3326		Other medium & long term bonds issued by UK residents	NNNU	4.5	4.7	4.9	5.1	5.3	5.5	5.7	5.9	6.1
AF.3329		Long term bonds issued by the rest of the world	NNNV	7.8	7.7	7.7	7.7	7.5	7.6	8.5	8.2	8.3
AF.34		Financial derivatives	NNNW	–	–	0.1	0.7	0.6	1.3	2.5	2.6	2.7
AF.3		Total securities other than shares	NNMY	55.7	50.6	47.0	53.8	35.8	32.5	34.6	32.9	34.7
AF.4		Loans										
AF.42		Long term loans										
AF.424		Other long-term loans by UK residents	NNOQ	6.7	6.8	7.0	7.0	7.3	9.9	18.2	18.3	18.4
AF.4		Total loans	NNOA	6.7	6.8	7.0	7.0	7.3	9.9	18.2	18.3	18.4
AF.5		Shares and other equity										
AF.51		Shares and other equity, excluding mutual funds' shares										
AF.514		Quoted UK shares	NNOX	164.7	196.9	203.6	214.5	224.8	192.8	119.3	153.6	172.6
AF.515		Unquoted UK shares	NNOY	122.5	135.1	139.8	164.7	151.4	161.1	126.1	220.5	225.5
AF.516		Other UK equity (including direct investment in property)	NNOZ	1.4	1.4	1.4	1.4	1.4	1.4	1.4	1.4	1.4
AF.517		UK shares and bonds issued by other UK residents	NSQR	–	–	–	–	–	–	–	–	–
AF.519		Shares and other equity issued by the rest of the world	NNPC	25.1	33.8	43.6	64.2	73.2	81.9	81.7	88.3	91.2
AF.52		Mutual funds' shares										
AF.521		UK mutual funds' shares	NNPG	108.3	118.9	138.2	139.7	164.1	162.9	76.9	101.9	142.7
AF.529		Rest of the world mutual funds' shares	NNPH	1.4	1.4	1.7	4.1	6.0	4.5	2.3	0.8	0.7
AF.5		Total shares and other equity	NNOS	423.4	487.5	528.3	588.4	620.8	604.6	407.6	566.5	634.0
AF.6		Insurance technical reserves										
AF.61		Net equity of households in life assurance and pension funds' reserves	NNPI	1 384.1	1 509.2	1 603.2	1 894.3	2 071.7	2 168.7	1 867.4	2 141.8	2 270.2
AF.62		Prepayments of insurance premiums and reserves for outstanding claims	NNPL	34.9	35.1	37.8	37.0	39.6	41.7	46.9	45.7	46.6
AF.6		Total insurance technical reserves	NPYL	1 419.0	1 544.3	1 641.0	1 931.3	2 111.3	2 210.3	1 914.3	2 187.5	2 316.7
AF.7		Other accounts receivable	NNPM	84.7	90.1	92.7	95.9	124.0	113.9	129.1	123.0	127.8
AF.A		**Total financial assets**	NNML	2 720.5	2 974.8	3 182.1	3 613.0	3 914.9	4 074.9	3 676.3	4 107.2	4 347.0

6.1.9 Households and non-profit institutions serving households
ESA95 sectors S.14 and S.15 Unconsolidated
continued

£ billion

				2002	2003	2004	2005	2006	2007	2008	2009	2010
IV.3	**FINANCIAL BALANCE SHEET** continued at end of period											
AF.L	**Financial liabilities**											
AF.3	Securities other than shares											
AF.331	Short term: money market instruments											
AF.3316	Issued by other UK residents	NNQO	0.2	0.1	0.1	0.1	0.8	1.2	1.3	0.4	0.5
AF.332	Medium (1 to 5 year) and long term (over 5 year) bonds											
AF.3326	Other medium & long term bonds issued by UK residents	NNQY	2.8	3.0	3.1	3.1	3.2	3.2	3.3	3.7	3.5
AF.34	Financial derivatives	NNRA	–	–	0.2	1.1	0.7	1.2	3.4	3.5	3.1
AF.3	Total securities other than shares	NNQC	3.0	3.1	3.4	4.4	4.6	5.6	8.0	7.6	7.1
AF.4	Loans											
AF.41	Short term loans											
AF.411	Loans by UK monetary financial institutions, excluding loans secured on dwellings & financial leasing	NNRG	148.5	152.4	169.7	179.3	185.6	191.5	191.8	181.2	173.4
AF.4112	o/w foreign currency loans	NNRI	0.6	0.6	0.8	0.9	1.4	1.4	2.1	1.7	1.5
AF.419	Loans by rest of the world monetary financial institutions	NNRK	8.3	13.0	18.5	19.9	26.4	26.0	32.6	25.9	31.8
AF.42	Long term loans											
AF.422	Loans secured on dwellings by UK monetary financial institutions	NNRP	669.4	772.9	881.1	938.3	1 046.3	1 146.8	1 185.7	1 191.4	1 198.3
AF.424	Other long-term loans by UK residents	NNRU	20.9	21.8	24.0	25.8	28.7	33.9	38.4	42.1	47.6
AF.4	Total loans	NNRE	847.1	960.1	1 093.4	1 163.3	1 287.0	1 398.2	1 448.5	1 440.6	1 451.1
AF.7	Other accounts payable	NNSQ	72.4	85.8	85.8	87.9	121.3	116.8	93.7	83.4	85.3
AF.L	**Total financial liabilities**	NNPP	922.5	1 049.1	1 182.5	1 255.6	1 412.9	1 520.6	1 550.1	1 531.6	1 543.6
BF.90	**Net financial assets / liabilities**											
AF.A	Total financial assets	NNML	2 720.5	2 974.8	3 182.1	3 613.0	3 914.9	4 074.9	3 676.3	4 107.2	4 347.0
-AF.L	*less* Total financial liabilities	-NNPP	–922.5	–1 049.1	–1 182.5	–1 255.6	–1 412.9	–1 520.6	–1 550.1	–1 531.6	–1 543.6
BF.90	**Net financial assets (+) / liabilities (-)**	NZEA	1 798.1	1 925.8	1 999.6	2 357.3	2 502.0	2 554.3	2 126.1	2 575.7	2 803.4
	Total net worth											
AN	Non-financial assets	CGCZ	3 135.1	3 491.1	3 902.2	4 047.2	4 471.4	4 917.6	4 451.7	4 621.5	4 881.3
BF.90	Net financial assets (+) / liabilities (-)	NZEA	1 798.1	1 925.8	1 999.6	2 357.3	2 502.0	2 554.3	2 126.1	2 575.7	2 803.4
BF.90	**Net worth**	CGRC	4 933.2	5 416.9	5 901.8	6 404.5	6 973.4	7 471.9	6 577.8	7 197.2	7 684.7

6.2 Household final consumption expenditure: classified by purpose
At current market prices

£ million

			2002	2003	2004	2005	2006	2007	2008	2009	2010
P.31	**FINAL CONSUMPTION EXPENDITURE OF HOUSEHOLDS**										
	Durable goods										
05.	Furnishings, household equipment and routine maintenance of the house	LLIJ	20 115	21 208	21 216	21 674	21 992	23 092	22 414	20 032	20 082
06.	Health	LLIK	2 399	2 719	2 513	2 420	2 801	2 969	3 034	3 135	2 872
07.	Transport	LLIL	37 100	37 997	39 024	38 422	38 238	40 247	36 652	36 977	38 888
08.	Communication	LLIM	630	732	684	728	760	717	761	839	714
09.	Recreation and culture	LLIN	16 473	17 065	19 211	20 210	21 846	22 647	23 444	22 887	24 047
12.	Miscellaneous goods and services	LLIO	4 428	4 540	4 976	4 828	5 394	5 140	5 108	4 761	5 521
D	Total durable goods	UTIA	81 145	84 261	87 624	88 282	91 031	94 812	91 413	88 631	92 124
	Semi-durable goods										
03.	Clothing and footwear	LLJL	37 600	39 819	41 775	43 120	46 027	47 424	48 271	47 040	49 760
05.	Furnishings, household equipment and routine maintenance of the house	LLJM	13 062	13 572	13 046	12 964	13 717	14 200	13 146	13 015	13 269
07.	Transport	LLJN	3 339	3 745	3 396	3 832	3 849	3 820	4 176	4 244	3 879
09.	Recreation and culture	LLJO	24 944	26 638	27 487	26 683	27 046	29 156	28 680	26 305	26 822
12.	Miscellaneous goods and services	LLJP	2 769	3 295	3 498	3 320	3 475	3 335	2 998	3 812	4 831
SD	Total semi-durable goods	UTIQ	81 714	87 069	89 202	89 919	94 114	97 935	97 271	94 416	98 561
	Non-durable goods										
01.	Food & drink	ABZV	62 360	64 712	66 362	69 547	72 202	75 706	79 790	81 185	83 401
02.	Alcohol & tobacco	ADFL	25 707	26 973	28 359	28 511	28 658	29 258	29 885	29 906	31 532
04.	Housing, water, electricity, gas and other fuels	LLIX	23 382	24 175	28 502	32 136	36 504	38 570	45 215	44 753	46 919
05.	Furnishings, household equipment and routine maintenance of the house	LLIY	3 263	3 388	3 564	3 609	3 813	3 772	3 770	4 088	4 061
06.	Health	LLIZ	4 105	4 057	4 285	4 371	4 513	4 715	4 765	4 949	5 070
07.	Transport	LLJA	19 457	20 345	22 579	24 695	25 846	28 090	30 665	27 884	32 503
09.	Recreation and culture	LLJB	13 316	13 155	14 105	14 615	15 594	15 793	16 143	14 889	14 884
12.	Miscellaneous goods and services	LLJC	11 654	12 989	13 503	13 726	14 763	15 383	15 101	14 586	14 681
ND	Total non-durable goods	UTII	163 244	169 794	181 259	191 210	201 893	211 287	225 334	222 240	233 051
	Total goods	UTIE	326 103	341 124	358 085	369 411	387 038	404 034	414 018	405 287	423 736
	Services										
03.	Clothing and footwear	LLJD	790	776	720	770	838	893	1 021	1 044	910
04.	Housing, water, electricity, gas and other fuels	LLJE	99 226	107 626	115 230	121 335	127 209	137 300	144 296	150 927	166 446
05.	Furnishings, household equipment and routine maintenance of the house	LLJF	5 293	5 621	5 731	5 976	6 037	6 021	6 439	5 916	7 695
06.	Health	LLJG	4 630	4 896	5 279	5 648	6 192	6 901	6 435	7 005	7 254
07.	Transport	LLJH	39 972	41 752	43 898	47 402	50 223	53 607	53 422	53 160	54 598
08.	Communication	LLJI	14 095	15 076	15 097	16 144	15 726	16 415	15 877	15 826	17 152
09.	Recreation and culture	LLJJ	24 029	25 578	27 180	29 215	30 782	32 651	32 636	33 155	34 393
10.	Education	ADIE	10 645	10 806	10 944	11 408	12 213	12 987	13 163	13 451	13 837
11.	Restaurants and hotels	ADIF	72 565	74 886	77 153	79 922	82 060	84 974	86 353	82 092	87 391
12.	Miscellaneous goods and services	LLJK	73 120	74 456	78 351	84 958	89 457	94 247	90 875	80 868	78 759
S	Total services	UTIM	344 365	361 473	379 583	402 778	420 737	445 996	450 517	443 444	468 435
0.	**Final consumption expenditure in the UK by resident and non-resident households (domestic concept)**	ABQI	670 468	702 597	737 668	772 189	807 775	850 030	864 535	848 731	892 171
P.33	Final consumption expenditure outside the UK by UK resident households	ABTA	23 967	25 984	27 547	29 026	30 388	31 701	33 286	29 063	29 203
-P.34	Less Final consumption expenditure in the UK by households resident in the rest of the world	CDFD	–13 786	–14 069	–15 608	–17 066	–18 999	–19 489	–19 797	–19 552	–21 170
P.31	**Final consumption expenditure by UK resident households in the UK and abroad (national concept)**	ABPB	680 649	714 512	749 607	784 149	819 164	862 242	878 024	858 242	900 204

Additional detail is published in *Consumer Trends* and table A7 of *UK Economic Accounts*, available from the ONS website
http://www.ons.gov.uk/ons/publications/all-releases.html?definition
=tcm%3A77-23619

6.3 Household final consumption expenditure: classified by purpose
Chained volume measures (Reference year 2008)

£ million

				2002	2003	2004	2005	2006	2007	2008	2009	2010
P.31	**FINAL CONSUMPTION EXPENDITURE OF HOUSEHOLDS**											
	Durable goods											
05.	Furnishings, household equipment and routine maintenance of the house	LLME		20 658	21 902	21 935	22 367	22 855	23 626	22 414	19 357	18 803
06.	Health	LLMF		2 436	2 749	2 544	2 448	2 864	3 000	3 034	3 124	2 832
07.	Transport	LLMG		37 757	37 956	38 054	37 511	37 381	39 166	36 652	37 860	36 490
08.	Communication	LLMH		565	653	619	676	706	695	761	833	678
09.	Recreation and culture	LLMI		7 507	8 656	10 801	13 058	16 033	19 247	23 444	24 910	27 653
12.	Miscellaneous goods and services	LLMJ		5 189	5 180	5 616	5 503	5 892	5 425	5 108	4 519	4 911
D	Total durable goods	UTIC		68 450	72 100	75 949	79 195	84 333	90 485	91 413	90 603	91 367
	Semi-durable goods											
03.	Clothing and footwear	LLNG		28 016	30 886	34 079	37 102	41 284	44 214	48 271	51 015	54 500
05.	Furnishings, household equipment and routine maintenance of the house	LLNH		11 839	12 613	12 249	12 612	13 656	14 163	13 146	12 795	12 709
07.	Transport	LLNI		3 678	4 072	3 641	4 034	3 948	3 903	4 176	4 110	3 607
09.	Recreation and culture	LLNJ		20 622	23 180	24 933	24 964	26 038	28 429	28 680	26 749	27 375
12.	Miscellaneous goods and services	LLNK		2 729	3 289	3 595	3 427	3 587	3 379	2 998	3 769	4 824
SD	Total semi-durable goods	UTIS		66 178	73 244	77 998	81 783	88 291	93 933	97 271	98 438	103 015
	Non-durable goods											
01.	Food & drink	ADIP		75 128	77 111	78 579	81 167	82 276	82 534	79 790	76 986	76 627
02.	Alcohol & tobacco	ADIS		29 574	29 992	31 203	30 973	30 317	30 215	29 885	28 701	29 087
04.	Housing, water, electricity, gas and other fuels	LLMS		40 291	41 002	46 036	47 186	45 487	44 596	45 215	41 632	44 270
05.	Furnishings, household equipment and routine maintenance of the house	LLMT		3 322	3 536	3 877	3 940	4 026	3 900	3 770	3 809	3 670
06.	Health	LLMU		4 130	4 060	4 315	4 448	4 611	4 756	4 765	4 871	4 909
07.	Transport	LLMV		28 818	29 032	30 536	30 818	30 650	32 371	30 665	30 142	29 249
09.	Recreation and culture	LLMW		14 849	14 381	15 210	15 680	16 350	16 345	16 143	14 322	13 721
12.	Miscellaneous goods and services	LLMX		11 664	13 235	14 095	14 464	15 322	15 635	15 101	14 202	13 949
ND	Total non-durable goods	UTIK		207 784	212 693	223 375	228 151	229 026	230 370	225 334	214 665	215 482
	Total goods	UTIG		336 404	353 846	373 219	385 673	399 890	414 189	414 018	403 706	409 864
	Services											
03.	Clothing and footwear	LLMY		959	913	824	847	891	920	1 021	1 022	872
04.	Housing, water, electricity, gas and other fuels	LLMZ		132 532	137 511	138 463	138 322	140 063	142 740	144 296	144 610	146 423
05.	Furnishings, household equipment and routine maintenance of the house	LLNA		6 975	7 036	6 816	6 807	6 611	6 292	6 439	5 808	7 395
06.	Health	LLNB		5 759	5 855	6 175	6 297	6 599	7 084	6 435	6 716	6 713
07.	Transport	LLNC		50 224	50 676	51 404	53 272	54 378	55 846	53 422	51 668	51 663
08.	Communication	LLND		13 051	13 879	13 998	15 331	14 875	16 019	15 877	15 651	16 185
09.	Recreation and culture	LLNE		29 450	30 350	31 501	32 666	32 948	33 646	32 636	31 902	31 866
10.	Education	ADMJ		17 128	16 159	15 621	15 522	15 525	14 508	13 163	12 480	12 190
11.	Restaurants and hotels	ADMK		88 762	89 128	89 557	89 403	88 453	88 342	86 353	80 131	83 473
12.	Miscellaneous goods and services	LLNF		88 851	88 781	89 254	92 002	91 918	94 337	90 875	86 745	84 068
S	Total services	UTIO		432 611	439 447	442 922	450 212	451 886	459 717	450 517	436 733	440 848
0.	Final consumption expenditure in the UK by resident and non-resident households (domestic concept)	ABQJ		765 392	790 906	815 148	835 256	851 605	873 882	864 535	840 439	850 712
P.33	Final consumption expenditure outside the UK by UK resident households	ABTC		32 663	32 840	35 235	34 807	35 813	37 327	33 286	25 932	25 140
-P.34	*Less* Final consumption expenditure in the UK by households resident in the rest of the world	CCHX		-15 738	-15 767	-17 202	-18 386	-19 950	-19 888	-19 797	-19 410	-20 550
P.3	Final consumption expenditure by UK resident households in the UK and abroad (national concept)	ABPF		781 860	807 653	832 690	851 338	867 082	890 872	878 024	846 961	855 302

Additional detail is published in *Consumer Trends* and table A7 of *UK Economic Accounts*, available from the ONS website
http://www.ons.gov.uk/ons/publications/all-releases.html?definition
=tcm%3A77-23619

6.4 Individual consumption expenditure at current market prices by households, non-profit institutions serving households and general government
Classified by function (COICOP/COPNI/COFOG)[1]

£ million

			2002	2003	2004	2005	2006	2007	2008	2009	2010
P.31	**FINAL CONSUMPTION EXPENDITURE OF HOUSEHOLDS**										
01.	**Food and non-alcoholic beverages**	ABZV	62 360	64 712	66 362	69 547	72 202	75 706	79 790	81 185	83 401
01.1	Food	ABZW	54 990	56 993	58 221	60 907	63 165	66 530	70 519	71 621	73 506
01.2	Non-alcoholic beverages	ADFK	7 370	7 719	8 141	8 640	9 037	9 176	9 271	9 564	9 895
02.	**Alcoholic beverages and tobacco**	ADFL	25 707	26 973	28 359	28 511	28 658	29 258	29 885	29 906	31 532
02.1	Alcoholic beverages	ADFM	11 148	11 710	13 062	13 146	13 034	13 596	14 146	14 159	14 510
02.2	Tobacco	ADFN	14 559	15 263	15 297	15 365	15 624	15 662	15 739	15 747	17 022
03.	**Clothing and footwear**	ADFP	38 390	40 595	42 495	43 890	46 865	48 317	49 292	48 084	50 670
03.1	Clothing	ADFQ	33 181	35 007	36 518	37 758	40 185	41 440	42 195	41 124	43 116
03.2	Footwear	ADFR	5 209	5 588	5 977	6 132	6 680	6 877	7 097	6 960	7 554
04.	**Housing, water, electricity, gas and other fuels**	ADFS	122 608	131 801	143 732	153 471	163 713	175 870	189 511	195 680	213 365
04.1	Actual rentals for housing	ADFT	27 141	30 005	32 878	33 975	35 486	39 532	42 055	43 303	47 796
04.2	Imputed rentals for housing	ADFU	63 397	68 567	73 067	77 440	80 707	86 265	91 054	96 593	107 612
04.3	Maintenance and repair of the dwelling	ADFV	12 072	12 623	13 804	13 734	13 737	13 719	13 904	13 297	13 057
04.4	Water supply and miscellaneous dwelling services	ADFW	5 304	5 599	5 884	6 366	6 905	7 517	7 455	7 741	8 202
04.5	Electricity, gas and other fuels	ADFX	14 694	15 007	18 099	21 956	26 878	28 837	35 043	34 746	36 698
05.	**Furnishings, household equipment and routine maintenance of the house**	ADFY	41 733	43 789	43 557	44 223	45 559	47 085	45 769	43 051	45 107
05.1	Furniture, furnishings, carpets and other floor coverings	ADFZ	15 268	16 387	16 186	16 241	16 559	17 527	16 454	15 057	14 663
05.2	Household textiles	ADGG	4 961	5 271	4 787	4 476	4 699	5 188	5 051	5 333	5 543
05.3	Household appliances	ADGL	5 732	5 589	6 117	6 357	6 385	6 290	6 308	5 770	6 358
05.4	Glassware, tableware and household utensils	ADGM	4 588	4 608	4 332	4 653	4 759	4 492	4 292	4 058	4 070
05.5	Tools and equipment for house and garden	ADGN	3 338	3 618	3 536	3 591	3 947	4 396	3 966	3 337	3 256
05.6	Goods and services for routine household maintenance	ADGO	7 846	8 316	8 599	8 905	9 210	9 192	9 698	9 496	11 217
06.	**Health**	ADGP	11 134	11 672	12 077	12 439	13 506	14 585	14 234	15 089	15 196
06.1	Medical products, appliances and equipment	ADGQ	6 504	6 776	6 798	6 791	7 314	7 684	7 799	8 084	7 942
06.2	Out-patient services	ADGR	2 449	2 591	2 923	3 145	3 567	4 188	3 639	3 889	4 123
06.3	Hospital services	ADGS	2 181	2 305	2 356	2 503	2 625	2 713	2 796	3 116	3 131
07.	**Transport**	ADGT	99 868	103 839	108 897	114 351	118 156	125 764	124 915	122 265	129 868
07.1	Purchase of vehicles	ADGU	37 100	37 997	39 024	38 422	38 238	40 247	36 652	36 977	38 888
07.2	Operation of personal transport equipment	ADGV	39 587	41 279	43 956	48 213	50 242	53 332	56 699	54 700	60 127
07.3	Transport services	ADGW	23 181	24 563	25 917	27 716	29 676	32 185	31 564	30 588	30 853
08.	**Communication**	ADGX	14 725	15 808	15 781	16 872	16 486	17 132	16 638	16 665	17 866
08.1	Postal services	CDEF	1 057	1 040	1 098	1 165	1 131	1 149	1 083	1 067	1 026
08.2	Telephone & telefax equipment	ADWO	630	732	684	728	760	717	761	839	714
08.3	Telephone & telefax services	ADWP	13 038	14 036	13 999	14 979	14 595	15 266	14 794	14 759	16 126
09.	**Recreation and culture**	ADGY	78 762	82 436	87 983	90 723	95 268	100 247	100 903	97 236	100 146
09.1	Audio-visual, photographic and information processing equipment	ADGZ	17 921	18 385	20 894	21 443	22 129	22 040	22 370	20 471	21 257
09.2	Other major durables for recreation and culture	ADHL	4 809	5 314	5 544	5 843	6 244	6 548	6 919	7 408	7 853
09.3	Other recreational items and equipment; flowers, garden and pets	ADHZ	23 585	24 906	24 942	24 763	25 518	28 683	28 765	27 578	28 554
09.4	Recreational and cultural services	ADIA	22 317	23 798	25 225	26 810	28 533	30 065	30 289	30 485	31 526
09.5	Newspapers, books and stationery	ADIC	10 130	10 033	11 378	11 864	12 844	12 911	12 560	11 294	10 956
09.6	Package holidays[2]	ADID	–	–	–	–	–	–	–	–	–
10.	**Education**										
10.	Education services	ADIE	10 645	10 806	10 944	11 408	12 213	12 987	13 163	13 451	13 837
11.	**Restaurants and hotels**	ADIF	72 565	74 886	77 153	79 922	82 060	84 974	86 353	82 092	87 391
11.1	Catering services	ADIG	62 797	64 893	67 275	69 418	71 091	73 024	73 878	70 330	73 874
11.2	Accommodation services	ADIH	9 768	9 993	9 878	10 504	10 969	11 950	12 475	11 762	13 517
12.	**Miscellaneous goods and services**	ADII	91 971	95 280	100 328	106 832	113 089	118 105	114 082	104 027	103 792
12.1	Personal care	ADIJ	16 903	18 615	19 819	20 084	21 122	21 734	21 369	21 111	21 675
12.3	Personal effects n.e.c.	ADIK	6 370	6 740	7 026	6 870	7 794	7 410	7 245	7 520	9 225
12.4	Social protection	ADIL	9 131	9 427	9 475	9 948	10 569	10 962	12 117	13 098	13 791
12.5	Insurance	ADIM	22 007	20 917	21 683	23 217	23 106	24 837	22 169	23 659	21 922
12.6	Financial services n.e.c.	ADIN	31 693	33 240	35 316	39 289	43 289	45 612	43 664	31 458	30 204
12.7	Other services n.e.c.	ADIO	5 867	6 341	7 009	7 424	7 209	7 550	7 518	7 181	6 975
0.	Final consumption expenditure in the UK by resident and non-resident households (domestic concept)	ABQI	670 468	702 597	737 668	772 189	807 775	850 030	864 535	848 731	892 171
P.33	Final consumption expenditure outside the UK by UK resident households	ABTA	23 967	25 984	27 547	29 026	30 388	31 701	33 286	29 063	29 203
-P.34	*less* Final consumption expenditure in the UK by households resident in the rest of the world	CDFD	-13 786	-14 069	-15 608	-17 066	-18 999	-19 489	-19 797	-19 552	-21 170
P.31	**Final consumption expenditure by UK resident households in the UK and abroad (national concept)**	ABPB	680 649	714 512	749 607	784 149	819 164	862 242	878 024	858 242	900 204

6.4 continued Individual consumption expenditure at current market prices by households, non-profit institutions serving households and general government
Classified by function (COICOP/COPNI/COFOG)[1]

£ million

			2002	2003	2004	2005	2006	2007	2008	2009	2010
P.31	**CONSUMPTION EXPENDITURE OF UK RESIDENT HOUSEHOLDS**										
P.31	Final consumption expenditure of UK resident households in the UK and abroad	ABPB	680 649	714 512	749 607	784 149	819 164	862 242	878 024	858 242	900 204
13.	**FINAL INDIVIDUAL CONSUMPTION EXPENDITURE OF NPISH**										
P.31	Final individual consumption expenditure of NPISH	ABNV	26 422	27 668	29 197	30 824	32 408	34 324	35 767	35 863	37 702
14.	**FINAL INDIVIDUAL CONSUMPTION EXPENDITURE OF GENERAL GOVERNMENT**										
14.1	Health	IWX5	63 219	69 838	76 027	81 733	89 403	94 233	101 562	109 958	112 717
14.2	Recreation and culture	IWX6	7 370	7 797	4 974	5 550	5 801	5 852	6 048	6 207	6 215
14.3	Education	IWX7	39 045	40 631	41 891	45 070	48 632	51 992	55 330	58 371	60 902
14.4	Social protection	IWX8	22 369	25 383	24 859	26 842	28 653	29 685	31 681	32 377	32 930
14.5	Housing	QYXO	–	–	–	–	–	–	–	–	–
P.31	Final individual consumption expenditure of general government	NNAQ	132 003	143 649	147 751	159 195	172 489	181 762	194 621	206 913	212 764
P.31 P.41	Total, individual consumption expenditure/ actual individual consumption	NQEO	839 074	885 829	926 555	974 168	1 024 061	1 078 328	1 108 412	1 101 018	1 150 670

1 "Purpose" or "function" classifications are designed to indicate the "socio-economic objectives" that institutional units aim to achieve through various kinds of outlays. COICOP is the Classification of Individual Consumption by Purpose and applies to households. COPNI is the Classification of the Purposes of Non-profit Institutions Serving Households and COFOG the Classification of the Functions of Government. The introduction of ESA95 coincides with the redefinition of these classifications and data will be available on a consistent basis for all European Union member states.

2 Package holidays data are dispersed between components (transport etc)

6.5 Individual consumption expenditure by households, NPISH and general government
Chained volume measures (Reference year 2008)
Classified by function (COICOP/COPNI/COFOG)[1]

£ million

			2002	2003	2004	2005	2006	2007	2008	2009	2010
P.31	**FINAL CONSUMPTION EXPENDITURE OF HOUSEHOLDS**										
01.	**Food and non-alcoholic beverages**	ADIP	75 128	77 111	78 579	81 167	82 276	82 534	79 790	76 986	76 627
01.1	Food	ADIQ	67 156	68 708	69 565	71 581	72 626	73 132	70 519	67 834	67 700
01.2	Non-alcoholic beverages	ADIR	8 043	8 452	9 022	9 574	9 643	9 415	9 271	9 152	8 927
02.	**Alcoholic beverages and tobacco**	ADIS	29 574	29 992	31 203	30 973	30 317	30 215	29 885	28 701	29 087
02.1	Alcoholic beverages	ADIT	11 467	11 882	13 413	13 719	13 438	13 986	14 146	13 461	13 611
02.2	Tobacco	ADIU	18 437	18 387	17 881	17 288	16 911	16 232	15 739	15 240	15 476
03.	**Clothing and footwear**	ADIW	28 854	31 720	34 878	37 936	42 172	45 135	49 292	52 037	55 372
03.1	Clothing	ADIX	24 525	26 984	29 695	32 353	35 840	38 509	42 195	44 834	47 497
03.2	Footwear	ADIY	4 340	4 746	5 191	5 587	6 345	6 630	7 097	7 203	7 875
04.	**Housing, water, electricity, gas and other fuels**	ADIZ	173 295	179 148	184 195	184 957	185 403	187 346	189 511	186 242	190 693
04.1	Actual rentals for housing	ADJA	34 418	37 005	38 048	37 899	38 486	40 354	42 055	41 448	41 977
04.2	Imputed rentals for housing	ADJB	86 365	88 792	88 988	88 921	89 431	90 298	91 054	92 383	93 737
04.3	Maintenance and repair of the dwelling	ADJC	14 630	14 876	15 870	15 422	15 054	14 417	13 904	12 831	12 100
04.4	Water supply and miscellaneous dwelling services	ADJD	7 704	7 833	7 821	7 692	7 809	8 001	7 455	7 359	7 713
04.5	Electricity, gas and other fuels	ADJE	29 314	29 368	33 049	35 361	34 767	34 276	35 043	32 221	35 166
05.	**Furnishings, household equipment and routine maintenance of the house**	ADJF	42 598	44 968	44 754	45 632	47 132	48 002	45 769	41 769	42 577
05.1	Furniture, furnishings, carpets and other floor coverings	ADJG	16 523	17 644	17 316	17 182	17 412	18 102	16 454	14 655	13 890
05.2	Household textiles	ADJH	4 229	4 584	4 172	4 070	4 479	5 079	5 051	5 320	5 463
05.3	Household appliances	ADJI	5 150	5 182	5 784	6 127	6 438	6 289	6 308	5 455	5 773
05.4	Glassware, tableware and household utensils	ADJJ	4 364	4 431	4 208	4 697	4 885	4 543	4 292	3 957	3 819
05.5	Tools and equipment for house and garden	ADJK	3 131	3 572	3 557	3 697	4 029	4 436	3 966	3 265	3 081
05.6	Goods and services for routine household maintenance	ADJL	9 354	9 704	9 901	10 006	9 955	9 563	9 698	9 117	10 551
06.	**Health**	ADJM	12 331	12 680	13 028	13 180	14 072	14 833	14 234	14 711	14 454
06.1	Medical products, appliances and equipment	ADJN	6 564	6 805	6 858	6 895	7 475	7 756	7 799	7 995	7 741
06.2	Out-patient services	ADJO	2 807	2 916	3 299	3 394	3 702	4 226	3 639	3 787	3 947
06.3	Hospital services	ADJP	3 016	2 991	2 897	2 922	2 904	2 849	2 796	2 929	2 766
07.	**Transport**	ADJQ	120 990	122 269	123 866	125 702	126 399	131 308	124 915	123 780	121 009
07.1	Purchase of vehicles	ADJR	37 757	37 956	38 054	37 511	37 381	39 166	36 652	37 860	36 490
07.2	Operation of personal transport equipment	ADJS	55 991	55 714	56 260	57 704	57 160	58 609	56 699	56 215	55 132
07.3	Transport services	ADJT	27 095	28 331	29 314	30 493	31 839	33 436	31 564	29 705	29 387
08.	**Communication**	ADJU	13 616	14 533	14 616	16 007	15 582	16 714	16 638	16 484	16 863
08.1	Postal services	CCGZ	1 486	1 418	1 454	1 486	1 329	1 223	1 083	979	889
08.2	Telephone & telefax equipment	ADQF	565	653	618	676	706	695	761	833	678
08.3	Telephone & telefax services	ADQG	11 713	12 559	12 651	13 929	13 597	14 808	14 794	14 672	15 296
09.	**Recreation and culture**	ADJV	66 888	71 924	78 879	83 799	89 923	97 013	100 903	97 883	100 615
09.1	Audio-visual, photographic and information processing equipment	ADJW	7 598	8 752	11 219	13 324	15 702	18 241	22 370	23 351	26 145
09.2	Other major durables for recreation and culture	ADJX	5 324	5 714	5 770	6 009	6 413	6 679	6 919	7 159	7 250
09.3	Other recreational items and equipment; flowers, gardens and pets	ADJY	20 650	22 888	23 607	23 881	25 158	28 514	28 765	27 079	27 774
09.4	Recreational and cultural services	ADJZ	27 406	28 278	29 258	29 983	30 521	30 933	30 289	29 353	29 234
09.5	Newspapers, books and stationery	ADKM	11 639	11 168	12 425	12 888	13 544	13 423	12 560	10 941	10 212
09.6	Package holidays[2]	ADMI	–	–	–	–	–	–	–	–	–
10.	**Education**										
10.	Education services	ADMJ	17 128	16 159	15 621	15 522	15 525	14 508	13 163	12 480	12 190
11.	**Restaurants and Hotels**	ADMK	88 762	89 128	89 557	89 403	88 453	88 342	86 353	80 131	83 473
11.1	Catering services	ADML	76 525	77 040	78 099	77 870	76 921	76 163	73 878	68 316	70 127
11.2	Accommodation services	ADMM	12 290	12 135	11 489	11 565	11 562	12 191	12 475	11 815	13 346
12.	**Miscellaneous goods and services**	ADMN	107 875	110 306	112 540	115 348	116 678	118 768	114 082	109 235	107 752
12.1	Personal care	ADMO	17 972	19 833	21 267	21 463	22 123	22 205	21 369	20 618	20 649
12.3	Personal effects n.e.c.	ADMP	7 052	7 355	7 686	7 571	8 358	7 719	7 245	7 260	8 659
12.4	Social protection	ADMQ	12 562	12 251	11 666	11 553	11 655	11 467	12 117	12 522	12 778
12.5	Insurance	ADMR	29 101	26 712	26 294	26 622	25 031	25 787	22 169	22 600	19 727
12.6	Financial services n.e.c.	ADMS	34 327	36 355	37 255	39 693	41 655	43 673	43 664	39 206	39 301
12.7	Other services n.e.c.	ADMT	8 519	8 821	9 148	9 066	8 159	8 067	7 518	7 029	6 638
0.	Final consumption expenditure in the UK by resident and non-resident households (domestic concept)	ABQJ	765 392	790 906	815 148	835 256	851 605	873 882	864 535	840 439	850 712
P.33	Final consumption expenditure outside the UK by UK resident households	ABTC	32 663	32 840	35 235	34 807	35 813	37 327	33 286	25 932	25 140
-P.34	*less* Final consumption expenditure in the UK by households resident in the rest of the world	CCHX	-15 738	-15 767	-17 202	-18 386	-19 950	-19 888	-19 797	-19 410	-20 550
P.31	**Final consumption expenditure by UK resident households in the UK and abroad (national concept)**	ABPF	781 860	807 653	832 690	851 338	867 082	890 872	878 024	846 961	855 302

6.5 continued Individual consumption expenditure by households, NPISH and general government
Chained volume measures (Reference year 2008)
Classified by function (COICOP/COPNI/COFOG)[1]

£ million

		2002	2003	2004	2005	2006	2007	2008	2009	2010
P.31 CONSUMPTION EXPENDITURE OF UK RESIDENT HOUSEHOLDS										
P.31 Final consumption expenditure of UK resident households in the UK and abroad	ABPF	781 860	807 653	832 690	851 338	867 082	890 872	878 024	846 961	855 302
13. FINAL INDIVIDUAL CONSUMPTION EXPENDITURE OF NPISH										
P.31 Final individual consumption expenditure of NPISH	ABNU	36 615	36 266	36 441	36 334	36 421	36 582	35 767	34 487	35 803
14. FINAL INDIVIDUAL CONSUMPTION EXPENDITURE OF GENERAL GOVERNMENT										
14.1 Health	K4CP	81 420	84 488	88 076	91 063	94 279	98 295	101 562	100 932	104 918
14.2 Recreation and culture	K4CQ	5 479	5 623	5 830	6 170	6 237	6 144	6 048	5 790	5 686
14.3 Education	K4CR	50 161	52 971	55 972	55 945	55 729	55 647	55 330	51 651	51 712
14.4 Social protection	K4CS	30 152	31 347	32 404	32 355	32 456	31 963	31 681	29 897	29 614
14.5 Housing	QYXN	–	–	–	–	–	–	–	–	–
P.31 Final individual consumption expenditure of general government	NSZK	172 082	176 681	181 706	185 163	188 485	191 998	194 621	188 270	191 930
P.31/P.41 Total, individual consumption expenditure/ actual individual consumption	YBIO	989 940	1 020 298	1 050 668	1 072 795	1 091 991	1 119 538	1 108 412	1 069 718	1 083 035

1 "Purpose" or "function" classifications are designed to indicate the "socio-economic objectives" that institutional units aim to achieve through various kinds of outlays. COICOP is the Classification of Individual Consumption by Purpose and applies to households. COPNI is the Classification of the Purposes of Non-profit Institutions Serving Households and COFOG the Classification of the Functions of Government. The introduction of ESA95 coincides with the redefinition of these classifications and data will be available on a consistent basis for all European Union member states.

2 Package holidays data are dispersed between components (transport etc)

Chapter 7

Rest of the world

7.1.0 Rest of the world
ESA95 sector S.2

£ million

			2002	2003	2004	2005	2006	2007	2008	2009	2010
V.I	**EXTERNAL ACCOUNT OF GOODS AND SERVICES**										
	Resources										
P.7	Imports of goods and services										
P.71	Imports of goods	LQBL	234 110	236 772	251 725	280 282	320 133	310 952	346 158	310 978	364 176
P.72	Imports of services	KTMR	74 378	79 750	84 530	93 489	99 689	105 729	115 830	110 247	112 304
P.7	Total resources, total imports	KTMX	308 488	316 522	336 255	373 771	419 822	416 681	461 988	421 225	476 480
	Uses										
P.6	Exports of goods and services										
P.61	Exports of goods	LQAD	186 443	188 241	190 786	211 498	243 564	220 347	251 977	228 126	265 714
P.62	Exports of services	KTMQ	94 011	101 966	112 826	119 569	135 527	153 685	170 887	167 462	171 082
P.6	Total exports	KTMW	280 454	290 207	303 612	331 067	379 091	374 032	422 864	395 588	436 796
B.11	**External balance of goods and services**	-KTMY	**28 034**	**26 315**	**32 643**	**42 704**	**40 731**	**42 649**	**39 124**	**25 637**	**39 684**
P.7	Total uses	KTMX	308 488	316 522	336 255	373 771	419 822	416 681	461 988	421 225	476 480

7.1.2 Rest of the world
ESA95 sector S.2

£ million

V.II EXTERNAL ACCOUNT OF PRIMARY INCOMES AND CURRENT TRANSFERS

Resources

Code	Description	Series	2002	2003	2004	2005	2006	2007	2008	2009	2010
B.11	External balance of goods and services	-KTMY	28 034	26 315	32 643	42 704	40 731	42 649	39 124	25 637	39 684
D.1	Compensation of employees										
D.11	Wages and salaries	KTMO	1 054	1 057	1 425	1 584	1 896	1 718	1 761	1 435	1 486
D.2	Taxes on production and imports, received										
D.21	Taxes on products										
D.211	Value added type taxes (VAT)	FJKM	2 808	2 740	1 789	1 999	2 167	2 319	2 270	1 593	2 253
D.212	Taxes and duties on imports excluding VAT										
D.2121	Import duties	FJWE	1 919	1 937	2 145	2 237	2 329	2 412	2 636	2 645	2 933
D.2122	Taxes on imports excluding VAT and duties	FJWF	–	–	–	–	–	–	–	–	–
D.214	Taxes on products excluding VAT and import duties	FJWG	25	18	25	24	–	–	–	–	–
D.2	Total taxes on production and imports, received	FJWB	4 752	4 695	3 959	4 260	4 496	4 731	4 906	4 238	5 186
-D.3	*less* Subsidies, paid										
-D.31	Subsidies on products	-FJWJ	−1 862	−2 099	−2 725	–	–	–	–	–	–
-D.39	Other subsidies on production	-NHQR	−519	−592	−592	−3 408	−3 221	−2 952	−3 051	−3 411	−3 032
-D.3	Total	-FJWI	−2 381	−2 691	−3 317	−3 408	−3 221	−2 952	−3 051	−3 411	−3 032
D.4	Property income, received										
D.41	Interest	QYNG	73 847	70 835	78 683	113 728	158 568	207 293	203 988	106 225	89 605
D.42	Distributed income of corporations	QYNH	23 417	24 851	30 515	37 813	45 229	38 167	22 620	37 502	48 762
D.43	Reinvested earnings on direct foreign investment	QYNI	3 647	7 429	8 558	10 501	22 195	23 276	1 542	4 148	−14
D.44	Property income attributed to insurance policy-holders	NHRM	1 196	1 243	1 101	1 102	1 043	775	841	782	585
D.4	Total	HMBO	102 107	104 358	118 857	163 144	227 035	269 511	228 991	148 657	138 938
D.5	Current taxes on income, wealth etc										
D.51	Taxes on income	FJWM	644	444	535	589	428	549	793	565	638
D.61	Social contributions										
D.611	Actual social contributions										
D.6112	Employees' social contributions	FJWQ	–	–	–	–	–	–	–	–	–
D.62	Social benefits other than social transfers in kind										
D.621	Social security benefits in cash	FJVZ	1 338	1 404	1 539	1 596	1 675	1 774	1 946	2 048	2 160
D.622	Private funded social benefits	QZEM	54	25	25	47	37	32	30	152	64
D.624	Social assistance benefits in cash	RNNF	50	48	57	54	46	55	53	51	–
D.62	Total	FJKO	1 442	1 477	1 621	1 697	1 758	1 861	2 029	2 251	2 224
D.7	Other current transfers										
D.71	Net non-life insurance premiums	FJKS	19	19	47	16	39	50	54	77	315
D.72	Non-life insurance claims	NHRR	3 008	2 208	3 181	6 133	6 530	3 148	4 477	4 148	4 295
D.74	Current international cooperation	FJWT	2 362	2 433	3 080	3 255	3 632	3 930	4 292	5 011	5 683
D.75	Miscellaneous current transfers	FJWU	8 878	10 610	11 631	13 354	13 176	13 191	13 539	15 891	16 358
	of which GNP based fourth own resource	NMFH	5 335	6 772	7 549	8 732	8 521	8 323	8 423	10 555	10 819
D.7	Total	FJWR	14 267	15 270	17 939	22 758	23 377	20 319	22 362	25 127	26 651
D.8	Adjustment for the change in net equity of households in pension funds	QZEP	−1	−4	−11	−55	−9	−37	−2	−41	−10
Total	Total resources	NSUK	149 918	150 921	173 651	233 273	296 491	338 349	296 913	204 458	211 765

7.1.2 Rest of the world
ESA95 sector S.2
continued

£ million

V.II EXTERNAL ACCOUNT OF PRIMARY INCOMES AND CURRENT TRANSFERS
continued

Uses

			2002	2003	2004	2005	2006	2007	2008	2009	2010
D.1	Compensation of employees										
D.11	Wages and salaries	KTMN	1 121	1 116	931	974	938	984	1 046	1 176	1 097
D.2	Taxes on production and imports, paid										
D.21	Taxes on products										
D.212	Taxes and duties on imports excluding VAT										
D.2121	Import duties	FJVQ	–	–	–	–	–	–	–	–	–
D.2122	Taxes on imports excluding VAT and duties	FJVR	–	–	–	–	–	–	–	–	–
D.214	Taxes on products excluding VAT and import duties	FJVS	–	–	–	–	–	–	–	–	–
D.21	Total taxes on products	FJVN	–	–	–	–	–	–	–	–	–
D.2	Total taxes on production and imports, paid	FJVM	–	–	–	–	–	–	–	–	–
D.4	Property income, paid										
D.41	Interest	QYNJ	59 788	57 624	64 486	92 491	136 026	177 827	172 590	84 537	67 193
D.42	Distributed income of corporations	QYNK	28 546	42 989	41 818	49 594	53 601	50 049	51 858	71 535	72 253
D.43	Reinvested earnings on direct foreign investment	QYNL	32 209	21 456	31 076	43 555	47 878	63 738	38 394	13 241	22 920
D.44	Property income attributed to insurance policy-holders										
D.4	Total	HMBN	120 543	122 069	137 380	185 640	237 505	291 614	262 842	169 313	162 366
D.5	Current taxes on income, wealth etc										
D.51	Taxes on income	NHRS	527	375	482	546	681	603	616	672	567
D.61	Social contributions										
D.6112	Employee's social contributions	FKAA	77	44	36	14	56	26	68	172	83
D.7	Other current transfers										
D.71	Net non-life insurance premiums	NHRX	3 008	2 208	3 181	6 133	6 530	3 148	4 477	4 148	4 295
D.72	Non-life insurance claims	FJTT	19	19	47	16	39	50	54	77	315
D.74	Current international cooperation	FJWA	3 112	3 570	3 673	3 726	3 674	3 684	4 996	5 522	3 179
D.75	Miscellaneous current transfers	NHSI	3 110	3 140	3 031	3 557	3 973	3 414	3 061	3 062	3 137
D.7	Total	NHRW	9 249	8 937	9 932	13 432	14 216	10 296	12 588	12 809	10 926
B.12	**Current external balance**	-HBOG	**18 401**	**18 380**	**24 890**	**32 667**	**43 095**	**34 826**	**19 753**	**20 316**	**36 726**
Total	Total uses	NSUK	149 918	150 921	173 651	233 273	296 491	338 349	296 913	204 458	211 765

7.1.7 Rest of the World
ESA95 sector S.2

£ million

			2002	2003	2004	2005	2006	2007	2008	2009	2010
V.III	**ACCUMULATION ACCOUNTS**										
V.III.1	**CAPITAL ACCOUNT**										
	Changes in liabilities and net worth										
B.12	**Current external balance**	-HBOG	**18 401**	**18 380**	**24 890**	**32 667**	**43 095**	**34 826**	**19 753**	**20 316**	**36 726**
D.9	Capital transfers receivable										
D.92	Investment grants	NHSA	263	345	389	396	388	449	491	264	239
D.99	Other capital transfers	NHSB	833	693	637	1 816	2 038	784	817	794	838
D.9	Total	NHRZ	1 096	1 038	1 026	2 212	2 426	1 233	1 308	1 058	1 077
-D.9	*less* Capital transfers payable										
-D.92	Investment grants	-NHQQ	−296	−624	−1 111	−1 482	−668	−857	−1 389	−855	−1 040
-D.99	Other capital transfers	-NHQS	−1 864	−1 951	−2 298	−2 491	−2 725	−2 953	−3 200	−3 467	−3 688
-D.9	Total	-NHSC	−2 160	−2 575	−3 409	−3 973	−3 393	−3 810	−4 589	−4 322	−4 728
B.10.1	Total, change in net worth due to saving (current external balance)and capital transfers	NHSD	17 337	16 843	22 507	30 906	42 128	32 249	16 472	17 052	33 075
	Changes in assets										
K.2	Acquisitions less disposals of non-produced non-financial assets	NHSG	−132	−71	−319	−258	8	−11	−40	373	57
B.9	**Net lending(+)/net borrowing(-)**	NHRB	**17 469**	**16 914**	**22 826**	**31 164**	**42 120**	**32 260**	**16 512**	**16 679**	**33 018**
Total	Total change in assets	NHSD	17 337	16 843	22 507	30 906	42 128	32 249	16 472	17 052	33 075

7.1.8 Rest of the world
ESA95 sector S.2 Unconsolidated

£ million

			2002	2003	2004	2005	2006	2007	2008	2009	2010
III.2	**FINANCIAL ACCOUNT**										
F.A	**Net acquisition of financial assets**										
F.1	Monetary gold and special drawing rights	NEWJ	240	2	37	8	−47	50	24	132	−18
F.2	Currency and deposits										
F.21	Currency	NEWN	86	81	113	64	73	45	−25	−167	63
F.22	Transferable deposits										
F.221	Deposits with UK monetary financial institutions	NEWP	88 772	171 703	288 554	279 648	333 915	681 049	−459 095	−323 972	62 153
F.2212	of which Foreign currency deposits	NFAS	77 472	148 376	261 474	232 399	276 414	471 475	−416 325	−265 205	90 035
F.29	Other deposits	NEWU	−24	232	−877	−57	474	−299	−282	201	293
F.2	Total currency and deposits	NEWM	88 834	172 016	287 790	279 655	334 462	680 795	−459 402	−323 938	62 509
F.3	Securities other than shares										
F.331	Short term: money market instruments										
F.3311	Issued by UK central government	NEWX	−180	2 150	1 974	−1 023	747	3 547	12 653	587	8 330
F.3315	Issued by UK monetary financial institutions	NEXC	18 960	335	7 977	−4 524	44 654	14 200	−34 641	85 994	−66 504
F.3316	Issued by other UK residents	NEXH	10 819	−4 323	93	−2 629	−3 498	2 922	3 137	−5 418	3 284
F.332	Medium (1 to 5 year) and long term (over 5 year) bonds										
F.3321	Issued by UK central government	NEXK	−3 636	11 197	12 607	30 661	24 923	27 237	28 535	23 529	78 490
F.3322	Issued by UK local authorities	NEXN	–	–	–	–	–	–	–	–	–
F.3325	Medium term bonds issued by UK monetary financial institutions	NEXO	1 775	13 871	18 747	22 738	26 035	36 499	−22 942	26 967	4 293
F.3326	Other medium & long term bonds issued by UK residents	NEXR	20 316	63 687	56 299	79 472	74 610	121 814	180 066	7 827	62 160
F.3	Total securities other than shares	NEWV	48 054	86 917	97 697	124 695	167 471	206 219	166 808	139 486	90 053
F.4	Loans										
F.41	Short term loans										
F.4191	Loans by rest of the world monetary financial institutions	NEYD	4 924	39 859	83 665	23 259	65 005	14 653	−43 778	−5 417	71 619
F.4192	Other short-term loans by rest of the world	ZMDZ	−38 798	30 857	52 108	198 664	−48 885	40 408	−232 686	−49 040	83 224
F.42	Long term loans										
F.4211	Outward direct investment	NEYG	39 286	12 453	18 815	30 025	29 320	4 247	67 075	−33 996	17 448
F.4212	Inward direct investment	NEYH	11 159	474	−461	14 383	8 017	4 449	19 673	−9 653	−96
F.429	Other long-term loans by the rest of the world	QYLT	−30	124	904	94	228	−25	414	405	−245
F.4	Total loans	NEXX	16 541	83 767	155 031	266 425	53 685	63 732	−189 302	−97 701	171 950
F.5	Shares and other equity										
F.51	Shares and other equity, excluding mutual funds' shares										
F.514	Quoted UK shares	NEYU	2 754	12 891	13 265	57 706	25 378	31 502	54 888	44 790	21 918
F.515	Unquoted UK shares	NEYV	13 849	18 691	20 315	41 477	41 129	88 705	36 493	48 313	13 305
F.516	Other UK equity (including direct investment in property)	NEYW	748	395	623	597	467	2 358	1 493	532	532
F.517	UK shares and bonds issued by other UK residents	NSPR	–	–	–	–	–	–	–	–	–
F.52	Mutual funds' shares										
F.521	UK mutual funds' shares	NEZD	8	4	28	49	50	21	11	35	44
F.5	Total shares and other equity	NEYP	17 359	31 981	34 231	99 829	67 024	122 586	92 885	93 670	35 799
F.6	Insurance technical reserves										
F.61	Net equity of households in life assurance and pension funds' reserves	NEZF	−1	−4	−11	−55	−9	−37	−2	−41	−10
F.62	Prepayments of insurance premiums and reserves for outstanding claims	NEZI	335	−1 371	1 324	2 675	4 423	−4 223	−3 914	−282	194
F.6	Total insurance technical reserves	NPWP	334	−1 375	1 313	2 620	4 414	−4 260	−3 916	−323	184
F.7	Other accounts receivable	NEZJ	−613	58	−158	158	57	245	175	108	814
F.A	**Total net acquisition of financial assets**	NEWI	170 749	373 366	575 941	773 390	627 066	1 069 367	−392 728	−188 566	361 291

7.1.8 Rest of the world
ESA95 sector S.2 Unconsolidated
continued

£ million

			2002	2003	2004	2005	2006	2007	2008	2009	2010
III.2	**FINANCIAL ACCOUNT** continued										
F.L	**Net acquisition of financial liabilities**										
F.2	Currency and deposits										
F.21	Currency	NEZR	54	30	44	14	124	34	−81	−64	−140
F.22	Transferable deposits										
F.229	Deposits with rest of the world monetary financial institutions[1]	NEZX	53 299	190 273	212 662	372 741	277 866	516 077	−486 838	−217 063	220 619
F.2	Total currency and deposits	NEZQ	53 353	190 303	212 706	372 755	277 990	516 111	−486 919	−217 127	220 479
F.3	Securities other than shares										
F.331	Short term: money market instruments										
F.3319	Issued by the rest of the world[1]	NFAM	−6 133	12 224	−2 473	7 274	14 806	−2 625	−22 891	14 204	−1 382
F.332	Medium (1 to 5 year) and long term (over 5 year) bonds										
F.3329	Issued by the rest of the world	NFAW	9 900	818	88 345	84 691	102 366	68 073	−43 385	148 024	79 734
F.34	Financial derivatives	NSUL	−1 159	5 211	6 752	−5 422	−20 911	26 969	121 491	−29 194	−32 597
F.3	Total securities other than shares	NEZZ	2 608	18 253	92 624	86 543	96 261	92 417	55 215	133 034	45 755
F.4	Loans										
F.41	Short term loans										
F.411	Short-term loans by UK monetary financial institutions	NFBD	17 517	70 991	112 036	134 808	119 836	226 527	−122 658	−117 400	17 089
F.4112	*of which* Foreign currency loans	NFBF	12 778	70 529	105 145	114 591	97 717	200 310	−128 655	−98 828	15 333
F.42	Long term loans										
F.4211	Outward direct investment	NFBK	16 530	11 961	18 059	13 657	356	41 060	88 181	−30 994	−10 731
F.4212	Inward direct investment	NFBL	10 054	−3 049	2 916	12 013	5 106	15 367	30 358	−13 241	3 878
F.423	Finance leasing	NFBQ	–	–	–	–	–	–	–	–	–
F.424	Other long-term loans by UK residents	NSRT	−1 458	−292	−69	−1 623	−3 171	−447	−335	−16	178
F.4	Total loans	NFBB	42 643	79 611	132 942	158 855	122 127	282 507	−4 454	−161 651	10 414
F.5	Shares and other equity										
F.51	Shares and other equity, excluding mutual funds' shares										
F.519	Shares and other equity issued by the rest of the world	NFCD	55 592	61 972	107 366	119 152	94 291	152 954	17 289	33 575	43 247
F.52	Mutual funds' shares										
F.529	Rest of the world mutual funds' shares	NFCI	−8	41	536	1 810	783	−110	−376	−1 544	−185
F.5	Total shares and other equity	NFBT	55 584	62 013	107 902	120 962	95 074	152 844	16 913	32 031	43 062
F.7	Other accounts payable	NFCN	357	625	304	−960	1 638	506	532	382	64
F.L	**Total net acquisition of financial liabilities**	NEZM	154 545	350 805	546 478	738 155	593 090	1 044 385	−418 713	−213 331	319 774
B.9	**Net lending / borrowing**										
F.A	Total net acquisition of financial assets	NEWI	170 749	373 366	575 941	773 390	627 066	1 069 367	−392 728	−188 566	361 291
-F.L	*less* Total net acquisition of financial liabilities	-NEZM	−154 545	−350 805	−546 478	−738 155	−593 090	−1 044 385	418 713	213 331	−319 774
B.9f	Net lending (+) / net borrowing (-), from financial account	NYOD	16 204	22 561	29 463	35 235	33 976	24 982	25 985	24 765	41 517
dB.9f	Statistical discrepancy	NYPO	1 265	−5 647	−6 637	−4 071	8 144	7 278	−9 473	−8 086	−8 499
B.9	**Net lending (+) / net borrowing (-), from capital account**	NHRB	17 469	16 914	22 826	31 164	42 120	32 260	16 512	16 679	33 018

1 There is a discontinuity in this series between 1995 and 1996 because an instrument breakdown of offical reserves is not available prior to 1996

7.1.9 Rest of the world
ESA95 sector S.2 Unconsolidated

£ billion

			2002	2003	2004	2005	2006	2007	2008	2009	2010
IV.3	**FINANCIAL BALANCE SHEET** at end of period										
AF.A	**Financial assets**										
AF.2	Currency and deposits										
AF.21	Currency	NLCW	1.2	1.3	1.4	1.4	1.5	1.5	1.5	1.4	1.4
AF.22	Transferable deposits										
AF.221	Deposits with UK monetary financial institutions	NLCY	1 439.4	1 605.3	1 855.2	2 199.8	2 370.7	3 143.4	3 597.2	2 976.3	3 068.6
AF.2212	of which Foreign curency deposits	NLDA	1 206.5	1 348.1	1 570.0	1 861.6	1 974.2	2 531.0	3 031.5	2 475.1	2 584.9
AF.29	Other deposits	NLDD	1.6	1.9	1.0	0.9	1.4	1.1	0.8	1.0	1.3
AF.2	Total currency and deposits	NLCV	1 442.2	1 608.4	1 857.6	2 202.1	2 373.6	3 146.1	3 599.5	2 978.7	3 071.4
AF.3	Securities other than shares										
AF.331	Short term: money market instruments										
AF.3311	Issued by UK central government	NLDG	0.2	1.9	3.8	2.8	3.5	7.2	21.0	19.4	27.9
AF.3315	Issued by UK monetary financial institutions	NLDL	140.3	130.6	130.7	136.1	162.0	183.7	202.3	267.8	206.0
AF.3316	Issued by other UK residents	NLDQ	30.6	23.7	22.5	22.2	16.3	19.1	29.9	21.5	25.4
AF.332	Medium (1 to 5 year) and long term (over 5 year) bonds										
AF.3321	Issued by UK central government	NLDT	56.4	66.1	83.8	110.7	135.5	160.2	203.6	224.3	309.2
AF.3322	Issued by UK local authorities	NLDW	–	–	–	–	–	–	–	–	–
AF.3325	Medium term bonds issued by UK monetary financial institutions	NLDX	43.6	53.7	70.9	95.5	114.9	167.0	200.2	208.0	204.0
AF.3326	Other medium & long term bonds issued by UK residents	NLEA	228.9	295.7	361.8	463.4	529.1	605.8	757.8	854.5	848.4
AF.34	Financial derivatives	J8XN	..	..	715.0	831.1	890.5	1 392.2	3 915.3	2 096.8	2 895.0
AF.3	Total securities other than shares	NLDE	499.9	571.8	1 388.6	1 661.8	1 851.6	2 535.2	5 330.1	3 692.3	4 515.8
AF.4	Loans										
AF.41	Short term loans										
AF.4191	Loans by rest of the world monetary financial institutions	NLEM	158.1	204.0	283.8	324.0	391.8	413.5	473.4	441.3	510.6
AF.4192	Other short-term loans by rest of the world	ZMEA	280.9	308.3	353.8	563.3	480.4	535.9	427.9	354.6	447.0
AF.42	Long term loans										
AF.4211	Outward direct investment	NLEP	128.4	127.7	149.0	184.5	194.2	178.2	253.8	260.2	277.6
AF.4212	Inward direct investment	NLEQ	155.6	152.9	156.1	174.2	182.6	160.3	171.8	161.7	161.6
AF.429	Other long-term loans by the rest of the world	NLEX	2.0	2.2	3.2	3.2	3.4	3.3	3.9	4.4	4.5
AF.4	Total loans	NLEG	725.0	795.0	945.9	1 249.2	1 252.4	1 291.2	1 330.8	1 222.2	1 401.3
AF.5	Shares and other equity										
AF.51	Shares and other equity, excluding mutual funds' shares										
AF.514	Quoted UK shares	NLFD	418.7	500.4	550.3	659.5	739.2	783.2	535.0	753.3	861.6
AF.515	Unquoted UK shares	NLFE	236.5	255.4	273.4	348.7	452.8	521.9	591.3	599.1	625.5
AF.516	Other UK equity (including direct investment in property)	NLFF	15.9	15.9	17.8	18.4	20.2	24.8	24.0	24.5	26.5
AF.517	UK shares and bonds issued by other UK residents	NSOP	–	–	–	–	–	–	–	–	–
AF.52	Mutual funds' shares										
AF.521	UK mutual funds' shares	NLFM	0.9	1.0	1.2	1.5	1.7	1.7	1.0	1.3	1.6
AF.5	Total shares and other equity	NLEY	671.9	772.8	842.6	1 028.0	1 213.9	1 331.7	1 151.2	1 378.3	1 515.3
AF.6	Insurance technical reserves										
AF.61	Net equity of households in life assurance and pension funds' reserves	NLFO	0.2	0.2	0.2	0.2	0.2	0.2	0.2	0.2	0.2
AF.62	Prepayments of insurance premiums and reserves for outstanding claims	NLFR	12.6	10.2	11.5	14.2	18.6	14.4	10.5	10.2	10.4
AF.6	Total insurance technical reserves	NPYF	12.9	10.4	11.7	14.4	18.8	14.6	10.7	10.4	10.6
AF.7	Other accounts receivable	NLFS	2.0	1.9	1.7	2.0	1.9	2.2	2.6	2.6	3.5
AF.A	**Total financial assets**	NLEF	3 353.9	3 760.3	5 048.2	6 157.5	6 712.4	8 320.9	11 425.0	9 284.5	10 517.8

7.1.9 Rest of the world
ESA95 sector S.2 Unconsolidated
continued

£ billion

				2002	2003	2004	2005	2006	2007	2008	2009	2010
IV.3	**FINANCIAL BALANCE SHEET** continued at end of period											
AF.L	**Financial liabilities**											
AF.2	Currency and deposits											
AF.21	Currency	NLGA		0.5	0.6	0.6	0.6	0.7	0.8	0.9	0.8	0.7
AF.22	Transferable deposits											
AF.229	Deposits with rest of the world monetary financial institutions[1]	NLGG		1 203.3	1 399.9	1 605.3	2 055.5	2 189.5	2 768.0	3 029.5	2 589.6	2 798.0
AF.2	Total currency and deposits	NLFZ		1 203.9	1 400.5	1 605.9	2 056.1	2 190.2	2 768.8	3 030.5	2 590.4	2 798.7
AF.3	Securities other than shares											
AF.331	Short term: money market instruments											
AF.3319	Issued by the rest of the world[1]	NLGV		48.7	62.0	58.3	63.8	75.5	76.4	72.2	85.2	87.7
AF.332	Medium (1 to 5 year) and long term (over 5 year) bonds											
AF.3329	Issued by the rest of the world	NLHF		538.2	550.1	611.3	717.2	798.3	903.5	1 076.0	1 176.1	1 304.2
AF.34	Financial Derivatives	NLEC		0.2	–	709.5	820.4	853.7	1 378.2	4 040.2	2 176.4	2 962.9
AF.3	Total securities other than shares	NLGI		587.1	612.1	1 379.1	1 601.4	1 727.5	2 358.1	5 188.4	3 437.7	4 354.9
AF.4	Loans											
AF.41	Short term loans											
AF.411	Short-term loans by UK monetary financial institutions	NLHM		328.4	398.4	496.3	642.0	709.1	955.9	1 127.8	903.5	971.2
AF.4112	*of which* Foreign currency loans	NLHO		290.9	358.3	448.9	575.1	621.3	842.8	1 010.0	806.9	867.9
AF.42	Long term loans											
AF.4211	Outward direct investment	NLHT		114.5	116.3	144.5	145.6	147.2	194.5	278.8	292.0	281.2
AF.4212	Inward direct investment	NLHU		61.6	59.0	61.0	77.0	76.9	75.5	97.3	77.7	81.6
AF.423	Finance leasing	NLHZ		–	–	–	–	–	–	–	–	–
AF.424	Other long-term loans by UK residents	NROS		7.3	7.2	7.3	7.3	5.4	5.2	7.0	5.9	6.1
AF.4	Total loans	NLHK		511.8	580.9	709.2	872.0	938.6	1 231.0	1 511.0	1 279.1	1 340.2
AF.5	Shares and other equity											
AF.51	Shares and other equity, excluding mutual funds' shares											
AF.519	Shares and other equity issued by the rest of the world	NLIM		931.3	1 049.0	1 128.8	1 348.3	1 459.0	1 620.1	1 596.0	1 648.7	1 799.3
AF.52	Mutual funds' shares											
AF.529	Rest of the world mutual funds' shares	NLIR		1.4	1.4	1.7	4.1	6.0	4.5	2.3	0.8	0.7
AF.5	Total shares and other equity	NLIC		932.7	1 050.4	1 130.5	1 352.4	1 465.0	1 624.6	1 598.3	1 649.5	1 800.0
AF.7	Other accounts payable	NLIW		4.1	4.8	3.6	2.7	3.8	5.7	6.8	8.0	8.7
AF.L	**Total financial liabilities**	NLHJ		3 239.6	3 648.6	4 828.4	5 884.7	6 325.1	7 988.1	11 334.9	8 964.7	10 302.4
BF.90	**Net financial assets / liabilities**											
AF.A	Total financial assets	NLEF		3 353.9	3 760.3	5 048.2	6 157.5	6 712.4	8 320.9	11 425.0	9 284.5	10 517.8
-AF.L	*less* Total financial liabilities	-NLHJ		–3 239.6	–3 648.6	–4 828.4	–5 884.7	–6 325.1	–7 988.1	–11 334.9	–8 964.7	–10 302.4
BF.90	**Net financial assets (+) / liabilities (-)**	NLFK		114.4	111.7	219.8	272.8	387.2	332.8	90.1	319.8	215.4

1 There is a discontinuity in this series between 1995 and 1996 because an instrument breakdown of official reserves is not available prior to 1996

Other analyses and derived statistics

Part 4

Chapter 8

Percentage distributions and growth rates

8.1 Composition of UK gross domestic product at market prices By category of expenditure[1]

Current prices

Percentage

		2002	2003	2004	2005	2006	2007	2008	2009	2010
	Gross domestic product: expenditure approach									
P.3	Final consumption expenditure									
P.41	Actual individual consumption									
P.3	Household final consumption expenditure	63.3	62.7	62.3	62.5	61.7	61.3	61.2	61.6	61.7
P.3	Final consumption expenditure of NPISH	2.5	2.4	2.4	2.5	2.4	2.4	2.5	2.6	2.6
P.31	Individual government final consumption expenditure	12.3	12.6	12.3	12.7	13.0	12.9	13.6	14.8	14.6
P.41	Total actual individual consumption	78.0	77.7	77.1	77.7	77.1	76.7	77.3	79.0	78.9
P.32	Collective government final consumption expenditure	7.5	7.8	8.6	8.7	8.5	8.1	8.4	8.6	8.6
P.3	Total final consumption expenditure	85.5	85.5	85.6	86.4	85.6	84.8	85.7	87.6	87.5
P.3	Households and NPISH	65.8	65.1	64.8	65.0	64.1	63.8	63.7	64.1	64.3
P.3	Central government	12.1	12.5	12.7	12.9	13.1	12.7	13.3	14.3	14.2
P.3	Local government	7.6	7.9	8.2	8.5	8.4	8.3	8.7	9.2	9.0
P.5	Gross capital formation									
P.51	Gross fixed capital formation	16.8	16.4	16.7	16.7	17.1	17.8	16.8	15.0	14.9
P.52	Changes in inventories	0.3	0.4	0.4	0.4	0.4	0.4	0.1	−0.8	0.5
P.53	Acquisitions less disposals of valuables	–	–	–	–	–	–	–	–	–
P.5	Total gross capital formation	17.1	16.8	17.1	17.0	17.5	18.3	17.0	14.2	15.4
P.6	Exports of goods and services	26.1	25.5	25.3	26.4	28.5	26.6	29.5	28.4	29.9
-P.7	less imports of goods and services	−28.7	−27.8	−28.0	−29.8	−31.6	−29.6	−32.2	−30.2	−32.7
B.11	External balance of goods and services	−2.6	−2.3	−2.7	−3.4	−3.1	−3.0	−2.7	−1.8	−2.7
de	Statistical discrepancy between expenditure components and GDP	–	–	–	–	–	–	–	–	−0.2
B.1*g	Gross domestic product at market prices	100.0	100.0	100.0	100.0	100.0	100.0	100.0	100.0	100.0

1 Based on table 1.2

8.2 Composition of UK gross domestic product at market prices by category of income[1,2]

Percentage

		2002	2003	2004	2005	2006	2007	2008	2009	2010
B.2g	Total gross operating surplus									
	Public non-financial corporations	0.6	0.6	0.6	0.7	0.7	0.7	0.6	0.7	0.6
	Private non-financial corporations	17.4	17.4	18.0	17.9	18.4	18.4	17.8	16.7	16.9
	Financial corporations	2.5	2.9	2.8	2.7	2.9	3.1	4.0	4.7	3.6
	Central government	0.5	0.5	0.5	0.5	0.5	0.5	0.5	0.5	0.5
	Local government	0.4	0.4	0.4	0.5	0.5	0.5	0.5	0.5	0.5
	Households and NPISH	5.2	5.4	5.5	5.4	5.3	5.5	5.2	4.1	4.9
B.2g	Total gross operating surplus	26.7	27.2	27.8	27.7	28.3	28.6	28.6	27.3	27.1
B.3	Mixed income	6.2	6.3	6.1	6.3	6.1	5.9	6.0	5.8	5.6
D.1	Compensation of employees	54.6	54.1	53.7	54.0	53.7	53.5	53.8	55.7	54.9
D.2	Taxes on production and imports[2]	13.3	13.2	13.2	12.9	12.9	12.8	12.4	12.0	13.2
-D.3	Subsidies on products	−0.7	−0.8	−0.8	−0.9	−0.9	−0.9	−0.8	−0.9	−0.9
di	Statistical discrepancy between income components and GDP	–	–	–	–	–	–	–	–	0.2
B.1*g	Gross domestic product	100.0	100.0	100.0	100.0	100.0	100.0	100.0	100.0	100.0

1 Based on table 1.2
2 Includes taxes on products

8.3 Gross value added at current basic prices analysed by industry[1,2,3]

Percentage

	2002	2003	2004	2005	2006	2007	2008	2009
Agriculture	0.9	1.0	0.9	0.7	0.7	0.7	0.7	0.6
Production	17.9	16.8	16.0	15.9	15.9	15.5	15.4	15.0
Construction	7.0	7.2	7.4	7.4	7.5	7.7	7.6	7.0
Distribution, transport, hotels and restaurants	20.2	19.9	19.8	19.6	19.3	19.2	18.7	18.7
Information and communication	6.2	6.3	6.4	6.3	6.1	6.2	6.2	6.1
Financial and insurance	6.6	7.0	7.1	7.2	7.7	7.9	8.9	10.1
Real estate	8.3	8.5	8.7	8.6	8.3	8.8	8.4	7.2
Professional and support	11.8	11.7	11.7	12.0	12.2	12.1	11.9	11.8
Government, health and education	17.7	18.1	18.5	19.0	19.0	18.6	18.9	20.1
Other services[4]	3.4	3.5	3.5	3.5	3.4	3.3	3.2	3.3
Gross value added at basic prices	100.0	100.0	100.0	100.0	100.0	100.0	100.0	100.0

1 Based on table 2.2.
2 Before providing for consumption of fixed capital.
3 See footnote 2 to table 2.3.
4 Comprising of sections R,S and T of the SIC2007.

8.4 Annual increases in categories of expenditure (chained volume measures)

Percentage increase over previous year

		2002	2003	2004	2005	2006	2007	2008	2009	2010
P.3	Household final consumption expenditure	4.5	3.3	3.1	2.2	1.8	2.7	−1.4	−3.5	1.0
P.3	NPISH final consumption expenditure	−1.1	−1.0	0.5	−0.3	0.2	0.4	−2.2	−3.6	3.8
P.3	General government final consumption	3.9	4.4	3.4	2.2	1.5	0.6	1.6	−0.1	1.5
P.5	Gross fixed capital formation:									
	Private sector	4.0	1.9	7.0	3.5	8.8	9.9	−7.5	−18.5	5.2
	Public non-financial corporations	20.3	−51.5	−32.1	1 532.9	−73.6	13.0	18.7	12.1	−0.4
	General government	14.2	32.7	13.2	−69.5	234.2	11.0	24.9	13.0	−1.9
	Total	3.6	1.1	5.1	2.4	6.4	8.1	−4.8	−13.4	2.6
P.6	Exports of goods and services	1.9	1.9	5.2	7.7	11.7	−1.3	1.3	−9.5	6.2
P.7	Imports of goods and services	5.3	1.9	6.7	7.4	10.2	−0.9	−1.2	−12.2	8.5
B.1*g	Gross domestic product at market prices	2.7	3.5	3.0	2.1	2.6	3.5	−1.1	−4.4	1.8

8.5 Aggregates related to gross national income[1]

Percentage of gross national income

		2002	2003	2004	2005	2006	2007	2008	2009	2010
D.2	Taxes on production and imports[2]	13.1	13.0	13.0	12.7	12.8	12.7	12.2	11.8	13.0
D.5	Current taxes on income wealth etc	15.3	14.7	14.9	15.8	16.7	16.3	16.5	15.6	15.4
D.61	Compulsory social contributions[3]	5.8	6.2	6.5	6.6	6.7	6.5	6.7	6.7	6.6
D.91	Capital taxes	0.2	0.2	0.2	0.2	0.3	0.3	1.7	0.3	0.2
	Paid to central government	32.4	32.2	32.7	33.4	34.5	33.8	35.1	32.3	33.0
	Paid to local government	1.5	1.6	1.7	1.7	1.7	1.7	1.7	1.8	1.8
	Paid to institutions of the European Union	0.4	0.4	0.3	0.3	0.3	0.3	0.3	0.3	0.4
	Total taxes	34.4	34.2	34.7	35.4	36.5	35.8	37.1	34.4	35.1
D.3	Subsidies	0.7	0.8	0.8	0.9	0.9	0.8	0.8	0.9	0.9

1 Based on tables 1.2, 11.1 and 7.1.8.
2 Including National Insurance surcharge.
3 Including employers', employees', self employed and non-employed persons contributions

8.6 Average rates of change of gross domestic product at current market prices ('money GDP')

Percentage change, at annual rate

Initial year	Terminal year 1969	1970	1971	1972	1973	1974	1975	1976	1977	1978	1979	1980	1981	1982	1983	1984	1985	1986	1987	1988	1989
1968	7.7	8.8	9.7	10.3	11.3	11.6	13.6	14.2	14.4	14.5	14.8	15.0	14.6	14.2	13.9	13.5	13.2	12.9	12.8	12.7	12.6
1969		9.9	10.7	11.2	12.2	12.4	14.6	15.2	15.3	15.3	15.5	15.7	15.2	14.7	14.3	13.9	13.6	13.2	13.1	13.0	12.8
1970			11.6	11.8	13.0	13.1	15.6	16.0	16.1	16.0	16.2	16.3	15.7	15.2	14.7	14.2	13.8	13.4	13.3	13.2	13.0
1971				12.1	13.7	13.6	16.6	17.0	16.9	16.6	16.8	16.8	16.1	15.5	15.0	14.4	14.0	13.6	13.4	13.3	13.1
1972					15.4	14.4	18.2	18.2	17.9	17.4	17.4	17.4	16.5	15.8	15.2	14.6	14.2	13.7	13.4	13.3	13.1
1973						13.4	19.6	19.2	18.5	17.8	17.8	17.7	16.7	15.9	15.2	14.5	14.1	13.6	13.3	13.2	13.0
1974							26.3	22.2	20.3	19.0	18.7	18.4	17.2	16.2	15.4	14.6	14.1	13.6	13.3	13.2	13.0
1975								18.3	17.4	16.6	16.9	16.9	15.7	14.8	14.1	13.4	13.0	12.5	12.3	12.2	12.1
1976									16.4	15.8	16.4	16.6	15.2	14.3	13.5	12.8	12.4	11.9	11.8	11.7	11.6
1977										15.2	16.4	16.6	14.9	13.8	13.1	12.2	11.9	11.4	11.3	11.3	11.2
1978											17.6	17.3	14.8	13.5	12.7	11.8	11.5	11.0	10.9	10.9	10.8
1979												17.0	13.4	12.2	11.4	10.6	10.5	10.0	10.1	10.2	10.2
1980													9.9	9.8	9.6	9.1	9.2	8.9	9.1	9.4	9.4
1981														9.7	9.5	8.8	9.0	8.7	9.0	9.3	9.4
1982															9.3	8.3	8.8	8.5	8.8	9.3	9.3
1983																7.4	8.5	8.2	8.7	9.3	9.4
1984																	9.7	8.6	9.1	9.7	9.7
1985																		7.6	8.9	9.8	9.8
1986																			10.2	10.9	10.5
1987																				11.6	10.7
1988																					9.8

Initial year	Terminal year 1990	1991	1992	1993	1994	1995	1996	1997	1998	1999	2000	2001	2002	2003	2004	2005	2006	2007	2008	2009	2010
1968	12.4	12.1	11.7	11.4	11.2	11.0	10.9	10.7	10.5	10.4	10.2	10.0	9.9	9.8	9.6	9.5	9.4	9.3	9.1	8.8	8.7
1969	12.6	12.3	11.9	11.6	11.4	11.1	11.0	10.8	10.6	10.5	10.3	10.1	9.9	9.8	9.7	9.6	9.5	9.4	9.2	8.8	8.7
1970	12.8	12.4	12.0	11.7	11.4	11.2	11.0	10.8	10.6	10.5	10.3	10.1	9.9	9.8	9.7	9.5	9.4	9.3	9.1	8.8	8.7
1971	12.8	12.4	12.0	11.7	11.4	11.2	11.0	10.8	10.6	10.4	10.2	10.1	9.9	9.8	9.6	9.5	9.4	9.3	9.1	8.7	8.6
1972	12.9	12.4	12.0	11.7	11.4	11.1	10.9	10.8	10.6	10.4	10.2	10.0	9.8	9.7	9.6	9.4	9.3	9.2	9.0	8.7	8.5
1973	12.7	12.3	11.8	11.5	11.2	11.0	10.8	10.6	10.4	10.2	10.0	9.8	9.6	9.5	9.4	9.2	9.1	9.0	8.8	8.5	8.4
1974	12.7	12.2	11.7	11.4	11.1	10.8	10.6	10.4	10.3	10.1	9.9	9.7	9.5	9.4	9.3	9.1	9.0	8.9	8.7	8.3	8.2
1975	11.8	11.4	10.9	10.6	10.3	10.1	9.9	9.8	9.6	9.4	9.3	9.1	8.9	8.8	8.7	8.6	8.5	8.4	8.2	7.9	7.8
1976	11.4	10.9	10.5	10.2	9.9	9.7	9.5	9.4	9.2	9.1	8.9	8.7	8.6	8.5	8.4	8.2	8.2	8.1	7.9	7.5	7.5
1977	11.0	10.6	10.1	9.8	9.6	9.3	9.2	9.0	8.9	8.7	8.6	8.4	8.3	8.2	8.1	8.0	7.9	7.8	7.6	7.3	7.2
1978	10.6	10.2	9.7	9.4	9.2	9.0	8.9	8.7	8.6	8.4	8.3	8.1	8.0	7.9	7.8	7.7	7.6	7.6	7.4	7.0	7.0
1979	10.0	9.6	9.2	8.9	8.7	8.5	8.4	8.3	8.1	8.0	7.9	7.7	7.6	7.5	7.5	7.3	7.3	7.2	7.0	6.7	6.6
1980	9.4	8.9	8.5	8.3	8.1	7.9	7.9	7.8	7.7	7.5	7.4	7.3	7.2	7.1	7.1	7.0	6.9	6.9	6.7	6.4	6.3
1981	9.3	8.9	8.4	8.1	8.0	7.8	7.7	7.6	7.5	7.4	7.3	7.2	7.1	7.0	7.0	6.8	6.8	6.8	6.6	6.2	6.2
1982	9.2	8.8	8.3	8.0	7.8	7.7	7.6	7.5	7.4	7.3	7.2	7.0	6.9	6.9	6.8	6.7	6.7	6.7	6.5	6.1	6.1
1983	9.2	8.7	8.2	7.9	7.7	7.5	7.4	7.4	7.3	7.2	7.0	6.9	6.8	6.8	6.7	6.6	6.6	6.5	6.4	6.0	5.9
1984	9.6	8.9	8.3	7.9	7.7	7.5	7.5	7.4	7.3	7.1	7.0	6.9	6.8	6.7	6.7	6.6	6.5	6.5	6.3	5.9	5.9
1985	9.5	8.8	8.1	7.7	7.5	7.3	7.3	7.2	7.1	7.0	6.8	6.7	6.6	6.6	6.5	6.4	6.4	6.4	6.2	5.8	5.7
1986	10.0	9.0	8.1	7.7	7.5	7.3	7.2	7.1	7.0	6.9	6.8	6.6	6.6	6.5	6.5	6.4	6.3	6.3	6.1	5.7	5.7
1987	10.0	8.7	7.7	7.3	7.1	6.9	6.9	6.8	6.7	6.7	6.5	6.4	6.3	6.3	6.3	6.1	6.1	6.1	5.9	5.5	5.5
1988	9.2	7.8	6.8	6.5	6.4	6.3	6.3	6.3	6.3	6.2	6.1	6.0	6.0	6.0	5.9	5.8	5.8	5.8	5.6	5.2	5.2
1989	8.6	6.8	5.8	5.6	5.7	5.7	5.8	5.9	5.9	5.9	5.8	5.7	5.7	5.7	5.7	5.6	5.6	5.6	5.4	5.0	5.0
1990		5.0	4.4	4.7	5.0	5.2	5.4	5.5	5.6	5.6	5.5	5.4	5.4	5.5	5.5	5.4	5.4	5.5	5.3	4.8	4.8
1991			3.9	4.5	5.0	5.2	5.5	5.6	5.6	5.6	5.5	5.5	5.5	5.5	5.5	5.4	5.5	5.5	5.3	4.8	4.8
1992				5.2	5.5	5.6	5.9	5.9	5.9	5.9	5.8	5.7	5.6	5.7	5.6	5.5	5.6	5.6	5.4	4.9	4.8
1993					5.9	5.9	6.1	6.1	6.1	6.0	5.9	5.7	5.7	5.7	5.7	5.6	5.6	5.6	5.4	4.8	4.8
1994						5.8	6.2	6.2	6.1	6.0	5.9	5.7	5.6	5.7	5.7	5.5	5.6	5.6	5.3	4.8	4.8
1995							6.6	6.4	6.2	6.1	5.9	5.7	5.6	5.7	5.6	5.5	5.6	5.6	5.3	4.7	4.7
1996								6.2	6.0	5.9	5.7	5.5	5.5	5.5	5.5	5.4	5.4	5.5	5.2	4.5	4.6
1997									5.9	5.8	5.6	5.3	5.3	5.4	5.4	5.3	5.4	5.4	5.1	4.4	4.4
1998										5.7	5.4	5.1	5.2	5.3	5.4	5.2	5.3	5.4	5.0	4.3	4.3
1999											5.1	4.9	5.0	5.2	5.3	5.1	5.2	5.3	4.9	4.1	4.2
2000												4.6	5.0	5.3	5.3	5.1	5.3	5.3	4.9	4.0	4.1
2001													5.3	5.6	5.6	5.3	5.4	5.5	5.0	4.0	4.0
2002														6.0	5.7	5.3	5.4	5.5	4.9	3.8	3.9
2003															5.5	4.9	5.3	5.4	4.7	3.4	3.6
2004																4.3	5.1	5.3	4.5	3.0	3.3
2005																	5.9	5.9	4.6	2.7	3.1
2006																		5.8	3.9	1.6	2.4
2007																			2.0	-0.4	1.2
2008																				-2.8	0.9
2009																					4.6

8.7 Average rates of change of gross domestic product (chained volume measures)

Percentage change, at annual rate

Initial year \ Terminal year	1969	1970	1971	1972	1973	1974	1975	1976	1977	1978	1979	1980	1981	1982	1983	1984	1985	1986	1987	1988	1989
1968	2.1	2.2	2.1	2.5	3.4	2.6	2.2	2.2	2.2	2.3	2.4	2.0	1.7	1.8	1.9	1.9	2.0	2.1	2.3	2.4	2.4
1969		2.2	2.2	2.7	3.8	2.7	2.2	2.2	2.3	2.4	2.4	2.0	1.7	1.7	1.9	1.9	2.0	2.1	2.3	2.4	2.4
1970			2.1	2.9	4.3	2.9	2.2	2.2	2.3	2.4	2.4	2.0	1.6	1.7	1.8	1.9	2.0	2.1	2.3	2.4	2.4
1971				3.7	5.4	3.1	2.2	2.3	2.3	2.4	2.4	1.9	1.6	1.6	1.8	1.9	2.0	2.1	2.3	2.4	2.4
1972					7.2	2.9	1.7	1.9	2.0	2.2	2.3	1.7	1.4	1.5	1.6	1.7	1.9	2.0	2.2	2.4	2.4
1973						-1.3	-1.0	0.2	0.8	1.2	1.5	1.0	0.7	0.8	1.1	1.2	1.4	1.6	1.8	2.1	2.1
1974							-0.6	1.0	1.5	1.9	2.1	1.3	1.0	1.1	1.4	1.5	1.7	1.9	2.1	2.3	2.3
1975								2.6	2.5	2.7	2.7	1.7	1.2	1.4	1.6	1.7	1.9	2.1	2.3	2.5	2.5
1976									2.4	2.8	2.8	1.5	1.0	1.1	1.5	1.6	1.9	2.1	2.3	2.5	2.5
1977										3.2	3.0	1.2	0.6	0.9	1.3	1.5	1.8	2.0	2.3	2.5	2.5
1978											2.7	0.3	-0.3	0.3	1.0	1.3	1.6	1.9	2.2	2.5	2.4
1979												-2.1	-1.7	-0.5	0.6	1.0	1.4	1.8	2.1	2.4	2.4
1980													-1.3	0.4	1.4	1.7	2.1	2.4	2.7	3.0	2.9
1981														2.1	2.9	2.8	3.0	3.2	3.4	3.7	3.5
1982															3.6	3.1	3.3	3.5	3.7	3.9	3.7
1983																2.7	3.1	3.4	3.7	4.0	3.7
1984																	3.6	3.8	4.1	4.3	3.9
1985																		4.0	4.3	4.5	4.0
1986																			4.6	4.8	4.0
1987																				5.0	3.6
1988																					2.3

Initial year \ Terminal year	1990	1991	1992	1993	1994	1995	1996	1997	1998	1999	2000	2001	2002	2003	2004	2005	2006	2007	2008	2009	2010
1968	2.3	2.2	2.1	2.1	2.2	2.2	2.2	2.3	2.3	2.4	2.4	2.4	2.4	2.5	2.5	2.5	2.5	2.5	2.4	2.2	2.2
1969	2.3	2.2	2.1	2.1	2.2	2.2	2.2	2.3	2.3	2.4	2.4	2.5	2.5	2.5	2.5	2.5	2.5	2.5	2.4	2.2	2.2
1970	2.3	2.2	2.1	2.1	2.2	2.2	2.2	2.3	2.3	2.4	2.4	2.5	2.5	2.5	2.5	2.5	2.5	2.5	2.4	2.2	2.2
1971	2.3	2.2	2.1	2.1	2.2	2.2	2.2	2.3	2.3	2.4	2.4	2.5	2.5	2.5	2.5	2.5	2.5	2.5	2.4	2.3	2.2
1972	2.3	2.1	2.0	2.0	2.1	2.1	2.2	2.2	2.3	2.3	2.4	2.4	2.4	2.5	2.5	2.5	2.5	2.5	2.4	2.2	2.2
1973	2.0	1.8	1.7	1.7	1.9	1.9	2.0	2.0	2.1	2.1	2.2	2.3	2.3	2.3	2.3	2.3	2.3	2.4	2.3	2.1	2.1
1974	2.2	2.0	1.9	1.9	2.0	2.1	2.1	2.2	2.2	2.3	2.4	2.4	2.4	2.4	2.5	2.5	2.5	2.5	2.4	2.2	2.2
1975	2.4	2.2	2.0	2.0	2.2	2.2	2.2	2.3	2.4	2.4	2.5	2.5	2.5	2.6	2.6	2.6	2.6	2.6	2.5	2.3	2.2
1976	2.4	2.1	2.0	2.0	2.1	2.2	2.2	2.3	2.3	2.4	2.5	2.5	2.5	2.6	2.6	2.6	2.6	2.6	2.5	2.3	2.2
1977	2.4	2.1	2.0	2.0	2.1	2.2	2.2	2.3	2.3	2.4	2.5	2.5	2.5	2.6	2.6	2.6	2.6	2.6	2.5	2.2	2.2
1978	2.3	2.0	1.9	1.9	2.1	2.1	2.2	2.2	2.3	2.4	2.5	2.5	2.5	2.5	2.6	2.5	2.5	2.6	2.4	2.2	2.2
1979	2.3	2.0	1.8	1.8	2.0	2.1	2.1	2.2	2.3	2.3	2.4	2.5	2.5	2.5	2.5	2.5	2.5	2.6	2.4	2.2	2.2
1980	2.7	2.3	2.2	2.2	2.3	2.4	2.4	2.5	2.5	2.6	2.7	2.7	2.7	2.7	2.7	2.7	2.7	2.7	2.6	2.4	2.3
1981	3.2	2.7	2.5	2.5	2.6	2.6	2.6	2.7	2.8	2.8	2.9	2.9	2.9	2.9	2.9	2.9	2.9	2.9	2.7	2.5	2.5
1982	3.3	2.8	2.5	2.5	2.6	2.7	2.7	2.7	2.8	2.9	2.9	3.0	2.9	3.0	3.0	2.9	2.9	2.9	2.8	2.5	2.5
1983	3.3	2.7	2.4	2.4	2.5	2.6	2.6	2.7	2.7	2.8	2.9	2.9	2.9	2.9	2.9	2.9	2.9	2.9	2.7	2.5	2.4
1984	3.4	2.7	2.4	2.3	2.5	2.6	2.6	2.7	2.8	2.8	2.9	2.9	2.9	2.9	2.9	2.9	2.9	2.9	2.7	2.4	2.4
1985	3.3	2.5	2.2	2.2	2.4	2.5	2.5	2.6	2.7	2.8	2.9	2.9	2.9	2.9	2.9	2.9	2.9	2.9	2.7	2.4	2.4
1986	3.1	2.2	1.9	1.9	2.2	2.3	2.4	2.5	2.6	2.7	2.8	2.8	2.8	2.8	2.8	2.8	2.8	2.8	2.6	2.3	2.3
1987	2.7	1.6	1.3	1.5	1.9	2.0	2.1	2.3	2.4	2.5	2.7	2.7	2.7	2.7	2.7	2.7	2.7	2.7	2.6	2.2	2.2
1988	1.5	0.5	0.4	0.8	1.4	1.6	1.8	2.0	2.1	2.3	2.5	2.5	2.5	2.6	2.6	2.6	2.6	2.6	2.4	2.1	2.1
1989	0.8	-0.3	-0.2	0.4	1.2	1.5	1.7	1.9	2.1	2.3	2.5	2.5	2.5	2.6	2.6	2.6	2.6	2.6	2.4	2.1	2.1
1990		-1.4	-0.6	0.3	1.3	1.6	1.8	2.1	2.3	2.4	2.6	2.7	2.7	2.7	2.8	2.7	2.7	2.8	2.5	2.2	2.1
1991			0.1	1.2	2.2	2.4	2.5	2.7	2.8	2.9	3.1	3.1	3.1	3.1	3.1	3.0	3.0	3.0	2.8	2.4	2.3
1992				2.2	3.2	3.2	3.1	3.2	3.3	3.3	3.5	3.4	3.4	3.4	3.3	3.2	3.2	3.2	2.9	2.5	2.5
1993					4.3	3.7	3.4	3.4	3.5	3.5	3.7	3.6	3.5	3.5	3.4	3.3	3.3	3.3	3.0	2.5	2.5
1994						3.1	3.0	3.1	3.3	3.4	3.6	3.5	3.4	3.4	3.4	3.2	3.2	3.2	2.9	2.4	2.4
1995							2.9	3.2	3.4	3.5	3.7	3.6	3.4	3.4	3.4	3.3	3.2	3.2	2.9	2.3	2.3
1996								3.4	3.6	3.6	3.8	3.7	3.5	3.5	3.5	3.3	3.2	3.3	2.9	2.3	2.3
1997									3.8	3.7	4.0	3.8	3.6	3.5	3.5	3.3	3.2	3.2	2.8	2.2	2.2
1998										3.7	4.1	3.8	3.5	3.5	3.4	3.2	3.1	3.2	2.7	2.1	2.0
1999											4.5	3.8	3.4	3.4	3.3	3.1	3.1	3.1	2.6	1.9	1.9
2000												3.2	2.9	3.1	3.1	2.9	2.8	2.9	2.4	1.6	1.6
2001													2.7	3.1	3.0	2.8	2.8	2.9	2.3	1.4	1.5
2002														3.5	3.2	2.9	2.8	2.9	2.2	1.3	1.3
2003															3.0	2.5	2.5	2.8	2.0	0.9	1.0
2004																2.1	2.3	2.7	1.7	0.5	0.7
2005																	2.6	3.0	1.6	0.1	0.4
2006																		3.5	1.2	-0.7	-0.1
2007																			-1.1	-2.8	-1.3
2008																				-4.4	-1.4
2009																					1.8

8.8 Average rates of change of GDP at market prices (current prices) per capita

Percentage change, at annual rate

Initial year	Terminal year 1990	1991	1992	1993	1994	1995	1996	1997	1998	1999	2000	2001	2002	2003	2004	2005	2006	2007	2008	2009	2010
1989	8.3	6.4	5.5	5.3	5.4	5.4	5.6	5.6	5.6	5.6	5.5	5.4	5.4	5.4	5.3	5.2	5.2	5.2	5.0	4.6	4.6
1990		4.6	4.1	4.4	4.7	4.9	5.1	5.2	5.3	5.3	5.2	5.1	5.1	5.1	5.1	5.0	5.1	5.1	4.8	4.4	4.4
1991			3.7	4.3	4.7	4.9	5.2	5.3	5.4	5.4	5.3	5.2	5.2	5.2	5.2	5.1	5.1	5.1	4.9	4.4	4.4
1992				4.9	5.3	5.4	5.6	5.7	5.7	5.6	5.5	5.4	5.3	5.3	5.3	5.2	5.2	5.2	4.9	4.4	4.4
1993					5.7	5.6	5.8	5.9	5.8	5.7	5.6	5.4	5.4	5.4	5.3	5.2	5.2	5.2	4.9	4.4	4.4
1994						5.5	5.9	5.9	5.8	5.7	5.6	5.4	5.3	5.3	5.3	5.2	5.2	5.2	4.9	4.3	4.3
1995							6.4	6.1	6.0	5.8	5.6	5.4	5.3	5.3	5.3	5.1	5.1	5.1	4.8	4.2	4.2
1996								5.9	5.8	5.6	5.4	5.2	5.1	5.2	5.2	5.0	5.0	5.0	4.7	4.1	4.1
1997									5.6	5.5	5.2	5.0	5.0	5.1	5.0	4.9	4.9	4.9	4.6	3.9	3.9
1998										5.3	5.0	4.8	4.8	4.9	4.9	4.8	4.8	4.9	4.5	3.8	3.8
1999											4.8	4.5	4.6	4.9	4.9	4.7	4.8	4.8	4.4	3.6	3.7
2000												4.2	4.6	4.9	4.9	4.7	4.8	4.8	4.4	3.5	3.6
2001													4.9	5.2	5.1	4.8	4.9	4.9	4.4	3.4	3.5
2002														5.5	5.3	4.7	4.9	4.9	4.3	3.2	3.3
2003															5.0	4.3	4.7	4.8	4.1	2.8	3.0
2004																3.6	4.5	4.7	3.8	2.3	2.7
2005																	5.3	5.2	3.9	2.0	2.5
2006																		5.1	3.2	0.9	1.8
2007																			1.3	-1.1	0.7
2008																				-3.4	0.4
2009																					4.3

8.9 Average rates of change of GDP at market prices (chained volume measures) per capita

Percentage change, at annual rate

Initial year	Terminal year 1990	1991	1992	1993	1994	1995	1996	1997	1998	1999	2000	2001	2002	2003	2004	2005	2006	2007	2008	2009	2010
1989	0.5	-0.6	-0.5	0.1	0.9	1.2	1.4	2.0	2.1	2.3	2.4	2.5	2.4	2.5	2.5	2.4	2.4	2.4	2.2	1.8	1.8
1990		-1.7	-0.9	0.0	1.0	1.4	1.6	2.2	2.4	2.5	2.6	2.6	2.6	2.6	2.6	2.6	2.5	2.5	2.3	1.9	1.9
1991			-0.1	0.9	2.0	2.2	2.3	2.9	3.0	3.0	3.1	3.1	3.0	3.0	3.0	2.9	2.8	2.8	2.5	2.1	2.1
1992				2.0	3.0	2.9	2.8	3.5	3.5	3.4	3.5	3.4	3.3	3.3	3.2	3.1	3.0	3.0	2.7	2.2	2.2
1993					4.0	3.4	3.1	3.8	3.8	3.7	3.8	3.6	3.5	3.4	3.4	3.2	3.1	3.1	2.7	2.2	2.2
1994						2.8	2.7	3.8	3.7	3.6	3.7	3.6	3.4	3.4	3.3	3.1	3.0	3.0	2.7	2.1	2.1
1995							2.6	4.3	4.0	3.8	3.9	3.7	3.5	3.5	3.3	3.1	3.0	3.0	2.6	2.1	2.0
1996								5.9	4.7	4.3	4.2	3.9	3.6	3.6	3.4	3.2	3.1	3.1	2.6	2.0	2.0
1997									3.6	3.4	3.6	3.4	3.2	3.2	3.1	2.9	2.8	2.8	2.4	1.7	1.7
1998										3.3	3.7	3.4	3.1	3.1	3.0	2.8	2.7	2.7	2.2	1.6	1.5
1999											4.1	3.4	3.0	3.1	2.9	2.7	2.6	2.6	2.1	1.4	1.4
2000												2.8	2.5	2.7	2.7	2.4	2.3	2.4	1.9	1.1	1.1
2001													2.3	2.7	2.6	2.3	2.3	2.3	1.8	0.9	0.9
2002														3.1	2.8	2.3	2.3	2.4	1.7	0.7	0.8
2003															2.5	1.9	2.0	2.2	1.4	0.3	0.4
2004																1.4	1.7	2.1	1.1	-0.1	0.1
2005																	2.0	2.4	1.0	-0.5	-0.1
2006																		2.8	0.5	-1.4	-0.7
2007																			-1.8	-3.4	-1.8
2008																				-5.0	-1.8
2009																					1.4

8.10 Average rates of change of household disposable income (chained volume measures) Total

Percentage change, at annual rate

Initial year	Terminal year 1969	1970	1971	1972	1973	1974	1975	1976	1977	1978	1979	1980	1981	1982	1983	1984	1985	1986	1987	1988	1989
1968	0.9	2.3	1.9	3.5	4.1	3.2	2.8	2.4	1.9	2.4	2.7	2.6	2.4	2.2	2.2	2.3	2.4	2.5	2.4	2.6	2.7
1969		3.7	2.4	4.4	4.9	3.7	3.2	2.6	2.0	2.6	2.9	2.8	2.5	2.3	2.3	2.4	2.5	2.6	2.5	2.7	2.8
1970			1.2	4.7	5.2	3.7	3.1	2.4	1.8	2.5	2.8	2.7	2.4	2.2	2.2	2.3	2.4	2.5	2.5	2.6	2.7
1971				8.4	7.3	4.5	3.5	2.7	1.9	2.6	3.0	2.9	2.5	2.3	2.3	2.4	2.5	2.6	2.5	2.7	2.8
1972					6.3	2.6	2.0	1.3	0.6	1.7	2.3	2.2	1.9	1.7	1.7	1.9	2.0	2.2	2.2	2.4	2.5
1973						-1.0	-0.1	-0.3	-0.7	0.8	1.6	1.6	1.4	1.2	1.3	1.5	1.7	1.9	1.9	2.1	2.3
1974							0.7	0.1	-0.7	1.3	2.2	2.1	1.7	1.5	1.6	1.8	1.9	2.1	2.1	2.3	2.5
1975								-0.6	-1.4	1.4	2.5	2.4	1.9	1.6	1.7	1.9	2.1	2.3	2.2	2.5	2.6
1976									-2.2	2.5	3.6	3.1	2.4	2.0	2.0	2.2	2.3	2.5	2.5	2.7	2.9
1977										7.3	6.6	4.9	3.5	2.8	2.7	2.8	2.9	3.1	2.9	3.2	3.3
1978											5.9	3.7	2.3	1.7	1.8	2.1	2.3	2.6	2.5	2.8	3.0
1979												1.6	0.6	0.4	0.8	1.4	1.7	2.1	2.0	2.4	2.7
1980													-0.4	-0.3	0.5	1.3	1.8	2.2	2.1	2.5	2.8
1981														-0.1	1.0	1.9	2.3	2.7	2.5	3.0	3.2
1982															2.1	3.0	3.1	3.4	3.1	3.5	3.7
1983																3.8	3.6	3.8	3.3	3.7	3.9
1984																	3.5	3.9	3.1	3.7	4.0
1985																		4.3	3.0	3.8	4.1
1986																			1.7	3.6	4.0
1987																				5.6	5.2
1988																					4.8

Initial year	Terminal year 1990	1991	1992	1993	1994	1995	1996	1997	1998	1999	2000	2001	2002	2003	2004	2005	2006	2007	2008	2009	2010
1968	2.8	2.7	2.7	2.8	2.7	2.7	2.7	2.8	2.8	2.8	2.8	2.9	2.9	2.9	2.8	2.8	2.8	2.7	2.7	2.7	2.6
1969	2.9	2.8	2.8	2.8	2.8	2.8	2.8	2.8	2.8	2.8	2.9	3.0	3.0	3.0	2.9	2.9	2.8	2.8	2.7	2.7	2.6
1970	2.8	2.8	2.8	2.8	2.7	2.7	2.7	2.8	2.8	2.8	2.9	2.9	2.9	2.9	2.9	2.9	2.8	2.8	2.7	2.7	2.6
1971	2.9	2.9	2.9	2.9	2.8	2.8	2.8	2.9	2.8	2.9	2.9	3.0	3.0	3.0	2.9	2.9	2.9	2.8	2.7	2.7	2.6
1972	2.6	2.6	2.6	2.6	2.6	2.6	2.6	2.6	2.6	2.7	2.7	2.8	2.8	2.8	2.8	2.7	2.7	2.7	2.6	2.6	2.5
1973	2.4	2.4	2.4	2.4	2.4	2.4	2.4	2.5	2.5	2.5	2.6	2.7	2.7	2.7	2.7	2.6	2.6	2.6	2.5	2.5	2.4
1974	2.6	2.6	2.6	2.6	2.6	2.6	2.6	2.6	2.6	2.7	2.7	2.8	2.8	2.8	2.8	2.7	2.7	2.7	2.6	2.6	2.5
1975	2.8	2.7	2.7	2.7	2.7	2.6	2.7	2.7	2.7	2.7	2.8	2.9	2.9	2.9	2.9	2.8	2.8	2.7	2.7	2.6	2.5
1976	3.0	2.9	2.9	2.9	2.8	2.8	2.8	2.9	2.9	2.9	3.0	3.1	3.1	3.1	3.0	2.9	2.9	2.8	2.8	2.7	2.6
1977	3.4	3.3	3.3	3.2	3.1	3.1	3.1	3.1	3.1	3.1	3.2	3.3	3.3	3.3	3.2	3.1	3.1	3.0	2.9	2.9	2.8
1978	3.1	3.0	3.0	3.0	2.9	2.9	2.9	2.9	2.9	2.9	3.0	3.1	3.1	3.1	3.0	3.0	2.9	2.9	2.8	2.7	2.7
1979	2.8	2.8	2.8	2.8	2.7	2.7	2.7	2.8	2.8	2.8	2.9	3.0	3.0	3.0	2.9	2.9	2.8	2.8	2.7	2.6	2.5
1980	3.0	2.9	2.9	2.9	2.8	2.7	2.8	2.8	2.8	2.8	2.9	3.1	3.0	3.0	3.0	2.9	2.9	2.8	2.7	2.7	2.6
1981	3.3	3.2	3.2	3.1	3.0	3.0	3.0	3.1	3.0	3.0	3.1	3.2	3.2	3.2	3.1	3.1	3.0	2.9	2.8	2.8	2.7
1982	3.8	3.6	3.5	3.4	3.3	3.2	3.2	3.3	3.2	3.2	3.3	3.4	3.4	3.4	3.3	3.2	3.1	3.0	2.9	2.9	2.8
1983	4.0	3.8	3.6	3.6	3.4	3.3	3.3	3.3	3.3	3.3	3.4	3.5	3.4	3.4	3.3	3.2	3.2	3.1	3.0	2.9	2.8
1984	4.1	3.8	3.6	3.6	3.3	3.3	3.3	3.3	3.3	3.3	3.4	3.5	3.4	3.4	3.3	3.2	3.1	3.1	2.9	2.9	2.8
1985	4.2	3.8	3.6	3.6	3.3	3.2	3.2	3.3	3.3	3.2	3.3	3.5	3.4	3.4	3.3	3.2	3.1	3.0	2.9	2.9	2.7
1986	4.1	3.7	3.5	3.5	3.2	3.1	3.1	3.2	3.2	3.2	3.3	3.4	3.4	3.4	3.2	3.1	3.1	3.0	2.9	2.8	2.7
1987	5.0	4.2	3.9	3.8	3.4	3.3	3.3	3.4	3.3	3.3	3.4	3.5	3.5	3.5	3.3	3.2	3.1	3.0	2.9	2.8	2.7
1988	4.7	3.8	3.5	3.4	3.1	3.0	3.0	3.1	3.1	3.1	3.2	3.4	3.3	3.3	3.2	3.1	3.0	2.9	2.8	2.7	2.6
1989	4.6	3.2	3.1	3.1	2.7	2.7	2.8	2.9	2.9	2.9	3.1	3.3	3.2	3.2	3.1	3.0	2.9	2.8	2.7	2.6	2.5
1990		1.9	2.3	2.6	2.3	2.3	2.5	2.7	2.7	2.7	2.9	3.2	3.1	3.1	3.0	2.9	2.8	2.7	2.6	2.5	2.4
1991			2.7	2.9	2.4	2.4	2.6	2.8	2.8	2.8	3.0	3.3	3.2	3.2	3.0	2.9	2.9	2.8	2.6	2.5	2.4
1992				3.0	2.2	2.3	2.5	2.8	2.8	2.8	3.1	3.3	3.3	3.3	3.1	3.0	2.9	2.8	2.6	2.5	2.4
1993					1.4	2.0	2.3	2.8	2.8	2.8	3.1	3.4	3.3	3.3	3.1	3.0	2.9	2.7	2.6	2.5	2.4
1994						2.6	2.8	3.2	3.1	3.1	3.4	3.7	3.5	3.5	3.2	3.1	3.0	2.8	2.7	2.6	2.4
1995							3.1	3.6	3.3	3.2	3.5	3.8	3.7	3.6	3.3	3.2	3.0	2.9	2.7	2.6	2.4
1996								4.1	3.4	3.3	3.7	4.0	3.8	3.7	3.3	3.2	3.0	2.8	2.6	2.5	2.4
1997									2.7	2.8	3.5	4.0	3.7	3.6	3.2	3.1	2.9	2.7	2.5	2.4	2.2
1998										3.0	3.9	4.4	4.0	3.8	3.3	3.1	2.9	2.7	2.5	2.4	2.2
1999											4.9	5.2	4.3	4.0	3.4	3.1	2.9	2.7	2.4	2.3	2.1
2000												5.4	4.1	3.7	3.0	2.8	2.6	2.4	2.1	2.1	1.9
2001													2.7	2.9	2.2	2.1	2.0	1.9	1.6	1.6	1.5
2002														3.0	2.0	1.9	1.8	1.7	1.5	1.5	1.3
2003															1.0	1.4	1.4	1.4	1.2	1.2	1.1
2004																1.8	1.7	1.5	1.2	1.3	1.1
2005																	1.5	1.4	1.0	1.2	0.9
2006																		1.2	0.7	1.0	0.8
2007																			0.3	0.9	0.6
2008																				1.6	0.8
2009																					0.1

8.11 Average rates of change of household disposable income (chained volume measures) per capita

Percentage change, at annual rate

Initial year	Terminal year 1969	1970	1971	1972	1973	1974	1975	1976	1977	1978	1979	1980	1981	1982	1983	1984	1985	1986	1987	1988	1989
1968	0.5	1.9	1.5	3.1	3.7	2.9	2.6	2.2	1.7	2.2	2.6	2.5	2.2	2.1	2.1	2.2	2.2	2.3	2.3	2.4	2.5
1969		3.4	2.0	4.0	4.5	3.4	2.9	2.4	1.8	2.4	2.8	2.6	2.4	2.2	2.2	2.3	2.3	2.4	2.4	2.5	2.6
1970			0.7	4.3	4.9	3.4	2.8	2.3	1.6	2.3	2.7	2.6	2.3	2.1	2.1	2.2	2.3	2.4	2.3	2.5	2.6
1971				8.0	7.0	4.3	3.4	2.6	1.8	2.6	3.0	2.8	2.5	2.2	2.2	2.3	2.4	2.5	2.4	2.6	2.7
1972					6.1	2.5	1.9	1.3	0.6	1.7	2.3	2.2	1.9	1.7	1.7	1.9	2.0	2.1	2.1	2.3	2.4
1973						-1.0	-0.1	-0.3	-0.7	0.8	1.6	1.6	1.3	1.2	1.3	1.5	1.6	1.8	1.8	2.0	2.2
1974							0.7	0.1	-0.6	1.3	2.2	2.0	1.7	1.5	1.5	1.7	1.9	2.1	2.0	2.2	2.4
1975								-0.5	-1.3	1.5	2.5	2.3	1.8	1.6	1.6	1.9	2.0	2.2	2.1	2.4	2.5
1976									-2.1	2.5	3.6	3.0	2.3	1.9	2.0	2.2	2.3	2.5	2.4	2.6	2.8
1977										7.3	6.5	4.8	3.5	2.8	2.7	2.8	2.8	3.0	2.8	3.1	3.2
1978											5.8	3.6	2.2	1.7	1.7	2.1	2.2	2.4	2.3	2.6	2.8
1979												1.5	0.5	0.3	0.8	1.3	1.6	2.0	1.9	2.3	2.5
1980													-0.5	-0.2	0.5	1.3	1.7	2.1	2.0	2.4	2.6
1981														0.0	1.1	1.9	2.2	2.6	2.4	2.8	3.0
1982															2.1	2.8	3.0	3.2	2.9	3.3	3.5
1983																3.6	3.4	3.6	3.1	3.5	3.7
1984																	3.2	3.6	2.9	3.5	3.7
1985																		4.0	2.7	3.6	3.8
1986																			1.4	3.4	3.8
1987																				5.4	5.0
1988																					4.5

Initial year	Terminal year 1990	1991	1992	1993	1994	1995	1996	1997	1998	1999	2000	2001	2002	2003	2004	2005	2006	2007	2008	2009	2010
1968	2.6	2.6	2.6	2.6	2.5	2.5	2.5	2.6	2.6	2.6	2.6	2.7	2.7	2.7	2.6	2.6	2.5	2.5	2.4	2.4	2.3
1969	2.7	2.7	2.7	2.7	2.6	2.6	2.6	2.6	2.6	2.6	2.7	2.8	2.8	2.7	2.7	2.6	2.6	2.5	2.5	2.4	2.4
1970	2.7	2.6	2.6	2.6	2.6	2.6	2.6	2.6	2.6	2.6	2.7	2.7	2.7	2.7	2.7	2.6	2.6	2.5	2.4	2.4	2.3
1971	2.8	2.7	2.7	2.7	2.7	2.6	2.6	2.7	2.7	2.7	2.7	2.8	2.8	2.8	2.7	2.7	2.6	2.6	2.5	2.4	2.4
1972	2.5	2.5	2.5	2.5	2.4	2.4	2.4	2.5	2.5	2.5	2.6	2.6	2.6	2.6	2.6	2.5	2.5	2.4	2.3	2.3	2.2
1973	2.3	2.3	2.3	2.3	2.2	2.2	2.3	2.3	2.3	2.3	2.4	2.5	2.5	2.5	2.5	2.4	2.4	2.3	2.2	2.2	2.1
1974	2.5	2.5	2.5	2.5	2.4	2.4	2.4	2.5	2.5	2.5	2.6	2.7	2.6	2.6	2.6	2.5	2.5	2.4	2.3	2.3	2.2
1975	2.6	2.6	2.6	2.6	2.5	2.5	2.5	2.6	2.6	2.6	2.6	2.7	2.7	2.7	2.6	2.6	2.5	2.5	2.4	2.3	2.3
1976	2.9	2.8	2.8	2.8	2.7	2.6	2.7	2.7	2.7	2.7	2.8	2.9	2.8	2.8	2.7	2.7	2.6	2.6	2.5	2.4	2.3
1977	3.3	3.1	3.1	3.1	3.0	2.9	2.9	3.0	2.9	2.9	3.0	3.1	3.0	3.0	2.9	2.9	2.8	2.7	2.6	2.6	2.5
1978	2.9	2.8	2.8	2.8	2.7	2.7	2.7	2.7	2.7	2.7	2.8	2.9	2.9	2.9	2.8	2.7	2.6	2.6	2.5	2.4	2.3
1979	2.7	2.6	2.6	2.6	2.5	2.5	2.5	2.6	2.6	2.6	2.7	2.8	2.7	2.7	2.6	2.6	2.5	2.5	2.4	2.3	2.2
1980	2.8	2.7	2.7	2.7	2.6	2.5	2.6	2.6	2.6	2.6	2.7	2.8	2.8	2.8	2.7	2.6	2.6	2.5	2.4	2.3	2.3
1981	3.2	3.0	3.0	2.9	2.8	2.8	2.8	2.8	2.8	2.8	2.9	3.0	3.0	2.9	2.8	2.8	2.7	2.6	2.5	2.4	2.3
1982	3.6	3.3	3.3	3.2	3.0	3.0	3.0	3.0	3.0	3.0	3.0	3.2	3.1	3.1	3.0	2.9	2.8	2.7	2.6	2.5	2.4
1983	3.8	3.5	3.4	3.3	3.1	3.1	3.0	3.1	3.0	3.0	3.1	3.2	3.2	3.1	3.0	2.9	2.8	2.7	2.6	2.6	2.4
1984	3.8	3.5	3.4	3.3	3.1	3.0	3.0	3.1	3.0	3.0	3.1	3.2	3.1	3.1	3.0	2.9	2.8	2.7	2.6	2.5	2.4
1985	3.9	3.5	3.4	3.3	3.1	3.0	3.0	3.0	3.0	3.0	3.1	3.2	3.1	3.1	3.0	2.9	2.8	2.7	2.5	2.5	2.4
1986	3.9	3.4	3.3	3.2	2.9	2.9	2.9	2.9	2.9	2.9	3.0	3.1	3.1	3.1	2.9	2.8	2.7	2.6	2.5	2.4	2.3
1987	4.7	3.9	3.6	3.5	3.2	3.0	3.0	3.1	3.0	3.0	3.1	3.3	3.2	3.2	3.0	2.9	2.8	2.7	2.5	2.5	2.3
1988	4.4	3.4	3.2	3.1	2.8	2.7	2.7	2.8	2.8	2.8	2.9	3.1	3.0	3.0	2.8	2.7	2.6	2.5	2.4	2.3	2.2
1989	4.3	2.9	2.8	2.8	2.4	2.4	2.5	2.6	2.6	2.6	2.8	3.0	2.9	2.9	2.7	2.6	2.5	2.4	2.3	2.2	2.1
1990		1.6	2.0	2.3	2.0	2.1	2.2	2.4	2.4	2.4	2.6	2.9	2.8	2.8	2.6	2.5	2.4	2.3	2.2	2.1	2.0
1991			2.4	2.6	2.1	2.2	2.3	2.5	2.5	2.5	2.8	3.0	2.9	2.9	2.7	2.6	2.5	2.4	2.2	2.1	2.0
1992				2.8	2.0	2.1	2.3	2.6	2.5	2.6	2.8	3.0	3.0	2.9	2.7	2.6	2.5	2.4	2.2	2.1	2.0
1993					1.1	1.7	2.1	2.5	2.5	2.5	2.8	3.1	3.0	3.0	2.7	2.6	2.5	2.3	2.1	2.1	1.9
1994						2.3	2.6	3.0	2.8	2.8	3.1	3.4	3.2	3.2	2.9	2.7	2.6	2.4	2.2	2.1	2.0
1995							2.8	3.3	3.0	2.9	3.2	3.5	3.4	3.3	2.9	2.8	2.6	2.4	2.2	2.1	2.0
1996								3.8	3.1	2.9	3.3	3.7	3.4	3.3	3.0	2.8	2.6	2.4	2.2	2.1	1.9
1997									2.4	2.5	3.2	3.6	3.4	3.2	2.8	2.6	2.4	2.3	2.0	1.9	1.8
1998										2.6	3.6	4.1	3.6	3.4	2.9	2.7	2.5	2.2	2.0	1.9	1.7
1999											4.5	4.8	4.0	3.6	3.0	2.7	2.4	2.2	1.9	1.8	1.6
2000												5.0	3.7	3.3	2.6	2.3	2.1	1.9	1.6	1.5	1.3
2001													2.3	2.5	1.8	1.6	1.5	1.3	1.1	1.1	0.9
2002														2.6	1.5	1.4	1.3	1.2	0.9	0.9	0.8
2003															0.5	0.8	0.9	0.8	0.5	0.6	0.5
2004																1.2	1.1	0.9	0.6	0.6	0.5
2005																	0.9	0.8	0.4	0.5	0.4
2006																		0.6	0.1	0.4	0.2
2007																			-0.4	0.3	0.1
2008																				1.0	0.3
2009																					-0.3

Chapter 9

Fixed capital formation supplementary tables

9.1 Gross fixed capital formation at current purchasers' prices[1]
Analysis by type of asset and sector
Total economy

£ million

			2002	2003	2004	2005	2006	2007	2008	2009	2010
	Dwellings, excluding land										
	Households and NPISH	DLWK	34 858	40 180	47 330	50 751	54 176	57 410	50 848	38 161	39 362
	Other	KNF7	1 924	1 307	1 195	3 683	3 016	3 701	4 601	4 522	4 570
	Total	DFDK	36 782	41 487	48 525	54 434	57 192	61 112	55 449	42 683	43 931
	Other buildings and structures										
	Total	DLWS	43 192	47 300	49 970	57 844	62 215	71 567	79 433	72 990	69 225
	Transport equipment										
	Total	DLWZ	17 703	16 204	14 128	13 582	14 435	14 110	13 721	12 398	17 215
	Other machinery and equipment and cultivated assets										
	Total	KNF8	54 682	53 135	53 253	48 556	53 402	59 284	59 389	51 905	54 146
	Intangible fixed assets										
	Total	DLXP	14 245	14 979	15 110	15 678	16 009	16 723	17 417	17 038	17 456
	Costs associated with the transfer of ownership of non-produced assets										
	Total	DFBH	12 410	12 059	17 452	16 925	21 566	24 053	13 963	10 855	15 134
P.51	**Gross fixed capital formation**										
S.11001	Public non-financial corporations	FCCJ	3 830	1 857	1 260	20 575	5 440	6 148	7 296	8 177	8 141
S.11002	Private non-financial corporations	FDBM	99 445	99 505	98 081	99 740	109 536	123 355	126 775	111 319	111 796
S.12	Financial corporations	NHCJ	8 025	6 717	6 398	8 744	7 106	8 048	8 704	6 230	7 578
S.1311	Central government	NMES	7 506	6 372	8 328	−6 425	9 894	11 977	15 643	18 476	17 896
S.1313	Local government	NMOA	7 946	14 137	14 891	13 516	13 807	14 329	17 217	18 649	18 538
S.14+S.15	Households and NPISH	NSSU	53 782	58 173	71 472	73 570	81 387	86 180	65 729	46 401	53 158
S.1, P.51	Total gross fixed capital formation	NPQX	180 533	186 759	200 430	209 722	227 172	250 036	241 364	209 253	217 108

1 Components may not sum to totals due to rounding.

9.2 Gross fixed capital formation at current purchasers' prices[1]
Analysis by broad sector and type of asset
Total economy
£ million

			2002	2003	2004	2005	2006	2007	2008	2009	2010
	Private sector										
	New dwellings, excluding land	DFDF	35 277	40 664	47 918	51 390	54 870	58 660	52 237	39 071	40 307
	Other buildings and structures	EQBU	30 534	30 784	32 118	35 668	40 949	47 937	50 499	41 015	39 425
	Transport equipment	EQBV	17 070	15 440	13 035	12 634	13 836	13 468	12 981	11 560	16 150
	Other machinery and equipment and cultivated assets	EQBW	51 352	49 740	49 187	49 153	50 319	55 672	54 021	44 973	46 410
	Intangible fixed assets	EQBX	13 590	14 321	14 468	14 716	15 124	15 816	16 415	15 863	16 050
	Costs associated with the transfer of ownership of non-produced assets	EQBY	13 427	13 444	19 227	18 495	22 933	26 031	15 055	11 469	14 190
P.51	Total	EQBZ	161 251	164 393	175 951	182 056	198 031	217 582	201 208	163 951	172 533
S.11001	**Public non-financial corporations**										
	New dwellings and transfer costs	KNG2	1 937	980	722	4 124	3 299	3 657	4 096	4 379	4 577
	Other buildings and structures	DEES	1 165	490	233	1 766	1 045	1 114	779	1 020	652
	Transport equipment	DEEP	56	28	30	280	103	95	222	231	416
	Other machinery and equipment and cultivated assets	DEEQ	398	227	163	13 790	563	793	1 539	1 774	1 699
	Intangible fixed assets	DLXJ	274	133	112	615	429	489	660	772	797
P.51	Total	FCCJ	3 830	1 857	1 260	20 575	5 440	6 148	7 296	8 177	8 141
S.13	**General government**										
	New dwellings and transfer costs	KNG3	69	55	103	53	9	3	15	1	−8
	Other buildings and structures	EQCH	11 493	16 026	17 619	20 410	20 220	22 517	28 155	30 955	29 148
	Transport equipment	EQCI	577	736	1 063	669	496	548	518	607	649
	Other machinery and equipment and cultivated assets	EQCJ	2 932	3 167	3 903	−14 388	2 519	2 821	3 829	5 159	6 037
	Intangible fixed assets	EQCK	381	525	531	348	457	417	342	402	608
P.51	Total	NNBF	15 452	20 509	23 219	7 091	23 701	26 306	32 860	37 125	36 434
P.51	Total gross fixed capital formation	NPQX	180 533	186 759	200 430	209 722	227 172	250 036	241 364	209 253	217 108

1 Components may not sum to totals due to rounding.

9.3 Gross fixed capital formation at current purchasers' prices[1]
Analysis by type of asset
Total economy
£ million

		2002	2003	2004	2005	2006	2007	2008	2009	2010
Tangible fixed assets										
New dwellings, excluding land	DFDK	36 782	41 487	48 525	54 434	57 192	61 112	55 449	42 683	43 931
Other buildings and structures	DLWS	43 192	47 300	49 970	57 844	62 215	71 567	79 433	72 990	69 225
Transport equipment	DLWZ	17 703	16 204	14 128	13 582	14 435	14 110	13 721	12 398	17 215
Other machinery and equipment and cultivated assets	KNF8	54 682	53 135	53 253	48 556	53 402	59 284	59 389	51 905	54 146
Total	EQCQ	155 527	160 790	168 799	178 447	190 137	209 415	209 672	176 617	184 518
Intangible fixed assets	DLXP	14 245	14 979	15 110	15 678	16 009	16 723	17 417	17 038	17 456
Costs associated with the transfer of ownership of non-produced assets	DFBH	12 410	12 059	17 452	16 925	21 566	24 053	13 963	10 855	15 134
P.51 Total gross fixed capital formation	NPQX	180 533	186 759	200 430	209 722	227 172	250 036	241 364	209 253	217 108

1 Components may not sum to totals due to rounding.

9.4 Gross fixed capital formation[1,2]
Chained volume measures (Reference year 2008)
Total economy: Analysis by broad sector and type of asset   £ million

			2002	2003	2004	2005	2006	2007	2008	2009	2010
	Private sector										
	New dwellings, excluding land	DFDP	46 314	49 745	54 867	54 711	56 941	59 423	52 237	40 362	40 755
	Other buildings and structures	EQCU	31 740	32 175	32 530	36 011	41 183	48 052	50 499	45 293	43 424
	Transport equipment	EQCV	18 569	16 714	14 040	13 438	14 546	14 155	12 981	10 381	13 912
	Other machinery and equipment and cultivated assets	EQCW	46 929	46 385	47 571	48 681	50 524	56 540	54 021	47 253	47 914
	Intangible fixed assets	EQCX	14 621	15 431	15 580	15 544	15 758	16 129	16 415	15 362	15 270
	Costs associated with the transfer of ownership of non-produced assets	EQCY	21 865	19 303	26 589	23 858	25 972	26 132	15 055	14 232	16 558
P.51	Total	EQCZ	177 994	178 088	187 997	190 429	203 294	219 316	201 208	172 882	177 833
S.11001	**Public non-financial corporations**										
	New dwellings and transfer costs	KNG7	2 458	1 174	855	4 772	3 696	3 785	4 096	−2 724	−2 911
	Other buildings and structures	DEEX	1 564	647	289	2 125	1 197	1 199	779	1 076	697
	Transport equipment	DEEU	57	27	30	284	103	93	222	230	384
	Other machinery and equipment and cultivated assets	DEEV	340	199	147	13 043	582	817	1 539	1 687	1 598
	Intangible fixed assets	EQDE	336	159	127	687	464	506	660	762	770
P.51	Total	EQDG	1 490	1 102	1 477	21 620	5 754	6 424	7 296	1 031	538
S.13	**General government**										
	New dwellings and transfer costs	KNG8	77	59	111	57	9	3	15	–	−9
	Other buildings and structures	EQDI	15 199	20 346	21 368	23 021	21 600	23 137	28 155	29 676	29 697
	Transport equipment	EQDJ	373	444	518	582	522	496	518	536	534
	Other machinery and equipment and cultivated assets	EQDK	2 356	2 566	3 251	−13 162	2 611	3 061	3 829	4 548	5 339
	Intangible fixed assets	EQDL	249	596	580	371	482	431	342	378	554
P.51	Total	EQDN	19 616	24 982	26 376	9 850	25 304	26 987	32 860	35 137	36 115
P.51	Total gross fixed capital formation	NPQR	202 615	204 883	215 291	220 497	234 572	253 562	241 364	209 051	214 486

1 For the years before 2008, totals differ from the sum of their components.
2 Components may not sum to totals due to rounding.

9.5 Gross fixed capital formation[1,2]
Chained volume measures (Reference year 2008)
Total economy: Analysis by type of asset   £ million

		2002	2003	2004	2005	2006	2007	2008	2009	2010
Tangible fixed assets										
New dwellings, excluding land	DFDV	47 526	49 782	54 746	58 044	59 068	61 630	55 449	44 119	44 450
Other buildings and structures	EQDP	48 503	53 167	54 188	61 158	63 979	72 388	79 433	76 045	73 818
Transport equipment	DLWJ	18 548	16 762	14 332	14 009	14 909	14 533	13 721	11 147	14 831
Other machinery and equipment and cultivated assets	KNG6	49 625	49 150	50 969	48 563	53 717	60 418	59 390	53 488	54 851
Total	EQDS	165 215	170 195	175 292	182 117	192 345	209 507	207 993	184 799	187 948
Intangible fixed assets	EQDT	15 032	15 988	16 083	16 388	16 531	16 923	17 417	16 502	16 593
Costs associated with the transfer of ownership of non-produced assets	DFDW	22 625	19 587	26 875	25 305	27 141	27 386	15 954	7 750	9 944
P.51 Total gross fixed capital formation	NPQR	202 615	204 883	215 291	220 497	234 572	253 562	241 364	209 051	214 486

1 For the years before 2008, totals differ from the sum of their components.
2 Components may not sum to totals due to rounding.

Chapter 10
Non-financial balance sheets

The non-financial balance sheets show the market value of non-financial assets in the UK. As such they are a measure of the wealth of the UK.

The non-financial balance sheets figures show that the most valuable asset continues to be housing with a total value of £4,260 billion in 2010. This is up 5 per cent on the previous year and equivalent to 58 per cent of the nation's total wealth. The housing stock belonging to the household and non-profit institutions serving households sector was worth £4,037 billion, up 5 per cent on the previous year.

When financial assets are added to the value of the non-financial assets, this results in the net worth of the UK being estimated at £7,333 billion in 2010. This is an increase of £695 billion on the previous year.

In 2005 it was announced that UK companies would be required to produce their accounts in line with the International Financial Reporting Standards (IFRS), and to be fully implemented by 2013. Companies have applied these changes at different times therefore the implementation of the IFRS has resulted in an upward revision on the valuation of some tangible assets, such as commercial industrial and other (CIO) buildings, civil engineering and plant and machinery. As there is no obligation for companies to apply IFRS retrospectively, these discontinuities are unavoidable and further information to accurately revise the back series is unavailable. Therefore it is advisable not to make year-on-year comparisons from 2005 for CIO assets, as these changes affect data series across this period.

Non-financial assets include both tangible and intangible assets. Tangible assets consist of property: plant and machinery; agricultural assets; vehicles; and also include certain types of farming stocks (mainly dairy cattle and orchards) and military equipment whose use is not solely destructive. Intangible assets consist of the value of computer software, patents, mineral exploration and artistic originals.

Data sources include:

- other government departments and agencies
- annual reports of public corporations and major businesses
- industry publications
- Chartered Institute of Public Finance and Accountancy report on Local Authority Assets

These sources are subject to IFRS

Where non-financial asset market valuations are not readily available, a proxy is used based on the UK net capital stocks data modelled in the Perpetual Inventory Method (PIM) within the Office for National Statistics. For central government, data are taken from returns made by government departments to HM Treasury. Central government assets also include the value of the electro-magnetic spectrum. The spectrum is treated as a tangible non-produced asset and the payments made by mobile phone companies as rent.

Local authority housing is shown in the public corporations sector. This is because government-owned market activities are always treated as being carried out by public corporations, either in their own right or via quasi-corporations.

Residential buildings in the non-financial balance sheets includes the value of the land that the residential buildings are situated on, as these cannot be separated out from our source data, which is housing valuations.

Revisions in the data are due to ongoing improvements in the non-financial balance sheets compilation process, the most prominent of these are agriculture and commercial, industrial and other buildings. Revisions to the financial accounts and balance sheets for this publication have also been incorporated into the overall values for net worth.

The non-financial balance sheet is available on the ONS website.

10.1 National Balance Sheet: by Sector[1,2] At Current Prices

£ billion at end year

				2002	2003	2004	2005	2006	2007	2008	2009	2010
	Non-financial corporations[3]											
S.11001	Public[4]		CGRW	60.1	59.8	61.7	51.0	54.2	61.6	59.2	63.4	64.0
S.11002	Private[3]		TMPN	64.1	−28.4	−75.4	−339.9	−474.2	−429.3	144.3	−307.8	−36.0
S.11	Total		CGRV	124.2	31.4	−13.7	−288.9	−420.0	−367.7	203.5	−244.4	28.0
S.12	**Financial corporations**		CGRU	−342.6	−309.2	−318.2	−404.4	−407.0	−397.8	−266.7	−396.8	−315.5
	General government[4]											
S.1311	Central government		CGRY	−104.4	−121.5	−161.5	−167.0	−169.4	−195.9	−260.6	−393.3	−547.1
S.1313	Local government		CGRZ	357.1	396.8	452.4	485.2	510.2	554.7	520.6	475.2	483.0
S.13	Total		CGRX	252.6	275.2	290.9	318.2	340.8	358.9	260.1	81.9	−64.1
S.14+S.15	**Households and NPISH[5]**		CGRC	4 933.2	5 416.9	5 901.8	6 404.5	6 973.4	7 471.9	6 577.8	7 197.2	7 684.7
S.1	**Total net worth[6]**		CGDA	4 967.4	5 414.3	5 860.8	6 029.4	6 487.2	7 065.4	6 774.7	6 637.9	7 333.0

1 Due to the introduction of IFRS, it is advisable not to make year on year comparisons from 2005 as the changes affect data series across the period.
2 See footnotes on net worth in tables 10.2 - 10.11 for asset allocation changes between sectors.
3 Including quasi-corporations.
4 Public sector (general government plus public non-financial corporations) is as shown below.
5 Non-profit institutions serving households.
6 Net worth was previously defined as *net wealth*.

10.2 National Balance Sheet: by Asset[1] At Current Prices

£ billion at end year

		2002	2003	2004	2005	2006	2007	2008	2009	2010
Non-financial assets										
Tangible assets:										
Residential buildings	CGLK	2 737.1	3 054.9	3 427.0	3 555.0	3 915.3	4 313.6	3 922.6	4 048.8	4 259.7
Agricultural assets	CGMP	53.8	53.7	53.8	54.1	54.3	54.0	53.0	52.3	51.4
Commercial, industrial and other buildings	CGMU	590.2	608.7	661.3	664.2	752.1	701.3	596.5	561.8	806.9
Civil engineering works	CGQZ	588.6	625.0	666.9	706.0	745.0	801.5	782.1	746.2	789.8
Plant and machinery	CGRA	368.9	373.7	386.9	403.0	414.5	432.8	459.6	476.0	496.8
Vehicles, including ships, aircraft, etc	CGRB	134.6	146.5	153.5	154.9	159.2	177.4	180.7	175.3	193.0
Inventories	CGRD	180.4	184.8	197.3	207.8	215.8	229.7	240.6	230.5	243.6
Spectrum[2]	ZLDX	21.9	21.9	21.9	21.9	21.9	21.9	21.9	21.9	21.9
Total tangible assets	CGRE	4 675.5	5 069.1	5 568.7	5 766.9	6 278.1	6 732.3	6 257.0	6 312.8	6 863.3
Intangible assets:										
Non-marketable tenancy rights	CGRF	365.3	413.5	466.1	486.9	545.1	611.5	549.3	574.7	610.1
Other intangible assets	CGRG	38.6	40.9	43.4	45.1	47.7	49.9	52.1	54.5	57.0
Total intangible assets	CGRH	403.9	454.4	509.5	532.1	592.9	661.5	601.5	629.2	667.0
Total non-financial assets	CGJB	5 079.4	5 523.5	6 078.1	6 299.0	6 871.0	7 393.8	6 858.5	6 942.0	7 530.3
Total net financial assets/liabilities	NQFT	−112.0	−109.2	−217.3	−269.6	−383.8	−328.4	−83.8	−304.1	−197.3
Total net worth[3]	CGDA	4 967.4	5 414.3	5 860.8	6 029.4	6 487.2	7 065.4	6 774.7	6 637.9	7 333.0

1 Due to the introduction of IFRS, it is advisable not to make year on year comparisons from 2005 as the changes affect data series across the period.
2 Following the grant of licences to mobile phone companies, the electromagnetic spectrum is included as an asset for the first time in 2000.
3 Net worth was previously defined as *net wealth*.

10.3 Non-Financial Corporations[1] At Current Prices

£ billion at end year

Non-financial assets		2002	2003	2004	2005	2006	2007	2008	2009	2010
Tangible assets:										
Residential buildings[2]	CGUT	164.8	182.0	200.9	214.2	212.8	228.4	219.7	211.1	208.5
of which Local Authority housing	CGWM	86.5	96.3	107.9	118.1	107.2	111.8	113.3	100.4	91.9
Agricultural assets	CGUU	4.1	4.0	4.0	4.1	4.2	4.1	3.8	3.7	3.5
Commercial, industrial and other buildings	CGUV	292.2	290.7	316.7	285.8	354.2	290.1	208.4	166.9	385.0
Civil engineering works	CGUW	272.8	284.0	287.5	298.6	306.7	321.9	333.5	340.0	378.4
Plant and machinery	CGUX	325.4	326.0	338.0	350.9	357.8	375.8	399.1	416.4	431.1
Vehicles, including ships, aircraft, etc	CGUY	60.6	68.6	71.3	69.5	72.9	89.2	100.9	90.6	101.2
Inventories	CGUZ	164.0	168.0	180.3	191.3	199.2	212.8	223.5	213.7	226.4
Total tangible assets	CGVA	1 284.0	1 323.3	1 398.8	1 414.5	1 507.8	1 522.3	1 489.0	1 442.3	1 733.9
Intangible non-financial assets										
Non-marketable tenancy rights	CGVB	–	–	–	–	–	–	–	–	–
Other intangible assets	CGVC	31.5	33.2	35.2	36.9	39.2	41.2	43.3	45.5	47.9
Total intangible assets	CGVE	31.5	33.2	35.2	36.9	39.2	41.2	43.3	45.5	47.9
Total non-financial assets	CGES	1 315.4	1 356.4	1 434.0	1 451.4	1 547.0	1 563.5	1 532.3	1 487.9	1 781.8
Total net financial assets/liabilities	NYOM	-1 191.2	-1 325.0	-1 447.7	-1 740.3	-1 967.0	-1 931.1	-1 328.8	-1 732.3	-1 753.9
Total net worth[3]	CGRV	124.2	31.4	-13.7	-288.9	-420.0	-367.7	203.5	-244.4	28.0

1 Due to the introduction of IFRS, it is advisable not to make year on comparisons from 2005 as the changes affect data series across the period.
2 Figures now include both council housing and Housing Association properties.
3 Net worth was previously defined as *net wealth*.

10.4 Public Non-Financial Corporations[1] At Current Prices

£ billion at end year

Non-financial assets		2002	2003	2004	2005	2006	2007	2008	2009	2010
Tangible assets:										
Residential buildings[2]	CGVF	91.0	101.1	111.9	122.3	111.8	116.7	117.9	105.1	96.6
of which Local Authority housing	CGWM	86.5	96.3	107.9	118.1	107.2	111.8	113.3	100.4	91.9
Agricultural assets	CGVG	0.9	0.9	0.9	1.0	1.0	0.9	1.0	1.1	1.1
Commercial, industrial and other buildings	CGVH	25.7	23.8	25.4	26.4	26.8	27.6	25.9	44.6	44.4
Civil engineering works	CGVI	22.4	15.9	15.5	15.7	17.2	19.0	23.0	24.8	25.6
Plant and machinery	CGVJ	7.6	8.1	8.7	8.8	8.6	8.9	9.6	10.5	10.7
Vehicles, including ships, aircraft, etc	CGVK	1.6	1.4	1.7	2.1	2.3	2.3	2.2	2.6	3.3
Inventories	CGVL	5.1	5.1	5.2	5.2	5.3	5.3	5.3	5.3	5.4
Total tangible assets	CGVM	154.4	156.5	169.4	181.4	173.0	180.7	184.9	194.0	187.1
Intangible non-financial assets										
Non-marketable tenancy rights	CGVN	–	–	–	–	–	–	–	–	–
Other intangible assets	CGVO	3.3	3.5	3.9	4.1	4.5	4.8	5.1	5.5	5.9
Total intangible assets	CGVP	3.3	3.5	3.9	4.1	4.5	4.8	5.1	5.5	5.9
Total non-financial assets	CGGN	157.7	160.0	173.3	185.6	177.4	185.5	190.1	199.5	193.0
Total net financial assets/liabilities	NYOP	-97.6	-100.2	-111.6	-134.6	-123.2	-123.9	-130.9	-136.1	-129.0
Total net worth[3]	CGRW	60.1	59.8	61.7	51.0	54.2	61.6	59.2	63.4	64.0

1 Due to the introduction of IFRS, it is advisable not to make year on year comparisons from 2005 as the changes affect data series across the period.
2 Figures now include council housing: these were formally included in table 10.9 (local government).
3 Net worth was previously defined as *net wealth*.

10.5 Private Non-Financial Corporations[1]
At Current Prices

£ billion at end year

Non-financial assets		2002	2003	2004	2005	2006	2007	2008	2009	2010
Tangible assets:										
Residential buildings[2]	TMPB	73.8	80.8	89.0	92.0	101.0	111.7	101.9	105.9	111.8
Agricultural assets	TMPC	3.1	3.1	3.1	3.2	3.2	3.1	2.8	2.6	2.4
Commercial, industrial and other buildings	TMPD	266.5	266.9	291.3	259.4	327.4	262.5	182.5	122.3	340.6
Civil engineering works	TMPE	250.4	268.0	272.0	282.9	289.5	302.9	310.5	315.2	352.8
Plant and machinery	TMPF	317.8	317.9	329.3	342.1	349.1	366.9	389.5	405.9	420.3
Vehicles, including ships, aircraft, etc	TMPO	59.0	67.2	69.5	67.5	70.7	87.0	98.7	87.9	97.8
Inventories	TMPG	158.9	162.9	175.1	186.1	193.9	207.5	218.2	208.3	221.0
Total tangible assets	TMPH	1 129.6	1 166.8	1 229.3	1 233.1	1 334.9	1 341.6	1 304.1	1 248.3	1 546.8
Intangible non-financial assets										
Non-marketable tenancy rights	TMPI	–	–	–	–	–	–	–	–	–
Other intangible assets	TMPJ	28.1	29.6	31.4	32.7	34.8	36.4	38.1	40.0	42.1
Total intangible assets	TMPK	28.1	29.6	31.4	32.7	34.8	36.4	38.1	40.0	42.1
Total non-financial assets	TMPL	1 157.7	1 196.4	1 260.7	1 265.9	1 369.6	1 378.0	1 342.2	1 288.4	1 588.8
Total net financial assets/liabilities	NYOT	–1 093.7	–1 224.9	–1 336.1	–1 605.8	–1 843.8	–1 807.2	–1 197.9	–1 596.1	–1 624.9
Total net worth[3]	TMPN	64.1	–28.4	–75.4	–339.9	–474.2	–429.3	144.3	–307.8	–36.0

1 Due to the introduction of IFRS, it is advisable not to make year on comparisons from 2005 as the changes affect data series across the period.
2 Figures now include Housing Association properties: these were formally included in table 10.10 (non-profit institutions serving households).
3 Net worth was previously defined as *net wealth*.

10.6 Financial Corporations[1]
At Current Prices

£ billion at end year

Non-financial assets		2002	2003	2004	2005	2006	2007	2008	2009	2010
Tangible assets:										
Residential buildings	CGUD	0.7	0.5	0.4	0.9	1.4	2.7	8.1	4.8	4.2
Agricultural assets	CGUE	0.8	0.8	0.8	0.9	0.9	0.9	0.8	0.8	0.8
Commercial, industrial and other buildings	CGUF	103.0	109.3	119.7	121.9	124.9	129.0	105.5	107.8	117.8
Civil engineering works	CGUG	–	–	–	–	–	–	–	–	–
Plant and machinery	CGUH	11.3	11.5	11.8	12.4	13.1	14.6	16.0	15.6	15.4
Vehicles, including ships, aircraft, etc	CGUI	0.7	0.5	0.6	0.5	0.2	0.3	0.1	0.3	0.2
Inventories	CGUO	–	–	–	–	–	–	–	–	–
Total tangible assets	CGUP	116.6	122.7	133.4	136.5	140.5	147.3	130.7	129.3	138.4
Intangible non-financial assets										
Non-marketable tenancy rights	CGUQ	–	–	–	–	–	–	–	–	–
Other intangible assets	CGUR	5.5	6.0	6.3	6.4	6.6	6.8	7.1	7.3	7.4
Total intangible assets	CGUS	5.5	6.0	6.3	6.4	6.6	6.8	7.1	7.3	7.4
Total non-financial assets	CGDB	122.1	128.7	139.7	142.9	147.1	154.1	137.8	136.6	145.9
Total net financial assets/liabilities	NYOE	–464.7	–437.8	–457.9	–547.3	–554.1	–551.9	–404.5	–533.4	–461.3
Total net worth[2]	CGRU	–342.6	–309.2	–318.2	–404.4	–407.0	–397.8	–266.7	–396.8	–315.5

1 Due to the introduction of IFRS, it is advisable not to make year on year comparisons from 2005 as the changes affect data series across the period.
2 Net worth was previously defined as *net wealth*.

10.7 General Government[1] At Current Prices

£ billion at end year

		2002	2003	2004	2005	2006	2007	2008	2009	2010
Non-financial assets										
Tangible assets:										
Residential buildings[2]	CGVQ	3.5	3.3	4.3	3.8	4.8	5.3	5.9	6.4	10.4
Agricultural assets	CGVR	2.0	2.0	2.0	2.0	2.0	2.0	2.0	1.9	1.9
Commercial, industrial and other buildings	CGVS	146.1	158.1	174.4	200.6	212.9	226.7	235.2	237.5	246.1
Civil engineering works	CGVT	313.6	338.9	377.4	405.4	436.4	477.7	446.6	404.2	409.2
Plant and machinery	CGVU	14.2	17.7	16.6	17.2	20.4	17.5	17.6	15.9	20.7
Vehicles, including ships, aircraft, etc	CGVV	4.4	4.3	4.5	5.6	5.8	6.5	6.5	7.2	10.3
Inventories	CGVW	0.1	0.2	0.2	0.2	0.2	0.1	0.1	0.2	0.2
Spectrum[3]	ZLDB	21.9	21.9	21.9	21.9	21.9	21.9	21.9	21.9	21.9
Total tangible assets	CGVX	505.8	546.3	601.3	656.5	704.5	757.7	736.0	695.3	720.7
Intangible non-financial assets										
Non-marketable tenancy rights	CGVY	–	–	–	–	–	–	–	–	–
Other intangible assets	CGVZ	0.9	1.0	1.0	0.9	1.0	0.9	0.8	0.7	0.6
Total intangible assets	CGWA	0.9	1.0	1.0	0.9	1.0	0.9	0.8	0.7	0.6
Total non-financial assets	CGIX	506.8	547.3	602.3	657.5	705.4	758.6	736.7	696.0	721.3
Total net financial assets/liabilities	NYOG	−254.1	−272.1	−311.4	−339.3	−364.6	−399.7	−476.6	−614.0	−785.5
Total net worth[4]	CGRX	252.6	275.2	290.9	318.2	340.8	358.9	260.1	81.9	−64.1

1 Due to the introduction of IFRS, it is advisable not to make year on year comparisons from 2005 as the changes affect data series across the period.
2 Council housing has now been transferred from general government to public non-financial corporations.
3 Following the grant of licences to mobile phone companies, the electro-magnetic spectrum is included as an asset for the first time in 2000.
4 Net worth was previously defined as *net wealth*.

10.8 Central Government[1] At Current Prices

£ billion at end year

		2002	2003	2004	2005	2006	2007	2008	2009	2010
Non-financial assets										
Tangible assets:[2]										
Residential buildings	CGWB	3.5	3.3	4.3	3.8	4.8	5.3	5.9	6.4	10.4
Agricultural assets	CGWC	0.1	0.1	0.1	0.1	0.1	0.1	0.1	0.1	0.1
Commercial, industrial and other buildings	CGWD	56.7	63.0	69.1	87.9	92.9	97.6	100.0	99.9	105.9
Civil engineering works	CGWE	100.1	105.2	109.9	121.1	130.2	139.9	147.4	151.0	149.5
Plant and machinery	CGWF	11.4	14.3	11.8	11.2	14.4	11.5	11.3	9.2	13.7
Vehicles, including ships, aircraft, etc	CGWG	3.6	3.6	3.6	4.3	4.4	4.8	5.0	5.3	8.3
Inventories	CGWH	0.1	0.2	0.2	0.2	0.2	0.1	0.1	0.2	0.2
Spectrum[3]	ZLDA	21.9	21.9	21.9	21.9	21.9	21.9	21.9	21.9	21.9
Total tangible assets	CGWI	197.6	211.6	220.9	250.5	269.0	281.3	291.8	294.0	310.0
Intangible non-financial assets										
Non-marketable tenancy rights	CGWJ	–	–	–	–	–	–	–	–	–
Other intangible assets	CGWK	0.2	0.2	0.2	0.1	0.1	0.1	0.1	0.1	0.1
Total intangible assets	CGWL	0.2	0.2	0.2	0.1	0.1	0.1	0.1	0.1	0.1
Total non-financial assets	CGIY	197.8	211.8	221.1	250.6	269.1	281.4	291.9	294.2	310.1
Total net financial assets/liabilities	NZDZ	−302.3	−333.3	−382.5	−417.7	−438.5	−477.2	−552.5	−687.4	−857.2
Total net worth[4]	CGRY	−104.4	−121.5	−161.5	−167.0	−169.4	−195.9	−260.6	−393.3	−547.1

1 Due to the introduction of IFRS, it is advisable not to make year on year comparisons from 2005 as the changes affect data series across the period.
2 UK national accounts classification excludes fighting equipment from tangible assets.
3 Following the grant of licences to mobile phone companies, the electro-magnetic spectrum is included as an asset for the first time in 2000.
4 Net worth was previously defined as *net wealth*.

10.9 Local Government[1] At Current Prices

£ billion at end year

		2002	2003	2004	2005	2006	2007	2008	2009	2010
Non-financial assets										
Tangible assets:										
Local Authority housing[2]	ZLCS	–	–	–	–	–	–	–	–	–
Agricultural assets	CGWN	1.9	1.9	1.9	1.9	1.9	1.9	1.9	1.8	1.8
Commercial, industrial and other buildings	CGWO	89.4	95.1	105.3	112.7	120.0	129.1	135.2	137.6	140.1
Civil engineering works	CGWP	213.5	233.7	267.5	284.3	306.2	337.8	299.3	253.2	259.7
Plant and machinery	CGWQ	2.8	3.4	4.8	5.9	5.9	6.0	6.3	6.7	7.0
Vehicles, including ships, aircraft, etc	CGWR	0.7	0.7	0.9	1.2	1.5	1.7	1.5	1.8	2.1
Inventories	CGWS	–	–	–	–	–	–	–	–	–
Total tangible assets	CGWT	308.2	334.7	380.4	406.0	435.5	476.4	444.1	401.2	410.8
Intangible non-financial assets										
Non-marketable tenancy rights	CGWU	–	–	–	–	–	–	–	–	–
Other intangible assets	CGWV	0.7	0.8	0.8	0.8	0.8	0.8	0.6	0.6	0.5
Total intangible assets	CGWW	0.7	0.8	0.8	0.8	0.8	0.8	0.6	0.6	0.5
Total non-financial assets	CGIZ	308.9	335.5	381.2	406.8	436.3	477.2	444.8	401.8	411.2
Total net financial assets/liabilities	NYOJ	48.2	61.3	71.1	78.4	73.8	77.5	75.8	73.4	71.7
Total net worth[3]	CGRZ	357.1	396.8	452.4	485.2	510.2	554.7	520.6	475.2	483.0

1 Due to the introduction of IFRS, it is advisable not to make year on year comparisons from 2005 as the changes affect data series across the period.
2 Figures for council housing are now included in table 10.4 (public non-financial corporations).
3 Net worth was previously defined as *net wealth*.

10.10 Households & Non-Profit Institutions Serving Households (NPISH)[1] At Current Prices

£ billion at end year

		2002	2003	2004	2005	2006	2007	2008	2009	2010
Non-financial assets										
Tangible assets:										
Residential buildings[2]	CGRI	2 568.1	2 869.0	3 221.3	3 336.2	3 696.3	4 077.3	3 688.8	3 826.5	4 036.7
Agricultural assets	CGRJ	46.9	46.9	47.0	47.1	47.3	47.1	46.3	45.9	45.2
Commercial, industrial and other buildings	CGRK	48.9	50.6	50.5	55.9	59.9	55.6	47.4	49.6	58.1
Civil engineering works	CGRL	2.2	2.1	2.0	2.0	2.0	2.0	1.9	1.9	2.3
Plant and machinery	CGRM	18.0	18.5	20.4	22.5	23.2	25.0	26.9	28.1	29.6
Vehicles, including ships, aircraft, etc	CGRN	68.8	73.1	77.1	79.3	80.2	81.4	73.1	77.2	81.3
Inventories	CGRO	16.2	16.7	16.8	16.3	16.4	16.7	16.9	16.6	17.0
Total tangible assets	CGRP	2 769.1	3 076.8	3 435.2	3 559.3	3 925.3	4 305.1	3 901.3	4 045.9	4 270.2
Intangible non-financial assets										
Non-marketable tenancy rights	CGRQ	365.3	413.5	466.1	486.9	545.1	611.5	549.3	574.7	610.1
Other intangible assets	CGRS	0.7	0.8	0.8	0.9	1.0	1.0	1.0	1.0	1.0
Total intangible assets	CGRT	366.0	414.2	467.0	487.8	546.1	612.5	550.4	575.7	611.1
Total non-financial assets	CGCZ	3 135.1	3 491.1	3 902.2	4 047.2	4 471.4	4 917.6	4 451.7	4 621.5	4 881.3
Total net financial assets/liabilities	NZEA	1 798.1	1 925.8	1 999.6	2 357.3	2 502.0	2 554.3	2 126.1	2 575.7	2 803.4
Total net worth[3]	CGRC	4 933.2	5 416.9	5 901.8	6 404.5	6 973.4	7 471.9	6 577.8	7 197.2	7 684.7

1 Due to the introduction of IFRS, it is advisable not to make year on year comparisons from 2005 as the changes affect data series across the period.
2 Figures for Housing Association properties are now included in table 10.5 (private non-financial corporations).
3 Net worth was previously defined as *net wealth*.

10.11 Public Sector[1] At Current Prices

£ billion at end year

		2002	2003	2004	2005	2006	2007	2008	2009	2010
Non-financial assets										
Tangible assets:										
Residential buildings	CGWX	94.5	104.4	116.3	126.0	116.6	122.0	123.8	111.5	107.0
Agricultural assets	CGWY	2.9	2.9	2.9	2.9	3.0	2.9	3.0	3.0	3.0
Commercial, industrial and other buildings	CGWZ	171.8	181.9	199.8	227.0	239.8	254.2	261.1	282.1	290.4
Civil engineering works	CGXA	336.0	354.9	392.9	421.1	453.5	496.7	469.7	429.0	434.8
Plant and machinery	CGXB	21.8	25.8	25.4	25.9	29.0	26.4	27.2	26.4	31.5
Vehicles, including ships, aircraft, etc	CGXC	6.0	5.7	6.2	7.6	8.1	8.8	8.7	9.8	13.7
Inventories	CGXD	5.3	5.2	5.4	5.4	5.5	5.4	5.5	5.5	5.6
Spectrum[2]	ZLDC	21.9	21.9	21.9	21.9	21.9	21.9	21.9	21.9	21.9
Total tangible assets	CGXE	660.2	702.8	770.7	837.9	877.4	938.3	920.9	889.2	907.8
Intangible non-financial assets										
Non-marketable tenancy rights	CGXF	–	–	–	–	–	–	–	–	–
Other intangible assets	CGXG	4.3	4.5	4.8	5.1	5.5	5.7	5.9	6.2	6.5
Total intangible assets	CGXH	4.3	4.5	4.8	5.1	5.5	5.7	5.9	6.2	6.5
Total non-financial assets	CGJA	664.5	707.3	775.6	843.0	882.9	944.1	926.8	895.5	914.3
Total net financial assets/liabilities	CGSA	−351.7	−372.2	−423.0	−473.8	−487.9	−523.6	−607.5	−750.1	−914.5
Total net worth[3]	CGTY	312.8	335.1	352.6	369.2	395.0	420.5	319.2	145.3	−0.2

1 Due to the introduction of IFRS, it is advisable not to make year on year comparisons from 2005 as the changes affect data series across the period.
2 Following the grant of licences to mobile phone companies, the electro-magnetic spectrum is included as an asset for the first time in 2000.
3 Net worth was previously defined as *net wealth*.

Chapter 11
Public sector supplementary tables

Introduction

The Government's fiscal policy rules rely on statistical measures based on the National Accounts framework. The speed with which revisions could be taken on in the National Accounts is not adequate for the purposes of fiscal policy, which is based on an economic cycle and requires up-to-date information over the entire cycle. This has led to a separate revisions policy for the *Public Sector Finances*[1], where revisions are immediately implemented, with the National Accounts catching up as soon as possible.

As a consequence of these different revisions policies, the version of Chapter 11 published here is consistent with the National Accounts, but not with the *Public Sector Finances*[1].

Table 11.2 (functional breakdown of General Government) was withdrawn from the *Blue Book* in 2007 as the majority of the data in this table, with consistent time series, are published elsewhere by ONS within ESA Table 11[2].

Table 11.3 (key fiscal aggregates) was also withdrawn from the *Blue Book* in 2007. The bulk of the data in this table are published in the *Public Sector Finances*[1]. These data are more up-to-date than is possible in a National Accounts publication as the *Public Sector Finances*[1] are not subject to the National Accounts revision policy (see above).

Tables 11.4 and 11.5 (reconciliation of financial balance sheets and transactions for the General Government sector and the Central and Local Government sub-sectors) and Table 11.7 (housing operating account) were withdrawn from the *Blue Book* in 2008. Table 11.6 was withdrawn from the *Blue Book* in 2009.

Taxes payable by UK residents (Table 11.1)

This table is consistent with the National Accounts. The table shows the taxes and national insurance contributions payable to central government, local government, and to the institutions of the European Union.

Taxes on production are included in GDP at market prices. Taxes on products are taxes levied on the sale of goods and services. Other taxes on production include taxes levied on inputs to production (for example non-domestic rates by businesses) and some compulsory unrequited levies that producers have to pay.

Taxes on income and wealth include income tax and corporation tax. Also included are some charges payable by households (for example local government taxes and motor vehicle duty), which are classified as taxes on production when payable by businesses. The totals are measured gross of any tax credits and reliefs recorded as expenditure in the National Accounts, such as working families and child tax credit.

The European System of Accounts 1995 (ESA95) has a category called compulsory social contributions. In the UK accounts this category includes all national insurance contributions. Details of total social contributions and benefits are shown in Tables 5.2.4S and 5.3.4S of Chapter 5.

Some UK taxes are recorded as the resources of the European Union. These include taxes on imports and an amount calculated as the hypothetical yield from VAT at a standard rate on a harmonised base across the EU.

References

1 Office for National Statistics/HM Treasury Public Sector Finances monthly statistical bulletin.
http://www.ons.gov.uk/ons/taxonomy/index.html?nscl=Public+Sector+Finance

2 Office for National Statistics/EU Government Debt and Deficit returns.
http://www.ons.gov.uk/ons/publications/re-reference-tables.html?edition=tcm%3A77-230219

11.1 Taxes paid by UK residents to general government and the European Union
Total economy sector S.1

£ million

Part			2002	2003	2004	2005	2006	2007	2008	2009	2010
	GENERATION OF INCOME										
	Uses										
D.2	Taxes on production and imports										
D.21	Taxes on products and imports										
D.211	Value added tax (VAT)										
	Paid to central government	NZGF	68 251	74 595	79 755	81 426	85 591	89 698	89 682	78 307	93 711
	Paid to the European Union	FJKM	2 808	2 740	1 789	1 999	2 167	2 319	2 270	1 593	2 253
D.211	Total	QYRC	71 059	77 335	81 544	83 425	87 758	92 017	91 952	79 900	95 964
D.212	Taxes and duties on imports excluding VAT										
D.2121	Paid to CG: import duties[1]	NMXZ	–	–	–	–	–	–	–	–	–
D.2121	Paid to EU: import duties	FJWE	1 919	1 937	2 145	2 237	2 329	2 412	2 636	2 645	2 933
D.212	Total	QYRB	1 919	1 937	2 145	2 237	2 329	2 412	2 636	2 645	2 933
D.214	Taxes on products excluding VAT and import duties										
	Paid to central government										
	Customs & excise revenue										
	Beer	GTAM	2 934	3 035	3 111	3 072	3 065	3 042	3 140	3 189	3 278
	Wines, cider, perry & spirits	GTAN	4 333	4 491	4 761	4 802	4 779	5 008	5 533	5 728	6 075
	Tobacco	GTAO	7 947	8 079	8 097	8 021	8 089	8 051	8 253	8 734	9 040
	Hydrocarbon oils	GTAP	22 070	22 476	23 412	23 346	23 448	24 512	24 790	25 894	27 013
	Car tax	GTAT	–	–	–	–	–	–	–	–	–
	Betting, gaming & lottery	CJQY	997	933	872	864	958	959	989	1 013	1 092
	Air passenger duty	CWAA	814	781	856	896	961	1 883	1 876	1 800	2 094
	Insurance premium tax	CWAD	2 138	2 294	2 359	2 343	2 314	2 306	2 281	2 259	2 402
	Landfill tax	BKOF	541	607	672	733	804	877	954	842	1 065
	Other	ACDN	–	–	–	–	–	–	–	–	–
	Fossil fuel levy	CIQY	32	–	–	–	–	–	–	–	–
	Gas levy	GTAZ	–	–	–	–	–	–	–	–	–
	Stamp duties	GTBC	7 432	7 256	8 885	9 910	13 070	14 633	9 497	7 138	9 098
	Levies on exports (Third country trade)	CUDF	–	–	–	–	–	–	–	–	–
	Camelot payments to National Lottery Distribution Fund	LIYH	1 452	1 293	1 342	1 349	1 440	1 310	1 405	1 553	1 625
	Purchase Tax	EBDB	–	–	–	–	–	–	–	–	–
	Hydro-benefit	LITN	44	44	40	10	–	–	–	–	–
	Aggregates levy	MDUQ	213	340	328	327	321	339	334	275	289
	Milk super levy	DFT3	35	56	69	19	1	–	–	–	–
	Climate change levy	LSNT	825	828	756	747	711	690	717	693	666
	Channel 4 funding formula	EG9G	–	–	–	–	–	–	–	–	–
	Renewable energy obligations	EP89	195	345	373	369	450	520	496	470	472
	Rail franchise premia	LITT	–	–	205	98	125	244	285	496	792
	Other taxes and levies	GCSP	–	–	–	–	–	–	–	–	–
	Total paid to central government	NMYB	52 002	52 858	56 138	56 906	60 536	64 374	60 550	60 084	65 001
	Paid to the European Union										
	Sugar levy	GTBA	25	18	25	24	–	–	–	–	–
	European Coal & Steel Community levy	GTBB	–	–	–	–	–	–	–	–	–
	Total paid to the European Union	FJWG	25	18	25	24	–	–	–	–	–
D.214	Total taxes on products excluding VAT & import duties	QYRA	52 026	52 876	56 162	56 930	60 536	64 375	60 550	60 084	65 001
D.21	Total taxes on products and imports	NZGW	125 004	132 148	139 851	142 592	150 623	158 804	155 138	142 629	163 898
D.29	Production taxes other than on products										
	Paid to central government										
	Consumer Credit Act fees	CUDB	190	208	220	197	223	281	328	435	480
	National non-domestic rates	CUKY	16 604	16 891	17 099	17 919	18 919	19 455	20 709	21 585	21 772
	Northern Ireland non-domestic rates	NSEZ	134	139	263	286	318	311	313	325	342
	Levies paid to CG levy-funded bodies	LITK	195	193	214	235	232	261	459	548	560
	Selective employment tax	CSAH	–	–	–	–	–	–	–	–	–
	National insurance surcharge	GTAY	–	–	–	–	–	–	–	–	–
	London regional transport levy	GTBE	–	–	–	–	–	–	–	–	–
	IBA levy	GTAL	–	–	–	–	–	–	–	–	–
	Motor vehicle duties paid by businesses	EKED	724	797	808	809	865	878	885	908	937
	Regulator fees	GCSQ	93	101	86	78	72	76	70	72	90
	Tithe Act payments[2]	EBDD	–	–	–	–	–	–	–	–	–
	Northern Ireland Driver Vehicle Agency	IY9N	–	–	–	–	–	3	4	4	4
	Bank Payroll Tax: Accrued receipts	JT2Q	–	–	–	–	–	–	–	–	3 417
	Total	NMBX	17 940	18 329	18 690	19 524	20 629	21 265	22 768	23 877	27 602
	Paid to local government										
	Non-domestic rates[3]	NMYH	173	188	163	182	202	267	301	317	329
D.29	Total production taxes other than on products	NMYD	18 113	18 517	18 853	19 706	20 831	21 532	23 069	24 194	27 931
D.2	Total taxes on production and imports, paid										
	Paid to central government	NMBY	138 193	145 782	154 583	157 856	166 756	175 337	173 000	162 268	186 314
	Paid to local government	NMYH	173	188	163	182	202	267	301	317	329
	Paid to the European Union	FJWB	4 752	4 695	3 959	4 260	4 496	4 731	4 906	4 238	5 186
D.2	Total	NZGX	143 117	150 665	158 704	162 298	171 454	180 335	178 207	166 823	191 829

1 These taxes existed before the UK's entry into the EEC in 1973
2 These taxes existed before 1969
3 From 1990/1991 onwards these series only contain rates paid in Northern Ireland

11.1 continued Taxes paid by UK residents to general government and the European Union
Total economy sector S.1

£ million

Part			2002	2003	2004	2005	2006	2007	2008	2009	2010
	SECONDARY DISTRIBUTION OF INCOME										
	Uses										
D.5	Current taxes on income, wealth etc											
D.51	Taxes on income											
	Paid to central government											
	Household income taxes	DRWH	109 358	111 559	117 481	128 098	137 156	147 951	150 257	138 403	143 695
	Corporation Tax	ACCD	28 866	28 489	31 160	37 820	47 108	43 912	46 487	35 402	41 253
	Petroleum revenue tax	DBHA	946	1 146	1 166	1 799	2 546	1 387	2 663	1 047	1 349
	Windfall tax	EYNK	–	–	–	–	–	–	–	–	–
	Other taxes on income	BMNX	3 672	3 040	4 320	4 781	5 790	6 601	8 190	10 308	5 045
D.51	Total	NMCU	142 842	144 234	154 127	172 498	192 600	199 851	207 597	185 160	191 342
D.59	Other current taxes											
	Paid to central government											
	Motor vehicle duty paid by households	CDDZ	3 570	3 923	3 955	3 953	4 145	4 506	4 639	4 722	4 903
	Northern Ireland domestic rates	NSFA	106	101	225	233	244	265	281	290	354
	Boat licences	NSNP	–	–	–	–	–	–	–	–	–
	Fishing licences	NRQB	–	–	19	20	20	20	20	20	20
	National non-domestic rates paid by non-market sectors[1]	BMNY	1 029	996	1 082	1 190	1 262	1 304	1 355	1 408	1 470
	Passport fees	E8A6	148	185	220	279	322	377	376	351	390
	Television licence fee	DH7A	2 280	2 329	2 490	2 655	2 696	2 862	2 949	3 009	3 088
	Northern Ireland Driver Vehicle Agency	IY9O	–	–	–	–	–	12	15	14	12
	Total	NMCV	7 133	7 534	7 991	8 330	8 689	9 346	9 635	9 814	10 237
	Paid to local government											
	Domestic rates[2]	NMHK	83	91	139	147	155	127	122	131	146
	Community charge	NMHL	–	–	–	–	–	–	–	–	–
	Council tax	NMHM	16 448	18 391	19 871	20 966	22 064	23 224	24 275	24 943	25 464
	Total	NMIS	16 531	18 482	20 010	21 113	22 219	23 351	24 397	25 074	25 610
D.59	Total	NVCM	23 664	26 016	28 001	29 443	30 908	32 697	34 032	34 888	35 847
D.5	Total current taxes on income, wealth etc											
	Paid to central government	NMCP	149 975	151 768	162 118	180 828	201 289	209 197	217 232	194 974	201 579
	Paid to local government	NMIS	16 531	18 482	20 010	21 113	22 219	23 351	24 397	25 074	25 610
D.5	Total	NMZL	166 506	170 250	182 128	201 941	223 508	232 548	241 629	220 048	227 189
D.61	Social contributions											
D.611	Actual social contributions											
	Paid to central government (National Insurance Contributions)											
D.61111	Employers' compulsory contributions	CEAN	35 735	39 890	43 874	46 824	49 568	53 765	57 080	54 387	56 089
D.61121	Employees' compulsory contributions	GCSE	25 357	29 055	32 623	34 810	37 052	36 584	38 186	37 179	38 500
D.61131	Self- and non-employed persons' compulsory contributions	NMDE	2 318	2 595	2 727	2 825	2 930	2 861	3 053	2 879	2 576
D.611	Total	AIIH	63 410	71 540	79 224	84 459	89 550	93 210	98 319	94 445	97 165
Part	**CAPITAL ACCOUNT**										
	Changes in liabilities and net worth										
D.91	Other capital taxes											
	Paid to central government											
	Inheritance tax	GILF	2 327	2 386	2 831	3 100	3 471	3 764	3 130	2 305	2 593
	Tax on other capital transfers	GILG	54	30	50	50	50	50	50	50	50
	Development land tax and other	GCSV	–	–	–	–	–	–	–	–	–
	Tax paid on LG equal pay settlements	C625	–	–	–	–	54	53	77	46	–
	FSCS levies on private sector[3]	HZQ4	–	–	–	–	–	–	21 816	1 805	–
D.91	Total	NMGI	2 381	2 416	2 881	3 150	3 575	3 867	25 073	4 206	2 643
	TOTAL TAXES AND COMPULSORY SOCIAL CONTRIBUTIONS										
	Paid to central government	GCSS	353 959	371 506	398 806	426 293	461 170	481 611	513 624	455 893	487 701
	Paid to local government	GCST	16 704	18 670	20 173	21 295	22 421	23 618	24 698	25 391	25 939
	Paid to the European Union	FJWB	4 752	4 695	3 959	4 260	4 496	4 731	4 906	4 238	5 186
	Total	GCSU	375 415	394 871	422 938	451 848	488 087	509 960	543 228	485 522	518 826

1 Up until 1995/96 these payments are included in national non-domestic rates under production taxes other than on products
2 From 1990/1991 onwards these series only contain rates paid in Northern Ireland
3 Financial Services Compensation Scheme

Chapter 12

Statistics for European Union purposes

The European Union uses National Accounts data for a number of administrative and economic purposes. Gross National Product (GNP), calculated in accordance with the European System of Accounts 1979 (ESA79), has been used in setting a ceiling on the EU budget and calculating part of Member States' contributions to the budget.

However from 2002, the calculation reflects the move to the new European System of Accounts 1995 (ESA95) and the progression to Gross National Income (GNI) from GNP.[1] ESA95 is the basis on which most UK statistical information is now supplied to the EU.

ESA95 differs from the ESA79 in a number of ways; for example, the recording of interest payments and the treatment of software in gross fixed capital formation, and roads and bridges in the consumption of fixed capital formation.[2]

Data supplied for EU budgetary purposes

The GNP/GNI measure[3] is one component in the calculation of Member States' contributions to the EU Budget.

GNP data up to and including 2001 have been frozen, or 'closed' in the calculation of UK contributions. In future, revisions will only be made due to methodological improvements to the transition mechanism (see note 2).

The years 2002 onwards remain 'open' years, reflecting any revisions to National Accounts. From 2002, UK contributions are calculated under the ESA95 framework as shown in Table 1.2.

UK transactions with the institutions of the EU

Table 12.1 shows the UK contribution to the budget under the four categories of revenue raising ('own resources'), and payments flowing into the UK in the form of EU expenditure and the UK budgetary rebate. UK GNP/GNI forms the basis of the 'Fourth Resource' contributions.

Data to monitor government deficit and debt

The convergence criteria for Economic and Monetary Union (EMU) are set out in the 1992 Treaty on European Union (The Maastricht Treaty).[4] The Treaty, plus the Stability and Growth Pact, requires Member States to avoid excessive government deficits – defined as general government net borrowing and gross debt as a percentage of GDP. Member States report their planned and actual deficits, and the levels of their debt, to the European Commission. Data to monitor excessive deficits are supplied in accordance with EU legislation.[5]

The Treaty does not determine what constitutes 'excessive'. This is agreed by the Economic and Finance Council (ECOFIN). However, a Protocol to the Treaty does provide a reference value of 3 per cent of GDP for net borrowing and 60 per cent of GDP for gross debt.

The United Kingdom submitted the estimates in the following table to the European Commission in September 2011.[6]

	2007/08	2008/09	2009/10	2010/11
General government deficit				
net borrowing (£bn)	39.7	98.5	162.8	140.0
as a percentage of GDP[6]	2.8	6.9	11.6	9.5
General government debt				
debt at nominal value (£bn)[7]	620.1	799.9	1001.6	1129.6
as a percentage of GDP[6]	43.6	55.8	71.2	76.7

References

1 The harmonisation of gross national income at market prices (GNI regulation) was adopted in July 2003 under Council Regulation (EC) No. 1287/2003.

2 Commission Decision 97/178 set down a transition mechanism for deriving ESA79 GNP figures from ESA95 for the purposes of the EC budget. The mechanism was extended following Commission Decision 98/501 and the July 2001 meeting of the GNP Committee.

3 Council Directive 89/130/EEC.

4 Treaty on European Union (Luxembourg, Office for Official Publications of the European Communities, 1992).

5 Council Regulation (EC) No. 3605/93.

6 Data were also published in calendar years in the March 2011 *Government deficit and debt under the Maastricht Treaty* statistical bulletin.

7 At end year.

12.1 UK official transactions with institutions of the EU
UK transactions with ESA95 sector S.212

£ million

			2002	2003	2004	2005	2006	2007	2008	2009	2010
	UK resources										
P.62	Exports of services										
	UK charge for collecting duties and levies(net)[1,2]	QWUE	487	489	543	565	583	603	660	661	733
D.31	Subsidies on products, paid (negative resources)										
	Agricultural guarantee fund	EBGL	2 381	2 691	3 315	3 408	3 221	2 952	3 051	3 411	3 032
	European Coal & Steel Community grants	FJKP	–	–	2	–	–	–	–	–	–
D.75	Social assistance										
	European Social Fund	HDIZ	412	427	433	900	1 305	795	608	609	777
D.74	Current international co-operation										
	Fontainebleau abatement[2]	FKKL	3 099	3 560	3 592	3 655	3 570	3 523	4 862	5 392	3 046
	Grants to research councils and miscellaneous[2]	GCSD	13	10	12	13	24	117	30	26	15
D.92	Capital transfers, payable										
	Agricultural guidance fund	FJXL	–	2	49	80	50	150	417	215	431
	European regional development fund	HBZA	296	622	1 062	1 402	618	707	972	640	609
D.99	Agricultural compensation scheme payments[5]	EBGO	–	–	–	–	–	–	–	–	–
	Total identified UK resources	GCSL	6 688	7 801	9 008	10 023	9 371	8 847	10 600	10 954	8 643
	UK uses										
D.21	Taxes on products										
	EU traditional own resources										
D.212	Import duties	FJWD	1 919	1 937	2 145	2 237	2 329	2 412	2 636	2 645	2 933
D.214	Sugar levy	GTBA	25	18	25	24	–	–	–	–	–
D.214	European Coal & Steel Community levy	GTBB	–	–	–	–	–	–	–	–	–
	Third own resource contribution										
D.211	VAT contribution	HCML	2 720	2 775	1 764	1 980	2 165	2 293	2 255	1 733	2 172
D.211	Adjustment to VAT contribution	FSVL	88	–35	25	19	2	26	15	–140	81
D.75	Miscellaneous current transfers										
	Fourth own resource contribution[3]										
	GNP fourth resource	HCSO	5 259	6 622	7 565	8 597	8 358	7 996	8 628	10 692	10 718
	GNP adjustment	HCSM	76	150	–16	135	163	327	–205	–137	101
	Total GNP based fourth own resource	NMFH	5 335	6 772	7 549	8 732	8 521	8 323	8 423	10 555	10 819
D.74	Other current transfers										
	JET contributions and miscellaneous[3]	GVEG	10	18	–3	106	8	6	5	–14	–18
	Inter-government agreements[3]	HCBW	–	–	–	–	–	–	–	–	–
	EU non-budget (miscellaneous)[3]	HRTM	–	–	–	–	–	–	–	–	–
	Total identified UK uses	GCSM	10 097	11 485	11 505	13 098	13 025	13 060	13 334	14 779	15 987
	Balance, UK net contribution to the EU[4]	BLZS	–3 409	–3 684	–2 497	–3 075	–3 654	–4 213	–2 734	–3 825	–7 344

1 Before 1989 this is netted off the VAT contribution but cannot be identfified separately.
2 UK central government resources.
3 UK central government uses.
4 As defined in pre-ESA95 Blue Books.
5 Before 1999 these have been included in Agricultural guarantee fund payments (series EBGL).

UK Environmental Accounts

Part 5

Chapter 13
The UK Environmental Accounts at a glance

Oil and gas reserves

Proven oil reserves (remaining) at the end of 2009 were 378 million tonnes, 30 million tonnes less than at the end of 2008. After accounting for production of 68 million tonnes in 2009, there has been a net transfer of 38 million tonnes from probable to proven oil reserves. However, probable oil reserves have increased from 361 to 390 million tonnes, reflecting a large reallocation of possible reserves to probable reserves in light of a number of successful appraisal wells during 2009. Possible reserves have decreased by 17 million tonnes to 343 million tonnes.

Maximum oil reserves (combining remaining proven, probable and possible reserves) have decreased by 19 million tonnes to 1,111 million tonnes in 2009.

Additionally, at the end of 2009 the estimate of undiscovered recoverable oil resources which may exist in areas of the UK continental shelf ranges between 397 and 1,477 million tonnes.

Estimates of the remaining UK oil reserves are therefore uncertain but estimated reserves show an overall decline between 1998 and 2009. This would be expected given the extraction of reserves over the period.

Estimates of gas reserves are made on the same basis as oil and as such are similarly uncertain, ranging from 556 to 1,789 billion cubic metres (bcm) at the end of 2009. This is down 8.3 per cent from 1,950 bcm in 2008. Proven reserves were also lower at 256 bcm in 2009 compared with 292 bcm a year earlier. Rates of gas extraction stood at 57 bcm in 2009, the lowest since 1992.

At the end of 2009, oil and gas reserves were valued at £182.4 billion. This is a decrease of 1.9 per cent since 2008, when the value of reserves stood at £185.9 billion.

The decrease is the result of the 5.2 per cent decline in expected level of reserves of oil and gas more than off-setting the increases in oil and gas prices in 2009.

Expressing UK oil and gas reserves in monetary terms allows these subsoil assets to be compared with other economic entities. This provides a means for the commercial depletion of subsoil assets to be set against national income.

Estimated remaining recoverable oil reserves at end of year, 1998–2009

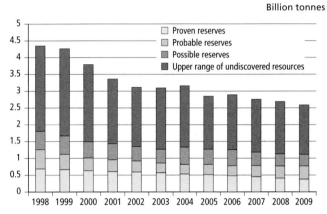

Source: ONS, DECC

Estimated remaining recoverable gas reserves at end of year, 1998–2009

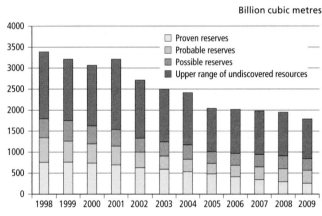

Source: ONS, DECC

Value of UK oil and gas reserves 1990–2009

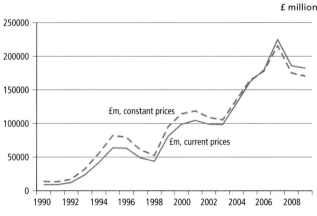

Source: ONS, DECC

Energy consumption

In 2009, total energy consumption from all sectors decreased to its lowest level since 1990.

Energy consumption, including energy from other sources decreased by 6.8 per cent between 2008 and 2009 to 210.8 million tonnes of oil equivalent, 3.5 per cent below the level it was in 1990.

This is the fourth consecutive year in which energy consumption has decreased. However, the decrease in the most recent year is considerably higher than that of previous years, suggesting that the economic downturn has had an effect on energy consumption.

In addition to the fall in energy consumption, economic output also decreased by 4.4 per cent between 2008 and 2009. Over the same period, energy consumption fell by 6.9 per cent meaning that energy intensity (energy consumed per unit of output) still decreased by 2.6 per cent.

Energy intensity decreased by 35.7 per cent between 1990 and 2009. This means that a greater amount of output is being produced for each unit of energy consumed.

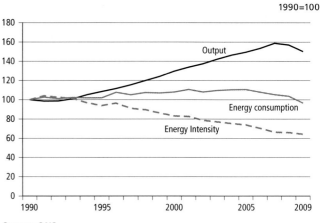

Energy consumption and Gross Domestic Product 1990–2009

Source: ONS

Atmospheric emissions

Greenhouse gas emissions in 2009 were 636 million tonnes of CO_2 equivalent. This was a decrease of 58.1 million tonnes or 8.4 per cent compared to 2008. The sectors with the biggest reductions in greenhouse gases in this period were:

- electricity, gas, steam and water supply, whose emissions decreased by 11.0 per cent or 23.3 million tonnes of CO_2 equivalent
- manufacturing, whose emissions decreased by 15.9 per cent or 17.1 million tonnes of CO_2 equivalent

The faster fall in greenhouse gas emissions compared to previous years reflects the contraction in economic activity seen in 2009.

Between 1990 and 2009 emissions of greenhouse gases fell 21.9 per cent or 178.7 million tonnes of CO_2 equivalent with the reduction being driven by:

- manufacturing, where emissions decreased by 47.5 per cent or 81.8 million tonnes of CO_2 equivalent
- electricity, gas, steam and water supply, where emissions decreased by 32.1 percent or 89.0 million tonnes of CO_2 equivalent

The sector that had the greatest absolute increase in CO_2 equivalent emissions was transport, which increased by 21.0 million tonnes of CO_2 equivalent or 32.1 per cent over the period.

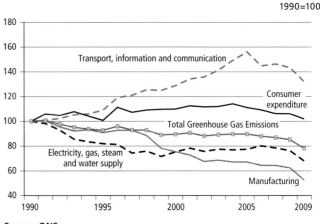

Greenhouse gas emissions by selected industries 1990–2009

Source: ONS

In *Environmental Accounts* comparisons are made with 1990 because this is the base year used for the Kyoto protocol targets. However, it should be noted that UK Environmental Accounts estimates are not on the same basis as estimates used to assess progress towards Kyoto targets. The National Accounts measure includes emissions by UK companies and households abroad and excludes emissions by foreign residents in the UK.

Emissions that cause acid rain fell by 67.6 per cent or 4.6 million tonnes of SO_2 equivalent between 1990 and 2009. Emissions generated by the electricity, gas, steam and water supply sector decreased by 89.1 per cent or 3.0 million tonnes of SO_2 equivalent. This accounted for 64.3 per cent of the total decline.

In 1990 the sector that produced the most acid rain precursor emissions – 3.3 million tonnes of SO_2 equivalent – was electricity, gas, steam and water supply. This was 306.7 per cent higher than the sector with the next highest level of emissions – transport. By 2009 acid rain precursor emissions from the transport sector were 85.8 per cent greater than those from the electricity, gas, steam and water supply sector.

The downward trend in total acid rain precursor emissions since 1990 is part of a longer term trend that began in the 1980s with the signing of international agreements to reduce emissions that cause acid rain.

Material flow accounting

In 2009, the sum of materials taken from the UK environment for economic use, total domestic extraction, was 458 million tonnes, down 12.5 per cent (66 million tonnes) from 2008.

Direct Material Input (DMI), which also includes imports to the UK, has fallen in every year since 2004 and by 18.3 per cent in total since 1990. It is now at the lowest level since records began (1970).

The largest fall in 2009 was in minerals extraction with a decrease of 51 million tonnes (19.6 per cent) driven by a sharp fall in the extraction of primary aggregates – crushed stone, sand and gravel – as demand was impacted by the economic downturn.

Between 2008 and 2009, the extraction of fossil fuels fell by 8.5 per cent to 147 million tonnes, largely as a result of lower volumes of natural gas extraction.

During the period extraction of biomass, including items such as crops, decreased by 0.6 per cent (0.6 million tonnes).

In 2009 the mass of imports fell by 3.7 per cent to 268 million tonnes. For the second year in a row imports decreased after four consecutive years of growth with volumes of imports at historically high levels. The fall was mainly driven by reduced

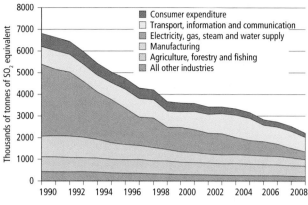

Acid rain precursor emissions for selected sectors 1990–2009

Source: ONS

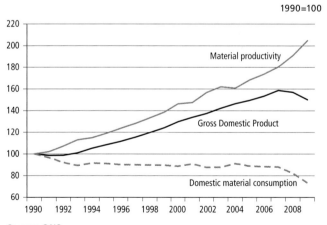

Material productivity, 1990–2009

Source: ONS

imports of minerals (6.4 per cent), biomass (5.6 per cent) and fossil fuels (2.5 per cent).

In 2009 Domestic Material Consumption (DMI less the mass of goods exported from the UK) decreased by 10.8 per cent from 634 million tonnes in 2008 to 566 million tonnes in 2009. Exports in the same period were down by 4.3 per cent (8 million tonnes).

Material productivity has increased between 1990 and 2009. This trend indicates that material use is falling in relation to the level of economic activity in the United Kingdom and supports evidence that domestic material use and economic growth have decoupled since 1990. However, levels of imports have generally risen over the same period suggesting that some of the environmental impacts associated with consumption are being transferred abroad.

Environmental protection expenditure

Please note that environmental protection expenditure statistics are not National Statistics.

In 2009 environmental protection expenditure by the extraction, manufacturing, energy production and water supply industries was estimated as £3.9 billion.

The industries where most environmental protection expenditure was made were:

- Electricity, gas and water which accounted for around 68 per cent
- Other manufacturing approximately 16 per cent
- Food products, beverages & tobacco around 8 per cent

The electricity, gas and water industry has the highest environmental protection expenditure. This could be due to implementation of the Water Framework Directive, implementing findings from the Pitt Review and tighter controls for emissions controls including carbon capture.

Environmental protection expenditure by industry 2009

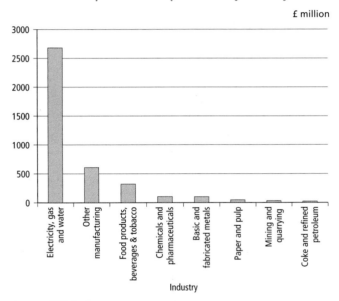

Source: ONS, Defra

UK Environmental Accounts

Environmental accounts provide information on the environmental impact of economic activity, on the use of resources from the environment in the economy, and on associated taxes and subsidies.

Environmental accounts are 'satellite accounts' to the main National Accounts. Satellite accounts are extensions to the National Accounts, which facilitate analysis of the wider impact of economic change. Environmental accounts use similar concepts and classifications of industries to those employed in the National Accounts, and they reflect the recommended European Union and United Nations frameworks for developing such accounts.

The accounts are used to inform sustainable development policy, to model impacts of fiscal or monetary measures and to evaluate the environmental performance of different sectors of the economy.

Most data are provided in units of physical measurement (volume or mass), although where appropriate some accounts are shown in monetary units.

This chapter includes information previously published in the 2011 edition of the *UK Environmental Accounts*[1], updated to be consistent with the UK National Accounts. More detailed industry statistics consistent with this publication will be made available on 30 November 2011 on the Environmental Accounts pages of the ONS website. http://www.ons.gov.uk/ons/taxonomy/index.html?nscl=Environmental+Accounts

The diagram below shows how the areas covered by environmental accounts relate to the economy as described by the National Accounts.

Economic activity and environmental impact

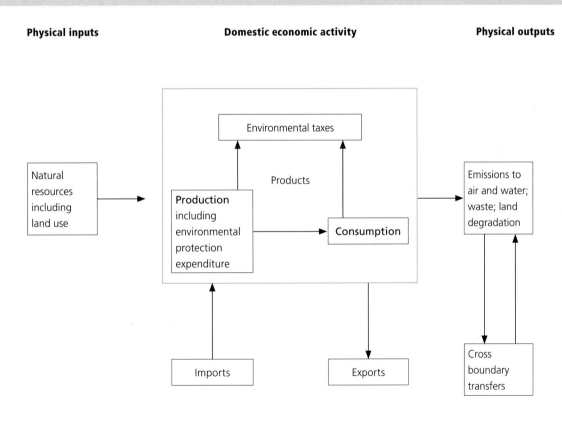

Oil and gas reserves (Tables 13.1 and 13.2)

Oil reserves include both oil and the liquids and liquefied products obtained from gas fields, gas-condensate fields and from the associated gas in oil fields. Gas reserves are the quantity of gas expected to be available for sale from dry gas fields, gas-condensate fields and oil fields with associated gas. Gas which is expected to be flared or used offshore is not included.

This publication uses terminology introduced by the Department for Energy and Climate Change (DECC) to describe UK reserves of oil and gas.[2] Descriptions are now more closely aligned to those used by the oil and gas industry in order to improve general understanding and ensure consistency. Reserves are classified into the following categories: reserves, potential additional reserves and undiscovered resources. Undiscovered resources relate to those resources as yet undiscovered but potentially recoverable in mapped leads. Potential additional reserves are defined as discovered reserves that are not currently technically or economically producible. Reserves are classified as discovered, remaining reserves which are recoverable and commercial. These can be subdivided into proven, probable or possible depending on confidence level.

Simulation models using Monte Carlo techniques have been used each year by DECC to assess the likely existence and size of undiscovered oil and gas fields on the UK Continental Shelf (UKCS). The assessments are presented as ranges, but the limits of the ranges should not be regarded as maxima or minima. Estimates of the volume of undiscovered reserves have fluctuated considerably in recent years as new areas of UKCS have been subjected to statistical analysis and older areas have been re-assessed.

The lower end of the range of total reserves shown in the table is the sum of estimated proven reserves and the lower end of the range of undiscovered resources for that year, net of cumulative production.

The upper end of the range of total reserves is the sum of estimated proven, possible and probable reserves, plus the upper-end range of undiscovered resources, for that year, net of cumulative production.

The expected level of reserves is calculated as the sum of proven and probable reserves and the lower end of the range of undiscovered resources.

Other volume changes are calculated as the difference between the expected level of reserves at the start of the year, less production within that year, and the estimated level of reserves at the start of the following year.

Monetary valuation of oil and gas reserves

The statistics presented in Table 13.2 are experimental. A methodological article[3] published with the *UK Environmental Accounts* in June 2011 provides more information on the monetary oil and gas valuation, including the oil and gas prices used.

Expressing UK oil and gas reserves in monetary terms allows these subsoil assets to be compared with other economic entities. This provides a means for the commercial depletion of subsoil assets to be set against national income.

Energy consumption (Table 13.3)

The Energy Consumption dataset gives estimates of total energy used by each industry and the proportion of total energy used from renewable resources.

Unit of measurement

The unit of measurement is tonne of oil equivalent (toe), which enables different fuels to be compared and aggregated. It should be regarded as a measure of energy content rather than a physical quantity. Standard conversion factors for each type of fuel are given in the *Digest of UK Energy Statistics* (DUKES)[4].

Consumption of carbon fuels, energy used in transformation processes and losses in distribution

The consumption of carbon fuels, and the related consumption of energy, can be analysed from a number of different perspectives. In terms of atmospheric emissions, it may be helpful to identify which sectors are actually consuming the carbon fuels that give rise to emissions. From this perspective, fuels used by the electricity generation sector are attributed entirely to that sector, even though some of the energy is transformed into electricity. This analysis is shown in the first section of the table showing Energy Consumption.

In terms of energy consumption, it is possible to attribute energy used during the process of transformation into electricity, and the energy lost in distributing electricity to end users, either directly to the electricity generation sector, or indirectly to the consumers of energy. The second and final sections of the Energy Consumption table consider energy consumption from both points of view. The second section allocates the consumption of energy directly to the immediate consumer of the energy, while the final section allocates these 'electricity overheads' of the major power producers to the user of the electricity.

Renewable energy sources

Renewable energy is defined to include solar power, energy from wind, wave and tide, hydroelectricity, and energy from wood, straw and sewage gas. Landfill gas and municipal solid waste combustion have been included with renewable energy for the purposes of defining energy sources in the context of sustainable development policy.

Understanding differences between energy accounts within a National Accounts framework and the DUKES energy balances

Energy consumption statistics are published in more than one form. The National Accounts measure puts energy consumption on a UK residents basis to allow for more consistent comparison with key National Accounts indicators such as gross domestic product and gross value added.

The National Accounts measure differs from the statistics presented in the DUKES in that:

- Only energy that leads to emissions is included whereas DUKES includes all energy.

- Fuels used by the UK fishing fleet, UK international shipping and aircraft operators and ships and aircraft used for UK military purposes, are included, whether or not they were purchased in the UK. Fuels purchased in the UK by non-resident operators are excluded.

- Purchases of petrol and diesel abroad by UK motorists and road hauliers are included whilst purchases of petrol and diesel in the UK by non-resident motorists and road hauliers are not.

- Some fuels such as gases used by the offshore industry are not treated as fuels by DUKES but are included in the Energy Account.

- The Energy account uses EU ETS data on petroleum coke burnt by refineries rather than sourcing DUKES.

- Any energy in fuels that is transformed into another fuel type is not included whereas both the primary fuel and the transformed fuel are included in the DUKES commodity balances.

- Tars and benzoles that are created as a by-product of coke ovens are treated as energy in DUKES but not in the greenhouse gas inventory or energy accounts.

- Non-energy uses of fuels for example, chemical feedstocks, solvents, lubricants and road-making material, are excluded. However, energy lost through gas leakage etc is included.

- Geothermal, solar etc gases are included in DUKES but not the Energy Account.

- The Energy Account does not include the losses of natural gas.

- Differences in publication times may result in minor reconciliation anomalies between ONS and DECC energy data.

A table which bridges the National Accounts measure of direct use of energy from fossil fuels with the equivalent figures in the DUKES publication is published every year with the *UK Environmental Accounts*.

http://www.ons.gov.uk/ons/rel/environmental/environmental-accounts/2011/rftenergybridge.xls

Sources and methods for estimating consumption of energy by industrial sector

The classification of industrial sectors used in environmental accounts differs from that used in DUKES. In particular, the transport sector is defined to include only enterprises that provide transport services to other consumers (i.e. public transport operators, freight haulage companies, etc.). The energy consumed by households' use of private cars is allocated to the domestic sector. The allocation of energy use to particular industries is primarily based on DUKES data. However, for certain industries better estimates are used as published by DECC in Energy Trends[5].

Atmospheric emissions (Tables 13.4 and 13.5)

The UK is required to report emissions under different international agreements for key air pollutants covered by the National Atmospheric Emissions Inventory (NAEI)[6] and greenhouse gases (GHG) covered by the UK GHG inventory.

There is a wide range of pollutants that contribute emissions to the atmosphere. They include greenhouse gases and substances that are directly toxic such as heavy metals. These pollutants can be grouped according to their contribution to environmental themes such as climate change and acid rain.

Each year the Environmental Accounts present estimates of pollutants directly emitted to the atmosphere by each industrial sector. The figures are on a National Accounts basis - they include emissions generated by UK households and companies in the UK and emissions from UK residents' transport and travel activities abroad. They exclude emissions generated by non-residents transport and travel in the UK. The data are therefore on a different basis from estimates published by the Department for Energy and Climate Change (DECC) under the UK's Kyoto Protocol obligations. The Kyoto basis covers emissions from UK territory only and excludes emissions from international aviation and shipping.

A table which bridges the National Accounts measure of greenhouse gas emissions with the other published measures is published every year with the *UK Environmental Accounts*.

http://www.ons.gov.uk/ons/publications/re-reference-tables.html?edition=tcm%3A77-227204

Changes in atmospheric emissions are compared to 1990 as this is the base year used in the Kyoto Protocol.

The Greenhouse effect (Climate change)

Greenhouse gases are transparent to natural light from the sun and relatively opaque to infra-red radiation from the Earth. Therefore, they trap some of the Earth's infra-red radiation and radiate it back to Earth. As a result, the Earth's temperature is kept at about 15°C by the atmospheric blanket. Without this naturally occurring greenhouse effect the Earth's temperature would be about minus 18°C – too cold for human life.

Although most greenhouse gas emissions occur naturally, some are man-made. Since the industrial revolution, human activity has led to an increase in both the natural and man-made gases, especially carbon dioxide. There is growing consensus that the rise in greenhouse gas emissions has led to changes in the global atmosphere, so called global warming. The greenhouse gases included in the atmospheric emissions accounts are those covered by the Kyoto Protocol:

Carbon dioxide, methane, nitrous oxide, hydrofluorocarbons, perfluorocarbons and sulphur hexafluoride.

To aggregate the greenhouse gases covered in the accounts, a weighting based on the relative global warming potential (GWP) of each of the gases is applied, using the effect of carbon dioxide over a 100 year period as a reference. This gives methane a weight of 21 relative to carbon dioxide and nitrous oxide a weight of 310 relative to carbon dioxide. Sulphur hexafluoride has a GWP of 23,900 relative to carbon dioxide. The GWP of the other fluorinated compounds varies according to the individual gas.

Greenhouse gas emissions are sometimes shown in terms of carbon equivalent rather than carbon dioxide equivalent. To convert from carbon dioxide equivalent to carbon equivalent it is necessary to multiply by 12/44.

Acid Rain Precursors

The term 'acid rain' describes the various chemical reactions acidic gases and particles undergo in the atmosphere and may be transported long distances before being deposited as wet or dry deposition. When deposited the hydrogen ions may be released causing acidification. These dilute acids damage ecosystems and buildings. The gases covered are sulphur dioxide, nitrogen oxides and ammonia.

Attributing emissions to industrial sectors

The emissions are weighted together using their relative acidifying effects. The weights, given relative to sulphur dioxide, are 0.7 for nitrogen oxides and 1.9 for ammonia. This is a simplification of the chemistry involved and there are a number of factors which can affect the eventual deposition and effect of acid rain. There may be an upward bias on the weights of the nitrogen-based compounds in terms of damage to ecosystems.

National Atmospheric Emissions Inventory (NAEI) projections of future emissions are an increasingly important requirement for UK government policy-making. National estimates of emissions are calculated across all economic sectors, e.g. industry, domestic use. The disaggregation of national estimates of emissions to industrial sectors is based upon an initial disaggregation provided by AEA Technology.

Emissions were estimated by multiplying fuel consumption by emissions factors and adding releases unrelated to fuel use such as methane arising from landfill and collieries.

The NAEI data is used to identify the main processes and industries responsible for the emissions. These are then allocated to individual sectors on the basis of information from a variety of sources. For example, emissions from diesel use by HGVs is allocated to sectors using vehicle mileage data from the Department for Energy and Climate Change (DECC). Expenditure information is also used, for example emissions arising from the use of various industrial coatings (e.g. general industrial, heavy duty and vehicle refinishing) are allocated to relevant sectors in proportion to each sector's expenditure on paints, varnishes and similar coatings, printing ink and mastics, using National Accounts Input-Output supply and use tables as the main source.

Material flows (Table 13.6)

Material flow accounts record the total mass of natural resources and products that are used by the economy, either directly in the production and distribution of products and services, or indirectly through the movement of materials which are displaced in order for production to take place.

A material flow account balances the inputs (extraction of natural resources from the UK environment, and imports of goods) with the outputs (wastes, emissions to air and water, exports) and accumulation (in terms of new buildings, etc) within the economy.

The direct input of materials into the economy derives primarily from domestic extraction, that is, from biomass (agricultural harvest, timber, fish and animal grazing); fossil fuel extraction (such as coal, crude oil and natural gas) and mineral extraction (metal ores, industrial minerals such as pottery clay; and construction material such as crushed rock, sand and gravel).

The direct input of materials from domestic sources is supplemented by the imports of products, which may be of raw materials such as unprocessed agricultural products, but can also be semi-manufactured or finished products. In a similar way the UK exports of raw materials, semi-manufactured and finished goods can be viewed as inputs to the production and consumption of overseas economies.

Water is used so widely and in such quantities that its inclusion in the accounts tends to obscure other resource use. For this reason, the accounts only include the water that is contained in products (for example, agricultural produce and imported beverages). Water for other consumptive uses (cleaning or irrigation) and *in situ* uses (such as hydroelectric power) is excluded from these accounts.

Hidden flows measure the quantity of material displaced by the process of extraction but not actually used in the production of goods and services. Indirect flows measure the quantity of material associated with imports of raw and semi-processed goods into the UK. Both hidden and indirect flows are measured indirectly by applying coefficients for particular materials and goods to the estimated levels of mass associated with domestic and overseas extraction. Therefore, there is a direct relationship between hidden flows and actual extraction. Levels are sensitive to assumptions embodied in the particular hidden or indirect flow coefficient used.

Examples of hidden flows are unused extraction from mining and quarrying (also known as overburden); discarded material from harvesting (for example, wood harvesting losses such as timber felled but left in the forests); and soil and rock moved as a result of construction and dredging.

Indicators

There are a number of indicators which can be used to summarise the flows of materials into and out of the economy. Material flows show three of the main indicators used to measure inputs.

Direct Material Input (DMI) measures the input of materials directly used by the economy. It is the sum of domestic extraction and imports.

Domestic material consumption (DMC) measures the total amount of material directly consumed by the economy. It is the sum of domestic extraction and imports *less* exports.

The **Total Material Requirement (TMR)** measures the total material basis of the economy, that is the total direct and indirect resource requirements of all the production and consumption activities. TMR includes the amount of used extraction in the UK, the imports into the UK and the resulting indirect or hidden flows associated with extraction in the UK and imports from other countries. Although TMR is widely favoured as a resource use indicator, the estimates of indirect flows are less reliable than those for materials directly used by the economy, and it can be argued that it double-counts trade flows, in that materials used both in the production of imports

and in the production of exports are included. The indicator therefore needs to be considered alongside other indicators.

The **Physical Trade Balance (PTB)** measures the difference between the total mass of exports and the total mass of imports. This can be used to understand the internal relationship of material use in the UK.

Sources and methods

Data on the yields of agriculture, forestry and fishing come from the Food and Agriculture Organization (FAO)[7]. Mineral extraction data have been taken from the UK Minerals Yearbook[8] and information on the mass of imports and exports has been taken from trade information compiled by HM Revenue and Customs[9].

Factors applied to give estimates of the amounts of unused material moved for each tonne of used material have been taken from research carried out by the Wuppertal Institute on behalf of the Department for Environment, Food and Rural Affairs (Defra)[10]. The methodology used to compile the account is also based upon the Wuppertal Institute's research.

Environmental protection expenditure (Table 13.7)

Estimates of environmental protection expenditure should be regarded as approximate orders of magnitude only. Because of this qualification, the estimates shown fall outside the scope of National Statistics.

Sources and comparisons with previous surveys

The information on spending by industries in 2009 comes from a regular series of surveys conducted by the URS Corporation on behalf of Defra[11]. Environmental protection expenditure in specified industries gives figures for spending by the extraction, manufacturing, energy production and water supply industries.

The estimates from this survey and the earlier surveys should be regarded as very approximate and any comparisons between the results should be treated with care.

Definition of expenditure

Environmental protection expenditure is defined as capital and operational expenditure incurred because of, and which can be directly related to, the pursuit of an environmental objective. Spending on installations and processes which are environmentally beneficial, but which also produce revenue (or savings) exceeding expenditures, are excluded on the grounds that they are likely to have been carried out for commercial not environmental reasons. Also excluded are expenditures on natural resource management (for example, fisheries and water resources), on the prevention of natural hazards (for example, flood defence), on the provision of access and amenities to

National Parks etc, and on the urban environment. The spending has been classified by the following groups of environmental concerns:

- Protection of ambient air and climate
- Waste water management
- Waste management
- Protection of biodiversity and landscapes
- Other abatement activities such as on the protection of soil and groundwater, protection against radiation, and noise and vibration abatement
- Other environmental expenditure, on research and development, education and administration

There are five main categories of spending in environmental protection expenditure by specified industries:

- End-of-pipe investment is defined as add-on installations and equipment which treats or controls emissions or reduces waste material generated by the plan, but which does not affect production processes
- Integrated processes are adaptation or changes to production processes in order to generate fewer emissions or waste materials
- In-house operating expenses cover operating costs necessary to run end-of-pipe or integrated facilities
- Current payments made to others include all payments to third parties for environmental services, including payments for the treatment or removal of solid waste; water service company charges for sewage treatment; payments to contractors for the removal or treatment of waste waters; and payments made to environmental regulatory authorities
- Research and development expenditure includes both in-house research and development and amounts paid to others such as trade associations and consultants.

References

1 Office for National Statistics (2011) *UK Environmental Accounts* 2011 edition

   http://www.ons.gov.uk/ons/rel/environmental/environmental-accounts/2011/environmental-accounts.pdf

2 Department for Energy and Climate Change Oil and Gas website

   https://www.og.decc.gov.uk/

3 Office for National Statistics (2011) Valuing the UN Continental Shelf's Oil and Gas Reserves

   http://www.ons.gov.uk/ons/rel/environmental/environmental-accounts/2011/artoilandgas.pdf

4 Department for Energy and Climate Change. *Digest of United Kingdom Energy Statistics*. Various issues, HMSO/TSO.

   http://www.decc.gov.uk/en/content/cms/statistics/publications/dukes/dukes.aspx

5 Department for Energy and Climate Change. *Energy Trends*. Various issues. Office for National Statistics (2002).

   http://www.decc.gov.uk/en/content/cms/statistics/publications/trends/trends.aspx

6 National Atmospheric Emissions Inventory

   http://naei.defra.gov.uk/

7 Food and Agricultural Organization (FAO)

   www.fao.org/

8 British Geological Survey *UK Minerals Yearbook*

   http://www.bgs.ac.uk/mineralsuk/statistics/UKStatistics.html

9 HM Revenue and Customs trade data.

   www.uktradeinfo.com

10 Department for Environment, Food and Rural Affairs (Defra) *Resource Use and Efficiency of the UK Economy: A study by the Wuppertal Institute*

11 Department for Environment Food and Rural Affairs, Environmental Protection Expenditure survey

   http://www.defra.gov.uk/statistics/environment/environmental-survey/

13.1 Estimates of remaining recoverable oil and gas reserves[1]

		2000	2001	2002	2003	2004	2005	2006	2007	2008	2009
Oil (Million tonnes)											
Reserves											
Proven	K7MI	630	605	593	571	533	516	479	452	408	378
Probable	K7MJ	380	350	327	286	283	300	298	328	361	390
Proven plus Probable	K7MK	1 010	955	920	857	816	816	776	780	770	769
Possible	K7ML	480	475	425	410	512	451	478	399	360	343
Maximum	K7MM	1 490	1 430	1 344	1 267	1 328	1 267	1 254	1 179	1 130	1 111
Range of undiscovered resources											
Lower	K7MN	225	205	272	323	396	346	438	379	454	397
Upper	K7MO	2 300	1 930	1 770	1 826	1 830	1 581	1 637	1 577	1 561	1 477
Range of total reserves											
Lower[2]	K7MP	855	810	865	894	929	862	917	831	862	775
Upper[3]	K7MQ	3 790	3 360	3 115	3 093	3 158	2 848	2 892	2 756	2 690	2 588
Expected level of reserves[4]											
Opening stocks	K7MR	1 370	1 235	1 160	1 192	1 180	1 212	1 162	1 215	1 159	1 223
Extraction[5]	K7MS	−126	−117	−117	−106	−95	−85	−77	−77	−72	−68
Other volume changes	K7MT	−9	42	149	94	127	35	130	21	136	10
Closing stocks	K7MU	1 235	1 160	1 192	1 180	1 212	1 162	1 215	1 159	1 223	1 165
Gas (billion cubic metres)											
Reserves											
Proven	K7MV	735	695	628	590	531	481	412	343	292	256
Probable	K7MW	460	445	369	315	296	247	272	304	309	308
Proven plus Probable	K7MX	1 195	1 140	998	905	826	728	684	647	601	564
Possible	K7MY	430	395	331	336	343	278	283	293	306	276
Maximum	K7MZ	1 630	1 535	1 329	1 241	1 169	1 006	967	940	907	840
Range of undiscovered resources											
Lower	K7N2	325	290	238	279	293	226	301	280	319	300
Upper	K7N3	1 440	1 680	1 386	1 259	1 245	1 035	1 049	1 039	1 043	949
Range of total reserves											
Lower[2]	K7N4	1 060	985	866	869	824	707	713	623	611	556
Upper[3]	K7N5	3 065	3 215	2 714	2 500	2 415	2 041	2 016	1 979	1 950	1 789
Expected level of reserves[4]											
Opening stocks	K7N6	1 615	1 520	1 430	1 235	1 184	1 120	954	985	927	920
Extraction[5]	K7N7	−108	−104	−102	−102	−95	−86	−78	−71	−68	−57
Other volume changes	K7N8	13	14	−93	51	31	−80	109	13	61	1
Closing stocks	K7N9	1 520	1 430	1 235	1 184	1 120	954	985	927	920	864

1 All data refer to end of year. Components may not sum to totals due to rounding.
2 The lower end of the range of total reserves has been calculated as the sum of proven reserves and the lower end of the range of undiscovered reserves.
3 The upper end of the range of total reserves is the sum of proven, probable and possible reserves and the upper end of the range of undiscovered reserves.
4 Expected reserves are the sum of proven reserves, probable reserves and the lower end of the range of undiscovered reserves.
5 Negative extraction is shown here for the purposes of the calculation only. Of itself, extraction should be considered as a positive value.

Source: ONS and Department of Energy and Climate Change

13.2 Oil and gas monetary balance sheet[1]

£ million

		2000	2001	2002	2003	2004	2005	2006	2007	2008	2009
Current Prices											
Opening stocks[2]	KI5I	80 964	98 891	104 644	98 977	98 561	129 922	162 243	179 864	224 910	185 865
Extraction[3]	KI5J	−11 134	−11 811	−11 598	−11 293	−14 022	−17 348	−17 451	−21 972	−17 131	−16 210
Revaluation due to time passing	KI5K	4 987	5 196	4 894	4 752	6 216	8 262	8 344	11 143	8 711	9 046
Other volume changes	KI5L	64	1 762	2 282	4 686	6 801	−2 004	13 953	2 570	12 026	740
Change in extraction path	KI5M	−427	−1 723	−226	−1 417	−3 234	−5 340	−5 044	−3 187	−3 285	−7 281
Change in rent	KI5N	24 437	12 329	−1 018	2 857	35 600	48 752	17 819	56 492	−39 364	10 251
Total changes	KI5O	17 927	5 753	−5 667	−416	31 361	32 321	17 620	45 046	−39 045	−3 453
Closing stocks[2]	KI5P	98 891	104 644	98 977	98 561	129 922	162 243	179 864	224 910	185 865	182 413
Constant Prices											
Opening stocks[2]	KI5Q	95 101	114 440	118 625	109 000	105 522	135 414	164 543	178 150	215 744	175 430
Extraction[3]	KI5R	−12 885	−13 389	−12 773	−12 091	−14 615	−17 594	−17 285	−21 076	−16 170	−15 148
Revaluation due to time passing	KI5S	5 771	5 891	5 389	5 087	6 479	8 379	8 264	10 689	8 222	8 454
Other volume changes	KI5T	74	1 997	2 513	5 017	7 089	−2 032	13 820	2 465	11 350	692
Change in extraction path	KI5U	−494	−1 954	−249	−1 517	−3 371	−5 416	−4 996	−3 057	−3 101	−6 804
Change in rent	KI5V	26 872	11 640	−4 505	26	34 310	45 792	13 804	48 574	−40 616	7 841
Total changes	KI5W	19 339	4 185	−9 625	−3 478	29 892	29 129	13 607	37 594	−40 314	−4 965
Closing stocks[2]	KI5X	114 440	118 625	109 000	105 522	135 414	164 543	178 150	215 744	175 430	170 465

1 These are experimental statistics
2 The estimated opening and closing stock values are based on the present value method - see Environmental Accounts on the ONS website for more detailed descriptions of the methodology used. The estimates are extremely sensitive to the estimated return to capital and to assumptions about future unit resource rents.
3 Negative extraction is shown here for the purposes of the calculation only. Of itself, extraction should be considered as a positive value.

Source: ONS, Department of Energy and Climate Change

13.3 Energy Consumption[1]

Million tonnes of oil equivalent

		1990	1995	2000	2005	2006	2007	2008	2009
Direct use of energy from fossil fuels									
Agriculture, forestry and fishing	K7YT	2.1	2.2	2.0	2.0	1.9	1.8	1.8	1.8
Mining and quarrying	K7YU	4.2	5.1	6.4	7.0	6.5	6.2	6.0	5.9
Manufacturing	K7YV	41.3	40.1	39.9	37.0	35.5	34.8	34.4	29.6
Electricity, gas, steam & air conditioning supply, water supply, sewerage, waste management activities & remediation services	K7YW	56.7	51.5	55.5	60.1	62.1	62.2	61.5	54.6
Construction	K7YX	2.8	3.0	3.4	3.5	3.5	3.6	3.5	3.2
Wholesale and retail trade, repair of motor vehicles & motorcycles	K7YY	4.8	5.3	5.4	4.8	4.7	4.8	4.6	4.7
Transport and storage; information and communication	K7YZ	22.2	24.3	28.7	34.5	32.1	32.4	31.8	29.3
Accommodation and food services	K7Z5	1.3	1.5	1.7	1.5	1.3	1.3	1.3	1.1
Financial and insurance activities	K8BZ	0.1	0.1	0.1	0.1	0.1	0.1	0.1	0.1
Real estate activities; professional scientific & technical activities; administrative and support service activities	K8C2	2.1	2.5	2.7	2.5	2.3	2.3	2.3	2.0
Public administration & defence; compulsory social security	K7Z3	4.1	3.9	3.3	3.0	2.9	2.8	2.7	2.5
Education	K7Z4	2.0	1.8	2.0	1.6	1.6	1.6	1.6	1.4
Human health and social work activities	K8C3	1.9	2.2	2.1	2.3	2.1	2.0	2.0	1.8
Arts, entertainment and recreation; other service activities	K8C4	1.3	1.5	1.4	1.3	1.2	1.1	1.1	1.1
Activities of households as employers, undifferentiated goods & services-producing activities of households for own use	K8C5	0.1	0.1	0.1	0.1	0.1	0.1	0.1	0.1
Total non-households	K7Z6	146.9	144.9	154.6	161.3	157.8	157.1	154.9	139.1
Households	K7Z7	53.8	54.7	59.8	60.6	59.3	57.5	57.6	55.0
Total use of energy from fossil fuels	K7Z8	200.7	199.6	214.4	221.9	217.2	214.6	212.5	194.1
Energy from other sources[2]	K7Z9	17.7	23.1	21.4	19.8	18.5	15.4	13.9	16.7
Total energy consumption of primary fuels and equivalents	K7ZA	218.4	222.7	235.8	241.7	235.7	230.0	226.4	210.8
Direct use of energy including electricity									
Agriculture, forestry and fishing	K7ZB	2.4	2.5	2.4	2.3	2.2	2.2	2.2	2.1
Mining and quarrying	K7ZC	4.4	5.3	6.7	7.2	6.7	6.4	6.2	6.1
Manufacturing	K7ZD	48.5	47.1	47.0	44.1	42.8	42.3	41.4	36.7
Electricity, gas, steam & air conditioning supply; water supply, sewerage, waste management activities and remediation services	K7ZE	52.2	50.9	51.5	52.9	53.7	50.7	48.9	45.6
of which - transformation losses by major producers	K7ZF	46.5	45.1	44.0	46.6	47.4	44.8	43.0	43.0
distribution losses of electricity supply	K7ZG	2.1	2.5	2.5	2.4	2.4	2.3	2.3	–
Construction	K7ZH	2.9	3.2	3.6	3.7	3.7	3.8	3.6	3.3
Wholesale and retail trade; repair of motor vehicles & motorcycles	K7ZI	6.4	7.1	7.7	7.3	7.1	7.2	7.0	7.0
Transport and storage; information and communication	K7ZJ	23.1	25.5	30.1	36.2	33.8	34.1	33.5	30.9
Accommodation and food services	K7ZN	1.7	1.9	2.1	2.0	1.9	1.9	1.9	1.7
Financial and insurance activities	K8C7	0.9	0.9	1.0	0.9	0.9	0.9	0.9	0.8
Real estate activities; professional scientific & technical activities; administrative and support service activities	K8C8	2.9	3.4	3.8	3.6	3.5	3.4	3.4	3.1
Public administration & defence; compulsory social security	K7ZL	4.5	4.6	3.6	3.2	3.1	3.0	2.8	2.3
Education	K7ZM	2.6	2.3	2.6	2.1	2.1	2.0	2.1	1.9
Human health and social work activities	K8C9	2.4	2.7	2.6	2.8	2.6	2.5	2.5	2.3
Arts, entertainment and recreation, other service activities	K8CA	1.8	1.9	1.7	1.7	1.6	1.5	1.6	1.4
Activities of households as employers; undifferentiated goods & services-producing activities of households for own use	K8CB	0.1	0.1	0.1	0.1	0.1	0.1	0.1	0.1
Total non-households	K7ZO	156.6	159.3	166.4	170.2	165.7	161.9	158.0	145.3
Households	K7ZP	61.8	63.5	69.4	71.4	70.0	68.1	68.4	65.5
Total energy consumption of primary fuels and equivalents	K7ZQ	218.4	222.7	235.8	241.7	235.7	230.0	226.4	210.8
Reallocated use of energy									
Energy industry electricity tranformation losses and distribution losses allocated to final consumer									
Agriculture, forestry and fishing	K7ZR	3.1	3.1	3.0	2.9	2.8	2.7	2.7	2.6
Mining and quarrying	K7ZS	4.7	5.6	7.0	7.7	7.0	6.7	6.5	6.4
Manufacturing	K7ZT	62.8	59.9	58.9	56.0	55.1	54.2	52.2	46.8
Electricity, gas, steam & air conditioning supply; water supply, sewerage, waste management activities and remediation services	K7ZU	7.8	7.3	8.8	8.0	8.3	7.7	7.4	9.2
Construction	K7ZV	3.1	3.4	3.8	4.0	3.9	4.0	3.9	3.5
Wholesale and retail trade; repair of motor vehicles and motorcycles	K7ZW	9.5	10.5	11.5	11.3	11.2	11.0	10.8	10.2
Transport and storage; information and communication	K7ZX	25.1	27.8	32.6	39.0	36.6	36.8	36.1	33.2
Accommodation and food services	K823	2.4	2.6	2.8	3.0	2.9	2.8	2.8	2.5
Financial and insurance activities	K8CD	2.4	2.3	2.7	2.3	2.3	2.2	2.2	1.9
Real estate activities; professional scientific & technical activities administration & support service activities	K8CE	4.5	5.0	5.6	5.5	5.4	5.2	5.2	4.6
Public administration & defence compulsory social security	K7ZZ	5.4	5.7	4.0	3.7	3.5	3.3	3.0	2.0
Education	K822	3.6	3.3	3.5	2.9	2.9	2.8	2.8	2.5
Human health and social work activities	K8CF	3.4	3.7	3.5	3.6	3.4	3.3	3.3	2.9
Arts, entertainment and recreation; other service activities	K8CG	2.6	2.8	2.4	2.4	2.3	2.2	2.2	2.0
Activities of households as employers; undifferentiated goods & services-producing activities of households for own use	K8CH	0.1	0.1	0.1	0.1	0.1	0.1	0.1	0.1
Total non-households	K824	140.5	143.1	150.2	152.3	147.6	145.0	141.1	130.4
Households	K825	77.9	79.6	85.5	89.4	88.1	85.0	85.3	80.4
Total energy consumption of primary fuels & equivalents	K826	218.4	222.7	235.8	241.7	235.7	230.0	226.4	210.8
Energy from renewable sources[3]	K827	1.8	2.3	2.7	4.0	4.1	4.5	4.9	5.4
Percentage from renewable sources	K828	0.8	1.1	1.2	1.6	1.8	1.9	2.2	2.6

Source: AEA Energy & Environment, DECC, ONS

1 Components may not sum to totals due to rounding.
2 Nuclear power, hydroelectric power and imports of electricty.
3 Renewable sources include solar power and energy from wind, wave and tide, hydroelectricity, wood, straw and sewage gas. Landfill gas and municipal solid waste combustion have also been included within this definition.

13.4 Atmospheric emissions 2009

	Total greenhouse gas emissions	Carbon Dioxide (CO2)	Methane (CH4)	Nitrous Oxide (N2O)	Hydrofluoro-carbons (HFCs)	Perfluoro-carbons (PFCs)	Sulphur hexafluoride (SF6)
Thousand tonnes CO2 equivalent							
Agriculture, forestry and fishing	51 042	5 680	17 934	27 381	47	–	–
Mining and quarrying	23 443	19 041	4 017	369	15	–	–
Manufacturing	90 583	86 862	331	1 885	1 172	144	189
Electricity, gas, steam & air conditioning supply; water supply, sewerage, waste management activities & remediation services	188 324	164 910	20 524	2 341	77	–	472
Construction	9 803	9 039	7	370	387	–	–
Wholesale & retail trade; repair of motor vehicles & motorcycles	16 405	12 773	14	176	3 440	3	–
Transport & storage; information & communication	86 438	84 930	36	1 099	373	–	–
Accommodation and food services	2 770	2 562	5	28	175	–	–
Financial and insurance activities	300	189	1	20	90	–	–
Real estate activities; professional scientific & technical activities; administrative & support service activities	5 639	5 072	6	39	521	–	–
Public administration & defence; compulsory social security	6 503	6 254	8	57	184	–	–
Education	3 518	3 267	6	21	225	–	–
Human health and social work activities	4 313	3 977	8	10	319	–	–
Arts, entertainment and recreation; other service activities	2 839	2 660	4	25	151	–	–
Activities of households as employers; undifferentiated goods & services-producing activities of households for own use	222	220	2	1	–	–	–
Households	144 329	139 547	525	585	3 672	–	–
Total	636 472	546 982	43 428	34 408	10 846	147	661
of which, emissions from road transport	114 392	113 319	89	983	–	–	–

	Total acid rain precursors	Sulphur Dioxide (SO2)	Nitrogen Oxides (NOx)	Ammonia (NH3)
Thousand tonnes SO2 equivalent				
Agriculture, forestry and fishing	475	2	26	446
Mining and quarrying	50	8	42	–
Manufacturing	304	162	133	9
Electricity, gas, steam & air conditioning supply; water supply, sewerage, waste management activities & remediation services	362	160	184	17
Construction	37	1	35	–
Wholesale & retail trade; repair of motor vehicles & motorcycles	43	2	41	–
Transport & storage; information & communication	672	254	416	1
Accommodation and food services	4	–	4	–
Financial and insurance activities	1	–	1	–
Real estate activities; professional scientific & technical activities; administrative & support service activities	9	–	8	–
Public administration and defence; compulsory social security	37	8	20	9
Education	6	3	4	–
Human health and social work activities	5	1	4	–
Arts, entertainment and recreation; other service activities	17	3	5	9
Activities of households as employers; undifferentiated goods & services-producing activities of households for own use	–	–	–	–
Households	190	36	105	48
Total (excluding Natural World)[1]	2 211	642	1 029	539
of which, emissions from road transport	278	–	256	21

	Thousand tonnes					Tonnes		
	PM10[2]	CO	NMVOC[3]	Benzene	Butadiene	Lead	Cadmium	Mercury
Agriculture, forestry and fishing	20.50	58.45	82.03	0.13	0.06	0.39	0.04	0.02
Mining and quarrying	8.70	30.64	95.63	0.24	0.01	0.18	0.05	0.01
Manufacturing	23.80	506.95	281.40	1.97	0.53	41.32	1.29	3.77
Electricity, gas, steam & air conditioning supply; water supply, sewerage, waste management activities & remediation services	7.51	86.56	51.56	1.37	0.03	2.99	0.22	2.35
Construction	5.46	54.37	48.02	0.20	0.09	0.36	0.04	0.01
Wholesale & retail trade; repair of motor vehicles & motorcycles	4.09	59.54	49.44	0.23	0.10	8.21	0.07	0.02
Transport & storage; information & communication	37.19	160.24	34.93	2.96	0.49	3.23	1.37	0.09
Accommodation and food services	0.39	11.73	1.27	0.04	0.01	0.03	–	–
Financial and insurance activities	0.16	7.27	0.57	0.02	0.01	0.02	–	–
Real estate activities; professional scientific & technical activities; administration & support service activities	1.01	29.56	2.95	0.13	0.04	0.05	0.01	–
Public administration & defence: compulsory social security	1.13	32.36	3.53	0.22	0.04	0.15	0.02	0.01
Education	0.57	6.82	0.56	0.02	–	0.74	0.01	0.07
Human health and social work activities	0.25	7.33	1.26	0.02	–	0.02	0.01	–
Arts, entertainment and recreation; other service activities	0.64	12.46	6.44	0.05	0.01	0.28	0.01	0.89
Activities of households as employers; undifferentiated goods & services-producing activities of households for own use	–	46.82	4.28	0.29	0.06	–	–	–
Households	49.85	1 217.21	245.63	11.73	0.83	4.93	0.39	0.18
Total (excluding Natural World)[1]	161.24	2 328.32	909.50	19.64	2.32	62.92	3.54	7.42
of which, emissions from road transport	27.47	1 080.27	87.27	3.81	1.21	1.61	–	–

1 Totals for ammonia, PM10, CO and NMVOC represent a small revision to the figures published in the UK Environmental Accounts in June 2011 and exclude emissions from the Natural World.
2 PM10 is particulate matter arising from various sources including fuel combustion, quarrying and construction, and formation of 'secondary' particles in the atmosphere from reactions involving other pollutants - sulphur dioxide, nitrogen oxides, ammonia and NMVOCs
3 Non-methane Volatile Compounds, including benzene and 1,3-butadiene.

Source: AEA Energy & Environment, ONS

13.5 Greenhouse gas and acid rain precursor emissions

Thousand tonnes CO2 equivalent

Greenhouse gases - CO2,CH4,N2O,HFC,PFCs and SF6[1]

		1990	1995	2000	2005	2006	2007	2008	2009
Agriculture, forestry and fishing	K8AQ	64 031	62 005	58 468	54 648	52 848	51 789	51 563	51 042
Mining and quarrying	K8AR	38 561	37 228	32 362	28 047	24 682	24 820	23 739	23 443
Manufacturing	K8AS	172 405	156 639	130 019	115 809	111 145	110 976	107 684	90 583
Electricity, gas, steam & air conditioning supply; water supply, sewerage, waste management activities & remediation services	K8AT	277 300	227 177	208 817	214 750	222 379	217 616	211 652	188 324
Construction	K8AU	8 307	9 074	10 309	10 739	10 809	11 155	10 760	9 803
Wholesale and retail trade; repair of motor vehicles & motorcycles	K8AV	13 010	14 858	16 893	16 383	16 234	16 583	16 115	16 405
Transport & storage; information & communication	K8AW	65 439	71 401	84 303	102 150	94 731	95 724	93 926	86 438
Accommodation and food services	K8AX	3 041	3 561	3 848	3 426	3 189	3 112	3 138	2 770
Financial and insurance activities	K8B2	241	223	212	277	297	322	328	300
Real estate activities; professional, scientific and technical activities; administration & support service activities	KI4H	5 280	6 248	6 831	6 530	6 335	6 325	6 269	5 639
Public administration & defence; compulsory social security	K8AY	11 446	10 525	8 577	7 653	7 469	7 232	7 167	6 503
Education	K8AZ	5 220	4 309	4 505	3 966	3 842	3 820	3 836	3 518
Human health and social work activities	KI4I	5 173	5 371	4 956	5 406	4 939	4 747	4 795	4 313
Arts, entertainment and recreation; other service activities	KI4J	3 814	4 130	3 559	3 363	3 067	2 933	3 007	2 839
Activities of households as employers; undifferentiated goods and services - producing activities of households for own use	KI4K	189	199	208	219	221	223	225	222
Total non-households	K8B3	673 457	612 949	573 868	573 365	562 187	557 378	544 203	492 143
Households	K8B4	141 704	142 746	155 843	157 636	154 925	150 641	150 413	144 329
Total greenhouse gas emissions	K8B5	815 161	755 695	729 711	731 000	717 112	708 019	694 615	636 472
of which, road transport emissions from all industries[2]	K8B6	111 657	113 701	119 806	122 615	122 943	124 007	119 242	114 392

Thousand tonnes SO2 equivalent

Acid rain precursor emissions - SO2,NOx,NH3[3]

		1990	1995	2000	2005	2006	2007	2008	2009
Agriculture, forestry and fishing	K8B9	684	625	566	524	516	501	475	475
Mining and quarrying	K8BA	73	58	55	56	48	55	55	50
Manufacturing	K8BB	957	775	478	416	400	397	368	303
Electricity, gas, steam & air conditioning supply; water supply, sewerage, waste management activities & remediation services	K8BC	3 319	1 984	1 132	683	668	569	436	362
Construction	K8BD	73	71	67	55	51	49	44	37
Wholesale and retail trade; repair of motor vehicles & motorcycles	K8BE	82	76	64	50	48	46	42	43
Transport & storage; information & communication	K8BF	816	778	725	1 023	762	787	793	672
Accommodation and food services	K8BG	8	8	6	5	5	5	5	4
Financial and insurance activities	K8BJ	2	2	2	2	2	2	2	1
Real estate activities; professional, scientific and technical activities; administrative & support service activities	KI4L	24	23	18	14	13	12	11	9
Public administration and defence; compulsory social security	KI4M	77	61	45	36	37	41	39	37
Education	KI4N	22	11	7	8	7	7	7	6
Human health and social work activities	KI4O	37	31	10	6	6	6	6	5
Arts, entertainment and recreation; other service activities	K8BH	34	31	21	19	20	17	17	17
Activities of households as employers; undifferentiated goods and services - producing activities of households for own use	K8BI	–	–	–	–	–	–	–	–
Total non-households	K8BK	6 208	4 532	3 198	2 897	2 581	2 493	2 298	2 021
Households	K8BL	604	499	401	264	250	234	225	190
Total acid rain precursor emissions	K8BM	6 812	5 031	3 599	3 161	2 831	2 727	2 523	2 211
of which, road transport emissions from all industries[2]	K8BN	817	709	586	434	406	376	339	278

1 Carbon dioxide, methane, nitrous oxide, hydrofluorocarbons, perfluorocarbon and sulphur hexafluoride expressed as thousand tonnes of carbon dioxide equivalent.
2 Includes emissions from all road transport sources (eg HGVs, LGVs, cars and motorcycles) across all industries
3 Sulphur dioxide, nitrogen oxides and ammonia expressed as thousand tonnes of sulphur dioxide equivalent.

Source: AEA Energy & Environment, ONS

13.6 Material Flows [1]

Million tonnes

		1970	1975	1980	1985	1990	1995	2000	2005	2006	2007	2008	2009
Domestic extraction													
Biomass													
Agricultural harvest	JKUN	42	38	47	47	46	47	51	48	46	43	49	48
Timber	JKUO	3	3	4	5	6	8	8	9	8	9	8	8
Animal grazing	JKUP	49	49	49	48	47	45	43	43	43	43	43	43
Fish	JKUQ	1	1	1	1	1	1	1	1	1	1	1	1
Total biomass	JKUR	96	92	101	100	101	101	103	100	98	96	101	101
Minerals													
Ores	JKUS	12	5	1	1	–	–	–	–	–	–	–	–
Clay	JKUT	38	33	25	23	21	18	15	14	13	13	11	7
Other industrial minerals	JKUU	12	11	11	11	11	10	8	8	8	8	8	8
Sand and gravel	JKUV	122	131	110	112	128	106	106	99	97	98	90	70
Crushed stone	JKUW	156	169	150	160	212	200	176	169	173	176	152	125
Total minerals	JKUX	340	349	297	307	373	334	305	290	292	295	262	210
Fossil fuels													
Coal	JKUY	149	129	130	94	94	53	31	20	19	17	18	18
Natural gas	JKUZ	17	54	55	37	42	71	108	88	80	72	70	60
Crude oil	JKVA	–	2	80	128	92	130	126	85	77	77	73	69
Total fossil fuels	JKVB	166	184	266	259	228	254	266	193	175	166	161	147
Total domestic extraction	JKVC	602	625	664	666	702	688	673	584	565	557	524	458
Imports													
Biomass	JKVD	38	33	30	32	39	41	46	54	54	54	52	50
Minerals	JKVE	30	32	24	36	43	53	52	59	60	64	57	54
Fossil fuels	JKVF	125	113	76	80	95	82	93	148	159	158	152	148
Other products	JKVG	4	5	10	9	10	11	16	16	16	16	16	16
Total imports	JKVH	197	184	141	157	187	188	208	278	290	292	278	268
Exports													
Biomass	JKVI	3	5	8	11	14	16	18	20	21	21	22	20
Minerals	JKVJ	18	21	26	22	26	39	45	49	51	50	48	44
Fossil fuels	JKVK	24	21	63	105	72	111	125	99	94	90	89	87
Other products	JKVL	2	3	4	7	5	8	9	9	9	9	9	9
Total exports	JKVM	47	51	101	146	117	173	197	177	174	171	168	160
Domestic Material Consumption (domestic extraction + imports - exports)	JKVU	752	758	704	677	772	704	685	686	682	679	634	566
of which													
Biomass	G9A8	131	120	123	121	126	126	130	134	132	129	132	130
Minerals	G9A9	353	361	296	320	390	348	312	301	301	309	271	220
Fossil fuels	G9AA	266	276	279	234	251	225	234	243	240	234	223	208
Indirect flows													
From domestic extraction (excl soil erosion)[2]	JKVN	575	581	643	635	703	642	576	519	487	493	494	471
of which													
Unused biomass	JKVO	25	23	32	36	37	37	41	38	36	34	39	38
Fossil fuels	JKVP	169	208	297	281	319	282	234	180	151	152	162	165
Minerals and ores	JKVQ	184	155	120	120	144	121	104	101	100	105	92	71
Soil excavation and dredging	JKVR	197	195	195	199	203	201	197	200	201	201	201	197
From production of raw materials and semi-natural products imported	JKVS	394	395	368	423	457	527	600	749	783	749	686	558
Other indicators													
Physical trade balance (imports - exports)[3]	DZ76	150	133	40	11	70	14	11	101	116	121	110	107
Direct Material Input (domestic extraction + imports)	JKVT	799	809	805	822	889	877	882	863	855	850	802	726
Total Material Requirement (direct material input + indirect flows)	JKVV	1 768	1 785	1 816	1 880	2 049	2 045	2 057	2 130	2 126	2 091	1 982	1 755

1 Components may not sum to totals due to rounding
2 Indirect flows from domestic extraction relate to unused material which is moved during extraction, such as overburden from mining and quarrying.
3 A positive physical trade balance indicates a net import of material into the UK. This calculation of the PTB differs from the National Accounts formula (exports-imports) because flows of materials and products are considered the inverse of the flows of money recorded in the National Accounts.

Source: ONS

13.7 Environmental protection expenditure in specified industries [1,2,3]
2009

£ million

	Protection of ambient air and climate	Waste water management	Waste management	Protection of bio-diversity and landscape	Other abatement activities	Research and development expenditure	Total environmental expenditure
Mining and quarrying	4	5	5	4	13	–	32
Food products, beverages & tobacco	23	151	98	2	45	2	322
Paper and pulp	6	27	12	1	2	–	48
Coke and refined petroleum	2	7	7	–	5	1	23
Chemicals and pharmaceuticals	19	26	45	–	11	2	105
Basic and fabricated metals	5	11	65	–	20	1	102
Electricity, gas and water	407	1 569	175	135	327	67	2 681
Other[4]	86	129	224	28	90	52	608
Total expenditure in extraction, manufacturing, energy and water supply industries[5]	553	1 925	633	172	513	124	3 920

Source: Department for Environment, Food and Rural Affairs

1 The figures in these tables fall outside the scope of National Statistics
2 The 2008 and 2009 surveys are based on the new SIC 2007 classifications. Previous surveys are based on SIC 2003
3 For 2009 the survey targeted a reduced number of industries. For more information please refer to the methodology section of the EPE Research Report 2009 at www.defra.gov.uk/statistics/files/EPE-Survey-2009_Final- report.pdf
4 These are estimates as the industries were not surveyed in 2009
5 Components may not sum to totals due to rounding

Supplementary Information

Glossary

Above the line
Transactions in the production, current and capital accounts which are above the Net lending (+)/Net borrowing (financial surplus or deficit) line in the presentation used in the economic accounts. The financial transactions account is below the line in this presentation.

Accruals basis
A method of recording transactions to relate them to the period when the exchange of ownership of the goods, services or financial asset applies (see also cash basis). For example, Value Added Tax accrues when the expenditure to which it relates takes place, but Customs and Excise receive the cash some time later. The difference between accruals and cash results in the creation of an asset and liability in the financial accounts, shown as amounts receivable or payable (F7).

Actual final consumption
The value of goods consumed by a sector but not necessarily purchased by that sector (see also Final consumption expenditure, Intermediate consumption).

Advance and progress payments
Payments made for goods in advance of completion and delivery of the goods. Also referred to as staged payments.

Asset boundary
Boundary separating assets included in creating core economic accounts (such as plant and factories, also including non-produced assets such as land and water resources) and those excluded (such as natural assets not managed for an economic purpose).

Assets
Entities over which ownership rights are enforced by institutional units, individually or collectively; and from which economic benefits may be derived by their owners by holding them over a period of time.

Assurance
An equivalent term to insurance, commonly used in the life insurance business.

Balancing item
A balancing item is an accounting construct obtained by subtracting the total value of the entries on one side of an account from the total value for the other side. In the sector accounts in the former system of UK economic accounts the term referred to the difference between the Financial Surplus or Deficit for a sector and the sum of the financial transactions for that sector, currently designated the statistical discrepancy.

Balance of payments
A summary of the transactions between residents of a country and residents abroad in a given time period.

Balance of trade
The balance of trade in goods and services. The balance of trade is a summary of the imports and exports of goods and services across an economic boundary in a given period.

Balance sheet
A statement, drawn up at a particular point in time, of the value of assets owned and of the financial claims (liabilities) against the owner of these assets.

Bank of England
This comprises S.121, the central bank sub-sector of the financial corporations sector.

Bank of England – Issue Department
This part of the Bank of England deals with the issue of bank notes on behalf of central government. It was formerly classified to central government though it is now part of the central bank/monetary authorities sector. It's activities include, inter alia, market purchases of commercial bills from UK banks.

Banks (UK)
Banks are defined as all financial institutions recognised by the Bank of England as UK banks. For statistical purposes, this includes institutions which have a permission under Part 4 of the Financial Services and Markets Act 2000 (FSMA) to accept deposits, other than;

– credit unions

– firms which have a permission to accept deposits only in the course of carrying out contracts of insurance in accordance with that permission

– friendly societies

– building societies

European Economic Area credit institutions with a permission under Schedule 3 to FSMA to accept deposits through a UK branch the Banking and Issue Departments of the Bank of England (the latter from April 1998)

Prior to December 2001, banks were defined as all financial institutions recognised by the Bank of England as UK banks for statistical purposes, including the UK offices of institutions authorised under the Banking Act 1987, the Banking and Issue Departments of the Bank of England (the latter from April 1988), and deposit-taking UK branches of 'European Authorised Institutions'. This includes UK branches of foreign banks, but not the offices abroad of these or of any British owned banks.

An updated list of banks appears regularly in the Bank of England's Monetary and Financial Statistics publication, available at: www.bankofengland.co.uk/statistics/ms

Basic prices
These prices are the preferred method of valuing gross value added and output. They reflect the amount received by the producer for a unit of goods or services minus any taxes payable plus any subsidy receivable on that unit as a consequence of production or sale (that is the cost of production including subsidies). As a result the only taxes included in the basic price are taxes on the production process – such as business rates and any vehicle excise duty paid by businesses – which are not specifically levied on the production of a unit of output. Basic prices exclude any transport charges invoiced separately by the producer.

Below the line
The financial transactions account which shows the financing of Net lending(+)/Net borrowing (–) (formerly financial surplus or deficit).

Bond
A financial instrument that usually pays interest to the holder. Bonds are issued by governments as well as companies and other institutions, for example local authorities. Most bonds have a fixed date on which the borrower will repay the holder. Bonds are attractive to investors since they can be bought and sold easily in a secondary market. Special forms of bonds include deep discount bonds, equity warrant bonds, Eurobonds, and zero coupon bonds.

British government securities
Securities issued or guaranteed by the UK government; also known as gilts.

Building society
Building societies are mutual institutions specialising in accepting deposits from members of the public and in long-term lending to members of the public, mainly to finance the purchase of dwellings; such lending being secured on dwellings. Their operations are governed by special legislation which places restrictions on their recourse to other sources of funding and other avenues of investment.

Capital
Capital assets are those which contribute to the productive process so as to produce an economic return. In other contexts the word can be taken to include tangible assets (for example buildings, plant and machinery), intangible assets and financial capital (see also fixed assets, inventories).

Capital formation
Acquisitions less disposals of fixed assets, improvement of land, change in inventories and acquisitions less disposals of valuables.

Capital Stock
Measure of the cost of replacing the capital assets of a country, held at a particular point in time.

Capital transfers
Transfers which are related to the acquisition or disposal of assets by the recipient or payer. They may be in cash or kind, and may be imputed to reflect the assumption or forgiveness of debt.

Cash basis

The recording of transactions when cash or other assets are actually transferred, rather than on an accruals basis.

Central monetary institutions (CMIs)

Institutions (usually central banks) which control the centralised monetary reserves and the supply of currency in accordance with government policies, and which act as their governments' bankers and agents. In the UK this is equivalent to the Bank of England. In many other countries maintenance of the exchange rate is undertaken in this sector. In the United Kingdom this function is undertaken by central government (part of HM Treasury) by use of the Exchange Equalisation Account.

Certificate of deposit

A short term interest-paying instrument issued by deposit-taking institutions in return for money deposited for a fixed period. Interest is earned at a given rate. The instrument can be used as security for a loan if the depositor requires money before the repayment date.

Chained volume measures

Chained volume measures are time series which measure GDP in real terms (that is excluding price effects). Series are calculated in the prices of the previous year and in current price, and all of these two-year series are then "chain-linked" together. The advantage of the chain-linking method is that the previous period's price structure is more relevant than the price structure of a fixed period from further into the past.

c.i.f. (cost, insurance and freight)

The basis of valuation of imports for Customs purposes, it includes the cost of insurance premiums and freight services. These need to be deducted to obtain the free on board (f.o.b.) valuation consistent with the valuation of exports which is used in the economic accounts.

COICOP (Classification of Individual Consumption by Purpose)

An international classification which groups consumption according to its function or purpose. Thus the heading clothing, for example, includes expenditure on garments, clothing materials, laundry and repairs.

Combined use table

Table of the demand for products by each industry group or sector, whether from domestic production or imports, estimated at purchaser's prices. It displays the inputs used by each industry to produce their total output and separates out intermediate purchases of goods and services. This table shows which industries use which products. Columns represent the purchasing industries: rows represent the products purchased.

Commercial paper

This is an unsecured promissory note for a specific amount and maturing on a specific date. The commercial paper market allows companies to issue short term debt direct to financial institutions who then market this paper to investors or use it for their own investment purposes.

Compensation of employees

Total remuneration payable to employees in cash or in kind. Includes the value of social contributions payable by the employer.

Consolidated Fund

An account of central government into which most government revenue (excluding borrowing and certain payments to government departments) is paid, and from which most government expenditure (excluding loans and National Insurance benefits) is paid.

Consumption

See Final consumption, Intermediate consumption.

Consumption of fixed capital

The amount of capital resources used up in the process of production in any period. It is not an identifiable set of transactions but an imputed transaction which can only be measured by a system of conventions.

Corporations

All bodies recognised as independent legal entities which are producers of market output and whose principal activity is the production of goods and services.

Counterpart

In a double-entry system of accounting each transaction gives rise to two corresponding entries. These entries are the counterparts to each other. Thus the counterpart of a payment by one sector is the receipt by another.

Debenture

A long-term bond issued by a UK or foreign company and secured on fixed assets. A debenture entitles the holder to a fixed interest payment or a series of such payments.

Depreciation

See Consumption of fixed capital.

Derivatives (F.34)

Financial instruments whose value is linked to changes in the value of another financial instrument, an indicator or a commodity. In contrast to the holder of a primary financial instrument (for example a government bond or a bank deposit), who has an unqualified right to receive cash (or some other economic benefit) in the future, the holder of a derivative has only a qualified right to receive such a benefit. Examples of derivatives are options and swaps.

DIM (Dividend and Interest Matrix)

The Dividend and Interest Matrix represents property income flows related to holdings of financial transactions. The gross flows are now shown in D.4.

Direct investment

Net investment by UK/foreign companies in their foreign/UK branches, subsidiaries or associated companies. A direct investment in a company means that the investor has a significant influence on the operations of the company, defined as having an equity interest in an enterprise resident in another country of 10 per cent or more of the ordinary shares or voting stock. Investment includes not only acquisition of fixed assets, stock building and stock appreciation, but also all other financial transactions such as: additions to, or payments of working capital; other loans and trade credit; and acquisitions of securities. Estimates of investment flows allow for depreciation in any undistributed profits. Funds raised by the subsidiary or associate company in the economy in which it operates are excluded as they are locally raised and not sourced from the parent company.

Discount market

That part of the market dealing with short-term borrowing. It is called the discount market because the interest on loans is expressed as a percentage reduction (discount) on the amount paid to the borrower. For example, for a loan of £100 face value when the discount rate is 5 per cent the borrower will receive £95 but will repay £100 at the end of the term.

Double deflation

Method for calculating value added by industry chained volume measures; which takes separate account of the differing price and volume movements of input and outputs in an industry's production process.

Dividend

A payment made to company shareholders from current or previously retained profits. Dividends are recorded when they become payable. See DIM.

ECGD

See Export Credit Guarantee Department.

Economically significant prices

These are prices whose level significantly affects the supply of the good or service concerned. Market output consists mainly of goods and services sold at 'economically significant' prices while non-market output comprises those provided free or at prices that are not economically significant.

Enterprise

An institutional unit producing market output. Enterprises are found mainly in the non-financial and financial corporations sectors but exist in all sectors. Each enterprise consists of one or more kind-of-activity units.

Environmental accounts

A satellite account describing the relationship between the environment and the economy.

Equity

Equity is ownership of a residual claim on the assets of the institutional unit that issued the instrument. Equities differ from other financial instruments in that they confer ownership of something more than a financial claim. Shareholders are owners of the company whereas bond holders are merely outside creditors.

ESA

European System of National and Regional Accounts. An integrated system of economic accounts which is the European version of the System of National Accounts (SNA).

European Investment Bank

This was set up to assist economic development within the European Union. It's members are the member states of the EU.

Exchange Cover Scheme (ECS)

A scheme first introduced in 1969 whereby UK public bodies raise foreign currency from overseas residents, either directly or through UK banks, and surrender it to the Exchange Equalisation Account in exchange for sterling for use to finance expenditure in the United Kingdom. HM Treasury sells the borrower foreign currency to service and repay the loan at the exchange rate that applied when the loan was taken out.

Exchange Equalisation Account (EEA)

The government account with the Bank of England in which transactions in reserve assets are recorded. These transactions are classified to the central government sector. It is the means by which the government, through the Bank of England, influences exchange rates.

Export credit

Credit extended abroad by UK institutions, primarily in connection with UK exports but also including some credit in respect of third-country trade.

Export Credit Guarantee Department (ECGD)

A non-ministerial government department, classified to the public corporations sector, the main function of which is to provide insurance cover for export credit transactions.

Factor cost

In the former system of national accounts this was the basis of valuation which excluded the effects of taxes on expenditure and subsidies.

Final consumption expenditure

The expenditure on goods and services that are used for the direct satisfaction of individual needs or the collective needs of members of the community as distinct from their purchase for use in the productive process. It may be contrasted with actual final consumption, which is the value of goods consumed but not necessarily purchased by that sector (see also Intermediate consumption).

Finance houses

Financial corporations that specialise in the financing of hire purchase arrangements.

Financial auxiliaries

Auxiliary financial activities are ones closely related to financial intermediation but which are not financial intermediation themselves, such as the repackaging of funds, insurance broking and fund management. Financial auxiliaries therefore include insurance brokers and fund managers.

Financial corporations

All bodies recognised as independent legal entities whose principal activity is financial intermediation and/or the production of auxiliary financial services.

Financial intermediation

Financial intermediation is the activity by which an institutional unit acquires financial assets and incurs liabilities on its own account by engaging in financial transactions on the market. The assets and liabilities of financial intermediaries have different characteristics so that the funds are transformed or repackaged with respect to; for example, maturity, scale, risk, in the financial intermediation process.

Financial leasing

A form of leasing in which the lessee contracts to assume the rights and responsibilities of ownership of leased goods from the lessor (the legal owner) for the whole (or virtually the whole) of the economic life of the asset. In the economic accounts this is recorded as the sale of the assets to the lessee, financed by an imputed loan (F.42). The leasing payments are split into interest payments and repayments of principal.

Financial surplus or deficit (FSD)

The former term for Net lending(+)/Net borrowing (−), the balance of all current and capital account transactions for an institutional sector or the economy as a whole.

FISIM

FISIM is an acronym for Financial Intermediation Services Indirectly Measured. It represents the implicit charge for the service provided by monetary financial institutions paid for by the interest differential between borrowing and lending rather than through fees and commissions.

Fixed assets

Produced assets that are themselves used repeatedly or continuously in the production process for more than one year. They comprise buildings and other structures, vehicles and other plant and machinery and also plants and livestock which are used repeatedly or continuously in production, for example fruit trees or dairy cattle. They also include intangible assets such as computer software and artistic originals.

Flows

Economic flows reflect the creation, transformation, exchange, transfer or extinction of economic value. They involve changes in the volume, composition or value of an institutional unit's assets and liabilities. They are recorded in the production, distribution and use of income and accumulation accounts.

F.o.b. (free on board)

An f.o.b. price excludes the cost of insurance and freight from the country of consignment but includes all charges up to the point of the exporting country's customs frontier.

Futures

Futures are forward contracts traded on organised exchanges. They give the holder the right to purchase a commodity or a financial asset at a future date.

GFCF

See Gross fixed capital formation.

Gilts

Bonds issued or guaranteed by the UK government. Also known as gilt-edged securities or British government securities.

Gold

The SNA and the IMF (in the 5th Edition of its Balance of Payments Manual) recognise three types of gold:

- monetary gold, treated as a financial asset
- gold held as a store of value, to be included in valuables
- gold as an industrial material, to be included in intermediate consumption or inventories

This is a significant change from previous UK practice and presents problems such that the United Kingdom has received from the European Union a temporary derogation from applying this fully.

The present treatment is as follows:

- In the accounts a distinction is drawn between gold held as a financial asset (financial gold) and gold held like any other commodity (commodity gold). Commodity gold in the form of finished manufactures together with net domestic and overseas transactions in gold moving into or out of finished manufactured form (i.e. for jewellery, dentistry, electronic goods, medals and proof – but not bullion – coins) is recorded in exports and imports of goods
- All other transactions in gold (that is those involving semi-manufactures for example rods, wire; or bullion, bullion coins or banking-type assets and liabilities denominated in gold, including official reserve assets) are treated as financial gold transactions and included in the financial account of the Balance of Payments

The United Kingdom has adopted different treatment to avoid distortion of its trade in goods account by the substantial transactions of the London bullion market.

Grants

Voluntary transfer payments. They may be current or capital in nature. Grants from government or the European Union to producers are subsidies.

Gross

Key economic series can be shown as gross (i.e. before deduction of the consumption of fixed capital) or net (i.e. after deduction). Gross has this meaning throughout this book unless otherwise stated.

Gross domestic product (GDP)

The total value of output in the economic territory. It is the balancing item on the production account for the whole economy. Domestic product can be measured gross or net. It is presented in the accounts at market (or purchasers') prices.

Gross fixed capital formation (GFCF)

Acquisitions less disposals of fixed assets and the improvement of land.

Gross national disposable income

The income available to the residents arising from GDP, and receipts from, less payments to, the rest of the world of employment income, property income and current transfers.

Gross value added (GVA)

The value generated by any unit engaged in production, and the contributions of individual sectors or industries to gross domestic product. It is measured at basic prices, excluding taxes less subsidies on products.

Hidden economy

Certain activities may be productive and also legal but are concealed from the authorities for various reasons – for example to evade taxes or regulation. In principle these, as well as economic production that is illegal, are to be included in the accounts but they are by their nature difficult to measure.

Holding gains or losses

Profit or loss obtained by virtue of the changing price of assets being held. Holding gains or losses may arise from either physical or financial assets.

Households (S.14)

Individuals or small groups of individuals as consumers and in some cases as entrepreneurs producing goods and market services (where such activities cannot be hived off and treated as those of a quasi corporation).

Imputation

The process of inventing a transaction where, although no money has changed hands, there has been a flow of goods or services. It is confined to a very small number of cases where a reasonably satisfactory basis for the assumed valuation is available.

Index-linked gilts

Gilts whose coupon and redemption value are linked to movements in the retail prices index.

Institutional unit

Institutional units are the individual bodies whose data is amalgamated to form the sectors of the economy. A body is regarded as an institutional unit if it has decision-making autonomy in respect of its principal function and either keeps a complete set of accounts or is in a position to compile, if required, a complete set of accounts which would be meaningful from both an economic and a legal viewpoint.

Institutional sector

See Sector.

Input–Output

A detailed analytical framework based on Supply and Use tables. These are matrices showing the composition of output of individual industries by types of product and how the domestic and imported supply of goods and services is allocated between various intermediate and final uses, including exports.

Intangible assets

Intangible fixed assets include mineral exploration, computer software and entertainment, literary or artistic originals. Expenditure on them is part of gross fixed capital formation. They exclude non-produced intangible assets such as patented entities, leases, transferable contracts and purchased goodwill, expenditure on which would be intermediate consumption.

Intermediate consumption

The consumption of goods and services in the production process. It may be contrasted with final consumption and capital formation.

International Monetary Fund (IMF)

A fund set up as a result of the Bretton Woods Conference in 1944 which began operations in 1947. It currently has 187 member countries including most of the major countries of the world. The fund was set up to supervise the fixed exchange rate system agreed at Bretton Woods and to make available to its members a pool of foreign exchange resources to assist them when they have balance of payments difficulties. It is funded by member countries' subscriptions according to agreed quotas.

Inventories

Inventories (known as stocks in the former system) consist of finished goods (held by the producer prior to sale, further processing or other use) and products (materials and fuel) acquired from other producers to be used for intermediate consumption or resold without further processing.

Investment trust

An institution that invests its capital in a wide range of other companies' shares. Investment trusts issue shares which are listed on the London Stock Exchange and use this capital to invest in the shares of other companies (see also Unit trusts).

Kind-of-activity unit (KAU)

An enterprise, or part of an enterprise, which engages in only one kind of non-ancillary productive activity, or in which the principal productive activity accounts for most of the value added. Each enterprise consists of one or more kind-of-activity units.

Liability

A claim on an institutional unit by another body which gives rise to a payment or other transaction transferring assets to the other body. Conditional liabilities, that is where the transfer of assets only takes place under certain defined circumstances, are known as contingent liabilities.

Liquidity

The ease with which a financial instrument can be exchanged for goods and services. Cash is very liquid whereas a life assurance policy is less so.

Lloyd's of London

The international insurance and reinsurance market in London.

Marketable securities

Securities which can be sold on the open market.

Market output

Output of goods and services sold at economically significant prices.

Merchant banks

These are monetary financial institutions whose main business is primarily concerned with corporate finance and acquisitions.

Mixed income

The balancing item on the generation of income account for unincorporated businesses owned by households. The owner or members of the same household often provide unpaid labour inputs to the business. The surplus is therefore a mixture of remuneration for such labour and return to the owner as entrepreneur.

Monetary financial institutions (MFIs)

Banks and building societies

Money market

The market in which short-term loans are made and short-term securities traded. 'Short–term' usually applies to periods under one year but can be longer in some instances.

NACE

The industrial classification used in the European Union. Revision 2 is the 'Statistical classification of economic activities in the European Community in accordance with Commission Regulation (EC) No. 1893/2006 of 20th December 2006'.

National income

See Gross national disposable income and Real national disposable income.

National Loans Fund

An account of HM Government set up under the National Loans Fund Act (1968) which handles all government borrowing and most domestic lending transactions.

Net

After deduction of the consumption of fixed capital. Also used in the context of financial accounts and balance sheets to denote, for example, assets less liabilities.

Non-market output

Output of own account production of goods and services provided free or at prices that are not economically significant. Non-market output is produced mainly by the general government and NPISH sectors.

NPISH

Non-profit institutions serving households (S.15). These include bodies such as charities, universities, churches, trade unions or member's clubs.

Operating surplus

The balance on the generation of income account. Households also have a mixed income balance. It may be seen as the surplus arising from the production of goods and services before taking into account flows of property income.

Glossary of terms

Operating leasing
The conventional form of leasing, in which the lessee makes use of the leased asset for a period in return for a rental while the asset remains on the balance sheet of the lessor. The leasing payments are part of the output of the lessor, and the intermediate consumption of the lessee (see also Financial leasing).

Ordinary share
The most common type of share in the ownership of a corporation. Holders of ordinary shares receive dividends (see also Equity).

Output for own final use
Production of output for final consumption or gross fixed capital formation by the producer. Also known as own-account production.

Own-account production
Production of output for final consumption or gross fixed capital formation by the producer. Also known as output for own final use.

Par value
A security's face or nominal value. Securities can be issued at a premium or discount to par.

Pension funds
The institutions that administer pension schemes. Pension schemes are significant investors in securities. Self-administered funds are classified in the financial accounts as pension funds. Those managed by insurance companies are treated as long-term business of insurance companies. They are part of S.125, the insurance corporations and pension funds sub-sector of the financial corporations sector within the National Accounts.

Perpetual Inventory Model (or Method) (PIM)
A method for estimating the level of assets held at a particular point of time by accumulating the acquisitions of such assets over a period and subtracting the disposals of assets over that period. Adjustments are made for price changes over the period. The PIM is used in the UK accounts to estimate the stock of fixed capital, and hence the value of the consumption of fixed capital.

Portfolio
A list of the securities owned by a single investor. In the Balance of Payments statistics, portfolio investment is investment in securities that does not qualify as direct investment.

Preference share
This type of share guarantees its holder a prior claim on dividends. The dividend paid to preference share holders is normally more than that paid to holders of ordinary shares. Preference shares may give the holder a right to a share in the ownership of the company (participating preference shares). However in the UK they usually do not, and are therefore classified as bonds (F.3).

Prices
See economically significant prices, basic prices, producers' prices.

Principal
The lump sum that is lent under a loan or a bond.

Private sector
Private non-financial corporations, financial corporations other than the Bank of England, households and the NPISH sector.

Production boundary
Boundary between production included in creating core economic accounts (such as all economic activity by industry and commerce) and production which is excluded (such as production by households which is consumed within the household).

Promissory note
A security which entitles the bearer to receive cash. These may be issued by companies or other institutions (see commercial paper).

Property income
Incomes that accrue from lending or renting financial or tangible non-produced assets, including land, to other units. See also Tangible assets.

Public corporations
These are public trading bodies which have a substantial degree of financial independence from the public authority which created them. A body is normally treated as a trading body when more than half of its income is financed by fees. A public corporation is publicly controlled to the extent that the public authorities appoint a majority of the board of management or when public authorities can exert significant control over general corporate policy through other means. Since the 1980s many public corporations, such as British Telecom, have been privatised and reclassified within the accounts as private non-financial corporations. Such bodies comprise much the greater part of sub-sector S.11001, public non-financial corporations.

Public sector
Central government, local authorities and public corporations.

Purchasers' prices
These are the prices paid by purchasers. They include transport costs, trade margins and taxes (unless the taxes are deductible by the purchasers from their own tax liabilities).

Quasi-corporations
Unincorporated enterprises that function as if they were corporations. For the purposes of allocation to sectors and sub-sectors they are treated as if they were corporations, that is separate units from those to which they legally belong. Three main types of quasi-corporation are recognised in the accounts: unincorporated enterprises owned by government which are engaged in market production, unincorporated enterprises (including partnerships) owned by households and unincorporated enterprises owned by foreign residents. The last group consists of permanent branches or offices of foreign enterprises and production units of foreign enterprises which engage in significant amounts of production in the territory over long or indefinite periods of time.

Real national disposable income (RNDI)
Gross national disposable income adjusted for changes in prices and in the terms of trade.

Related companies
Branches, subsidiaries, associates or parents.

Related import or export credit
Trade credit between related companies, included in direct investment.

Rental
The amount payable by the user of a fixed asset to its owner for the right to use that asset in production for a specified period of time. It is included in the output of the owner and the intermediate consumption of the user.

Rents (D.45)
The property income derived from land and sub-soil assets. It should be distinguished in the current system from rental income derived from buildings and other fixed assets, which is included in output (P.1).

Repurchase agreement (Repo)/reverse repo
This is short for 'sale and repurchase agreement'. One party agrees to sell bonds or other financial instruments to other parties under a formal legal agreement to repurchase them at some point in the future – usually up to six months – at a fixed price. Reverse repos are the counterpart asset to any repo liability. Repo/reverse repo transactions are generally treated as borrowing/lending within other investment, rather than as transactions in the underlying securities. The exception being for banks, where repos are recorded as deposit liabilities. Banks' reverse repos are recorded as loans, the same as for all other sectors. Legal ownership does not change under a 'repo' agreement. It was previously treated as a change of ownership in the UK financial account but under the SNA is treated as a collateralised deposit (F.22).

Reserve assets
Short-term assets which can be very quickly converted into cash. They comprise the UK's official holdings of gold, convertible currencies, Special Drawing Rights and changes in the UK reserve position in the IMF. Also included between July 1979 and December 1998 are European Currency Units acquired from swaps with the European Co-operation Fund, EMI and the ECB.

Residents
These comprise general government, individuals, private non-profit-making bodies serving households and enterprises within the territory of a given economy.

Residual error
The term used in the former accounts for the difference between the measures of gross domestic product from the expenditure and income approaches.

Resources and Uses
The term resources refers to the side of the current accounts where transactions which add

to the amount of economic value of a unit or sector appear. For example, wages and salaries are a resource for the unit or sector receiving them. Resources are by convention put on the right side, or at the top of tables arranged vertically. The left side (or bottom section) of the accounts, which relates to transactions that reduce the amount of economic value of a unit or sector, is termed uses. To continue the example, wages and salaries are a use for the unit or sector that must pay them.

Rest of the world

This sector records the counterpart of transactions of the whole economy with non-residents.

Satellite accounts

Satellite accounts describe areas or activities not dealt with by core economic accounts. These areas/activities are considered to require too much detail for inclusion in the core accounts or they operate with a different conceptual framework. Internal satellite accounts re-present information within the production boundary. External satellite accounts present new information not covered by the core accounts.

Saving

The balance on the use of income account. It is that part of disposable income which is not spent on final consumption, and may be positive or negative.

Sector

In the economic accounts the economy is split into different institutional sectors, that is groupings of units according broadly to their role in the economy. The main sectors are non-financial corporations, financial corporations, general government, households and non-profit institutions serving households (NPISH). The rest of the world is also treated as a sector for many purposes within the accounts.

Secondary market

A market in which holders of financial instruments can re-sell all or part of their holding. The larger and more effective the secondary market for any particular financial instrument the more liquid that instrument is to the holder.

Securities

Tradable or potentially tradable financial instruments.

SIC

Standard Industrial Classification. The industrial classification applied to the collection and publication of a wide range of economic statistics. The current version, SIC 2007, is consistent with NACE, rev.2.

SNA

System of National Accounts, the internationally agreed standard system for macroeconomic accounts. The latest version is described in System of National Accounts 1993.

Special Drawing Rights (SDRs)

These are reserve assets created and distributed by decision of the members of the IMF. Participants accept an obligation to provide convertible currency, when designated by the IMF to do so, to another participant, in exchange for SDRs equivalent to three times their own allocation. Only countries with a sufficiently strong balance of payments are so designated by the IMF. SDRs may also be used in certain direct payments between participants in the scheme and for payments of various kinds to the IMF.

Staged payments

See Advance and progress payments.

Stocks, stockbuilding

The terms used in the former system corresponding to inventories and changes in inventories.

Subsidiaries

Companies owned or controlled by another company. Under Section 1159 of the Companies Act (2006) this means, broadly speaking, that another company either holds a majority of the voting rights in it or is a member of it and has the right to appoint or remove a majority of its board of directors, or is a member of it and controls alone, pursuant to an agreement with other members, a majority of the voting rights in it. The category also includes subsidiaries of subsidiaries.

Subsidies (D.3)

Current unrequited payments made by general government or the European Union to enterprises. Those made on the basis of a quantity or value of goods or services are classified as 'subsidies on products' (D.31). Other subsidies based on levels of productive activity (for example numbers employed) are designated 'Other subsidies on production' (D.39).

Suppliers' credit

Export credit extended overseas directly by UK firms other than to related concerns.

Supply table

Table of estimates of domestic industries' output by type of product. Compiled at basic prices and includes columns for imports of goods and services, for distributors' trading margins and for taxes less subsidies on products. The final column shows the value of the supply of goods and services at purchaser's prices. This table shows which industries make which products. Columns represent the supplying industries: rows represent the products supplied.

Tangible assets

These comprise produced fixed assets and non-produced assets. Tangible fixed assets, the acquisition and disposal of which are recorded in gross fixed capital formation (P.51), comprise buildings and other structures (including historic monuments), vehicles, other machinery and equipment and cultivated assets in the form of livestock and trees yielding repeat products (for example dairy cattle, orchards). Tangible non-produced assets are assets such as land and sub-soil resources that occur in nature over which ownership rights have been established. Similar assets to which ownership rights have not been established are excluded as they do not qualify as economic assets. The acquisition and disposal of non-produced assets in principle is recorded separately in the capital account (K.2). The distinction between produced and non-produced assets is not yet fully possible for the United Kingdom.

Taxes

Compulsory unrequited transfers to central or local government or the European Union. Taxation is classified in the following main groups: taxes on production and imports (D.2), current taxes on income wealth, etc (D.5) and capital taxes (D.91).

Technical reserves (of insurance companies)

These reserves consist of pre-paid premiums, reserves against outstanding claims, actuarial reserves for life insurance and reserves for with-profit insurance. They are treated in the economic accounts as the property of policy-holders.

Terms of trade

Ratio of the change in export prices to the change in import prices. An increase in the terms of trade implies that the receipts from the same quantity of exports will finance an increased volume of imports. Thus measurement of real national disposable income needs to take account of this factor.

Transfers

Unrequited payments made by one unit to another. They may be current transfers (D.5–7) or capital transfers (D.9). The most important types of transfers are taxes, social contributions and benefits.

Treasury bills

Short-term securities or promissory notes which are issued by government in return for funding from the money market. In the United Kingdom every week the Bank of England invites tenders for sterling Treasury bills from the financial institutions operating in the market. ECU/euro-denominated bills were issued by tender each month but this programme has now wound down; the last bill was redeemed in September 1999. Treasury bills are an important form of short-term borrowing for the government, generally being issued for periods of 3 or 6 months.

Unit trusts

Institutions within sub-sector S.123 through which investors pool their funds to invest in a diversified portfolio of securities. Individual investors purchase units in the fund representing an ownership interest in the large pool of underlying assets, that is they have an equity stake. The selection of assets is made by professional fund managers. Unit trusts therefore give individual investors the opportunity to invest in a diversified and professionally managed portfolio of securities without the need for detailed knowledge of the individual companies issuing the stocks and bonds. They differ from investment trusts in that the latter are companies in which investors trade shares on the Stock Exchange, whereas unit trust units are issued and bought back on demand by the managers of the trust. The prices of unit trust units thus reflect the value of the underlying pool of securities, whereas the price of shares in investment trusts are affected by the usual market forces.

Uses
See Resources and Uses.

Use Table
See Combined Use Table.

United Kingdom
Broadly, in the accounts, the United Kingdom comprises Great Britain plus Northern Ireland and that part of the continental shelf deemed by international convention to belong to the UK. It excludes the Channel Islands and the Isle of Man.

Valuables
Goods of considerable value that are not used primarily for production or consumption but are held as stores of value over time. They consist of, for example, precious metals, precious stones, jewellery, works of art. As a new category in the accounts the estimates for them are currently fairly rudimentary, though transactions are likely to have been recorded elsewhere in the accounts.

Valuation
See Basic prices, Purchasers' prices, Factor cost.

Value added
The balance on the production account: output less intermediate consumption. Value added may be measured net or gross.

Value Added Tax (VAT) (D.211)
A tax paid by enterprises. In broad terms an enterprise is liable for VAT on the total of its taxable sales but may deduct tax already paid by suppliers on its inputs (intermediate consumption). Thus the tax is effectively on the value added by the enterprise. Where the enterprise cannot deduct tax on its inputs the tax is referred to as non-deductible. VAT is the main UK tax on products (D.21).